PRE-ALGEBRA
A TEACHING TEXTBOOK

Greg Sabouri
Shawn Sabouri

Pre-Algebra: A Teaching Textbook™
Second Edition
Greg Sabouri and Shawn Sabouri

Copyright © 2011 by Teaching Textbooks, LLC

Printed in the United States of America.

ISBN: 978-0-9835812-2-2

Teaching Textbooks, LLC
6501 Broadway Extension Suite 300
Oklahoma City, OK 73116
www.teachingtextbooks.com

Acknowledgements

The authors would like to thank the following individuals for their invaluable contributions to this product: Jeremiah Alcorn, Tyler Ball, Tina Kugler, Justin Lacy, Yen Soon Low, Andrew Martin, Sam Martindale, Thanh Nguyen, Vikas Patel, Eric Sandhop, and Austin Taylor.

"An investment in knowledge pays the best interest."--Benjamin Franklin

Table of Contents

Chapter 1: Arithmetic Basics ———————————————— 5
Lesson 1—Number Beginnings   6
Lesson 2—Adding and Subtracting Whole Numbers   11
Lesson 3—Multiplying Whole Numbers   16
Lesson 4—Dividing Whole Numbers   21
Lesson 5—Divisibility   25

Chapter 2: Rational Numbers ———————————————— 31
Lesson 6—Fractions   32
Lesson 7—Equivalent Fractions   39
Lesson 8—Factoring and Canceling   46
Lesson 9—Prime Numbers   50
Lesson 10—Adding and Subtracting Fractions   55
Lesson 11—Finding the Lowest Common Denominator   61
Lesson 12—Mixed Numbers   65
Lesson 13—Multiplying and Dividing Fractions   70
Lesson 14—Fractions and Whole Numbers   75

Chapter 3: Decimals ———————————————— 83
Lesson 15—Ill-Fitting Fractions   84
Lesson 16—Hundredths, Thousandths …   88
Lesson 17—Adding and Subtracting Decimals   92
Lesson 18—Filling the Holes   96
Lesson 19—Money and Decimals   99
Lesson 20—Multiplying Decimals   102
Lesson 21—Dividing Decimals   107
Lesson 22—Decimal Remainders   111
Lesson 23—Converting Fractions to Decimals   115
Lesson 24—Never-Ending Decimals   119

Chapter 4: Percents ———————————————— 123
Lesson 25—Percents   124
Lesson 26—Calculating Percents   127
Lesson 27—Percent of Any Number   131
Lesson 28—Fractional Percents   134
Lesson 29—Percents and Banking   138
Lesson 30—Finding the Percent   141
Lesson 31—Calculating a Grade   145

Chapter 5: Measuring Length ———————————————— 149
Lesson 32—Units of Measurement   150
Lesson 33—Unit Conversions   154
Lesson 34—Skipping Around   158
Lesson 35—Making a Table   161
Lesson 36—The Metric System   165
Lesson 37—It's All in a Name   170

Lesson 38—Converting in Metric 174
Lesson 39—Converting Between Common and Metric 178

Chapter 6: Measuring Area and Volume — 183
Lesson 40—Little Squares 184
Lesson 41—Area Unit Conversions 188
Lesson 42—Area in the Metric System 192
Lesson 43—Little Cubes 196
Lesson 44—Volume Unit Conversions 199
Lesson 45—Liquid Measures of Volume 203
Lesson 46—Volume in the Metric System 207

Chapter 7: Simple Algebraic Equations — 213
Lesson 47—Advanced Arithmetic 214
Lesson 48—What's it for Anyway? 218
Lesson 49—The Golden Rule of Algebra 222
Lesson 50—Undoing Multiplication and Division 227
Lesson 51—Changing Places 231
Lesson 52—New Symbols 234
Lesson 53—Undoing the Algebra Way 238
Lesson 54—Solving Percent Problems with Algebra 243
Lesson 55—Solving Distance Problems with Algebra 247

Chapter 8: Integers — 251
Lesson 56—Less Than Zero 252
Lesson 57—The Number Line 255
Lesson 58—How Negatives are Used 259
Lesson 59—Addition with Negatives 262
Lesson 60—Subtraction with Negatives 267
Lesson 61—Multiplication with Negatives 271
Lesson 62—Division with Negatives 275
Lesson 63—Undoing Equations with Negatives—Part 1 279
Lesson 64—Undoing Equations with Negatives—Part 2 284
Lesson 65—Negatives and Fractions 287
Lesson 66—Handling a -x 291
Lesson 67—Dealing with -x in a Fraction 295

Chapter 9: Longer Algebraic Equations — 299
Lesson 68—Order Matters 300
Lesson 69—Writing Equations in Order 305
Lesson 70—Order and the Fraction Bar 309
Lesson 71—Using the Fraction Bar in Equations 314
Lesson 72—Undoing in Reverse—Part 1 318
Lesson 73—Undoing in Reverse—Part 2 323
Lesson 74—Simplifying First 327
Lesson 75—More Simplifying First 331

Chapter 10: Combining Like Terms — 337
Lesson 76—Adding x's 338

Lesson 77—Subtracting x's   342
Lesson 78—x and 1x   346
Lesson 79—Work Problems   350
Lesson 80—Fancy Distance Problems   354
Lesson 81—x's on Both Sides   358
Lesson 82—Refrigerator Repairs   362

Chapter 11: Rational Expressions   367
Lesson 83—Reducing Fractions with x's   368
Lesson 84—Canceling x's   372
Lesson 85—Fractions and Parentheses—Part 1   376
Lesson 86—Fractions and Parentheses—Part 2   381
Lesson 87—Multiplying Fractions with x's   386
Lesson 88—Dividing Fractions with x's   391
Lesson 89—Adding Fractions with x's   396
Lesson 90—Subtracting Fractions with x's   402

Chapter 12: Powers, Polynomials, and Radicals   409
Lesson 91—Raising a Number to a Power   410
Lesson 92—Scientific Notation   415
Lesson 93—Order and Powers   420
Lesson 94—Adding and Subtracting Powers   424
Lesson 95—Multiplying Powers   428
Lesson 96—Multiplying Powers: Tougher Cases   433
Lesson 97—Dividing Powers   438
Lesson 98—Fractions with Powers   443
Lesson 99—Taking a Root   448
Lesson 100—Undoing Powers and Roots   452
Lesson 101—An Exponent of 1   457
Lesson 102—An Exponent of 0   462

Chapter 13: Geometry   467
Lesson 103—Points, Lines, and Planes   468
Lesson 104—Angles   475
Lesson 105—Pairs of Angles   483
Lesson 106—Line and Angle Relationships   491
Lesson 107—Triangles   496
Lesson 108—Pythagorean Theorem   504
Lesson 109—Quadrilaterals   511
Lesson 110—Polygons   518

Chapter 14: More on Geometry   525
Lesson 111—Congruent Figures   526
Lesson 112—Similar Figures   532
Lesson 113—Perimeter, Symmetry, and Reflections   539
Lesson 114—Area Calculations   547
Lesson 115—Circles   556
Lesson 116—Solids   566

Lesson 117—More on Volume and Surface Area 576

Chapter 15: Relations, Functions, and Graphing ——— 587
Lesson 118—Relations and Functions 588
Lesson 119—More on Functions 595
Lesson 120—Functional Notation 602
Lesson 121—The Coordinate Plane 607
Lesson 122—Graphing Equations 615
Lesson 123—More on Graphing 623
Lesson 124—The Slope of a Line 634
Lesson 125—Slope-Intercept Form 643
Lesson 126—Horizontal and Vertical Lines 653

Chapter 16: Statistics, Probability, and Inequalities ——— 661
Lesson 127—Measures of Central Tendency 662
Lesson 128—Range and Stem-and-Leaf Plots 669
Lesson 129—Histograms and Scatter Plots 675
Lesson 130—Probability 684
Lesson 131—Tree Diagrams 691
Lesson 132—Fundamental Counting Principle 698
Lesson 133—Inequalities 703
Lesson 134—Undoing Inequalities 709
Lesson 135—Undoing Inequalities in Reverse Order 717

Chapter 17: Additional Topics ——— 723
Lesson 136—Equations and the Distributive Property 724
Lesson 137—Absolute Value 730
Lesson 138—Distance Formula 736
Lesson 139—More on Formulas 744

Appendix ——— 751
Appendix A—Basic Math 752
Appendix B—Geometry 756
Appendix C—Algebra, Etc. 764

Index ——— 771

CHAPTER 1:
ARITHMETIC BASICS

Lesson 1—Number Beginnings

A long time ago, people counted with their fingers. For instance, to tell somebody that there were 5 sheep in the backyard, a person would just hold up 5 fingers. That was the simplest way to communicate numbers.

From Fingers to Words

Eventually, people began to use words instead of fingers to indicate a number. Rather than hold up a hand to communicate the number 5, they would just say "hand." In that way, the word for hand (in their language) came to mean 5. Other numbers were dealt with in the same way. For example, to communicate the number 11, instead of holding up a bunch of fingers, people just said "two hands and a finger." And so "two hands and a finger" came to mean 11. After awhile, a whole system of words for numbers grew up. And the system was based on the words for fingers and hands. This is how words for numbers were born. Actually, words for feet were also used since some people counted with their toes too. Even our modern languages show evidence of this history. For example in English, the word **digit** is used to mean a single number. (The number 25 has two digits: 2 and 5.) But digit comes from an old Latin word that means finger. So in English, the word for a single number is really Latin for finger!

Up to 10 and Start Over Again

Fingers also affected our numbers in a different way. Since people first counted with their fingers, it was natural to start their numbers over after they had gone through all the fingers on both hands. And that's the method we still use today. If that surprises you, think about it. When counting, we first go to 10, and then we start over with 11. That's because 11 really just means 10 and 1 left over. From 11, we go to 12, which means 10 and 2 left over and then on to 13, which means 10 and 3 ("thir" stands for three and "teen" for ten). Then once we get to 20, which means two 10s, we start over again. Twenty-one means two 10s and 1, twenty-two means two 10s and 2, and so on. Therefore, our numbers basically start over every time we get to 10. And the reason it works this way is that people used to always count with their fingers! In fact, if humans had 7 fingers instead of 10, we might count by starting over after every seventh number instead of after every tenth.

Written Numbers

As time progressed, people needed to do more with numbers than just talk about them. They needed to write numbers down in order to keep records for things like taxes. A lot of different kinds of written number symbols were developed around the world: Roman, Greek, Sumerian, and so on. In fact, Roman numbers (or "numerals") are still used occasionally today, mainly on clocks, buildings, and in book headings. Here are the major Roman numerals.

I	V	X	L	C	D	M
one	five	ten	fifty	one hundred	five hundred	one thousand

Roman Numerals

To show 1 using Roman numerals, we just write the symbol I. To show 2 we write II. Three is III. Since the symbol V is used as 5, the Roman system sort of starts over at 5, except that there's no new symbol after 10 until you get to 50, so it's a little confused. In the old days, the Romans would write 4 as IIII. But later on, people got into the habit of writing 4 as IV, which is shorter. With the I to the left of the V, you're supposed to subtract 1 from 5 to get 4. To show 6, they would write VI. Since the I is to the right of the V, this means to add 5 and 1 to get 6. Here are some other examples of Roman numerals.

VIII = 8	XI = 11	XV = 15
LXXV = 75	CCCXXII = 322	

Our Modern Numbers

The bad thing about Roman numerals is they're hard to calculate with. That's why Roman numerals aren't used much anymore. The number symbols we use today actually came all the way from India and were brought to Europe by Arabs. They're called **Hindu-Arabic numbers**. (Many Hindus live in India.) Hindu-Arabic numbers are so easy to calculate with that they're used by practically everybody—all over the world. Basically, Hindu-Arabic numbers drove all the other numbers out of existence.

What makes Hindu-Arabic or "modern" numbers easy to calculate with is that they use the **place value system**. The way it works is all numbers are written using only ten symbols (or digits) which you're already familiar with. Of course these symbols are 0, 1, 2, 3, 4, 5, 6, 7, 8, and 9. The value of each of these symbols depends on its "place" or position within the number. So the number four hundred thirty-two is written as 432.

And notice that the 2 represents ones, because it's on the far right, the 3 comes next and it represents tens. The 4 is last, and it represents hundreds. Since each symbol or digit has a different value depending on its place, writing numbers this way is called the place value system. Also, with this system we can write numbers as large as we want using only 0, 1, 2, 3, 4, 5, 6, 7, 8, and 9.[1] Compare that with Roman numerals. Using them, if we wanted to write a number very far above 1,000, we would need to use lots of different letters.

What happens when a number doesn't have any ones or tens or hundreds? Well, then we put a 0 in that position. For instance, the number seven hundred four has 7 hundreds and 4 ones, but no tens. And the number is written like this: 704. The 0 in the tens position shows that there are no tens.

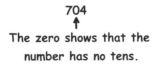

Imagine how confusing numbers would be without 0. If there were no digit to go in an empty place, we would just have to leave a blank spot. Then, the number seven hundred four would have to be written like this.

7   4
seven hundred four?

But it's really easy to confuse this with the number 74. So it's much better to have 0s to go in the empty places.

---

[1] As you know, when writing larger numbers, we put a comma after every third number starting from the right: 2,345,211,018.

Writing Numbers in Words

Sometimes it's necessary to write a number out in words. It turns out that there's a whole system of rules for doing this. Fortunately, they aren't too complicated. There are really only two things to remember. First, when we write a number in words, we should put the commas in the same places that they appear in the number. For example, if we wanted to write 45,238 in words, we'd write it like this.

Forty-five thousand, two hundred thirty-eight

Another way to think about this rule is just to remember that we should always put commas after the words "trillion," "billion," "million," and "thousand." One more thing. Did you notice that the "forty-five" had a dash between the forty and the five? The "thirty-eight" also had a dash. That's because we're supposed to use a dash on all numbers between 20 and 100 that have two words (fifty-six is another example).

Practice 1

a.
(1) Tell what number MCVIII represents.

b.
(1) Write five million, six hundred thirty thousand, two (using modern numbers).

c.
(1) Select the correct word phrase for the number 150,088,341.

    A. fifteen million, eight hundred eighty thousand, three hundred forty-one
    B. one fifty thousand, eighty-eight hundred, three hundred forty-one
    C. one hundred five million, eight hundred eight thousand, three forty-one
    D. one hundred fifty million, eighty-eight thousand, three hundred forty-one
    E. one million fifty, eighty-eight thousand, three hundred forty-one

d.
(1) Rearrange the digits in 2,548,796 so that the number is as large as possible.

e.
(1) Answer the question below.

A page in a book is numbered XI. What will the number on the next page be? Write your answer in Roman numbers.

Problem Set 1

Tell whether each sentence below is True or False.

1.
(1) Roman numbers are hard to calculate with.

2.
(1) With only ten symbols, Hindu-Arabic (modern) numbers can be used to represent any number, no matter how large.

Complete each sentence below with the best of the choices given.

3.
(1) A number system that starts over every 10 numbers became popular because _____.

    A. it was simpler than other systems mathematically
    B. humans have 10 fingers
    C. ancient astronomers believed there were 10 planets
    D. 10 was believed to be a divine number
    E. the ancient world was divided into 10 nations

4. Our modern numbers were invented in _____.
(1)

      A. America   B. Greece   C. India

      D. Rome   E. England

5. Under the _____, the value of a number symbol depends on its position.
(1)

      A. place value system   B. binary system   C. Greek alphabet

      D. latest scientific discoveries   E. Egyptian number system

6. If our modern number system did not have a symbol for _____, it would be easy to confuse one
(1) written number with another.

      A. plus   B. zero   C. minus

      D. three   E. equal

Tell what number each Roman numeral below represents.

7. XIII   **8.** DCLXXI   **(a) 9.** MCCLXII
(1)   (1)   (1)

Write the Roman numeral for each number below.

10. 73   **11.** 206   **12.** 3,721
(1)   (1)   (1)

Complete the following.

13. 7,891 = ____ thousands ____ hundreds ____ tens ____ ones
(1)

14. 4,862,357 = ____ millions ____ hundred thousands ____ ten thousands
(1)

                     ____ thousands ____ hundreds ____ tens ____ ones

Rewrite each number below with commas in the proper places.

15. 58162840   **16.** 8150276150938
(1)   (1)

Write each number below (using modern numbers).

17. twenty-seven thousand, six hundred thirty-two
(1)

(b) 18. fourteen million, three hundred eleven thousand, four
(1)

Select the correct word phrase for each number below.

19. 46,867
(1)

    A. forty thousand six hundred, eighty-six and seven
    B. forty-six thousand, eight hundred sixty-seven
    C. four million six thousand, eight hundred sixty-seven
    D. four hundred six thousand, eight sixty-seven
    E. forty-six hundred, eight sixty-seven

(c) 20. 520,075,998
(1)

    A. five hundred two million, seven hundred five thousand, nine ninety-eight
    B. five million twenty, seventy-five thousand, nine hundred ninety-eight
    C. five twenty thousand, seventy-five hundred, nine hundred ninety-eight
    D. fifty-two million, seven hundred fifty thousand, nine hundred ninety-eight
    E. five hundred twenty million, seventy-five thousand, nine hundred ninety-eight

Rearrange the digits in each number below so that it is as large as possible.

21. 204,913
(1)

(d) 22. 4,356,872
(1)

Answer the question below.

(e) 23. A page in a book is numbered XXII. What will the number on the next page be? Write your answer in
(1) Roman numbers.

Lesson 2—Adding and Subtracting Whole Numbers

Now that we've introduced modern numbers, let's go over the methods for calculating with them. We'll start with addition and subtraction. This is all review for you, so we'll go over it quickly.

You know that **whole numbers are just the numbers 0, 1, 2, 3, and on up**. When the numbers are larger, we add vertically. For instance, we add 5,243 and 1,605 like this.

$$\begin{array}{r} 5,243 \\ +1,605 \\ \hline \mathbf{6,848} \end{array}$$

Notice we put one number on top of the other and line up ones with ones, tens with tens, hundreds with hundreds, and thousands with thousands. Then we add each of the columns, starting with the ones column on the far right. The answer or sum turns out to be 6,848. The reason lining up the columns works so well is the place value system. All the digits in a column have the same value. You're always adding ones to ones, tens to tens, hundreds to hundreds, and so on. That makes addition really easy. Remember, the big advantage of modern (Hindu-Arabic) numbers is that they're easy to calculate with.

On some addition problems, we have to carry. You've done that for years. But just to refresh your memory, let's do a carrying example. Let's add 2,138,457 and 975,606. As always, we line up the numbers vertically, ones over ones, tens over tens, hundreds over hundreds, and on up.

$$\begin{array}{r} 2,138,457 \\ +975,606 \end{array}$$

Now we add the columns. Only, when a column adds to 10 or more, we have to put the ones digit below and carry the tens digit to the next column. That's how carrying works (as you know). After going through the entire process, the finished problem looks like this.

$$\begin{array}{r} \mathbf{1\,111\ 1} \\ 2,138,457 \\ +\ 975,606 \\ \hline \mathbf{3,114,063} \end{array}$$

All of our examples have had just two numbers added. But longer strings of whole numbers can be added in the same way—by adding vertically. Here's an addition problem with four numbers added.

$$\begin{array}{r} \mathbf{2\,2\,1} \\ 5,081 \\ 1,973 \\ 652 \\ +2,457 \\ \hline \mathbf{10,163} \end{array}$$

Subtraction

Those are the basics of addition of whole numbers. Now let's talk about subtraction. As you already know, subtraction works in basically the same way. We line up the numbers vertically with the larger number on top. Only we subtract the columns. Let's look at an example. We'll do 7,895 minus 4,671.

$$\begin{array}{r} 7,895 \\ -4,671 \\ \hline \mathbf{3,224} \end{array}$$

Notice ones are over ones, tens over tens, and so on. And then to complete the process, you start on the right with the ones and subtract each column. The answer or **difference—that's the technical name for the answer to a subtraction problem**—comes out to 3,224.

Some subtraction problems are a little more complicated, because a column will have a bigger number on top than on bottom. If that happens, you have to regroup or "borrow," as it's sometimes called. Basically, **regrouping is just moving a number from one column to another**. Here's a regrouping example.

$$8,291$$
$$-5,746$$

Notice in the ones column there's a 1 on top and a 6 on bottom. Since 1 is smaller than 6, we have to "borrow" from the 9 in the tens column and bring that ten over into the ones column. When that 10 is added to the 1 that's already there, we get 11 on top.

$$\begin{array}{r} \overset{8\ 11}{8,29\!\!\!/1} \\ -5,746 \end{array}$$

Now we can subtract in the ones column: $11-6=5$. From there, we can subtract in all of the other columns to get our final answer of 2,545.

$$\begin{array}{r} \overset{7}{}\overset{12\,8\ 11}{8,29\!\!\!/1} \\ -5,746 \\ \hline \mathbf{2,545} \end{array}$$

Notice that we had to regroup again in the third column. The reason is that the 2 on top was smaller than the 7 on bottom. So we borrowed 1 from the next column over (leaving just 7 in the top of the thousands column) and when moved over, the 1 became a 10 and was added to the 2.

Some Basic Rules

We should also go over a few basic rules. You learned these in earlier math courses, so this will just be a quick review. When you're adding two numbers, the order of the numbers doesn't matter. For instance, $3+8$ is the same as $8+3$. This rule is called the **commutative property of addition**. To show that it works for any two numbers, the commutative property is written like this.

$$a+b=b+a$$

The letters a and b stand for any two numbers. There's actually a technical name for numbers that are added. They're called **addends**. So a and b stand for addends. And you already know that the answer to an addition problem is called the **sum**. That means another way of stating the commutative property of addition is to say that the order of the addends doesn't affect the sum.

There's another addition rule called the **associative property of addition**. This says basically that three numbers can be added in any order. For instance, what if we had the problem $4+8+7$? We could add 4 and 8 first and then add 7 to that total. Or we could add 8 and 7 first and then add 4 to that.

$4+8+7$	$4+8+7$
$12+7$	$4+15$
19	19

Notice that we get the same answer, 19, each way. So that's an example of the associative property of addition.

What about basic rules for subtraction? Well, there's not a commutative property of subtraction. For example, 9 – 2 is not the same as 2 – 9.

$$9 - 2 \neq 2 - 9$$

That's one big difference between addition and subtraction. There's also no associative property of subtraction.

Practice 2

a.
(1)
Write twelve billion, three hundred forty-two million, sixty-five using modern numbers.

b.
(2)
Write a number that is 700,000 less than 5,849,812.

c.
(2)
Add
$$\begin{array}{r} 6,568 \\ 345 \\ +4,029 \\ \hline \end{array}$$

d. Subtract
(2)
$$\begin{array}{r} 841 \\ -352 \\ \hline \end{array}$$

e.
(2)
Translate the word problem below into math; then solve.

John owns 432 finger puppets. If he gives away 257 of these to his friend Billy, how many will he have left?

Problem Set 2

Tell whether each sentence below is True or False.

1.
(2)
The commutative property of addition says that the order in which any two numbers are added can be changed without changing the sum (answer).

2.
(2)
In some subtraction problems, a column might have a bigger number on bottom than on top.

Complete the following.

3.
(1)
28,765 = ____ ten thousands ____ thousands ____ hundreds ____ tens

____ ones

4.
(1)
45,893,239 = ____ ten millions ____ millions ____ hundred thousands

____ ten thousands ____ thousands ____ hundreds ____ tens ____ ones

13

Write each number below (using modern numbers).

5.
(1)
two million, six thousand

(a) 6.
(1)
fourteen billion, eight hundred sixty-one million, forty-seven

Select the correct word phrase for each number below.

7.
(1)
3,578,213

       A. three thousand, five hundred seventy-eight, two hundred thirty
       B. three million, fifty-seven thousand, eight hundred twenty-three
       C. three million, five hundred seventy-eight thousand, two hundred thirteen
       D. three hundred million, five hundred seventy-eight thousand, twenty-three
       E. thirty-five million, seventy-eight thousand, two hundred thirteen

8.
(1)
286,170,094

       A. two million eighty-six, one hundred seventy thousand, nine hundred four
       B. two hundred eighty-six million, one hundred seventy thousand, ninety-four
       C. two hundred eighty-six thousand, one hundred seventy, ninety-four
       D. two thousand eighty-six million, one hundred seven thousand, ninety-four
       E. two eighty-six million, one hundred seven thousand, nine hundred and four

Rearrange the digits in each number below so that it is as small as possible.

9.   3,278
(1)

10.   8,231,457
(1)

Answer each question below.

11.
(2)
Write a number that is 90,000 greater than 8,304,088.

12.
(2)
Write a number that is 500,000 greater than 8,304,088.

(b) 13.
(2)
Write a number that is 400,000 less than 1,585,302.

Add each group of numbers below.

14.   427   **15.**   3,999   **16.**   54,087
(2)   +362   (2)   +3,824   (2)   +81,890

17.   895   **(c) 18.**   9,541
(2)   17   (2)   239
       +725   +1,083

Subtract each group of numbers below.

19.
(2)
$$\begin{array}{r} 85 \\ -15 \\ \hline \end{array}$$

20.
(2)
$$\begin{array}{r} 485 \\ -352 \\ \hline \end{array}$$

21.
(2)
$$\begin{array}{r} 83 \\ -54 \\ \hline \end{array}$$

22.
(2)
$$\begin{array}{r} 954 \\ -65 \\ \hline \end{array}$$

(d) 23.
(2)
$$\begin{array}{r} 623 \\ -234 \\ \hline \end{array}$$

Translate the word problem below into math; then solve.

(e) 24. The first version of the garbage sculpture weighed 2,653 pounds, but then El Magnifico, the great
(2)   artist/composer, decided to eliminate another 385 pounds (this time for good). How much does the
sculpture weigh now?

15

Lesson 3—Multiplying Whole Numbers

You probably learned in previous math courses that **multiplication** is really just a short way to write the same number added to itself over and over—a repeated addition, in other words. For instance, 4×6 just means four 6s added or 6+6+6+6.

4×6 is the same as 6+6+6+6.

The only reason people would write a problem as a multiplication rather than a repeated addition is that multiplication is shorter. For example if you needed to show the sum of seven 2s, it would certainly be shorter and faster to write 7×2 instead of seven 2s added together.

7×2 is shorter and faster to write than 2+2+2+2+2+2+2.

Since multiplication is used so often, people are required to memorize the basic multiplication facts, which are just multiplication answers for small numbers. Those facts are usually presented in a **multiplication table**. And, hopefully, you've already memorized the entire table. The nice thing about memorizing your multiplication facts, though, is that it allows you to do small multiplications in your head.

Multiplication with Zeros

It's actually possible to use the multiplication facts to multiply larger numbers in your head, as long as the numbers end in 0s. Take 9,000×70 as an example. To multiply these in your head, you first multiply 9 and 7 to get 63. Next, you count the number of zeros in both numbers. Since 9,000 has three 0s and 70 has one 0, that's a total of four 0s. The last step is to put four 0s after 63 to get 630,000. So 9,000×70 = 630,000.

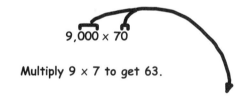

Multiply 9 × 7 to get 63.

Then put all four 0s on the end to get 630,000.

Here's another example where the numbers are even larger: 80,000×4,000. Since these numbers also end with 0s, we can multiply these in our heads as well. First, we multiply 8 times 4, which is 32. Next, we count the 0s. There are four 0s in 80,000 and three 0s in 4,000. That's a total of seven 0s. Finally, we put those seven 0s after 32, which gives us 320,000,000. So 80,000×4,000 = 320,000,000.

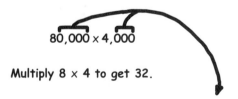

Multiply 8 × 4 to get 32.

Then put all seven 0s on the end to get 320,000,000.

Long Multiplication

Unfortunately, most big numbers don't end with 0s, which means we can't multiply them in our head. An example would be the problem 765×3. In a case like this, we have to multiply on paper using long multiplication. You've done plenty of long multiplication problems, but let's go through the steps just to refresh your memory. The first step is to line the numbers up vertically. In other words, we put one number on top of the other. And the number with more digits (765) should be on top.

$$
\begin{array}{r}
765 \\
\times\ 3 \\
\hline
\end{array}
$$

Notice that the 3 is lined up underneath the 5. That's because—as you know—the digits should always be lined up, ones should be lined up with ones, tens with tens, and so on. Now that the numbers are on top of each other and in the proper position, all we have to do is multiply the digit on bottom by each of the digits on top. Going through that process gives us this.

$$
\begin{array}{r}
1\ 1 \\
765 \\
\times\ 3 \\
\hline
2{,}295 \\
\end{array}
$$

Notice that we had to carry. Anytime multiplying a column gives an answer that's 10 or greater, the ones digit goes below and the tens digit gets "carried" over to the next column.

In some long multiplication problems, we have to multiply by a two-digit number. Let's go through an example like that. Here's 1,856 times 64.

$$
\begin{array}{r}
1{,}856 \\
\times\ 64 \\
\hline
\end{array}
$$

The numbers are already on top of each other. Ones are lined up with ones, and tens with tens, so we're ready to multiply. We just multiply each of the digits on top by each of the digits on bottom. Only since we're multiplying by a two-digit number, there are a few complications. We have to put the results of multiplying each digit in its own row below. In other words, when multiplying everything on top by 4, the results should be in the first row below. And when multiplying each of the digits on top by 6, those results should be in a separate row below that. Here's what it looks like.

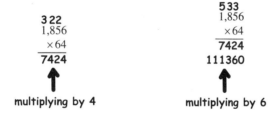

$\begin{array}{r} 3\ 2\ 2 \\ 1{,}856 \\ \times\ 64 \\ \hline 7424 \end{array}$	$\begin{array}{r} 5\ 3\ 3 \\ 1{,}856 \\ \times\ 64 \\ \hline 7424 \\ 111360 \end{array}$
↑	↑
multiplying by 4	multiplying by 6

Notice also that we put a 0 in the ones place in the second row. That's because you're supposed to skip that place and move over 1. So when we multiply 6 times 6 to get 36, we put the 6 in the *tens* place (in the second row) and carry the 3. The reason for skipping over the ones place is that we're really multiplying the top number by 60 (not 6). Remember, the 6 in 64 is in the tens place, so it represents 60. The last step of the whole process is to add the two rows. The final answer comes out to 118,784.

$$
\begin{array}{r}
1{,}856 \\
\times\ 64 \\
\hline
7424 \\
111360 \\
\hline
118784 \\
\end{array}
$$

We could follow the same basic approach to multiply by a three-digit number. For instance, to multiply 3,412 and 143, we line the numbers up vertically and then multiply each of the digits on top by each of the digits on bottom.

multiplying by 3	multiplying by 4	multiplying by 1	adding the three rows
1 3,412 ×143 ‾‾‾‾‾ 10236	1 3,412 ×143 ‾‾‾‾‾ 10236 136480	3,412 ×143 ‾‾‾‾‾ 10236 136480 341200	3,412 ×143 ‾‾‾‾‾ 10236 136480 341200 ‾‾‾‾‾ 487916

However, since 143 has three digits, notice there are three rows below instead of two. The first row has the results of multiplying each of the digits on top by 3. The second row has the results of multiplying each of the digits on top by 4. Then, the third row has the results of multiplying each of the digits by 1. In the bottom row, instead of skipping over 1 place (and putting a 0 in the empty spot), we skip over two places (and put a 0 in each). Of course, the last step is to add the three rows to get the final answer of 487,916. That's how you multiply by a three-digit number. Multiplying by numbers with 4 digits, 5 digits or even more works the same way. There are just more rows and you have to skip over more places before starting to multiply.

Basic Rules

In the last lesson, we learned about the basic rules for addition: the commutative and associative properties. It turns out that there are also basic rules for multiplication. There's a **commutative property of multiplication**, which says that you can multiply two numbers in any order. This is the rule which tells you that 6×8 is the same as 8×6. Here it is written to show that the rule applies to any two numbers.

$$a\times b = b\times a$$

There's also an **associative property of multiplication**, which says that three numbers can be multiplied in any order. For example, in the problem $2\times4\times9$, we can multiply 2 and 4 first and then multiply that result by 9. Or we can choose a different order; we can multiply 4 and 9 first and multiply that result by 2. Either way we get the same answer.

$2\times4\times9$	$2\times4\times9$
8×9	2×36
72	72

Another simple multiplication rule is that any number times 1 equals the number itself. This is the rule which tells us that $385\times1 = 385$. And another rule is that any number times 0 equals 0. That's how we know that $43\times0 = 0$. Here are these two rules written in a way that shows they work for any number.

$$a\times1 = a \qquad\qquad a\times0 = 0$$

There are also a couple of technical terms used a lot with multiplication. Numbers that are multiplied are called **factors**. So in the problem $8\times9 = 72$, the numbers 8 and 9 are factors. The answer to a multiplication problem is called the **product**, which means 72 is the product of that problem.

Practice 3

a.
(1)   Select the correct word phrase for the number 200,005,885.

      A.   two hundred million, fifty thousand, eighty hundred eight fifteen
      B.   two hundred million, five thousand, eight hundred eighty-five
      C.   twenty million, five hundred thousand, eight hundred eighty-five
      D.   two million, five thousand, eight hundred eighty-five
      E.   two hundred million, five hundred thousand, eight hundred eighteen-five

b.
(3)   Write a multiplication problem to represent 6 groups of 2.

c. Multiply $\begin{array}{r} 8,421 \\ \times\ \ 6 \\ \hline \end{array}$
(3)

d. Multiply $\begin{array}{r} 545 \\ \times 35 \\ \hline \end{array}$
(3)

e.
(3)   Translate the word problem below into math; then solve.

The director has sat through 27 auditions a day for each of the last 3 days. How many auditions is this altogether?

Problem Set 3

Tell whether each sentence below is True or False.

1.
(3)   Multiplication is really just a shortcut for repeated subtraction.

2.
(3)   When multiplying numbers, the order doesn't affect the answer.

Fill in the blanks to tell what each number below stands for.

3.
(1)   4,510 = ____ thousands ____ hundreds ____ tens ____ ones

4.
(1)   6,200,700 =   ____ millions ____ hundred thousands ____ ten thousands

                ____ thousands ____ hundreds ____ tens ____ ones

Add each group of numbers below.

5. $\begin{array}{r} 347 \\ +853 \\ \hline \end{array}$
(2)

6. $\begin{array}{r} 5,045 \\ +4,994 \\ \hline \end{array}$
(2)

7. $\begin{array}{r} 48,786 \\ 123 \\ +5,348 \\ \hline \end{array}$
(2)

Subtract each group of numbers below.

8. $\begin{array}{r} 75,595 \\ -310 \\ \hline \end{array}$
(2)

9. $\begin{array}{r} 844 \\ -696 \\ \hline \end{array}$
(2)

Select the correct word phrase for each number below.

10. 43,799
(1)

    A. forty-three million, seven thousand ninety-nine
    B. four million three thousand, seven hundred ninety-nine
    C. four hundred three thousand, seventy-nine nine
    D. forty-three thousand, seven hundred ninety-nine
    E. fourteen thousand three hundred, seven ninety-nine

(a) 11. 600,003,119
(1)

    A. sixty million, three hundred thousand, one hundred nineteen
    B. six hundred million, three thousand, one hundred nineteen
    C. six million, three thousand, one hundred nineteen
    D. six hundred million, thirty thousand, eleven hundred nineteen
    E. six hundred million, three thousand, one hundred ninety

Answer each question below.

12. Write $5 + 5 + 5 + 5$ as a multiplication.
(3)

13. Write $3 + 3 + 3 + 3 + 3 + 3 + 3$ as a multiplication.
(3)

(b) 14. Write a multiplication problem to represent 14 groups of 3.
(3)

Multiply each pair of numbers below in your head.

15. 5×9 **16.** 42×10 **17.** 400×500
(3)   (3)   (3)

18. 300×20 **19.** $3,000 \times 100$
(3)   (3)

Multiply each pair of numbers below.

20. $\begin{array}{r} 43 \\ \times\, 2 \\ \hline \end{array}$ **21.** $\begin{array}{r} 572 \\ \times\, 6 \\ \hline \end{array}$ **(c) 22.** $\begin{array}{r} 9,563 \\ \times\quad 2 \\ \hline \end{array}$
(3)   (3)   (3)

23. $\begin{array}{r} 76 \\ \times 32 \\ \hline \end{array}$ **(d) 24.** $\begin{array}{r} 395 \\ \times 65 \\ \hline \end{array}$
(3)   (3)

Translate the word problem below into math; then solve.

(e) 25. Joey can make 21 free throws in a single minute. How many free throws can he make in 5 minutes?
(3)

Lesson 4—Dividing Whole Numbers

In the last lesson, we reviewed some of the basics of multiplication with whole numbers. Now let's turn to division with whole numbers. **Division** is basically the reverse of multiplication. When multiplying, you're adding the same number over and over. But when dividing, you're taking a total and breaking it down into smaller equal groups.

Just as you memorize the facts in the multiplication table, you should also memorize the basic division facts. These are just problems involving division with smaller numbers, such as $18 \div 3 = 6$ and $24 \div 6 = 4$. The nice thing about the division facts, though, is that if you forget them you can use your knowledge of the multiplication facts to come up with the answer. For example, what if you forgot the answer to $56 \div 7$? If you can remember from the multiplication table that $7 \times 8 = 56$, then you know automatically that $56 \div 7$ must equal 8.

You can even divide some larger whole numbers in your head using the division facts—as long as the larger numbers end with zeros. The process is a lot like multiplication of larger numbers that end with zeros. Only instead of adding the zeros, you subtract them. Here's an example.

$$8,000 \div 20$$

To divide these, we first do $8 \div 2$ to get 4. Then notice that 8,000 has three 0s and 20 has one 0. Then, three 0s minus one 0 equals two 0s. So we take those two 0s and put them after 4 to get 400.

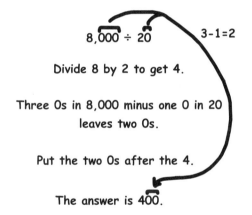

$8,000 \div 20$ 3-1=2

Divide 8 by 2 to get 4.

Three 0s in 8,000 minus one 0 in 20 leaves two 0s.

Put the two 0s after the 4.

The answer is 400.

Of course, not all division problems with larger numbers can be done in your head. The really tough ones have to be done on paper using long division. (Assuming you're not allowed to use a calculator!) Even though you've done long division for years, let's go through an example: $11,297 \div 3$. First, we need to put 11,297 inside a division box and 3 goes outside.

$$3\overline{)11,297}$$

In a division problem, the number being divided is called the **dividend** and the number you're dividing by is called the **divisor**. So 11,297 is the dividend and 3 is the divisor in this problem. The first step is to try to divide 3 into the first 1 on the left. But since 1 is too small we have to divide 3 into 11. That goes 3 times, so we put a 3 on top. Then we multiply, subtract, and bring down the next digit. We keep going through the process—divide, multiply, subtract, and bring down—until there are no more digits left. Here's the entire problem worked out.

```
        3765
   3)11,297
   - 9
     22
    -21
     19
    - 18
      17
     -15
       2
```

The final answer is 3,765 with a remainder of 2. That means 11,297 can be broken down into 3,765 groups of 3, with 2 left over. The answer to a division problem is also called the **quotient**, by the way. So 3,765 R2 is the quotient of 11,297 divided by 3.

Let's do one more long division example. In this one, we'll divide by a two-digit number.

$$14\overline{)3,851}$$

We can't divide 14 into 3, but we can divide it into 38. From there we multiply, subtract, and bring down the next digit. Then we start over again. That process is repeated until there are no digits left to bring down. Here's the finished problem.

```
        275
   14)3,851
    -28
     105
    - 98
      71
     - 70
        1
```

You can see the quotient is 275 with a remainder of 1. Of course, we could use long division to divide by a three-digit (or even higher) divisor by following the same basic process: divide, multiply, subtract, and bring down.

Basic Rules

As with the other operations, there are a few basic rules of division. And we should quickly review those. The first rule is that any number divided by 1 equals the number itself. For example, $94 \div 1 = 94$. The second rule is that 0 divided by any number equals 0. An example of this rule is that $0 \div 18 = 0$. Or we could write it as a fraction: $\frac{0}{18} = 0$. The last rule is that dividing *by* 0 is not allowed. For instance, a problem like $21 \div 0$ doesn't have an answer. We just say that the answer is undefined. Here are these rules written to show that they're true for any number.

$$a \div 1 = a \qquad\qquad 0 \div a = 0 \qquad\qquad a \div 0 = \text{undefined}$$

Just remember that when writing division using a fraction bar, you can't have 0 in the bottom of the fraction. You can have 0 in the top of the fraction, because that's dividing 0 by something else. In that case, the problem does have an answer (0). But if 0 is in the bottom, there is no answer.

$$\frac{0}{21} = 0 \qquad\qquad \frac{21}{0} = \text{undefined}$$

Practice 4

a.
(3)   Multiply $\begin{array}{r} 732 \\ \times\,201 \\ \hline \end{array}$

b.
(4)   Divide $3,600,000 \div 4,000$

c.
(4)   Divide $16\overline{)6,256}$. Write any remainder next to your answer.

d.
(4)   Divide $19\overline{)8,592}$. Write any remainder next to your answer.

e.
(4)   Translate the word problem below into math; then solve.

In a rare kind-hearted moment, the ruthless queen decided to give away 234 of her silk shawls—all the ones with out-of-date colors or not enough purple—to 3 people: her breakfast carrier, her head flower arranger, and her chief pillow fluffer. Assuming each person received the same number of shawls, how many did each get?

Problem Set 4

Tell whether each sentence below is True or False.

1.
(4)   Any number divided by 0 is equal to 0.

2.
(4)   It is possible to divide large numbers that end with zeros, using only a knowledge of the division table.

Write each number below (using modern numbers)

3.
(1)   eighteen thousand, four hundred twenty

4.
(1)   forty million, twenty-five thousand, eleven

Answer each question below.

5.
(2)   Write a number that is 10,000 less than 312,019.

6.
(3)   Write a multiplication problem to represent 100 groups of 17.

7.
(4)   Write a division problem to represent 72 marbles divided into so many groups of 9.

8.
(4)   When dividing 80 by 9, what is the remainder?

Add or subtract each group of numbers below.

9.
(2)
$$\begin{array}{r} 57 \\ 97 \\ +55 \\ \hline \end{array}$$

10.
(2)
$$\begin{array}{r} 3,685 \\ 4,997 \\ +4,085 \\ \hline \end{array}$$

11.
(2)
$$\begin{array}{r} 7,802 \\ -988 \\ \hline \end{array}$$

12.
(2)
$$\begin{array}{r} 59,146 \\ -43,899 \\ \hline \end{array}$$

Multiply each pair of numbers below.

13.
(3)
$$\begin{array}{r} 219 \\ \times 5 \\ \hline \end{array}$$

14.
(3)
$$\begin{array}{r} 25 \\ \times 78 \\ \hline \end{array}$$

15.
(3)
$$\begin{array}{r} 807 \\ \times 62 \\ \hline \end{array}$$

(a) 16.
(3)
$$\begin{array}{r} 925 \\ \times 304 \\ \hline \end{array}$$

Divide each pair of numbers below in your head.

17. $2,700 \div 90$
(4)

18. $15,000 \div 300$
(4)

(b) 19. $4,200,000 \div 6,000$
(4)

Divide each pair of numbers below. Write any remainders next to your answer.

20. $7\overline{)917}$
(4)

21. $4\overline{)2,720}$
(4)

22. $3\overline{)2,384}$
(4)

(c) 23. $25\overline{)7,950}$
(4)

(d) 24. $22\overline{)9,750}$
(4)

Translate the word problem below into math; then solve.

(e) 25. On last week's episode of Designer Closets, the contractor created 4 identical "sweater spaces" for a
(4)   total cost of $580. How much did it cost to create each sweater space?

Lesson 5—Divisibility

We've been learning about division. And so far our goal has always been to find the answer to every one of our problems. But sometimes, we don't need to know the actual answer to a division problem. We just need to know whether one number can be divided by another number evenly—whether it's **divisible** by the other number. That just means whether it can be divided with a remainder of 0. For instance, 12 can be divided evenly by 3 because we get an answer of 4 with a remainder of 0. So we say that 12 is divisible by 3. There are a lot of situations where you might just want to know whether a number can be divided evenly by another. Here's a not-so-realistic example.

The ruthless queen's younger sister, Madame Pompadour, is so crazy about poodles that she treats them as if they were real people. For example, next week she's holding a tea party for her poodle and his five best friends. At the party, Madame P. is planning to serve a tray of doggie biscuits, but she wants to make sure that each poodle receives the same number. If she serves 80 biscuits in total, can each of the poodles be given an equal amount or will one of them (sadly) get shortchanged?

In this problem, Madame Pompadour doesn't really care how many biscuits each poodle is going to get. She just wants to make sure that they all get the same number. That means she needs to know whether 80 can be divided evenly by 6. (The poodle plus its 5 friends makes 6.) If there's no remainder, then every poodle has to get the same number of doggie biscuits. If there is a remainder, then some poodles will get more doggie biscuits than others. You might think that the only way to figure this out is to go through the entire division problem of $80 \div 6$. But actually we don't have to work out the whole problem. There are rules that will tell us very quickly whether one number can be divided evenly by another. These are called the **divisibility rules**.

The number 80 is small enough that the divisibility rules wouldn't be that much of a time saver. It just takes a few seconds, after all, to figure out that $80 \div 6$ gives you 13 plus a remainder of 2. (So some poodle is going to get shortchanged.) But what if the problem were $85,254 \div 6$? Then it would take a long time to do the division. That's where the divisibility rules are really helpful.

Divisibility Rules for 2, 5, and 10

We'll go through all of the major divisibility rules, starting with the simplest. One rule that almost everybody knows about is the divisibility rule for 2. To see how that one works, look at the list of numbers below.

Even numbers can all be divided evenly by 2.

0, 2, 4, 6, 8, 10, 12, 14, 16, 18, 20, 22, 24, 26, 28, 30, 32….

Every one of these numbers can be divided evenly by 2. Can you see the pattern in the numbers? The last digit on the right is always 0, 2, 4, 6, or 8. As you probably know, numbers ending in 0, 2, 4, 6, or 8 are called **even numbers**. And the rule is that every even number can be divided evenly by 2. All other numbers are called **odd numbers**, by the way, and they can't be divided evenly by 2. So, for example, the number 324 ends with the digit 4. That makes it an even number, which tells us immediately that 324 can be divided evenly by 2. However, the number 1,407 ends in 7, so it has to be odd. From that, we know it won't divide evenly by 2. Sometimes people will say that 1,407 is not "divisible" by 2. It means the same thing.

What about dividing evenly by 5? That rule is easy too. Look at this list.

Numbers ending in 0 or 5 can all be divided evenly by 5.

0, 5, 10, 15, 20, 25, 30, 35, 40, 45, 50, 55….

Every one of these numbers can be divided evenly by 5. And if you look closely, you'll see that they all end in either 5 or 0. The general rule is that no matter how big or small a number is, as long as it ends in 5 or 0, the number can be divided evenly by 5. And, once again, divisibility rules are most helpful when working with really big numbers. What if we had a number like 237,815? Does that divide evenly by 5? Yes it does, because the last digit (the number in the ones place) is 5.

The rule for divisibility by 10 is even easier than the one for 5. You've known this rule for years. Any number that can be divided evenly by 10 has to end in 0. Here are some examples.

Numbers ending in 0 can all be divided evenly by 10.

0, 10, 20, 30, 40, 50, 60, 70, 80, 90, 100, 110, 120 ….

The pattern continues all the way up. As long as the last (ones) digit is 0, then it has to work.[1]

Divisibility Rules for 4 and 8

The rules for 2, 5, and 10 are simple, because we only have to look at the last digit. The rule for dividing by 4 is a little tougher. To tell whether a number can be divided by 4 evenly, we have to look at the last *two* digits. If those two digits are divisible by 4, then so is the entire number. An example is 7,324. Focus on the last two digits of 7,324, which are 24. Since the number 24 divides evenly by 4 (to get 6 and no remainder), we know that the entire number 7,324 must be divisible by 4 as well. If you do the calculation, you'll see that $7,324 \div 4$ equals 1,831 with no remainder. Here's the divisibility rule for 4.

For a number to be divisible by 4, the last two digits must divide evenly by 4.

---

[1] Notice that every list starts with 0. That's because 0 can be divided evenly by *any* number. Remember, 0 divided by any number always equals 0.

What about dividing by 8? There we have to look at the last *three* digits. If they can be divided by 8 evenly, then so can the entire number. For example, 10,888 can be divided evenly by 8 because 888 divided by 8 equals 111 (with no remainder). If you go through the long division, $10,888 \div 8$ actually comes out to 1,361 with no remainder.

**For a number to be divisible by 8,
the last three digits must divide evenly by 8.**

Divisibility Rules for 3, 9, and 6

For some divisibility rules, we have to look at all of the digits. Take dividing by 3, for instance. To figure out whether a number can be divided evenly by 3, we have to add up all the digits of the number. If that sum can be divided evenly by 3, then so can the entire number. Let's figure out whether 414 can be divided by 3. The first step is to add the digits: $4+1+4=9$. Next, we take that sum, which is 9, and divide it by 3. Since 9 divided by 3 equals 3, with no remainder, we know automatically that 414 divides evenly by 3 too. It turns out that $414 \div 3$ equals 138 with no remainder. Here is the divisibility rule for 3.

**For a number to be divisible by 3,
the sum of the number's digits must divide evenly by 3.**

Let's do one more example to see if a number is divisible by 3. This time we'll use the large number 7,234,209. It would take quite awhile to divide this by 3 using long division. But with our divisibility rule, we just add up the digits: $7+2+3+4+2+0+9=27$. Then, since 27 divides evenly by 3 (for an answer of 9, with no remainder), we know that 7,234,209 must divide evenly by 3 as well. In fact, when you do the division, $7,234,209 \div 3$ comes out to 2,411,403 with no remainder.

7,234,209 divides evenly by 3, since
$7+2+3+4+2+0+9=27$
and 27 divides evenly by 3.

What about dividing evenly by 9? This rule works just like the divisibility rule for 3. We just add up all the digits and see whether the sum can be divided by 9. If it can, then so can the entire number. To go through an example, we'll use a big number again: 9,273,618. Adding all of the digits gives us $9+2+7+3+6+1+8$ which equals 36. And since 36 divides evenly by 9 (for an answer of 4 with no remainder), we know that 9,273,618 must divide evenly by 9 as well.

9,273,618 divides evenly by 9, since
$9+2+7+3+6+1+8=36$
and 36 divides evenly by 9.

It turns out that 9,273,618 divided by 9 equals 1,030,402 with no remainder. Here is the divisibility rule for 9.

**For a number to be divisible by 9,
the sum of the number's digits must divide evenly by 9.**

The divisibility rule for 9 even comes up in the multiplication table. Some people learn their 9s by memorizing that any number in the table times 9 has to equal a number whose digits add up to 9.[2] For instance, $9 \times 2 = 18$ and $1+8$ equals 9, $9 \times 3 = 27$ and $2+7$ equals 9, $9 \times 4 = 36$ and $3+6$ equals 9, etc. That's consistent with our rule, because 9 can obviously be divided evenly by itself.

_____

[2] This rule works up through 9×10.

27

There is also a rule for dividing by 6. This one is pretty complicated. The easiest way to explain it is to go through an actual example first. We'll use the number 1,356. First, we need to add up all the digits: $1+3+5+6=15$. Now we see if that sum, 15, can be divided evenly by 3 (not 6). Since $15 \div 3$ 15 equals 5 with no remainder, that works. But we're not done yet. The next step is to see if 1,356 is an even number. Since the last digit of 1,356 is 6, it is even. That means 1,356 is divisible by 6. You can also check this one for yourself. ($1,356 \div 6 = 226$ with no remainder)

1,356 divides evenly by 6, since
it's even and $1 + 3 + 5 + 6 = 15$
and 15 divides evenly by 3.

The interesting thing about this rule is that if the number had been odd, no matter what the sum of the digits turned out to be, then it would not have been divisible by 6. So the number has to be even and the sum of the digits has to divide evenly by 3, not 6. It's a tricky rule. Here's the complete rule for dividing evenly by 6.

For a number to be divisible by 6,
the number must be even and
the sum of the number's digits must
equal a number that's divisible by 3.

What about figuring out whether a number can divide evenly by 7? Well, there's really not a good rule for 7. There aren't any good rules for numbers greater than 10 either, because they're a lot more complicated. So the rules that we've covered are the main ones that you need to remember.

Practice 5

a.
(5) Use the divisibility rules to tell whether 262 can be divided evenly by 2.

b.
(5) Use the divisibility rules to tell whether 184,824 can be divided evenly by 9.

c.
(3) Multiply $\begin{array}{r} 6,057 \\ \times\ 2,840 \\ \hline \end{array}$

d.
(4) Divide $16\overline{)5,235}$. Write any remainders next to your answer.

e.
(3) Translate the word problem below into math; then solve.

Claude Ebair, the legendary French fashion designer, expects his rattlesnake high-tops to be a huge hit, so last week he shipped out 70 crates of them. If each crate contained 200 pairs, how many pairs did Monsieur Ebair ship in all?

Problem Set 5

Tell whether each sentence below is True or False.

1.
(5) Any number that ends in 0, 2, 4, 6, or 8 is called an even number and can be divided evenly by 2.

2.
(5)
A number can be divided evenly by 3 if the sum of its digits can be divided evenly by 3.

3.
(5)
A number can be divided evenly by 9 if the sum of its digits can be divided evenly by 9.

Select the correct word phrase for each number below.

4. 99,875
(1)

    A. ninety-nine hundred, eighty-seven five
    B. nine thousand nine, eight hundred seventy five
    C. nine thousand nine, eighty-seven hundred five
    D. ninety-nine thousand, eight hundred seventy-five
    E. nine million nine thousand, eight hundred seventy-five

5. 560,001
(1)

    A. five hundred six thousand, one hundred
    B. five hundred sixty thousand, one
    C. five thousand six hundred, ten
    D. fifty-six thousand, one
    E. five hundred six thousand, one

Do each calculation below in your head.

6. Multiply $100,000 \times 237,000$
(3)

7. Divide $238,000,000 \div 100,000$
(4)

Use the divisibility rules to answer each question below.

(a) 8. Tell whether 382 can be divided evenly by 2.
(5)

(b) 9. Tell whether 198,936 can be divided evenly by 9.
(5)

10. Tell whether 2,000,005 can be divided evenly by 10.
(5)

Add or subtract each group of numbers below.

11.
(2)

$$\begin{array}{r} 8,000 \\ 3,768 \\ 4,469 \\ +903 \\ \hline \end{array}$$

12.
(2)

$$\begin{array}{r} 5,269 \\ 874 \\ 7,210 \\ +7,025 \\ \hline \end{array}$$

13.
(2)

$$\begin{array}{r} 636 \\ -257 \\ \hline \end{array}$$

14.
(2)

$$\begin{array}{r} 47,368 \\ -14,379 \\ \hline \end{array}$$

Multiply each pair of numbers below.

15.
(3)
$$9,739 \times 4$$

16.
(3)
$$1,021 \times 900$$

(c) **17.**
(3)
$$8,093 \times 4,570$$

Divide each pair of numbers below. Write any remainders next to your answer.

18.
(4)
$8\overline{)275}$

19.
(4)
$6\overline{)2,334}$

20.
(4)
$8\overline{)3,771}$

21.
(4)
$25\overline{)8,075}$

(d) **22.**
(4)
$19\overline{)7,306}$

Translate the word problem below into math; then solve.

(e) **23.**
(3)
Madame Pompadour recently ordered her servants to dig 30 tunnels underneath her winter hideaway (all so her pet poodle could avoid the frigid weather while stretching his little legs). If each tunnel took 400 hours to create, how many hours did it take to complete the entire project?

CHAPTER 2:
RATIONAL NUMBERS

Lesson 6— Fractions

So far in this book, we've been learning about whole numbers. And whole numbers work really well when we need to count things. For example, to count the number of people at a party, we just need whole numbers like 1, 2, 3, 4, and on up. There might be 18 people at the party or 19 people, but there can't be between 18 and 19 people. A half person doesn't make any sense. That's why whole numbers work fine for counting.

One Becomes Two Halves

But sometimes instead of counting, we need to measure. The problem is that whole numbers don't work very well for measurement. For example, what if Farmer Brown needed to measure the length of one of his fields? Would it be possible for his field to be between 172 and 173 yards? Sure. But if that were the length, then whole numbers wouldn't work. We would need a new kind of number that was between 172 and 173. The way it's done is to "break up" the whole numbers into pieces.

These broken numbers are called **fractions**, of course. You've been learning about fractions for years.[1] But let's go through a quick review of the basics. When we break a whole number into 2 equal pieces, we get 2 halves.

half

half

A whole is broken into 2 equal halves.

Mathematically, we can view each half as 1 divided by 2 ($1 \div 2$). Since 1 is smaller than 2, there's no need to carry out the division, though. We just leave it alone. And, actually, instead of using the division symbol, we write 1 divided by 2 with a fraction bar: $\frac{1}{2}$. So $\frac{1}{2}$ represents one-half of a whole.

A Couple of Terms

The top number of a fraction is called the **numerator** and the bottom number is called the **denominator**. The denominator tells us how many pieces the whole has been broken into. The numerator tells us how many of those pieces we have. So $\frac{1}{2}$ means the whole has been divided into 2 equal pieces and we have 1 of them.

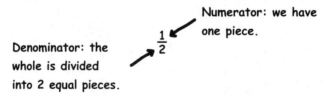

Numerator: we have one piece.

Denominator: the whole is divided into 2 equal pieces.

$\frac{1}{2}$

Thirds Too

Of course, a whole doesn't have to be broken into 2 equal pieces. It could be broken into 3 equal pieces. If we sawed a board into three equal pieces, each of those pieces would be "a third."

---

[1] The word fraction actually comes from a Latin word meaning "broken."

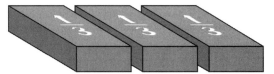

A board sawed into thirds (3 equal pieces).

Mathematically a third is written as $\frac{1}{3}$. The denominator is 3 because the whole is broken (or sawed, in this case) into 3 equal pieces. And the numerator is 1 because $\frac{1}{3}$ represents 1 of those pieces.

Now let's go back to measuring Farmer Brown's field. The field was between 172 and 173 yards, which means that whole numbers won't allow us to get a precise measurement. But with fractions we can do the measurement easily. What if the field turns out to be 172 yards plus an extra half of a yard?

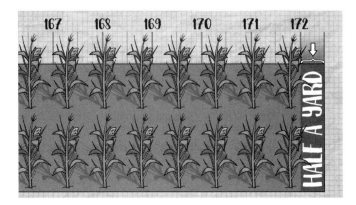

$172\frac{1}{2}$ yards long

All we have to do is use the number $\frac{1}{2}$ to measure the extra. That would make the field 172 and $\frac{1}{2}$ yards long, which is written as $172\frac{1}{2}$ yards. But what if the extra length was a third of a yard more than 172? Then we could use $\frac{1}{3}$ to measure the extra. In that case, the field would be $172\frac{1}{3}$ yards long.

Fourths, Fifths, and on Up

It's actually possible to break a whole number into as many pieces as you need in order to do a proper measurement. In other words, we're not limited to halves or third. For example, what if we need to break a whole into 4 equal pieces? Then we end up with fourths, and that's written as $\frac{1}{4}$, as you know. Here's a board sawed into fourths.

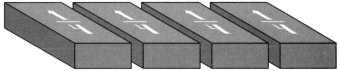

Each of these pieces represents $\frac{1}{4}$ of the whole. The 4 in the denominator tells how many pieces the board was sawed into, and the 1 in the numerator says that we have just 1 of those pieces.

Of course, we could have just as easily sawed the board into five equal pieces. That would have given us fifths ($\frac{1}{5}$). Or we could have sawed it into six equal pieces to get sixths ($\frac{1}{6}$). There's really no end to the process. The point is that we can saw the board into as many pieces as we want and there will be a fraction to represent the pieces, no matter how small they are.

More than One Piece

The other interesting thing is that we don't always have to focus on just one of the pieces. For instance, if a whole is broken up into 3 equal pieces (thirds), we might need two of those to make a measurement. What if the extra amount of Farmer Brown's field were equal to exactly 2 of those thirds? In that case, we would need the fraction "two-thirds," which is written as $\frac{2}{3}$. The 3 in the denominator shows that we've still broken up the whole into 3 equal pieces. And the 2 in the numerator shows that we're taking 2 of those pieces instead of just 1.

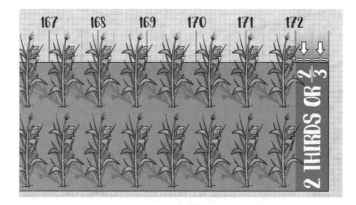

$172\frac{2}{3}$ yards long

There are lots of other possibilities. For example, we could break a stick into 5 equal pieces and take 3 of them. Then we would have three-fifths, which is written as $\frac{3}{5}$. The shaded parts below show $\frac{3}{5}$ of the stick.

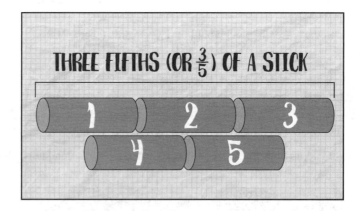

Some other possibilities are $\frac{2}{7}$, where a whole is broken into 7 equal pieces and we have 2 of them, and $\frac{5}{9}$, where a whole is broken into 9 equal pieces and we have 5 of them. We can have any number we want in the top or bottom of a fraction. The bottom always tells the number of pieces the whole has been broken into, and the top tells the number of pieces that we have.

Improper Fractions

If it's possible to have any number in the top or bottom of a fraction, what about the fraction $\frac{3}{3}$? This has the same number in the top (numerator) and bottom (denominator). Or what about the fraction $\frac{4}{3}$? It has a bigger number in the top than in the bottom. Are these fractions legal?

Same on Top and Bottom

Absolutely. The fraction $\frac{3}{3}$ just means that the whole has been divided into 3 equal pieces and we have 3 of them. Here's a picture of a pie (don't ask what kind) that's divided into 3 pieces.

Three pieces
equals the
entire whole.

Since all 3 pieces are shaded, the entire pie is shaded. That just means we have the entire whole. So $\frac{3}{3} = 1$.

It works the same way for any fraction where the numbers in the top and bottom are the same: $\frac{2}{2}, \frac{4}{4}, \frac{7}{7}$ all equal 1. In every case, we have all the pieces that the whole has been divided into, so we must have the entire whole.

Bigger on Top than Bottom

What about $\frac{4}{3}$? This means that the whole has been divided into 3 equal pieces again, but we have 4 of them! Let's draw a picture of this one.

$\frac{4}{3}$ is greater than 1.

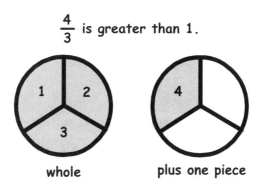

whole   plus one piece

We have 1 more than the 3 pieces of the pie, which means we have more than the whole. The fraction $\frac{4}{3}$ must be greater than 1. In fact, any time the top of a fraction is bigger than its bottom, the fraction has to be greater than 1. Here are a few more examples.

$$\frac{3}{2} \qquad\qquad \frac{7}{6} \qquad\qquad \frac{5}{3}$$

A fraction that has the same or greater number on top than it has on bottom is called an **improper fraction**. The name "improper" comes from the fact that some people used to think that improper fractions were kind of weird or abnormal. They thought of fractions that have a smaller number on top than on bottom as being "normal." In fact, they called those "proper" fractions. The "normal" fractions—the ones with tops smaller than their bottoms—are called **proper fractions**. But there's actually nothing wrong with improper fractions. Mathematically, they're as normal and acceptable as proper fractions. It's just that proper fractions are used more often than improper fractions, so people have gotten more comfortable with them.

Improper Fraction	A fraction with the same top and bottom. It always equals 1. A fraction where the top is bigger than the bottom. It is always greater than 1.
Proper Fraction	A fraction where the top is smaller than the bottom. It is always less than 1.

Practice 6

a.
(5)
Use the divisibility rules to tell whether 1,152 can be divided evenly by 6.

b.
(6)
A whole has been divided into 4 equal parts. Write a fraction to show that you have 5 of those parts.

c.
(3)
Multiply $\begin{array}{r} 6,050 \\ \times 739 \\ \hline \end{array}$

d.
(4)
Divide $63\overline{)9,545}$. Write any remainders next to your answer.

e.
(4)
Translate the word problem below into math; then solve.

The Noble Savage decided to share his coconuts equally with his two best friends. If he had 105 coconuts in all, how many did each of the 3 get?

Problem Set 6

Tell whether each sentence below is True or False.

1.
(6)
The denominator tells you how many pieces into which the whole has been broken.

2.
(6)
The numerator tells you how many pieces you have of a whole that's been divided into equal groups.

3.
(6)
Any fraction whose numerator and denominator are the same is equal to 0.

Do each calculation below in your head.

4.
(3)
Multiply $2,000 \times 900$

5.
(4)
Divide $42,000,000 \div 6,000$

Use the divisibility rules to answer each question below.

6.
(5)
Tell whether 75,231 can be divided evenly by 3.

(a) 7.
(5)
Tell whether 2,412 can be divided evenly by 6.

Answer each question below.

8.
(6)
A whole has been divided into 17 equal parts. Write a fraction to show that you have 3 of those parts.

(b) 9.
(6)
A whole has been divided into 2 equal parts. Write a fraction to show that you have 3 of those parts.

10.
(6)
Write a fraction to represent the diagram below.

11.
(6)   Write a fraction to represent the diagram below.

Add or subtract each group of numbers below.

12.
(2)
$$976$$
$$43$$
$$+88$$

13.
(2)
$$7,364$$
$$2,581$$
$$2,479$$
$$+6,846$$

14.
(2)
$$578$$
$$-199$$

15.
(2)
$$3,005$$
$$-2,346$$

16.
(2)
$$68,444$$
$$-24,468$$

Multiply each pair of numbers below.

17.
(3)
$$937$$
$$\times 7$$

18.
(3)
$$497$$
$$\times 76$$

(c) 19.
(3)
$$4,030$$
$$\times 946$$

Divide each pair of numbers below. Write any remainders next to your answer.

20.
(4) $7)\overline{339}$

21.
(4) $5)\overline{419}$

22.
(4) $56)\overline{8,176}$

23.
(4) $84)\overline{9,492}$

(d) 24.
(4) $63)\overline{9,835}$

Translate the word problem below into math; then solve.

(e) 25.
(4)   Lawrence of Siberia has 68 ounces of frozen water in his canteen. If he and his three companions agree to share this amount equally, how many ounces will each of the 4 get?

38

Lesson 7—Equivalent Fractions

We talked in the last lesson about how fractions represent parts of a whole. Interestingly, a part of a whole can be represented by more than one fraction. As an example, the circle on the left below has one-half shaded. We could represent the shaded part of this circle with the fraction $\frac{1}{2}$. But now look at the fraction on the right below. This is the same circle but it's been divided into 4 equal parts instead of 2. We could represent the shaded part as $\frac{2}{4}$ now, because the circle is divided into 4 equal parts and 2 of those are shaded.

$$\frac{1}{2} = \frac{2}{4}$$

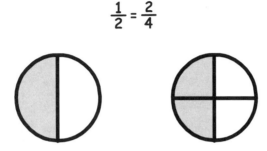

They represent the same part of the whole.

But think about it. This is the same part of the whole that was shaded before. It's still just half the circle. The only difference is the number of pieces that the whole was divided into. This shows that $\frac{1}{2}$ and $\frac{2}{4}$ represent the same amount of the whole. The two fractions are equal.

Actually, there are other fractions that could also represent this same part of the whole. For instance, we could slice the circle into 8 equal pieces. We could represent this part of the whole with the fraction $\frac{4}{8}$, because the circle has been divided into 8 equal pieces and 4 of those are shaded.

$$\frac{4}{8} = \frac{1}{2}$$

But it's still half the circle that's shaded, so $\frac{4}{8}$ must also equal $\frac{1}{2}$. Fractions such as $\frac{1}{2}$ and $\frac{2}{4}$ and $\frac{4}{8}$ are called equivalent fractions. **Equivalent fractions** are fractions that have the same value. They're equal to each other.

Multiplying Top and Bottom by the Same Number

There's actually an easier way to create equivalent fractions without having to slice up circles. Starting with a fraction like $\frac{1}{2}$, we can create an equivalent (equal) fraction by just multiplying the top and bottom by the same number. Let's multiply the top and bottom of $\frac{1}{2}$ by 2.

$$\frac{1 \times 2}{2 \times 2} = \frac{2}{4}$$

We end up with $\frac{2}{4}$, which we already know is equivalent to $\frac{1}{2}$. It turns out that no matter what number you multiply the top and bottom by, as long as it's the same number, you'll end up with an equivalent fraction. Let's multiply the top and bottom of $\frac{2}{4}$ by 4.

$$\frac{2 \times 4}{4 \times 4} = \frac{8}{16}$$

We end up with $\frac{8}{16}$, which tells us that $\frac{8}{16}$ and $\frac{2}{4}$ must be equivalent. They represent the same part of the whole.

Dividing Top and Bottom by the Same Number

This rule also works in reverse. If we start with a fraction and *divide* the top and bottom by the same number, we'll always end up with an equivalent fraction. Let's take $\frac{3}{6}$ and divide the top and bottom by 3.

$$\frac{3 \div 3}{6 \div 3} = \frac{1}{2}$$

We end up with $\frac{1}{2}$, which means that $\frac{3}{6}$ and $\frac{1}{2}$ must be equivalent fractions. They represent the same part of the whole. The picture below shows that that's true.

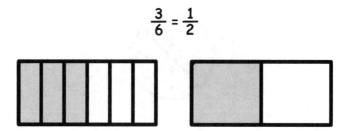

$$\frac{3}{6} = \frac{1}{2}$$

The box on the left is a picture of the fraction $\frac{3}{6}$, since it's divided into 6 equal pieces and 3 of those are shaded.

The box on the right is a picture of the fraction $\frac{1}{2}$, because it's divided into 2 equal pieces and one of those is shaded. But it's pretty obvious that the same part of the whole—half the box—is shaded in both.

The main point of the lesson is that we can either multiply the top and bottom of a fraction by the same number or divide the top and bottom of a fraction by the same number and we'll always end up with a fraction that's equivalent to what we started with. It won't change the value of the fraction at all. This is called **the Law of Equivalent Fractions**.

Law of Equivalent Fractions	We can either multiply or divide the top and bottom of a fraction by the same number (except 0) and always get an equivalent fraction.

Comparing Fractions

The Law of Equivalent Fractions can help you compare the value of two fractions. Comparing fractions is easy when their denominators are the same. We just compare the numerators. For instance, $\frac{5}{6}$ is obviously greater than $\frac{1}{6}$, because $\frac{5}{6}$ has a bigger numerator. The pieces are the same size for both fractions (they're both sixths). So 5 of those pieces is more than just 1.

$$\frac{5}{6} > \frac{1}{6}$$

You probably know that > is called an **inequality symbol**. The pointed end always goes toward the smaller number and the big end—the open end—always goes toward the greater number.

When two fractions have different denominators comparing their value is more difficult. Take $\frac{3}{5}$ and $\frac{2}{3}$, for example. We can't just compare the numerators because the sizes of the pieces are different. Here's a circle divided into 5 equal pieces (on the left). And another one divided into 3 equal pieces (on the right).

The pieces are different sizes.

The pieces are different sizes. So we can't just say that 3 pieces are more than 2 pieces. To compare fractions in a case like this, we must first make the denominators the same. And we can do that with the Law of Equivalent Fractions. First, we multiply the top and bottom of $\frac{3}{5}$ by 3.

$$\frac{3 \times 3}{5 \times 3} = \frac{9}{15}$$

The fraction $\dfrac{9}{15}$ must have the same value as $\dfrac{3}{5}$, because we multiplied the top and bottom by the same number. We can also give $\dfrac{2}{3}$ a denominator of 15 using the Law of Equivalent Fractions. We just need to multiply the top and bottom of that fraction by 5. That gives us $\dfrac{10}{15}$, which means that $\dfrac{2}{3}$ and $\dfrac{10}{15}$ have the same value.

$$\frac{2\times5}{3\times5}=\frac{10}{15}$$

We've changed the two original fractions to $\dfrac{9}{15}$ and $\dfrac{10}{15}$. Since their denominators are now the same (the slices of the pie are the same size), it's easy to see that $\dfrac{9}{15}$ is less than $\dfrac{10}{15}$.

$$\frac{9}{15}<\frac{10}{15}$$

And since these fractions are the same as $\dfrac{3}{5}$ and $\dfrac{2}{3}$, we know that $\dfrac{3}{5}$ has to be less than $\dfrac{2}{3}$.

$$\frac{3}{5}<\frac{2}{3}$$

That's how you can compare fractions using the Law of Equivalent Fractions. Just make the denominators the same, and then compare the numbers on top.

Reducing a Fraction

The Law of Equivalent Fractions is also used to reduce fractions. Reducing a fraction is really just making the fraction as simple as possible. Let's go through a quick example by reducing $\dfrac{6}{8}$. For this fraction, the whole has been divided into 8 equal pieces and we have 6 of them (6 are shaded, in other words). But we can reduce $\dfrac{6}{8}$ (make it simpler) by dividing the top and bottom by 2.

$$\frac{6\div2}{8\div2}=\frac{3}{4}$$

Since the top and bottom were divided by the same number, we know that $\dfrac{3}{4}$ has the same value as $\dfrac{6}{8}$. But $\dfrac{3}{4}$ is simpler since the numbers are smaller. Most people would rather use $\dfrac{3}{4}$ than $\dfrac{6}{8}$. To reduce a fraction, then, we divide the top and bottom by the same number to make the numerator and denominator as small as possible.

Let's reduce the fraction $\dfrac{25}{75}$. The numbers on top and bottom are bigger, but the process is the same. We can divide the top and bottom by 5.

$$\frac{25 \div 5}{75 \div 5} = \frac{5}{15}$$

That gives us $\frac{5}{15}$. But $\frac{5}{15}$ can also be reduced by dividing the top and bottom by 5 again.

$$\frac{5 \div 5}{15 \div 5} = \frac{1}{3}$$

We end up with $\frac{1}{3}$, which is fully reduced. Technically, a fraction is fully reduced when you can't divide the top and bottom evenly by any whole number. That's the situation with $\frac{1}{3}$. Since we divided the top and bottom by the same number both times, we know that $\frac{25}{75}$, $\frac{5}{15}$, and $\frac{1}{3}$ are all equivalent fractions. But, obviously, $\frac{1}{3}$ is the simplest one to work with.

We could have fully reduced $\frac{25}{75}$ in just one step. Instead of dividing the top and bottom by 5, we could have divided the top and bottom by 25.

$$\frac{25 \div 25}{75 \div 25} = \frac{1}{3}$$

That takes us straight to $\frac{1}{3}$ in a single step. The way to fully reduce a fraction all at once is to think of the largest possible whole number that will divide the top and bottom evenly. When you divide by that number, the answer will always be fully reduced.

Practice 7

a. Tell whether <, >, or = should go between these fractions: $\frac{3}{8}$ ____ $\frac{1}{2}$.
(7)

b. Tell whether <, >, or = should go between these fractions: $\frac{2}{5}$ ____ $\frac{3}{7}$.
(7)

c. Write a fraction to represent the diagram below.
(6)

d. Fully reduce the fraction $\frac{20}{35}$.
(7)

43

e. Translate the word problem below into math; then solve.
(3)

Podunk University is offering a new course called Baby Gibberish. If 12 people have signed up and the course costs $399, how much money did the university take in?

Problem Set 7

Tell whether each sentence below is True or False.

1. Multiplying the top and bottom of a fraction by the same number will change the fraction's value.
(7)

2. The Law of Equivalent Fractions can be used to reduce fractions.
(7)

Tell whether <, >, or = should go between these fractions.

3. $\dfrac{3}{4}$ —— $\dfrac{5}{4}$
(7)

(a) 4. $\dfrac{3}{10}$ —— $\dfrac{1}{5}$
(7)

(b) 5. $\dfrac{3}{4}$ —— $\dfrac{7}{9}$
(7)

Use the divisibility rules to answer each question below.

6. Tell whether 4,687,405 can be divided evenly by 5.
(5)

7. Tell whether 3,286 can be divided evenly by 3.
(5)

Answer each question below.

8.
(6) A whole has been divided into 11 equal parts. Write a fraction to show that you have 6 of those parts.

(c) 9.
(6) Write a fraction to represent the diagram below.

Add or subtract each group of numbers below.

10.
(2)
5,885
2,526
1,928
+6,447

11.
(2)
468
−426

12.
(2)
70,035
−56,279

Multiply each pair of numbers below.

13.
(3)
947
×27

14.
(3)
142
×104

15.
(3)
931
×603

Divide each pair of numbers below. Write any remainders next to your answer.

16.
(4) 9)1,856

17.
(4) 43)2,150

18.
(4) 20)1,386

19.
(4) 37)2,621

Fully reduce each fraction below.

20.
(7) $\frac{2}{10}$

(d) 21.
(7) $\frac{8}{24}$

22.
(7) $\frac{10}{12}$

Translate the word problem below into math; then solve.

(e) 23.
(3) Encouraged by the success of its Baby Gibberish course, Podunk U. decided to offer three new classes: Scientific Mumbo Jumbo, Surfer Slang, and Office Lingo. How much money did the university take in from their Surfer Slang course, if the course costs $450 and 28 people signed up?

Lesson 8—Factoring and Canceling

In the previous lesson we learned to reduce fractions by dividing the top and bottom by the same number. Well, it turns out that there's another method for reducing fractions. Take a look at this example.

El Magnifico, the great artist/composer, plans to produce 21 spectacular laser light shows at various points on the equator. Five minutes after he announced the shows, 14 of them sold out. What fraction sold out? Make sure your answer is fully reduced.

All we have to do is take the number of shows produced (21) and make that the denominator of the fraction. And the number of shows that sold out (14) should be the numerator of the fraction. That gives us $\frac{14}{21}$, which is the fraction of shows that sold out. But the problem says that the answer should be fully reduced. So we need to reduce $\frac{14}{21}$.

Factoring: Writing a Number as a Multiplication

We could reduce the fraction by dividing the top and bottom by 7. We know that's legal according to the Law of Equivalent Fractions. But instead of dividing top and bottom by 7, let's do something different. Let's first write the 14 and 21 as multiplications. We'll change 14 to 2×7 and 21 to 3×7.

$$\frac{2 \times 7}{3 \times 7}$$

Rewriting a number as a multiplication is called **factoring**. So we say the number 14 was "factored" as 2×7, and 21 was factored as 3×7. The numbers 2 and 7 are also called **factors** of 14, and 3 and 7 are factors of 21.

Canceling: Marking Out Common Factors

Next, to reduce, all we have to do is mark out the numbers on the top and bottom that are the same. That means we mark out the 7s, like this.

$$\frac{2 \times \cancel{7}}{3 \times \cancel{7}} = \frac{2}{3}$$ Canceling the 7s

Marking out factors is called **canceling**. Canceling the 7s leaves us with a 2 on top and a 3 on bottom for the fraction $\frac{2}{3}$. And that's fully reduced. So another method for reducing fractions is by **factoring and canceling.** The procedure is to write the top and bottom as multiplications (factor), and then mark out the factors that are the same on top and bottom (cancel). Whatever is left becomes the numerator and denominator of the reduced fraction. Here's a summary.

Reducing a Fraction by Factoring and Canceling

1.	Factor the top and bottom of the fraction, which just means to write each as a multiplication.
2.	Cancel (mark out) the factors that are the same on the top and bottom.
3.	The factors that are left become the numerator and denominator of the reduced fraction.

How Does Factoring and Canceling Work?

Factoring and canceling is a nice method for reducing fractions. But you may be wondering how the method works. Is it legal to mark out numbers? Actually, it is. That's because canceling is really just a shortcut for dividing the top and bottom by the same number. Think about it. When we divide the top of the fraction $\frac{14}{21}$ by 7, we get $14 \div 7$ or 2. If we have the top factored (as 2×7), why not just mark out the 7? That will leave a 2 by itself on top, which is right. And when we divide the bottom of $\frac{14}{21}$ by 7, we get $21 \div 7$ or 3. So why not mark out the 7 in 3×7 so that a 3 is left by itself on bottom?

$$\frac{2 \times \cancel{7}}{3 \times \cancel{7}} = \frac{2}{3} \quad \text{is just a shortcut for} \quad \frac{14 \div 7}{21 \div 7} = \frac{2}{3}$$

It always works this way. When we divide by one of the factors (dividing 2×7 by 7, for instance), we always get the other factor as the answer. So we can just mark out the factor that we're dividing by. That's why factoring and canceling really is just another way to divide the top and bottom of a fraction by the same number. And according to the Law of Equivalent Fractions that's perfectly legal.

Why Bother?

If both methods (dividing and factoring/canceling) are the same is there any reason to use one rather than another? Well, the advantage of factoring and canceling is that with everything factored, it's easy to see what numbers will go evenly into the top and bottom. For instance, with $\dfrac{14}{21}$ written as $\dfrac{2\times7}{3\times7}$, it's obvious that both 14 and 21 can be divided evenly by 7, because those 7s are staring right at us. Basically, any time the same number is a factor of both the top and bottom of a fraction, we know automatically that that number will divide evenly into both. And to do the division, we can just mark those out.

Of course, not every fraction can be reduced. What happens when we factor a non-reducible fraction? Check out this example.

$$\frac{14}{15}$$

We can factor the top as 2×7 and the bottom as 3×5 to get this.

$$\frac{2\times7}{3\times5}$$

But notice that the numbers on top are all different from the numbers on bottom, which doesn't leave us anything to cancel. That's how we know that $\dfrac{14}{15}$ is already fully reduced. It always works that way when we factor a fully-reduced fraction. All the factors in the top will be different from those in the bottom.

Practice 8

a.
(7) Tell whether <, >, or = should go between these fractions: $\dfrac{4}{9}$ _____ $\dfrac{5}{11}$.

b.
(4) Divide $18\overline{)2,228}$. Write any remainders next to your answer.

c.
(8) Fully reduce the fraction $\dfrac{6}{14}$ by factoring and canceling.

d.
(8) Fully reduce the fraction $\dfrac{15}{10}$ by factoring and canceling.

e.
(4) Translate the word problem below into math; then solve.

The Do-Nothing Duo never forgets to fulfill their quota of 5 pea knuckle matches each day. If the Duo has had 900 matches this year, how many days have there been so far in the year?

Problem Set 8

Tell whether each sentence below is True or False.

1.
(8) Rewriting a number as a multiplication is called factoring.

2.
(8) Canceling is just a shortcut for dividing the top and bottom of a fraction by the same number.

Tell whether <, >, or = should go between these fractions.

3. $\frac{5}{7}$ _____ $\frac{12}{14}$
(7)

(a) 4. $\frac{3}{8}$ _____ $\frac{2}{7}$
(7)

Use the divisibility rules to answer each question below.

5. Tell whether 2,121,121 can be divided evenly by 2.
(5)

6. Tell whether 2,781 can be divided evenly by 9.
(5)

Add each group of numbers below.

7. 2,346
(2) 8,532
+6,291

8. 4,957
(2) 9,578
3,373
+8,733

Subtract each pair of numbers below.

9. 8,592
(2) −3,657

10. 6,173
(2) −1,846

11. 71,943
(2) −24,086

Multiply each pair of numbers below.

12. 380
(3) × 55

13. 209
(3) ×38

14. 406
(3) ×951

Divide each pair of numbers below. Write any remainders next to your answer.

15. 8)395
(4)

16. 6)2,740
(4)

(b) 17. 23)1,162
(4)

Fully reduce each fraction below by factoring and canceling.

18. $\frac{6}{10}$
(8)

(c) 19. $\frac{10}{22}$
(8)

(d) 20. $\frac{21}{15}$
(8)

Translate the word problem below into math; then solve.

(e) 21. Every day since his accounting class started, Dylan has read 7 pages out of his accounting textbook
(4) (because he knows that at this rate he will finish the book by the last day of class). If Dylan has read 504 pages out of the text, how many days ago did class start?

Lesson 9—Prime Numbers

We've been learning to reduce fractions by factoring and canceling. Let's try to reduce the fraction $\frac{18}{30}$ with that method. We can factor the 18 on top as 2 times 9 and the 30 on bottom as 3 times 10 to get this.

$$\frac{2\times9}{3\times10}$$

The factors on top are all different from the factors on bottom. In the last lesson, we learned that fractions where all the factors on top are different from those on bottom are already fully reduced. So apparently, $\frac{18}{30}$ is fully reduced.

But 2 and 9 aren't the only pair of numbers that multiply to equal 18. And 3 and 10 aren't the only pair of numbers that multiply to equal 30. What if we factored $\frac{18}{30}$ like this?

$$\frac{3\times6}{5\times6}$$

This works, because $3\times6=18$ and $5\times6=30$. But look at the factors now. The top and bottom have a pair of 6s in common, and those can be canceled.

$$\frac{3\times\cancel{6}}{5\times\cancel{6}}=\frac{3}{5}\qquad\textbf{Canceling the 6s}$$
$$\textbf{reduces the fraction.}$$

Factoring this way, the fraction reduces to $\frac{3}{5}$. So $\frac{18}{30}$ wasn't fully reduced after all.

Factoring the Right Way

This example raises a really important question. How can we be sure we've factored a fraction in the right way so the factors that can be canceled will show up? Simple. We just factor the top and bottom into as many numbers as possible; then we can see *all* the factors. As an example, let's go back to the fraction $\frac{18}{30}$. Originally, we factored $\frac{18}{30}$ like this.

$$\frac{2\times9}{3\times10}$$

But instead of giving up here, we could have taken one more step and factored the 9 as 3×3 and the 10 as 2×5. That would have given us

$$\frac{2\times3\times3}{3\times2\times5}.$$

Now we can see that the top and bottom actually have two factors in common (a 2 and a 3). Let's cancel both of these.

$$\frac{\cancel{2} \times \cancel{3} \times 3}{\cancel{3} \times \cancel{2} \times 5} = \frac{3}{5}$$

Canceling 2s and 3s reduces the fraction.

We end up with $\frac{3}{5}$, which is fully reduced.

Of course, canceling is just a shortcut for dividing the top and bottom by the number being marked out. So what we really just did was divide the top and bottom of $\frac{18}{30}$ by 2 (when canceling the 2s). Then we also divided the top and bottom by 3 (when canceling the 3s). That's the same thing as dividing by 2×3 or 6, if you think about it.

The main point is that factoring the numerator and denominator as far as possible will always show every factor. Then if you cancel *all* the factors that are the same in the top and bottom, you'll know for sure that the fraction is fully reduced.

Factoring into Prime Numbers

In our example, once we got down to just 2s, 3s, and 5s there was no way to factor further. Numbers like 2, 3, and 5, which can't be broken down any more as multiplications of smaller whole numbers, are called **prime numbers** ("primes" for short).[1] So when reducing fractions by factoring and canceling, we should really factor the numerator and denominator into prime numbers; then cancel everything possible.

Let's do another example that's kind of interesting. Let's reduce the fraction below by factoring and canceling.

$$\frac{9}{27}$$

The first step is to factor the top and bottom into prime numbers. On top, 9 can be broken down to 3×3. Since 3 is a prime number, that's as far as we can go on top. As for the bottom, 27 can be broken down as 3×9. But then 9 can be factored further as 3×3. So that gives us $3 \times 3 \times 3$ on bottom.

$$\frac{3 \times 3}{3 \times 3 \times 3}$$

Factoring the top and bottom into primes

The next step is to cancel. We have to make sure to cancel *every* possible pair of factors, though. There are two pairs of 3s that can be canceled here.

$$\frac{\cancel{3} \times \cancel{3}}{\cancel{3} \times \cancel{3} \times 3}$$

Canceling the factors in top and bottom

After canceling, look what happened. There's nothing left on top. What should go in the numerator of the answer then? Should the numerator be 0? No. Think about what canceling really means. It's just a shortcut for division. By canceling the 3s, we were really dividing the top and bottom of the fraction by 3 twice, which is the same as dividing by 9. The original numerator was 9. So what's 9 divided by 9? It's 1. That means the numerator of the answer has to be 1.

$$\frac{1}{3}$$

Fully reduced answer

---

[1] We could write 2 as 2×1 and 3 as 3×1. That doesn't count, though, because it really doesn't break the number down any further. Technically, a number is prime if it cannot be written as a multiplication of whole numbers any way other than the number itself times 1.

The rule is that anytime everything cancels, we have to put a 1 in place of the canceled factors. And once again, that's because canceling is really just a shortcut for dividing. So by canceling the 3s, we were really dividing the top by 9.

It's possible for everything to cancel on the bottom too. Let's quickly look at an example like that.

$$\frac{14}{7}$$

Step one is to factor the top and bottom into prime numbers or **prime factors**, as they're also called. On top, 14 factors as 2×7. On bottom, 7 is a prime number, so it can't be broken down any further.

$$\frac{2 \times 7}{7}$$ Factoring the top and bottom into primes

Step two is to cancel every factor possible. There's just one pair of 7s that will cancel.

$$\frac{2 \times \cancel{7}}{\cancel{7}} = \frac{2}{1} = 2$$ Canceling the 7s leaves a 1 on bottom.

Notice that everything on the bottom canceled this time. By canceling, all we really did was divide the top and bottom of the fraction by 7. And on bottom 7 divided by 7 is 1. So we just put a 1 in the bottom. The answer, then, is $\frac{2}{1}$, which equals 2 (since any number over 1 is just equal to itself).

The main point of the lesson is that to make sure a fraction is fully reduced you should factor the top and bottom into prime numbers and then cancel every possible factor.

Practice 9

a.
(5)   Use the divisibility rules to tell whether 7,264 can be divided evenly by 4.

b.
(4)   Divide $24\overline{)2,019}$. Write any remainders next to your answer.

c.
(9)   Fully reduce the fraction $\frac{81}{243}$ by factoring and canceling.

d.
(9)   Fully reduce the fraction $\frac{28}{32}$ by factoring and canceling.

e.
(4)   Translate the word problem below into math; then solve.

Mrs. Ritter put 4 smiley faces on each of her students' penmanship papers. If Mrs. Ritter gave out 76 smiley face stickers in all, how many penmanship papers did she grade?

Problem Set 9

Tell whether each sentence below is True or False.

1. A prime number cannot be factored into smaller whole numbers (other than itself and 1).
(9)

2. When reducing a fraction, it's best to factor the numerator and denominator into prime numbers.
(9)

3. If all the factors on top or bottom cancel, then a 1 should go in their place.
(9)

Tell whether <, >, or = should go between these fractions.

4. $\dfrac{5}{11}$ —— $\dfrac{9}{22}$
(7)

5. $\dfrac{5}{8}$ —— $\dfrac{3}{5}$
(7)

Use the divisibility rules to answer each question below.

6. Tell whether 5,331 can be divided evenly by 3.
(5)

(a) 7. Tell whether 9,932 can be divided evenly by 4.
(5)

Answer each question below.

8. Write a fraction to represent the diagram below.
(6)

9. Write a fraction to represent the diagram below.
(6)

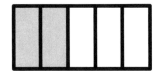

Add each group of numbers below.

10.
(2)
$$\begin{array}{r} 1{,}321 \\ 6{,}053 \\ +9{,}672 \\ \hline \end{array}$$

11.
(2)
$$\begin{array}{r} 6{,}826 \\ 1{,}335 \\ 2{,}476 \\ +1{,}637 \\ \hline \end{array}$$

Subtract each pair of numbers below.

12.
(2)
$$\begin{array}{r} 6{,}014 \\ -3{,}549 \\ \hline \end{array}$$

13.
(2)
$$\begin{array}{r} 12{,}365 \\ -8{,}975 \\ \hline \end{array}$$

Multiply each pair of numbers below.

14.
(3)
$$\begin{array}{r} 129 \\ \times 37 \\ \hline \end{array}$$

15.
(3)
$$\begin{array}{r} 406 \\ \times 58 \\ \hline \end{array}$$

16.
(3)
$$\begin{array}{r} 780 \\ \times 490 \\ \hline \end{array}$$

Divide each pair of numbers below. Write any remainders next to your answer.

17.
(4)
$9\overline{)388}$

18.
(4)
$5\overline{)1{,}974}$

(b) 19.
(4)
$24\overline{)1{,}996}$

Fully reduce each fraction below by factoring and canceling.

20.
(9)
$\dfrac{14}{12}$

(c) 21.
(9)
$\dfrac{16}{32}$

(d) 22.
(9)
$\dfrac{20}{32}$

Translate the word problem below into math; then solve.

(e) 23.
(4)
Millicent Fenwick gives Major Beauregard, her pet parrot, 3 pellets of food every time he makes a negative comment about a bad guy on TV. If Major Beauregard has received 894 pellets of food this way, how many negative comments has he made about bad guy characters?

Lesson 10—Adding and Subtracting Fractions

We've been reducing fractions in the last few lessons. But sometimes it's necessary to add fractions. Here's an example.

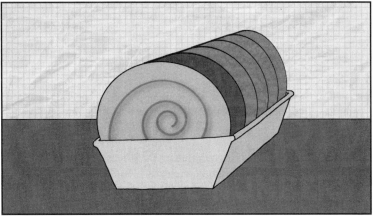

You ate one-fifth of a cinnamon-sugar loaf on Monday morning, and then ate another two-fifths of the loaf on Tuesday morning. What fraction of the loaf did you eat in total?

Adding Fractions

If we just use common sense, the answer is obvious. One-fifth plus another two-fifths has to equal three-fifths. And so you must have eaten three-fifths of the loaf in total. But now look at the same problem in numbers.

$$\frac{1}{5} + \frac{2}{5} = \frac{3}{5}$$ **Add the tops and keep the bottom the same.**

Notice that we can get the right answer by just adding the tops and then keeping 5 in the bottom. It turns out, that's the rule for adding fractions. You've been adding fractions for years, so this isn't new to you. We're just reviewing the basics. The rule is that to add fractions, you add the numerators and keep the denominator the same.

Why Does It Work?

The rule works because of the meaning of the numerator and denominator. Remember, the bottom of a fraction tells you how big the piece of the whole is. In the last problem we were working with fifths, which is why both fractions had a 5 in the bottom. The top of a fraction tells you how many of those pieces you have. So if one piece that's one-fifth in size is add to another piece that's two-fifths in size, the result is a piece that is three-fifths in size. The pieces don't change their size just because you added them together; they're still fifths. That's why we keep the 5 in the bottom the same when adding.

As another example, let's add $\frac{2}{7}$ and $\frac{3}{7}$. These pieces are all sevenths; they have the same size. We have two-sevenths added to three more sevenths. To do the calculation, we just add the tops and keep the bottom as 7. The answer comes out to $\frac{5}{7}$.

$$\frac{2}{7} + \frac{3}{7} = \frac{5}{7}$$

Subtracting Fractions

Subtracting fractions works in much the same way. To show you, let's go through a subtraction example.

Mom served five-eighths of her hot, steaming apple pie to the kids. But after just a few minutes, two-eighths had already been eaten. How much of Mom's pie was left?

If we start with five-eighths and then take away two-eighths, that leaves us with three-eighths. So three-eighths of the pie was left. But here's what it looks like with numbers.

$$\frac{5}{8} - \frac{2}{8} = \frac{3}{8}$$

You can see that we just need to subtract the tops and keep the bottoms the same. That's because the bottoms just tell the size of the slices. The slices that are left over are still eighths.

As another quick example, let's subtract $\frac{5}{6}$ and $\frac{1}{6}$. The bottoms are the same, which means the slices are the same size; they're both sixths. All we have to do is subtract the tops and keep the 6 on bottom.

$$\frac{5}{6} - \frac{1}{6} = \frac{4}{6}$$

We end up with $\frac{4}{6}$. But this can be reduced. When adding or subtracting fractions, it's always important to fully reduce your answers. We'll use the factor and cancel method. On top, 4 factors into the prime numbers as 2 times 2. And on bottom, 6 factors as 2 times 3.

$$\frac{4}{6} = \frac{2 \times 2}{2 \times 3}$$

Now we're ready to cancel. We can cancel one pair of 2s.

$$\frac{\cancel{2} \times 2}{\cancel{2} \times 3} \qquad \text{Cancel the 2s.}$$

The last step is to write down what's left.

$$\frac{4}{6} = \frac{\cancel{2} \times 2}{\cancel{2} \times 3} = \frac{2}{3}$$

So the fully reduced answer to $\frac{5}{6} - \frac{1}{6}$ is $\frac{2}{3}$.

Different Denominators

So far, all of our examples have had fractions where the denominators are the same. Sometimes, however, we have to add or subtract fractions with different denominators. Let's go through an example like that.

$$\frac{1}{2}+\frac{1}{4}$$

We can't just add the tops here, because the slices have different sizes. The first fraction is one-*half* of the whole and the second fraction is one-*fourth* of the whole. Halves are bigger than fourths. Before adding, we need to make the denominators the same. Then the slices will be the same size. We can change the denominator of $\frac{1}{2}$ from 2 to 4 by multiplying both the bottom and top by 2. We have to multiply both the bottom and the top, because we don't want to violate the Law of Equivalent Fractions and accidentally change the value of the fraction.

$$\frac{1\times 2}{2\times 2}=\frac{2}{4}$$

Since $\frac{1}{2}$ is the same as $\frac{2}{4}$, we can change our problem to this.

$$\frac{2}{4}+\frac{1}{4}$$

Now we're adding fourths to fourths, and we can add the fractions in the normal way. We just add the tops and keep the bottom the same (as 4).

$$\frac{2}{4}+\frac{1}{4}=\frac{3}{4}$$

We end up with $\frac{3}{4}$. Since it can't be reduced any further, $\frac{3}{4}$ is our final answer.

Changing Both Denominators

Let's do one more example: a subtraction problem where we have to change *both* denominators.

$$\frac{3}{4}-\frac{1}{3}$$

We can't subtract the tops, because the slices have different sizes. We're subtracting fourths and thirds. The first step, then, is to make the denominators the same. This time, though, we can't just change one denominator. We have to change both. We can multiply the top and bottom of $\frac{3}{4}$ by 3 and the top and bottom of $\frac{1}{3}$ by 4. This will change both denominators to 12.

$$\frac{3\times 3}{4\times 3}=\frac{9}{12} \qquad\qquad \frac{1\times 4}{3\times 4}=\frac{4}{12}$$

Replacing the original fractions with $\frac{9}{12}$ and $\frac{4}{12}$ gives us this.

$$\frac{9}{12}-\frac{4}{12}$$

The denominators are the same now, so we can just subtract the tops.

$$\frac{9}{12} - \frac{4}{12} = \frac{5}{12}$$

So $\frac{3}{4} - \frac{1}{3}$ equals $\frac{5}{12}$, which is fully reduced. You can check for yourself by factoring it. The top and bottom won't have anything that can be canceled.

Practice 10

a.
(9) Fully reduce the fraction $\frac{54}{6}$ by factoring and canceling.

b.
(10) Add $\frac{1}{18} + \frac{5}{18}$. Make sure your answer is fully reduced.

c.
(10) Subtract $\frac{7}{9} - \frac{1}{3}$. Make sure your answer is fully reduced.

d.
(10) Add $\frac{3}{4} + \frac{1}{3}$. Make sure your answer is fully reduced.

e.
(10) Translate the word problem below into math; then solve.

A lot of the rhubarb pie, $\frac{8}{9}$ to be exact, was left. That is, until Moose, the all-star defensive lineman, discovered it. Now, only $\frac{1}{9}$ of the pie is left. What fraction of the pie did Moose eat? Make sure your answer is fully reduced.

Problem Set 10

Tell whether each sentence below is True or False.

1.
(10) To add two fractions, you should add their tops and bottoms.

2.
(10) When subtracting fractions with different denominators, the denominators have to be made the same before subtracting.

Tell whether <, >, or = should go between these fractions.

3.
(7) $\frac{3}{4} \underline{\qquad} \frac{36}{48}$

4.
(7) $\frac{4}{7} \underline{\qquad} \frac{7}{12}$

Use the divisibility rules to answer each question below.

5.
(5)   Tell whether 24,681 can be divided evenly by 2.

6.
(5)   Tell whether 7,235 can be divided evenly by 5.

Answer each question below.

7.
(6)   Write a fraction to represent the diagram below.

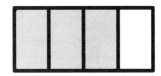

8.
(6)   Write a fraction to represent the diagram below.

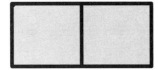

Add or subtract each group of numbers below.

9.
(2)
    4,667
  − 859

10.
(2)
   34,478
    8,509
   56,091
  +18,403

11.
(2)
   83,500
  −3,672

Multiply each pair of numbers below.

12.
(3)
    926
   ×46

13.
(3)
    805
   ×319

Divide each pair of numbers below. Write any remainders next to your answer.

14.
(4)   8)4,664

15.
(4)   21)7,255

Fully reduce each fraction below by factoring and canceling.

16.
(9) $\dfrac{4}{18}$

17.
(9) $\dfrac{3}{27}$

(a) **18.**
(9) $\dfrac{24}{6}$

Add or subtract each pair of fractions below. Make sure your answers are fully reduced.

19.
(10) $\dfrac{1}{7}+\dfrac{3}{7}$

20.
(10) $\dfrac{4}{9}-\dfrac{2}{9}$

21.
(10) $\dfrac{10}{11}-\dfrac{8}{11}$

(b) **22.**
(10) $\dfrac{1}{8}+\dfrac{3}{8}$

(c) **23.**
(10) $\dfrac{5}{8}-\dfrac{1}{4}$

(d) **24.**
(10) $\dfrac{1}{2}+\dfrac{2}{3}$

Translate the word problem below into math; then solve.

(e) **25.**
(10) The beaker was $\dfrac{12}{13}$ full; then Igor, the lab assistant, mistakenly poured out some of its contents. Now the beaker is only $\dfrac{3}{13}$ full. What fraction of the beaker was poured out? Make sure your answer is fully reduced.

Lesson 11—Finding the Lowest Common Denominator

We just finished learning how to add and subtract fractions that have different denominators. We have to make the denominators the same before doing the addition or subtraction, remember. That means we have to find a **common denominator**, which is just a whole number that we can change both denominators to.

Multiplying the Denominators Together

But sometimes it's pretty hard to find a common denominator. Take a look at this example.

$$\frac{11}{30} - \frac{1}{20}$$

We need to make both denominators the same, but what should we do? We can't multiply just one of the denominators. That won't work. But it's not easy to see how we can make the denominators the same even if we multiply both of them.

One method that will always give us a common denominator is to multiply the two denominators together. We can take 30×20 to get 600. That's a common denominator. And the great thing about this method is that it's easy to make both denominators equal 600. All we have to do is multiply the 30 by 20 and the 20 by 30.

$$\frac{11 \times 20}{30 \times 20} - \frac{1 \times 30}{20 \times 30} \qquad \textbf{Making the bottoms the same}$$

Notice we've multiplied the tops of each fraction by the same number to avoid violating the Law of Equivalent Fractions. But here's what we get.

$$\frac{220}{600} - \frac{30}{600}$$

Now we can subtract the numerators and put that result over 600.

$$\frac{190}{600}$$

This is the answer, but look at how huge the numbers are. This is the big drawback of finding a common denominator by just multiplying the bottoms together. If the original fractions have big numbers in them, the common denominator will be really big. And then it could take a long time to reduce the answer.[1]

The Lowest Common Denominator

Instead of just multiplying the denominators together, a better approach is to find the **lowest common denominator** (or LCD for short). That's the smallest number that both denominators will divide into evenly. By using the lowest common denominator, we can keep the numbers in our fraction as small as possible.

But how do we find the LCD? Do we just come up with a bunch of common denominators and pick the lowest one? No. There's actually a method for finding the LCD which will work every time.

---

[1] Actually, the fraction $\frac{190}{600}$ isn't all that hard to reduce. It reduces to $\frac{19}{60}$.

We'll show you how the method works on $\dfrac{11}{30}-\dfrac{1}{20}$. Step one is to factor each denominator into prime numbers. The 30 factors as $2\times3\times5$, and the 20 factors as $2\times2\times5$.

$$\dfrac{11}{2\times3\times5}-\dfrac{1}{2\times2\times5}$$ **Factor the bottoms into prime numbers.**

Now here's an important fact. An LCD has to include all of the factors from each denominator, with no extras. So step two is to list all of the factors in the two denominators. Starting with the first denominator, 30 contains one 2, one 3, and one 5. That means our LCD needs to have one 2, one 3, and one 5. We'll list those and show them multiplied together.

$$LCD = 2\times3\times5 \ ...$$

The second denominator, 20, contains two 2s and one 5. We already have one 2, but since the second denominator has two 2s, our LCD needs another one. So we include it in the list.

$$LCD = 2\times3\times5\times2$$ **Include another 2**

The second denominator also has a 5. But since our LCD already has one 5, there's no need to include another one. That's what it means to say that the LCD can't have any extra factors. Step three of the process is just to multiply all those factors together.

$$LCD = 2\times3\times5\times2 = 60$$ **Multiply the factors**

We end up with a lowest common denominator (LCD) of 60. That's a lot smaller than 600. (Remember, that's the common denominator we got by multiplying 30 and 20.) So 60 is going to be a lot easier to work with.

From here, subtracting the fractions is easy. We need to make both denominators equal 60. Here are the fractions again.

$$\dfrac{11}{30}-\dfrac{1}{20}$$

To change 30 to 60, we just need to multiply by 2. Of course, we have to multiply the bottom and the top by 2. To make 20 equal to 60, we need to multiply the top and bottom by 3.

$$\dfrac{11\times2}{30\times2}-\dfrac{1\times3}{20\times3}$$ **Making the bottoms equal 60 (the LCD)**

Calculating everything gives us this.

$$\dfrac{22}{60}-\dfrac{3}{60}$$

Finally, the denominators are the same. We're subtracting sixtieths from sixtieths. The last step is to subtract the tops.

$$\dfrac{22}{60}-\dfrac{3}{60}=\dfrac{19}{60}$$

We get $\dfrac{19}{60}$, which is fully reduced.

There's one last point we should make. From time to time, you may hear people refer to the lowest common denominator as **the least common multiple**. That's the lowest number that a group of numbers will divide into evenly. If that sounds familiar, it's because it's just our definition of lowest common denominator. But when adding or subtracting fractions, instead of saying they're finding the lowest common denominator, some people will say they're finding the least common multiple of the denominators. But the two terms mean pretty much the same thing. And you can use the same method to find the least common multiple of a group of numbers that you do to find the lowest common denominator.

Practice 11

a. Find the least common multiple of 18 and 45.
(11)

b. Find the lowest common denominator of $\frac{1}{4}$, $\frac{2}{7}$, and $\frac{1}{8}$.
(11)

c. Add $\frac{6}{7} + \frac{6}{9}$. Make sure your answer is fully reduced.
(11)

d. Subtract $\frac{3}{10} - \frac{1}{8}$. Make sure your answer is fully reduced.
(11)

e. Translate the word problem below into math; then solve.
(11)

Michael drank $\frac{1}{9}$ of the can of pop during his first gulp and $\frac{1}{12}$ during his second. What fraction of the can has Michael drunk? Make sure your answer is fully reduced.

Problem Set 11

Tell whether each sentence below is True or False.

1. The lowest common denominator (LCD) is the smallest number that the denominators will divide into
(11) evenly.

2. The lowest common denominator must include all of the factors in each of the denominators and no
(11) extras.

Add or subtract each group of numbers below.

3.
(2)
$$\begin{array}{r} 1,902 \\ 2,355 \\ 4,874 \\ +5,009 \\ \hline \end{array}$$

4.
(2)
$$\begin{array}{r} 65,563 \\ -9,924 \\ \hline \end{array}$$

5. (2)
$$43,573$$
$$23,497$$
$$17,943$$
$$+3,759$$

6. (2)
$$38,225$$
$$-27,870$$

Multiply each pair of numbers below.

7. (3)
$$574$$
$$\times 28$$

8. (3)
$$412$$
$$\times 532$$

Divide each pair of numbers below. Write any remainders next to your answer.

9. (4) $4\overline{)7,929}$

10. (4) $25\overline{)5,075}$

Fully reduce each fraction below by factoring and canceling.

11. (9) $\dfrac{15}{25}$

12. (9) $\dfrac{20}{24}$

Find the least common multiple for each pair of numbers below.

13. (11) $2\,,\,5$

(a) 14. (11) $12\,,\,20$

Find the lowest common denominator for each group of fractions below.

15. (11) $\dfrac{2}{3}\,,\,\dfrac{1}{6}$

16. (11) $\dfrac{3}{4}\,,\,\dfrac{1}{2}\,,\,\dfrac{5}{6}$

(b) 17. (11) $\dfrac{1}{8}\,,\,\dfrac{7}{9}\,,\,\dfrac{1}{6}$

Add or subtract each pair of fractions below. Make sure your answers are fully reduced.

18. (10) $\dfrac{3}{4}+\dfrac{1}{4}$

19. (10) $\dfrac{5}{11}-\dfrac{2}{11}$

20. (10) $\dfrac{1}{3}+\dfrac{2}{9}$

21. (10) $\dfrac{9}{10}-\dfrac{3}{5}$

(c) 22. (11) $\dfrac{5}{6}+\dfrac{3}{8}$

(d) 23. (11) $\dfrac{5}{8}-\dfrac{7}{12}$

Translate the word problem below into math; then solve.

(e) 24. (11) The Do-Nothing Duo spent $\dfrac{1}{3}$ of last weekend whistling their favorite tunes and $\dfrac{1}{2}$ blowing bubbles. What fraction of the weekend did the Duo spend doing these activities? Make sure your answer is fully reduced.

Lesson 12—Mixed Numbers

We've been adding and subtracting fractions, but what about adding or subtracting a whole number and a fraction? Here's an example.

$$5 + \frac{1}{3}$$

Put the Whole Number Over 1

Although this may seem tricky, it's actually pretty easy. The first step is to turn the whole number 5 into a fraction. Remember, any whole number can be turned into a fraction by putting it over 1. So putting 5 over 1 gives us this.

$$\frac{5}{1} + \frac{1}{3}$$

That changes the problem into an addition of two fractions, which is something we know how to do. Since these fractions have different denominators, we need to find the lowest common denominator (LCD). Our two denominators are really small, so we can find the LCD in our head: it's 3.

Now we need to make both denominators equal to 3. The second fraction, $\frac{1}{3}$, already has a denominator of 3. To make the first denominator equal to 3, we just multiply the bottom and the top (as always) by 3.

$$\frac{5 \times 3}{1 \times 3} + \frac{1}{3} \qquad \textbf{Multiplying top}$$
$$\textbf{and bottom by 3}$$

$$\frac{15}{3} + \frac{1}{3}$$

Next, we add the fractions by adding their tops and putting the result over 3 to get $\frac{16}{3}$.

$$\frac{15}{3} + \frac{1}{3} = \frac{16}{3} \qquad \textbf{Add the tops and keep}$$
$$\textbf{the bottom the same.}$$

Since $\frac{16}{3}$ is fully reduced, that's our final answer. So $5 + \frac{1}{3}$ is equal to $\frac{16}{3}$. Of course, if we were subtracting a fraction from a whole number we'd follow the same process.

Being Lazy with Mixed Numbers

People tend to be a little lazy when it comes to adding a whole number and a fraction. A lot of times they won't even bother doing the addition. For instance, they might just leave $5 + \frac{1}{3}$ as $5 + \frac{1}{3}$. In fact, this happens so often that people no longer even bother writing the + sign (which is really lazy). They just squeeze the numbers together like this.

$$5 + \frac{1}{3} \textbf{ is often written as } 5\frac{1}{3}$$

So $5\frac{1}{3}$ and $5+\frac{1}{3}$ mean the same thing. As you probably already know, $5\frac{1}{3}$ is called a mixed number. **A mixed number is just a whole number plus a fraction with the plus sign left out.** None of this is new to you, because mixed numbers are used a lot in arithmetic. But one thing you might not know is that mixed numbers aren't used as much in higher math. In more advanced courses, improper fractions (like $\frac{16}{3}$) are used a lot more often.

Converting a Mixed Number to an Improper Fraction

Now that we've mentioned mixed numbers, let's talk about how to change or "convert" (that's the technical term) a mixed number to a single fraction.[1] Take $4\frac{1}{2}$ for example. Since a mixed number is just a whole number plus a fraction, $4\frac{1}{2}$ really means $4+\frac{1}{2}$. So all we have to do is add these two.

$$4+\frac{1}{2} \qquad \textbf{Just add them.}$$

The first step is to just change 4 to $\frac{4}{1}$.

$$\frac{4}{1}+\frac{1}{2}$$

Now we add the fractions normally. The LCD is 2. And we can make the denominators the same by multiplying the top and bottom of $\frac{4}{1}$ by 2.

$$\frac{4\times 2}{1\times 2}+\frac{1}{2} \qquad \begin{array}{l}\textbf{Multiplying top}\\ \textbf{and bottom by 2}\end{array}$$

$$\frac{8}{2}+\frac{1}{2}$$

Now we can add the tops to get $\frac{9}{2}$, which is fully reduced. So the mixed number $4\frac{1}{2}$ converts into the improper fraction $\frac{9}{2}$.

A Neat Shortcut

There is also a shortcut for converting a mixed number to an improper fraction. Almost everybody learns it in arithmetic. To refresh your memory, we'll show you how it works on $4\frac{1}{2}$. The first step is to take the denominator of the fraction part of the mixed number and multiply it by the whole number part. So we take 2 (the denominator of $\frac{1}{2}$) and multiply it by 4 (the whole number part) to get 8. The next step is to add the numerator (1) to that result: $8+1$ equals 9. Then we put 9 on top of 2 (which is the denominator of $\frac{1}{2}$) to get our improper fraction.

---

[1] When you change a mixed number to a fraction, the fraction will be an improper fraction because the numerator (top) will be bigger than the denominator (bottom).

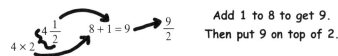

Add 1 to 8 to get 9.
Then put 9 on top of 2.

We end up with $\frac{9}{2}$, which is the same answer we got before. Here are the steps for the shortcut summarized.

Shortcut for Converting Mixed Number to Improper Fraction

1.	Multiply the denominator of the fraction part by the whole number and add the numerator.
2.	Put the result over the denominator.

The interesting thing about the shortcut is that it's actually the same thing as adding 4 and $\frac{1}{2}$ normally. Remember, when we added $\frac{4}{1}$ and $\frac{1}{2}$, we had to multiply 2 by the 4 on top to change $\frac{4}{1}$ to $\frac{8}{2}$. Then we added 8 and 1 to add the numerators ($\frac{8}{2} + \frac{1}{2}$). So the shortcut is just a fast way of adding the whole number to the fraction.

Converting the other Way

What about converting the other way by changing an improper fraction into a mixed number? That's easy. We just divide the denominator into the numerator and put the remainder over the denominator. For example, to convert $\frac{9}{2}$ back to a mixed number, we divide 2 into 9.

$$
\begin{array}{r}
4 \\
2\overline{)9} \\
-\underline{8} \\
1
\end{array}
$$

That gives us 4 with a remainder of 1. So 4 is the whole number part. And to get the fraction part, we put the remainder 1 over 2 (the divisor) to get $4\frac{1}{2}$. That's all there is to it.

Practice 12

a.
(11)   Find the lowest common denominator of $\frac{1}{6}$, $\frac{7}{12}$, and $\frac{11}{18}$.

b.
(12)   Add $3 + \frac{4}{7}$ to get an improper fraction. Make sure your answer is fully reduced.

c.
(12)   Change $\frac{17}{6}$ to a mixed number. Make sure the fraction part of your answer is fully reduced.

d. Add $1\dfrac{1}{4}+\dfrac{1}{12}$. Make sure your answer is fully reduced.
(12)

e. Translate the word problem below into math; then solve.
(11)

Farmer Brown has an artistic streak. He likes to paint the spots on his cows different shades of blue. If he painted $\dfrac{1}{4}$ of his cows with navy spots, $\dfrac{1}{3}$ of his cows with indigo spots, and $\dfrac{1}{6}$ of his cows with cobalt spots, what fraction of his cows were painted one of these three colors? Be sure to reduce your answer fully.

Problem Set 12

Tell whether each sentence below is True or False.

1. A mixed number is just a whole number plus a fraction with the plus sign left out.
(12)

2. It's better to change improper fractions to mixed numbers before adding or subtracting.
(12)

Add or subtract each group of numbers below.

3.
(2)
$$\begin{array}{r}7,342\\240\\3,398\\+1,432\\\hline\end{array}$$

4.
(2)
$$\begin{array}{r}12,886\\-4,592\\\hline\end{array}$$

5.
(2)
$$\begin{array}{r}983\\5,002\\14,280\\+6,793\\\hline\end{array}$$

Multiply or divide each pair of numbers below.

6.
(3)
$$\begin{array}{r}721\\\times85\\\hline\end{array}$$

7. $27\overline{)83,421}$
(4)

8.
(3)
$$\begin{array}{r}504\\\times433\\\hline\end{array}$$

Fully reduce each fraction below by factoring and canceling.

9. $\dfrac{8}{30}$
(9)

10. $\dfrac{28}{21}$
(9)

Find the lowest common denominator for each group of fractions below.

11. $\dfrac{1}{12},\dfrac{5}{4},\dfrac{3}{7}$
(11)

(a) 12. $\dfrac{2}{7},\dfrac{5}{21},\dfrac{9}{14}$
(11)

Add each pair of numbers below to get an improper fraction. Make sure your answer is fully reduced.

13.
(12) $4 + \dfrac{1}{3}$

(b) 14.
(12) $7 + \dfrac{2}{9}$

Change each improper fraction below into a mixed number. Make sure the fraction part of your answer is fully reduced.

15.
(12) $\dfrac{22}{7}$

(c) 16.
(12) $\dfrac{11}{4}$

Add or subtract each pair of numbers below. Make sure your answers are fully reduced.

17.
(10) $\dfrac{6}{8} + \dfrac{5}{8}$

18.
(10) $\dfrac{9}{10} - \dfrac{3}{10}$

19.
(10) $\dfrac{3}{5} + \dfrac{4}{15}$

20.
(11) $\dfrac{5}{7} - \dfrac{1}{8}$

(d) 21.
(12) $1\dfrac{1}{2} + \dfrac{1}{6}$

Translate the word problem below into math; then solve.

(e) 22.
(11)   When Farmer Jones found it hard to keep some of his cows from getting onto the highway after dark, Farmer Brown (see practice problem e) suggested that he paint their spots bright colors. Now $\dfrac{1}{6}$ of Farmer Jones' cows have neon pink spots, $\dfrac{1}{8}$ have glow-in-the-dark yellow spots, and $\dfrac{1}{12}$ have spots that are safety orange. What fraction of his cows did Farmer Jones protect with paint? Be sure to reduce your answer fully.

Lesson 13—Multiplying and Dividing Fractions

We've been reviewing how to add and subtract fractions. Now let's shift to multiplying and dividing them. The rule is pretty simple. We just multiply the tops and bottoms. We'll start out with a simple example.

$$\frac{1}{5} \times \frac{1}{3} = \frac{1}{15}$$

Here we multiply the numerators: 1×1 equals 1. Then we multiply the denominators: 5×3 equals 15. So we end up with $\frac{1}{15}$, which is fully reduced.

Canceling First

On some multiplying fractions problems, you actually have to reduce the answer. An example is $\frac{5}{9} \times \frac{3}{10}$. We could just multiply the tops and bottoms, the way we did in the previous example.

$$\frac{5}{9} \times \frac{3}{10} = \frac{15}{90}$$

We end up with $\frac{15}{90}$. But this answer can be reduced. On top, 15 factors as 3×5, and on bottom, 90 factors as 9×10 (although it can be broken down further).

$$\frac{15}{90} = \frac{3 \times 5}{9 \times 10}$$

But notice something. The factoring step is like going backwards. We got to 15 in the first place by multiplying 3 and 5. Now we're going back to 3×5. And we got a denominator of 90 by multiplying 9×10. After factoring, we've gone right back to where we started: 9×10. Continuing with the problem, we should factor the bottom all the way down to prime numbers. The 9 factors as 3×3 and the 10 as 2×5.

$$\frac{15}{90} = \frac{3 \times 5}{3 \times 3 \times 2 \times 5}$$

Now we can cancel. There's a pair of 3s and a pair of 5s that will cancel.

$$\frac{15}{90} = \frac{\cancel{3} \times \cancel{5}}{3 \times \cancel{3} \times 2 \times \cancel{5}} \qquad \textbf{Canceling 3s and 5s}$$

That leaves us with 1 on top—since everything's canceled up there. And then there's a 3×2 left on bottom, which is equal to 6.

$$\frac{15}{90} = \frac{\cancel{3} \times \cancel{5}^{\,1}}{3 \times \cancel{3} \times 2 \times \cancel{5}} = \frac{1}{6}$$

So the fully reduced answer comes out to $\frac{1}{6}$.

The only bad thing about our method for solving this problem is we wasted time and effort by going backwards. We multiplied the tops and bottoms, but then when we factored them both. Factoring is essentially "unmultiplying." So that's going backwards.

$$\frac{5}{9} \times \frac{3}{10} = \frac{15}{90} \qquad\qquad \frac{15}{90} = \frac{3 \times 5}{9 \times 10} = \frac{3 \times 5}{3 \times 3 \times 2 \times 5}$$

We multiplied,   **but then "unmultiplied."**

A better way to do the problem is to factor and cancel before multiplying. Then you don't have to go backwards.

Avoiding Extra Work

Let's do $\frac{5}{9} \times \frac{3}{10}$ again. Only this time, the very first step—before multiplying the tops and bottoms—is to factor the top and bottom of both fractions. The numerators are already prime numbers, so nothing can be done with the 5 and the 3. The denominators can be factored further, though: 9 factors as 3×3 and 10 factors as 2×5.

$$\frac{5}{3 \times 3} \times \frac{3}{2 \times 5}$$

The next step is to cancel. And here's the key point. With this method, we can cancel any factor on top of either fraction with the same factor on the bottom of either fraction. For instance, even though the 5s are in different fractions, we can still cancel them like this.

$$\frac{\cancel{5}^{1}}{3 \times 3} \times \frac{3}{2 \times \cancel{5}}$$

We can also cancel a pair of 3s even though they're in different fractions.

$$\frac{\cancel{5}^{1}}{3 \times \cancel{3}} \times \frac{\cancel{3}^{1}}{2 \times \cancel{5}}$$

This works because when we multiply the fractions, everything will end up in one fraction anyway. All we're doing is canceling first, before the multiplying step. It's perfectly legal.

Now that we're finished factoring, we can multiply. And we still just multiply the tops and bottoms of the factors that are left.

$$\frac{1}{3} \times \frac{1}{2} = \frac{1}{6}$$

We end up with $\frac{1}{6}$, the same answer as before. But the second method was faster because we didn't have to multiply and then "unmultiply" again. The main point is that when multiplying fractions, you should always factor and cancel first. Then you can multiply the tops and bottoms normally. The other nice thing about factoring and canceling first is that by using that method your answer will always be fully reduced. You don't have to worry about reducing at the end.

Dividing Fractions

Now let's focus on dividing with fractions. Here's an example.

$$\frac{5}{2} \div \frac{1}{2}$$

All we have to do is turn the second fraction upside down and change the division to multiplication. So we change $\frac{1}{2}$ to $\frac{2}{1}$ and multiply.

$$\frac{5}{2} \times \frac{2}{1}$$

Now we have two fractions multiplied, and we should follow our normal method. But we should factor and cancel first. In this case, there's actually nothing to factor because everything is a prime number.[1] The next step, then, is to cancel. Remember, we're allowed to cancel anything on top of either fraction with the same factor on the bottom of either fraction. Here, we can cancel a pair of 2s (even though they're in different fractions).

$$\frac{5}{\cancel{2}_{1}} \times \frac{\cancel{2}^{1}}{1}$$

The last step is to multiply what's left in the top and bottom. So we end up with $\frac{5}{1}$ or just 5.

$$\frac{5}{1} \times \frac{1}{1} = \frac{5}{1} = 5$$

$\frac{5}{2} \div \frac{1}{2}$ is equal to 5. The main point is that to divide fractions you flip the second fraction upside down and change the division to multiplication. The process is actually called **inverting and multiplying**. Invert just means to flip the fraction over. And there's another technical word you should know. When turning a number upside down, we get the **reciprocal** of the original number. So $\frac{1}{2}$ and $\frac{2}{1}$ are reciprocals, and so are $\frac{3}{4}$ and $\frac{4}{3}$, $\frac{5}{6}$ and $\frac{6}{5}$, and $\frac{4}{1}$ and $\frac{1}{4}$. Another way to say the rule for dividing fractions, then, is that you have to take the reciprocal of the second number and multiply it by the first number.

Practice 13

a.
(12)   Change $\frac{36}{8}$ to a mixed number. Make sure the fraction part of your answer is fully reduced.

b.
(13)   Multiply $\frac{7}{9} \times \frac{3}{5}$. Make sure your answer is fully reduced.

c.
(13)   Divide $\frac{4}{7} \div \frac{4}{21}$. Make sure your answer is fully reduced.

---

[1] 5 and 2 are prime numbers. Technically, 1 is not considered to be a prime number, but it can't be factored either.

d. Divide $\dfrac{3}{4} \div \dfrac{6}{20}$. Make sure your answer is fully reduced.
(13)

e. Translate the word problem below into math; then solve.
(11)

If Suzy combined a ketchup bottle that was $\dfrac{1}{3}$ full with a ketchup bottle that was $\dfrac{1}{6}$ full, what fraction of a bottle does she have now? Make sure your answer is fully reduced.

Problem Set 13

Tell whether each sentence below is True or False.

1. To multiply fractions, multiply their tops and bottoms.
(13)

2. To divide fractions, change the division to multiplication by the reciprocal.
(13)

Add or subtract each group of numbers below.

3.
(2)
$$\begin{array}{r} 756 \\ 9,348 \\ 845 \\ +6,432 \\ \hline \end{array}$$

4.
(2)
$$\begin{array}{r} 64,914 \\ -42,856 \\ \hline \end{array}$$

Multiply or divide each pair of numbers below.

5. $9\overline{)2,837}$
(4)

6.
(3)
$$\begin{array}{r} 279 \\ \times 822 \\ \hline \end{array}$$

Fully reduce each fraction below by factoring and canceling.

7. $\dfrac{13}{26}$
(9)

8. $\dfrac{25}{35}$
(9)

Find the lowest common denominator for each group of fractions below.

9. $\dfrac{9}{8}, \dfrac{5}{6}, \dfrac{1}{10}$
(11)

10. $\dfrac{2}{9}, \dfrac{4}{15}, \dfrac{9}{10}$
(11)

Change each improper fraction below into a mixed number. Make sure the fraction part of your answer is fully reduced.

11. $\dfrac{29}{7}$
(12)

(a) **12.** $\dfrac{38}{6}$
(12)

Add or subtract each pair of fractions below. Make sure your answers are fully reduced.

13.
(10) $\dfrac{5}{3}+\dfrac{2}{3}$

14.
(10) $\dfrac{7}{8}-\dfrac{1}{4}$

15.
(12) $9+\dfrac{2}{5}$

16.
(11) $\dfrac{1}{3}-\dfrac{3}{10}$

Multiply each pair of numbers below. Make sure your answers are fully reduced.

17.
(13) $\dfrac{1}{4}\times\dfrac{1}{3}$

(b) 18.
(13) $\dfrac{5}{4}\times\dfrac{2}{3}$

19.
(13) $\dfrac{2}{5}\times\dfrac{5}{3}$

20.
(13) $\dfrac{10}{3}\times\dfrac{1}{5}$

Divide each pair of numbers below. Make sure your answers are fully reduced.

21.
(13) $\dfrac{2}{5}\div\dfrac{1}{3}$

(c) 22.
(13) $\dfrac{3}{5}\div\dfrac{3}{10}$

23.
(13) $\dfrac{1}{2}\div\dfrac{2}{9}$

(d) 24.
(13) $\dfrac{2}{7}\div\dfrac{4}{21}$

Translate the word problem below into math; then solve.

(e) 25. Super Duper Saver Grocery has decided to offer partially-consumed boxes of chocolates. If Vicki bought
(11) $\dfrac{1}{4}$ of a box of cherry chocolates and $\dfrac{1}{8}$ of a box of assorted chocolates, what fraction of a whole box did she buy? Make sure your answer is fully reduced.

Lesson 14—Fractions and Whole Numbers

In the last lesson, we reviewed how to multiply and divide with fractions. In all of our examples, both of the numbers were fractions. But sometimes a problem will have a whole number and a fraction that are multiplied or divided.

Multiplying with a Whole Number and Fraction

Here's a simple example.

$$15 \times \frac{2}{9}$$

The first step is to turn 15 into a fraction by putting it over 1.

$$\frac{15}{1} \times \frac{2}{9}$$

Now we have two fractions multiplied. And we just follow the method from the last lesson. We should factor and cancel first. Fifteen factors as 3×5 and 9 factors as 3×3.

$$\frac{3 \times 5}{1} \times \frac{2}{3 \times 3}$$

Everything is factored as far as possible, so we can cancel. We're allowed to cancel anything on top of either fraction with the same factor on the bottom of either fraction. There's a pair of 3s that can be canceled.

$$\frac{\cancel{3} \times 5}{1} \times \frac{2}{\cancel{3} \times 3}$$

The next step is to multiply the tops and bottoms of what's left.

$$\frac{5}{1} \times \frac{2}{3} = \frac{10}{3}$$

So we end up with $\frac{10}{3}$. And since we canceled before multiplying, we know that this is already fully reduced. That's the method for multiplying a whole number and a fraction. Here are the steps written out formally.

Multiplying a Whole Number and Fraction

1.	Turn the whole number into a fraction by putting it over 1.
2.	Multiply the tops and bottoms of the two fractions.

Dividing with a Whole Number and Fraction

Now let's review how to divide a whole number and a fraction.

$$20 \div \frac{4}{5}$$

The first step is to turn 20 into a fraction by putting it over 1.

$$\frac{20}{1} \div \frac{4}{5}$$

That gives us two fractions that are divided. From here, we can just divide normally. We invert the second fraction and multiply.

$$\frac{20}{1} \times \frac{5}{4}$$

To carry out the multiplication, we should factor and cancel first. 20 factors as 4×5. But 4 can be factored further as 2×2. So 20 factors into primes as $2 \times 2 \times 5$. The 4 on the bottom of $\frac{5}{4}$ factors as 2×2.

$$\frac{2 \times 2 \times 5}{1} \times \frac{5}{2 \times 2}$$

Now we're ready to cancel. As it turns out, we can cancel two pairs of 2s.

$$\frac{\cancel{2} \times \cancel{2} \times 5}{1} \times \frac{5}{\cancel{2} \times \cancel{2}_1}$$

The next step is to multiply the tops and bottoms of what's left.

$$\frac{5}{1} \times \frac{5}{1} = \frac{25}{1} = 25$$

The final answer is 25. The method for dividing a whole number and a fraction, then, is to put the whole number over 1 and then divide the two fractions normally.

The process would have been the same if the problem had been a fraction divided by a whole number—in other words, if the order had been reversed. Here's the problem only with the fraction, $\frac{4}{5}$, in the first position.

$$\frac{4}{5} \div 20$$

We still go through the same process. We turn 20 into a fraction by putting it over 1.

$$\frac{4}{5} \div \frac{20}{1}$$

Now we divide the fractions in the normal way—by inverting and multiplying. Here are the steps.

$$\frac{4}{5} \times \frac{1}{20}$$ inverting and multiplying

$$\frac{2 \times 2}{5} \times \frac{1}{2 \times 2 \times 5}$$ factoring

$$\frac{\cancel{2} \times \cancel{2}^{\,1}}{5} \times \frac{1}{\cancel{2} \times \cancel{2} \times 5}$$ cancelling

$$\frac{\cancel{2} \times \cancel{2}^{\,1}}{5} \times \frac{1}{\cancel{2} \times \cancel{2} \times 5} = \frac{1}{25}$$ multiplying

The answer comes out to $\frac{1}{25}$.

Fractions in the Real World

Now let's go through a real world example that requires us to multiply a fraction and a whole number.

A florist has 450 bouquets set out for Valentine's Day, but $\frac{3}{5}$ of them are wilting. How many bouquets are wilting?

In this problem, we need to find $\frac{3}{5}$ of 450. This is a "fraction of a number" problem. To solve these, we need to multiply the fraction and the number.

$$\frac{3}{5} \times 450$$

Some people like to put "multiply" in place of the word "of." If you're trying to find $\frac{3}{5}$ of 450, that's the same thing as $\frac{3}{5} \times 450$. That's one way to remember to multiply on problems like this. To carry out the multiplication, we first put the fraction over 1.

$$\frac{3}{5} \times \frac{450}{1}$$

Now we multiply the two fractions. To factor 450 all the way down to prime numbers would take quite a bit of time, since 450 is large. We can see from the problem that the only way to cancel anything is if 450 has a factor 5, because there's just a 5 and 1 in the bottom of the fractions. So we can save some time by factoring 450 partially—until we see a 5 that can be canceled. The easiest way to start is to write 450 as 45×10.

$$\frac{3}{5} \times \frac{45 \times 10}{1}$$

Of course, 10 can be factored as 2×5.

$$\frac{3}{5} \times \frac{45 \times 2 \times 5}{1}$$

That gives us our 5. Now we can cancel the 5 on top with the 5 on bottom.

$$\frac{3}{\cancel{5}_1} \times \frac{45 \times 2 \times \cancel{5}}{1}$$

Now we multiply what's left in the tops and bottoms.

$$\frac{3}{1} \times \frac{45 \times 2}{1} = \frac{270}{1} = 270$$

That means 270 of the bouquets are wilting.

The main point is that to find a fraction of a number, you multiply. Also, to find the fraction of a big number like 450, you may not have to factor it all the way down to prime numbers. You may be able to factor it part way until you identify enough factors to cancel all the factors in the bottom of the fractions.

Some real world problems require finding a fraction of a fraction. Here's an example like that.

Betty gave $\frac{1}{3}$ of a delicious pan of lasagna to her mother. But her mother gave $\frac{1}{5}$ of that to the cat. What fraction of the lasagna pan did the cat get?

This problem is asking us to find $\frac{1}{5}$ of $\frac{1}{3}$ of the lasagna pan. This is a "fraction of a fraction" problem. All you have to remember is that "of" means "multiply." So $\frac{1}{5}$ of $\frac{1}{3}$ is calculating like this.

$$\frac{1}{5} \times \frac{1}{3}$$

There isn't anything to factor and cancel, so all we have to do is multiply the tops and bottoms.

$$\frac{1}{5} \times \frac{1}{3} = \frac{1}{15}$$

The cat must have eaten $\frac{1}{15}$ of the lasagna pan.

What about real world problems where you have to divide with fractions? These are a somewhat tougher. Here's an example.

> Only $\frac{1}{3}$ of the cake was left, but Jack and his brother Joe wanted to share it equally. What fraction of the cake should each brother get?

To solve this problem, we need to take $\frac{1}{3}$ and divide it in half, since the two brothers are sharing the cake equally. That gives us this.

$$\frac{1}{3} \div 2$$

First, we should change 2 into a fraction by putting it over 1.

$$\frac{1}{3} \div \frac{2}{1}$$

Now we just invert and multiply.

$$\frac{1}{3} \times \frac{1}{2}$$

$$\frac{1}{3} \times \frac{1}{2} = \frac{1}{6}$$

So each brother should get $\frac{1}{6}$ of the original cake.

Here's a real world problem that requires us to divide a whole number by a fraction.

> The coach bought 7 pizzas for the victory party. If he gave each person $\frac{1}{4}$ of a pizza, how many people were at the victory party?

Since there are 7 pizzas and each player is supposed to get $\frac{1}{4}$ of a pizza, we need to figure out how many $\frac{1}{4}$s are in 7. This seems hard. But what if the problem involved simpler numbers? For instance, what if there were 10 pizzas and the players were supposed to get 2 pizzas each? With simpler numbers, it's pretty obvious that we would need to divide: $10 \div 2$. There would have to be 5 players. Well, we should do the same thing with the actual numbers in the problem. We need to divide 7 by $\frac{1}{4}$.

$$7 \div \frac{1}{4}$$

That's a good strategy when solving a word problem that contains fractions. If you're having trouble figuring out which operation to do, just replace the numbers with simpler whole numbers and decide on the correct operation that way. Then use the same operations with the fractions. Now let's do the calculation for our problem. First, we turn 7 into a fraction by putting it over 1.

$$\frac{7}{1} \div \frac{1}{4}$$

Now we just divide the fractions normally by inverting and multiplying.

$$\frac{7}{1} \times \frac{4}{1}$$

The last step is to multiply the tops and bottoms.

$$\frac{7}{1} \times \frac{4}{1} = \frac{28}{1} = 28$$

There must have been 28 people at the victory party. That's another example of dividing with fractions in the real world.

Practice 14

a.
(14)   Multiply $2 \times \frac{3}{10}$. Make sure your answer is fully reduced.

b.
(14)   Divide $21 \div \frac{3}{5}$. Make sure your answer is fully reduced.

c.
(14)   What is $\frac{2}{9}$ of 990? Make sure your answer is fully reduced.

d.
(14)   50 has how many $\frac{1}{2}$s in it? Make sure your answer is fully reduced.

e.
(14) Translate the word problem below into math; then solve.

Everybody loves Fiona's banana cream pie, but she never makes enough. For example, yesterday only $\frac{1}{4}$ of the pie was left, but 10 family members still wanted a piece. What fraction of the whole pie will each of the 10 family members have to settle for? Make sure your answer is fully reduced.

Problem Set 14

Tell whether each sentence below is True or False.

1.
(14) Multiplying a whole number by a proper fraction will always make the whole number larger.

2.
(14) To multiply a whole number and fraction, turn the whole number into a fraction first; then multiply the two fractions normally.

Add or subtract each group of numbers below.

3.
(2)
$$\begin{array}{r} 436 \\ 5,232 \\ 6,948 \\ +733 \\ \hline \end{array}$$

4.
(2)
$$\begin{array}{r} 54,934 \\ -23,007 \\ \hline \end{array}$$

Multiply or divide each pair of numbers below.

5.
(3)
$$\begin{array}{r} 1,045 \\ \times 802 \\ \hline \end{array}$$

6.
(4) $18\overline{)17,389}$

Fully reduce each fraction below by factoring and canceling.

7.
(9) $\frac{56}{24}$

8.
(9) $\frac{36}{81}$

Add or subtract each pair of fractions below. Make sure your answers are fully reduced.

9.
(10) $\frac{1}{7}+\frac{4}{7}$

10.
(10) $\frac{2}{3}-\frac{5}{9}$

11.
(11) $\frac{7}{5}-\frac{3}{4}$

12.
(12) $11+\frac{3}{10}$

13.
(12) $1\frac{1}{2}+\frac{1}{6}$

Multiply each pair of numbers below. Make sure your answers are fully reduced.

14.
(13) $\dfrac{2}{15} \times \dfrac{5}{4}$

15.
(13) $\dfrac{6}{35} \times \dfrac{7}{3}$

16.
(14) $6 \times \dfrac{2}{11}$

(a) 17.
(14) $4 \times \dfrac{5}{12}$

18.
(14) $\dfrac{7}{8} \times 16$

Divide each pair of numbers below. Make sure that your answers are fully reduced.

19.
(13) $\dfrac{3}{7} \div \dfrac{1}{5}$

20.
(13) $\dfrac{3}{5} \div \dfrac{3}{10}$

21.
(14) $8 \div \dfrac{1}{3}$

(b) 22.
(14) $15 \div \dfrac{3}{4}$

Answer each question below. Make sure your answer is fully reduced.

(c) 23.
(14) What is $\dfrac{3}{8}$ of 136?

(d) 24.
(14) 100 has how many $\dfrac{1}{2}$ s in it?

Translate the word problem below into math; then solve.

(e) 25.
(14) Wendy has been pouring coffee refills all morning. If only $\dfrac{1}{5}$ of her decaf pitcher is left, and 7 people are asking for an immediate decaf refill, what fraction of the pitcher should each of the 7 get? Make sure your answer is fully reduced.

CHAPTER 3:
DECIMALS

Lesson 15—Ill-Fitting Fractions

In the last few chapters, we've been learning all about fractions. And it turns out that fractions are a big advantage of our number system. That's because, unlike whole numbers, which can only be used for counting, fractions are good for measuring. However, there is one problem with fractions that you may not have noticed. They don't fit into the place value system. In that system, remember, each place (or digit) equals ten times the place to the right. Take the number 247, for instance. We have 2 in the hundreds place, 4 in the tens place; and 7 in the ones place. And of course hundreds have ten times the value of tens and tens have ten times the value of ones. Everything works perfectly.

But now look at the mixed number $247\frac{3}{4}$. This number has hundreds, tens, ones, but then *fourths*. The fraction doesn't fit. A one is not ten times the value of a fourth. It's actually only four times the value.

Fitting Fractions In

Wouldn't it be nice if we could get fractions to fit with all the whole numbers? The mathematicians thought so, and that's why they invented a new kind of fraction that would fit into the place value system. These new fractions are called decimal fractions, or **decimals** for short.[1] Regular fractions like $\frac{3}{4}$ are technically called common fractions to distinguish them from decimal fractions. Of course, you've worked with decimals for years. But you may not have realized that the real difference between fractions (the regular kind) and decimals is that fractions don't fit in with 10-based place value system but decimals do.

Here's how decimals work. To continue the place value system with numbers less than one (fractions), we have to add another place to the right of the ones place, and ones have to be ten times the size of the numbers in that place. One is ten times bigger than $\frac{1}{10}$, so the place to the right of the ones is the tenths place. Next, we need to include another place to the right of the tenths. Tenths need to be ten times the size of the numbers in this place. The numbers in this place, then, need to be hundredths ($\frac{1}{100}$).[2] And we can keep adding places as long as we want, just as we can add as many places on the left as we want for the whole numbers.

···	100s	10s	1s	$\frac{1}{10}$	$\frac{1}{100}$	···
←	3	2	6	☐	☐	→

Once we have all these new places, it's usually easy to fit fractions into them. Take the number $326\frac{1}{2}$ as an example. It has 3 hundreds, 2 tens, 6 ones, and one *half*. Obviously, the half doesn't fit. Ones aren't ten times the size of halves. So to use decimals here, we need to change halves to tenths. All we have to do is multiply the top and

---

[1] The word decimal is from a Latin word for 10.

[2] Ones are ten times as big as tenths because 10 times $\frac{1}{10}$ equals 1. And tenths are ten times as big as hundredths because 10 times $\frac{1}{100}$ equals $\frac{1}{10}$.

bottom of $\frac{1}{2}$ by 5. We know from the Law of Equivalent Fractions that that won't change the value of the fraction at all. But it will change the denominator to 10, which turns $\frac{1}{2}$ into five tenths.

$$\frac{1 \times 5}{2 \times 5} = \frac{5}{10}$$

Multiplying top and bottom of $\frac{1}{2}$ by 5

Now our number is $326\frac{5}{10}$. The fraction is a tenth and it's in the tenth place, where it should be. But wait a minute. We don't write hundreds next to the 3 or tens next to the 2. So why do we need the denominator in $\frac{5}{10}$? The denominator is telling us that the 5 is a tenth. But we already know that, since the place next to ones always stands for tenths. So we can just put in a 5 to stand for 5 tenths and leave the denominator out.

The 5 stands for tenths.

3265

There's still a problem with this, though. How do we tell which place is which? Somebody might think that 3265 means "three thousand two hundred sixty-five" mistaking the 5 for ones instead of tenths. We could try to fix this problem in several different ways. We could put a space between the 6 and 5, to show that the 5 stands for tenths.

326 5

But that might get confusing because people with sloppy handwriting might not make the space big enough. Another approach would be to put a slash between the two.

326/5

That would work okay. But, in the end, the mathematicians decided to use a dot instead of a slash. So in decimal form, $326\frac{1}{2}$ is written as 326.5.

The dot separates whole numbers from decimals

326.5

This number means 3 hundreds, 2 tens, 6 ones, and 5 tenths (which is the same as $\frac{1}{2}$). The dot shows very clearly which place is which, because the dot always goes between the ones and tenths place. As you know, the dot is actually called a **decimal point**.

By turning $\frac{1}{2}$ into $\frac{5}{10}$ and fitting it into the tenths place to get 326.5, we've made the number $326\frac{1}{2}$ fit perfectly into the place value system, where each place is worth ten times as much as the place to the right of it.

Leaving Off the Whole Numbers

Of course, decimals aren't always used to write numbers that are greater than one. We can also convert a pure fraction like $\frac{2}{5}$ (which doesn't have a whole number attached) into a decimal fraction. We just need to change $\frac{2}{5}$ to tenths. This is done by multiplying top and bottom by 2.

$$\frac{2 \times 2}{5 \times 2} = \frac{4}{10} \qquad \text{Multiplying top and bottom of } \frac{2}{5} \text{ by 2}$$

That gives us $\frac{4}{10}$. But we want to write this as a decimal, so we don't need the denominator of the fraction. All we have to do is put 4 in the tenths place. The decimal point should go to the left of it, like this: .4. But since the decimal point is hard to see, most people add a 0 in the ones column.

$$0.4$$

The 0 doesn't change the value of the number, but it keeps people from confusing four tenths with four. When they see the 0, they realize that 0.4 doesn't have 4 ones it has 0 ones and 4 tenths. The main point is that $\frac{2}{5}$ written as a decimal is 0.4.

Practice 15

a.
(14)
400 has how many $\frac{4}{3}$ s in it?

b.
(15)
Write $\frac{3}{10}$ as a decimal.

c.
(15)
Write $\frac{3}{5}$ as a decimal.

d.
(15)
Write $3\frac{4}{5}$ as a decimal.

e.
(14)
Translate the word problem below into math; then solve.

Only $\frac{1}{2}$ of a slice of pizza was left and the 3 college roommates agreed to split it equally. What fraction of the entire slice did each get? Make sure your answer is fully reduced.

Problem Set 15

Tell whether each sentence below is True or False.

1.
(15)
Decimals are special fractions that have been designed to fit into our modern number system.

2.
(15)
A decimal point separates the ones column from the tenths column.

Add or subtract each group of numbers below.

3.
(2)
$$
\begin{array}{r}
8,025 \\
3,671 \\
4,054 \\
+1,239 \\
\hline
\end{array}
$$

4.
(2)
$$
\begin{array}{r}
89,705 \\
-47,846 \\
\hline
\end{array}
$$

Multiply or divide each pair of numbers below.

5.
(3)
$$
\begin{array}{r}
8,308 \\
\times 101 \\
\hline
\end{array}
$$

6.
(4)
$32\overline{)24,389}$

Add or subtract each pair of numbers below. Make sure your answers are fully reduced.

7.
(10)
$\dfrac{5}{9} + \dfrac{4}{9}$

8.
(11)
$\dfrac{19}{20} - \dfrac{7}{10}$

9.
(11)
$\dfrac{9}{14} + \dfrac{5}{12}$

10.
(12)
$1\dfrac{1}{8} - \dfrac{2}{3}$

11.
(12)
$4\dfrac{3}{4} + 5\dfrac{1}{2}$

Multiply or divide each pair of numbers below. Make sure your answers are fully reduced.

12.
(14)
$120 \times \dfrac{2}{5}$

13.
(14)
$\dfrac{2}{11} \div 5$

14.
(13)
$\dfrac{3}{8} \times \dfrac{4}{9}$

15.
(13)
$\dfrac{5}{3} \div \dfrac{2}{3}$

Answer each question below. Make sure your answer is fully reduced.

16.
(13)
What is $\dfrac{6}{7}$ of $\dfrac{1}{12}$?

(a) 17.
(14)
300 has how many $\dfrac{2}{3}$s in it?

(b) 18.
(15)
Write $\dfrac{1}{10}$ as a decimal.

(c) 19.
(15)
Write $\dfrac{2}{5}$ as a decimal.

(d) 20.
(15)
Write $14\dfrac{1}{2}$ as a decimal.

Translate the word problem below into math; then solve.

(e) 21.
(14)
The 87 person rescue squadron was stuck in the middle of the desert with only $\dfrac{1}{2}$ of a water cooler left. What fraction of the water cooler should each member of the squadron get? Make sure your answer is fully reduced.

Lesson 16—Hundredths, Thousandths ...

In the last lesson, we learned about decimals. To refresh your memory, the main advantage of decimals is that they allow us to fit fractions into our place value system in the same way as whole numbers.

Going Beyond Tenths

We changed a couple of fractions into tenths in the previous lesson. And it was a pretty simple process. Sometimes, though, a fraction can't be written with a denominator of 10, which means that it just won't fit into the tenths place. Here's an example.

$$28\frac{3}{4}$$

To make this a tenth, we would need to multiply the top and bottom of $\frac{3}{4}$ by some number that would change the 4 into a 10. The problem is that there's no whole number that will do that. So we can't change $\frac{3}{4}$ into a tenth.

That's no big deal, though. Not all whole numbers will fit into the ones place either. For instance, the number 28 can't be written with just ones. It uses the tens place too. It works the same way with some fractions. When a fraction can't be written as a tenth, we have to use the next place over, which is the hundredths place.

So to change $\frac{3}{4}$ to a decimal, instead of thinking of a number that we can multiply 4 by to get 10, let's think of a number we can multiply 4 by to get 100. That number is 25. So we should multiply the top and bottom of $\frac{3}{4}$ by 25.

$$\frac{3\times 25}{4\times 25} = \frac{75}{100}$$

Multiplying top and bottom of $\frac{3}{4}$ by 25

That gives us $\frac{75}{100}$. Notice that the number on top has two digits instead of one, so it won't fit into a single place. How do we handle that? What we can do is split $\frac{75}{100}$ into two separate fractions.

$$\frac{75}{100} = \frac{70}{100} + \frac{5}{100}$$

Split $\frac{75}{100}$ into two fractions.

Then, since $\frac{70}{100}$ reduces to $\frac{7}{10}$, that means $\frac{75}{100} = \frac{7}{10} + \frac{5}{100}$. But that's just 7 tenths and 5 hundredths. Both of those fit perfectly into our decimal number system, with 7 going in the tenths place and 5 in the hundredths place. So $28\frac{3}{4}$ becomes 28.75.

We wanted to show you the splitting-the-fraction step because that explains why $\frac{3}{4}$ is the same as 7 tenths and 5 hundredths. But it would be a real hassle to have to split a fraction every time we change one to a decimal.

Fortunately, there's a shorter way to do it. Once we make the denominator of a fraction equal to 100 (like $\frac{75}{100}$), then if the numerator has two numbers (as in 75), we know automatically that the first digit is the tenth and the second is the hundredth. If the numerator has just one digit (like $\frac{2}{100}$), then that digit is a hundredth, and a zero needs to go in the tenths place (0.02). With this shortcut, we know immediately that $\frac{43}{100}$ means 4 tenths and 3 hundredths (0.43). And we know that $\frac{7}{100}$ means 7 hundredths (0.07). No fraction splitting is necessary.

Going Beyond Hundredths

Some fractions won't fit completely into the tenths and the hundredths place. Even some simple fractions can't be squeezed into those two positions. Take $\frac{1}{8}$, for instance. It won't fit into tenths and hundredths, because there's no whole number that can be multiplied by 8 to get 10 or 100. What we have to do is go to the next place over, which is thousandths. To make the denominator of $\frac{1}{8}$ equal 1,000, we just have to multiply top and bottom by 125.

$$\frac{1 \times 125}{8 \times 125} = \frac{125}{1,000} \qquad \textbf{Multiplying top and bottom of } \frac{1}{8} \textbf{ by 125.}$$

To turn $\frac{125}{1,000}$ into a decimal, we could break it down into three fractions: $\frac{100}{1,000} + \frac{20}{1,000} + \frac{5}{1,000}$. Then, the first two fractions can be reduced to get $\frac{1}{10} + \frac{2}{100} + \frac{5}{1,000}$. That comes out to 1 tenth, 2 hundredths, and 5 thousandths. All three of these fit into our number system, so $\frac{1}{8}$ becomes 0.125.

As before, we can change $\frac{125}{1,000}$ to a decimal without any fraction splitting. Here's the shortcut for a denominator of 1,000. If the numerator has three digits (like 125), the first digit is the tenth, the second digit is the hundredth, and the third digit is the thousandth. If the numerator has two digits (like $\frac{21}{1,000}$), then the first digit is the hundredth and the second digit is the thousandth. There's no tenth, so a zero goes in the tenths place. So $\frac{21}{1,000}$ actually equals 0.021. If the numerator has just one digit (like $\frac{3}{1,000}$), then that digit goes in the thousandths place, with zeros in the tenths and hundredths place. Therefore, $\frac{3}{1,000}$ equals 0.003. Of course, there are some fractions that require places even farther to the right than thousandths, such as ten thousandths, hundred thousandths, and on up. The method for converting them to decimal form is exactly the same.

Practice 16

a.
(16) Write $14\frac{9}{100}$ as a decimal.

b.
(13) $\frac{3}{8}$ has how many $\frac{1}{4}$s in it? Make sure your answer is fully reduced.

c.
(16) Write $2\frac{5}{8}$ as a decimal.

d.
(16) Write $\frac{1}{5}$ as a decimal.

e.
(13) Translate the word problem below into math; then solve.

One-half of the motocross racers said they had banged up their shins. One-fifth of those said they had bruised their elbows too. What fraction of the racers had banged up their shins <u>and</u> bruised their elbows? Make sure your answer is fully reduced.

Problem Set 16

Tell whether each sentence below is True or False.

1.
(16) Some fractions cannot fit in the tenths column alone.

2.
(16) All fractions can fit into either the tenths or hundredths column.

Add or subtract each group of numbers below.

3.
(2)
$$\begin{array}{r} 899 \\ 2,212 \\ 3,923 \\ +1,205 \\ \hline \end{array}$$

4.
(2)
$$\begin{array}{r} 65,134 \\ -33,201 \\ \hline \end{array}$$

Multiply or divide each pair of numbers below.

5.
(3)
$$\begin{array}{r} 4,008 \\ \times 305 \\ \hline \end{array}$$

6.
(4) $14\overline{)28,764}$

Add or subtract each pair of fractions below. Make sure your answers are fully reduced.

7.
(10) $\frac{2}{3}+\frac{1}{6}$

8.
(10) $\frac{3}{4}-\frac{1}{7}$

9.
(10) $\frac{3}{8}+\frac{5}{9}$

10.
(12) $6\frac{1}{2}-3\frac{2}{5}$

Multiply or divide each pair of numbers below. Make sure your answers are fully reduced.

11.
(13) $\dfrac{1}{3} \times \dfrac{3}{11}$

12.
(14) $\dfrac{3}{7} \div 6$

13.
(13) $1\dfrac{1}{4} \times \dfrac{8}{9}$

14.
(13) $\dfrac{9}{10} \div \dfrac{1}{2}$

Answer each question below. Make sure your answer is fully reduced.

15.
(14) What is $\dfrac{1}{5}$ of 320?

16.
(14) 150 has how many $\dfrac{2}{7}$ s in it?

(a) 17.
(16) Write $24\dfrac{7}{100}$ as a decimal.

(b) 18.
(13) $\dfrac{7}{9}$ has how many $\dfrac{1}{3}$ s in it?

(c) 19.
(16) Write $10\dfrac{3}{8}$ as a decimal.

(d) 20.
(16) Write $\dfrac{1}{4}$ as a decimal.

Translate the word problem below into math; then solve.

(e) 21.
(13) One-fourth of the villains nabbed by the Second-Rate Superhero were jaywalkers. One-ninth of those were illegal double parkers too. What fraction of the nabbed villains were both jaywalkers and illegal double parkers? Make sure your answer is fully reduced.

Lesson 17—Adding and Subtracting Decimals

For the last few lessons, you may have been asking yourself why anyone would bother changing regular fractions to decimals (like $\frac{1}{8}$ to 0.125). Maybe the mathematicians get excited about putting all numbers (whole and fractional) into the place value system, but is there any practical reason for doing it? Absolutely. The reason for making the change is that fractions become much easier to add and subtract when they're written as decimals. It's a lot like going from Roman numerals (which are hard to add and subtract) to our modern numbers (which are easy to add and subtract). Let us explain.

Lining Up the Decimal Points

You know what a pain it is to add mixed numbers with different denominators. An example would be something like $4\frac{2}{5} + 3\frac{1}{2}$. First, you have to convert each mixed number to an improper fraction. Then you have to find a lowest common denominator (LCD). After that, you have to change both of the denominators to the LCD and add their numerators. Finally, you might even have to reduce the answer. That's a lot of work.

But what if $4\frac{2}{5} + 3\frac{1}{2}$ were converted to decimals first? We know that $4\frac{2}{5}$ is 4.4 and $3\frac{1}{2}$ is 3.5, so that gives us $4.4 + 3.5$. With both numbers in decimal form, they can be added vertically, just like whole numbers.

$$\begin{array}{r} 4.4 \\ + \ 3.5 \\ \hline \mathbf{7.9} \end{array}$$

Add vertically and bring the decimal point down.

The answer is 7.9.[1] See how easy that was? That's the big advantage of converting fractions to decimals. By making fractions fit into the number system, they can be added or subtracted using the same basic methods that you've already learned for whole numbers. Even though you learned how to add decimals years ago, you may not have known their true purpose. Notice also that the decimal points in 4.4 and 3.5 are lined up. And the decimal point in the answer 7.9 is directly below them. That's important because that's how we make sure we're adding ones to ones and tenths to tenths, and so on. When adding and subtracting decimals, then, the decimal points must always be lined up.

Carrying with Decimals

Occasionally, when adding decimals, the tenths or hundredths (or some column even further to the right) will add to equal a number more than 10. Here's an example.

$$\begin{array}{r} 25.81 \\ + 14.73 \\ \hline \end{array}$$

Both of these numbers have fractional parts (0.81 and 0.73). But since the fractions are written as decimals, we can add the two numbers as if they were whole numbers. We just add the columns vertically. But notice below that when adding the tenths column, we get 15. All we have to do, though, is put the 5 down below and carry the 1, just as we do with whole numbers. From there we finish by adding the other columns in the normal way. And, of course, the decimal points need to be all lined up.

---

[1] The answer 7.9 could be changed back to a mixed number to get $7\frac{9}{10}$. But it isn't necessary to do this.

$$
\begin{array}{r}
\mathbf{1\,1} \\
25.81 \\
+ \; 14.73 \\
\hline
40.54
\end{array}
$$

Add vertically and
carry when necessary.

Even though adding decimals is so easy that you can do it without thinking, it's helpful to understand how the process actually works. When we added the tenths column to get 15, that was really 15 tenths or $\frac{15}{10}$. That's the same as $1\frac{5}{10}$. We then wrote down the 5 in the tenths column and carried the 1 into the ones column. The system worked perfectly. That's the beauty of decimals. We can handle fractions as easily as whole numbers.

A Subtraction Example

Here's a subtraction example.

$$
\begin{array}{r}
887.616 \\
-352.372
\end{array}
$$

First, we have to make sure that the decimal points are all lined up vertically, with hundreds over hundreds, tens over tens, ones over ones, and tenths over tenths, etc. Next, we just subtract each column. The procedure is exactly the same as with whole numbers. When a number on top is smaller then the one below it, we have to regroup. In this problem, we need to regroup in the hundredths column by bringing over 1 tenth.

$$
\begin{array}{r}
\mathbf{5\,11} \\
887.6\cancel{1}6 \\
- \; 352.372 \\
\hline
535.244
\end{array}
$$

Subtract vertically and
regroup when necessary.

Make sure you understand what we did in the regrouping step. We had 1 hundredth minus 7 hundredths. But then we brought 1 tenth over, which makes 11 hundredths. And that left only 5 tenths on top in the tenths column. But, once again, the great thing about decimals is that you don't even have to think about whether you're subtracting tenths, hundredths, or anything else. It all works just like whole numbers.

We don't have room to show any more examples, but it's possible to add more than 2 numbers with decimals. And the procedure is exactly the same as the one we use for whole numbers, except for making sure that the decimal points are lined up.

Practice 17

a.
(16) Write $2\frac{7}{1,000}$ as a decimal.

b.
(15) Write $\frac{3}{5}$ as a decimal.

c.
(17) Subtract
$$
\begin{array}{r}
68.742 \\
-35.393
\end{array}
$$

d.
(17) Add
$$
\begin{array}{r}
456.923 \\
+138.729
\end{array}
$$

e.
(13)   Translate the word problem below into math; then solve.

One fourth of the Thai recipes were too spicy for Brenda's taste buds and $\frac{1}{2}$ of the ones that were too spicy for Brenda were also too spicy for her husband. What fraction of the recipes were too spicy for Brenda's husband? Make sure your answer is fully reduced.

Problem Set 17

Tell whether each sentence below is True or False.

1.
(17)   Fractions are easier to add and subtract when they are written as decimals.

2.
(17)   When adding or subtracting decimals, the decimal points of the numbers should always be lined up.

Write each number below as a decimal.

3.
(16) $12\frac{7}{100}$

(a) 4.
(16) $3\frac{5}{1,000}$

(b) 5.
(15) $\frac{2}{5}$

Add or subtract each pair of numbers below.

6.
(17)
$$\begin{array}{r} 25.13 \\ +43.62 \\ \hline \end{array}$$

7.
(17)
$$\begin{array}{r} 9.75 \\ -3.23 \\ \hline \end{array}$$

8.
(17)
$$\begin{array}{r} 464.15 \\ +302.71 \\ \hline \end{array}$$

(c) 9.
(17)
$$\begin{array}{r} 46.563 \\ -24.275 \\ \hline \end{array}$$

(d) 10.
(17)
$$\begin{array}{r} 526.663 \\ +193.478 \\ \hline \end{array}$$

Multiply or divide each pair of numbers below.

11.
(3)
$$\begin{array}{r} 864 \\ \times 92 \\ \hline \end{array}$$

12.
(4) $18\overline{)9,846}$

Add or subtract each pair of fractions below. Make sure your answers are fully reduced.

13.
(10) $\frac{1}{8} + \frac{3}{4}$

14.
(10) $\frac{4}{5} - \frac{2}{3}$

15.
(12) $5\frac{1}{4} + 2\frac{1}{6}$

16.
(12) $7 - \frac{1}{5}$

Multiply or divide each pair of numbers below. Make sure your answers are fully reduced.

17.
(13) $\dfrac{2}{5}\times\dfrac{10}{12}$

18.
(14) $5\div\dfrac{2}{7}$

19.
(13) $\dfrac{2}{9}\div\dfrac{4}{3}$

Answer each question below. Make sure your answers are fully reduced.

20.
(14) What is $\dfrac{3}{4}$ of 264?

21.
(13) $\dfrac{5}{6}$ has how many $\dfrac{1}{12}$ s in it?

Translate the word problem below into math; then solve.

(e) 22.
(13) After seventy-seven failed attempts, the hockey team finally won the championship. Now $\dfrac{1}{2}$ of the fans think the city should name a street after the winning coach, and $\dfrac{1}{12}$ of those believe he should also be appointed mayor. What fraction of the fans believe the coach should be appointed mayor as well as have a street named after him? Make sure your answer is fully reduced.

Lesson 18—Filling the Holes

In the last lesson, we learned how to add and subtract decimals. But here's an addition problem that's a little different. Suppose we tried to add the decimals 79.2 and 82.43.

$$79.2$$
$$+\ 82.43$$

Filling Holes when Adding

We've got the decimal points lined up vertically, as we should. But notice that there's a hole in the hundredths column. Is that a problem? Not really. It just means that 79.2 doesn't have any hundredths. But just so we have a number in every place, it's a good idea to fill the hole with a 0.

$$79.20 \longleftarrow \text{Fill in the}$$
$$+\ 82.43 \qquad \text{hole with a 0.}$$

The extra zero makes it clear that the hundredths column is being treated just like all the others. Even more importantly, it helps us avoid the mistake of getting the decimal points out of line. For instance, without that extra 0, we might have mistakenly written the problem like this.

$$\text{The decimal points}$$
$$\text{aren't lined up.}$$
$$\downarrow$$
$$79.2$$
$$+\ 82.43$$

These decimal points are out of line, and that could cause us to add tenths with hundredths or tenths with ones, which would be totally wrong. Putting in that extra zero is kind of like putting a zero in front of .7 to get 0.7. It doesn't change the value of the number, it just makes things easier. But here's our problem worked out correctly (with the extra 0).

$$\overset{1}{79.20}$$
$$+\ 82.43 \qquad \text{Adding normally}$$
$$\overline{161.63}$$

Filling Holes when Subtracting

Filling the holes with an extra 0 is even more important when we're subtracting decimals. For example, to subtract 23.14 from 85.7 vertically, we really need to put a zero in the hundredths place of 85.7 to get 85.70.

$$85.70$$
$$-\ 23.14$$

What makes the 0 really necessary here is that we're going to have to regroup to subtract the hundredths (since 0 is smaller than 4). Without the 0, regrouping would be kind of tough. Here's the way it should work.

$$85.\overset{6\ 10}{\cancel{70}}$$
$$-\ 23.14 \qquad \text{The 0 helps}$$
$$\overline{62.56} \qquad \text{with regrouping.}$$

Filling More than One Hole

Sometimes, we have to fill more than one hole. Look at this problem.

$$896.9$$
$$- 53.324$$

We have two holes to fill here. One in the hundredths place and one in the thousandths place. All we do is put an extra 0 in each place and subtract normally.

$$
\begin{array}{r}
896.900 \\
- 53.324 \\
\hline
843.576
\end{array}
$$

Subtract normally,
regrouping twice.

We could have even filled the hole in the hundreds column of 53.324. Then the problem would have looked like this.

$$896.900$$
$$-053.324$$

But we're so used to working with whole numbers that it's not really necessary to fill in a hole to the left of the decimal point. It's probably enough just to fill in the holes on the right side of the point.

Practice 18

a.
(16)   Write $\dfrac{189}{1,000}$ as a decimal.

b.
(16)   Write $6\dfrac{5}{8}$ as a decimal.

c.
(18)   Add $\begin{array}{r} 649.58 \\ +285.4 \\ \hline \end{array}$

d.
(18)   Subtract $\begin{array}{r} 67.8 \\ -53.43 \\ \hline \end{array}$

e.
(13)   Translate the word problem below into math; then solve.

One half of the Tech All-Star League had air-conditioned helmets and $\dfrac{1}{15}$ of that group also had foot-massage cleats. What fraction of the league had both air-conditioned helmets and foot-massage cleats? Make sure your answer is fully reduced.

Problem Set 18

Tell whether each sentence below is True or False.

1.
(18)   When adding numbers, putting zeros in for empty places helps avoid getting the decimal points out of line.

2.
(18)   It is never necessary to put in extra zeros when subtracting decimals.

Write each number below as a decimal.

(a) 3.
(16) $\dfrac{142}{1,000}$

4.
(16) $7\dfrac{23}{100}$

(b) 5.
(16) $10\dfrac{3}{8}$

Add or subtract each pair of numbers below.

6.
(17)
$$\begin{array}{r} 46.95 \\ +21.62 \\ \hline \end{array}$$

7.
(17)
$$\begin{array}{r} 8.63 \\ -4.81 \\ \hline \end{array}$$

(c) 8.
(18)
$$\begin{array}{r} 573.68 \\ +391.6 \\ \hline \end{array}$$

(d) 9.
(18)
$$\begin{array}{r} 89.7 \\ -65.25 \\ \hline \end{array}$$

10.
(17)
$$\begin{array}{r} 57.346 \\ +33.579 \\ \hline \end{array}$$

Multiply or divide each pair of numbers below.

11.
(3)
$$\begin{array}{r} 1,708 \\ \times 130 \\ \hline \end{array}$$

12.
(4) $22\overline{)15,432}$

Add or subtract each pair of fractions below. Leave your answer in fractional form, but make sure the fraction is fully reduced.

13.
(10) $\dfrac{5}{11}+\dfrac{4}{11}$

14.
(12) $8\dfrac{1}{3}-2\dfrac{1}{7}$

15.
(12) $5+\dfrac{9}{4}$

16.
(12) $3-\dfrac{6}{5}$

Multiply or divide each pair of numbers below. Make sure your answer is fully reduced.

17.
(13) $\dfrac{1}{9}\times\dfrac{3}{5}$

18.
(14) $\dfrac{7}{8}\div 14$

19.
(13) $\dfrac{3}{2}\div\dfrac{1}{8}$

Answer each question below.

20.
(14) What is $\dfrac{1}{8}$ of 480?

21.
(14) 56 has how many $\dfrac{2}{3}$ s in it?

Translate the word problem below into math; then solve.

(e) 22.
(13) One half of the genius islanders had hammocks and $\dfrac{1}{7}$ of that group also had wind-resistant grass huts.

What fraction of the genius islanders had both hammocks and wind-resistant grass huts? Make sure your answer is fully reduced.

Lesson 19—Money and Decimals

In this lesson, we're going to talk about one of the most common ways that people use decimals, and that's to work with money. You may have never thought of this, but everybody uses decimals when money is involved.

Quarters and Nickels and Decimals

As an example, what if we wanted to add a $5 bill and a quarter to a $10 bill and a nickel? A quarter is the same as 25 cents and that's written as 0.25. A nickel is the same as 5 cents or 0.05. What we would probably do is combine the 5 dollars and the quarter to get 5.25. Then we would combine the 10 dollars and the nickel to get 10.05. Since these are decimals, we would add them vertically, making sure to line up the decimal points like this.

$$\begin{array}{r} \overset{1}{5.25} \\ +\,10.05 \\ \hline \mathbf{15.30} \end{array}$$

Convert cents to decimal and add vertically.

The answer comes out to 15.30, which is just 15 dollars and 30 cents.

Everybody knows how to add money in that way. But if you think about it, the whole procedure was designed to avoid using fractions with different denominators. After all, a quarter is a fourth of a dollar (that's where the name "quarter" comes from), and a nickel is a twentieth of a dollar. (It takes 20 nickels to make $1.) So we could have done the problem like this instead.

$$5\frac{1}{4}+10\frac{1}{20}$$

It would have been a lot harder, though, because we would have had to find a lowest common denominator, and so on. By converting the quarter and nickel into decimal form, we avoided the messy fractions entirely. And since we're so used to working with quarters and nickels, we even did the conversions in our head. (You were probably required to memorize those in earlier basic math courses.) But no one would ever dream of doing a money calculation using $\frac{1}{4}$ for a quarter and $\frac{1}{20}$ for a nickel, because decimals are so much easier. So money is just another example of why decimals are so helpful.

A Handy Table

Just as a review, here are the most common amounts of money and their decimal forms. You can look back at this whenever you're doing money problems in your assignments.

Common Money Amounts in Dollars

amount	fraction	decimal
half dollar	$\frac{1}{2}$	0.5
quarter	$\frac{1}{4}$	0.25
dime	$\frac{1}{10}$	0.10
nickel	$\frac{1}{20}$	0.05
penny	$\frac{1}{100}$	0.01

Practice 19

a.
(16) Write $\dfrac{23}{1,000}$ as a decimal.

b.
(19) Write the following amount of money as a decimal number (in dollars): two $5 bills, three $1 bills, two quarters, and two dimes.

c.
(19) Write the following amount of money as a decimal number (in dollars): two quarters, one dime, four nickels, and three pennies.

d.
(18) Add $\begin{array}{r} 88.37 \\ +43.945 \\ \hline \end{array}$

e.
(19) Translate the word problem below into math; then solve.

Just before heading off to her palatial winter getaway, Madame Pompadour purchased her 43rd pair of mink earmuffs for $3,900.45 and her 27th pair of mink leg warmers for $5,230.58. What was the total bill for these two items?

Problem Set 19

Tell whether each sentence below is True or False.

1.
(19) We use decimal numbers when doing calculations with money.

2.
(19) It helps to memorize what a quarter, a dime, and a nickel all stand for when written as decimals.

Write each number below as a decimal.

3.
(16) $\dfrac{17}{100}$

(a) 4.
(16) $\dfrac{52}{1,000}$

5.
(16) $18\dfrac{3}{10,000}$

Write each amount of money as a decimal number (in dollars).

(b) 6.
(19) three $5 bills, two $1 bills, one quarter, and one dime

(c) 7.
(19) one quarter, two dimes, three nickels, and four pennies

Add or subtract each pair of numbers below.

8.
(17)
$$11.25$$
$$+6.76$$

9.
(17)
$$36.61$$
$$-15.72$$

10.
(17)
$$467.58$$
$$-56.19$$

(d) 11.
(18)
$$99.05$$
$$+37.211$$

Multiply or divide each pair of numbers below.

12.
(3)
$$3,200$$
$$\times 405$$

13.
(4)
$$26\overline{)20,384}$$

Add or subtract the fractions below. Leave your answer in fractional form, but make sure the fraction is fully reduced.

14.
(10)
$\dfrac{1}{2}+\dfrac{5}{2}$

15.
(11)
$\dfrac{5}{6}-\dfrac{7}{9}$

16.
(12)
$12\dfrac{3}{4}-11\dfrac{3}{8}$

Multiply or divide each pair of numbers below. Make sure your answer is fully reduced.

17.
(14)
$6\times\dfrac{7}{12}$

18.
(13)
$\dfrac{7}{8}\div\dfrac{1}{4}$

19.
(13)
$\dfrac{2}{5}\times 4\dfrac{1}{2}$

Answer each question below. Make sure your answer is fully reduced.

20.
(13)
What is $\dfrac{1}{4}$ of $\dfrac{2}{3}$?

21.
(13)
$\dfrac{3}{4}$ has how many $\dfrac{1}{16}$s in it?

Translate the word problem below into math; then solve.

(e) 22.
(19)
Madame Pompadour recently purchased a velvet-lined doggie basket and a diamond-studded flea collar as birthday gifts for her beloved pet poodle. If the two items cost \$3,215.90 and \$5,850.25 respectively, what was the total bill?

Lesson 20—Multiplying Decimals

Now that we've learned about adding and subtracting decimals, let's talk about multiplying them. Take a look at this example.

$$1.25 \times 7.5$$

Since 1.25 is the same as $1\frac{1}{4}$ and 7.5 is the same as $7\frac{1}{2}$, we could multiply these as mixed numbers. But that would be pretty messy. Multiplying them as decimals is actually much easier, because decimals can be multiplied using basically the same method we use for multiplying whole numbers. The tenths and hundredths can be treated just like the ones. So it's not just addition and subtraction that are made easier by using decimals, but multiplication too.

That's another advantage of using decimals to make fractions (like $\frac{1}{4}$ and $\frac{1}{2}$) fit into our number system.

Just Like Whole Numbers Again

Let's go through the steps for multiplying 1.25 and 7.5. First, we need to write the numbers vertically (just as with long multiplication of whole numbers).

```
   ↓
  1.25
× 7.5
```

Just line the numbers
up on the right.

Notice, though, that the decimal points aren't lined up. That's one of the differences between addition and subtraction with decimals and multiplication with decimals. When multiplying, we don't have to worry about lining up the decimal points. All we have to do is make the digits that are farthest to the right line up (the 5s, in this case) and let the rest of the digits (and the decimal points) take care of themselves. The next step is to multiply the numbers normally, completely ignoring the decimal points. We just pretend they aren't even there at this point.

```
    3
  1 2
  1.25
× 7.5
 1 625
  8750
 9375
```

Multiply normally,
ignoring the decimal
points.

We end up with 9375. But that isn't the final answer, because we still need to place the decimal point. Where should it go? We can't write it underneath the other decimal points, because they aren't lined up. Here's how we figure out where to put the decimal point.

Counting the Digits

We count the number of digits to the right of the decimal point in each of the numbers being multiplied. In 1.25, there are two digits to the right of the decimal point (2 and 5). In 7.5, there is one digit to the right of the decimal point (5). Then we add up the total number of digits: 2+1 equals 3.

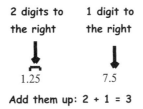

2 digits to   1 digit to
the right   the right

1.25   7.5

Add them up: 2 + 1 = 3

Next comes the key step. We go to 9375 (our answer) and put the decimal point in a position so that there are exactly 3 digits to the right of it. That means the decimal point needs to go between the 9 and 3 like this.

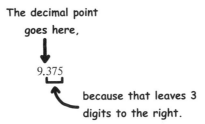

The decimal point
goes here,

9.375

because that leaves 3
digits to the right.

So our final answer is 9.375. That's all there is to it.

Decimal Times Whole Number

To multiply a decimal by a whole number, we use the exact same method. Here's a simple example.

$$7.4$$
$$\times 8$$

We already have the numbers lined up along the right. So the first step is to multiply, ignoring the decimal point.

$$
\begin{array}{r}
^{3}\,7.4 \\
\times\ 8 \\
\hline
592
\end{array}
$$

Multiply normally,
ignoring the decimal
point.

Now to place the decimal point in the answer, we just count the number of digits to the right of the decimal points in 7.4 and 8. There's 1 digit to the right of the point in 7.4. What about 8, though? No decimal point is showing. But, remember, every whole number actually has a decimal point on the far right, even if it isn't shown. Since there's no digit to the right of the point, we get 0 digits for 8.[1] Next, we need to add those digits up: 1+0 equals 1. The final step is to place the decimal point in 592 so that there is 1 digit to the right of it. That means the point goes between the 9 and 2.

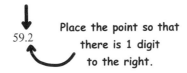

59.2

Place the point so that
there is 1 digit
to the right.

---

[1] It's wrong to write 8 as 8.0 and then say there's 1 digit to the right of the decimal point. With that method, you could create as many digits to the right of the point as you wanted: 8.00 or 8.000 or 8.0000 and so on.

No Hole Filling

Another nice thing about multiplication is that we don't have to fill up holes with zeros (the way we do when adding and subtracting decimals). For example, when multiplying 5.34 times 2.2, we can just write the problem like this.

$$5.34$$
$$\times 2.2$$

We don't have to fill the hundredths place in 2.2 to get 2.20. That's not necessary because we're not lining up the decimal points. All we have to do is line the numbers up on the right and start multiplying. Here's this problem all worked out.

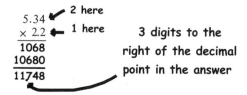

Since there are 2 digits to the right of the decimal point in 5.34 and 1 digit to the right of the point in 2.2, we place the decimal point so that there are 3 digits to the right in the answer. That gives us 11.748.

Practice 20

a.
(16)   Write $\dfrac{409}{10,000}$ as a decimal.

b.
(20)   Multiply
$$3.8$$
$$\times 0.77$$

c.
(20)   Multiply
$$0.547$$
$$\times 2.6$$

d.
(20)   Multiply
$$422.4$$
$$\times 23$$

e.
(20)   Translate the word problem below into math; then solve.

Rocky Raccoons were on sale for $3.30 per pound. If Mrs. Gargantua bought 4.5 pounds worth for tonight's dinner, what was her total bill?

Problem Set 20

Tell whether each sentence below is True or False.

1.
(20)   Decimals can be multiplied with the same basic method that is used for multiplying whole numbers.

2.
(20)   When multiplying decimals, both decimal points must be lined up.

Write each number below as a decimal.

(a) 3.
(16) $\dfrac{101}{10,000}$

4.
(16) $\dfrac{11}{50}$

Write each amount of money as a decimal number (in dollars).

5.
(19)   one $10 bill, one $1 bill, two quarters, two dimes, and four pennies

6.
(19)   three quarters, three dimes, five nickels, and one penny

Add or subtract each group of numbers below.

7.
(17)
$$\begin{array}{r} 86.32 \\ -8.25 \\ \hline \end{array}$$

8.
(17)
$$\begin{array}{r} 156.3 \\ 54.8 \\ +8.9 \\ \hline \end{array}$$

9.
(17)
$$\begin{array}{r} 24.402 \\ -5.285 \\ \hline \end{array}$$

10.
(18)
$$\begin{array}{r} 738.254 \\ +95.05 \\ \hline \end{array}$$

Multiply or divide each pair of numbers below.

11.
(20)
$$\begin{array}{r} 27.657 \\ \times 0.8 \\ \hline \end{array}$$

(b) 12.
(20)
$$\begin{array}{r} 2.4 \\ \times 0.99 \\ \hline \end{array}$$

(c) 13.
(20)
$$\begin{array}{r} 0.839 \\ \times 1.9 \\ \hline \end{array}$$

14.
(4) $9\overline{)47,106}$

(d) 15.
(20)
$$\begin{array}{r} 251.7 \\ \times 12 \\ \hline \end{array}$$

Add or subtract each pair of fractions below. Make sure your answers are fully reduced.

16.
(10) $\dfrac{2}{14}+\dfrac{3}{7}$

17.
(11) $\dfrac{7}{18}-\dfrac{1}{12}$

Multiply or divide each pair of numbers below. Make sure your answer is fully reduced.

18.
(14) $10\times\dfrac{4}{5}$

19.
(14) $\dfrac{8}{15}\div 4$

20.
(14) $\dfrac{2}{9}\times 3\times\dfrac{1}{4}$

Answer each question below.

21.
(14) What is $\dfrac{3}{8}$ of 256?

22.
(14) 500 has how many $\dfrac{5}{9}$ s in it?

Translate the word problem below into math; then solve.

(e) 23.
(20) Hippo lard sells for $1.20 per ounce. If Mrs. Gargantua bought 8.5 ounces worth for her Saturday brunch, what was her total bill?

Lesson 21—Dividing Decimals

We covered multiplication of decimals in the last lesson. What about division? Well, it turns out that decimals can be divided in basically the same way we divide whole numbers. So decimals allow us to add, subtract, multiply, and divide fractions as if they were plain old whole numbers. Pretty amazing.

Turning the Divisor into a Whole Number

Let's go through a division example.

$$2.5\overline{)15.75}$$

We could just divide the numbers by ignoring the decimal points at first and then figuring out where to put the decimal in our answer. Doing the problem that way, the rule is the reverse of the rule for multiplying. Instead of adding up the digits to the right of the decimal points, we would have to subtract them. But we won't show you that method because nobody actually divides decimals that way.[1]

There's an easier method that everybody uses. With this one, the first step is to make a change to the decimal points. This change is easier to understand if the problem is written as a fraction, so let's do that.

$$\frac{15.75}{2.5}$$

We multiply the bottom number by 10 or 100 or 1,000, or etc. in order to turn it into a whole number. In this case, we need to multiply 2.5 by 10 to make it 25. To avoid changing the value of the fraction, we have to multiply the top by 10 as well.

$$\frac{15.75 \times 10}{2.5 \times 10} = \frac{157.5}{25}$$

Make the number
on bottom
a whole number.

The important thing to understand is that the answer to the problem hasn't changed. We've just made the denominator a whole number. That will make the division a little easier.

The next step is to write the problem as a normal long division problem again and then carry out the division.[2] And we don't need to pay any attention to the decimal point in 157.5 at this stage.

$$
\begin{array}{r}
63 \\
25\overline{)157.5} \\
\underline{150\downarrow} \\
75 \\
\underline{75} \\
0
\end{array}
$$

Divide normally, ignoring
the decimal point.

---

[1] However, it is kind of interesting that this method is the reverse of the one for multiplying with decimals.

[2] Keep in mind that $25\overline{)157.5}$ has the same answer as $2.5\overline{)15.75}$, so whatever answer we get here will also be the answer to our original problem.

That gives us 63, but we still have to figure out where to put the decimal point. Since we changed 2.5 to 25 (and 15.75 to 157.5), all we have to do is put the decimal point directly above the point in 157.5. That means the point goes directly between the 6 and 3 to get 6.3.

$$25 \overline{)157.5} \quad \begin{array}{r} 6.3 \\ \hline \end{array}$$

$$\begin{array}{r} \underline{150} \\ 75 \\ \underline{75} \\ 0 \end{array}$$

The point goes directly above the point in 157.5.

If we hadn't changed 2.5 to 25, then we would have had to count the number of digits to the right of the decimal point in both numbers and subtract the digits and so on. But this method is a lot easier. Here are all the steps again for dividing with decimals.

Dividing with Decimals

1.	Multiply top and bottom by 10, 100, 1,000 or etc. to make the bottom number (divisor) a whole number.
2.	Do normal long division, ignoring the decimal point.
3.	Put the decimal point in the answer directly above the point in the number underneath (dividend).

Doing it in Your Head

Let's do one more example.

$$0.18 \overline{)9.36}$$

The first step is to write the problem as a fraction ($\frac{9.36}{0.18}$) and turn 0.18 (the divisor) into a whole number. We can do that by multiplying 0.18 and 9.36 by 100, which will change the bottom to 18 and the top to 936. You probably know that most people don't bother writing the problem as a fraction. They do this step in their head. They just move the decimal point in 0.18 until it's all the way to the right (to become 18) and then move the decimal point in 9.36 the same number of places, which is 2 places to the right, for 936. But this is the same thing as multiplying the top and bottom of $\frac{9.36}{0.18}$ by 100 (even though most people don't know it). By the way, an easy way to multiply and divide numbers by 10, 100, 1,000, and so on is to just move the decimal point. You may remember these shortcuts from earlier math courses but here they are again.

Multiplying and Dividing by Moving the Decimal Point

1.	When multiplying a decimal by 10, 100, 1,000, etc., move the decimal point in the number to the right as many places as there are 0s.
2.	When dividing a decimal by 10, 100, 1,000, etc., move the decimal point in the number to the left as many places as there are 0s.

When people move the decimal point in 0.18 as many places as in 9.36, they're just using shortcut number 1.

But getting back to our problem, we now have it in the form $18\overline{)936}$. This is now a really easy problem, because it's just division of two whole numbers. We won't even bother working it out. The answer is 52. Make sure you understand, though, that since $18\overline{)936}$ and $0.18\overline{)9.36}$ are the same, 52 is also the answer to $0.18\overline{)9.36}$, which was our original problem.

Practice 21

a.
(16) Write $\dfrac{8}{25}$ as a decimal.

b.
(18) Add
$$\begin{array}{r} 0.24 \\ 9.3 \\ +15.87 \\ \hline \end{array}$$

c.
(21) Divide $0.5\overline{)11.85}$

d.
(21) Divide $0.12\overline{)6.24}$

e.
(21) Translate the word problem below into math; then solve.

Pretty in Pink Lemonade costs $1.24 per bottle. If Shirley bought $19.84 worth, how many bottles did she buy?

Problem Set 21

Tell whether each sentence below is True or False.

1.
(21) When dividing two decimals, the first step is to change the divisor to a whole number.

2.
(21) When dividing a decimal number by a whole number, the decimal point stays in the same spot in the answer.

Write each number below as a decimal.

3.
(15) $\dfrac{9}{10}$

(a) 4.
(16) $\dfrac{1}{25}$

Add or subtract each group of numbers below.

5.
(17)
12.96
+11.07

6.
(17)
125.145
−33.268

(b) 7.
(18)
0.88
5.1
+18.56

8.
(17)
72.427
−43.634

Multiply or divide each pair of numbers below.

(c) 9.
(21) $0.4\overline{)31.24}$

10.
(20)
801.7
×2.3

11.
(21) $1.2\overline{)6,278.4}$

12.
(20)
35.01
×0.75

(d) 13.
(21) $0.15\overline{)7.245}$

Add or subtract each pair of fractions below. Make sure your answers are fully reduced.

14.
(11) $\dfrac{1}{3}+\dfrac{2}{3}+\dfrac{1}{4}$

15.
(11) $\dfrac{2}{33}+\dfrac{4}{11}+\dfrac{1}{3}$

Multiply or divide each pair of numbers below. Make sure your answer is fully reduced.

16.
(13) $\dfrac{1}{6}\times\dfrac{3}{7}$

17.
(14) $1\dfrac{1}{2}\div 4$

18.
(14) $3\times\dfrac{1}{5}\times\dfrac{2}{3}$

Answer each question below. Make sure your answer is fully reduced.

19.
(13) What is $\dfrac{2}{3}$ of $\dfrac{3}{14}$?

20.
(13) $10\dfrac{1}{2}$ has how many $\dfrac{1}{2}$'s in it?

Translate the word problem below into math; then solve.

(e) 21.
(21) Redder than Red Cranberry Juice costs \$1.56 per bottle. If Amanda bought \$10.92 worth, how many bottles did she buy?

Lesson 22—Decimal Remainders

When dividing whole numbers, a lot of answers have a remainder. For example, when dividing 125 by 4, we get 31 with a remainder of 1.

$$
\begin{array}{r}
31 \\
4\overline{)125} \\
-12 \\
\hline
05 \\
4 \\
\hline
1
\end{array}
$$

The answer is 31
with a remainder of 1.

One way to show an answer with a remainder is to put the answer followed by the letter R and then the remainder: 31 R1. Another way to show a remainder, though, is with a fraction. What we do is put the remainder over the number we're dividing by (the divisor). For our example problem, $4\overline{)125}$, the remainder is 1 and the divisor is 4, so that gives us this.

$31\frac{1}{4}$ ← Remainder on top

← Divisor on bottom

Put in a Decimal Point and Zero

There is a third way to show a remainder. It's to turn it into a decimal. And the great thing about this approach is that all we have to do is keep dividing. We'll show you how it works on $4\overline{)125}$. After we've brought down the last number and subtracted to get the remainder, we put in a decimal point to the right of 125 (the dividend) and write a zero after it. This is perfectly legal because it doesn't change the value of 125.

$$
\begin{array}{r}
31. \\
4\overline{)125.0} \\
-12 \\
\hline
05 \\
4 \\
\hline
1
\end{array}
$$

Put a decimal
point after 31.

Put a decimal point
and 0 after 125.

The next step is to put a decimal point in 31 (our answer) directly above the point in 125 (the dividend), as we always do when dividing a decimal by a whole number.

Just Keep Dividing

From here, we just continue the division process by bringing down the 0, as if it were part of the original division problem. And since we already have the decimal point properly positioned in the answer, there's no need to worry about it anymore.

$$
\begin{array}{r}
31. \\
4\overline{)125.0} \\
-12 \\
\hline
05 \\
4 \\
\hline
10
\end{array}
$$

Bring down the 0
and keep dividing.

Now we divide 4 into 10 to get 2. The 2 goes on top above the 0. Then since 2×4 equals 8, we put an 8 below the 10 and subtract. That gives us a remainder of 2, though. We can't allow that, because we're converting the remainder into a decimal. So we have to put another 0 after 125.0 and bring it down. And the division process continues until we finally end up with a remainder of 0.

$$\begin{array}{r} 31.25 \\ 4\overline{)125.00} \\ -12 \\ \hline 05 \\ 4 \\ \hline 10 \\ 8 \\ \hline 20 \\ 20 \\ \hline 0 \end{array}$$

Keep bringing down 0s until the remainder comes out 0.

As you can see, it took two more steps to get to that point. The answer comes out to 31.25. That makes sense, because $31\frac{1}{4}$ is the same as 31.25. So by continuing to divide (bringing down another 0 each step) we automatically turned $\frac{1}{4}$ into its decimal form, 0.25. Here are all the steps for turning a remainder into a decimal.

Turning a Remainder into a Decimal

1.	Put a decimal after the number being divided (dividend) and write a 0 after it.
2.	Put a decimal point directly above in the answer.
3.	Keep dividing (and bringing down more 0s) until you get a 0 remainder.

Practice 22

a.
(22)   Divide $6\overline{)723}$. Write any remainder in decimal form.

b.
(22)   Divide $8\overline{)6,269}$. Write any remainder in decimal form.

c.
(22)   Divide $12\overline{)2,793}$. Write any remainder in decimal form.

d.
(13)   What is $\frac{1}{4}$ of $13\frac{1}{3}$? Make sure your answer is fully reduced.

e.
(21)   Translate the word problem below into math; then solve.

The Golden Spud restaurant sells plain baked potatoes for $1.82 each. If the restaurant sold $203.84 worth of plain baked potatoes at lunchtime, how many of them did they sell?

Problem Set 22

Tell whether the sentence below is True or False.

1. A remainder can be turned into a decimal by just continuing the long division process.
(22)

2. A remainder can be turned into a fraction by putting it over the divisor.
(22)

Add or subtract each group of numbers below.

3.
(18)
$$\begin{array}{r} 248.3 \\ +69.92 \\ \hline \end{array}$$

4.
(17)
$$\begin{array}{r} 7.325 \\ -0.142 \\ \hline \end{array}$$

5.
(17)
$$\begin{array}{r} 551.34 \\ +924.06 \\ \hline \end{array}$$

Multiply or divide each pair of numbers below. Write any remainders in decimal form.

(a) 6.
(22)
$4\overline{)526}$

7.
(20)
$$\begin{array}{r} 4.25 \\ \times 6.1 \\ \hline \end{array}$$

(b) 8.
(22)
$8\overline{)7,325}$

9.
(20)
$$\begin{array}{r} 387.6 \\ \times 0.15 \\ \hline \end{array}$$

(c) 10.
(22)
$16\overline{)4,054}$

11.
(20)
$$\begin{array}{r} 5.03 \\ \times 2.4 \\ \hline \end{array}$$

Add or subtract each pair of fractions below. Make sure your answers are fully reduced.

12. $\dfrac{3}{7}+\dfrac{1}{4}$
(10)

13. $\dfrac{7}{10}-\dfrac{1}{6}$
(11)

Multiply or divide each pair of numbers below. Make sure your answer is fully reduced.

14. $18\div\dfrac{2}{9}$
(14)

15. $\dfrac{3}{5}\times\dfrac{5}{2}$
(13)

16. $\dfrac{1}{8}\div\dfrac{7}{4}$
(13)

Answer each question below. Make sure your answer is fully reduced.

17. What is $\dfrac{9}{11}$ of $\dfrac{5}{18}$?
(13)

18. 24 has how many $\dfrac{3}{4}$'s in it?
(14)

(d) 19. What is $\dfrac{1}{5}$ of $52\dfrac{1}{2}$?
(13)

Translate the word problem below into math; then solve.

(e) 20.
(21) Hamster Accessories Incorporated sells eight-inch skateboards for $6.75 each. If the company sold $317.25 worth of eight-inch skateboards, how many did they sell?

Lesson 23—Converting Fractions to Decimals

Now that you know all about division with decimals, we can show you a quick way to change a fraction to decimal form. Take the fraction $\frac{1}{5}$ as an example. We've learned to convert $\frac{1}{5}$ to a decimal by multiplying the top and bottom of the fraction by 2 to get $\frac{2}{10}$, or 0.2. This method works fine, but another way to do it is to use the methods for dividing decimals that we've been reviewing.

Divide the Bottom into the Top

With this method, the first step is to change the 1 in the numerator to 1.0 to get $\frac{1.0}{5}$. Basically, we've just turned the numerator into a decimal. The next step is to divide the bottom (5) into the top (1.0), according to the rules for dividing decimals. The decimal point in the answer has to be directly above the point in 1.0. So we put the point in the proper position and then divide, ignoring the decimal points completely. And we just keep dividing until we get a 0 remainder.

$$
\begin{array}{r}
.2 \\
5\overline{)1.0} \\
-\underline{10} \\
0
\end{array}
$$

Divide the bottom
into the top.

The result comes out to .2 (or 0.2 to show the decimal point more clearly), which is the same answer we got by multiplying the top and bottom by 2.

So now we have two methods for converting a fraction to a decimal. The first is to multiply the top and bottom by the same number to make the denominator equal to 10, 100, 1,000, etc. The second is to make the numerator a decimal by putting a point to its right, and then divide the bottom of the fraction into the top, using long division.

Dividing Is Often Easier

Since $\frac{1}{5}$ is a simple fraction, it's just about as easy to convert it by multiplying the top and bottom of the fraction (by 2) as it is to use long division. But for some fractions, the division approach is a lot easier. For example, remember that to convert $\frac{1}{8}$ the old way, we have to change the denominator to 1,000. Figuring out what number to multiply the bottom by to make it equal 1,000 can take awhile. It's actually 125. After multiplying the top and bottom of $\frac{1}{8}$ by 125 the fraction becomes $\frac{125}{1,000}$. That turns out to be 0.125 in decimal form. But the process is pretty long.

It's faster to convert $\frac{1}{8}$ using long division. All we have to do is change the 1 on top to 1.0 and then divide until we get a 0 remainder (bringing down more 0s as necessary).

$$8\overline{)1.000} \quad \overset{.125}{}$$

```
      .125
  8)1.000
    -8↓
     20↓
    -16↓
      40
     -40
       0
```

Keep dividing until
the remainder is 0.

We end up with 0.125, which is the same answer we got by multiplying the top and bottom of $\frac{1}{8}$. But the long division approach was faster, because we didn't have to brainstorm about what number to multiply 8 (and 1) by.

Big, Messy Numbers Mean It's Better to Divide

Here's another example of a fraction that's a whole lot easier to convert using long division: $\frac{128}{4,096}$. Think of how hard it would be to convert this fraction into decimal form using the old method. We'd have to change the denominator to some huge number like 10000000000.... And how would we ever figure out what number to multiply the top and bottom by? But by using long division, we could change the fraction to a decimal fairly quickly. We would just put a decimal point after 128, and another point directly above that one, in the answer. And it would probably make sense to stick in several zeros at the end, since the division is likely to take several steps.[1]

$$4,096\overline{)128.0000}\,\overset{.}{}$$

The next step would be to divide normally, ignoring the decimal points, until we get a 0 remainder. We won't show you the steps, but the answer turns out to be 0.03125. That's the decimal form of $\frac{128}{4,096}$. The main point, though, is that whenever the numerator and denominator of a fraction are large, it's almost always easier to convert it to a decimal by using long division.

Converting Decimals into Fractions

We've been converting fractions into decimals, but what about converting a decimal back into a regular (common) fraction? We already learned how to do that. Say, for example, that we want to change 0.42 to a fraction. We just rewrite the decimal as a fraction with a denominator of 100. The digits 42 go on top and the 100 on bottom to get $\frac{42}{100}$. But then we have to make sure that the answer is fully reduced. For $\frac{42}{100}$, we can factor and cancel to reduce it down to $\frac{21}{50}$. So $\frac{21}{50}$ is the fraction form of 0.42.

Generally, to convert decimals into fractions we can just look at the last digit in the decimal. If the last digit is tenths, then the denominator will be 10, if it's hundredths, the denominator will be 100, and so on. Once we have the denominator, we write the digits that make up the decimal in the numerator (forgetting about any zeros to the left). So, in the last example, since the 2 in 0.42 is in the hundredths spot, that means that the denominator has to equal 100 and the numerator has to equal 42.

---

[1] Since 4,096 is so much bigger than 128, we have to add at least 2 zeros to 128 because the smallest whole number that 4,096 can divide into in this problem is 12,800.

Here's another quick one. To convert 0.051 to a fraction, we first need to recognize that the 1 is in the thousandths place, which means that the denominator has to equal 1,000. Then we ignore zeros to the left and write 51 in the numerator to get $\dfrac{51}{1,000}$.

Practice 23

a.
(22)   Divide $4\overline{)4,973}$. Write any remainder in decimal form.

b.
(13)   Multiply $\dfrac{5}{27} \times \dfrac{9}{25} \times \dfrac{5}{9}$. Make sure your answer is fully reduced.

c.
(23)   Convert $\dfrac{7}{8}$ into decimal form using long division.

d.
(23)   Convert 0.295 into a fraction. Make sure your answer is fully reduced.

e.
(17)   Translate the word problem below into math; then solve.

Big Hans is 188.5 cm (or 6 ft. 2 in.) tall. Little Hans is 94 cm (or 3 ft. 1 in.) tall. How many centimeters taller is Big Hans than Little Hans?

Problem Set 23

Tell whether each sentence below is True or False.

1.
(23)   A fraction can be converted into decimal form using long division.

2.
(23)   It is not possible to convert decimals into fractions.

Add or subtract each group of numbers below.

3.
(17)
```
  36.005
+18.756
```

4.
(17)
```
 157.24
-104.51
```

5.
(18)
```
 23.65
 14.72
+30.9
```

6.
(17)
```
 903.75
-646.32
```

117

Multiply or divide each pair of numbers below. Write any remainders in decimal form.

7.
(21) $3.2\overline{)13.76}$

8.
(20) $\begin{array}{r} 75.4 \\ \times 9.6 \\ \hline \end{array}$

9.
(21) $2.4\overline{)300.48}$

10.
(20) $\begin{array}{r} 77.42 \\ \times 0.52 \\ \hline \end{array}$

(a) 11.
(22) $4\overline{)5,235}$

Add or subtract each group of fractions below. Make sure your answers are fully reduced.

12.
(11) $\dfrac{1}{2}+\dfrac{3}{4}+\dfrac{1}{5}$

13.
(10) $\dfrac{5}{14}-\dfrac{2}{7}$

Multiply or divide each group of numbers below. Make sure your answer is fully reduced.

14.
(14) $24\times\dfrac{5}{6}$

15.
(14) $\dfrac{4}{5}\div 8$

(b) 16.
(13) $\dfrac{3}{8}\times\dfrac{4}{9}\times\dfrac{3}{4}$

Convert each fraction below into decimal form using long division.

17.
(23) $\dfrac{2}{5}$

(c) 18.
(23) $\dfrac{3}{8}$

Convert each decimal below into a fraction. Make sure your answers are fully reduced.

19.
(23) 0.23

(d) 20.
(23) 0.145

Translate the word problem below into math; then solve.

(e) 21.
(17)   In early August, the bag where the Happy Valley Post Office keeps all the letters to Santa weighed only 2.8 pounds, but by late September it weighed 4.7 pounds. How many pounds were added in between?

Lesson 24—Never-Ending Decimals

For quite a few lessons now, we've been telling you how great decimals are. But the truth is decimals do have some drawbacks.

It Just Keeps Going and Going ...

To show you, let's convert the fraction $\frac{1}{3}$ into decimal form. We'll use the long division method. We change the 1 on top to 1.0 and then divide. A decimal point should be placed in the answer (above the point in 1.0).

$$
\begin{array}{r}
.\overline{333}... \\
3\overline{)1.000} \\
\underline{-9}\!\downarrow\,| \\
10 \\
\underline{-\ 9}\!\downarrow \\
10 \\
\underline{-\ 9} \\
1
\end{array}
$$

We never get
a remainder of 0.

As always, we need to divide until the remainder comes out 0. But notice that we've gotten into a pattern. Every time we bring down another 0, 3 goes into 10 3 times, and 3 times 3 is 9, which leaves a remainder of 1 (not 0). So we're never going to get a 0 remainder. It will just be 3s forever. What does this mean? It means that the only way to get a decimal fraction that is exactly equal to $\frac{1}{3}$ is to let the 3s go on without stopping. In other words, $\frac{1}{3}$ is exactly equal to $\frac{3}{10}+\frac{3}{100}+\frac{3}{1,000}+\frac{3}{10,000}$ and on and on forever. Believe it or not, there's no simpler way to fit $\frac{1}{3}$ into our modern number system.[1]

$$
\frac{1}{3} = \frac{3}{10} + \frac{3}{100} + \frac{3}{1,000} + \frac{3}{10,000} + \frac{3}{100,000} + \cdots \text{ forever}
$$

Since we can't keep writing numbers forever, we write a line over the 3 like this: $0.\overline{3}$.

0.3333... is written as $0.\overline{3}$

The line simply means that the digit 3 repeats forever. Decimals like $0.\overline{3}$ are called **repeating decimals**, and decimals that stop (like 0.5) are called **terminating decimals.**

Lots of Repeaters

So the one big drawback of decimals is that not all fractions will fit nicely into the decimal system. There are some fractions where the digits have to go on forever to fit. It's kind of surprising that a fraction as simple as $\frac{1}{3}$ is like that. Even worse, there are a lot of other repeating decimals and many of them are also simple fractions. For instance, if we try to convert $\frac{2}{9}$ into decimal form, we get 0.222..... (In other words, $\frac{2}{9}$ is equal to $\frac{2}{10}+\frac{2}{100}+\frac{2}{1,000}+\frac{2}{10,000}$ and on and on.) Of course, the proper way to write 0.222... is $0.\overline{2}$.

---

[1] That just means there's no number that you can multiply by 3 to get 10, 100, 1,000, etc.

Here's another repeater: $\frac{1}{6}$. If we try to convert this one into a decimal using long division, the result is 0.1666.... Notice that there's a 1 in the tenths place, but then it's 6s forever after that. So $\frac{1}{6}$ actually equals $\frac{1}{10} + \frac{6}{100} + \frac{6}{1,000} + \frac{6}{10,000}$ and on and on. The short way to write 0.1666... is $0.1\overline{6}$. The line goes over only the repeating digit, the 6.

Sometimes more than one digit repeats. For example, if we try to convert $\frac{1}{7}$ into a decimal by long division, we'll get this: 0.142857142857142857.... There are actually six digits that are repeating. And they just go on and on. The correct way to write this is to put a line over all six digits like this: $0.\overline{142857}$. Even though repeating decimals can be a pain, they're worth it, because they allow us to add, subtract, multiply, and divide fractions in the same way as whole numbers. That's a huge advantage, especially when solving practical problems.

Rounding Off Repeating Decimals

But that raises an important question. How do we handle a repeating decimal if it pops up as the answer to a practical problem? For instance, what if we were measuring something and ended up with 0.333... feet? We wouldn't want to wrestle with never ending digits on a practical problem. One way out would be just to use the fraction form, $\frac{1}{3}$. But what if we wanted to work the decimal form to make our calculations simpler? Then we could use a decimal estimate by rounding off 0.333....

Here's the way rounding works. Instead of writing $\frac{1}{3}$ as 0.333333...., we first decide how many digits we really need. That's determined by how accurate the answer needs to be. The more 3s we use, the more accurate the estimate is (because the closer the decimal's value gets to $\frac{1}{3}$). The number 0.33333 is closer to $\frac{1}{3}$ than the number 0.333. But neither one is exactly equal to $\frac{1}{3}$. That would require 3s going on forever. But let's say we only need an answer accurate to tenths. Then we can just use 0.3. That's not equal to $\frac{1}{3}$ (it's actually equal to $\frac{3}{10}$), but it may be close enough for our problem. If we need the answer to be a little more accurate, then we could use an estimate to hundredths. That would be 0.33 (which isn't exactly right either).

Actually, to be technically correct when rounding a number, we have to look at the digit to the right of the one we're rounding to. For instance, if we want to round 0.166666..., which is the decimal form of $\frac{1}{6}$, to the hundredths place, we look at the thousandths place. If that digit is 5 or greater, then we increase the hundredths digit by 1. In 0.166666...., there's a 6 in the thousandths place, so we need to change 0.16 to 0.17 to correctly round.

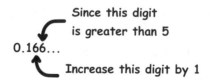

Since this digit
is greater than 5

0.166...

Increase this digit by 1

That means 0.1666 rounded to hundredths (2 decimal places) = 0.17

If the digit to the right (of the spot we're rounding to) is less than 5, then we leave the digit we're rounding to alone. An example is $\frac{2}{9}$, which equals 0.2222…. To round this to tenths (1 place), we look at the hundredths place. Since it's below 5, we keep the tenths digit the same, leaving us with 0.2. Here are the formal rules for rounding.

Rounding a Decimal

1.	When the digit to the right of the one you're rounding to is 5 or greater, round up (increase by 1).
2.	When the digit to the right of the one you're rounding to is less than 5, leave the number alone.

One more point. Rounding is really common when dealing with money. Nobody wants to mess with a fraction of a cent. For instance, if a money calculation resulted in an answer like $14.166666…., we would round it off to the nearest hundredths place, because a penny is the smallest kind of coin (it equals $\frac{1}{100}$ of a dollar). But since the number next to the hundredths place is greater than 5, we have to round up, which means the answer would have to be $14.17.

Practice 24

a.
(21)   Divide $0.22\overline{)48.4}$

b.
(22)   Divide $18\overline{)7,842}$. Write any remainder in decimal form.

c.
(24)   Convert $\frac{4}{9}$ into decimal form.

d.
(24)   Round $0.2\overline{8}$ to two digits (hundredths).

e.
(20)   Translate the word problem below into math; then solve.

Howie has decided to grow a beard. If his beard grows at a rate of 0.001 inches each week, how many inches long will it be in 12 weeks?

Problem Set 24

Tell whether each sentence below is True or False.

1.
(24)   A decimal that goes on forever is called a terminating decimal.

2.
(24)   When solving a practical problem, repeating decimals are often rounded.

Add or subtract each group of numbers below.

3.
(17)
909.64
+132.15

4.
(18)
42.89
−21.375

5.
(17)
576.5
149.7
+250.9

Multiply or divide each pair of numbers below. Write any remainders in decimal form.

6.
(20)
128.1
×0.5

(a) 7.
(21)
$0.25\overline{)75.5}$

8.
(20)
6.806
×4.3

(b) 9.
(22)
$12\overline{)5,648}$

10.
(20)
504.1
×0.07

Add or subtract each pair of fractions below. Make sure your answers are fully reduced.

11.
(12)
$4\frac{2}{3}+\frac{8}{9}$

12.
(10)
$\frac{5}{3}-\frac{3}{2}$

Multiply or divide each pair of numbers below. Make sure your answer is fully reduced.

13.
(13)
$\frac{3}{7}\div\frac{9}{14}$

14.
(14)
$\frac{5}{8}\times56$

15.
(14)
$\frac{6}{7}\div3$

Convert each fraction below into decimal form.

16.
(23)
$\frac{7}{20}$

(c) 17.
(24)
$\frac{1}{9}$

Convert each decimal below into a fraction. Make sure your answers are fully reduced.

18.
(23)
0.62

19.
(23)
0.008

Round each decimal below to two digits (hundredths).

20.
(24)
$0.\overline{4}$

(d) 21.
(24)
$0.5\overline{7}$

Translate the word problem below into math; then solve.

(e) 22.
(20)
Howie's hero, his uncle Thornton, has a beard that grows at a rate of 0.075 inches per week. How many inches will Thornton's beard grow in 12 weeks?

CHAPTER 4:
PERCENTS

Lesson 25—Percents

We've studied fractions and decimals pretty thoroughly, so now it's time to turn to percents. And even though you did percents in earlier math courses, we'll try to give you a better understanding of the concept.

For Each Hundred

The word **percent** actually means "per hundred." Or another way of saying it is "for each hundred."[1] For example, one percent of a number means 1 for each hundred in the number. So 1 percent of 500 is 5, since there are 5 hundreds in 500, and we're taking 1 in each of those 5 hundreds. Using the same logic, one percent of 900 has to be 9.

Percent really means "for each hundred."

You can also take more than one percent of a number. For instance, two percent just means 2 for each hundred, and since there are 2 hundreds in 200, 2 percent of 200 is $2+2$ or 4. Likewise, ten percent of 200 means 10 for every hundred, and since there are 2 hundreds in 200, 10 percent of 200 is $10+10$ or 20. Another example is 30 percent of 200. That would have to be $30+30$ or 60.

You may be wondering why we even need percents. After all, we already have fractions and decimals. Why do we need percents too? Mainly it's because people find it easy to think in 100s (which is what we do with percents). For example, what if there is a big political meeting and 10 out of every 25 people present are Democrats. Instead of talking about 10 out of 25, most people think it's easier to talk about 40 out of every 100 (which is the same thing). And that's 40 percent.

Writing Percents

It's important to know how to write a percent. Fortunately, we don't have to actually write out the word percent. That would take a long time. But since mathematicians like symbols better than words, they came up with a symbol for percent. Of course, you've used it for years. Here it is.

%   Symbol for "percent"

All we do is put the number of the percent and then the symbol goes right after it (as you know). So one percent is written as 1%, 2 percent is written as 2%, 30 percent is written as 30%, and so on.

Practice 25

a.
(24)   Convert the fraction $\dfrac{1}{7}$ into decimal form. If it's a repeating decimal, round to two digits (hundredths).

b.
(24)   Convert the fraction $\dfrac{13}{14}$ into decimal form. If it's a repeating decimal, round to two digits (hundredths).

c.
(23)   Convert 0.017 into a fraction. Make sure your answer is fully reduced.

---

[1] "Cent" is from a Latin word for hundred.

124

d. What is 2% of 300?
(25)

e. Translate the word problem below into math; then solve.
(14)

A rickshaw is a small, two-wheeled carriage that is pulled by a human being instead of a horse. Some rickshaw drivers in other countries get paid an amount equal to only $\frac{1}{2}$ of a penny for every block they travel. How many pennies will a driver earn after he travels 94 blocks?

Problem Set 25

Tell whether each sentence below is True or False.

1. The word percent means "per hundred."
(25)

2. A percent is shown using the symbol "&."
(25)

Add or subtract each group of numbers below.

3.
(17)
$$\begin{array}{r} 99.35 \\ +75.82 \\ \hline \end{array}$$

4.
(18)
$$\begin{array}{r} 503.2 \\ -14.19 \\ \hline \end{array}$$

5.
(17)
$$\begin{array}{r} 8.034 \\ +4.125 \\ \hline \end{array}$$

Multiply or divide each pair of numbers below. Write any remainders in decimal form.

6.
(20)
$$\begin{array}{r} 18.75 \\ \times 4.3 \\ \hline \end{array}$$

7. $1.5\overline{)4.575}$
(21)

8.
(20)
$$\begin{array}{r} 542.1 \\ \times 0.7 \\ \hline \end{array}$$

9. $9\overline{)6,333}$
(24)

10.
(20)
$$\begin{array}{r} 73.8 \\ \times 12 \\ \hline \end{array}$$

Add or subtract each pair of numbers below. Make sure your answers are fully reduced.

11. $11 - \frac{9}{2}$
(12)

12. $3\frac{3}{10} + \frac{5}{2}$
(12)

Multiply or divide each pair of numbers below. Make sure your answers are fully reduced.

13. $\frac{2}{11} \times 22$
(14)

14. $\frac{1}{3} \div \frac{1}{2}$
(13)

Convert each fraction below into decimal form. Round any repeating decimals to two digits (hundredths).

15. $\dfrac{3}{5}$
(23)

(a) 16. $\dfrac{4}{7}$
(24)

(b) 17. $\dfrac{11}{14}$
(24)

Convert each decimal below into a fraction. Make sure your answers are fully reduced.

18. 0.8
(23)

(c) 19. 0.029
(23)

Answer each question below.

20. What is 1% of 600?
(25)

(d) 21. What is 3% of 700?
(25)

Translate the word problem below into math; then solve.

(e) 22. In some countries, a shoe shine boy might earn an amount equal to only $\dfrac{1}{4}$ of a penny for each shoe he
(14)
shines. How many pennies will the boy earn after shining 128 shoes?

Lesson 26—Calculating Percents

In the last lesson we started learning about percents. We only did a few simple calculations, which is why we were able to do all of them in our heads. But there's also a pencil and paper way to calculate a percent. This method comes in handy when doing tougher percent problems.

Calculating a Percent Using a Fraction

To show you how the method works, let's go through an example.

Find 2% of 400.

The first step is to turn the percent into a fraction. All we have to do is drop the percent symbol, and then put 2 in the top (numerator) and 100 in the bottom (denominator) of the fraction.

$$2\% \text{ equals } \frac{2}{100} \text{ as a fraction}$$

The next step is to multiply the fraction by the number (400).

$$\frac{2}{100} \times 400$$

Let's put 400 over 1. Then, we can factor and cancel. We really only need to factor 400 as $4 \cdot 100$ because that will allow us to cancel the 100s.

$$\frac{2}{100} \times \frac{400}{1} \text{ equals } \frac{2}{100} \times \frac{4 \cdot 100}{1} \text{ equals } \frac{2}{\cancel{100}_{1}} \times \frac{4 \cdot \cancel{100}}{1}$$

After multiplying, we end up with this.

$$\frac{8}{1} = 8$$

That makes sense, if you think about it. Percent means "out of one hundred," and 1% of 400 is 4 (1 for each 100), so 2% must be 8. So to find the percent of a number, we can change the percent to a fraction and then multiply the fraction by the number normally.

Calculating a Percent Using a Decimal

We can also calculate a percent using a decimal. Going back to the problem 2% of 400, instead of using $\frac{2}{100}$, we just use the decimal form, which is 0.02.

$$\frac{2}{100} \text{ written as a decimal is } 0.02.$$

Next, we multiply the decimal (0.02) by 400 to get 8, which is the same answer we got before.

$$0.02 \times 400 = 8$$

Actually, there's a quick way to change a percent to a decimal, without having to write it as a fraction first. You probably remember the method from early math courses, but we'll go over it quickly.

Every whole number has a decimal point. So 2% is the same as 2.0%. But compare 2.0% with the decimal form 0.02. The only difference is that the percent symbol has been dropped and the decimal point has been moved two places to the left. That's always the way it works, which means that to change a percent to a pure decimal all we have to do is drop the percent symbol and move the decimal point 2 places to the left.[1]

**Move the decimal point
two places to the left.**

2.0% equals 0.02

Converting percents into decimals is important because most people think it's easier to calculate the percent of a number using a decimal (instead of a fraction). That's particularly true now that we all have calculators. With a calculator, you can punch in a decimal really fast.

A Quick Example

Just to make sure you're understanding the concept, let's do a quick example.

Lower Transylvania had never witnessed bravery equal to that displayed by the Seventeenth Brigade's Third Battalion. Amazingly, 17% of the Battalion's 800 men were awarded their country's highest military honor. How many received the honor?

To solve this, we need to find 17% of 800. Let's go through the formal method. The first step is to change 17% to a decimal. We could change it into a fraction, but a decimal is probably easier (as we said). All we have to do is drop the percent symbol and move the decimal point 2 places to the left. That turns 17% into 0.17.

17% equals 0.17

Next, we just multiply 0.17 by 800.

$$0.17 \times 800 = 136$$

That gives us 136, which means that 136 soldiers must have received the country's highest military honor.

---

[1] By the way, the reason this works is that dividing by 100 always moves the decimal point 2 places to the left.

Practice 26

a.
(24)
Divide $6\overline{)1,271}$. Write any remainders in decimal form.

b.
(24)
Convert $\dfrac{7}{11}$ into decimal form. If your answer is a repeating decimal, round to two digits (hundredths).

c.
(23)
Convert 0.64 into a fraction. Make sure your answer is fully reduced.

d.
(26)
What is 18% of 900?

e.
(26)
Translate the word problem below into math; then solve.

All the clowns who were surveyed said they had dreamed of becoming a clown when they grew up, but only 15% said they had dreamed of becoming a rodeo clown. If 200 clowns were surveyed, how many of those said they had dreamed of becoming a rodeo clown?

Problem Set 26

Tell whether each sentence below is True or False.

1.
(26)
To calculate the percent of a number, change the percent to a fraction or decimal and multiply.

2.
(26)
The shortcut for changing a percent to a decimal is to drop the percent symbol and move the decimal point two places to the left.

Add or subtract each group of numbers below.

3.
(17)
$$\begin{array}{r} 306.74 \\ +265.81 \\ \hline \end{array}$$

4.
(18)
$$\begin{array}{r} 8.214 \\ -3.93 \\ \hline \end{array}$$

5.
(17)
$$\begin{array}{r} 68.6 \\ 73.1 \\ +90.5 \\ \hline \end{array}$$

Multiply or divide each pair of numbers below. Write any remainders in decimal form.

6.
(21)
$2.4\overline{)134.4}$

7.
(20)
$$\begin{array}{r} 2.465 \\ \times 3.7 \\ \hline \end{array}$$

(a) 8.
(24)
$6\overline{)1,885}$

9.
(22)
$14\overline{)1,197}$

CHAPTER 4: PERCENTS

Add or subtract each pair of fractions below. Make sure your answers are fully reduced.

10.
(10)
$\dfrac{5}{7}-\dfrac{5}{14}$

11.
(11)
$\dfrac{7}{8}+\dfrac{1}{6}$

Multiply or divide each pair of numbers below. Make sure your answers are fully reduced.

12.
(14)
$\dfrac{3}{5}\times 95$

13.
(14)
$12\div\dfrac{4}{9}$

Convert each fraction below into decimal form. Round any repeating decimals to two digits (hundredths).

14.
(23)
$\dfrac{7}{8}$

15.
(23)
$\dfrac{5}{6}$

(b) 16.
(24)
$\dfrac{9}{11}$

Convert each decimal below into a fraction. Make sure your answers are fully reduced.

17.
(23)
0.11

(c) 18.
(23)
0.32

19.
(23)
0.701

Answer each question below.

20.
(26)
What is 14% of 300?

(d) 21.
(26)
What is 22% of 800?

Translate the word problem below into math; then solve.

(e) 22.
(26)
All the sailors who were surveyed said they had dreamed of crossing the ocean when they grew up, but only 5% said they had dreamed of crossing the ocean in a submarine. If 400 sailors were surveyed, how many of those said they had dreamed of crossing the ocean in a submarine?

130

Lesson 27—Percent of Any Number

We've been learning how to figure the percent of a number. But you may have noticed that all the numbers in our examples were simple ones that ended with zeros—like 400 and 800. Most of these calculations can be done in your head.

Percent of an Ordinary Number

But what about finding a percent of an ordinary number like 82 or 25 or 46? These are often too hard to do in your head, and that's when the method we showed you in the last lesson comes in really handy. Let's go through one of these harder examples.

Find 25% of 85.

The first step is to change the percent into a fraction or decimal. Since the decimal is easier, we'll use that. There's actually a decimal point after the 25 in 25%, so it could be written as 25.0%. But to change the percent to a decimal, what we do is drop the percent symbol and move the decimal point two places to the left.

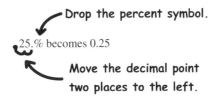

Drop the percent symbol.

25.% becomes 0.25

Move the decimal point two places to the left.

So the decimal form of 25% is 0.25. (We put the 0 in just to make it easier to see the point.) The next step is to multiply 0.25 by the number, which is 85.

$$\begin{array}{r} 85 \\ \times\,0.25 \\ \hline 425 \\ 1700 \\ \hline 21.25 \end{array}$$

25% of 85 is 21.25.

The answer turns out to be 21.25, so that's 25% of 85. If we had tried to do that in our heads it probably would have taken awhile.

Percent of a Fraction

This method for finding a percent of a number works on even the toughest problems. For instance, what if we needed to find the percent of a fraction? That may sound kind of tricky. But we can just apply the same method that we've been using. Here's an example.

Find 40% of $\frac{1}{2}$.

We could write 40% as the fraction $\frac{40}{100}$ and then multiply it by $\frac{1}{2}$. That turns out to equal $\frac{1}{5}$ (since $\frac{40}{100}$ reduces to $\frac{2}{5}$ and $\frac{2}{5} \times \frac{1}{2}$ equals $\frac{1}{5}$). So that works. But, as we've said, decimals are usually easier to use. And that's probably true even in this case, where the number is a fraction. But to use decimals on this problem, we have to change both 40% and $\frac{1}{2}$ into decimal form. To convert 40%, we go through the usual procedure. We drop the percent symbol and move the decimal point two places to the left. That gives us 0.40. Then $\frac{1}{2}$ as a decimal is 0.5.

Change both to decimal form.

40% is the same as 0.40 $\frac{1}{2}$ is the same as 0.5

Now we just multiply 0.40 and 0.5. We won't show the calculation, but it turns out to equal 0.2. But interestingly, 0.2 is the same as $\frac{2}{10}$, which reduces to $\frac{1}{5}$. So using decimals, we ended up with the decimal form of $\frac{1}{5}$, which is the same answer we got before.

Practice 27

a.
(24)
Convert $\frac{11}{12}$ into decimal form. If your answer is a repeating decimal, round to two digits (hundredths).

b.
(27)
What is 20% of 34?

c.
(27)
What is 45% of 18?

d.
(27)
What is 30% of $\frac{2}{5}$? Write your answer as a decimal.

e.
(27)
Translate the word problem below into math; then solve.

Salespeople at Silky Shiny Wigs Incorporated earn a 25% commission. How much will Suzanne make in commission if she sells a wig for $98?

Problem Set 27

Tell whether each sentence below is True or False.

1.
(27)
It is possible to calculate the percent of numbers that do not end in zeros.

2.
(27)
It is not possible to calculate the percent of a number that is less than one.

Add or subtract each group of numbers below.

3.
(18)
205.9
+732.24
_____

4.
(18)
64.5
−17.325
_____

5.
18)
5.14
+9.703
_____

Multiply or divide each pair of numbers below. Write any remainders in decimal form.

6.
(21) $5.3\overline{)445.2}$

7.
(20) $\begin{array}{r} 92.37 \\ \times 4.1 \\ \hline \end{array}$

8.
(22) $12\overline{)582}$

9.
(24) $9\overline{)2,279}$

Add or subtract each pair of fractions below. Make sure your answers are fully reduced.

10.
(10) $\dfrac{7}{9} - \dfrac{2}{3}$

11.
(11) $\dfrac{3}{10} + \dfrac{8}{15}$

Multiply or divide each pair of numbers below. Make sure your answers are fully reduced.

12.
(13) $\dfrac{7}{8} \times \dfrac{4}{14}$

13.
(13) $\dfrac{1}{6} \div \dfrac{1}{12}$

Convert each fraction below into decimal form. Round any repeating decimals to two digits (hundredths).

14.
(23) $\dfrac{1}{16}$

(a) 15.
(24) $\dfrac{5}{12}$

Convert each decimal below into a fraction. Make sure your answers are fully reduced.

16.
(23) 0.012

17.
(23) 0.65

Answer each question below. Write your answer as a whole number or decimal.

18.
(27) What is 12% of 500?

(b) 19.
(27) What is 30% of 28?

(c) 20.
(27) What is 65% of 16?

(d) 21.
(27) What is 20% of $\dfrac{3}{4}$?

Translate the word problem below into math; then solve.

(e) 22.
(27) The salespeople at the Livin' Doll Cosmetics Company get paid a 15% commission on everything they sell. How much will Linda make in commission if she sells $275 worth of cosmetics?

Lesson 28—Fractional Percents

In the last lesson, we learned that we can calculate the percent of all sorts of numbers, even whole numbers that don't end in zero and fractions. But is it possible for a percent itself to be fractional? For example, does it make sense to have something like $4\frac{1}{2}\%$? There's nothing wrong with that at all. Actually, $4\frac{1}{2}\%$ just means "four and one half for each hundred." So $4\frac{1}{2}\%$ of 100 is $4\frac{1}{2}$, and $4\frac{1}{2}\%$ of 200 is $4\frac{1}{2}+4\frac{1}{2}$ or 9.

Calculating Fractional Percents

Here's another important question: can we calculate the percent of a number even when the percent has a fraction in it? Fortunately, yes. We'll show you how with an example.

$$\text{What's } 4\frac{1}{2}\% \text{ of 88?}$$

The basic method is the same. We want to multiply the percent by the number. Before moving the decimal point, we should change $4\frac{1}{2}\%$ to 4.5%. Now we drop the percent symbol and move the decimal point two places to the left to get 0.045.

$$4.5\% \;=\; {}_\bullet04.5 \;=\; 0.045$$

Next, we multiply 0.045 and 88 to get 3.96. That's $4\frac{1}{2}\%$ of 88. So we can calculate the fractional percent of a number in basically the same way that we calculate regular percents. We just need to change $4\frac{1}{2}\%$ to 4.5% first.

And to be honest, we didn't have to change $4\frac{1}{2}\%$ to 4.5%. We could change $4\frac{1}{2}\%$ to a fraction. All we have to do is put $4\frac{1}{2}$ over 100 to get $\dfrac{4\frac{1}{2}}{100}$. The mixed number on top can then be changed to an improper fraction: $\dfrac{\frac{9}{2}}{100}$. From here, we invert and multiply to get $\dfrac{9}{2}\times\dfrac{1}{100}$ or $\dfrac{9}{200}$. So $4\frac{1}{2}\%$ written as a fraction is $\dfrac{9}{200}$. Then we can just multiply $\dfrac{9}{200}$ and 88 to get 3.96, which is the same answer as before. But notice that this second method is more complicated. That's why most people prefer to change a fractional percent (like $4\frac{1}{2}\%$) to a decimal. There are lots of other examples of fractional percents. Here are a few.

$15\frac{1}{4}\%$ is the same as 15.25%

$36\frac{1}{5}\%$ is the same as 36.2%

$75\frac{5}{8}\%$ is the same as 75.625%

Repeating Decimals Again

Sometimes, the fractional part of a percent is a repeating decimal. An example is $12\frac{1}{3}\%$. Since $\frac{1}{3}$ is the same as 0.333..., $12\frac{1}{3}\%$ is equal to 12.333...% or $12.\overline{3}\%$. But what if we need to do a calculation with this? How do we handle the repeating decimal? Well, one option is to round it. That's a good option if the answer doesn't need to be exact (as with many practical problems). Rounding $12.\overline{3}\%$ to tenths would give us 12.3%.

$12.\overline{3}\%$ rounded to tenths equals 12.3%   **You can round repeaters.**

That might be close enough. Or if we wanted to round to hundredths, we could use 12.33%.

But if the answer had to be exact, we could change the percent to a fraction (as we did with $4\frac{1}{2}\%$ above). We just drop the percent symbol in $12\frac{1}{3}\%$ and put $12\frac{1}{3}$ over 100.

$$12\frac{1}{3}\% \quad = \quad \frac{12\frac{1}{3}}{100} \qquad \textbf{Drop percent symbol and put over 100.}$$

But $\dfrac{12\frac{1}{3}}{100}$ is the same as $\dfrac{\frac{37}{3}}{100}$. Then inverting and multiplying gives us $\dfrac{37}{3}\times\dfrac{1}{100}$, or $\dfrac{37}{300}$. From there, we could multiply $\dfrac{37}{300}$ by whatever number we were trying to find $12\frac{1}{3}\%$ of. Using the fractional form is more complicated than rounding, but it does give an exact answer. So here are the two ways of dealing with a percent that contains a repeating decimal.

Can Handle a Percent with a Repeating Decimal in Two Ways

1.	Round off the repeating decimal to the right digit (depending on required accuracy).
2.	Turn the percent into a fraction by dropping the percent symbol and putting over 100. (Make sure to reduce the fraction before using.)

Practice 28

a.
(23) Convert 3.5 into a fraction. Make sure your answer is fully reduced.

b.
(28) Convert $8\frac{1}{2}\%$ into decimal form.

c.
(27) What is 40% of $\frac{3}{5}$? Write your answer as a decimal.

d.
(28) What is $2\frac{1}{4}\%$ of 80? Write your answer as a decimal.

e.
(28) Translate the word problem below into math; then solve.

Sales tax in The Land of the Burgeoning Bureaucrats is $18\frac{1}{2}\%$. If Burl buys a stereo system for $974, how much will he have to pay in sales tax?

Problem Set 28

Tell whether each sentence below is True or False.

1.
(28) It is possible for percents to contain fractions.

2.
(28) Fractional percents can be converted into fractions but not into decimals.

Add or subtract each group of numbers below.

3.
(17)
$$\begin{array}{r} 73.48 \\ +25.13 \\ \hline \end{array}$$

4.
(17)
$$\begin{array}{r} 825.75 \\ -433.82 \\ \hline \end{array}$$

Multiply or divide each pair of numbers below. Write any remainders in decimal form.

5.
(21) $0.21\overline{)15.435}$

6.
(20)
$$\begin{array}{r} 45.8 \\ \times 6.2 \\ \hline \end{array}$$

7.
(22) $5\overline{)2{,}113}$

Add or subtract each pair of numbers below. Make sure your answers are fully reduced.

8.
(11) $\frac{4}{5}+\frac{2}{7}$

9.
(12) $7-\frac{9}{2}$

Multiply or divide each pair of numbers below. Make sure your answers are fully reduced.

10.
(14) $24 \times \dfrac{3}{8}$

11.
(14) $\dfrac{7}{11} \div 21$

Convert each fraction below into decimal form. Round any repeating decimals to two digits (hundredths).

12.
(23) $\dfrac{9}{20}$

13.
(24) $\dfrac{8}{9}$

Convert each decimal below into a fraction. Make sure your answers are fully reduced.

14.
(23) 0.205

(a) 15.
(23) 2.5

Convert each percent below into decimal form.

16.
(26) 15%

(b) 17.
(28) $6\dfrac{1}{2}\%$

Answer each question below. Write your answer as a whole number or decimal.

18.
(27) What is 35% of 220?

(c) 19.
(27) What is 60% of $\dfrac{4}{5}$?

(d) 20.
(28) What is $7\dfrac{1}{4}\%$ of 56?

Translate the word problem below into math; then solve.

(e) 21.
(28) Sales tax in The Land of Contradictions is $6\dfrac{1}{2}$ %. If Connie buys a toothless comb for $8, how much will she have to pay in sales tax?

Lesson 29—Percents and Banking

We've been learning about percents, but how are they actually used in the real world? Well, it turns out that percents are used all the time, especially in areas where money is involved, like banking.

How a Bank Works

A bank will pay you to keep your money. You probably know that. But you might not know that the amount the bank agrees to pay is always a percent of the amount of money put in. Let's say we put $100 in a bank. The bank will pay us **interest** (that's what the payments are called) while it has our money, and if, for example, the bank pays a $5\frac{1}{2}$% interest rate, that means they'll pay $5\frac{1}{2}$% of what we have in the bank every year. So for $100, they'll pay $5\frac{1}{2}$% of that each year (in interest).

To calculate how much that is, we just change $5\frac{1}{2}$% to 5.5%. Then we drop the percent symbol and move the decimal point two places to the left to get 0.055. Finally, we multiply 0.055 by 100 to get 5.5. Since 100 was in dollars, that means the bank would pay us $5.50 each year.[1] We could also take our $100 out at the end of the year if we wanted to.

Interest Rate	×	Amount in Bank	=	Interest
$5\frac{1}{2}$% (0.055)	×	100	=	$5.50

Here's another example. Say we put $1,640 in a bank that pays a $3\frac{1}{4}$% interest rate. To calculate the amount of interest we'd get after a year, we change $3\frac{1}{4}$% to 3.25% and then to 0.0325. Then, we multiply 0.0325 by 1,640 to get 53.3. So the amount of interest comes out to $53.30.

Interest on Interest

Here's something else that's interesting (no pun intended!). What if we want to leave our money in the bank for *more than* one year? Let's say we have $1,000 and want to put it in the bank for 3 years at a 5% interest rate. In the first year, we'd earn 5% on the 1,000, which is $0.05\times1,000$ or $50. But at the end of the year, we wouldn't take our money out. We would just leave the $1,000 in the bank. And let's assume that we're going to leave the $50 in interest in the bank too. That means for the second year, instead of having $1,000, we would have $1,000 + $50 or $1,050 in the bank. So how much interest would we earn in that year? Well, we'd make 5% of $1,050, which is $0.05\times1,050$. That's equal to 52.5, or $52.50.

1st Year Interest	2nd Year Interest
5% of $1,000 = $50	5% of $1,050 = $52.50

Notice what happened, we earned more interest in the second year than we did in the first. That's because we earned "interest on our interest." This is called **compound interest**, actually.

What about the third year? Well, the answer depends on whether we keep our interest in the bank again. If we did, we'd have $1,050 + $52.50, or $1,102.50 in the bank after the second year. So in the third year, we would earn

---

[1] You may be wondering why the bank is willing to pay us for letting them hold our money. Well, it's because they're going to lend our money out to someone else and charge them even more interest. The bank will then keep the difference between what it pays us and what it earned from the amount it lent.

0.05 times 1,102.50, which equals 55.125, or $55.13 when it's rounded to cents. Notice that in the third year our interest is even higher. Of course, if we kept this up, our savings would grow faster and faster. This is why people always talk about how fast money can grow in the bank (or when it's invested somewhere else). The fast growth is caused by compound interest (interest on interest).

Practice 29

a.
(28) Convert $55\frac{1}{8}\%$ into decimal form.

b.
(26) Convert 28% into a fraction. Make sure your answer is fully reduced.

c.
(28) Convert $3\frac{1}{3}\%$ into a fraction. Make sure your answer is fully reduced.

d.
(28) What is $12\frac{3}{5}\%$ of 320? Write your answer as a decimal.

e.
(29) Translate the word problem below into math; then solve.

Mr. Stallworthy opened up a college savings account for his daughter at the local bank. He put $1,750 in the account, which pays $5\frac{1}{2}\%$ in yearly interest.

i.) How much will Mr. Stallworthy have earned in interest one year from now?

ii.) If he leaves his money <u>and</u> interest in the bank for another year, how much interest will he earn for the 2nd year? Round your answer to the nearest hundredths place.

Problem Set 29

Tell whether each sentence below is True or False.

1.
(29) Percents are used a lot in banking.

2.
(29) The "interest rate" is the percent the bank will pay you each year of the money they are holding for you.

3.
(29) "Compound interest" is interest earned on interest that you've already been paid.

Add or subtract each group of numbers below.

4.
(18)
$$\begin{array}{r} 6.145 \\ +17.82 \\ \hline \end{array}$$

5.
(17)
$$\begin{array}{r} 93.22 \\ -48.65 \\ \hline \end{array}$$

Multiply or divide each pair of numbers below. Write any remainders in decimal form.

6.
(20)
$$\begin{array}{r} 29.1 \\ \times 0.64 \\ \hline \end{array}$$

7.
(24)
$$15\overline{)1,280}$$

Add or subtract each pair of fractions below. Make sure your answers are fully reduced.

8.
(10) $\dfrac{3}{20} + \dfrac{1}{20}$

9.
(10) $\dfrac{6}{5} - \dfrac{7}{10}$

Multiply or divide each pair of numbers below. Make sure your answers are fully reduced.

10.
(13) $\dfrac{2}{9} \times \dfrac{3}{8}$

11.
(13) $\dfrac{5}{6} \div \dfrac{1}{2}$

Convert each fraction below into decimal form. Round any repeating decimals to two digits (hundredths).

12.
(24) $\dfrac{1}{15}$

13.
(23) $\dfrac{4}{25}$

Convert each decimal below into a fraction. Make sure your answers are fully reduced.

14.
(23) 0.085

15.
(23) 4.2

Convert each percent below into decimal form.

16.
(28) $14\dfrac{2}{5}\%$

(a) 17.
(28) $75\dfrac{1}{8}\%$

Convert each percent below into a fraction. Make sure your answers are fully reduced.

(b) 18.
(26) 38%

(c) 19.
(28) $5\dfrac{1}{3}\%$

Answer each question below. Write your answer as a whole number or decimal.

20.
(27) What is 62% of 980?

(d) 21.
(28) What is $15\dfrac{3}{5}\%$ of 250?

Translate the word problem below into math; then solve.

(e) 22.
(29) Albert is trying to save enough money to buy his uncle's classic Thunderbird. Although he still has a long way to go, he now has $1,500 in a bank account that pays $6\dfrac{1}{2}\%$ in yearly interest.

 i.) How much will Albert have earned in interest one year from now?

 ii.) If he leaves his money <u>and</u> interest in the bank for another year, how much interest will he earn for the 2nd year? Round your answer to the nearest hundredths place.

Lesson 30—Finding the Percent

We've learned how to find the percent of a number. But what if we have two numbers and want to know what percent one is of the other? Here's an example.

What percent of 100 is 30?

This one is easy enough to do in your head: it's 30%. But how do we do the formal calculation? Well, we just put 30 over 100 and then convert the fraction to a percent by getting rid of the denominator and putting in the percent symbol.

$$\frac{30}{100} \text{ is equal to } 30\%$$

Put 30 over 100 and change to a percent.

By the way, it's important to make sure to get the right numbers on top and bottom. How did we know to put 30 on top and 100 on bottom? Well, the "of" number always goes on bottom and the "is" number always goes on top. That's the easy way to remember.

Using a Decimal

We used a fraction to figure out our example problem. But it's also possible to do the problem with a decimal. We still start with $\frac{30}{100}$. But then we divide 100 into 30 using long division to get 0.30. Next, we convert the decimal to a percent. But how do we do that? We know that a percent can be converted into a decimal by dropping the percent symbol and moving the decimal point two places to the left. It shouldn't surprise you that to convert a decimal into a percent, we just go backwards: we move the decimal point two places to the *right* (in the other direction) and put the percent symbol back in again. So 0.30 becomes 30%.

To convert a decimal to a percent.

0.30. ⟵ **Move the decimal 2 places to the right.**

30% ⟵ **Put % back in.**

It's pretty easy to convert a fraction with a denominator of a 100 into a percent (whatever method we use). But on tougher problems, decimals are almost always easier to use than fractions. Here's an example.

What percent of 40 is 15?

The first step is to figure out what goes on top and what goes on bottom. Remember the rule: the "of" number goes on bottom and the "is" number goes on top. The "of" number is 40 because it immediately follows the word "of." The "is" number is 15 because it immediately follows the word "is." So it's 15 over 40.

"of" number goes $\frac{15}{40}$ ⟵ **"is" number goes**
on bottom ⟶   **on top**

Since this fraction doesn't have a denominator of 100, it's not clear what the percent is. What we need to do is convert it into a decimal by dividing 40 into 15.

$$\begin{array}{r} .375 \\ 40\overline{)15.000} \end{array}$$ Convert $\frac{15}{40}$ into a decimal.

That gives us 0.375. Now we can move the decimal point two places to the right and put in the percent symbol for an answer of 37.5% or $37\frac{1}{2}\%$. So 15 is $37\frac{1}{2}\%$ of 40.

Even with Fractions

This method will even work with fractions. Take this example.

What percent of $\frac{1}{2}$ is $\frac{1}{4}$?

This problem would stump a lot of people. But now that you understand the method, it's actually not that tough. The "of" number is $\frac{1}{2}$, so that goes on bottom. The "is" number is $\frac{1}{4}$, which goes on top.

$$\frac{\frac{1}{4}}{\frac{1}{2}}$$ **"Of" on bottom
and "is" on top.**

Inverting and multiplying, we get $\frac{1}{4}\times\frac{2}{1}$ or $\frac{2}{4}$, which reduces to $\frac{1}{2}$. Next, we could convert $\frac{1}{2}$ to a percent by changing it to $\frac{50}{100}$. That's the same as 50%. But most people would just use long division. They would divide 2 into 1 to get 0.5. (Actually, it's so simple they would do it in their heads.) But from 0.5, they would move the decimal point two places to the right for 50% again.

$$\frac{1}{2} = 0.5 = 50\%$$

Decimals Too

We can also find what percent one decimal is of another. Let's do this one.

What percent of 0.8 is 0.2?

The "of" number is 0.8, so it goes on bottom. The "is" number is 0.2, which goes on top.

$$\frac{0.2}{0.8} = 0.25$$ **Just divide.**

Then carrying out the division gives us 0.25. The next step is to change 0.25 to a percent by moving the decimal point two places to the right and putting the percent symbol back in.

$$0.25 = 25\%$$ **Change decimal
to percent**

So 0.2 is 25% of 0.8.

The main point of this lesson is that the best way to find what percent one number is of another is to divide the numbers to get a decimal and then change the decimal to a percent.

Practice 30

a.
(23) Convert $\frac{6}{5}$ into decimal form. If your answer is a repeating decimal, round to two digits (hundredths).

b.
(14) What is $\frac{2}{5}$ of 450?

c.
(30) What percent of 40 is 12?

d.
(30) What percent of $\frac{4}{5}$ is $\frac{1}{5}$?

e.
(30) Translate the word problem below into math; then solve.

Gus thinks he can juggle 5 bottles of ketchup at once. Right now, he is juggling 3. What percent of his goal has been achieved?

Problem Set 30

Add or subtract each group of numbers below.

1.
(17)
$\begin{array}{r} 48.03 \\ +21.55 \\ \hline \end{array}$

2.
(17)
$\begin{array}{r} 502.9 \\ -126.4 \\ \hline \end{array}$

Multiply or divide each pair of numbers below. Write any remainders in decimal form.

3.
(20)
$\begin{array}{r} 0.375 \\ \times 0.25 \\ \hline \end{array}$

4.
(22) $4\overline{)3{,}931}$

5.
(22) $25\overline{)962}$

Add or subtract each pair of numbers below. Make sure your answers are fully reduced.

6.
(12) $5\frac{1}{2} - 3\frac{2}{3}$

7.
(12) $6\frac{2}{5} + 2\frac{3}{10}$

Multiply or divide each pair of numbers below. Make sure your answers are fully reduced.

8.
(13) $\frac{3}{7} \times \frac{14}{18}$

9.
(14) $15 \div \frac{5}{8}$

Convert each fraction below into decimal form. Round any repeating decimals to two digits (hundredths).

10.
(24) $\frac{7}{12}$

(a) **11.**
(23) $\frac{5}{4}$

Convert each decimal below into a fraction. Make sure your answers are fully reduced.

12.
(23)
    0.024

13.
(23)
    0.48

Convert each percent below into decimal form.

14.
(26)
    67%

15.
(28)
    $98\frac{1}{10}\%$

Answer each question below. Write your answer as a whole number or decimal.

(b) 16.
(14)
    What is $\frac{3}{5}$ of 550?

17.
(27)
    What is 47% of 70?

18.
(27)
    What is 32.5% of 225?

(c) 19.
(30)
    What percent of 60 is 15?

(d) 20.
(30)
    What percent of $\frac{1}{2}$ is $\frac{2}{5}$?

Translate the word problem below into math; then solve.

(e) 21.
(30)
    Arnie plans to eat 4 Twinkies during his lunch break. So far he has eaten 3. What percent of his goal has been achieved?

Lesson 31—Calculating a Grade

Finding the percent one number is of another is something that most people need to do all the time in the real world. As a student, you've probably had to use this technique when calculating your grade on an assignment.

Grades Are Based on Percents

That's because most grading systems are based on percents. If you get $100-90\%$ of the questions right you get an A. If you get $89-80\%$ right, you get a B, $79-70\%$ equals a C, $69-60\%$ equals a D, and 59% and below equals an F.

Just to show you how it works, let's do an example. What if you take a test that has 25 questions and get 20 of them right? What should your grade be? Well, to figure this one out, all you have to do is calculate what percent of 25 is 20. The "of" number is 25, which goes on bottom. The "is" number is 20, so it goes on top.

$$\frac{20}{25} \qquad \textbf{"of" on bottom; "is" on top}$$

Next, we divide 25 into 20 using long division to get 0.8.

$$\frac{20}{25} = 0.8 \qquad \textbf{Divide to get a decimal.}$$

Now we just change 0.8 to a percent by moving the decimal point two places to the right and putting in the percent symbol to get 80%. That's just barely a B. Of course, as you probably know, instead of saying 80%, some people will just say "I got an 80." But that means 80 out of 100, which is 80 percent.

Worth More than One Point?

Sometimes each question on an assignment is worth more than one point. That tends to confuse people, but it really shouldn't, because the method for calculating the grade is basically the same. Say you did an assignment that had 50 questions and each one was worth 3 points. If you got 45 right, then you could calculate your percentage grade in one of two ways. First, you could just divide the number of questions you got right by the total number of questions. Since $\frac{45}{50}$ is equal to 0.90, or 90%, your grade would be an A (That's the same method we used above). That method will work just fine, as long as each question is worth the same number of points. The second method is to do the calculation using points. Since you got 45 right and each problem counted for 3 points, you earned 45 times 3, or 135 points out of a total of 50 times 3, or 150 points. So dividing the two point totals leaves $\frac{135}{150}$ (with the "of" number on bottom and the "is" number on top). That comes out to 0.90, which converts to 90%, the same answer we got with the first method. The two methods are the same if the problems are all worth the same amount. The point method is the one to use if the problems are worth different amounts. We won't do an example like that. But all you do is add up the points you got and divide that by the total points possible.

Practice 31

a. Convert 2.16 into a fraction. Make sure your answer is fully reduced.
(23)

b. Convert 110% into decimal form.
(26)

c. What is $8\frac{2}{5}\%$ of 75? Write your answer as a decimal.
(28)

d. What percent of $\frac{1}{3}$ is $\frac{1}{6}$?
(30)

e. Translate the word problem below into math; then solve.
(30)

The toddler only got 1 out of 3 questions right on his "Stop, Drop, and Roll" test. What percentage of the questions did he get right? Write your answer as a fractional percent.

Problem Set 31

Tell whether each sentence below is True or False.

1. Percents are never used in grading.
(31)

2. To calculate a grade, divide the number of questions answered correctly by the total number of
(31) questions (and convert the answer into a percent).

Add or subtract each group of numbers below.

3.
(17)
$$\begin{array}{r} 19.25 \\ 27.39 \\ +14.52 \\ \hline \end{array}$$

4.
(17)
$$\begin{array}{r} 24.65 \\ -14.38 \\ \hline \end{array}$$

Multiply or divide each pair of numbers below. Write any remainders in decimal form.

5.
(20)
$$\begin{array}{r} 1.825 \\ \times 0.4 \\ \hline \end{array}$$

6. $0.22\overline{)14.19}$
(22)

7.
(20)
$$\begin{array}{r} 6.58 \\ \times 1.2 \\ \hline \end{array}$$

Add or subtract each pair of fractions below. Make sure your answers are fully reduced.

8. $\frac{7}{8}+\frac{1}{4}$
(10)

9. $\frac{9}{14}-\frac{1}{14}$
(10)

Multiply or divide each pair of numbers below. Make sure your answers are fully reduced.

10. $\frac{5}{12}\times 144$
(14)

11. $\frac{3}{2}\div\frac{3}{16}$
(13)

Convert each fraction below into decimal form. Round any repeating decimals to two digits (hundredths).

12.
(23) $\dfrac{17}{20}$

13.
(24) $\dfrac{7}{6}$

Convert each decimal below into a fraction. Make sure your answers are fully reduced.

14.
(23) 0.45

(a) 15.
(23) 4.12

Convert each percent below into decimal form.

16.
(28) $62\dfrac{1}{4}\%$

(b) 17.
(26) 120%

Answer each question below. Write your answer as a whole number or decimal.

18.
(14) What is $\dfrac{2}{7}$ of 490?

(c) 19.
(28) What is $4\dfrac{1}{5}\%$ of 50?

(d) 20.
(30) What percent of $\dfrac{2}{3}$ is $\dfrac{1}{6}$?

Translate the word problem below into math; then solve.

(e) 21.
(30) The trainer kept trying to teach her dolphins how to play baseball, but after a year's worth of practice, only 4 out of 15 knew the difference between a "strike" and a "ball." What percentage of the dolphins knew the difference between a "strike" and a "ball"? Write your answer as a fractional percent.

CHAPTER 5:
MEASURING LENGTH

Lesson 32—Units of Measurement

We learned that you only need whole numbers to count but that measuring requires fractions. Actually, though, it takes more than fractions to measure things in the real world. We also need **units**. Examples of units would be miles, yards, feet, and inches. We're going to learn all about units over the next two chapters.

How Units Got Started

How did units ever get started? Well, the first people to do much measuring were farmers who needed to measure their land. This was no easy thing way back when. Imagine how hard it might be to measure the length of a field if nobody had taught you how to do it. If you didn't know much about math, you might try to "count" the length of your field (since counting worked so well on other problems). But how could you count a length? A length isn't broken up into pieces the way a basket of apples is.

So units probably first started when some clever farmer figured out a way to "count" the length of his field, even though it wasn't broken into pieces. In all likelihood, the farmer just measured how many times his foot would fit along the length of the field. If it fit 252 times, then his field was 252 "feet" long. That's where the unit feet came from. It's a way to measure by counting, even though a length can't be split up the way a bunch of apples can.

Actually, feet turned out to be good units to use, because they're with a person all the time. They never go away (hopefully). Other body parts, such as the hand and arm, began to be used for the same reason. The hand is still used today as a unit to measure the height of horses.

Why More than One?

But here's an interesting question? Why did people need to have more than one kind of unit to measure? Why not just always use your feet? Well, there are two reasons. First, some units are easier to use for certain measurements than others. For example, you wouldn't want to measure the length of a tilled garden with your arm. You'd have to crawl around on the ground, which would make you really dirty. Your foot would be far better for that kind of job. However, if you were measuring fabric, your arm would work much better than your foot because you can just pull the fabric alongside your arm to measure it. If you used your foot to measure fabric, you'd have to walk all over it.

The second reason we need different units is that some lengths are much longer than others. The longer the length, the longer the unit you want to use. You wouldn't want to measure the distance from New York to California in inches. That would be crazy. The measurement would turn out to equal a gigantic number, which would be really hard to work with. And you wouldn't want to measure the length of an atom in miles. It would be such a tiny number that it would be hard to work with.

Standard Measures

People eventually realized that even using different body parts for measuring wasn't so great. One drawback was that everyone has a different shaped body. How can we ever agree on the exact measurement of a field if my foot is bigger than your foot?

People got around this problem by creating **standard measures**. A standard measure is a physical object like a stick that represents a unit of measurement. Then everybody agrees that the stick is the correct length of the unit, which eliminates all the confusion.

The King's Foot

But how did people decide what the standard should be? Interestingly, the first standards were based on a King's body parts. For example, the first "foot" was the length of the great French King Charlemagne's foot, and (supposedly) the length of the yard was first determined by the distance between the nose and fingertip of Henry I of England.

Even after people came up with standard units, there was still a problem. Everybody couldn't share one single measuring stick. That's why a lot of copies of the standard stick had to be made and passed around so everybody could use them. These copies are called **secondary standards**. For instance, you probably own a ruler or a yardstick. Those are secondary standards. The original standard is kept safely under lock and key to make sure that nobody tampers with it. In fact, there are government officials who make sure that secondary standards (copies) are made properly. Otherwise, it would be really tempting for some people to whittle down the length of their yardsticks a bit. They could use the shorter yardsticks to cheat customers who bought goods (like fabric) by the yard.

Feet and Inches on the Same Stick

Eventually somebody got the idea of putting more than one unit on the secondary standards. That meant a yardstick would have marks for feet and inches on it. Here's why that's useful. With different units on the same stick, fractional measurements are easier to make. For example, if you're measuring something that's over 2 feet long, you can just read off your yardstick that the object is 2 feet and so many inches.

Adjusting the Units

There was one drawback of putting more than one unit on a single yardstick, though. What if the smaller unit didn't divide into the larger one evenly? Not surprisingly, this was pretty common. After all, why should the length of Charlemagne's foot divide evenly into the length from Henry I's nose to his fingertip? The way around the problem was to adjust the units a bit. For instance, you can make the inch a little smaller or larger until a certain number of inches equals a foot exactly. This is why there are exactly 12 inches in a foot and exactly 3 feet in a yard today.

Practice 32

a.
(24) Convert $\frac{1}{7}$ into decimal form. If your answer is a repeating decimal, round to two digits (hundredths).

b.
(28) Convert $2\frac{1}{4}\%$ into a fraction. Make sure your answer is fully reduced.

c.
(27) What is 12.5% of 42? Write your answer as a decimal.

d.
(30) What percent of 4 is $\frac{3}{5}$?

e.
(27) Translate the word problem below into math; then solve.

Of the 400 people who were surveyed, only 20% said the governor should not sign the bill against lobbying. How many of those surveyed thought the governor should not sign the bill against lobbying?

Problem Set 32

Tell whether each sentence below is True or False.

1.
(32) A standard measure is a physical object like a stick or rod that represents a unit of measurement.

2.
(32) The first standards for units of measure were based on the body parts of kings.

3.
(32) There is no good reason why we have more than one unit of measurement.

Add or subtract each group of numbers below.

4.
(17)
```
  709.02
+552.16
```

5.
(18)
```
 8.125
-4.03
```

Multiply or divide each pair of numbers below. Write any remainders in decimal form.

6.
(3)
```
 850
×42
```

7.
(24) $0.3\overline{)758}$

8.
(20)
```
 2.21
×0.8
```

Add or subtract each pair of numbers below. Make sure your answers are fully reduced.

9.
(10) $\frac{7}{3}+\frac{1}{2}$

10.
(12) $2-\frac{6}{5}$

Multiply or divide each pair of fractions below. Make sure your answers are fully reduced.

11. $\frac{1}{3} \times \frac{9}{10}$
(13)

12. $\frac{2}{5} \div \frac{4}{5}$
(13)

Convert each fraction below into decimal form. Round any repeating decimals to two digits (hundredths).

13. $\frac{7}{8}$
(23)

(a) 14. $\frac{2}{7}$
(24)

Convert each decimal below into a fraction. Make sure your answers are fully reduced.

15. 0.95
(23)

16. 0.2
(23)

Convert each percent below into a fraction. Make sure your answers are fully reduced.

17. 26%
(26)

(b) 18. $3\frac{1}{4}\%$
(28)

Convert each percent below into decimal form.

19. $18\frac{1}{10}\%$
(28)

20. 225%
(26)

Answer each question below. Write your answer as a whole number or decimal.

21. What is $\frac{2}{9}$ of 180?
(14)

(c) 22. What is 15.5% of 36?
(27)

(d) 23. What percent of 2 is $\frac{2}{5}$?
(30)

Translate the word problem below into math; then solve.

(e) 24. Of the 1,250 people who were surveyed, only 30% said the longtime city councilman should not run for mayor. How many of those surveyed thought the councilman should not run for mayor?
(27)

Lesson 33—Unit Conversions

We've been learning about units of measurements. Sometimes we have to add or subtract two measurements. What do we do with the units in a case like that? Well, the rule is that we can always add or subtract two measurements, as long as the units are the same for both. Here's a simple example.

$$2 \text{ feet} + 7 \text{ feet}$$

We have feet added to feet; the units are the same. All we have to do, then, is add the numbers and keep the units in feet to get 9 feet.

$$9 \text{ feet}$$

Feet to Inches

But what if the units are different? For example, what if we need to add 3 feet and 24 inches?

$$3 \text{ feet} + 24 \text{ inches}$$

Since one measurement is in feet and the other is in inches, we can't add the measurements the way they are right now. Adding 3 feet to 24 inches to get 27 feet (or 27 inches) is obviously wrong. What we do is change one unit into another, so that the units are the same. Then they can be added. Changing or "converting" one unit into another is actually called a **unit conversion**.

To do a unit conversion, we have to know how the two units are related. For example, we know that there are 12 inches in 1 foot. Using that knowledge, we can convert 3 feet to inches. Since there are 12 inches in each of the 3 feet, we *multiply* 3 by 12 to get 36 inches.

$$3 \times 12 = 36$$ **Multiply by 12 to convert feet to inches.**

Next, we put 36 inches in for 3 feet in our problem. With both measurements in the same units (inches), we can add normally.

$$36 \text{ inches} + 24 \text{ inches} = 60 \text{ inches}$$

Inches to Feet

As you probably know, that's not the only way to do the problem.

$$3 \text{ feet} + 24 \text{ inches}$$

Instead of converting everything into inches, we can convert into feet. Since there are 12 inches in a foot, we can convert 24 inches into feet by *dividing* 24 by 12 to get 2 feet.

$$24 \div 12 = 2$$ **Divide by 12 to convert inches to feet.**

With the units the same, we can add normally.

$$3 \text{ feet} + 2 \text{ feet} = 5 \text{ feet}$$

These may seem like different answers to the same problem, but they're really the same. If we convert 5 feet into inches by multiplying by 12 we get 60 inches ($5 \times 12 = 60$), which is the same answer we got by doing the problem in inches.

When to Multiply/When to Divide

Did you notice that in going from feet to inches, we multiplied, but in going from inches to feet, we divided? Those are really important rules. We always convert larger units (like feet) into smaller units (like inches) by multiplying. It doesn't matter what the units are. That's because multiplying increases the number, and there are always more smaller units in any measurement than there are larger units. (A yardstick has just 3 feet, but it has 36 inches).

Going in the other direction, we always convert smaller units (like inches) into larger units (like feet) by dividing. This also works no matter what units are involved. That's because dividing decreases the number, and there are always fewer larger units in any measurement than there are smaller units.

Rules for Unit Conversions

1.	When converting larger units to smaller units *multiply*.
2.	When converting smaller units to larger units *divide*.

Conversion Factors

Unit conversions are easy as long as we know how the units relate. In math, the numbers telling us how the units relate are called **conversion factors**. Here are the conversion factors between the major units of length.

Some Conversion Factors
(for lengths)

12 inches = 1 foot
3 feet = 1 yard
1,760 yards = 1 mile

Practice 33

a.
(33) Convert 5 feet into inches.

b.
(33) Convert 70 yards into feet.

c.
(33) Convert 6 miles into yards.

d.
(30) What percent of 12.5 is 4?

e.
(33) Translate the word problem below into math; then solve.

Mr. Shaw is 6 feet tall, and the stool he is standing on is 36 inches. How many *inches* high is Mr. Shaw plus the stool?

Problem Set 33

Tell whether each sentence below is True or False.

1.
(33) Changing or "converting" one unit into another is called a unit conversion.

2.
(33) Larger units (like feet) are always converted into smaller units (like inches) by dividing.

Add or subtract each group of numbers below.

3.
(2)
$$24,381$$
$$+92,903$$

4.
(17)
$$44.75$$
$$-28.29$$

Multiply or divide each pair of numbers below. Write any remainders in decimal form.

5.
(22) $3.2\overline{)52}$

6.
(20)
$$4.7$$
$$\times 7.5$$

7.
(22) $12\overline{)8,025}$

Add or subtract each group of fractions below. Make sure your answers are fully reduced.

8.
(11) $\frac{1}{2}+\frac{2}{5}+\frac{1}{4}$

9.
(10) $\frac{11}{14}-\frac{2}{7}$

Multiply or divide each pair of numbers below. Make sure your answers are fully reduced.

10.
(14) $8\times\frac{3}{16}$

11.
(14) $6\div\frac{2}{5}$

Convert each fraction below into decimal form. Round any repeating decimals to two digits (hundredths).

12.
(23) $\frac{9}{5}$

13.
(24) $\frac{1}{3}$

Convert each percent below into decimal form.

14.
(28) $12\frac{4}{5}\%$

15.
(26) 340%

Do each unit conversion below. (Conversion factors: 12 inches = 1 foot; 3 feet = 1 yard; 1,760 yards = 1 mile.)

(a) 16.   Convert 6 feet into inches.
(33)

(b) 17.   Convert 80 yards into feet.
(33)

(c) 18.   Convert 2 miles into yards.
(33)

Answer each question below. Write your answer as a whole number or decimal.

19.   What is 22% of 480?
(27)

(d) 20.   What percent of 12.5 is 8?
(30)

Translate the word problem below into math; then solve.

(e) 21.   The 5 foot tall circus performer is balancing a stack of containers on her head. If the stack is 24 inches
(33)   high, how many *inches* high is the woman plus the stack?

Lesson 34—Skipping Around

In the last lesson, we learned how to convert a measurement from one unit to another. The main thing we need to know is the proper conversion factor. That's the number that tells us how the units relate. Here are the conversion factors for the major units of length again.

12 inches = 1 foot   3 feet = 1 yard   1,760 yards = 1 mile

Miles to Feet and Back

Using these conversion factors, it's easy to convert between inches and feet, or between feet and yards, or between yards and miles. But what if we need to convert from miles all the way down to feet? The list of conversion factors doesn't tell us how many feet are in a mile. Is there a good way to do the conversion? Yes. Let's look at a specific example.

How many feet are in 4 miles?

We can do this problem in steps. The first step is to figure out how many yards are in 4 miles. Since we know that 1,760 yards = 1 mile , that's easy. We just multiply 4 by 1,760. (Remember, we multiply since we're going from larger to smaller units.)

$$4 \times 1,760 = 7,040 \qquad \textbf{Converting miles to yards}$$

That gives us 7,040 yards. We're not finished, because we're trying to find how many feet are in 4 miles. The second step, then, is to convert 7,040 yards to feet. Since we know that 3 feet = 1 yard , this is easy too. We just have to multiply 7,040 by 3. (We multiply, because we're going from larger to smaller units again.)

$$7,040 \times 3 = 21,120 \qquad \textbf{Converting yards to feet}$$

Our answer is 21,120 feet. That's how many feet are in 4 miles. The main point is that we converted miles into feet by going in steps: from miles to yards and then from yards to feet.

Inches to Miles

Let's do one more tough example where the units are far apart.

How many *miles* are in 76,032 *inches*?

We're skipping units again. We're going from miles all the way to inches. Only this time, we're starting with smaller units and going to larger units. That means we have to *divide* each time.

The first step is to convert inches to feet by dividing 76,032 by 12.

$$76,032 \div 12 = 6,336 \qquad \textbf{Converting inches to feet}$$

That gives us 6,336 feet. The second step is to convert feet to yards by dividing 6,336 by 3.

$$6,336 \div 3 = 2,112 \qquad \textbf{Converting feet to yards}$$

We end up with 2,112 yards. The last step is to convert yards to miles by dividing 2,112 by 1,760.[1]

---

[1] Since the divisor 1,760 is so large, it's okay to use a calculator on a problem like this.

$$2,112 \div 1,760 = 1.2$$ **Converting yards to miles**

We get 1.2, which means that 76,032 inches equals 1.2 miles.

The main point of this lesson, then, is that we can skip around between units that are far apart in size by going in steps. We just convert one unit at a time.

Practice 34

a.
(26)   Convert 0.45% into decimal form.

b.
(34)   How many inches are in 8 yards?

c.
(34)   Convert 6 miles into feet.

d.
(34)   How many miles are in 95,040 inches?

e.
(34)   Translate the word problem below into math; then solve.

It is 671 miles from Paris to Berlin. How far is this in feet?

Problem Set 34

Add or subtract each group of numbers below.

1.
(17)
$$\begin{array}{r} 80.57 \\ +46.11 \\ \hline \end{array}$$

2.
(2)
$$\begin{array}{r} 6,004 \\ -2,573 \\ \hline \end{array}$$

Multiply or divide each pair of numbers below. Write any remainders in decimal form.

3.
(24) $9\overline{)1,708}$

4.
(20)
$$\begin{array}{r} 520 \\ \times 7.3 \\ \hline \end{array}$$

5.
(22) $0.25\overline{)3.65}$

Add or subtract each pair of fractions below. Make sure your answers are fully reduced.

6.
(10) $\dfrac{3}{2} + \dfrac{1}{2}$

7.
(11) $\dfrac{5}{6} - \dfrac{3}{4}$

Multiply or divide each pair of numbers below. Make sure your answers are fully reduced.

8.
(13) $\dfrac{6}{5} \times \dfrac{10}{9}$

9.
(13) $\dfrac{1}{4} \div \dfrac{7}{8}$

Convert each fraction below into decimal form. Round any repeating decimals to two digits (hundredths).

10.
(23) $\dfrac{35}{10}$

11.
(24) $\dfrac{1}{6}$

Convert each decimal below into a fraction. Make sure your answers are fully reduced.

12.   0.05
(23)

13.   0.14
(23)

Convert each percent below into decimal form.

14. $8\frac{1}{2}\%$
(28)

(a) 15.   0.75%
(26)

Do each unit conversion below. (Conversion factors: 12 inches = 1 foot; 3 feet = 1 yard; 1,760 yards = 1 mile.)

(b) 16.   How many inches are in 9 yards?
(34)

(c) 17.   Convert 5 miles into feet.
(34)

(d) 18.   How many miles are in 158,400 inches?
(34)

Answer each question below. Write your answer as a decimal.

19.   What is 32% of 60?
(27)

20.   What percent of 40 is 5?
(30)

Translate the word problem below into math; then solve.

(e) 21.   It is 800 miles from Seattle to San Francisco. How far is this in feet?
(34)

Lesson 35—Making a Table

In the last lesson, we learned a method for converting units that aren't right next to each other (like going from miles all the way down to inches). We just do the conversion in steps. The only drawback of this method is that it takes a long time, especially when the units are very different in size.

Converting in a Single Step

There's actually a faster way to do conversions between units that are really far apart. Instead of going step by step from inches to miles, we can figure out the conversion factor for inches to miles directly. And we can do the same thing for miles to feet, inches to yards, and all of the other combinations. That allows us to convert between any two units in a single step. It helps to write all these conversion factors down neatly. Most people put them in a table, called (not surprisingly!) a **unit conversion table**. A unit conversion table for all of the major units of length is shown below.

Unit Conversion Table (for lengths)

	mile	yard	foot	inch
mile	1	1,760	5,280	63,360
yard	$\frac{1}{1,760}$	1	3	36
foot	$\frac{1}{5,280}$	$\frac{1}{3}$	1	12
inch	$\frac{1}{63,360}$	$\frac{1}{36}$	$\frac{1}{12}$	1

Here's how this table is used. Say we want to convert 4 yards to inches. Instead of having to convert yards to feet first and then feet to inches, all we have to do is look at our table for the yards to inches conversion factor. When looking up a conversion factor, we always begin on the left. Since we're starting with yards, we go to the yard row. Then we move to the right until we run into the inch column. The number in that spot is the conversion factor for yards to inches. It happens to be 36 because there are 36 inches in 1 yard. So all we have to do is multiply 4 by 36 to get 144 inches and we're done!

The Table Tells it All

The other neat thing about this table is that when using it, we don't have to worry about whether we should multiply or divide when converting from one unit to another. Assume, for example, that we want to convert feet to miles. That's going from smaller to larger units, which means we should divide. But watch what happens when we use the conversion table. To find the conversion factor, we start on the left and then go down to the foot row. Next, we move to the right until we hit miles. The number in that box is the fraction $\frac{1}{5,280}$. That's the conversion factor we need. Now all we have to do is *multiply* by $\frac{1}{5,280}$ to convert feet to miles.

But wait a minute. Aren't we supposed to divide when going from smaller to larger units? Well, yes, but we haven't broken any rules, because multiplying by $\frac{1}{5,280}$ is actually the same as dividing by 5,280. For instance, if we were converting 10,000 feet to miles, multiplying 10,000 by $\frac{1}{5,280}$ would give us this: $\frac{10,000}{1} \times \frac{1}{5,280}$ or

$\frac{10,000}{5,280}$. But 10,000 over 5,280 is the same as dividing by 5,280. The main point is that when using the table, we multiply every time—whether we're going from larger to smaller units or from smaller to larger units. Since the table has fractions in all the right places, it decides whether the number should be multiplied or divided for us.[1] We don't have to remember a thing.

It Pays to Memorize

Of course, you won't always have a unit conversion table in front of you when doing a unit conversion. So it's still smart to memorize as many conversion factors as possible. And it's definitely still worth remembering the rule about multiplying when going from larger to smaller units and dividing when going from smaller to larger units. If you're without a conversion table, that rule really helps.

Practice 35

a.
(35)   Convert 10 yards into inches. Use the table below problem 18.

b.
(35)   Convert 16,896 feet into miles. Use the table below problem 18.

c.
(35)   Convert 6.4 miles into inches. Use the table below problem 18.

d.
(30)   What percent of 3.4 is 1.7?

e.
(35)   Translate the word problem below into math; then solve.

The team had only 9 inches to go to get a first down. How many yards is that?

Problem Set 35

Tell whether each sentence below is True or False.

1.
(35)   A unit conversion table contains the conversion factors between all units.

2.
(35)   A unit conversion table tells what number to multiply by to do a particular conversion.

Add or subtract each group of numbers below.

3.
(17)
```
  573.1
 +98.9
```

4.
(17)
```
  901.42
 −854.26
```

---

[1] If you look closely, you'll see that every box that has a fraction in it is a case of converting from smaller to larger units. And when we multiply by that fraction, we're really dividing by the number on the bottom of the fraction.

Multiply or divide each pair of numbers below. Write any remainders in decimal form.

5.
(20)

$$13.4 \\ \times 2.1$$

6.
(22)

$$0.8\overline{)235}$$

7.
(3)

$$390 \\ \times 61$$

Add or subtract each pair of numbers below. Make sure your answers are fully reduced.

8.
(10)

$$\frac{3}{7} + \frac{4}{7}$$

9.
(12)

$$6\frac{2}{5} - 2\frac{9}{10}$$

Multiply or divide each pair of fractions below. Make sure your answers are fully reduced.

10.
(13)

$$\frac{3}{8} \times \frac{4}{5}$$

11.
(13)

$$\frac{5}{16} \div \frac{5}{4}$$

Convert each fraction below into decimal form. Round any repeating decimals to two digits (hundredths).

12.
(23)

$$\frac{5}{8}$$

13.
(24)

$$\frac{5}{6}$$

Convert each percent below into decimal form.

14.
(28)

$$77\frac{1}{4}\%$$

15.
(25)

$$500\%$$

Do each unit conversion below using the unit conversion table:

(a) 16. Convert 12 yards into inches.
(35)

(b) 17. Convert 18,480 feet into miles.
(35)

(c) 18. Convert 7.2 miles into inches.
(35)

	mile	yard	foot	inch
mile	1	1,760	5,280	63,360
yard	$\frac{1}{1,760}$	1	3	36
foot	$\frac{1}{5,280}$	$\frac{1}{3}$	1	12
inch	$\frac{1}{63,360}$	$\frac{1}{36}$	$\frac{1}{12}$	1

Answer each question below. Write your answer as a whole number or decimal.

19.
(27)   What is 25% of 14?

(d) 20.
(30)   What percent of 7.5 is 1.5?

Translate the word problem below into math; then solve.

(e) 21.
(35)   The man with the largest bicep in the world has a bicep which measures 30 inches when cold. How many yards is this?

Lesson 36—The Metric System

The units of length that we've been studying so far are all part of what's called the **English system** or **common system** of measurements. So inches, feet, yards, miles, etc. all go together. This system is called "English" because it originated in England, and it's called "common" because for a long time, units like inches, feet, yards, and miles were the ones most often used in "common," everyday measurements. But today only English speaking countries, like the U.S., Britain, Australia, and New Zealand, still use the common system at all. The other 200 or more countries in the world use a different system, which we're going to start learning about in this lesson.

Too Complicated

Why isn't the common system more popular? Well, since the common system was the first system of measurement, it arose gradually. And the original units were based on body parts. Remember, the foot was actually set to equal the length of the French King Charlemagne's foot. The original yard was based on the distance between the nose and fingertip of King Henry I of England. And the other units are just as random. With such weird beginnings, it's not surprising that the whole system turned out to be pretty complicated. Even though some of the units were later adjusted a bit so that they would fit together better (the foot was made to equal 12 inches exactly instead of $11\frac{1}{2}$ or $12\frac{1}{2}$ inches), that still didn't help all that much.

Too Much to Memorize

For example, think of how many different numbers we have to memorize when using the common system of measurements. There are 12 inches in a foot, so we need to remember the number 12. But then there are only 3 feet in a yard, so we have to remember the number 3 as well. There are 1,760 yards in a mile, and we wouldn't want to forget that. Then it also makes sense to remember that there are 5,280 feet in a mile. So with only a handful of units, we have to do a lot of memorizing. The other problem is that since everything is based on body parts, the numbers aren't related to one another in any simple way. No wonder we need a table to remember all of the conversion factors! The main point is the common system isn't all that popular because it's so complex. Wouldn't it be nice if there were a simpler system where all the numbers fit together nicely? Then there wouldn't be so much to memorize.

Based on Nature

In the 17th and 18th centuries—a time of great scientific discoveries—people began to wonder about whether such a system could actually be created. With so much science going on, there was a need for more accurate measurements than you could get by using the common system. (Scientists usually want their measurements to be as precise as possible.) People were also getting frustrated with having to remember all those conversion factors: 12 inches to a foot, 3 feet to a yard, and so on.

There was another reason that many of the scientifically-minded intellectuals of Europe wanted to dump the common system. They thought that units of measure should be based not on the length of a dead King's foot but on a fact of nature. Thomas Jefferson (the 3rd president of the U.S.) agreed with this thinking and was interested in creating a new system of units for America too. The only problem was that people had gotten so used to the old common units that changing to something new seemed really hard.

It wasn't until after the French Revolution (when the French king was thrown out and killed) that a new system was actually invented. The revolutionaries who took over from the king decided to recruit a group of scientists and give them the assignment of creating a complete new system of measurement. They asked the scientists to make the new system as logical as possible.

Finding the Basic Unit

The scientists first had to decide on a basic unit for their system. It would be the unit that all the other units are based upon. (The basic unit of the common system is the foot.) As we said, they wanted this unit to come from nature, because that seemed more logical and intelligent to them. After doing quite a bit of thinking, they ended up choosing the distance around the earth itself. Actually, instead of the distance all the way around the earth, they measured from the equator to the North Pole, which is a fourth of the way around.

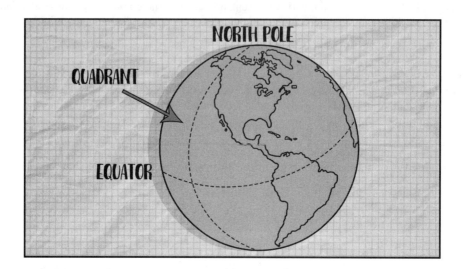

This length is called a **quadrant** ("quad" means four). Since the scientists were French, they measured along a line that ran right through the city of Paris (from the equator to the North Pole).

The only problem with the quadrant is that it's too long to be used in everyday measurements. A basic unit really should be short enough to fit on a stick. So the last step for the scientists was to divide the quadrant into 10 million pieces. One 10 millionth of the quadrant then became the basic unit of measure. This unit was given the name **meter**, and it's only a little longer than a yard (which is a great length for a stick).[1]

Of course, if the scientists' measurements had been exact, it would take precisely 10 million meters to go from the equator to the North Pole through Paris, and the distance all the way around the earth would be 4 times that or 40 million meters. But those first measurements were a little off, so today's meter is not precisely equal to this length, even though it's very close.

Giving the System a New Name

Once the meter was decided upon, the French scientists created other units to go along with it. All of these were fit together into a new system of measurement that was extremely logical, and since the meter was its basic unit, the new set of measurements was called the **metric system**. We'll learn more about the metric system in the next few lessons.

---

[1] There isn't enough room on the page to show the entire stick.

Practice 36

a.
(35)
Convert 504 inches into yards. Use the table below problem 17.

b.
(35)
How many feet are in $5\frac{1}{2}$ miles? Use the table below problem 17.

c.
(13)
$\frac{7}{2}$ has how many $\frac{1}{8}$ s in it?

d.
(33)
Add 47 inches and 6 feet and put your answer in inches.

e.
(29)
Translate the word problem below into math; then solve.

Mr. and Mrs. Gibbons are trying to save enough money to buy their daughter a harp. They have already saved $1,200 and it still isn't enough. (Harps are expensive!) If their $1,200 in savings is sitting in a bank account that pays $5\frac{1}{2}\%$ in yearly interest.

i.) How much will Mr. and Mrs. Gibbons have earned in interest one year from now?

ii.) If they leave their money <u>and</u> interest in the bank for another year, how much interest will they earn for the 2nd year? Round your answer to the nearest hundredths place.

Problem Set 36

Tell whether each sentence below is True or False.

1.
(36)
The English or common system of units is still used for everyday measurements in English-speaking countries (like the U.S. and Britain).

2.
(36)
The common system of units is not popular today because it is too logical and scientific.

3.
(36)
The basic unit of measurement in the metric system is the inch.

Add or subtract each group of numbers below.

4.
(2)
$$\begin{array}{r} 1,850 \\ +7,042 \\ \hline \end{array}$$

5.
(17)
$$\begin{array}{r} 9.056 \\ -4.135 \\ \hline \end{array}$$

Multiply or divide each pair of numbers below. Write any remainders in decimal form.

6.
(20)
$$\begin{array}{r} 236 \\ \times 4.2 \\ \hline \end{array}$$

7.
(21)
$0.5\overline{)11.75}$

8.
(20)
$$\begin{array}{r} 8.5 \\ \times 1.7 \\ \hline \end{array}$$

Add or subtract each pair of numbers below. Make sure your answers are fully reduced.

9.
(12) $1\dfrac{1}{4}+2\dfrac{5}{6}$

10.
(10) $\dfrac{8}{9}-\dfrac{2}{3}$

Multiply or divide each pair of fractions below. Make sure your answers are fully reduced.

11.
(13) $\dfrac{17}{18}\times\dfrac{18}{17}$

12.
(13) $\dfrac{9}{10}\div\dfrac{1}{5}$

Convert each fraction below into decimal form. Round any repeating decimals to two digits (hundredths).

13.
(23) $\dfrac{3}{5}$

14.
(24) $\dfrac{6}{11}$

Do each unit conversion below using the unit conversion table:

15.
(35)   How many inches are in 34 feet?

(a) 16.
(35)   Convert 612 inches into yards.

(b) 17.
(35)   How many feet are in $4\dfrac{1}{2}$ miles?

	mile	yard	foot	inch
mile	1	1,760	5,280	63,360
yard	$\dfrac{1}{1,760}$	1	3	36
foot	$\dfrac{1}{5,280}$	$\dfrac{1}{3}$	1	12
inch	$\dfrac{1}{63,360}$	$\dfrac{1}{36}$	$\dfrac{1}{12}$	1

Answer each question below. Write your answer as a whole number or decimal.

(c) 18.
(13) $\dfrac{5}{2}$ has how many $\dfrac{1}{4}$ s in it?

19.
(14)   What is $\dfrac{2}{5}$ of 205?

20.
(27)   What is 14.5% of 30?

(d) 21.
(33)   52 inches + 8 feet (Put your answer in inches.)

168

Translate the word problem below into math; then solve.

(e) 22.
(29)
Mr. Randall opened up a college savings account for his son at the local bank. He put $3,000 in the account, which pays $7\frac{1}{2}$ % in yearly interest.

    i.)   How much will Mr. Randall have earned in interest one year from now?

    ii.) If he leaves his money and interest in the bank for another year, how much interest will he earn for the 2nd year? Round your answer to the nearest hundredths place.

Lesson 37—It's All in a Name

As we talked about in the last lesson, the metric system is based on the meter. But there are also lots of other units of different sizes in the metric system. We'll learn about the major ones in this lesson.

Finally, a Simple System

Before getting into the names of the other units, though, we should talk a little about how they're all related. The common system's biggest weakness is that the conversion factors are hard to remember. You have to remember that there are 12 inches in a foot, 3 feet in a yard, 1,760 yards in a mile, and so on. Since the metric system was created from scratch (by logically-minded scientists), its units are related in a much simpler way. In the metric system, each unit is 10 times (or one tenth of) the next unit. So, for example, the meter is 10 times the unit that is just smaller than it in size. And the unit that is just bigger than the meter is 10 times the meter's length. All the units are related this way. Everything goes up by 10s. As we'll see later, this makes a huge difference in doing unit conversions.

Smaller than a Meter

What about the names of these other units? Let's start with the smaller ones. These come from breaking down the meter into smaller lengths. The unit that is one tenth of the meter is called the **decimeter**. It's about 4 inches long. And since the decimeter is one tenth of the meter, it takes 10 decimeters to equal 1 meter.

To get the unit just smaller than the decimeter, we have to break it down into ten pieces. This gives us the **centimeter**. It takes 10 centimeters to equal 1 decimeter and 100 centimeters to equal 1 meter. The centimeter is less than half an inch in length.

Next in line comes the **millimeter**, which as you might expect is one tenth of a centimeter. The millimeter is only about as wide as a pinhead. It takes 1,000 millimeters to equal 1 meter.

Bigger than a Meter

The decimeter, centimeter, and millimeter are units that are smaller than a meter—and the ones used most often. But what about the units that are bigger than a meter? Well, the first one is 10 times the meter in length, and it's called the **dekameter**. Notice that everything is still by 10s. That holds true for all the units of the metric system (small and large). The dekameter is over 30 feet long.

The next bigger unit is the **hectometer**, and it is 10 times the dekameter, which means that it's equal to 100 meters. A hectometer is longer than a football field.

Following the hectometer, we have the **kilometer**, which is 10 times the hectometer. The kilometer is equal to 1,000 meters and is over half a mile in length. Here are all of the major units of the metric system shown together.

Major Metric Units (for length)

1,000 meters = 1 kilometer
100 meters = 1 hectometer
10 meters = 1 dekameter
1 meter = 10 decimeters
1 meter = 100 centimeters
1 meter = 1,000 millimeters

The important point to remember is that each unit is 10 times as big as the one below it. The kilometer is the largest on the list, so it's 10 times as big as the hectometer. The hectometer is 10 times as big as the dekameter, and so on. That's what makes the metric system so simple.

The Name Tells the Size

The other big advantage of the metric system is that the names of the units tell you how big they are compared to the meter. The prefix "kilo" means 1,000, and a kilometer is 1,000 times a meter. The prefix "hecto" means 100, and the hectometer is 100 times the size of the meter. "Deka" means 10, because a dekameter is 10 times the meter. For the smaller units, "deci" means $\frac{1}{10}$, because a decimeter is $\frac{1}{10}$ the length of a meter. "Centi" means $\frac{1}{100}$, since a centimeter is $\frac{1}{100}$ the length of a meter. And "milli" means $\frac{1}{1,000}$, since a millimeter is $\frac{1}{1,000}$ as long as a meter. The whole system is set up to be as simple as possible, so that we don't have to memorize so much. It's totally different from the common system, where the word inch, for example, doesn't tell us anything about the size of that unit.

Practice 37

a.
(26) Convert 0.65% into decimal form.

b.
(35) Convert 7 yards 3 feet into inches. (Conversion factors: 12 inches = 1 foot; 3 feet = 1 yard; 1,760 yards = 1 mile.)

c.
(33) 14 feet 6 inches + 10 feet 3 inches (Put your answer in feet and as a decimal.)

d.
(35) 3 miles + 7,568 yards + 1,056 feet (Put your answer in miles and as a decimal.)

171

e. Translate the word problem below into math; then solve.
(33)

By the most exact measurements, the Empire State Building is said to be 1,453 feet 9 inches high. If a (very brave) person 5 feet 6 inches tall stood on the very tip of the building's antenna, how many <u>feet</u> high would the person plus the building be?

Problem Set 37

Tell whether each sentence below is True or False.

1. In the metric system, each unit is ten times the size of the next (smaller) unit.
(37)

2. In the metric system, the size of each unit can be determined by the prefix of its name.
(37)

Complete each sentence below with the best of the choices given.

3. A meter is equal to 10 _____.
(37)

    A. kilometers   B. hectometers   C. dekameters
    D. decimeters   E. centimeters

4. 1,000 millimeters equals 1 _____.
(37)

    A. kilometer   B. dekameter   C. meter
    D. decimeter   E. centimeter

5. A kilometer is equal to 10 _____.
(37)

    A. hectometers   B. dekameters   C. meters
    D. decimeters   E. centimeters

Add or subtract each group of numbers below.

6. $\begin{array}{r} 31.25 \\ +9.375 \\ \hline \end{array}$
(18)

7. $\begin{array}{r} 85,204 \\ -23,810 \\ \hline \end{array}$
(17)

Multiply or divide each pair of numbers below. Write any remainders in decimal form.

8. $\begin{array}{r} 0.58 \\ \times 0.12 \\ \hline \end{array}$
(20)

9. $4\overline{)372.5}$
(22)

Add or subtract each pair of fractions below. Make sure your answers are fully reduced.

10. $\dfrac{3}{8}+\dfrac{1}{4}$
(10)

11. $\dfrac{4}{5}-\dfrac{1}{2}$
(10)

Multiply or divide each pair of numbers below. Make sure your answers are fully reduced.

12.
(14)
$21 \times \dfrac{5}{7}$

13.
(14)
$32 \div \dfrac{8}{9}$

Convert each percent below into decimal form.

14.
(28)
$52\dfrac{1}{2}\%$

(a) 15.
(26)
0.75%

Answer each question below. (Conversion factors: 12 inches = 1 foot; 3 feet = 1 yard; 1,760 yards = 1 mile.) Write your answer as a whole number or decimal.

16.
(33)
How many feet are in 1,800 inches?

(b) 17.
(35)
Convert 6 yards 5 feet to inches.

(c) 18.
(33)
11 feet 6 inches + 12 feet 3 inches (Put your answer in feet.)

(d) 19.
(35)
6 miles + 9,152 yards + 1,320 feet (Put your answer in miles.)

Translate the word problem below into math; then solve.

(e) 20.
(33)
The limo measured 19 feet 6 inches; then the driver added a special back bumper that was 1 foot 3 inches long (just to keep the photographers even farther back). How many <u>feet</u> long is the limo now if you include the new back bumper?

Lesson 38—Converting in Metric

Just as we sometimes have to convert feet to inches (or yards), it's also often necessary to convert from one metric unit into another. But it's in converting units that the metric system is at its best. That's because the whole system is based on the number 10 (just like our number system), and this makes converting from one unit to another incredibly easy.

Just Move the Decimal Point

For example, let's say we want to change 5.2 dekameters into meters. Since the dekameter is the next bigger unit after the meter, we just need to multiply by 10. Since $5.2 \times 10 = 52$, we know that 5.2 dekameters equals 52 meters.

Actually, we don't even need to go through the formal multiplication process. Since multiplication by 10 only affects the position of the decimal point, 5.2 dekameters can be converted to meters just by moving the decimal point one place to the right to get 52.0 meters.

$$5.2 \text{ dekameters} = 52.0 \text{ meters}$$ **Move decimal point one place to the right.**

Converting from a smaller unit to a larger one is just as easy. For instance, to change 18 decimeters into meters, all we have to do is divide by 10. And we can do that by moving the decimal point (after the 8) one place to the left to get 1.8.

$$18.0 \text{ decimeters} = 1.8 \text{ meters}$$ **Move decimal point one place to the left.**

Larger to Smaller Still Means Multiply

Notice that the same rules about when to multiply and when to divide also apply to the metric system. When converting larger units (dekameters) into smaller units (meters), we multiply by 10, but when converting smaller units (meters) to larger units (dekameters), we divide by 10. It's just that with the metric system, multiplying and dividing are a lot easier, because it's always by 10. The table below shows a complete list of all the metric units that we've learned about. To go up a level on the list, we move the decimal point one place to the left, and to go down a level, we move the decimal point one place to the right.

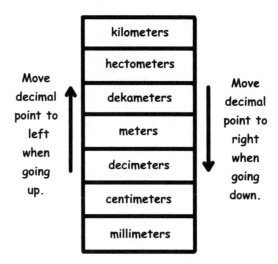

174

From Kilometers to Millimeters

Just to prove to you once and for all how much better the metric system is, let's convert 1.4 kilometers (because kilometers is at the top of the list) to millimeters, which is all the way at the bottom. We have to do the same kind of thing sometimes with common units. For example, we might have to convert miles (which are really long) into inches (which are really short). And you remember that that can be pretty tough.

But watch how much easier it is to go from kilometers all the way down to millimeters. All we have to do is count how many unit conversions are needed to go from kilometers to millimeters. Starting on top with kilometers, we need to make 6 conversions to get to millimeters. Next, we just move the decimal point that many places. Since we're going down, we move the decimal point 6 places to the right.[1]

1.400000 kilometers   **Move decimal point 6**

= 1,400,000 millimeters   **places to the right.**

So 1.4 kilometers equals 1,400,000 millimeters.

Going from really small units to really large units is just as easy. We just move the decimal point a certain number of places to the *left*. For example, to convert 950 centimeters to hectometers, we would need 4 conversions (count them yourself in the chart above). That means we need to move the decimal point 4 places to the left to get 0.095 hectometers. It's that easy.

The Not-So-Useful Table

As with the common system (with miles, yards, feet, and inches), it's also possible to create a unit conversion table for the metric system. Here's the part of the metric conversion table that includes units from meters on up.

Metric Conversion Table (for lengths)

	kilo	hecto	deka	meter
kilo	1	10	100	1,000
hecto	$\frac{1}{10}$	1	10	100
deka	$\frac{1}{100}$	$\frac{1}{10}$	1	10
meter	$\frac{1}{1,000}$	$\frac{1}{100}$	$\frac{1}{10}$	1

Notice the difference between this table and the unit conversion table for the common system. Everything is based on 10s here. It's all 1, 10, 100, 1,000 and fractions with 10, 100, and 1,000 on bottom. We can use this table in the same way as the common system table. We find the unit we're starting with on the left, and then move to the right to find the direct unit conversion. Next, we multiply by the number in the box. Of course, when the conversion factor is a fraction, that's actually the same as dividing by the denominator.

This section is titled "The Not-So-Useful Table." Why isn't the table useful? There's nothing wrong with it, really. It works just like our other table. But the metric system is so simple that we don't really need a unit

---

[1] We've added some zeros to the right of 1.4 to make it easier to move the decimal point.

conversion table. The easiest way to convert from one unit to another in the metric system is just by moving the decimal point. What more could anybody ask for?

Practice 38

a.
(34)
42 yards 2 feet + 37 yards 1 foot (Put your answer in feet.)

b.
(38)
How many centimeters are in 5 dekameters?

c.
(38)
Convert 415 meters to kilometers.

d.
(38)
How many hectometers are in 292 meters?

e.
(38)
Translate the word problem below into math; then solve.

Some South American plants have leaves so big that their leaf blades are 20 meters long. How many centimeters is this?

Problem Set 38

Tell whether each sentence below is True or False.

1.
(38)
Converting from one unit to another is more difficult in the metric system than it is in the common system.

2.
(38)
The old rules about when to multiply and divide when doing unit conversions do not apply in the metric system.

Complete each sentence below with the best of the choices given.

3.
(38)
A kilometer is equal to 10,000 _____.

A. hectometers	B. dekameters	C. meters
D. decimeters	E. centimeters	

4.
(38)
100 centimeters equals 1 _____.

A. kilometer	B. dekameter	C. meter
D. decimeter	E. millimeter	

5.
(38)
10,000 millimeters is equal to 1 _____.

A. kilometer	B. dekameter	C. meter
D. decimeter	E. centimeter	

Add or subtract each group of numbers below.

6.
(2)
$$
\begin{array}{r}
5,231 \\
+970 \\
\hline
\end{array}
$$

7.
(17)
$$
\begin{array}{r}
7.884 \\
-0.952 \\
\hline
\end{array}
$$

Multiply or divide each pair of numbers below. Write any remainders in decimal form.

8.
(20)
$$
\begin{array}{r}
620 \\
\times 3.4 \\
\hline
\end{array}
$$

9.
(22)
$0.6\overline{)3.207}$

Add or subtract each pair of numbers below. Make sure your answers are fully reduced.

10. $7\dfrac{1}{2}+\dfrac{5}{6}$
(12)

11. $\dfrac{4}{9}-\dfrac{5}{12}$
(11)

Multiply or divide each pair of fractions below. Make sure your answers are fully reduced.

12. $\dfrac{2}{3}\times\dfrac{9}{14}$
(13)

13. $\dfrac{1}{2}\div\dfrac{1}{6}$
(13)

Convert each fraction below into decimal form. Round any repeating decimals to two digits (hundredths).

14. $\dfrac{1}{50}$
(23)

15. $\dfrac{7}{11}$
(24)

Answer each question below.

(a) 16. 52 yards 2 feet + 47 yards 1 foot (Put your answer in feet.)
(34)

(b) 17. How many centimeters are in 8 dekameters?
(38)

(c) 18. Convert 245 meters to kilometers.
(38)

(d) 19. How many hectometers are in 374 meters?
(38)

Translate the word problem below into math; then solve.

(e) 20. A man in Indonesia claims to have made the world's tallest wedding cake. His cake is 24 meters tall.
(38) How tall is this in centimeters?

Lesson 39—Converting Between Common and Metric

In the last lesson, we learned to convert from one unit to another in the metric system. But what about converting between a metric unit and a common (English) unit, such as between inches and meters? Since a lot of people still use common units, especially in the U.S., it's important to be able to do that. The problem is that the common system is complicated, while the metric system is simple and based on the number 10. So the two systems don't fit well together, which makes the conversion factors between the two really messy.

Meters to Inches and Back

The common-metric unit conversion most often used is between the meter and the inch. It turns out that there are 39.37 inches in 1 meter.

$$39.37 \text{ inches} = 1 \text{ meter}$$

See what we mean about messy? This conversion factor isn't even a whole number. Let's go through a specific example, though, to show you how this factor is used.

How many inches are in 2 meters?

Since meters are longer than inches, we're going from larger to smaller units. That means we need to multiply. Specifically, we multiply 2 by 39.37.

$$2 \times 39.37 = 78.74$$

Multiply to convert meters to inches.

That gives us 78.74 inches, which is equal to 2 meters.

Let's do another example.

Convert 551 inches to meters.

Since we're going from smaller units (inches) to larger units (meters), this time we should divide. And we need to divide by 39.37, of course, since that's the conversion factor.

$$\frac{551}{39.37} = 14$$

Divide to convert inches to meters.

That leaves us with an answer of about 14 meters. (It's rounded.)

Amazingly, we only need this one conversion factor (39.37 inches = 1 meter) to do any other common-metric unit conversion we want. For example, what if we wanted to convert feet to meters, but didn't have that particular conversion factor? We could still do the calculation. All we would have to do is convert feet to inches first, and then we could use 39.37 inches = 1 meter to get the answer. And it would work the same way if we needed to convert between any other two units (common and metric). All it takes is 39.37 inches = 1 meter.

Other Conversion Factors

Even though technically we only need the meters to inches conversion factor, it speeds things up to know a few other ones. Below is a list of other common-metric conversions that are used pretty often.

Some Common-Metric Conversion Factors

1 inch (in) = 2.54 centimeters (cm)
1.0936 yards (yd) = 1 meter (m)
1 mile (mi) = 1.609 kilometers (km)

Let's do an example with one of these other conversion factors. Let's convert 18 inches to centimeters. Since there are 2.54 centimeters in 1 inch, we know that inches are larger than centimeters (because it takes more than 1 centimeter to make 1 inch). That means in converting 18 inches to centimeters, we're going from larger to smaller units. So we should multiply 18 by 2.54.

$$18 \times 2.54 = 45.72$$

Converting inches to centimeters.

The answer turns out to be 45.72 centimeters.

Let's do one more common-metric conversion.

Convert 5 yards to meters.

Since 1 meter = 1.0936 yards, a meter must be larger than a yard. (It takes more than 1 yard to equal 1 meter.) That means in converting 5 yards to meters, we're going from smaller to larger units. We should therefore divide 5 by 1.0936.

$$\frac{5}{1.0936} = 4.57$$

Converting yards to meters.

We get about 4.57 meters. Those are a few examples of how we convert between metric and common units.

Practice 39

a. How many meters are in 380 centimeters?
(38)

b. Convert 5 meters to inches. (Common conversion factors: 39.37 inches = 1 meter; 1 inch = 2.54 centimeters; 1.0936 yards = 1 meter; 1 mile = 1.609 kilometers)
(39)

c. Convert 13 meters to yards. Round your answer to two digits (hundredths).
(39)

d. What percent of 180 is 126?
(30)

e. Translate the word problem below into math; then solve.
(39)

In 1988, a man from France "walked" across the Atlantic Ocean on skis that were almost fourteen feet long and could float. The trip took two months and he survived by eating plankton along the way. If the man walked a total distance of 5,636 km, how many miles did he walk? Round your answer to two digits (hundredths).

Problem Set 39

Add or subtract each group of numbers below.

1.
(17)
$$\begin{array}{r} 46.57 \\ +39.18 \\ \hline \end{array}$$

2.
(17)
$$\begin{array}{r} 502.8 \\ -364.5 \\ \hline \end{array}$$

Multiply or divide each pair of numbers below. Write any remainders in decimal form.

3.
(20)
$$\begin{array}{r} 48.9 \\ \times 1.5 \\ \hline \end{array}$$

4.
(4)
$15\overline{)10,080}$

Add or subtract each pair of fractions below. Make sure your answers are fully reduced.

5.
(10)
$\dfrac{5}{18} + \dfrac{7}{18}$

6.
(11)
$\dfrac{3}{4} - \dfrac{1}{6}$

Multiply or divide each pair of numbers below. Make sure your answers are fully reduced.

7.
(13)
$\dfrac{3}{10} \times \dfrac{5}{4}$

8.
(14)
$\dfrac{3}{14} \div 3$

Convert each decimal below into a fraction. Make sure your answers are fully reduced.

9.
(23)
0.65

10.
(23)
0.004

Convert each percent below into decimal form.

11.
(28)
$7\dfrac{2}{5}\%$

12.
(26)
124%

Do each unit conversion below. (Common conversion factors: 12 inches = 1 foot; 3 feet = 1 yard; 1,760 yards = 1 mile.)

13.
(35)
Convert 2 miles 327 yards to feet.

(a) 14.
(38)
How many meters are in 420 centimeters?

Do each unit conversion below. (Common conversion factors: 39.37 inches = 1 meter; 1 inch = 2.54 centimeters; 1.0936 yards = 1 meter; 1 mile = 1.609 kilometer)

(b) 15. Convert 8 meters to inches.
(39)

(c) 16. Convert 17 meters to yards. Round your answer to two digits (hundredths).
(39)

Answer each question below. Write your answer as a whole number or decimal.

17. What is $\dfrac{8}{9}$ of 45?
(14)

18. What is 25% of 78?
(27)

(d) 19. What percent of 140 is 112?
(30)

Translate the word problem below into math; then solve.

(e) 20. The longest distance that anyone has ever walked on their hands is 1,400 km. How far is this in miles?
(39) Round your answer to two digits (hundredths).

CHAPTER 6:
MEASURING AREA AND VOLUME

Lesson 40—Little Squares

We've been learning about measurement. And, as you know, we use "units" such as inches, feet, yards, meters, and kilometers. But have you ever noticed that all the units we've studied so far, whether from the common or metric system, are lengths? In this lesson, we're going to switch gears and learn how to measure flat surfaces, like the top of a table or a backyard. As it turns out, there are also units for those kinds of measurements.

Measuring a Flat Surface

Let's use a rectangle as our first example.

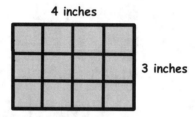

4 inches

3 inches

Notice that the rectangle is 4 inches long and 3 inches wide. Here's how we measure the space inside the rectangle. We figure out how many little squares with 1 inch sides will fit inside of it. One way to do this would be to draw little squares in rows until the entire rectangle is filled up. Then we could count the squares. If you count the little squares above, you'll see that there are 12 of them. But there's a faster way to do it. Instead of counting squares, we can just multiply the rectangle's length by its width. The length is 4 inches and the width is 3 inches, so the total amount of space inside the rectangle has to be 12 squares or 12 "square inches."

$$4 \times 3 = 12 \text{ square inches}$$ **Multiply length by width.**

Twelve square inches is called the **area** of the rectangle. And, once again, it just means that 12 squares, each with 1 inch sides, will fit inside the rectangle exactly. That's the way we measure surfaces. Instead of inches, it's "square" inches. But the other important point is that to calculate the area of a rectangle, instead of having to draw a bunch of little squares, we can just multiply its length by its width.

Let's do another example. Let's calculate the area of a big rectangle with a length of 7 feet and a width of 3 feet. Instead of drawing a picture and counting squares, all we have to do is multiply the length by the width.

$$7 \times 3 = 21 \text{ square feet}$$

This means that 21 squares with 1 foot sides will fit inside the rectangle exactly.

Larger Areas Need Larger Units

Notice that when the sides are measured in inches, the area is in square inches, and if the sides are measured in feet, the area is in square feet. So we can measure area in different units just as we measure length in different units. It's smart to always use the units that are the easiest. For smaller surfaces, like a piece of paper, units such as square inches work better.[1] For bigger surfaces, like a backyard, square yards would work a whole lot better. To measure the area of an entire city, we would need square miles. For example, the city of Los Angeles has an area of 498 square miles, which means that 498 squares with sides 1 mile long could fit on the ground inside L.A.

---

[1] By the way, a regular size sheet of paper turns out to have an area of over 93 square inches.

To make sure we have enough square units to measure any size surface, we should take all four major units of length from the common system—inches, feet, yards, and miles—and turn them into square inches, square feet, square yards, and square miles.

Units of Length	Units of Area
inches	square inches
feet	square feet
yards	square yards
miles	square miles

There's also one other unit for measuring areas in the common system that is popular. You've probably heard of it. It's called an **acre**. The acre is a very old unit that was used for measuring land. It was originally the amount of land 1 yoke of oxen could plow in one morning. Because of tradition, we still use acres to measure land surfaces, even though not many of us plow fields with oxen anymore. An acre is much smaller than a square mile. A good size yard might be about $\frac{1}{2}$ acre.

Converting Units to Find Area

What if we want to calculate an area, but the length and width are in different units? For example, here's a rectangle with a length of 3 feet and a width of 24 inches.

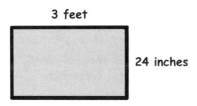

The problem is that we can't multiply when the units are different. But it's easy to see what to do. We can just convert one of the measurements into different units. We can either convert 3 feet to inches or 24 inches to feet. Let's convert 24 inches to feet by dividing by 12. We get $24 \div 12 = 2$, which means 24 inches equals 2 feet. And from there, we just multiply to find the area.

$$3 \text{ feet} \times 2 \text{ feet} = 6 \text{ square feet}$$

Convert inches to feet and multiply.

Since both length and width are now in feet, the answer is 6 square feet.

So to calculate areas, the length and width have to be in the same units. It's no different from calculating lengths. Before we can add feet to inches, we have to convert so that the units are the same. But when calculating areas, the answer comes out to square units. And it could be square feet, square inches, square miles, or anything else, depending on the specific problem.

Practice 40

a.
(34) How many inches are in 11 yards?   (Common conversion factors: 12 inches = 1 foot; 3 feet = 1 yard; 1,760 yards = 1 mile.)

b.
(38) How many centimeters are in 7.5 meters?

c.
(39) Convert 4 inches to centimeters. (Common conversion factors: 39.37 inches = 1 meter; 1 inch = 2.54 centimeters; 1.0936 yards = 1 meter; 1 mile = 1.609 kilometer)

d.
(39) Convert 4 yards to meters. Round your answer to two digits (hundredths).

e.
(39) Translate the word problem below into math; then solve.

Leeches are bloodsucking worms that live in water. Some are 8 inches long. How long is this in centimeters?

Problem Set 40

Tell whether each sentence below is True or False.

1.
(40) Flat surfaces or "areas" are measured by determining how many little squares will fit on them.

2.
(40) Several units used to measure area are square inches, square feet, square yards, square miles, and acres.

Complete each sentence below with the best of the choices given.

3.
(38) A dekameter is equal to 100 _____.

    A. kilometers   B. hectometers   C. meters
    D. decimeters   E. centimeters

4.
(38) 10 decimeters equals 1 _____.

    A. kilometer   B. hectometer   C. dekameter
    D. meter   E. centimeter

Add or subtract each group of numbers below.

5.
(2)
$$\begin{array}{r} 35,009 \\ +12,571 \\ \hline \end{array}$$

6.
(18)
$$\begin{array}{r} 7.5 \\ -3.875 \\ \hline \end{array}$$

Multiply or divide each pair of numbers below. Write any remainders in decimal form.

7.
(20)
$$\begin{array}{r} 0.42 \\ \times 3.1 \\ \hline \end{array}$$

8.
(22) $2.4\overline{)675}$

Add or subtract each pair of fractions below. Make sure your answers are fully reduced.

9.
(10) $\dfrac{1}{12} + \dfrac{7}{12}$

10.
(10) $\dfrac{2}{5} - \dfrac{1}{3}$

Multiply or divide each pair of fractions below. Make sure your answers are fully reduced.

11.
(13) $\dfrac{2}{9} \times \dfrac{3}{8}$

12.
(13) $\dfrac{4}{7} \div \dfrac{2}{14}$

Convert each percent below into decimal form.

13.
(28) $21\dfrac{1}{5}\%$

14.
(26) 375%

Do each unit conversion below. (Common conversion factors: 12 inches = 1 foot; 3 feet = 1 yard; 1,760 yards = 1 mile.)

(a) 15. How many inches are in 12 yards?
(34)

(b) 16. How many centimeters are in 8.6 meters?
(38)

Do each unit conversion below. (Common-metric conversion factors: 39.37 inches = 1 meter; 1 inch = 2.54 centimeters; 1.0936 yards = 1 meter; 1 mile = 1.609 kilometer)

(c) 17. Convert 3 inches to centimeters.
(39)

(d) 18. Convert 5 yards to meters. Round your answer to two digits (hundredths).
(39)

Answer each question below.

19. What is 40% of 730?
(27)

20. What percent of 56 is 14?
(30)

Translate the word problem below into math; then solve.

(e) 21. The nightstand was 36 inches tall. How tall is this in centimeters? (1 inch = 2.54 centimeters)
(39)

Lesson 41—Area Unit Conversions

In the last lesson, we learned how to calculate area. Remember, that's just the way we measure a flat surface like a rectangle. The method was to multiply the length by the width. And if you'll recall, we calculated the area of a rectangle that was 3 feet by 24 inches. Here it is again.

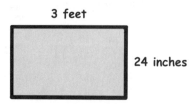

3 feet

24 inches

To do the calculation, we converted 24 inches to 2 feet and then multiplied to get 6 square feet. But what if we wanted to know the area in square inches? One way to do this would be to go back to the rectangle and convert 3 feet to inches and then multiply length times width again in inches. Doing that would give us 36 inches, and then $36 \times 24 = 864$ square inches.

The Conversion Factor Multiplied Twice

That's quite a bit of work to go from square feet to square inches. Is there any way to convert from one to the other, without going back and multiplying again? Yes, there is. To see how it works let's look at a single square foot.

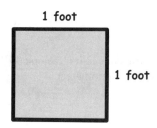

1 foot

1 foot

This obviously has an area of 1 square foot, and we get that answer by multiplying its length by its width ($1 \times 1 = 1$). But now let's convert the side lengths to inches. That gives us a 12 inch length and a 12 inch width. Next, let's calculate the area in square inches. We get $12 \times 12 = 144$ square inches. Notice that after converting from feet to inches, the side lengths went from 1 to 12, but the area went from 1 to 144. That's because in calculating area we multiply the length and width. So if both are 12 times bigger than they were before, the answer has to be 12×12 or 144 times bigger.

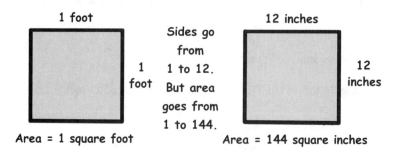

1 foot

Sides go from 1 to 12. But area goes from 1 to 144.

1 foot

Area = 1 square foot

12 inches

12 inches

Area = 144 square inches

This always happens when converting area units. The conversion factor is multiplied twice. For example, when dealing with lengths, the conversion factor for going from yards to feet is 3 (since there are 3 feet in a yard).

We have to multiply by 3 to make the conversion, in other words. But to convert from square yards to square feet, we have to multiply by 3×3 or 9. A picture will show why this is true. On the left is 1 square yard. But when we change the units from yards to feet (on the right), we get a length of 3 feet and a width of 3 feet.

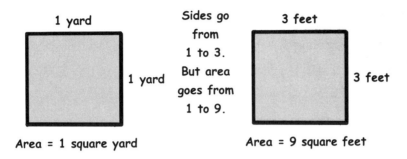

Since the sides go from 1 to 3, the areas go from 1 to 3×3 or 9 to get 9 square feet.

Smaller to Larger Means Divide

In both of our examples, we went from larger square units to smaller square units (from square feet to square inches and from square yards to square feet). What about going the other way, from smaller square units to larger square units? Well, then we would have to divide.

For example, if we want to convert 144 square inches into square feet, we should divide. But instead of dividing by 12, we divide by 12×12 or 144. Since 144÷144 equals 1, we end up with an answer of 1 square foot, which we know is right. And to go from 9 square feet to square yards, we divide by 3×3 or 9, to get 1 square yard.

More Examples

Let's do a few more examples to make sure you're getting it. Let's convert 7 square yards to square feet. Since we're going from larger to smaller units, we need to multiply. But instead of multiplying by 3, we multiply by 3×3 or 9. So we get 7×9 = 63 square feet.

How about converting 578 square inches to square feet? This is going from smaller to larger units, so we need to divide. But instead of dividing by 12, we need to divide by 12×12 or 144. Since 578÷144 equals a little over 4, the answer is about 4 square feet.

What about converting between square units that are far apart, like square yards to square inches? Let's convert 2 square yards to square inches. Since we're going from square yards all the way down to square inches, we need to do the conversion in steps. First, we convert square yards to square feet. Instead of multiplying by 3, though, we need to multiply by 3×3, or 9. And since 2×9 equals 18, we end up with 18 square feet. Next, we convert square feet to square inches by multiplying by 12×12, or 144 to get 18×144 = 2,592 square inches. That means 2 square yards equals 2,592 square inches. In other words, 2 squares with sides equaling 1 yard, take up the same amount of space as 2,592 squares with only 1 inch sides.

Practice 41

    a. 3 meters + 10 dekameters (Put your answer in meters.)
(38)

    b. Convert 9 square feet to square inches.
(41)

c.
(41) Convert 63 square feet to square yards.

d.
(14) 22 has how many $\frac{2}{7}$ s in it?

e.
(41) Translate the word problem below into math; then solve.

The world's largest T-shirt is approximately 7,470 square inches. How many square feet is this? Write your answer as a decimal.

Problem Set 41

Tell whether each sentence below is True or False.

1.
(41) To convert square feet to square inches, you should multiply by 144.

2.
(41) To convert square feet to square yards, you should divide by 9.

Complete each sentence below with the best of the choices given.

3.
(38) 1 kilometer is equal to 10 _____.

    A. hectometers   B. dekameters   C. meters
    D. decimeters   E. centimeters

4.
(38) 10 millimeters equals 1 _____.

    A. kilometer   B. dekameter   C. meter
    D. decimeter   E. centimeter

Add or subtract each group of numbers below.

5.
(17)
$$2.875$$
$$+3.104$$

6.
(2)
$$653$$
$$-229$$

Multiply or divide each pair of numbers below. Write any remainders in decimal form.

7.
(20)
$$6.7$$
$$\times 5.4$$

8.
(22) $0.5\overline{)8.24}$

Add or subtract each pair of fractions below. Make sure your answers are fully reduced.

9.
(10) $\frac{5}{6} + \frac{4}{3}$

10.
(10) $\frac{2}{5} - \frac{4}{15}$

Multiply or divide each pair of numbers below. Make sure your answers are fully reduced.

11.
(14) $\dfrac{4}{7} \times 21$

12.
(14) $35 \div \dfrac{5}{6}$

Convert each percent below into decimal form.

13.
(28) $3\dfrac{1}{2}\%$

14.
(26) 98%

Answer each question below.

15.
(33) 17 feet 9 inches + 8 feet 9 inches (Put your answer in feet.)

(a) 16.
(38) 5 meters + 11 dekameters (Put your answer in meters.)

Do each unit conversion below.

(b) 17.
(41) Convert 8 square feet to square inches.

(c) 18.
(41) Convert 72 square feet to square yards.

Answer each question below.

19.
(27) What is 40% of 730?

(d) 20.
(14) 38 has how many $\dfrac{2}{5}$s in it?

Translate the word problem below into math; then solve.

(e) 21.
(41) The largest finger painting in the world is 141,120 square inches. How many square feet is this?

Lesson 42—Area in the Metric System

We've been learning how to calculate areas and convert them between different square units. But did you notice how complicated the conversions were? It's hard to remember that we have to multiply by 12×12, or 144, to go from square feet to square inches, or that we have to multiply by 3×3, or 9, to go from square yards to square feet.

It's Easier with Metric

Why can't we do areas with metric units? They're all based on the number 10, which makes conversions much easier. The good news is we can. To show you how it works, look at the square meter on the left.

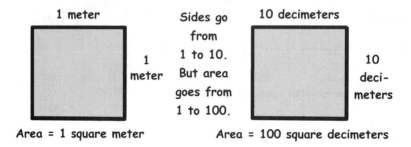

1 meter

1 meter

Area = 1 square meter

Sides go from 1 to 10. But area goes from 1 to 100.

10 decimeters

10 deci-meters

Area = 100 square decimeters

It has sides of 1 meter, of course. But when we convert the side lengths to decimeters (on the right), they're each 10 decimeters long (because 1 meter = 10 decimeters). Then look what happens to the area. Since 10×10 equals 100, the area is 100 square decimeters. So 1 square meter = 100 square decimeters. Here's the neat thing, though, about doing areas in metric. Since the units for length go up by 10s, all the square units (for area) go up by 10×10 or 100. So there's not as much to remember when doing area conversions in metric. Here are the major units for area in metric.

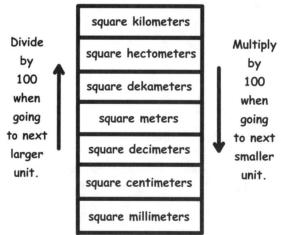

Divide by 100 when going to next larger unit.

| square kilometers |
| square hectometers |
| square dekameters |
| square meters |
| square decimeters |
| square centimeters |
| square millimeters |

Multiply by 100 when going to next smaller unit.

Just Move the Decimal Point

Now we'll do a few examples. Let's convert 3 square centimeters to square millimeters. We're going from larger units to smaller units, so we need to multiply, and there are 10 millimeters in 1 centimeter. However, since we're dealing with square units, we need to multiply not by 10 but by 10×10 or 100. That gives us this.

$$3\times100 = 300 \text{ square millimeters} \qquad \textbf{Multiply by 100}$$

So 3 square centimeters = 300 square millimeters. Notice how easy the multiplication was. All we really had to do was move the decimal point two places to the right (since we multiplied by 100).

What about converting 450 square hectometers (better known as hectares) to square kilometers? This time, we're going from smaller to larger units, so we need to divide. But since we're dealing with square units, we divide not by 10 but by 10×10 or 100. Rather than go through a complete division, we can just move the decimal point two places to the left to get 4.5 square kilometers.[1]

$$\frac{450}{100} = 4.5 \text{ square kilometers} \qquad \textbf{Divide by 100}$$

Finally, let's convert 17 square meters to square centimeters. What's different about this example is that we're skipping a unit (square decimeters). So what we have to do is multiply by 100 *twice*. The easiest way to do that is to move the decimal point 4 places to the right (2 places for each multiplication of 100). That gives us an answer of 170,000 square centimeters.

$$17 \times 100 \times 100 =$$
$$170,000 \text{ square centimeters} \qquad \textbf{Multiply by 100 twice}$$

Practice 42

a.
(41) Convert 2 square miles to square yards.

b.
(42) How many square decimeters are in 14 square meters?

c.
(41) Convert 3,888 square inches to square yards.

d.
(42) How many square meters are in 67,000 square centimeters?

e.
(42) Translate the word problem below into math; then solve.

A mosaic is a picture or design made with colored pieces, such as glass or tile, set in mortar. In 2000, a group of school children in New York City created a 29 square meter mosaic with jellybeans. How many square centimeters is this?

Problem Set 42

Tell whether each sentence below is True or False.

1.
(42) Converting from one square unit to another is easier in the metric system than it is in the common system.

2.
(42) To convert square millimeters to square centimeters, you divide by 100.

---

[1] Remember, the decimal point goes to the right when multiplying and to the left when dividing.

Complete each sentence below with the best of the choices given.

3.
(38)   1 dekameter is equal to 1,000 _____.

     A. kilometers   B. hectometers   C. meters
     D. decimeters   E. centimeters

4.
(38)   100,000 centimeters equals 1 _____.

     A. kilometer   B. dekameter   C. meter
     D. decimeter   E. centimeter

Add or subtract each group of numbers below.

5. (17)
$$9.83 + 7.06$$

6. (2)
$$74,981 - 35,026$$

Multiply or divide each pair of numbers below. Write any remainders in decimal form.

7. (20)
$$0.551 \times 0.7$$

8. (22) $14\overline{)7,329}$

Add or subtract each pair of numbers below. Make sure your answers are fully reduced.

9. (10) $\frac{7}{16}+\frac{5}{16}$

10. (12) $3-\frac{7}{6}$

Multiply or divide each pair of fractions below. Make sure your answers are fully reduced.

11. (13) $\frac{1}{2}\times\frac{3}{11}$

12. (13) $\frac{2}{9}\div\frac{3}{4}$

Convert each fraction below into decimal form. Round any repeating decimals to two digits (hundredths).

13. (24) $\frac{1}{3}$

14. (23) $\frac{21}{30}$

Answer each question below.

15. (33)   3 miles 440 yards + 6 miles 880 yards (Put your answer in miles.)

16. (38)   2.4 kilometers + 18 hectometers (Put your answer in hectometers.)

Do each unit conversion below.

(a) **17.**   Convert 3 square miles to square yards.
(41)

(b) **18.**   How many square decimeters are in 12 square meters?
(42)

(c) **19.**   Convert 5,184 square inches to square yards.
(41)

(d) **20.**   How many square meters are in 82,000 square centimeters?
(42)

Translate the word problem below into math; then solve.

(e) **21.**   In 1998, a company in Utah created the world's largest Twister™ mat—one big enough for hundreds of
(42)   people to play the game. If the mat measured about 108 square meters, how many square centimeters is this?

Lesson 43—Little Cubes

We've learned how to measure lengths and flat surfaces. But we haven't yet talked about measuring 3 dimensional (3-D) spaces, like the inside of a box.

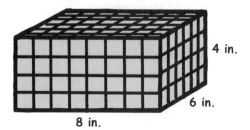

Lengths are measured with straight lines, like rulers, and flat surfaces are measured with little squares. What about 3-D spaces? As it turns out, they're measured with little cubes. In other words, if we want to know how big the box above is, we need to figure out how many little cubes will fit inside it.

Length x Width x Height

Fortunately, we don't have to count all the little cubes to come up with an answer. We can just multiply the box's length, width, and height. Notice how similar this is to the way we calculate the area of a rectangle. With areas, we multiply length and width.[1] With 3-D spaces, it's length, width, as well as height. As you can see, our box has a length of 8 inches, a width of 6 inches, and a height of 4 inches, and since all the measurements are in the same units (inches), we can go ahead with the multiplication.

$$8 \times 6 \times 4 = 192 \text{ cubic inches}$$

Multiply length, width, and height.

The answer comes out to 192 cubic inches. "Cubic inches" means that 192 little cubes, each with 1 inch sides, will fit exactly inside our box. Actually, the technical term for 3-D space is **volume**. So we should say that the box has a volume of 192 cubic inches.

Choose Big Units for Big Stuff

Now we have inches, square inches, and cubic inches, depending on whether we're measuring a length, a flat surface (area), or a 3-D space (volume). So it shouldn't surprise you that it's also possible to have cubic feet, cubic yards, or even cubic miles. As always, we should choose the units based on the size of the space we're measuring. For example, the space inside a refrigerator is usually measured in cubic feet.[2] Cubic miles, on the other hand, should only be used for really big spaces. An example would be the inside of the moon, which happens to be over 5 billion cubic miles. That means that we could fit

over 5 billion cubes, each with 1 mile long sides, inside the moon. In fact, the moon's volume is so big that a unit even bigger than cubic miles might be better to use.

---

[1] That's because a flat surface is two-dimensional.
[2] By the way, an average size refrigerator might have a volume of about 20 cubic feet.

Practice 43

a.
(38)
Subtract 60 hectometers – 5,400 meters. (Put your answer in hectometers.)

b.
(39)
How many centimeters are in 13 inches? (39.37 inches = 1 meter; 1 inch = 2.54 centimeters; 1.0936 yards = 1 meter; 1 mile = 1.609 kilometer)

c.
(41)
Convert 360 square inches to square feet. Write your answer as a decimal.

d.
(42)
How many square kilometers are in 1,420,000 square meters?

e.
(43)
Translate the word problem below into math; then solve.

Baby Gargantua's lunch box is 3 feet long, 2 feet wide, and 2 feet high. What is the lunch box's volume in cubic feet?

Problem Set 43

Tell whether each sentence below is True or False.

1.
(43)
A three-dimensional space is measured by figuring out how many little cubes will fit inside of it.

2.
(43)
The three-dimensional space inside a box is calculated by multiplying its length by its width.

3.
(43)
The technical word for a three-dimensional space is "volume."

Complete each sentence below with the best of the choices given.

4.
(38)
10 hectometers equals 1 _____.

    A. kilometer   B. hectometer   C. meter
    D. decimeter   E. centimeter

5.
(38)
1 meter is equal to 1,000 _____.

    A. kilometers   B. dekameters   C. decimeters
    D. centimeters   E. millimeters

Add or subtract each group of numbers below.

6.
(18)
$$\begin{array}{r} 5.23 \\ 4.1 \\ +8.17 \\ \hline \end{array}$$

7.
(18)
$$\begin{array}{r} 13.6 \\ -9.04 \\ \hline \end{array}$$

Multiply or divide each pair of numbers below. Write any remainders in decimal form.

8.
(20)
$$\begin{array}{r} 43.5 \\ \times 1.8 \\ \hline \end{array}$$

9.
(22)
$0.9\overline{)52}$

Add or subtract each pair of numbers below. Make sure your answers are fully reduced.

10.
(10)
$\dfrac{2}{3} + \dfrac{1}{5}$

11.
(12)
$\dfrac{14}{2} - 4$

Multiply or divide each pair of numbers below. Make sure your answers are fully reduced.

12.
(13)
$\dfrac{7}{8} \times \dfrac{2}{21}$

13.
(14)
$18 \div \dfrac{3}{5}$

Convert each decimal below into a fraction. Make sure your answers are fully reduced.

14.
(23)
0.6

15.
(23)
0.52

Answer each question below.

16.
(33)
7 feet − 54 inches (Put your answer in feet.)

(a) 17.
(38)
50 hectometers − 4,500 meters (Put your answer in hectometers.)

18.
(14)
What is $\dfrac{3}{7}$ of 56?

Do each unit conversion below. (39.37 inches = 1 meter; 1 inch = 2.54 centimeters; 1.0936 yards = 1 meter; 1 mile = 1.609 kilometer) Write your answer as a whole number or decimal.

(b) 19.
(39)
How many centimeters are in 11 inches?

(c) 20.
(41)
Convert 504 square inches to square feet.

(d) 21.
(42)
How many square kilometers are in 1,750,000 square meters?

Translate the word problem below into math; then solve.

(e) 22.
(43)
If a ballroom is 200 feet long, 140 feet wide, and 30 feet high, what is its volume in cubic feet?

Lesson 44—Volume Unit Conversions

In the last lesson, we learned how to calculate the volume (size) of a 3-D space like a box. All we do is multiply the length by the width by the height of the space and that gives us an answer in cubic inches, cubic feet, or whatever (depending on the units that are used for length, width, and height).

Not Once, Not Twice, but...

Sometimes, though, if an answer is in cubic feet, we might want to convert it to cubic inches. How is that done? Well, let's say we want to convert 32 cubic feet into cubic inches. We know that to convert a length from feet to inches, we multiply by 12, and to convert an area from square feet to square inches, we multiply by 12×12 or 144. What should we multiply by to convert cubic feet to cubic inches? If you guessed $12 \times 12 \times 12$ which comes to 1,728, you're right! Here's why that works. Take a cube with 1 foot sides

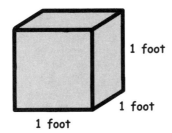

Obviously, this has a volume of 1 cubic foot. If you want to waste time calculating it, just multiply its length, width, and height: $1 \times 1 \times 1$ equals 1. But what if we were to convert those measurements into inches? Then the length, width, and height would each be 12. Multiplying those together gives us $12 \times 12 \times 12$ or 1,728 cubic inches.

$$1 \times 1 \times 1 = 1 \text{ cubic foot} \qquad 12 \times 12 \times 12 = 1,728 \text{ cubic inches}$$

So 1 cubic foot equals 1,728 cubic inches. That's why we multiply by 1,728 to convert cubic feet to cubic inches. For every cube with 1 foot sides, there have to be 1,728 cubes with 1 inch sides.

The same thing happens if we convert cubic yards to cubic feet. Instead of multiplying by 3 or by 3×3, we have to multiply by $3 \times 3 \times 3$ or 27. To do an actual example, let's convert 11 cubic yards to cubic feet. Even though 1 yard equals 3 feet, we don't multiply by 3, because we're not dealing with a length here. We don't multiply by 3×3 or 9 either, because we aren't dealing with an area. Since this is a volume (involving cubic units) we need to multiply by $3 \times 3 \times 3$ or 27. That makes sense, because a cube with sides that are 1 yard long is the same as a cube with 3 feet sides, and 3 feet by 3 feet by 3 feet comes to a volume of 27 cubic feet.

$$11 \times 27 = 297 \text{ cubic feet} \qquad \textbf{Multiply by 27}$$

We end up with 297 cubic feet. That's how many cubes with 1 foot sides will fit inside 11 cubic yards of space.

The basic rule, then, is that we multiply by the proper number three times when converting cubic units. Of course, if we're going from smaller to larger units we need to divide instead of multiply. The rules about when to multiply and divide work the same with cubic units as they do with lengths and areas.

From Smaller to Larger Units

Let's go through an actual example that requires dividing. This time let's convert 54 cubic feet to cubic yards. We have to divide here because we're going from smaller to larger units, but we don't divide by 3 or even by 9. Instead we have to divide by $3 \times 3 \times 3$ or 27 to get 2 cubic yards.

$$54 \div 27 = 2 \text{ cubic yards} \qquad \textbf{Divide by 27}$$

Skipping Again

It's actually possible to convert between any two cubic units. For instance, we can convert 5 cubic yards all the way down to cubic inches. But when skipping units we do it in steps. The first step is to convert 5 cubic yards to cubic feet. To do that we multiply by $3 \times 3 \times 3$ or 27 square feet to get 5×27, or 135 cubic feet. The second step is to convert 135 cubic feet to cubic inches. To make that conversion, we multiply by $12 \times 12 \times 12$ or 1,728 to get $135 \times 1,728 = 233,280$ cubic inches . So 5 square yards is the same as 233,280 cubic inches.

Converting cubic yards to cubic inches in two steps.

$$5 \times 27 = 135 \text{ cubic feet} \qquad 135 \times 1,728 = 233,280 \text{ cubic inches}$$

That means 5 cubes with sides equaling 1 yard takes up the same amount of space as 233,280 one-inch-sided cubes.

Practice 44

a.
(30)   What percent of 50 is 35?

b.
(44)   How many cubic inches are in 6 cubic feet?

c.
(44)   Convert 189 cubic feet to cubic yards.

d.
(42)   How many square centimeters are in 4 square meters?

e.
(44)   Translate the word problem below into math; then solve.

The owner of Carlisle Construction is a little overprotective of his brand new cement mixer, so each night, he parks it in a storage facility that is 120 feet long, 45 feet wide, and 45 feet high. What is the facility's volume in cubic yards?

Problem Set 44

Tell whether each sentence below is True or False.

1. To convert cubic feet to cubic inches, you should multiply by 1,728.
(44)

2. To convert cubic feet to cubic yards, you should divide by 27.
(44)

Complete each sentence below with the best of the choices given.

3. 1,000 decimeters equals 1 _____.
(38)

    A. kilometer   B. hectometer   C. dekameter

    D. meter   E. centimeter

4. 1 kilometer is equal to 100 _____.
(38)

    A. hectometers   B. dekameters   C. decimeters

    D. centimeters   E. millimeters

Add or subtract each group of numbers below.

5.
(2)
$$\begin{array}{r} 8,049 \\ +657 \\ \hline \end{array}$$

6.
(17)
$$\begin{array}{r} 0.386 \\ -0.097 \\ \hline \end{array}$$

Multiply or divide each pair of numbers below. Write any remainders in decimal form.

7.
(20)
$$\begin{array}{r} 250 \\ \times 0.8 \\ \hline \end{array}$$

8. $2.5\overline{)453}$
(22)

Add or subtract each pair of fractions below. Make sure your answers are fully reduced.

9. $\dfrac{7}{20}+\dfrac{7}{20}$
(10)

10. $\dfrac{8}{9}-\dfrac{2}{3}$
(10)

Multiply or divide each pair of numbers below. Make sure your answers are fully reduced.

11. $64\times\dfrac{5}{4}$
(14)

12. $\dfrac{4}{3}\div\dfrac{2}{7}$
(13)

Convert each percent below into decimal form.

13. 0.5%
(26)

14. 189%
(26)

Answer each question below.

15.
(33) $3\frac{1}{2}$ miles − 3,520 yards (Put your answer in miles.)

16.
(38)   7 kilometers − 2,000 meters (Put your answer in kilometers.)

(a) 17.
(30)   What percent of 75 is 60?

Do each unit conversion below.

(b) 18.
(44)   How many cubic inches are in 5 cubic feet?

(c) 19.
(44)   Convert 216 cubic feet to cubic yards.

(d) 20.
(42)   How many square centimeters are in 3 square meters?

Translate the word problem below into math; then solve.

(e) 21.
(44)   Super entrepreneur Freddie Fandango thinks his latest product might set the world on fire (hopefully not literally). It's basically a giant microwave oven that cooks lots of whole hams and turkeys in just a few seconds (so Freddie claims). If the microwave is 9 feet long, 6 feet wide, and 3 feet high, what is its volume in cubic yards?

Lesson 45—Liquid Measures of Volume

We've learned to measure volume in cubic feet, cubic inches, and so on. But here's some bad news. Cubic units aren't actually used much in the common system. In fact, about the only things measured in cubic feet are the insides of refrigerators and freezers. That's because there are other units of volume that were created long ago that are even more popular.

Just Weigh It

Before mathematical knowledge was very developed, people hadn't figured out how to calculate cubic units. Yet they still needed to measure volumes, so they found a nonmathematical way to do it. To measure the volume of a pot, for instance, they would just fill it to the brim with water.

Then they would pour the water back out and weigh it. The weight of the water served as a measure for what the pot could hold. The great thing about this approach is that water, or any other liquid, fills a container it's poured into completely, no matter what the shape of the container. And so, with this approach, you never have to calculate anything. (But you do have to pour a lot of water!) Water measurement became so widespread that today most of our common units for volume are still based on water or "liquid" measurements.[1]

Gallon, Quart, Pint, and Ounce

The four best known liquid units for volume are the **gallon, quart, pint**, and **fluid ounce**. A gallon is a volume that (whatever the specific shape of the container) will hold 8.337 pounds of water. The gallon was first used in Britain, and it was equal to 10 pounds of water. That's still the size of the gallon in Britain today. But the U.S. gallon is only 8.337 pounds.

To measure a U.S. gallon of volume, then, we just pour 8.337 pounds of water into a container and mark the water's height on the container's side. From that point down is equal to 1 gallon.

---

[1] These are often called units of "capacity," because they're based on how much a container will hold instead of a direct calculation of a space.

What about the other liquid units? Well, there are 4 quarts in a gallon, so 4 quarts = 1 gallon.[2] That means to convert between quarts and gallons, we multiply or divide by 4. The next smaller unit is the pint. There are two pints in a quart, so 2 pints = 1 quart. And the conversion factor between a pint and quart is 2. Then there are 16 fluid ounces in a pint: 16 fluid ounces = 1 pint. The conversion factor between a fluid ounce and a pint is therefore 16. Here is the list of the units and their relationships in a table.

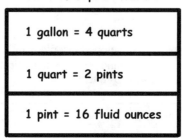

Units of Liquid Measure

1 gallon = 4 quarts
1 quart = 2 pints
1 pint = 16 fluid ounces

These units probably look more familiar to you than cubic inches or cubic feet. That's because, as we said, these are used much more often (at least in English speaking countries) than cubic units for measuring volume. That's why you buy a gallon of milk at the grocery store instead of a cubic foot of milk!

Practice 45

a.
(34)   How many inches are in 12 yards?

b.
(45)   How many pints are in 14 quarts?

c.
(44)   How many cubic feet are in 31 cubic yards?

d.
(39)   Convert 3 miles to kilometers. (1 mile = 1.609 kilometers)

e.
(45)   Translate the word problem below into math; then solve.

Lucy, the health food fanatic, drinks 7 sixteen ounce glasses of raisin juice each day. How many pints (not ounces) of raisin juice does she consume each day?

Problem Set 45

Tell whether each sentence below is True or False.

1.
(45)   People first measured the space inside a container (its volume) by pouring liquid inside of it and then weighing the liquid.

2.
(45)   The most popular units for measuring volume in the common system are the gallon, quart, pint, and fluid ounce.

---

[2] The word "quart" comes from a Latin word for 4.

Complete each sentence below with the best of the choices given.

3.
(42) 1 *square* meter equals 100 _____.

    A. square kilometers   B. square hectometers   C. square dekameters
    D. square decimeters   E. square centimeters

4.
(42) 100 *square* millimeters equals 1 _____.

    A. square kilometer   B. square hectometer   C. square dekameter
    D. square decimeter   E. square centimeter

Add or subtract each group of numbers below.

5.
(18)
$$\begin{array}{r} 52.7 \\ +3.59 \\ \hline \end{array}$$

6.
(18)
$$\begin{array}{r} 8.25 \\ -4.178 \\ \hline \end{array}$$

Multiply or divide each pair of numbers below. Write any remainders in decimal form.

7.
(20)
$$\begin{array}{r} 46.1 \\ \times 3.5 \\ \hline \end{array}$$

8.
(21) $0.3\overline{)759}$

Add or subtract each pair of numbers below. Make sure your answers are fully reduced.

9.
(10) $\dfrac{1}{8}+\dfrac{5}{4}$

10.
(12) $4-2\dfrac{2}{5}$

Multiply or divide each pair of fractions below. Make sure your answers are fully reduced.

11.
(13) $\dfrac{2}{6}\times\dfrac{3}{10}$

12.
(13) $\dfrac{1}{3}\div\dfrac{2}{9}$

Convert each fraction below into decimal form. Give exact answers (no rounding).

13.
(23) $\dfrac{7}{8}$

14.
(24) $\dfrac{6}{11}$

Answer each question below. Write your answer as a whole number or decimal.

15.
(14) What is $\dfrac{2}{3}$ of 126?

16.
(27) What is 14% of 57?

Do each unit conversion below.

(a) 17.
(34)
How many inches are in 15 yards?

(b) 18.
(45)
How many pints are in 12 quarts? (1 quart = 2 pints)

(c) 19.
(44)
How many cubic feet are in 28 cubic yards?

(d) 20.
(39)
Convert 2 miles to kilometers. (1 mile = 1.609 kilometers)

Translate the word problem below into math; then solve.

(e) 21.
(45)
Mr. Le Grand owns a worldwide chain of European-style coffee shops. Every time he visits a shop, he purchases a 16 ounce café au lait (coffee with steamed milk). If Mr. Le Grand visits 5 stores each day, what is his daily consumption of café au laits in pints (not ounces)?

Lesson 46—Volume in the Metric System

We've learned about volume in the common system. What about volume in the metric system? Not surprisingly, doing volume with metric units is a lot easier. That's because everything in the metric system goes by 10s. Let's go over some of the details.

First of all, we know that the metric units for length like meters and decimeters all differ by 10 times. In other words, the next larger unit is always 10 times the previous one. That means to go up from one unit to the next, we can always just multiply or divide by 10.

A meter is 10 times a decimeter in length.

meter

decimeter

The metric units for area like square meters and square decimeters all differ by 100 times. So to go from one area unit to the next, we have to multiply or divide by 100.[1]

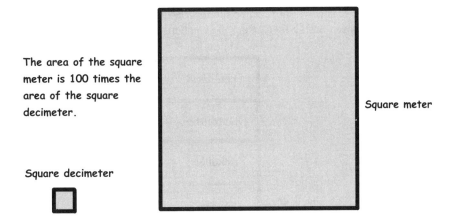

The area of the square meter is 100 times the area of the square decimeter.

Square meter

Square decimeter

What about cubic metric units like cubic meters and cubic decimeters? These units are used for measuring volume. A cubic meter has a volume the size of a cube with sides that are 1 meter long, and a cubic decimeter is the size of a cube with 1 decimeter sides. How do these volumes differ? Well, if lengths go up by 10 times and areas go up by 100 times, it stands to reason that volumes would go up by 1,000 times ($10 \times 10 \times 10$). That means when converting from one cubic unit to the next larger one, we have to divide by 1,000. And when converting from a larger cubic unit to the next smaller one, we need to multiply by 1,000.

Converting in Metric

As an example, let's convert 4 cubic meters to cubic decimeters. Since these are cubic units, the conversion factor is 1,000. And since we're going from larger to smaller units, we need to multiply by 1,000.

$$4 \times 1,000 = 4,000$$

So we get 4,000 cubic decimeters.

---

[1] Of course, these drawings aren't actual size.

Let's do another example. This time we'll convert 800 cubic meters to cubic dekameters. These are cubic units again, which means that our conversion factor is 1,000. But in this case we're going from smaller to larger units, so we should divide by 1,000.

$$800 \div 1,000 = 0.8$$

The answer to this one is 0.8 cubic dekameters.

Inventing the Liter

Actually, there is one change that's been made to volumes in the metric system. But unlike the changes that were made (through the years) to gallons, quarts, pints, and the other common units, this change is very logical.

It turns out there's a problem with cubic meters, cubic decimeters, and all the other cubic units in the metric system. They're too far apart. A cubic meter is 1,000 times as large as a cubic decimeter, and a cubic decimeter is 1,000 times as large as a cubic centimeter, and so on. That means even units that are right next to each other are incredibly far apart. It's like trying to cook a meal with measuring cups that all differ in size by 1,000 times.

Fortunately, the scientists who designed the metric system realized that it would be better if the units were closer together. That's why they created a new unit which is exactly the same size as the cubic decimeter (because it's a good size for everyday use). This new unit is called the liter. So 1 liter = 1 cubic decimeter. Then the scientists created larger and smaller units based on the liter, using the standard metric system prefixes (which are shown on the next page).

Units based on the liter

kiloliter
hectoliter
dekaliter
liter
deciliter
centiliter
milliliter

The key point, though, is that these units all differ only by 10s. A liter is 10 times the size of a deciliter, a deciliter is 10 times the size of a centiliter, and so on. That makes the units for volume a lot closer in size and more convenient to use. With this change, metric units of volume are just as close together as metric units for length, which is really useful. By the way, if you're having trouble picturing how large a liter is, just remember that soda is often sold in 2 liter bottles. So a liter is half a big bottle of soda.

Converting with Liters

Finally, let's work a couple of examples with liters. Let's say we have a container that is 7.5 liters in size. How many deciliters is that?

Since we're going from larger to smaller units, we need to multiply. Also, since liters are 10 times the size of deciliters, we should multiply by 10.

$$7.5 \times 10 = 75$$

That gives us 75 deciliters. The main point is that we convert by multiplying only by 10, even though we're working with volume units.

Here's one more quick example. Let's convert 825 liters to hectoliters. Since we're going from smaller to larger units, we need to divide this time. But liters and hectoliters are two steps apart (look back at the table). So what we have to do is divide by 10 twice.

$$825 \div 10 = 82.5 \quad \text{and} \quad 82.5 \div 10 = 8.25$$

We could have done the calculation even faster by just moving the decimal point two places to the left. But whatever method you use, the answer is 8.25 hectoliters.

Practice 46

a.
(30) What percent of 120 is 30?

b.
(41) How many square yards are in 675 square feet?

c.
(46) Convert 26 liters to deciliters.

d.
(45) How many gallons are in 20 quarts? (1 gallon = 4 quarts)

e.
(44) Translate the word problem below into math; then solve.

The largest cargo aircraft has a volume of 1,400 cubic meters. How many cubic decimeters is this?

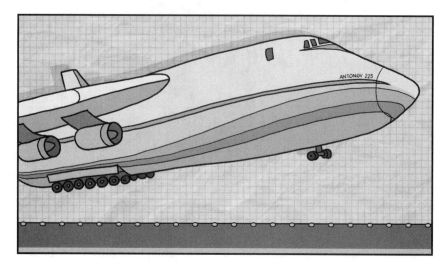

Problem Set 46

Tell whether each sentence below is True or False.

1.
(46) To convert from cubic meters to cubic decimeters, you have to multiply by 10.

2.
(46) The designers of the metric system created a new unit called the liter to make the units of volume closer together in size.

Complete each sentence below with the best of the choices given.

3.
(44) 1 *cubic* kilometer equals 1,000 _____.

    A. cubic kilometers   B. cubic hectometers   C. cubic dekameters
    D. cubic decimeters   E. cubic centimeters

4.
(44) 1,000 *cubic* millimeters equals 1 _____.

    A. cubic kilometer   B. cubic hectometer   C. cubic dekameter
    D. cubic decimeter   E. cubic centimeter

5.
(46) 10 liters equals 1 _____.

    A. kiloliter   B. hectoliter   C. dekaliter
    D. deciliter   E. centiliter

Add or subtract each group of numbers below.

6.
(2)
$$\begin{array}{r} 12{,}053 \\ +14{,}780 \\ \hline \end{array}$$

7.
(18)
$$\begin{array}{r} 0.782 \\ -0.54 \\ \hline \end{array}$$

Multiply or divide each pair of numbers below. Write any remainders in decimal form.

8.
(20)
$$\begin{array}{r} 9.30 \\ \times 6.1 \\ \hline \end{array}$$

9.
(22)
$8\overline{)586}$

Add or subtract each pair of fractions below. Make sure your answers are fully reduced.

10.
(10)
$\dfrac{4}{15} + \dfrac{6}{15}$

11.
(10)
$\dfrac{8}{5} - \dfrac{3}{4}$

Multiply or divide each pair of numbers below. Make sure your answers are fully reduced.

12.
(14)
$\dfrac{5}{12} \times 60$

13.
(14)
$14 \div \dfrac{7}{9}$

Convert each fraction below into decimal form. Give exact answers (no rounding).

14.
(23)
$\dfrac{9}{20}$

15.
(24)
$\dfrac{1}{18}$

Answer each question below.

16.
(14)
What is $\dfrac{3}{4}$ of 80?

17.
(14)
How many $\dfrac{1}{2}$ s are in 17?

(a) 18.
(30)
What percent of 150 is 45?

Do each unit conversion below.

(b) 19.
(41)
How many square yards are in 765 square feet?

(c) 20.
(46)
Convert 24 liters to deciliters.

(d) 21.
(45)
How many gallons are in 16 quarts? (1 gallon = 4 quarts)

Translate the word problem below into math; then solve.

(e) 22. The largest blimps ever built could carry 200,000 cubic meters of hydrogen gas. How many cubic
(44) decimeters is this?

CHAPTER 7:
SIMPLE ALGEBRAIC EQUATIONS

Lesson 47—Advanced Arithmetic

So far this book has been all about arithmetic, which is just basic math. But this is a pre-algebra book, after all, so let's move on to algebra.

Finding Missing Numbers

What is algebra, anyway? You've probably heard about it. In fact, a lot of people say it's difficult. But what is it really? Well, despite the scary stories, algebra is actually not that different from arithmetic. You might even say that algebra is just a more advanced version of arithmetic. To explain, let's do a comparison. Here are several simple arithmetic problems.

$$19 + 42 = \textbf{?} \qquad 23 \times 15 = \textbf{?} \qquad 128 \div 4 = \textbf{?}$$

To work these, we only need to find the missing numbers by doing the calculations. Putting in the missing numbers, we get this.

$$19 + 42 = \textbf{61} \qquad 23 \times 15 = \textbf{345} \qquad 128 \div 4 = \textbf{32}$$

Now let's compare these arithmetic problems to three *algebra* problems.

$$19 + \textbf{?} = 61 \qquad 23 \times \textbf{?} = 345 \qquad 128 \times \textbf{?} = 32$$

To solve these, we just find the missing numbers again.

$$19 + \textbf{42} = 61 \qquad 23 \times \textbf{15} = 345 \qquad 128 \times \textbf{4} = 32$$

Do you see how similar arithmetic and algebra are? They're both about finding missing numbers. So what makes algebra harder? Well, notice that the arithmetic problems all have the missing number on one side by itself. That makes the answer easy to find. But algebra problems have the missing number mixed together with other numbers (through addition, subtraction, etc.). And that makes finding the answer more difficult.

Other Differences

Here are some other differences between arithmetic and algebra. Arithmetic problems usually have only one operation. Remember, addition, subtraction, multiplication, and division are called **operations**. Arithmetic problems usually have only one operation, which keeps them fairly simple. Algebra problems, on the other hand, often involve several operations, which makes the process of finding the missing number quite a bit more complicated. Here's an example of an algebra problem with lots of operations.

$$4 \times \textbf{?} + 3 - 1 = 5 \times 2$$

The answer to this problem is still the number that makes the two sides equal when it's put in for the question mark. (It's 2, in case you're wondering.)

Another difference between algebra and arithmetic is that in arithmetic problems, the missing number appears only once. (There's just one question mark, in other words.) But in algebra problems, it can appear many times. Here is an example of an algebra problem that has several question marks.

$$\textbf{?} \times 7 + \textbf{?} - 4 = 3 \times \textbf{?} + 11$$

The correct answer here is the number which makes the sides equal when put in for *all three* question marks. (This answer turns out to be 3.)

These last two examples may look tough, and finding the answers does require some skill. But notice that in each example, the name of the game is still finding the missing number. And that's why algebra and arithmetic are so much the same.

x's and y's

There's one other difference between algebra and arithmetic that's worth mentioning. Instead of using question marks to stand for missing numbers, algebra uses letters—especially the letters x, y, and z. That's why everybody talks about algebra being full of letters instead of numbers. But there's actually nothing strange about it if you realize that the letters are just missing numbers. The letter most commonly used is x. Here are the last two problems we showed with x's in place of the question marks.

$$4 \times x + 3 - 1 = 5 \times 2 \qquad\qquad x \times 7 + x - 4 = 3 \times x + 11$$

Before reading this lesson, these problems might have seemed confusing. But now you know that algebra problems are just a more complicated game of finding the missing number—an advanced form of arithmetic.

Practice 47

a.
(47)
Tell whether $x \times 3 - 2 + x = 11 + x - 5$ is an algebra or arithmetic problem.

b.
(47)
Find the missing number in the problem $x \times 11 = 55$.

c.
(47)
Find the missing number in the problem $13 \div x = 13$.

d.
(47)
Find the missing number in the problem $x - \dfrac{1}{5} = \dfrac{2}{5}$.

e.
(46)
Translate the word problem below into math; then solve.

Eric is homeschooled, and whenever he goes to the grocery store with his mom, she turns the trip into a math lesson. Today, one of the questions was "How many deciliters are in a 2 liter bottle of grape soda?" Eric got it right. What was his answer?

Problem Set 47

Tell whether each sentence below is True or False.

1.
(47)
Algebra and arithmetic problems can be described as "games," where the goal is to find the missing number.

2.
(47)
In arithmetic problems, the missing number appears by itself on one side of the equals sign.

3.
(47)
In algebra problems, the missing number is mixed together with other numbers.

Complete each sentence below with the best of the choices given.

4.
(47)   In algebra, letters are used in place of _____.

      A. missing numbers   B. operations   C. calculations
      D. words   E. people

5.
(47)   Addition, subtraction, multiplication, and division are called _____.

      A. answers   B. operations   C. missing numbers
      D. calculations   E. letters

6.
(47)   _____ problems usually contain only one operation.

      A. Algebra   B. Difficult   C. Medical
      D. Arithmetic   E. Geometry

7.
(47)   _____ problems usually have several operations.

      A. Algebra   B. Arithmetic   C. Simple
      D. Medical   E. Subtraction

Add or subtract each group of numbers below.

8.
(17)
$$\begin{array}{r} 9.35 \\ +7.18 \\ \hline \end{array}$$

9.
(17)
$$\begin{array}{r} 63.1 \\ -52.9 \\ \hline \end{array}$$

Multiply or divide each pair of numbers below. Write any remainders in decimal form.

10.
(20)
$$\begin{array}{r} 8.02 \\ \times 0.9 \\ \hline \end{array}$$

11.
(21) $1.4\overline{)124.6}$

Add or subtract each pair of fractions below. Make sure your answers are fully reduced.

12.
(10) $\dfrac{1}{3} + \dfrac{1}{5}$

13.
(10) $\dfrac{9}{14} - \dfrac{1}{2}$

Multiply or divide each pair of fractions below. Make sure your answer is fully reduced.

14.
(13) $\dfrac{4}{9} \times \dfrac{18}{20}$

15.
(13) $\dfrac{7}{3} \div \dfrac{5}{6}$

Tell whether these are arithmetic or algebra problems.

16.
(47) $x \div 7 = 3$

17.
(47) $4 \times 9 = x$

(a) 18.
(47) $x \times 4 - 6 + x = 5 + x - 2$

Find the missing number in each problem below. Make sure your answer is fully reduced.

(b) 19. $x \times 12 = 48$
(47)

(c) 20. $15 \div x = 15$
(47)

(d) 21. $x - \dfrac{1}{7} = \dfrac{2}{7}$
(47)

Translate the word problem below into math; then solve.

(e) 22. Super Duper Saver Mart is selling 5 liter jugs of a new item called *Tastes as Good as Maple Syrup*. How many deciliters are in the jug?
(46)

Lesson 48—What's it for Anyway?

Now you know that algebra is in many ways just a game of finding missing numbers. But if algebra were only a game, you wouldn't be forced to learn it. So what's the purpose of algebra? Well, it turns out that algebra is used to find answers to real-life problems. That's what makes it really valuable. Here's a simple example.

Mike Gleason is a football fanatic. Naturally, when Mike's hometown pro football team made it to the Super Bowl, he had to take his whole family to the game. If Mike took 11 people (Mike plus his wife, Sherry, and their five kids along with Mike's Dad and his three brothers) and if the total bill for the tickets was $3,025, how much did each ticket cost?

Some Important Terms

Before we try to figure this out, you should realize that answering a real-life problem with algebra involves several steps. The most difficult one is translating the problem into a mathematical statement called an equation. All of the examples in the previous problem set were actually equations, even though we didn't use that word. An equation is just two groups of numbers (and maybe x's) with an equal sign between them. Here are a couple of the equations from the last problem set to refresh your memory.

$$15 \times x = 45 \qquad\qquad x - \frac{2}{3} = \frac{1}{3}$$

The equals signs say that what's on the left is supposed to equal what's on the right, when the proper number is put in for x. By the way, the groups of numbers and x's on either side of each equals sign are actually called **expressions**. So a more precise definition for an **equation** is two expressions that have an equals sign between them.

Setting up the Equation

Now let's translate our Super Bowl problem into an equation. The first step is to make x represent the thing that we're trying to find. This is critical, so you should always write out what x means on paper. Since we're trying to find the price of each Super Bowl ticket, that's what we'll set equal to x.

$$x = \text{price of each Super Bowl ticket}$$

The next step is to pick out two things from the facts of the problem that are supposed to be equal. In this case, if you study the problem carefully, you may realize that the price of each ticket multiplied by the number of people in Mike's family should equal the total cost. This idea should be written out in a word equation like this.

$$\text{Price of each ticket} \quad\times\quad \text{Number in family} \quad=\quad \text{Total spent}$$

The third step is to turn the word equation into a math equation. We know that the price of each ticket is x, the number of people in the family is 11, and the total spent is $3,025. So we replace the words with x's and numbers, like this.

$$\text{Price of each ticket} \quad\times\quad \text{Number in family} \quad=\quad \text{Total spent}$$
$$\downarrow \qquad\qquad \downarrow \qquad\qquad \downarrow$$
$$x \quad\times\quad 11 \quad=\quad 3{,}025$$

Here's the same equation, without the extra spaces.

$$x \times 11 = 3{,}025$$

Notice that the equation doesn't include dollar signs. That's because equations should have only numbers, never symbols like dollar signs, cent signs, inches, feet, minutes, etc.

Solving the Equation

After we've translated the problem into an equation, our fourth step is to find the missing number, which, of course, is the answer to the equation. That's the number that when put in for x makes both sides equal. You probably know that the formal name for answer is **solution**. Finding the answer to an equation is also called "solving" the equation. So to sound mathematical, we would say that by "solving the equation $x \times 11 = 3,025$, we found its solution to be 275." And it turns out that 275 is the correct missing number on this one.

Interpreting the Solution

The fifth and final step of the whole process is to interpret the meaning of the answer (solution). The equation itself doesn't tell us what the solution, 275, stands for. That's because equations just have numbers in them, nothing else. The 275 could mean anything: 275 turnips, 275 potato chips, or 275 tennis balls. We need to look back to see what x means in this particular case. In our problem, x represents the price of each Super Bowl ticket, so 275 means "275 dollars for each ticket," and this is the answer to our problem.[1] Here, again, are all the steps for finding the answer to a problem using algebra.

Solving a Problem with Algebra

1.	Make x stand for whatever you're trying to find.
2.	Study the facts to find two things that must be equal; then write a word equation.
3.	Turn the word equation into an algebra equation, with numbers and an x.
4.	Find the solution (answer) which when put in for x makes both sides equal.
5.	Interpret the meaning of the solution.

Practice 48

a.
(46) Convert 18 cubic centimeters to cubic millimeters.

b.
(34) How many miles are in 22,176 feet?

c.
(48) Write an equation to represent the problem below. Don't solve the problem.

The sum of 25 and what number is 62?

A. $x + 62 = 25$ B. $25 - x = 62$ C. $25 + 62 = x$

D. $25 + x = 62$ E. $25 + x + 62$

---

[1] Of course, $275 is a lot of money to spend on a football game (way too much, actually), but Mike felt he had to do it.

d.
(48)
Write an equation to represent the problem below. Don't solve the problem.

What number minus 17 is equal to 34?

A. $x+17=34$ B. $34-17=x$ C. $x-17=34$
D. $x-17-34$ E. $17-x=34$

e.
(21)
Translate the word problem below into math; then solve.

Karen likes to buy silly little gifts for her employees to cheer them up during especially hectic times. For example, yesterday she bought each of them a court jester hat with bells. If each hat costs $3.50, and she bought $63 worth of hats, how many employees does Karen have?

Problem Set 48

Tell whether each sentence below is True or False.

1.
(48)
The main purpose of algebra is to find answers to real-life problems.

2.
(48)
An equation is just two groups of numbers (and maybe x's) with an equal sign between them.

3.
(48)
Addition, subtraction, multiplication, and division are called solutions.

Complete each sentence below with the best of the choices given.

4.
(48)
A group of numbers and x's is called a (or an) _____.

A. equation   B. solution   C. paragraph
D. expression   E. multiplication

5.
(48)
The answer to an equation is also called the _____.

A. expression   B. tabulation   C. exception
D. solution   E. sum

6.
(46)
1,000 centiliters equals 1 _____.

A. kiloliter   B. hectoliter   C. dekaliter
D. deciliter   E. centiliter

Multiply or divide each pair of numbers below. Write any remainders in decimal form.

7.
(20)
$$8,070 \times 0.2$$

8.
(22)
$6.2\overline{)522.35}$

Add or subtract each pair of numbers below. Make sure your answers are fully reduced.

9.
(12)
$7\frac{1}{2}+4\frac{7}{8}$

10.
(12)
$3-1\frac{2}{3}$

Convert each fraction below into decimal form. Give exact answers (no rounding).

11.
(24) $\dfrac{1}{9}$

12.
(23) $\dfrac{3}{16}$

Do each unit conversion below.

(a)13.
(46) Convert 14 cubic centimeters to cubic millimeters.

(b)14.
(34) How many miles are in 20,064 feet?

15.
(41) Convert 68 square feet to square inches.

Write an equation to represent each problem below. Don't solve the problem.

(c)16.
(48) The sum of 23 and what number is 51?

   A. $x+51=23$ B. $23+x=51$ C. $23+x+51$
   D. $23+51=x$ E. $23-x=51$

(d)17.
(48) What number minus 19 is equal to 27?

   A. $x+19=27$ B. $19-x=27$ C. $x-19-27$
   D. $x-19=27$ E. $27-19=x$

18.
(48) $\dfrac{1}{2}$ multiplied by what number equals 14?

   A. $x=\dfrac{1}{2}\times14$ B. $\dfrac{1}{2}\times x\times14$ C. $14\times x=\dfrac{1}{2}$
   D. $\dfrac{1}{2}+x=14$ E. $\dfrac{1}{2}\times x=14$

Find the solution (missing number) in each equation below. Make sure your answer is fully reduced.

19.
(47) $x+\dfrac{1}{4}=\dfrac{1}{2}$

20.
(47) $x\times14=28$

21.
(47) $x-39=72$

Translate the word problem below into math; then solve.

(e) 22.
(21) When Moose's mom saw that her butcher shop was having a sale on T-Bone steaks, she thought she'd better buy all she could with the money she had on her, which happened to be $27. If the steaks were on sale for $4.50 per pound, how many pounds did she buy?

Lesson 49—The Golden Rule of Algebra

We've learned about algebra equations and how they're used. But have you noticed that finding that missing number can be pretty hard? That's because, in the last two problem sets, you've had to solve all the equations in your head. Don't get stressed out, though, because algebra equations aren't really supposed to be solved that way. Algebra actually has step-by-step procedures for solving equations that are simple to learn and that give you the right answer every time. In fact, this is the first of many lessons where we show you how these methods work. And after you've had some practice, you'll be able to solve equations that would have been impossible to do in your head. To get started, let's compare the two equations below.

$$x = 63 - 25 \qquad\qquad x + 25 = 63$$

Which of these seems easier to you? Most people would say the one on the left is easier, because it's just an arithmetic problem. To find its solution (answer), we just subtract: 63 minus 25 gives 38. The equation on the right looks harder, even though it involves the same numbers. That's because it's in algebra form, where x is not already by itself on one side. If asked to find its solution, we might have to shuffle things around in our heads, like this:

"Let's see, if $x + 25$ is equal to 63, then x has to be $63 - 25$."

But notice something about this mental process. We ended up turning the algebra equation $x + 25 = 63$ into the arithmetic equation $x = 63 - 25$. That tells us two things. It tells us that both equations have the same answer, and more importantly, it tells us that we can get the answer to the harder equation by solving the easy equation.

Undoing Addition

As it turns out, that's how the equation-solving methods of algebra work. They help us turn a hard algebra equation into a simple arithmetic equation that has the same answer. But instead of having to do everything in your head, the process is done one step at a time on paper. Now let's actually go through the solving steps on another example.

$$x + 5.14 = 13.86$$

This is an algebra equation, and our goal is to turn it into an easy arithmetic equation, where x is by itself on the left side. The question is how can we get rid of the 5.14? Simple. We just *subtract* 5.14, like this.

$$x + 5.14 - 5.14$$

Here's why subtracting works. If we add 5.14 to any number, then take away 5.14, we end up with the original number again. It's as if your best friend gave you $5.14, but then, two seconds later, took the $5.14 back—you have the same amount of money you did before. So after subtracting 5.14, the left side of the equation is equal to just x, which is what we wanted.

$$x + 5.14 - 5.14 \text{ equals } x$$

This process of subtracting a number to get rid of an addition is called **undoing**. By subtracting 5.14, we are reversing or "undoing" the addition of 5.14 to get x by itself. In fact, any addition can be undone by subtracting the very same number that was added.

The Golden Rule of Algebra

There's one catch, however. Subtracting a number from one side could spoil an equation entirely and give us a wrong answer.[1] To avoid this, we have to follow the most important rule of algebra—so important, in fact, that it's called the **golden rule of algebra**. The rule is that if we change the value of one side of an equation, we must change the other side by the same amount.

The golden rule is pretty obvious, really. If the two sides of an equation are supposed to be equal to start, then they should still be equal after changing the value of each side by the same amount. It's a little bit like a scale. If both sides are in balance to begin with, then they should still be in balance after we subtract the same amount from both sides.

Getting back to our example, let's follow the golden rule and subtract 5.14 from *both sides* of the equation.

$$x + 5.14 - 5.14 = 13.86 - 5.14$$

The left side is now equal to just x.

$$x = 13.86 - 5.14$$

And notice what's happened. By undoing, we've turned our tough algebra equation into a simple arithmetic equation (with the x on one side by itself and the numbers on the other). And since we followed the golden rule in the process, the equation hasn't been spoiled. From here, we can find the solution by simply subtracting the numbers on the right.

$$x = 8.72$$

The solution (answer) is 8.72.

Checking the Answer

It turns out a solution (answer) can always be checked by putting it in for x in the original equation to see if the two sides are made equal. Let's try that with the equation we just solved. Remember, this is what the equation looked like originally.

$$x + 5.14 = 13.86$$

If we put in (or "substitute" as it's also called) 8.72 for x, we get this.

---

[1] The equation gets "spoiled" because the solution changes. For example, the equation $x + 5 = 8$ has an answer of 3. But if we subtract 2 from the left side, without doing anything to the right side, the equation becomes $x + 3 = 8$. This equation has been spoiled because it now has an answer of 5 instead of 3.

$$8.72 + 5.14 = 13.86$$

All that's left now is to do the calculation on the left side.

$$13.86 = 13.86$$

Since the sides are equal, our answer of 8.72 is correct.

Undoing Subtraction

Many equations have a number *subtracted* from x. How do we handle these? Take the equation $x - \frac{1}{4} = \frac{1}{2}$ as an example. To undo the subtraction, we *add* $\frac{1}{4}$ to each side.

$$x - \frac{1}{4} + \frac{1}{4} = \frac{1}{2} + \frac{1}{4}$$

The left side now has $\frac{1}{4}$ taken away from x, then another $\frac{1}{4}$ added back again. By the same logic we used before, this makes the left side equal to just x.

$$x = \frac{1}{2} + \frac{1}{4}$$

Again, by undoing we have turned our algebra equation into a far simpler arithmetic equation. From here we can find the solution by just adding on the right.

$$x = \frac{3}{4}$$

This answer can also be checked by putting in $\frac{3}{4}$ for x in the original equation. We won't bother showing the steps this time, but you can do them on your own if you like.

Inverse Operations

Notice that we eliminated the subtraction of $\frac{1}{4}$ by *adding* $\frac{1}{4}$. In fact, we can undo any subtraction by adding back the same number. So not only can subtraction undo addition, but addition can also undo subtraction. Two operations that undo each other are called **inverse operations**. Since addition and subtraction are inverse operations, we can solve any equation where a number is added to or subtracted from an x (even a really tough case like $x + 8.003067 = 17.432995$) by undoing.

Practice 49

   a. How many fluid ounces are in 3 gallons? (1 gallon = 4 quarts; 1 quart = 2 pints; 1 pint = 16 fluid ounces)
(45)

b. Convert 370 square meters to square dekameters.
(42)

c. What must be done to the expression $x - 145$ to make it equal x?
(49)

    A. Divide by 145   B. Subtract x C. Subtract 145
    D. Add 145   E. Multiply by 145

d. Solve the equation $x + 49 = 75$ by undoing.
(49)

e. Translate the word problem below into an equation; then solve.
(48)

On a cold January afternoon, workers at a local charity distributed 12.7 gallons of beef vegetable soup. If they had 2.3 gallons leftover, how many gallons did they start with?

Problem Set 49

Tell whether each sentence below is True or False.

1. Any addition can be undone by subtracting the very same number.
(49)

2. Any subtraction can be undone by adding the very same number.
(49)

3. The golden rule of algebra says that if you change the value of one side of an equation the value of the
(49) other side must be changed by the same amount.

Complete each sentence below with the best of the choices given.

4. If the same number is added to both sides of an equation, the solution to the equation will _____.
(49)

    A. stay the same   B. increase   C. decrease
    D. equal zero   E. be spoiled

5. Algebra equations are solved by turning them into _____ that have the same answer.
(49)

    A. solutions   B. expressions   C. algebra equations
    D. inverse operations   E. arithmetic equations

6. Two operations that can undo each other are called _____ operations.
(49)

    A. solution   B. expression   C. algebra
    D. inverse   E. arithmetic

Add or subtract each group of numbers below.

7.   632
(2)   917
     +546

8.   635.1
(17)   −98.6

Add or subtract each pair of numbers below. Make sure your answers are fully reduced.

9. $1\frac{4}{5}+1\frac{3}{5}$
(12)

10. $\frac{4}{6}-\frac{2}{3}$
(10)

Multiply or divide each pair of numbers below. Make sure your answer is fully reduced.

11. $24\times\frac{1}{6}$
(14)

12. $\frac{4}{7}\div2$
(14)

Convert each percent below into decimal form.

13. $82\frac{3}{4}\%$
(28)

14. 105%
(26)

Do each unit conversion below.

(a) 15. How many fluid ounces are in 2 gallons? (1 gallon = 4 quarts; 1 quart = 2 pints; 1 pint = 16 fluid ounces)
(45)

(b) 16. Convert 490 square meters to square dekameters.
(42)

Answer each question below.

17. What must be done to the expression $x+92$ to make it equal x?
(49)
    A. Subtract x B. Subtract 92   C. Add 92
    D. Divide 92   E. Multiply 92

(c) 18. What must be done to the expression $x-115$ to make it equal x?
(49)
    A. Subtract 115   B. Divide 115   C. Subtract x
    D. Multiply 115   E. Add 115

Solve each equation below by undoing.

19. $x+5=28$
(49)

20. $x-13=36$
(49)

(d) 21. $x+57=81$
(49)

Translate the word problem below into an equation; then solve.

(e) 22. Clement lost the bet. Now he has to drink the entire jar of lukewarm milk. So far, he has drunk only 2.4
(48) ounces. If he has 9.6 ounces to go, how many ounces were in the jar to begin with?

Lesson 50—Undoing Multiplication and Division

We just learned to undo addition and subtraction in an equation. In this lesson, we'll learn how to undo multiplication and division.

Undoing Multiplication

Let's start with a multiplication example.

$$x \times 6 = 84$$

Remember how this works. To solve here, we need to change the algebra equation into an easy arithmetic equation. So on this one, we have to get rid of (undo, in other words) the multiplication by 6 to get x by itself on the left.

The question is how do we undo multiplication? Well, let's do a little experiment. Say the number 2 is multiplied by 5 to get 10. What must be done to turn the result back into 2? Subtracting 5 doesn't work because $2 \times 5 - 5$ is equal to $10 - 5$ or 5. That's not 2. Adding 5 is no good either because $2 \times 5 + 5$ is $10 + 5$ or 15. That's not 2 either. Actually, to return to 2, we have to *divide* by 5. See, if we take $2 \times 5 \div 5$, that equals $10 \div 5$ or 2. In fact, if you try this on other numbers, you'll find that a multiplication can always be undone by dividing by the very same number.

Now you can see how to undo the multiplication by 6 in the equation. We just divide by 6. But we can't forget the golden rule of algebra. We have to divide the right side by 6 too.

$$x \times 6 \div 6 = 84 \div 6$$

This makes the left side equal to just x.

$$x = 84 \div 6$$

That turns the algebra equation into an arithmetic equation, which is exactly what we wanted. From here we can solve easily by just doing the division on the right.

$$x = 14$$

The Answer is a Fraction

Notice that the answer in that last example was a whole number. But a lot of times dividing both sides of an equation can give a fraction or decimal answer. For instance, look at this problem.

$$x \times 4 = 9$$

To solve it we have to divide both sides by 4.

$$x \times 4 \div 4 = 9 \div 4$$

Dividing by 4 after multiplying by 4 leaves just x on the left side.

$$x = 9 \div 4$$

But since 4 doesn't divide into 9 evenly, we end up with the fraction $\dfrac{9}{4}$ (or 2.25 in decimal form) on the right side.

$$x = \frac{9}{4} \quad \text{or} \quad x = 2.25$$

Undoing Division

What about undoing division? Take a look at this one.

$$x \div 7 = 15$$

We need to turn this algebra equation into an arithmetic equation by getting x by itself on one side of the equals sign. To do that, we have to undo the division by 7. You can probably guess the method. Division is undone by multiplication. For example, if we have $8 \div 2$ and want to undo the division to get back to 8, we multiply by 2. That gives us $8 \div 2 \times 2$, which is the same as 4×2 or 8. So for $x \div 7 = 15$, we undo by multiplying both sides by 7.

$$x \div 7 \times 7 = 15 \times 7$$

That leaves us with just x on the left side.

$$x = 15 \times 7$$

And once again we've changed our algebra equation into an arithmetic equation. To get the answer from here, all we have to do is multiply on the right.

$$x = 105$$

Since multiplication and division undo each other, they too are inverse operations, just like addition and subtraction. So every one of the four major operations of arithmetic—addition, subtraction, multiplication, and division—has an inverse operation that will undo it.

Practice 50

a.
(50) What must be done to the expression $x \times 14$ to make it equal x?

      A. Add 14   B. Multiply by 14   C. Divide by 14
      D. Divide by x E. Subtract 14

b.
(50) What must be done to the expression $x \div 25$ to make it equal x?

      A. Subtract 25   B. Divide by 25   C. Multiply by x
      D. Multiply by 25   E. Add 25

c.
(50) Solve the equation $x \times 6 = 186$ by undoing.

d.
(50) Solve the equation $x \div 5.5 = 7.3$ by undoing.

e.
(43) Translate the word problem below into math; then solve.

      If a brick is 2 inches wide, 4 inches tall, and 8 inches long, what is its volume in cubic inches?

Problem Set 50

Tell whether each sentence below is True or False.

1.
(50) A multiplication can be undone by dividing by the very same number.

2.
(50) A division can be undone by dividing by the very same number.

Complete each sentence below with the best of the choices given.

3.
(45) 1 gallon equals 4 _____.

    A. quarts   B. pints   C. fluid ounces
    D. cubic inches   E. liters

4.
(45) 1 pint equals 16 _____ .

    A. gallons   B. quarts   C. fluid ounces
    D. cubic inches   E. liters

5.
(38) 100 centimeters equals 1 _____ .

    A. kilometer   B. hectometer   C. dekameter
    D. meter   E. millimeter

Add or subtract each group of numbers below.

6.
(18)
$$\begin{array}{r} 8.9 \\ 12.8 \\ +1.76 \\ \hline \end{array}$$

7.
(17)
$$\begin{array}{r} 300.5 \\ -231.8 \\ \hline \end{array}$$

Add or subtract each pair of fractions below. Make sure your answers are fully reduced.

8.
(10) $\dfrac{7}{12} - \dfrac{5}{12}$

9.
(10) $\dfrac{7}{9} + \dfrac{2}{3}$

Multiply or divide each pair of fractions below. Make sure your answers are fully reduced.

10.
(13) $\dfrac{2}{5} \times \dfrac{3}{8}$

11.
(13) $\dfrac{1}{7} \div \dfrac{11}{14}$

Do each unit conversion below.

12.
(38) How many millimeters are in 87 decimeters?

13.
(41) Convert 1,152 square inches to square feet.

Answer each question below.

(a) 14.
(50) What must be done to the expression $x \times 17$ to make it equal x?

      A. Subtract 17   B. Add 17   C. Divide by x
      D. Divide by 17   E. Multiply by 17

(b) 15.
(50) What must be done to the expression $x \div 35$ to make it equal x?

      A. Multiply by 35   B. Add 35   C. Multiply by x
      D. Divide by 35   E. Subtract 35

Solve each equation below by undoing.

16.
(49) $x + 4.2 = 19$ **17.**
(49) $x - 38 = 65$ **(c) 18.**
(50) $x \times 7 = 161$

19.
(50) $x \div 9 = 21$ **(d) 20.**
(50) $x \div 6.5 = 8.2$

Translate the word problem below into math; then solve.

(e) 21.
(43) Concrete blocks are typically 8 inches wide, 8 inches tall, and 16 inches long. How many cubic inches is this?

Lesson 51—Changing Places

By now, you're probably getting better and better at solving equations. But take a look at this one.

$$4 + x = 25$$

We could figure out the answer in our heads, but what is the proper way to undo the addition? In all of the equations we've solved so far, x was on the outside. Here it's on the inside, next to the equals sign. Wouldn't it be easier to undo if we could make the 4 and the x change places? Is this allowed?

Flip 'Em Around

Yes, we can change these numbers around, because a basic rule of arithmetic says that two numbers can be added in any order, and their sum will be the same. It's called the commutative property of addition, and we talked about it way back in Chapter 1. This is the rule that says that $4+6$ equals $6+4$, $1+7$ equals $7+1$, and so on. But the important thing to know is that we can use this rule even when an x is involved. So in our example we can change $4+x$ to $x+4$.

$$x + 4 = 25$$

Now we can solve in the normal way.

$$x + 4 - 4 = 25 - 4$$

$$x = 25 - 4$$

$$x = 21$$

Next, let's take a look at another equation where it's helpful to make a number and an x change places.

$$8 \times x = 72$$

Here it would be nice to switch the 8 and the x to make the undoing step easier. And this is legal, because there's another arithmetic rule which says that two numbers can be multiplied in any order, and their answer (product) will be the same. We already talked about this rule too. It's called the commutative property of multiplication, remember. It tells us that 8×5 is the same as 5×8. But the key point is that it can be used when an x is involved. So we can change $8 \times x$ to $x \times 8$.

$$x \times 8 = 72$$

Now it's easy to see how to undo. We just divide both sides by 8 like this.

$$x \times 8 \div 8 = 72 \div 8$$

The left side is equal to just x.

$$x = 72 \div 8$$

And doing the division on the right gives us the answer.

$$x = 9$$

These arithmetic rules work for all numbers. So anytime we have two numbers added or multiplied, no matter what they are—even if one of them is an x—we're free to switch their positions. When we change an expression around like this, we say that we are **rewriting** the expression. But make sure that you always follow one of the basic rules of arithmetic we talked about when rewriting.

It Won't Work for Subtraction and Division

One more thing. The rules about changing places only work for addition and multiplication. They do *not* work for subtraction or division. That means $5-x$ cannot be changed to $x-5$. And $4 \div x$ cannot be changed to $x \div 4$. Don't forget that.

Practice 51

a.
(46) Convert 2.3 liters to milliliters.

b.
(51) Tell whether the expressions $x-9$ and $9-x$ are equivalent.

c.
(51) Solve the equation $10.7 + x = 54.6$.

d.
(51) Solve the equation $53 \times x = 424$.

e.
(48) Translate the word problem below into an equation; then solve.

A whopping 3,289 people attended the power tool convention. Of these, 3,172 were men. How many were women?

Problem Set 51

Tell whether each sentence below is True or False.

1.
(51) According to the commutative property of addition, two numbers can be added in any order and their sum will be the same.

2.
(51) According to the commutative property of addition , two numbers can be divided in any order and their quotient will be the same.

Complete each sentence below with the best of the choices given.

3.
(38) 1 hectometer equals 10,000 _____ .

    A. millimeters   B. dekameters   C. meters
    D. centimeters   E. decimeters

4.
(34) 1 mile equals 5,280 _____ .

    A. yards   B. feet   C. inches
    D. kilometers   E. meters

Multiply or divide each pair of numbers below. Write any remainders in decimal form.

5.
(20)
$$\begin{array}{r} 345 \\ \times 1.7 \\ \hline \end{array}$$

6.
(22) $0.12 \overline{)5.61}$

Add or subtract each pair of numbers below. Make sure your answers are fully reduced.

7. $3\frac{1}{4} + 2\frac{1}{2}$
(12)

8. $\frac{11}{5} - 1\frac{3}{5}$
(12)

Convert each fraction below into decimal form. Give exact answers (no rounding).

9. $\frac{3}{8}$
(23)

10. $\frac{1}{6}$
(24)

Do each unit conversion below.

(a) 11. Convert 3.8 liters to milliliters.
(46)

12. How many yards are in 54 feet?
(33)

Tell whether each pair of expressions below is equivalent.

(b) 13. $x - 5$ and $5 - x$
(51)

14. $7 + x$ and $x + 7$
(51)

Solve each equation below by undoing. Make sure your answer is fully reduced.

(c) 15. $12.4 + x = 78.3$
(51)

16. $x - \frac{1}{5} = \frac{3}{5}$
(49)

(d) 17. $61 \times x = 549$
(51)

18. $x \div \frac{2}{7} = \frac{1}{2}$
(50)

19. $x \div 32 = 1.5$
(50)

20. $x \times \frac{1}{4} = \frac{1}{3}$
(50)

Translate the word problem below into an equation; then solve.

(e) 21. There were 5,642 participants in last year's antique and custom car show. Of these, 4,398 were from
(48) California. How many were *not* from California?

Lesson 52—New Symbols

You know that multiplication is shown with the $\times$ symbol and division with the $\div$ symbol, but you may be surprised to find out that those symbols are really only used in arithmetic. In algebra and all the more advanced math subjects, multiplication and division are actually written differently.

Writing Multiplication the Algebra Way

Here's how it works. To write "2 multiplied by x" the algebra way, we just put the 2 and x right next to each other, like this.

$$2x \qquad\qquad \textbf{"2 multiplied by x"}$$

So in algebra we write the equation $2 \times x = 40$ as $2x = 40$. You may be wondering, what difference it makes. Well, there are several reasons for writing multiplication differently in algebra. Eliminating the $\times$ symbol and pushing the 2 and x up against each other takes up less space. And, as you know, algebra problems can be a lot longer than arithmetic problems. So extra space is helpful. Another reason is that the symbol $\times$ looks a lot like an x. And so getting rid of the $\times$ symbol avoids a lot of confusion.

Another thing to keep in mind is that the number is always shown first when writing a multiplication with an x. That means to write the equation $x \times 5 = 13$ correctly, the x and 5 should not only be pushed completely together, but the order should also be changed to get $5x = 13$. Of course, mathematically it doesn't matter which number is listed first in a multiplication. But everybody has gotten into the habit of always putting the number first, so you should too.

The only problem is that pushing together won't work when you're multiplying two numbers instead of a number and an x. For example, if we try to write 5×6 by taking out the $\times$ symbol and pushing the numbers together, we get 56, which looks just like the number "fifty–six." So when multiplying two numbers we put parentheses around each number. The algebra way to write 5×6, then, is like this.

$$(5)(6) \qquad\qquad \textbf{"5 multiplied by 6"}$$

The numbers are still pushed together, but the parentheses show that 5 and 6 are actually two different numbers. Actually, we only need one set of parentheses to separate the 5 and 6. So 5×6 can also be written as $(5)6$ or $5(6)$. There's even another way to show two numbers multiplied. We can use a dot. Here's 5 times 6 written with a dot.

$$5 \cdot 6 \qquad\qquad \textbf{also "5 multiplied by 6"}$$

The dot can be used to show 5 multiplied by x too: $5 \cdot x$. But notice that the dot takes up some extra space, and since the 5 and x can be pushed completely together without causing any problems, the dot isn't usually used to show a number multiplied by an x.[1]

Writing Division the Algebra Way

We said that division is also shown differently in algebra. What takes the place of the $\div$ symbol then? Actually, it's the fraction bar. This makes sense if you think about it, because the fraction bar is used to stand for division even in basic math. For example, $\dfrac{12}{2}$ is the same as $12 \div 2$.

$$\frac{12}{2} \qquad\qquad \textbf{"12 divided by 2"}$$

---

[1] The dot is actually used quite a bit when factoring. People will factor $5x$ like this: $5 \cdot x$. You'll see more of this later.

In arithmetic, the fraction bar isn't used nearly as often as the ÷ sign. But in algebra, the fraction bar is used almost always. That means an algebra equation like $x \div 9 = 15$ is actually written as $\dfrac{x}{9} = 15$. The fraction bar not only saves space but also has some other advantages that we'll talk about later.

Practice 52

a.
(52)
Write "x times 7" the algebra way. Select the best possible choice.

    A. $x7$ B. $7x$ C. $\dfrac{x}{7}$

    D. $7(x)$ E. $7 \times x$

b.
(52)
Write "x divided by 3" the algebra way. Select the best possible choice.

    A. $3x$ B. $x3$ C. $\dfrac{x}{3}$

    D. $x \div 3$ E. $\dfrac{3}{x}$

c.
(42)
Convert 6 square meters to square decimeters. *60?*

d.
(52)
Tell whether the expressions $\dfrac{x}{11}$ and $\dfrac{11}{x}$ are equivalent. *No*

e.
(49)
Translate the word problem below into an equation; then solve.

Today alone, the cafeteria worker has dipped $1\dfrac{3}{5}$ gallons of Jell-O™. If there is still $\dfrac{9}{10}$ of a gallon left in her Jell-O™ tub, how many gallons were in the tub to start with? Write your answer as a fraction.

Problem Set 52

$\dfrac{3}{5} \times 2$ $\dfrac{16}{10} + \dfrac{9}{10} = \dfrac{25}{10}$ = $2\frac{1}{2}$

Tell whether each sentence below is True or False.

1.
(52)
Multiplication is written differently in algebra than it is in basic math. ✓

2.
(52)
Division is written differently in algebra than it is in basic math. ✓

Complete each sentence below with the best of the choices given.

3.
(38)
1,000 meters equals 1 _____ .

    A. kilometer   B. hectometer   C. dekameter

    D. meter   E. decimeter

4.
(34) 1 yard equals 36 _____ .

    A. miles   B. feet   C. inches

    D. decimeters   E. centimeters

Add or subtract each group of numbers below.

5.
(2)
$$\begin{array}{r} 8,467 \\ +4,320 \\ \hline \end{array}$$
12787

6.
(17)
$$\begin{array}{r} 2.875 \\ -1.309 \\ \hline \end{array}$$
4184

Add or subtract each pair of fractions below. Make sure your answers are fully reduced.

7.
(10) $\dfrac{12}{18} + \dfrac{3}{18}$ = $\dfrac{15}{18}$ = $\dfrac{5}{6}$

8.
(10) $\dfrac{2}{3} - \dfrac{1}{7}$ = $\dfrac{14}{21} - \dfrac{3}{21}$ = $\dfrac{11}{21}$

Convert each percent below into decimal form.

9.
(25) 78%   0.7 6

10.
(26) 103.75%   .0375

Answer each question below.

(a) 11.
(52) Write "x times 8" the algebra way. Select the best possible choice.

    A. $x \times 8$ B. $8(x)$ C. $x8$

    D. $\dfrac{x}{8}$ (E. $8x$)

(b) 12.
(52) Write "x divided by 2" the algebra way. Select the best possible choice.

    (A. $\dfrac{x}{2}$)   B. $x \div 2$ C. $\dfrac{2}{x}$

    D. $x2$ E. $2x$

Do each unit conversion below.

(c) 13.
(42) Convert 4 square meters to square decimeters.

14.
(34) How many yards are in 720 inches?

Answer each question below.

15.
(49)
What must be done to the expression $x + \dfrac{1}{3}$ to make it equal x?

    A. Subtract $\dfrac{1}{3}$ B. Add $\dfrac{1}{3}$ C. Multiply by $\dfrac{1}{3}$

    D. Subtract x E. Divide by $\dfrac{1}{3}$

16.
(50)
What must be done to the expression $\dfrac{x}{4.5}$ to make it equal x?

    A. Multiply by x B. Add 4.5   C. Multiply by 4.5

    D. Subtract 4.5   E. Divide by 4.5

Tell whether each pair of expressions below is equivalent.

(d) 17.
(52)
$\dfrac{x}{12}$ and $\dfrac{12}{x}$ **18.**
(52)
    $x29$ and $29x$

Solve each equation below by undoing. Make sure your answer is fully reduced.

19.
(51)
  $0.8 + x = 1.5$ **20.**
(49)
  $x - \dfrac{1}{9} = \dfrac{2}{3}$ **21.**
(49)
  $x - 2{,}500 = 1{,}760$

Translate the word problem below into an equation; then solve.

(e) 22.
(49)
Yesterday, the cafeteria worker dipped $1\dfrac{1}{4}$ gallons of potato salad. If she had $\dfrac{1}{2}$ of a gallon left, how many gallons did she start with? Write your answer as a fraction.

Lesson 53—Undoing the Algebra Way

What happens when we try to solve equations written in the new algebra style? Here's an example.

$$11x = 44$$

Undoing Multiplication

The 11 and x are pushed together, so this means 11 times x equals 44. To solve the equation we need to undo the multiplication by 11. As you know, that's done by dividing both sides by 11. But since division is shown with a fraction bar in algebra, we have to write the undoing step like this.

$$\frac{11x}{11} = \frac{44}{11}$$

Even though this may look funny, the left side is still saying that x is multiplied by 11 and then the result is divided by 11. So the left side is still equal to just x.

$$x = \frac{44}{11}$$

Now we've turned the equation into an arithmetic problem. The last step is to divide 44 by 11 to get 4.

$$x = 4$$

Here's an example of an equation where x is multiplied by a fraction.

$$\frac{1}{3}x = 24$$

How can we show the undoing step on this one? It's pretty simple, really. We just draw a fraction bar underneath everything on each side and divide by $\frac{1}{3}$.

$$\frac{\frac{1}{3}x}{\frac{1}{3}} = \frac{24}{\frac{1}{3}}$$

On the left side, x is multiplied by $\frac{1}{3}$ and then this result is divided by $\frac{1}{3}$. That makes that side equal just x.

$$x = \frac{24}{\frac{1}{3}}$$

Now, to get the answer, we still need to do the division on the right. To divide 24 by $\frac{1}{3}$, we invert the bottom fraction and multiply. Also, remember that the multiplication can be written with parentheses or with a dot. Here are both methods.

$$x = (24)\left(\frac{3}{1}\right) \quad \text{or} \quad x = 24 \cdot \frac{3}{1}$$

The answer is 72.

$$x = 72$$

What about Division?

Let's do one where the x is divided by a number.

$$\frac{x}{8} = 17$$

There's nothing too complicated here. To undo the division, we multiply both sides by 8. Either the dot or parentheses can be used. (Putting $\frac{x}{8}$ and 8 right next to each other without a dot or parentheses is not allowed, because it might look like x divided by 88.)

$$\frac{x}{8} \cdot 8 = 17 \cdot 8 \quad \text{or} \quad \left(\frac{x}{8}\right)(8) = (17)(8)$$

Since we can multiply two numbers in any order, we also could have put the 8s on the left side like this.

$$8 \cdot \frac{x}{8} = 8 \cdot 17 \quad \text{or} \quad (8)\left(\frac{x}{8}\right) = (8)(17)$$

And since multiplication undoes division, we end up with the following.

$$x = 8 \cdot 17 \quad \text{or if you prefer} \quad x = (8)(17)$$

The solution is 136.

$$x = 136$$

A Messy One

Equations where x is divided by a fraction are handled in the same way. Take this example.

$$\frac{x}{\frac{2}{3}} = 9$$

We undo by multiplying both sides by $\frac{2}{3}$.

$$\frac{x}{\frac{2}{3}} \cdot \frac{2}{3} = 9 \cdot \frac{2}{3}$$

(We could have done this step with parentheses just as easily.)

The multiplication by $\frac{2}{3}$ undoes the division by $\frac{2}{3}$, leaving x by itself on the left.

$$x = 9 \cdot \frac{2}{3}$$

Carrying out the multiplication gives us 6.

$$x = 6$$

Practice 53

a.
(52)   Write "3 times 5" the algebra way. Select the best possible choice.

     A. 3(5)   B. (3)(5)   C. (3)5

     D. $3 \cdot 5$ E. All of the above

b.
(53)   Solve the equation $12x = 180$.

c.
(53)   Solve the equation $\frac{x}{9} = 5.4$.

d.
(53)   Solve the equation $\frac{x}{\frac{2}{5}} = 20$.

e.
(53)   Translate the word problem below into an equation; then solve.

The largest elephants weigh 30.25 times as much as the largest gorillas, so if the largest elephants weigh 14,520 pounds, how much do the largest gorillas weigh?

Problem Set 53

Tell whether each sentence below is True or False.

1.
(53) To undo $3x = 12$ the algebra way, you write $3x \div 3 = 12 \div 3$.

2.
(53) To undo $\dfrac{x}{5} = 16$ the algebra way, you write $\dfrac{x}{5} \cdot 5 = 16 \cdot 5$.

Complete each sentence below with the best of the choices given.

3.
(45) 2 pints equal 1 _____ .

    A. gallon   B. quart   C. fluid ounce
    D. cubic inch   E. liter

4.
(34) 1,760 yards equals 1 _____ .

    A. mile   B. foot   C. inch
    D. kilometer   E. hectometer

Multiply or divide each pair of numbers below. Write any remainders in decimal form.

5.
(20)
$$\begin{array}{r} 0.64 \\ \times 0.23 \\ \hline \end{array}$$

6.
(24) $9\overline{)2{,}856}$

Add or subtract each pair of numbers below. Make sure your answers are fully reduced.

7.
(12) $14 + \dfrac{8}{5}$

8.
(12) $9 - 7\dfrac{3}{4}$

Convert each fraction below into decimal form. Give exact answers (no rounding).

9.
(23) $\dfrac{7}{5}$

10.
(24) $\dfrac{1}{11}$

Do each unit conversion below.

11.
(38) How many centimeters are in 9 meters?

12.
(34) Convert 3,520 yards into miles.

Answer each question below.

(a) 13.
(52)
Write "2 times 6" the algebra way. Select the best possible choice.

    A. (2)6   B. 2(6)   C. $2 \cdot 6$

    D. (2)(6)   E. All of the above

14.
(49)
What must be done to the expression $x - \dfrac{4}{9}$ to make it equal x?

    A. Divide by $\dfrac{4}{9}$ B. Add $\dfrac{4}{9}$ C. Subtract x

    D. Multiply by $\dfrac{4}{9}$ E. Subtract $\dfrac{4}{9}$

15.
(50)
What must be done to the expression $1{,}250x$ to make it equal x?

    A. Add 1,250   B. Divide by x C. Subtract 1,250

    D. Multiply by 1,250   E. Divide by 1,250

Solve each equation below by undoing. Make sure your answer is fully reduced.

(b) 16.
(53)
$13x = 156$

(c) 17.
(53)
$\dfrac{x}{6} = 7.5$

18.
(51)
$\dfrac{1}{8} + x = \dfrac{1}{2}$

19.
(53)
$\dfrac{1}{5}x = \dfrac{3}{10}$

(d) 20.
(53)
$\dfrac{x}{\frac{3}{4}} = 24$

Translate the word problem below into an equation; then solve.

(e) 21.
(53)
The longest tapeworms in the world are actually 1.65 times as long as the tallest giraffes. If the longest tapeworms measure 33 feet, how many feet tall are the tallest giraffes?

Lesson 54—Solving Percent Problems with Algebra

You already know how to find the percent of a number—we've been doing that for awhile. Take this problem, for example: What is 45% of 28? All we have to do is multiply 0.45 (which is 45% written as a decimal) and 28 to get 12.6.

Finding the Missing Number

But what if the question were asked backwards? What if it were "12.6 is 45% of what number?" Of course, we know the answer is 28, but it would be pretty hard to figure out if you didn't know that in advance. It turns out the easiest way to find the answer to a backwards percent problem is to use an algebra equation. Let's start by letting x represent the missing number.

$$x = \text{missing number}$$

Then since 45% of x equals 12.6, our equation needs to be

$$0.45x = 12.6$$

This equation makes perfect sense when you think about it. We know that there is a missing number, and that 45% of it equals 12.6. If that's true, then when we multiply the missing number by 0.45, shouldn't we get 12.6? Yes. And that's exactly what this equation does.

Solving the equation from here is easy. We just have to undo the multiplication by dividing both sides by 0.45.

$$\frac{0.45x}{0.45} = \frac{12.6}{0.45}$$

On the left we have x multiplied by 0.45 and then divided by 0.45, so that side becomes just x.

$$x = \frac{12.6}{0.45}$$

That's turned our algebra equation into a simple arithmetic problem, and now we can do the calculation on the right side to get the answer.

$$x = 28$$

Do you see the advantage of algebra? This example makes it clear. If we hadn't written an algebra equation, you probably wouldn't have known how to solve the problem because it was a pretty hard one. But by using our knowledge about how to find the percent of a number, we were able to set up an equation and get the answer just by undoing with division. We didn't have to know anything else.

Finding the Missing Percent

Let's try another example with percents.

What percent of 70 is 14?

We've done problems like this before. Do you remember how they work? We use division. The "of" number (70 in this case) goes on bottom and the "is" number (14) goes on top. That gives us this.

$$\frac{14}{70} = 0.2$$

We end up with 0.2. The last step is to change the decimal to a percent by moving the decimal two places to the right and putting the percent symbol back in.

$$\frac{14}{70} = 0.2 = 20\%$$

So the answer is 20%.

That's the way we learned to solve the problem with arithmetic. But this problem can also be solved with an algebra equation. Since we're looking for the missing percent, we'll let that be x.

$$x = \text{missing percent}$$

We know that the percent of a number can be found by multiplication, so since some % of 70 is 14, x times 70 should equal 14. When we write that out in an equation it looks like this.

$$x70 = 14$$

But since the number should always be to the left of the x, let's change $x70$ to $70x$.

$$70x = 14$$

From here all we have to do is solve normally. We undo the multiplication by dividing both sides by 70.

$$\frac{70x}{70} = \frac{14}{70}$$

On the left, x is multiplied by 70 and then divided by 70. That leaves just x (since the division undoes the multiplication).

$$x = \frac{14}{70}$$

Does this look familiar? It's the same calculation we got before when we solved the problem the arithmetic way. But this time we didn't have to remember to divide, or that the "of" number goes on bottom and the "is" number on top. All we had to know was the basic rule about multiplying to find a percent of a number. To finish solving our equation, we divide 14 by 70 on the right.

$$x = 0.2$$

Finally, we change the decimal back to a percent to get the answer.

$$x = 0.2 = 20\%$$

But that raises an important point. Whenever percents are put in equations, they're always in decimal form. That means we have to change them back to a percent after we have the answer. Once you get used to using equations, you'll probably think percent problems are easier to solve with algebra than they are with arithmetic, because you don't have to remember as much. And the harder the problem, the better it is to use algebra.

Practice 54

a.
(42)   How many square meters are in 350 square centimeters?

b.
(46)   Convert 2.6 liters to milliliters.

c.
(53)   Solve the equation $\frac{5}{4}x = \frac{1}{8}$. Make sure your answer is fully reduced.

d.
(53)   Solve the equation $\frac{x}{\frac{3}{2}} = \frac{4}{9}$. Make sure your answer is fully reduced.

e.
(54)   Translate the word problem below into an equation; then solve.

Harold paid 5% in sales tax on his new "smart fabric" warm-ups. (Smart fabrics can, for example, be made of threads that automatically tighten to block a cold breeze or loosen to release body heat.) If Harold paid \$37.25 in sales tax on the warm-ups, what was their pre-tax price?

Problem Set 54

Complete each sentence below with the best of the choices given.

1.
(42)   1 square kilometer equals 100 _____ .

   A. square hectometers   B. square dekameters   C. square meters
   D. square decimeters   E. square centimeters

2.
(41)   1 square yard equals 9 _____ .

   A. square miles   B. square feet   C. square inches
   D. square kilometers   E. square meters

Add or subtract each group of numbers below.

3.
(17)

```
   36.0
   67.5
 +90.2
```

4.
(17)

```
   98.5
 −79.1
```

Add or subtract each pair of fractions below. Make sure your answers are fully reduced.

5.
(10) $\frac{5}{6} + \frac{3}{6}$

6.
(11) $\frac{4}{7} - \frac{1}{2}$

Convert each percent below into decimal form.

7. $12\frac{1}{4}\%$
(28)

8. 150%
(26)

Do each unit conversion below.

(a) 9. How many square meters are in 280 square centimeters?
(42)

(b) 10. Convert 1.2 liters to milliliters.
(46)

Answer each question below.

11. Write "x times 15" the algebra way. Select the best possible choice.
(53)

    A. $\dfrac{15}{x}$ B. $x\times15$ C. $15x$

    D. $x15$ E. $x(15)$

12. Write "x divided by 3" the algebra way. Select the best possible choice.
(53)

    A. $\dfrac{x}{3}$ B. $x(3)$ C. $\dfrac{3}{x}$

    D. $3x$ E. $x\div3$

Tell whether each pair of expressions below is equivalent.

13. $x+\dfrac{4}{7}$ and $\dfrac{4}{7}+x$
(51)

14. $x0.03$ and $0.03x$
(51)

Solve each equation below by undoing. Make sure your answer is fully reduced.

15. $x-3.5=18.7$
(53)

16. $52x=676$
(53)

17. $\dfrac{x}{21}=0.5$
(53)

18. $x+\dfrac{2}{3}=\dfrac{4}{3}$
(53)

(c) 19. $\dfrac{6}{5}x=\dfrac{1}{10}$
(53)

(d) 20. $\dfrac{x}{\frac{4}{3}}=\dfrac{7}{8}$
(53)

Translate the word problem below into an equation; then solve.

(e) 21. Molly paid 8% in sales tax on her holophone, a phone that shows the person you're talking to in 3-D. If
(54) Molly paid $416 in sales tax on the phone, what was its pre-tax price?

246

Lesson 55—Solving Distance Problems with Algebra

In the last lesson, we learned how to handle percent problems using algebra. Now we're going to tackle distance problems with algebra. Distance problems are very common, and they always involve speed. People talk about speeds in daily life all the time. They say things like, "I was driving about 50 mph down the road when my tire blew out," or "That bicycle can go 50 mph!"

But what does "50 miles per hour" really mean? It just means that a car (or bicycle, or anything else) which travels that fast for 1 hour will go a total distance of 50 miles. After 2 hours, it will go a total distance of 100 miles. After 3 hours it will go a total distance of 150 miles, and so on. The word "per" means "each", so when we say "50 miles per hour," we really mean "50 miles each hour."

Finding the Distance

Once you understand the meaning of "miles per hour," it's easy to solve distance problems. Let's start with a really simple one.

How far will a car traveling 60 mph go in 3 hours?

All we have to do is multiply the speed by the time to get the distance: $(60)(3) = 180$. And that makes sense when you think about it. If a car covers 60 miles *each* hour, and it goes for 3 hours, then it will go a total of 60 times 3 or 180 miles. So 180 miles is our answer. And all we needed to do was multiply the speed and time to get the distance. That's an important rule, so remember it!

$$\text{speed} \times \text{time} = \text{distance}$$

This rule always works no matter how fast the car is moving. So we can use it to solve just about any distance problem we come across.

Finding the Time

What if we know the speed and the total distance, but don't know the time? Here's an example like that.

A car drove 50 mph to Pleasantville, which is 450 miles away. How long did the trip take?

We know the speed (50 miles per hour) and we know the distance (450 miles), but we don't know how long it took. This is easy enough to solve using arithmetic, but it's even easier with an algebra equation. All we need to set up the equation is the fact that speed multiplied by time equals distance. Since we're trying to find the time, we'll let that equal x.

$$x = \text{number of hours of trip}$$

Next, we just multiply the speed (50 mph) by the time (x), to equal the distance (450 miles). We put the 50 and the x right beside each other to show that they're multiplied and set that equal to the distance, 450.

$$50x = 450$$

To solve we just undo the multiplication by dividing both sides by 50.

$$\frac{50x}{50} = \frac{450}{50}$$

247

On the left, x is multiplied by 50 and then divided by 50. Since division undoes multiplication we're left with just x on that side.

$$x = \frac{450}{50}$$

Once again we've turned the algebra equation into a simple arithmetic problem. From here, all we have to do is divide 450 by 50 to get an answer of 9.

$$x = 9$$

Since x represents the number of hours, it must have taken 9 hours to get to Pleasantville. The important thing to notice, though, is that even simple problems can be made easier with algebra. We could have solved this problem with arithmetic, but it would have been harder. We would have had to figure out whether to divide or multiply. If we had decided to divide, we would have then had to figure out whether to divide 450 by 50, or 50 by 450. With algebra, all we need to know is that speed multiplied by time equals distance. Then we can make x equal the thing we're trying to find and set up the equation. Solving the equation is easy, because we can just undo it.

Finding the Speed

We can also use algebra to solve problems where we know the distance and the time but not the speed. Here's an example of a problem like that.

> If you ride a bicycle for 3 hours and go a total of 54 miles, what was your speed?

To use algebra on this one, all we need to know is that speed multiplied by time equals distance. Since we're looking for speed, we make x equal that.

$$x = \text{speed}$$

Now we multiply speed (x) by time (3) and set that equal to the distance (54) to get the following equation.

$$x3 = 54$$

Since the number should always be in front of the x, we should rewrite the left side, like this.

$$3x = 54$$

To solve, we just undo the multiplication by dividing both sides by 3.

$$\frac{3x}{3} = \frac{54}{3}$$

The left side becomes just x.

$$x = \frac{54}{3}$$

That turned our equation into an arithmetic problem. From here, we can find the answer by dividing 54 by 3 to get 18.

$$x = 18$$

Your speed on the bicycle must have been 18 miles per hour. The main thing to remember is that algebra makes it easier to solve distance problems whether we're looking for the speed, the time, or the distance. All we have to know to set up the equation is that speed × time = distance.

Practice 55

a.
(42)   Convert 32 square meters to square decimeters.

b.
(55)   How far will a cyclist riding at 30 miles per hour travel in 2 hours?

c.
(55)   How far will a race car going 120 miles per hour travel in 3 hours?

d.
(53)   Solve the equation $\dfrac{6}{7}x = \dfrac{3}{14}$. Make sure your answer is fully reduced.

e.
(55)   Translate the word problem below into an equation; then solve.

The fastest that anyone has ever ridden a motorcycle is 322 miles per hour. At this speed, how many hours would it take to travel 2,576 miles?

Problem Set 55

Tell whether each sentence below is True or False.

1.
(55)   A car that is going "50 miles per hour" will travel 50 miles each hour.

2.
(55)   Speed multiplied by time equals the total distance traveled.

Complete each sentence below with the best of the choices given.

3.
(38)   1 kilometer equals 10,000 _____ .

    A. hectometers   B. dekameters   C. meters
    D. decimeters   E. centimeters

4.
(34)   1 mile equals 5,280 _____ .

    A. yards   B. feet   C. inches
    D. kilometers   E. meters

Multiply or divide each pair of numbers below. Write any remainders in decimal form.

5.
(20)
$$\begin{array}{r} 29.5 \\ \times 3.4 \\ \hline \end{array}$$

6.
(24) $1.2\overline{)8,530}$

Add or subtract each pair of fractions below. Make sure your answers are fully reduced.

7.
(11) $\dfrac{5}{6} + \dfrac{1}{4}$

8.
(11) $\dfrac{5}{7} - \dfrac{1}{2}$

Convert each fraction below into decimal form. Give exact answers (no rounding).

9.
(23) $\dfrac{1}{4}$

10.
(24) $\dfrac{2}{15}$

Do each unit conversion below.

11.
(33) How many yards are in 39 feet?

(a) 12.
(42) Convert 42 square meters to square decimeters.

Answer each question below.

13.
(53) Write "x times $\dfrac{1}{3}$" the algebra way. Select the best possible choice.

    A. $\dfrac{1}{3}x$ B. $x \times \dfrac{1}{3}$ C. $x\dfrac{1}{3}$

    D. $x\left(\dfrac{1}{3}\right)$ E. $\dfrac{1}{3}+x$

14.
(53) Write "x divided by 7" the algebra way. Select the best possible choice.

    A. $x7$ B. $x \div 7$ C. $7x$

    D. $\dfrac{7}{x}$ E. $\dfrac{x}{7}$

15.
(53) What must be done to the expression $\dfrac{x}{24}$ to make it equal x?

    A. Add 24   B. Multiply by 24   C. Subtract 24
    D. Multiply by x E. Divide by 24

(b) 16.
(55) How far will a cyclist riding at 40 miles per hour travel in 2 hours?

(c) 17.
(55) How far will a race car going 110 miles per hour travel in 3 hours?

Solve each equation below by undoing. Make sure your answer is fully reduced.

18.
(53) $48x = 672$

19.
(53) $\dfrac{x}{18} = 11$

(d) 20.
(53) $\dfrac{3}{7}x = \dfrac{5}{14}$

Translate the word problem below into an equation; then solve.

(e) 21.
(55) The fastest that anyone has ever driven a vehicle on land is 763 mph. At this speed, how many hours would it take to drive 24,416 miles, which is just about equal to the distance around the earth at the equator?

CHAPTER 8:
INTEGERS

Lesson 56—Less Than Zero

We've learned how to solve any equation with an x and a number added, subtracted, multiplied, or divided. But now take a look at this equation.

$$x + 10 = 5$$

It *seems* pretty simple. The first solving step is easy. We just undo the addition of 10 by subtracting 10 from both sides.

$$x + 10 - 10 = 5 - 10$$

Then the subtraction undoes the addition on the left side, leaving x.

$$x = 5 - 10$$

And that turns the algebra equation into a simple arithmetic problem. From here all we have to do is calculate the right side: 5 minus 10.

"Less than Zero" Numbers

But what's 5 minus 10? That doesn't make much sense. How can we take away 10 apples from 5 apples or 10 from 5 of any other object? For a long time, mathematicians naturally assumed that it wasn't possible to subtract 10 from 5, and that equations like $x + 10 = 5$ just didn't have solutions. Then one day a brilliant mathematician came up with a bright idea. He invented a new category of numbers that could be solutions to equations like $x + 10 = 5$. You might call them "less than zero numbers." Here's how they work. To calculate $5 - 10$ we first take away 5, and that gets us down to zero. But we're supposed to take away 10, not 5. So, for the next step, we just keep going and take away the other 5, which gives an answer of "5 less than zero."

$$5 - 10 = 5 \text{ less than zero}$$

The great thing about less than zero numbers is that they allow us to subtract any larger number from any smaller number. Let's try another example.

$$3 - 6$$

First we take away 3, which gets us to zero; then we keep going and take away the other 3 to get "3 less than zero." So the answer to $3 - 6$ is "3 less than zero." We can do this no matter what numbers are involved. As long as the number we're subtracting is larger, we will end up with a less than zero number for the answer. Obviously, less than zero numbers can be solutions to any equation that requires us to subtract a larger number from a smaller number.

Negative and Positive Numbers

You probably have heard of less than zero numbers before. They're actually called **negative numbers**, and instead of writing the words "less than zero" beside them, we use a little minus sign. So "5 less than zero" is actually called "negative 5." Written with the little minus sign, it looks like this: -5.

$$5 \text{ less than zero} = -5$$

Since this is a negative number, the little minus sign is actually called a "negative sign". From now on, the ordinary numbers that you've always used will be called **positive numbers**, just to avoid confusion. The only exception is zero, which isn't positive or negative.

When negatives are mixed together with positive (ordinary) numbers, a plus sign (or positive sign) is sometimes used in front of the positive numbers. So 2 can be written as +2. But since positives are used so much more often than negatives, the plus sign is usually left off. That means a number without a sign is assumed to be positive. If we see the number "2," we know it means positive 2, not negative 2. So if we want to use a negative number, we have to include the negative sign or it will be assumed to be positive. Now that we have *both* positive numbers (the numbers we've been using all along) and negative numbers, we really can solve any equation with an x and a number added, subtracted, multiplied, or divided.

Practice 56

a.
(45)
Convert 10 gallons to quarts.

b.
(33)
How many miles are in 10,560 yards?

c.
(51)
Tell whether the expressions $x \div \dfrac{1}{5}$ and $\dfrac{1}{5} \div x$ are equivalent.

d.
(56)
Write the answer to $3 - 8$ as a negative number.

e.
(54)
Translate the word problem below into an equation; then solve.

Jenkins bought some driving moccasins at a 25% discount. If the discount saved him $17.50, what was the moccasins original price?

Problem Set 56

Tell whether each sentence below is True or False.

1.
(56)
Numbers that are less than zero are called negative numbers.

2.
(56)
The ordinary numbers that you learned about in arithmetic, which are greater than zero, are called positive numbers.

Add or subtract each group of numbers below.

3.
(18)
$$\begin{array}{r} 8.9 \\ 12.8 \\ +1.76 \\ \hline \end{array}$$

4.
(17)
$$\begin{array}{r} 300.5 \\ -231.8 \\ \hline \end{array}$$

Multiply or divide each pair of fractions below. Make sure your answers are fully reduced.

5.
(13)
$\dfrac{5}{2} \times \dfrac{2}{7}$

6.
(13)
$\dfrac{4}{9} \div \dfrac{16}{3}$

Do each unit conversion below.

(a) 7. Convert 12 gallons to quarts.
(45)

(b) 8. How many miles are in 8,800 yards?
(33)

Tell whether each pair of expressions below is equivalent.

9. $x - \dfrac{3}{5}$ and $\dfrac{3}{5} - x$
(51)

(c) 10. $x \div \dfrac{1}{9}$ and $\dfrac{1}{9} \div x$
(51)

Answer each question below.

11. What must be done to the expression $x + 158$ to make it equal x?
(53)

A. Add 158   B. Multiply by 158   C. Subtract 158
D. Subtract x E. Divide by 158

12. How far will a go cart moving at 30 miles per hour travel in 3 hours?
(55)

13. How far will an exercise fanatic walking at 5 miles per hour travel in 4 hours?
(55)

Write the answer to each problem below as a negative number.

(d) 14. $4 - 7$
(56)

15. $1 - 9$
(56)

16. $3 - 15$
(56)

Solve each equation below by undoing. Make sure your answer is fully reduced.

17. $\dfrac{2}{5} + x = 1$
(53)

18. $x - 14.2 = 36.8$
(53)

19. $\dfrac{1}{3} x = \dfrac{1}{6}$
(53)

20. $\dfrac{x}{\frac{3}{8}} = 24$
(53)

Translate the word problem below into an equation; then solve.

(e) 21. Raquel bought an insanely expensive espresso machine at a 60% discount. If the discount saved her
(54) $270, what was the machine's original price?

Lesson 57—The Number Line

One way to picture the negative numbers that we learned about in the last lesson is with a number line. The number line is just a simple line with numbers on it.

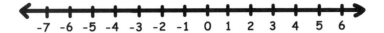

Notice that the positive numbers are on the right side and the negative numbers are on the left. Zero is right in the middle. The arrows on either end show that the number line goes on forever in both directions. Of course, we only use the arrows because there's not enough space on the page to keep going on and on. And we really would have to go on forever in both directions, because there are an infinite number of positive numbers and an infinite number of negative numbers. We could keep going to the left, beyond −7 to −8, −9, and so on, all the way up to −28,000,000 if we wanted (or even higher)!

You probably know that we show a number on the number line with a dot. (Technically, it's called a point.) For example, we can show the number −2 like this.

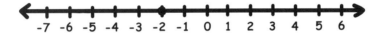

Which Negative is Greater?

The number line is really helpful for figuring out which of two negative numbers is greater. That can be confusing sometimes. For instance, which is greater, −2 or −7? At first, you might think it's −7 (since you're used to thinking that 7 is greater than 2) but it's not. Actually, −2 is greater because it's not as much "less than zero" as −7. But it's much easier to figure out which is greater when we put both numbers on the number line (using points).

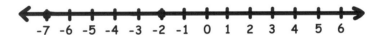

The greater number is always the one that's farther to the right on the number line. So since −2 is to the right of −7, we know that −2 has to be the greater number. This works because on the number line, the numbers always get larger as we move to the right and smaller as we move to the left. The positive numbers increase as they get farther and farther from zero, and the negative numbers increase as they get closer and closer to zero.

Negative Fractions and Decimals

So far we've only talked about negative whole numbers like −1, −2, −3, and so on. But there are also negative fractions and decimals, like $-\frac{1}{4}$, $-\frac{5}{8}$, $-7\frac{1}{2}$, −2.5, and −0.4.[1] The negative fractions and decimals haven't been labeled on any of our number lines, but they're still there. We just didn't have enough room to put them in. Negative fractions and decimals lie in between the negative whole numbers. For example, the decimal −2.5 is between −2 and −3, and the fraction $-\frac{1}{4}$ is between 0 and −1.

---

[1] As we mentioned earlier in the course, fractions and also decimals are called rational numbers. That's their technical name.

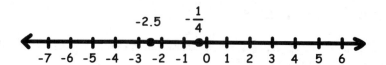

Positive fractions and decimals are also on the number line. The decimal 4.5, for example, is between the 4 and the 5.

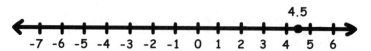

So the number line has positive and negative whole numbers, positive and negative fractions and decimals, and zero. There's also an important term that you should be aware of. Positive and negative whole numbers and zero are all called **integers**. People usually only label the integers on the number line because they don't have room for the fractions and decimals.

Opposites

There's something else important that we can see by looking at a number line. It shows us that every number (except 0) has an opposite. An **opposite** is the same number but with an opposite sign. For example, 3 and −3 are opposites; so are 1.4 and −1.4 and $\frac{3}{8}$ and $-\frac{3}{8}$. And the interesting thing about opposites is that they're always the same distance from zero. We can see this if we look at the example of 3 and −3 below.

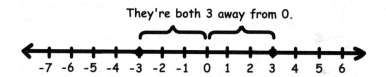

Practice 57

a.
(27) What is 35% of 240?

b.
(55) How far will a mouse running at 6 inches per second travel in 3 seconds?

c.
(57) Find −3.5 on the number line below.

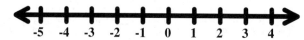

d.
(53) Solve the equation $\frac{2}{9}y = \frac{7}{18}$. Make sure your answer is fully reduced.

e.
(55) Translate the word problem below into an equation; then solve.

If a cyclist is traveling at 20 miles per hour, how many hours will it take him to travel 15 miles? Round your answer to the nearest hundredths place (two decimal places).

Problem Set 57

Tell whether each sentence below is True or False.

1.
(57)
A number line can be used to show both positive and negative numbers.

2.
(57)
The positive whole numbers, negative whole numbers, and zero are together called "integers."

3.
(57)
The opposite of 5 is -5.

Multiply or divide each pair of numbers below. Write any remainders in decimal form.

4.
(3)
$$\begin{array}{r} 295 \\ \times 71 \\ \hline \end{array}$$

5.
(4)
$11\overline{)2,541}$

Add or subtract each pair of fractions below. Make sure your answers are fully reduced.

6.
(10)
$\dfrac{6}{20} + \dfrac{4}{20}$

7.
(11)
$\dfrac{7}{8} - \dfrac{5}{6}$

Answer each question below.

8.
(14)
What is $\dfrac{3}{4}$ of 60?

(a) 9.
(27)
What is 28% of 250?

10.
(55)
How far will a jet flying at 550 miles per hour travel in 6 hours?

(b) 11.
(55)
How far will an unidentified furry object running at 7 inches per second travel in 4 seconds?

Find each number below on a number line.

12.
(57)
-3

(c) 13.
(57)
-4.5

Write the answer to each problem below as a negative number.

14. $2-8$
(56)

15. $5-21$
(56)

16. $3-4$
(56)

Solve each equation below by undoing. Make sure your answer is fully reduced.

17. $x-\dfrac{1}{4}=\dfrac{3}{8}$
(53)

18. $7x=154$
(53)

19. $\dfrac{x}{6.5}=2.3$
(53)

(d) 20. $\dfrac{4}{9}y=\dfrac{5}{27}$
(53)

Translate the word problem below into an equation; then solve.

(e) 21. If a go-cart rider is traveling at 12 miles per hour, how many hours will it take him to travel 3 miles?
(55) Round your answer to the nearest hundredths place (two decimal places).

258

Lesson 58—How Negatives Are Used

We've been focusing a lot on negative numbers, but you may have been wondering whether they have any use in real life? Actually, negative numbers are very practical. If they weren't, they probably would never have become so popular.

In Business

Negatives are used all the time in business. Imagine you're a stock trader and need to keep track of all of your profits and losses. Say you made a $650 profit and a $320 loss. You could just write it down like this.

650 **profit**

320 **loss**

But there's a faster way: make profits be positive and losses negative. Then you just write them with positive and negative signs.

+650

−320

This not only takes up less space on the page, but it makes adding and subtracting the numbers easier too. Adding and subtracting negative numbers is something we'll learn more about in the next lesson.

In Lots of Other Places

Negatives are also used when measuring temperatures. For example, when somebody says "It's −15 degrees Fahrenheit," that just means 15 degrees below zero. A navigator of a ship could also use negative numbers too. He could make distances to the north positive and distances to the south negative. Then it would be easier to calculate the position and direction of the ship. Generally speaking, negative numbers are helpful in any situation that involves two opposite kinds of numbers, like profits and losses, temperatures above zero and below zero, and directions like north and south.

Practice 58

a.
(38)
How many dekameters are in 59,000 centimeters?

b.
(55)
How far could a cheetah running at 60 miles per hour travel in $\frac{1}{2}$ hour?

c.
(58)
Use a positive or negative number to represent this quantity: A loss of 20 yards in football.

d.
(53)
Solve the equation $\dfrac{x}{\frac{5}{8}} = \dfrac{4}{15}$. Make sure your answer is fully reduced.

e.
(54)
Translate the word problem below into an equation; then solve.

Larry sells above ground swimming pools, and he receives a 15% commission on all the pools he sells. If Larry received $9,000 in commissions last year, how many dollars worth of pools did he sell?

Problem Set 58

Tell whether each sentence below is True or False.

1.
(58)   Negative numbers are never used in business.

2.
(58)   Negative numbers are useful in situations involving two opposite kinds of numbers, like north and south.

Add or subtract each group of numbers below.

3.
(2)
$$\begin{array}{r} 55,740 \\ +34,825 \\ \hline \end{array}$$

4.
(2)
$$\begin{array}{r} 7,923 \\ -4,296 \\ \hline \end{array}$$

Multiply or divide each pair of numbers below. Make sure your answers are fully reduced.

5.
(14) $18 \times \dfrac{5}{9}$

6.
(14) $\dfrac{20}{\frac{4}{5}}$

Do each unit conversion below.

7.
(34)   Convert 12 yards to inches.

(a) 8.
(38)   How many dekameters are in 75,000 centimeters?

Answer each question below.

9.
(53)   What must be done to the expression $x - 5,924$ to make it equal x?

   A. Add 5,924   B. Multiply by 5,924   C. Subtract 5,924
   D. Divide by 5,924   E. Subtract x

(b) 10.
(55)   How far will a horse running at 20 miles per hour travel in $\dfrac{1}{2}$ hour?

11.
(55)   How far will a blue shark swimming at 30 miles per hour travel in $1\dfrac{1}{2}$ hours?

Show each number below on a number line.

12.
(57) -5

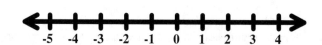

13.
(57) $-\dfrac{1}{2}$

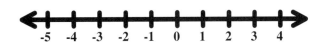

Tell which of each pair of numbers below is greater.

14.   −9 and 6
(57)

15.   −4 and −11
(57)

Use a positive or negative number to represent each quantity below.

(c) 16.   A loss of 12 yards in football.
(58)

17.   A temperature of 17 below zero.
(58)

18.   A $2,000 profit in the stock market.
(58)

Solve each equation below by undoing. Make sure your answer is fully reduced.

19. $\dfrac{2}{5} + x = \dfrac{7}{10}$
(53)

20. $290x = 1,160$
(53)

21. $x - 72.5 = 28.4$
(53)

(d) 22. $\dfrac{x}{\frac{5}{6}} = \dfrac{3}{10}$
(53)

Translate the word problem below into an equation; then solve.

(e) 23.   Larry has decided that the above ground swimming pools business is not the best way to earn a living
(54)   (see practice problem e). He now thinks the big money is in rowing machines. If Larry switches jobs, he
will earn a 12% commission on all the machines he sells. For Larry to receive $15,000 in commissions,
how many dollars worth of machines must he sell?

Lesson 59—Addition with Negatives

Now that we know what negative numbers are and a little bit about how they're used, it's time to talk about how to add, subtract, multiply, and divide them. That's important, because if we can't do that, we won't be able to use negatives to solve practical problems. In this lesson, we'll start with adding negatives.

Adding Losses

Let's say we want to add -2 and -3. We can write it out to get this.

$$-2 + -3$$

The easiest way to do the calculation is to think of the negatives as losses: -2 is like a loss of 2, and -3 is like a loss of 3. If you lose \$2 and then you lose \$3 more, how much have you lost in total? Obviously, you've lost \$5. So a loss of 2 plus a loss of 3 equals a loss of 5, which is another way of saying that $-2 + -3$ is -5.

$$-2 + -3 = -5$$

Another thing to keep in mind is that most people put parentheses around the second negative number.

$$-2 + (-3)$$

The parentheses show that the minus is actually a negative sign attached to the number 3. It you avoid getting the negative sign and the plus sign (right before it) confused. We don't need parentheses around the first number because there's no other symbol in front of the negative sign on -2. Now let's try another example. This time we'll put the parentheses around the second number to show that the minus is actually a negative sign.

$$-8 + (-7)$$

Once again, we just need to think of negatives as losses. If we lose \$8 and then lose another \$7, we've lost \$15 in total. So -8 plus -7 has to equal -15.

$$-8 + (-7) = -15$$

Finally, let's try adding -4 and -5.

$$-4 + (-5)$$

Thinking of the negatives as losses again, we have a loss of 4 added to another loss of 5, which equals a loss of 9. That gives us this.

$$-4 + (-5) = -9$$

Are you starting to get the idea? One negative plus another negative equals an even bigger (in magnitude) negative.

Adding on the Number Line

We can also show addition of negatives on the number line. Let's try this with our first example, $-2 + (-3)$. To show -2 we draw an arrow that starts at 0 and goes two places to the left.

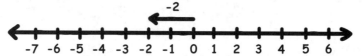

To add −3 we draw another arrow. This one starts where the first arrow ended, and goes three places to the left.

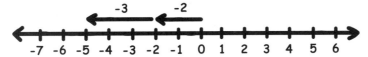

Combining the two, we end up with an arrow to the left that's five places long. That's −5.

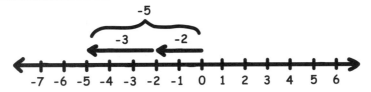

So the answer to $-2 + (-3)$ is −5.

Negative + Positive

We've covered adding a negative to a negative. Now let's add a negative to a positive number. We'll start by adding −3 and +7.

$$-3 + 7$$

Notice that there is no positive sign in front of the 7. Remember we don't have to include a positive sign because everybody assumes a number is positive unless it has a negative sign. But we could have shown the positive sign like this: $-3 + (+7)$. The best way to add a negative and a positive is to think of the negative as a loss (as usual) and the positive as a gain. So $-3 + 7$ is a loss of 3 plus a gain of 7. Now imagine that you lose $3 but then find $7. How much better off are you? You're $4 better off. That means −3 plus +7 has to equal +4 (since a gain is positive).

$$-3 + 7 = 4$$

Here's another example of a negative added to a positive.

$$-11 + 3$$

We should think of this as a loss of 11 added to a gain of 3. If you lose $11 and then gain $3, are you better off or worse off? You're $8 worse off. That's a loss of 8, which is −8.

$$-11 + 3 = -8$$

On the Number Line Again

It's also possible to show a positive added to a negative on a number line. For $-3 + 7$, we just show −3 as an arrow starting at 0 and going three places to the left. (Remember, negatives always have an arrow going to the left.)

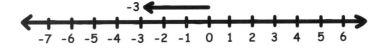

But the next step is a little tricky. Since 7 is positive, its arrow needs to go to the right. So we start the second arrow at the tip of the first arrow, and stretch it seven places to the right.

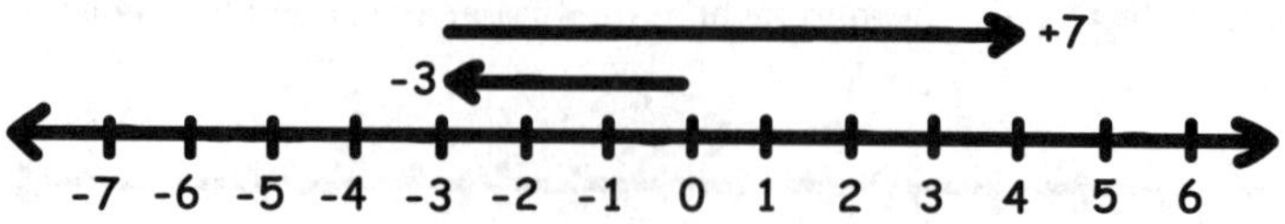

What's our final answer then? Well, we started at 0 and now we find ourselves four places to the right at +4. That means the answer is +4, which is what we got before.

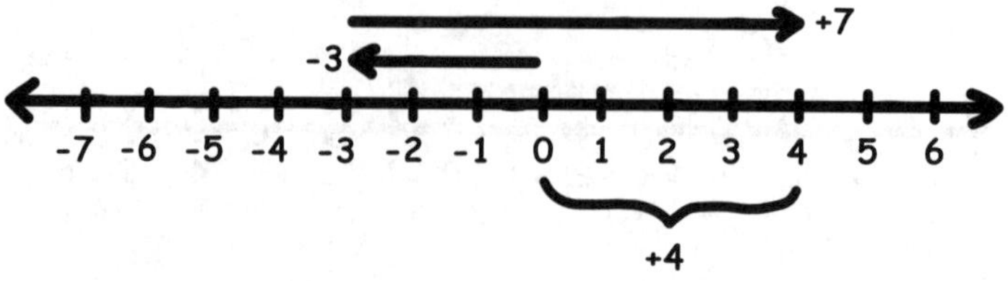

Some people like to use number lines when adding negatives. But you don't have to use them. Just remember to think of negatives as losses and positives as gains and you can usually figure out the answer in your head.

Practice 59

a. (59) Add $-2+(-6)$

b. (59) Add $8+(-3)$

c. (59) Show $-4+(-1)$ on a number line.

A. 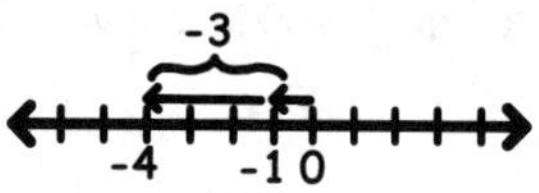

B. 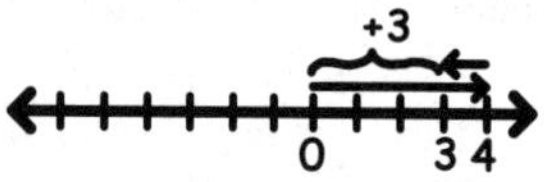

C. 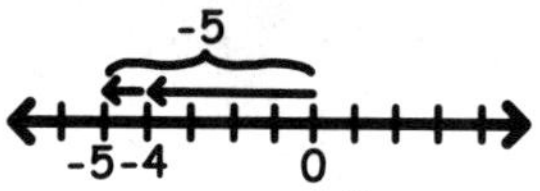

D. 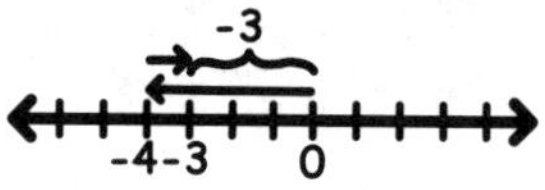

E. 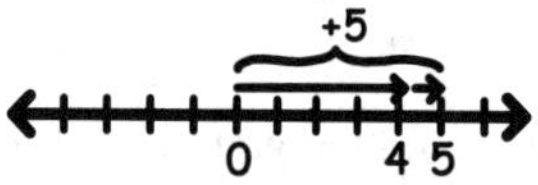

d. (59) Show $4+(-2)$ on a number line.

A. 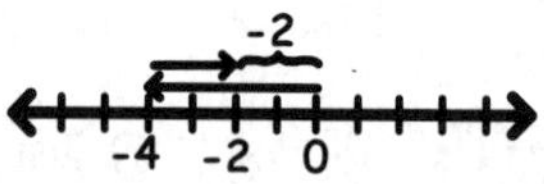

B. 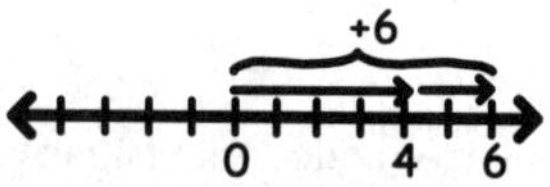

C. 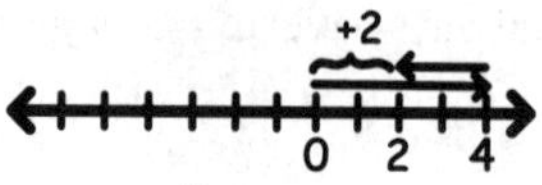

D. 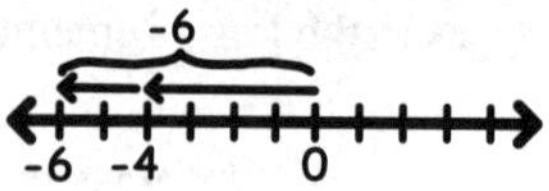

E. 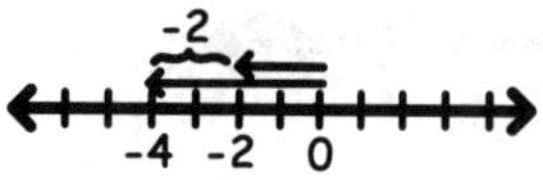

e. Translate the word problem below into an equation; then solve.
(55)

If a bird flew for 2 hours at a constant speed and traveled a distance of 74 miles, what was her speed?

Problem Set 59

Tell whether each sentence below is True or False.

1. When adding a negative number to a negative number, the answer is always negative.
(59)

2. When adding a negative number to a positive number, the answer is always positive.
(59)

Multiply or divide each pair of numbers below. Write any remainders in decimal form.

3.
(20)
$$\begin{array}{r} 0.85 \\ \times 2.1 \\ \hline \end{array}$$

4. $0.14\overline{)9.24}$
(21)

Add or subtract each pair of numbers below. Make sure your answers are fully reduced.

5. $8\frac{2}{9}+2\frac{1}{9}$
(12)

6. $6-4\frac{1}{5}$
(12)

Convert each fraction below into decimal form. Give exact answers (no rounding).

7. $\frac{3}{10}$
(23)

8. $\frac{8}{9}$
(24)

Answer each question below. Write your answer as a whole number or decimal.

9. What is $\frac{2}{7}$ of 112?
(14)

10. What is $14\frac{1}{2}\%$ of 80?
(28)

Use a positive or negative number to represent each quantity below.

11. A gain of 35 yards in football.
(58)

12. 3 miles to the south. (Assume north is positive and south negative.)
(58)

Tell which of each pair of numbers below is *smaller*.

13. −1 and 0
(57)

14. −3.2 and −5.7
(57)

Add each pair of numbers below.

(a) 15. −2 + (−4)
(59)

(b) 16. 9 + (−2)
(59)

17. 5 + (−14)
(59)

Show each addition below on a number line (using arrows).

(c) 18. −3 + (−1)
(59)

A.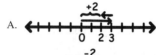

B.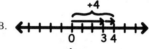

C.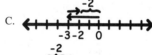

D.

E.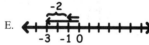

(d) 19. 5 + (−3)
(59)

A.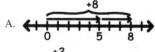

B.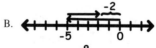

C.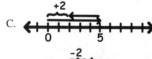

D.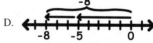

E.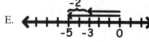

Solve each equation below by undoing.

20. $x + 83 = 95$
(53)

21. $7.5x = 51$
(53)

22. $\dfrac{x}{6.4} = 13$
(53)

Translate the word problem below into an equation; then solve.

(e) 23. If a bird flew for 4 hours at a constant speed and traveled a distance of 76 miles, what was his speed?
(55)

266

Lesson 60—Subtraction with Negatives

In the last lesson, we learned how to add with negatives. But what about subtracting with negatives? How do we do that? Let's look at an example.

$$8 - (-3)$$

First, we'll go through the calculation, and then we'll talk about why it works. It's going to seem pretty strange at first, but just hold on.

Adding the Opposite

Here's what we do. First, we change the subtraction to an addition. So instead of 8 minus something we have 8 plus something. Next, we change -3 (the second number) to its opposite, which is $+3$.

$$8 + (+3)$$

Since we don't have to write the positive sign in front of the 3, we can shorten the expression to this.

$$8 + 3$$

Now all we have to do is add 8 and 3 to get positive 11.

$$8 + 3 = 11$$

So 11 is the answer to our original problem.

$$8 - (-3) = 11$$

This method works every time. To subtract a negative, we change the subtraction to addition. Next, we change the negative number to its opposite. Then, we just add normally.

Let's do another one. We'll do another positive minus a negative.

$$9 - (-5)$$

The process is exactly the same. We change the subtraction to addition; then we change -5 to its opposite, $+5$.

$$9 + 5$$

Now we add to get 14.

$$9 + 5 = 14$$

So $9 - (-5)$ equals 14.

When the First Number Is Negative

It turns out that our method also works when the first number is negative. Let's try one like that.

$$-7 - (-2)$$

Again, we change subtraction to addition and then change the second number, -2, to its opposite, $+2$.

$$-7+2$$

Now, as always, we add normally. Remember from the last lesson that to add a negative and a positive, we should think of the negative as a loss and the positive as a gain. So in this example we have a loss of 7 added to a gain of 2. That equals a loss of 5, which is -5.

$$-7+2=-5$$

It Works with Positives Too

We can even use our new method to subtract positive numbers. Look at this example.

$$12-8$$

The answer is 4, of course, because all we have to do is subtract the numbers as they are. But what if we wanted to get fancy? We could change subtraction to addition and then change $+8$ to its opposite, which is -8.

$$12+(-8)$$

Next, we just add: a gain of 12 added to a loss of 8 equals a gain of 4. Our answer, then, is $+4$, which is right!

$$12+(-8)=4$$

We would never want to use this method on such a simple problem. The only time it makes sense to change a subtraction to an addition of the opposite is when negative numbers are involved. But to review, the basic rule is that we change subtraction to addition, and then change the second number—the one that was being subtracted—to its opposite. If the second number is negative, change it to a positive, and if the second number is positive, change it to a negative.

Taking Away a Loss

Now let's talk about why this rule works. Adding a negative is like adding a loss, remember. So subtracting a negative should be the same as subtracting or taking away a loss. But if a loss is taken away, are you worse off or better off? If you had a loss of $5, but then that loss was eliminated, you're better off. You got your $5 back. It's as if you owed a friend some money and then he said "Don't worry about it. You don't have to pay me back." That would make you better off. So subtracting, or taking away, a loss (a negative) is the same as adding a gain (a positive). And that's why we can subtract a negative by adding the opposite, which is a positive. And that's the easiest way to subtract with negatives. So any time you have to do a subtraction which involves negative numbers, immediately change the subtraction to addition of the opposite of the second number. And it may seem weird at first, but after some practice it will start to sink in.

Practice 60

    a.   How many miles are in 18,480 feet?
(34)

    b.   Tell which of the following numbers is greater: $-\dfrac{1}{5}$ and $-\dfrac{1}{2}$.
(57)

    c.   Subtract $-3-(-4)$ **d.**   Subtract $-6-17$
(60)   (60)

e. Translate the word problem below into an equation; then solve.
(29)

Mr. and Mrs. Simmons are trying to save enough money to buy a Steinway™ grand piano. They have already saved $15,000 but that is nowhere close to enough. If their $15,000 in savings is sitting in a bank account that pays 6% in yearly interest.

i.) How much will Mr. and Mrs. Simmons have earned in interest one year from now?

ii.) If they leave their money *and* interest in the bank for another year, how much interest will they earn for the 2nd year?

Problem Set 60

Tell whether each sentence below is True or False.

1. $10 - (-4)$ is the same as $10 + 4$.
(60)

2. The way we subtract negative numbers is to change the subtraction to an addition.
(60)

Add or subtract each group of numbers below.

3.   25.31
(18)   +9.248

4.   21.7
(18)   −13.54

Multiply or divide each pair of fractions below. Make sure your answers are fully reduced.

5. $\dfrac{5}{2} \cdot \dfrac{4}{25}$
(13)

6. $\dfrac{\frac{1}{12}}{\frac{2}{3}}$
(13)

269

Do each unit conversion below.

7. Convert 5.4 meters to millimeters.
(38)

(a) 8. How many miles are in 13,200 feet?
(34)

Answer each question below.

9. How far will a speed boat going 64 miles per hour travel in $2\frac{1}{2}$ hours?
(55)

10. How far will a spider crawling at 2 inches per second travel in 25 seconds?
(55)

Tell which of each pair of numbers below is greater.

11. 3 and −4
(57)

(b) 12. $-\frac{1}{4}$ and $-\frac{1}{2}$
(57)

Add each pair of numbers below.

13. −7 + (−4)
(59)

14. 6 + (−13)
(59)

15. −3 + (−3) + (−3)
(59)

Subtract each pair of numbers below.

16. 6 − (−2)
(60)

(c) 17. −2 − (−5)
(60)

(d) 18. −4 − 15
(60)

Solve each equation below by undoing.

19. $\frac{1}{2} + x = 1\frac{1}{2}$
(53)

20. $13x = 351$
(53)

21. $x - 91.8 = 125.4$
(53)

Translate the word problem below into an equation; then solve.

(e) 22. Mr. Noonan opened up a college savings account for his daughter at the local bank. He put $8,000 in the account, which pays 5% in yearly interest.
(29)

i.) How much will Mr. Noonan have earned in interest one year from now?

ii.) If he leaves his money <u>and</u> interest in the bank for another year, how much interest will he earn for the 2nd year?

Lesson 61—Multiplication with Negatives

Now that we've covered addition and subtraction with negatives, it's time to talk about multiplication. As in the last lesson, we'll learn the rules first; then we'll look at why they work.

Signs Are Different

Here's our first example.

$$(2)(-5)$$

We have a positive times a negative here, which means the signs of the numbers being multiplied are different. To handle a problem like this, the first step is to multiply the numbers without paying any attention to the signs. So for $(2)(-5)$, we forget for a minute that the 5 is negative and just multiply 2 and 5 to get 10.

$$(2)(5) = 10$$

This isn't the final answer, though. We still have one more step. Since the numbers being multiplied have opposite signs, we make the answer negative.

$$(2)(-5) = -10$$

Our answer, then, is -10.

Let's do another one.

$$(-4)(3)$$

We have a negative times a positive, which means the two numbers have different signs again. So our first step is to multiply not paying attention to the signs.

$$(4)(3) = 12$$

Next, since the signs are opposite, we make the answer negative.

$$(-4)(3) = -12$$

The answer to this one is -12. Are you getting the idea? When the signs of the two numbers being multiplied are different, the answer will *always* be negative.

Signs Are the Same

What about when the signs are the same? Here's an example like that.

$$(-2)(-7)$$

Even though this time, two negatives are being multiplied, the first step is still to multiply the numbers not paying attention to the signs.

$$(2)(7) = 14$$

But since the signs are the same, we have to make the answer positive.

$$(-2)(-7) = 14$$

In fact, it turns out, that the answer to a multiplication where both signs are the same will *always* be positive.

There's one last case we should show you, even though it's an obvious one. When both numbers are positive, the answer is always positive. For instance, in 5×6 both the 5 and 6 are positive, which is why the answer is positive 30 (but you already knew that!)

$$(5)(6) = 30$$

The main point is that even this simple example fits with our rules for multiplying with negatives. When the signs are different, the answer is always negative. And when the signs are the same, the answer is always positive. And that's true even in a simple case like 5×6.

Here are the official rules for multiplication with negatives.

Multiplying with Negatives

negative ✘ positive = negative
positive ✘ negative = negative
negative ✘ negative = positive
positive ✘ positive = positive

Why It Works: Positive x Negative

Now that we've covered the rules, let's talk about why they work. We'll go back to the example $(2)(-5)$. Think for a second about what multiplication really means. When we multiply two positive numbers in arithmetic, like $(2)(5)$, that's the same as adding 5 two times.

$$(2)(5) = 5 + 5$$

Since $5 + 5$ equals 10, $(2)(5)$ also equals 10. So multiplication is just a short way to write a number added to itself several times. If the example had been $(3)(5)$, the answer would have been $5 + 5 + 5$ or 15.

But now it's easy to see why $(2)(-5)$ has to equal -10. It's because $(2)(-5)$ is just -5 added two times, or $-5 + (-5)$ and we know that equals -10.

$$(2)(-5) = -5 + (-5) = -10$$

The same thing happens anytime we have a positive times a negative, no matter what numbers are involved. It's always like adding a negative number to itself several times (a loss plus a loss plus a loss, and so on). Take the example of $(3)(-2)$. That's the same as $-2 + (-2) + (-2)$, and we know that adds up to -6.

Or look at the example of $(-8)(2)$. The negative comes first this time, but don't let that throw you off. Remember, we can always switch the order of numbers that are multiplied. So let's think of $(-8)(2)$ as $(2)(-8)$. That tells us that $(-8)(2) = -8 + (-8)$, which equals -16. Finally, let's look at one more problem: $(4)(-6)$. This is the same as -6 added 4 times, or $-6 + (-6) + (-6) + (-6)$, and that comes out to -24. So a negative times a positive (or a positive times a negative) must always have a negative answer because it's really just a negative added to itself over and over again. And that always has to come out negative.

Why It Works: Negative x Negative

What about a negative times a negative? Why does that rule work? This one's a little more difficult to explain. We can think of a negative times a negative as taking away a negative number several times. For instance, look at the problem $(-2)(-7)$. We can't think of this as adding -7 two times because -2 isn't the same as 2. But we can think of it as taking away -7 twice. If we take away a loss of 7 twice, we're 14 better off. That's why a negative times a negative equals a positive. That may not be a very satisfying explanation, but it's the best one there is.

Practice 61

a.
(59)   Add $-\frac{2}{3} + \left(-\frac{1}{3}\right)$

b.
(60)   Subtract $29 - (-33)$

c.
(61)   Multiply $(-4)(8)$

d.
(61)   Multiply $(-2)(-6)$

e.
(54)   Translate the word problem below into an equation; then solve.

Dave wants to buy a classic leather flight jacket that is being sold for $60 less than the normal price. If the jacket normally costs $300, by what percent is it being discounted? (The answer to your equation will be a decimal. Don't forget to convert it to a percent.)

Problem Set 61

Tell whether each sentence below is True or False.

1.
(61)   When multiplying with negatives, if the signs are different, the answer is always negative.

2.
(61)   When multiplying with negatives, if the signs are the same, the answer is always positive.

Multiply or divide each pair of numbers below. Write any remainders in decimal form.

3.
(20)
$$\begin{array}{r} 3.9 \\ \times 7.5 \\ \hline \end{array}$$

4.
(24) $0.6 \overline{)83.5}$

Add or subtract each pair of fractions below. Make sure your answers are fully reduced.

5.
(10)
$$\frac{4}{12} + \frac{3}{4}$$

6.
(10)
$$\frac{2}{3} - \frac{1}{7}$$

Convert each percent below into decimal form.

7.
(26)
32%

8.
(28)
$54\frac{1}{8}\%$

Answer each question below. Make sure your answer is fully reduced.

9.
(14)
What is $\frac{5}{9}$ of 351?

10.
(13)
What is $\frac{1}{2}$ of $\frac{1}{4}$?

Add each pair of numbers below.

11.
(59)
$-17 + (-25)$

12.
(59)
$-11 + 15$

(a) **13.**
(59)
$-\frac{3}{4} + \left(-\frac{1}{4}\right)$

Subtract each pair of numbers below.

14.
(60)
$-9 - 7$

15.
(60)
$-12 - (-6)$

(b) **16.**
(60)
$32 - (-41)$

Multiply each pair of numbers below.

17.
(61)
$(+6)(-4)$

(c) **18.**
(61)
$(-5)(7)$

(d) **19.**
(61)
$(-3)(-9)$

Solve each equation below by undoing. Make sure your answer is fully reduced.

20.
(53)
$x + 4.7 = 16.3$

21.
(53)
$31x = 589$

22.
(53)
$$\frac{x}{\frac{2}{5}} = \frac{10}{11}$$

Translate the word problem below into an equation; then solve.

(e) **23.**
(54)
Suzy wants to buy a Navy pea coat that is being sold for $30 less than the normal price. If the coat normally costs $75, by what percent is it being discounted? (The answer to your equation will be a decimal. Don't forget to convert it to a percent.)

Lesson 62—Division with Negatives

So far, we've talked about addition, subtraction, and multiplication with negatives. But we still have division left. The good news is that dividing with negatives is incredibly easy, once you know how to multiply with negatives. That's because the rules are exactly the same. Specifically, when dividing with negatives, if the signs of the numbers are different, the answer is negative. If the signs of the numbers are the same, the answer is positive. Some people actually write the division rules as fractions.

Dividing with Negatives

$\dfrac{\text{negative}}{\text{positive}} = \text{negative}$	$\dfrac{\text{positive}}{\text{negative}} = \text{negative}$
$\dfrac{\text{negative}}{\text{negative}} = \text{positive}$	$\dfrac{\text{positive}}{\text{positive}} = \text{positive}$

Signs Are Different

Now let's go through some examples to make sure you can actually use these rules. We'll start with -25 divided by $+5$.

$$\frac{-25}{+5}$$

We have a negative divided by a positive. And since the signs are different, we know the answer has to be negative. The first step, though, is to divide the numbers not paying attention to their signs.

$$\frac{25}{5} = 5$$

Now we make the answer negative, which gives us a final answer of -5.

$$\frac{-25}{+5} = -5$$

Let's try another one.

$$\frac{18}{-6}$$

This time, the negative is on the bottom and the positive is on the top. But the signs are still different, so we know the answer has to be negative again. To do the calculation, we first divide the numbers not paying attention to their signs.

$$\frac{18}{6} = 3$$

Then we make the answer negative.

$$\frac{18}{-6} = -3$$

That's all there is to it.

275

Signs Are the Same

Now let's do a negative divided by another negative.

$$\frac{-42}{-7}$$

The signs are the same here, which means that the answer has to be positive. But, as always, we start by dividing the numbers not paying attention to their signs.

$$\frac{42}{7} = 6$$

Now since the signs are the same, we make sure the answer is positive, which leaves us with 6.

$$\frac{-42}{-7} = 6$$

We don't need to go through an example of a positive divided by a positive. That's just basic arithmetic. But following our rules, the answer has to be positive because the signs are the same.

Why It Works

Now let's talk about why these rules for division work. Think about how we come up with the answer to a simple division problem, like $\frac{72}{9}$. What we usually do is ask ourselves, "9 times what number equals 72?" Since 9×8 equals 72, then $\frac{72}{9} = 8$. In other words, we often figure out division problems using our knowledge of multiplication.

But now let's go through the same process on a division with a negative.

$$\frac{-24}{8}$$

We start by asking, "8 times what number equals -24?" Since a positive times a negative equals a negative, 8 has to be multiplied by a *negative* number to get -24, and that number turns out to be -3. So the answer to the division problem is -3.

$$\frac{-24}{8} = -3$$

This also works when the negative is on bottom. Let's do one like that.

$$\frac{14}{-7}$$

First, we ask the question, "-7 times what number equals $+14$?" Since a negative times a negative equals a positive, -7 has to be multiplied by *negative* 2 to get $+14$. So -2 is the answer to the division problem.

$$\frac{14}{-7} = -2$$

This way of thinking will also explain why a negative divided by a negative has to be positive. Here's an example.

$$\frac{-15}{-3}$$

Again, we start with the question, "-3 times what number equals -15?" Since a negative times a positive equals a negative, -3 has to be multiplied by *positive* 5 to get -15. So that explains why $+5$ is the answer.

$$\frac{-15}{-3} = 5$$

The main point of the lesson is that the rules for dividing with negatives are the same as those for multiplying with negatives: If the signs are different the answer is negative, and if the signs are the same, the answer is positive.

Practice 62

a.
(41) How many square yards are in 2,700 square feet?

b.
(60) Subtract $\frac{5}{7} - \left(-\frac{1}{7}\right)$. Make sure your answer is fully reduced.

c.
(62) Divide $\frac{63}{-7}$

d.
(62) Divide $\frac{-30}{-5}$

e.
(53) Translate the word problem below into an equation; then solve.

Mr. Morris would probably be the most boring man on Earth were it not for his eclectic collection of tweed driving caps, which he usually purchases on his trips to England. On his last trip, he bought 8 caps, spending a total of $167.60. What was the average price of each cap?

Problem Set 62

Tell whether each sentence below is True or False.

1.
(62) When dividing with negatives, if the signs are different, the answer is always negative.

2.
(62) When dividing with negatives, if the signs are the same, the answer is always positive.

Add or subtract each group of numbers below.

3.
(2)

```
  8,060
+9,127
```

4.
(17)

```
 659.25
-296.75
```

Multiply or divide each pair of numbers below. Make sure your answers are fully reduced.

5.
(14) $24 \cdot \dfrac{7}{8}$

6.
(14) $\dfrac{8}{9} \div 16$

Do each unit conversion below.

7.
(38)   Convert 8 kilometers to hectometers.

(a) 8.
(41)   How many square yards are in 1,800 square feet?

Add each pair of numbers below.

9.
(59) $-9 + (-14)$

10.
(59) $82 + (-57)$

Subtract each pair of numbers below. Make sure your answer is fully reduced.

11.
(60) $7 - (-7)$

12.
(60) $-13 - 5$

(b) 13.
(60) $\dfrac{3}{5} - \left(-\dfrac{1}{5}\right)$

Multiply each pair of numbers below.

14.
(61) $(6)(-9)$

15.
(61) $(-12)(+5)$

16.
(61) $(-7)(-4)$

Divide each pair of numbers below.

17.
(62) $\dfrac{-36}{+6}$

(c) 18.
(62) $\dfrac{56}{-7}$

(d) 19.
(62) $\dfrac{-40}{-8}$

Solve each equation below by undoing.

20.
(53) $\dfrac{3}{5} + x = 1\dfrac{1}{5}$

21.
(53) $9x = 2,052$

22.
(53) $\dfrac{x}{21.8} = 5.3$

Translate the word problem below into an equation; then solve.

(e) 23.
(53)   Katy loves shoes, especially velvet slippers with embroidered patterns. On her last trip to Paris, she bought 5 pairs of these slippers, spending a total of $328.75. What was the average price of each pair of slippers?

Lesson 63—Undoing Equations with Negatives—Part 1

Now that we've learned how to add, subtract, multiply, and divide with negatives, it's time to talk about how to handle negatives in equations. This is important because if we're going to use negatives to solve real problems, they're bound to pop up in equations.

Undoing a Subtracted Negative

We'll start by learning how to undo some simple equations that have negatives in them. Here's our first example.

$$x - (-3) = 8$$

Notice that a negative number is being subtracted from x. How do we undo this? There are actually two methods. One method is just to add the very same number, in this case -3, to both sides.

$$x - (-3) + (-3) = 8 + (-3)$$

The addition undoes the subtraction on the left side, leaving x.

$$x = 8 + (-3)$$

That's turned our algebra equation into a simple arithmetic equation. From here, we just add on the right. A gain of 8 added to a loss of 3 is equal to a gain of 5.

$$x = 5$$

So our answer is 5.

A Faster Method

But there's another, easier method for undoing $x - (-3) = 8$. Remember that subtraction is the same as adding the opposite. For instance, $10 - (-3)$ is the same as $10 + 3$. That's how we always subtract negatives. But we can use this fact to change the left side of the equation *before* undoing. Since subtracting is the same as adding the opposite, we can change the subtraction of -3 to an addition of $+3$. In other words, $x - (-3) = 8$ can be changed to $x + (+3) = 8$, which is just the same as $x + 3 = 8$.

$$x - (-3) = 8 \quad \Longrightarrow \quad x + (+3) = 8 \quad \Longrightarrow \quad x + 3 = 8$$

Now the equation is really easy to undo. No more negatives to worry about. We just have to subtract 3 from both sides.

$$x + 3 - 3 = 8 - 3$$

The left side equals x because the subtraction undoes the addition, leaving us with this.

$$x = 8 - 3$$

Finally, we subtract on the right to get the answer.

$$x = 5$$

And it's the same answer we got before. But it was much simpler to undo because we didn't have to mess with negatives. So an easier method for undoing the subtraction of a negative is to change the subtraction to an addition of the opposite (a positive) first. Then undo normally. You can use this method every time.

Undoing an Added Negative

Here's another example of a negative in an equation.

$$x+(-5)=7$$

This time, we have a negative number added to x. How do we undo this one? Again, there are two methods. The first one is just to undo the addition by subtracting the same number, -5, from both sides.

$$x+(-5)-(-5)=7-(-5)$$

The equation looks pretty messy now, but it's really not that hard. The subtraction of -5 undoes the addition of -5, leaving just x on the left.

$$x=7-(-5)$$

To do the calculation on the right, we can change subtraction to addition of the opposite (Remember, we always subtract with negatives this way.) That gives us this.

$$x=7+5$$

Now, all that's left is to add 7 and 5 on the right.

$$x=12$$

So the first method is the same one we've always used to undo addition: just subtract the very same number from both sides.

The Simpler Approach

But there's another, easier method for undoing $x+(-5)=7$. Instead of subtracting negative 5 from both sides, we add a positive 5 to both sides. This may seem weird, but just watch.

$$x+(-5)+5=7+5$$

On the left side, we have $-5+5$. Think about it. That just equals 0. So the left side becomes $x+0$ or just x.

$$x+0=7+5 \qquad \longrightarrow \qquad x=7+5$$

Now x is by itself, which is exactly what we wanted! We undid the addition of -5 with the addition of $+5$. In other words, instead of undoing the addition with a subtraction, we were able to undo it with another addition. From here, all we have left is to add 7 and 5 on the right.

$$x=12$$

That gives us 12 for the answer, which is exactly what we got before.

Why Adding the Opposite Works

Let's talk about why adding +5 to both sides worked. Here's the original equation again.

$$x + (-5) = 7$$

Remember that subtraction and adding the opposite are the same thing. So instead of subtracting −5 from both sides, it's legal to add the opposite of −5 (+5) to both sides. Mathematically, the two are the same.

$$x + (-5) + 5 = 7 + 5$$

The only difference is that adding 5 is easier, because notice that on the right side all we have to do is add 7 and 5, which is really simple. Doing it the other way forces us to subtract a negative on the right, which is a little harder. And the great thing is that any addition can be undone this way. Instead of subtracting the same number, we can always undo by adding the opposite.

Let's look at another example.

$$x + (-7) = 3$$

We could undo this by subtracting −7 from both sides, but subtracting a negative is messy (and can even seem a little confusing). So instead, let's add +7 to both sides.

$$x + (-7) + 7 = 3 + 7$$

Since $-7 + 7$ equals 0, x is now by itself on the left.

$$x = 3 + 7$$

All we need to do from here is add on the right to get an answer of 10.

$$x = 10$$

Let's finish with one more example.

$$x + (-2) = 11$$

Again, we could undo the addition by subtracting −2 from both sides. But since that would involve subtracting a negative, it's easier to add +2 to both sides instead.

$$x + (-2) + 2 = 11 + 2$$

Because $-2 + 2$ is 0, we end up with x all by itself on the left.

$$x = 11 + 2$$

Next, we just add 11 and 2 to get an answer of 13.

$$x = 13$$

Get into the Habit

We can undo *any* addition by adding the opposite instead of subtracting. But there's no reason to get fancy when x just has a positive number added to it. For example, in an equation like $x+3=9$, we could undo by adding -3 to both sides. Why bother, though? It's easier to subtract 3 from both sides instead. However, when a negative number is added to x, it is easier to undo by adding the opposite to both sides. So get in the habit of using the second method when x has a negative number added to it.

Practice 63

a. (61) Multiply $(-2.5)(8)$

b. (62) Divide $\dfrac{-171}{-3}$

c. (63) Solve the equation $x-(-6)=22$

d. (63) Solve the equation $x+(-12)=15$

e. (55) Translate the word problem below into an equation; then solve.

The young newlyweds decided to explore the countryside together on a two-seater bike. If they traveled 7 hours for a total of 98 miles, how fast did they go in miles per hour?

Problem Set 63

Tell whether each sentence below is True or False.

1. (63) It is easier to undo in the equation $x-(-5)=11$ if you change the subtraction of -5 to addition of $+5$ first.

2. (63) Another method for undoing addition in the equation $x+(-4)=9$ is to add $+4$ to both sides.

Multiply or divide each pair of numbers below. Write any remainders in decimal form.

3. (20)
$$\begin{array}{r} 9.24 \\ \times 3.7 \\ \hline \end{array}$$

4. (22) $5\overline{)2{,}596}$

Add or subtract each pair of fractions below. Make sure your answers are fully reduced.

5. (10) $\dfrac{2}{10}+\dfrac{3}{5}$

6. (11) $\dfrac{5}{6}-\dfrac{1}{9}$

Convert each fraction below into decimal form. Give exact answers (no rounding).

7. (24) $\dfrac{1}{18}$

8. (24) $\dfrac{2}{15}$

Add each pair of numbers below.

9.
(59) $-12+(-37)$

10.
(59) $26+(-26)$

Subtract each pair of numbers below.

11.
(60) $19-(-52)$

12.
(60) $-31-(-29)$

Multiply each pair of numbers below.

13.
(61) $(10)(-8)$

14.
(61) $(-1)(-14)$

(a) 15.
(61) $(-3.5)(6)$

Divide each pair of numbers below.

16.
(62) $\dfrac{-50}{5}$

17.
(62) $\dfrac{60}{-12}$

(b) 18.
(62) $\dfrac{-118}{-2}$

Solve each equation below by undoing. Make sure your answer is fully reduced.

19.
(53) $35x=420$

20.
(53) $\dfrac{x}{3}=\dfrac{7}{9}$

(c) 21.
(63) $x-(-9)=24$

(d) 22.
(63) $x+(-11)=13$

Translate the word problem below into an equation; then solve.

(e) 23.
(55) The lonely hitchhiker has walked 187 hours for a total of 374 miles. How fast is he going in miles per hour?

Lesson 64—Undoing Equations with Negatives—Part 2

In the last lesson, we learned how to undo equations where negative numbers were added to and subtracted from x. In this lesson, we'll learn how to undo when x has been multiplied or divided by a negative.

x Divided by a Negative

We'll start with a division example.

$$\frac{x}{-3} = 7$$

This one is probably easier than you think. There are no new rules or shortcuts to learn, and there's just one method. All we have to do is multiply both sides by -3.

$$(-3)\left(\frac{x}{-3}\right) = (7)(-3)$$

The multiplication undoes the division on the left, leaving x by itself on one side.

$$x = (7)(-3)$$

The last step is to do the multiplication on the right. Since a positive times a negative is a negative, we know the answer has to be -21.

$$x = -21$$

Believe it or not, that's all there is to know about undoing division by a negative.

x Multiplied by a Negative

Now let's go through an example where x is multiplied by a negative.

$$-2x = -12$$

There's really nothing new to learn here either. We just undo the multiplication by dividing both sides by -2.

$$\frac{-2x}{-2} = \frac{-12}{-2}$$

It's the same thing we've always done when undoing multiplication. The division undoes the multiplication on the left, leaving us with this.

$$x = \frac{-12}{-2}$$

Now we divide on the right. Since a negative divided by a negative is a positive, the answer is 6.

$$x = 6$$

So when it comes to undoing equations where x is multiplied or divided by a negative number, we use exactly the same methods we covered earlier (for positive numbers).

Practice 64

a.
(62)   Divide $\dfrac{-72}{-6}$

b.
(63)   Solve the equation $x-(-13)=-14$

c.
(64)   Solve the equation $-7x=91$

d.
(64)   Solve the equation $\dfrac{x}{-3}=-15$

e.
(54)   Translate the word problem below into an equation; then solve.

In a recent poll, 28% of the lifeguards who were surveyed said they thought body surfing should be an Olympic sport. If 126 lifeguards gave this response, how many were surveyed in total?

Problem Set 64

Add or subtract each group of numbers below.

1.
(17)
$$\begin{array}{r} 0.465 \\ +0.829 \\ \hline \end{array}$$

2.
(17)
$$\begin{array}{r} 18.54 \\ -9.92 \\ \hline \end{array}$$

Multiply or divide each pair of fractions below. Make sure your answers are fully reduced.

3.
(13) $\dfrac{2}{3}\cdot\dfrac{9}{24}$

4.
(13) $\dfrac{10}{12}\div\dfrac{5}{8}$

Answer each question below.

5.
(55)   How far will a tank moving at 18 miles per hour travel in 6 hours?

6.
(55)   How far will a satellite orbiting at 1,000 miles per hour travel in 12 hours?

Add each pair of numbers below.

7.
(59) $-11+(-29)$

8.
(59) $0+(-100)$

Subtract each pair of numbers below.

9.
(60) $7-(-3)$

10.
(60) $-9-13$

Multiply each pair of numbers below.

11. (1)(−94)
(61)

12. (−6)(13)
(61)

13. (−2)(−52)
(61)

Divide each pair of numbers below.

14. $\dfrac{-27}{9}$
(62)

15. $\dfrac{112}{-8}$
(62)

(a) **16.** $\dfrac{-84}{-4}$
(62)

Solve each equation below by undoing.

17. $x+(-2)=9$
(63)

(b) **18.** $x-(-17)=-18$
(63)

(c) **19.** $-5x=95$
(64)

(d) **20.** $\dfrac{x}{-4}=-12$
(64)

Translate the word problem below into an equation; then solve.

(e) **21.** In a recent poll, 32% of the referees who were surveyed said that ejecting angry coaches was their
(54) favorite thing to do. If 152 referees gave this response, how many were surveyed in total?

Lesson 65—Negatives and Fractions

In the last lesson, we learned how to undo equations where x is multiplied by a negative number. Our example was $-2x = -12$. And, remember, after undoing we ended up with $x = \dfrac{-12}{-2}$. That made things pretty easy, since -12 can be divided evenly by -2 (to get 6). But sometimes, when undoing a multiplication of a negative, we end up with a division that doesn't come out even. In this lesson we'll learn how to deal with that.

Converting to a Decimal

For starters, take a look at this example.

$$-5x = 3$$

We know how to undo the multiplication by -5. We just divide both sides by -5.

$$\frac{-5x}{-5} = \frac{3}{-5}$$

The division undoes the multiplication on the left side, leaving x by itself.

$$x = \frac{3}{-5}$$

But this is where it gets a little tricky. On the right side, -5 won't go into 3 evenly. How should we write the answer? There are actually two ways to do it. The first is to convert the answer into a decimal. To do that we ignore the signs and divide 5 into 3 with long division to get 0.6. Then, to figure out the sign of the answer, we use the rule that says a positive divided by a negative equals a negative. That gives us an answer of -0.6.

$$x = \frac{3}{-5} = -0.6$$

That's how we convert fractions with negatives into decimals. We first use long division (which is the normal way of converting fractions to decimals), and then apply the rules for dividing negatives to figure out the sign of the decimal answer.

Leaving it as a Fraction

The second way of dealing with $\dfrac{3}{-5}$ is to leave it as a fraction. But we have to do something about that negative sign in the bottom. If we want the answer to be a fraction, we have to figure out the sign of the *entire* fraction. And that requires us to use the rules for dividing negative numbers again. The fraction $\dfrac{3}{-5}$ is a positive divided by a negative, which we know must equal a negative. So we make the entire fraction negative by just putting the negative sign out in front like this.

$$x = -\frac{3}{5}$$

Positive divided by negative equals negative

In fact, any time you have a fraction with a negative number in either the top or the bottom, you should figure out the sign of the entire fraction. For example, what if the answer to our equation had been $\frac{-3}{5}$? This is a negative on top and a positive on bottom. Again we just need to use the rules for dividing negatives. A negative divided by a positive equals a negative. So, just as in the last example, we should put the negative sign out in front of the entire fraction.

$$\frac{-3}{5} = -\frac{3}{5}$$

Negative divided by positive equals negative

What if the fraction had a negative in both the top *and* the bottom?

$$\frac{-3}{-5}$$

We still need to find the sign of the entire fraction. Applying the rules for dividing negatives, we know that a negative divided by a negative equals a positive. That means $\frac{-3}{-5}$ is actually equal to $+\frac{3}{5}$. But we really don't need the positive sign in front because everybody knows that $+\frac{3}{5}$ is the same as $\frac{3}{5}$.

$$\frac{-3}{-5} = \frac{3}{5}$$

Negative divided by negative equals positive

Let's quickly go back over all the different possibilities for signs in fractions, so you won't forget them. Actually, we never went over the first case—a positive divided by a positive—because you already know that it equals a positive. Here are all four possibilities.

Negatives in Fractions

$\frac{+3}{+5} = +\frac{3}{5}$	$\frac{+3}{-5} = -\frac{3}{5}$
$\frac{-3}{+5} = -\frac{3}{5}$	$\frac{-3}{-5} = +\frac{3}{5}$

The main point is that when the answer to an equation is a division that doesn't come out even, you have two options. You can convert the answer into a decimal and then use the rules for dividing with negatives to figure out what the sign of the decimal should be. Or you can leave the answer as a fraction. But you'll still need to figure out the sign of the entire fraction by using the rules for dividing with negatives.

Practice 65

a.
(44)
How many cubic inches are in 16 cubic feet?

b.
(65)
Tell whether $\dfrac{-5}{8}$ and $-\dfrac{5}{8}$ are equivalent.

c.
(63)
Solve the equation $x-(-5)=-11.2$.

d.
(63)
Solve the equation $x+(-81)=-157$.

e.
(55)
Translate the word problem below into an equation; then solve.

Phil and Leslie spent all of Saturday on their new motorboat. If they traveled 9 hours for a total of 144 miles, how fast did they go in miles per hour?

Problem Set 65

Multiply or divide each pair of numbers below. Write any remainders in decimal form.

1.
(20)
$$\begin{array}{r} 58.2 \\ \times 4.9 \\ \hline \end{array}$$

2.
(4)
$15\overline{)38,925}$

Add or subtract each pair of fractions below. Make sure your answers are fully reduced.

3.
(10)
$\dfrac{7}{8}+\dfrac{3}{4}$

4.
(10)
$\dfrac{6}{5}-\dfrac{2}{3}$

Do each unit conversion below.

5.
(45)
Convert 14 gallons to quarts.

(a) 6.
(44)
How many cubic inches are in 14 cubic feet?

Add each pair of numbers below.

7.
(59)
$-92+(-37)$

8.
(59)
$-11+75$

Subtract each pair of numbers below.

9.
(60)
$-13-8$

10.
(60)
$24-(-16)$

Multiply each pair of numbers below.

11. $(-7)(13)$
(61)

12. $(-5)(-19)$
(61)

Divide each pair of numbers below.

13. $\dfrac{21}{-7}$
(62)

14. $\dfrac{-84}{-12}$
(62)

Tell whether each of the following pairs of fractions is equivalent.

(b) 15. $\dfrac{-7}{9}$ and $-\dfrac{7}{9}$
(65)

16. $\dfrac{-2}{-3}$ and $\dfrac{2}{3}$
(65)

Solve each equation below by undoing.

(c) 17. $x-(-8)=-15.6$
(63)

18. $\dfrac{x}{-12}=34$
(64)

19. $19x=209$
(53)

(d) 20. $x+(-73)=-141$
(63)

Translate the word problem below into an equation; then solve.

(e) 21. Bill lost his bet with his buddy Tom. As a result, Bill now has to drive all the way back from the
(55) stadium to his house with the score of the game emblazoned in shoe polish on his back windshield. If Bill drives 11 hours for a total of 715 miles, how fast will he be traveling in miles per hour?

Lesson 66—Handling a -x

Here's an equation that we learned how to solve a while ago.

$$5.8 + x = 26.3$$

Notice that the x isn't in its usual place on the far left. Remember, we've been handling these situations by switching $5.8 + x$ to $x + 5.8$.

$$x + 5.8 = 26.3$$

That's perfectly legal, of course. There's a basic rule of arithmetic (the commutative property of addition), which allows us to add two numbers in any order. By moving the x to the far left, where we're used to seeing it, the equation is easier to undo.

Now check out this equation.

$$8.1 - x = 13.7$$

The x is on the inside again. And it would be nice to move it to the left to make this equation easier to undo. The problem is that we can't switch the order of numbers that are subtracted. Switching only works for addition and multiplication, remember.

Flipping Around a Subtraction

So what do we do in a case like this? We just use our knowledge of negative numbers. Any subtraction can be changed to an addition of the opposite. Well, the opposite of x is $-x$, so we can change $8.1 - x$ to $8.1 + (-x)$.

$$8.1 - x = 13.7 \quad \longrightarrow \quad 8.1 + (-x) = 13.7$$

Now the left side is an addition, which means that the order *can* be switched to get $-x$ on the far left.

$$-x + 8.1 = 13.7$$

From here, we can undo the addition in the usual way, by subtracting 8.1 from both sides.

$$-x + 8.1 - 8.1 = 13.7 - 8.1$$

That makes the left side equal to $-x$.

$$-x = 13.7 - 8.1$$

Next, we subtract on the right.

$$-x = 5.6$$

Changing a -x to x

Are we done? No, not yet. We have $-x$ on the left, but that's not what we're looking for. We need the value of plain old x. So we have to get rid of the negative sign on the x. It's not as hard as it might seem. All we have to do is multiply $-x$ by -1. To see why this works, take a close look at these multiplications.

$$(-1)(-2) = +2 \qquad (-1)(+8) = -8$$

$$(-1)(-4) = +4 \qquad (-1)(+10) = -10$$

Do you see the pattern? A -1 multiplied by any number equals the number's opposite. That's always true, because of the rules for multiplying with negatives. So using this rule, we can change $-x$ to its opposite, which is just x. But we have to remember to avoid violating the golden rule. In other words, if we multiply one side of the equation by -1 we have to multiply the other side by -1 too.

$$(-1)(-x) = (-1)(5.6)$$

The left side is now a plain x, which is exactly what we wanted. The right side is -5.6, which is our final answer.

$$x = -5.6$$

The main thing to remember is that we can get rid of a $-x$ in an equation by multiplying both sides by -1.

Checking a Negative Answer

There's one more important point we need to cover: how to check a negative answer to an equation. To show you how it works, let's check -5.6. We need to put -5.6 back in for x in the original equation. Here's the original equation again.

$$8.1 - x = 13.7$$

But the best way to put a negative answer back in is to put parentheses around it, like this.

$$8.1 - (-5.6) = 13.7$$

The parentheses help us to remember the negative sign on the 5.6. Without the parentheses, it's easy to confuse the minus sign and the negative sign. We might end up leaving out the negative sign and just writing $8.1 - 5.6 = 13.7$, which is wrong. That's putting positive 5.6 in for x. So always put parentheses around a negative number when putting it in for x to check an answer. To finish the checking process, though, we just calculate the value of the left side. Putting a number in for x in an expression and then calculating the expression's value is called **evaluating** the expression, by the way. So we need to evaluate $8.1 - x$ for $x = -5.6$. All we have to do is change the subtraction to addition of the opposite on the left side and then add.

$$8.1 - (-5.6) = 13.7$$

$$8.1 + 5.6 = 13.7$$

$$13.7 = 13.7$$

Since both sides end up equal, our solution -5.6 is correct.

Practice 66

a.
(66)   Tell whether $9 - x$ and $-x + 9$ are equivalent.

b.
(66)   Tell whether $(-1)(-y)$ and y are equivalent.

c.
(66)   Solve the equation $3.5 - x = 17.6$.

d. Solve the equation $-4 - x = 16$.
(66)

e. Translate the word problem below into an equation; then solve.
(54)

John just bought the woman of his dreams an engagement ring for $720 less than the normal price. If the ring normally costs $2,400, by what percent is it being discounted? (The answer to your equation will be a decimal. Don't forget to convert it to a percent.)

Problem Set 66

Tell whether each sentence below is True or False.

1. To change a $-x$ to x in an equation, multiply both sides by -1.
(66)

2. It's best to put parentheses around a negative number when putting it in for an x in an equation.
(66)

Add or subtract each group of numbers below.

3. $\begin{array}{r} 82,216 \\ +29,253 \\ \hline \end{array}$
(2)

4. $\begin{array}{r} 4,073 \\ -2,869 \\ \hline \end{array}$
(2)

Multiply or divide each pair of numbers below. Make sure your answers are fully reduced.

5. $\dfrac{3}{14} \cdot \dfrac{7}{9}$
(13)

6. $24 \div \dfrac{3}{5}$
(14)

Add each pair of numbers below.

7. $-107 + (-113)$
(59)

8. $25 + (-94)$
(59)

Subtract each pair of numbers below.

9. $-28 - (-17)$
(60)

10. $-32 - 9$
(60)

Multiply each pair of numbers below.

11. $(-1)(10)$
(61)

12. $(47)(\ 8)$
(61)

Divide each pair of numbers below.

13. $\dfrac{-140}{70}$
(62)

14. $\dfrac{-36}{-4}$
(62)

Tell whether each pair of expressions below is equivalent.

(a) 15. $7-x$ and $-x+7$
(66)

(b) 16. $(-1)(-x)$ and x
(66)

Solve each equation below by undoing. Make sure your answer is fully reduced.

17. $\dfrac{3}{5}x=\dfrac{7}{10}$
(53)

(c) 18. $2.5-x=19.3$
(66)

19. $\dfrac{x}{4.1}=-6$
(53)

(d) 20. $-3-x=12$
(66)

21. $\dfrac{x}{\frac{3}{4}}=12$
(53)

Translate the word problem below into an equation; then solve.

(e) 22. John thought that after he bought the woman of his dreams that beautiful engagement ring (see practice
(54) problem e) she would surely say "Yes." She didn't. Now John plans (mistakenly) to win her charms by buying her a diamond necklace too! If the necklace is being sold for $600 less than the normal price of $1,500, by what percent is it being discounted? (The answer to your equation will be a decimal. Don't forget to convert it to a percent.)

Lesson 67—Dealing with -x in a Fraction

We can change $-x$ to x by multiplying both sides of an equation by -1. But what if $-x$ is inside a fraction in an equation? Here's a problem like that.

$$\frac{-x}{7.9} = -1.5$$

There are two basic ways to handle this situation.

Multiplying by -1

The first method is just to undo the division by multiplying both sides by 7.9.

$$(7.9)\left(\frac{-x}{7.9}\right) = (7.9)(-1.5)$$

That leaves $-x$ on the left.

$$-x = (7.9)(-1.5)$$

On the right side, we have a positive multiplied by a negative, which equals a negative. So the right side becomes -11.85.

$$-x = -11.85$$

But -11.85 isn't the answer to the equation. We're not trying to find $-x$; we need just plain x. As we learned in the last lesson, though, $-x$ can be changed to x by multiplying both sides by -1.

$$(-1)(-x) = (-1)(-11.85)$$

That makes the left side plain x and the right side turns out to be 11.85, which is our final answer.

$$x = 11.85$$

So the first method for dealing with a $-x$ in a fraction is to undo normally. We'll end up with a $-x$ on one side, which we can get rid of by multiplying both sides by -1 at the end.

Moving the Sign

The other method for eliminating a $-x$ inside a fraction is to use the rules for dividing negatives. To show you how it works, let's go back to our original equation.

$$\frac{-x}{7.9} = -1.5$$

The fraction is a negative divided by a positive, which means that the whole fraction has to be negative. We could put a negative sign out in front of the entire fraction, if we wanted. But wouldn't a positive divided by a negative make the whole fraction negative too? Yes, it would. So why can't we move the negative sign from the x on top to the 7.9 on bottom?

$$\frac{x}{-7.9}$$

This is perfectly legal, because both $\frac{-x}{7.9}$ and $\frac{x}{-7.9}$ are the same as $-\frac{x}{7.9}$. Whether the negative is on the top or on the bottom, the value of the whole fraction is the same.

$$\frac{-x}{7.9} = \frac{x}{-7.9} = -\frac{x}{7.9}$$

Moving the negative sign to the bottom helps us because it gets rid of the $-x$. Now our equation looks like this.

$$\frac{x}{-7.9} = -1.5$$

From here, we can undo the division by multiplying both sides by -7.9.

$$(-7.9)\left(\frac{x}{-7.9}\right) = (-7.9)(-1.5)$$

That leaves us with just plain x on the left side, which is what we wanted.

$$x = (-7.9)(-1.5)$$

Finally, since a negative times a negative equals a positive, the answer comes out to 11.85. And that's the same thing we got using our first method.

$$x = 11.85$$

The main point is that there are two ways to undo an equation that has a $-x$ in a fraction. We can undo normally and then multiply both sides by -1, or we can move the negative sign to the other half of the fraction. Most people like the second method better, because you don't have to multiply both sides by -1.

Practice 67

a.
(65)   Tell whether $\frac{-1}{-5}$ and $-\frac{1}{5}$ are equivalent.

b.
(67)   Tell whether $\frac{-x}{3}$ and $\frac{x}{-3}$ are equivalent.

c.
(67)   Solve the equation $\frac{-x}{15} = -8$.

d.
(66)   Solve the equation $17 - x = -31$.

e.
(54)

Translate the word problem below into an equation; then solve.

Mr. and Mrs. Thompson are trying to save enough money to go on an extended island vacation. They have already saved $800 but that is still not enough. If their $800 in savings is sitting in a bank account that pays 6% in yearly interest.

i.) How much will Mr. and Mrs. Thompson have earned in interest one year from now?

ii.) If they leave their money and interest in the bank for another year, how much interest will they earn for the 2nd year?

Problem Set 67

Multiply or divide each pair of numbers below. Write any remainders in decimal form.

1.
(20)
$$\begin{array}{r} 0.839 \\ \times 5.3 \\ \hline \end{array}$$

2.
(22)
$0.4\overline{)12.62}$

Add or subtract each pair of numbers below. Make sure your answers are fully reduced.

3.
(10)
$\dfrac{3}{16} + \dfrac{7}{16}$

4.
(12)
$2\dfrac{1}{5} - \dfrac{4}{5}$

Convert each percent below into decimal form.

5.
(25)
2.25%

6.
(28)
$46\dfrac{1}{5}\%$

Add each pair of numbers below.

7.
(59)
$-22 + (-15)$

8.
(59)
$-7 + 9$

Subtract each pair of numbers below.

9.
(60)
$0 - (-4)$

10.
(60)
$-16 - (-12)$

Multiply each pair of numbers below.

11.
(61)
$(30)(-6)$

12.
(61)
$(-14)(-19)$

Divide each pair of numbers below.

13.
(62)
$\dfrac{33}{-3}$

14.
(62)
$\dfrac{-56}{8}$

Tell whether each of the following pairs of expressions is equivalent.

(a) 15.
(65)
$\dfrac{-1}{-4}$ and $-\dfrac{1}{4}$

(b) 16.
(67)
$\dfrac{-x}{5}$ and $\dfrac{x}{-5}$

Solve each equation below by undoing.

17.
(63)
$x + (-72) = -49$

(c) 18.
(67)
$\dfrac{-x}{23} = -7$

19.
(53)
$\dfrac{3}{7}x = 27$

(d) 20.
(66)
$14 - x = -28$

21.
(53)
$10.5x = 131.25$

Translate the word problem below into an equation; then solve.

(e) 22.
(54)
Mr. Macmillan opened up a college savings account for his son at the local bank. He put $12,100 in the account, which pays 5% in yearly interest.

i.) How much will Mr. Macmillan have earned in interest one year from now?

ii.) If he leaves his money <u>and</u> interest in the bank for another year, how much interest will he earn for the 2nd year?

CHAPTER 9:
LONGER ALGEBRAIC EQUATIONS

Lesson 68—Order Matters

So far all of the equations we've looked at have had only one operation done to x. For instance, we've had equations like $x+5=18$, with a number added to x. And we've had others, such as $x-7=29$, where a number is subtracted from x. We've also worked on equations where a number was multiplied by x (like $-3x=-12$) and divided into x (like $\dfrac{x}{6}=-4.1$). But in every equation so far, there's just been one operation done to x.

More Than One Operation

As it turns out, algebra also has equations with more than one operation done to x. And we're going to start learning to solve those in this lesson. What makes these equations a little harder is that we have to figure out the order in which the operations are supposed to be done. We'll explain what we mean with a simple arithmetic example.

$$8+3\cdot2$$

Notice that we have two operations here: an addition and a multiplication. If we wanted to do this calculation, it would seem natural to add the 8 and 3 first (since they're on the left) to get this.

$$11\cdot2 \qquad\qquad \textbf{Adding first}$$

Then we would multiply the 11 and 2 to get 22.

$$22$$

But we could also do the calculation another way. We could multiply the 3 and 2 first.

$$8+6 \qquad\qquad \textbf{Multiplying first}$$

And then we could add second to get 14.

$$14$$

Do you see what just happened? We did the operations in a different order and got different answers. We got 22 when we added first and multiplied second. And we got 14 when we multiplied first and added second. This is why it's so important to get the order right in equations that have more than one operation. If we don't, the whole equation will be spoiled and we'll get the wrong answer.

The Order of Operations Rules

Since getting the order right is so important, the mathematicians have set up rules for figuring out the correct order of operations in any situation. The rules below are extremely important, so be sure to memorize them.

Order of Operations Rules

1.	All multiplications and divisions are done first.
2.	All additions and subtractions are done second.
3.	If a different order is needed, the operations that are supposed to be done first must be put in parentheses.

Here's what the rules mean. If we have a calculation that mixes multiplication and addition (like in our example) the multiplication should be done first. So according to the rules, the right way to calculate $8 + 3 \cdot 2$ is to multiply first, even though the multiplication is to the right of the addition, and it might feel unnatural. Doing this gives us $8 + 6$. The second step is to add the 8 and 6 to get 14. So 14 is the one and only correct answer because of the rules for the order of operations. If we wanted to describe the meaning of $8 + 3 \cdot 2$ in words, we would say "multiply 3 and 2 *first*, and add the result to 8 *second*." The order of operations has to be included.

Using Parentheses

But what if we want the addition to be done first? Does multiplication always have to come before addition? Let's look again at our example.

$$8 + 3 \cdot 2$$

What do the order of operations rules tell us? Rule 3 says that if we want to change the usual order of multiplication first and addition second, we have to put parentheses around the addition. So if we want our problem to show that 8 and 3 should be added first, we would have to write it like this.

$$(8 + 3) \cdot 2$$ **Parentheses mean add first.**

The proper way to calculate $(8 + 3) \cdot 2$ is to add 8 and 3 first to get 11. Then we multiply 11 and 2 second to get 22. That's the only correct answer to this one. Those parentheses tell us that the addition has to be first. The meaning of $(8 + 3) \cdot 2$ in words is "add 8 and 3 first, and multiply the result by 2 second."

Subtraction Too

Here's an example with subtraction. Let's multiply 2 and 4 then subtract the total from 9. In this case multiplication is supposed to be first and subtraction second. To show the correct order, we should write it like this.

$$9 - 2 \cdot 4$$

According to the rules, unless there are parentheses, multiplication is always done before subtraction. So $9 - 2 \cdot 4$ means "multiply 2 and 4 first, then subtract the total from 9." Here's the actual calculation, which has an answer of 1.

$$9 - 2 \cdot 4 \quad \longrightarrow \quad 9 - 8 \quad \longrightarrow \quad 1$$

Let's do one more. Let's subtract 7 from 12 and then multiply that total by 5. The order of operations rules tell us that without parentheses we always do multiplication first. So to show that subtraction should be done before multiplication, we need to use rule 3 and put parentheses around the subtraction, like this.

$$(12 - 7) \cdot 5$$ **Parentheses mean subtract first.**

This means "do $12 - 7$ first, then multiply the total by 5." Here's the complete calculation.

$$(12 - 7) \cdot 5 \quad \longrightarrow \quad 5 \cdot 5 \quad \longrightarrow \quad 25$$

The main point of this lesson is that when we're working with more than one operation, we have to make sure to do those operations in the correct order. And the mathematicians created rules for writing the order correctly.

Once again, the rules are that multiplication and division are always done before addition and subtraction, unless the addition or subtraction is put inside parentheses.

Practice 68

a. Calculate the value of the expression $5 \cdot 3 + 6$.
(68)

b. Calculate the value of the expression $3 \cdot (5 + 1)$.
(68)

c. Translate the following phrase into a mathematical expression: 5 and 6 multiplied together first, and then
(68) 4 added to that total. (Don't calculate the answer.)

      A. $5 + 6 \cdot 4$ B. $(5 + 6) \cdot 4$ C. $5 \cdot 6 + 4$

      D. $5 \cdot 6 \cdot 4$ E. $5 + 6 + 4$

d. Translate the following phrase into a mathematical expression: 2 and 7 added together first, and that total
(68) multiplied by 4. (Don't calculate the answer.)

      A. $2 \cdot (7 + 4)$ B. $(2 + 7) \cdot 4$ C. $2 \cdot 7 \cdot 4$

      D. $2 + 7 \cdot 4$ E. $2 \cdot 7 + 4$

e. Translate the word problem below into an equation; then solve.
(55)

    If Randy is driving at 25 miles per hour, how many hours will it take him to travel 20 miles? Round your answer to the nearest tenths place (one decimal place).

Problem Set 68

Tell whether each sentence below is True or False.

1. The first order of operations rule states: All multiplications and divisions are done first.
(68)

2. The second order of operations rule states: All additions and subtractions are done second.
(68)

3. The third order of operations rule states: If a different order is needed, the operations that are supposed
(68) to be first must be put inside parentheses.

Add or subtract each group of numbers below.

4.   68.24
(17)   +35.17

5.   53.49
(17)   −26.03

Do each unit conversion below.

6. Convert 28 yards to inches.
(34)

7. How many meters are in 125 decimeters?
(38)

Add each pair of numbers below.

8. $-\dfrac{1}{2}+\left(-\dfrac{1}{2}\right)$
(59)

9. $84+(-49)$
(59)

Subtract each pair of numbers below.

10. $7-(-15)$
(60)

11. $-63-71$
(60)

Multiply each pair of numbers below.

12. $(-21)(4)$
(61)

13. $(-7)(-5)$
(61)

Divide each pair of numbers below.

14. $\dfrac{-24}{8}$
(62)

15. $\dfrac{-63}{-9}$
(62)

Calculate the value of each expression below. (Make sure to do the operations in the correct order.)

(a) 16. $6\cdot2+7$
(68)

(b) 17. $2\cdot(3+4)$
(68)

Translate each of the following phrases into a mathematical expression. (Don't calculate the answer.)

(c) 18. 3 and 2 multiplied together first and then 5 added to that total.
(68)

    A. $3\cdot2+5$ B. $3+2+5$ C. $3\cdot2\cdot5$

    D. $(3+2)\cdot5$ E. $3+2\cdot5$

(d) 19. 5 and 9 added first, and that total multiplied by 3.
(68)

    A. $5\cdot(9+3)$ B. $5+9\cdot3$ C. $5\cdot9\cdot3$

    D. $5\cdot9+3$ E. $(5+9)\cdot3$

Solve each equation below by undoing.

20.
(53)
$x + (-10) = 24$

21.
(53)
$\dfrac{5}{6}x = 20$

22.
(67)
$\dfrac{-x}{12} = 9$

23.
(66)
$-5 - x = -3$

Translate the word problem below into an equation; then solve.

(e) 24.
(55)
If Brett is riding his mountain bike at 15 miles per hour, how many hours will it take him to travel 9 miles? Round your answer to the nearest tenths place (one decimal place).

Lesson 69—Writing Equations in Order

In the last lesson, we learned rules for the order of operations. But we kept things pretty simple and only worked with arithmetic problems, like $(12-7)\cdot 5$. Now we're going to apply the order of operations rules to real algebra equations.

Multiplication First

Here's our first example.

There's some number that if we multiply it by 2 first, and then add 5 to the total we get 27. What's the number?

We need to translate this into an equation, and since we're trying to find the missing number, that's what x has to represent.

$$x = \text{missing number}$$

Notice the problem involves *two* operations—multiplication and addition—and that the multiplication is supposed to be done first. So we have to make the equation show that order. Let's start by just putting in the numbers and x. Then we'll figure out the right order of operations.

$$2x+5 = 27$$

We have x multiplied by 2 and we have 5 added for a result of 27. Now what about the order? Is it right? Well, remember the rules. They say that multiplication is done before addition unless there are parentheses around the addition. Here we *want* multiplication to be first because that's what the problem says. So there shouldn't be any parentheses in this equation. We've got it exactly right: $2x+5 = 27$ means what we want it to mean. It says "If the missing number x is multiplied by 2 *first* and then 5 is added *second*, the result is equal to 27."

So when writing an equation for a problem with more than one operation, we have more to worry about than just getting the numbers and the x right. We have to get the order of operations right too. Otherwise the equation won't really represent the problem, and the answer will turn out wrong (even if we undo everything correctly).

Addition or Subtraction First

Let's try another one.

There's some number that if we subtract 22 from it and then multiply that total by 7, the result is -42. What's the number?

To write the equation, we first let x stand for the missing number:

$$x = \text{missing number.}$$

Since there are two operations (subtraction and multiplication), we have to make sure to get the order right. According to the problem, the subtraction is supposed to be done first. You may be wondering, though, how we were able to tell. Well, you have to read the problem carefully. It says "subtract 22 and *then* multiply." That little word "then" is what tells us the subtraction comes first and the multiplication second. Another clue is the phrase "multiply *that total*." If we're supposed to multiply the total from the subtraction, then obviously we have to do the subtraction first. Let's start by putting in the numbers and x.

$$x-22\cdot 7 = -42$$

Next, we need to make sure that the correct order of operations is shown. With the way the equation is written now, the order is wrong. Remember, our rules tell us to do multiplication first unless there are parentheses. So this equation says to multiply 22 and 7 first, and subtract that total from x second. But our problem is telling us we're supposed to subtract 22 first, and then that total should be multiplied by 7 second. So we need to put parentheses in like this.

$$(x-22)\cdot 7 = -42$$

Now the equation says "there's a missing number x and if we subtract 22 from it first and multiply that total by 7 second, the result is -42." That's exactly what we want.

Write It Right

One last thing. There's actually no reason to use the dot to show multiplication in this equation. Remember, we can show multiplication with parentheses too. Since $x-22$ already has parentheses around it, we could write the equation as $(x-22)7 = -42$. But since everybody puts the 7 first, the proper way to write it is actually like this.

$$7(x-22) = -42$$

Mathematically, it doesn't make any difference whether the 7 goes before or after $x-22$, because multiplication can be done in any order. But everybody always puts the number before the parentheses. It's like writing $3x$ instead of $x3$.

Practice 69

a.
(68)
Calculate the value of the expression $-5(3-6)$.

b.
(68)
Translate the following phrase into a mathematical expression: 5 and 6 multiplied together first and then subtracted -9 from that total. (Don't calculate the answer.)

A. $5\cdot(6-9)$ B. $5-6\cdot(-9)$ C. $5\cdot 6-(-9)$

D. $5\cdot 6+(-9)$ E. $9-5\cdot 6$

c.
(69)
Translate the following word problem into an equation: There's some number that if you multiply it by 5 first and then add 4 to the total you get 24. (Don't solve.)

A. $5(x+4)=24$ B. $5x+4+24$ C. $5+4x=24$

D. $(5+4)x=24$ E. $5x+4=24$

d.
(69)
Translate the following word problem into an equation: There's some number that if you subtract 7 from it and then multiply that total by 3, the result is -15. (Don't solve.)

A. $3x-7=-15$ B. $3(x-7)-15$ C. $x-7\cdot 3=-15$

D. $(7-3)x=-15$ E. $3(x-7)=-15$

e.
(54)
Translate the word problem below into an equation; then solve.

Maggie bought a designer cotton vest at a 30% discount. If the discount saved her $27, what did the vest cost originally?

Problem Set 69

Multiply or divide each pair of fractions below. Make sure your answers are fully reduced.

1.
(13) $\dfrac{4}{14} \cdot \dfrac{7}{8}$

2.
(13) $\dfrac{6}{10} \div \dfrac{2}{5}$

Convert each fraction below into decimal form. Give exact answers (no rounding).

3.
(23) $\dfrac{6}{5}$

4.
(24) $\dfrac{9}{11}$

Add each pair of numbers below.

5.
(59) $-45 + (-17)$

6.
(59) $-23 + 19$

Subtract each pair of numbers below.

7.
(60) $2.5 - (-1)$

8.
(60) $-8 - 13$

Multiply each pair of numbers below.

9.
(61) $(6)(-7)$

10.
(61) $(-9)(-9)$

Divide each pair of numbers below.

11.
(62) $\dfrac{52}{-13}$

12.
(62) $\dfrac{-45}{-5}$

Tell whether each of the following pairs of expressions is equivalent.

13.
(65) $\dfrac{-9}{10}$ and $-\dfrac{9}{10}$

14.
(66) $(-1)(-x)$ and $-x$

Calculate the value of each expression below. (Make sure to do the operations in the correct order.)

15.
(68) $9 - 5 \cdot 3$

(a) **16.**
(68) $-4(2 - 8)$

Translate each of the following phrases into a mathematical expression. (Don't calculate the answer.)

(b) 17.
(68)
7 and 4 multiplied together first and then -3 subtracted from that total.

    A. $7 \cdot 4 - (-3)$ B. $7 \cdot 4 + (-3)$ C. $7 \cdot (4-3)$

    D. $7 - 4 \cdot (-3)$ E. $3 - 7 \cdot 4$

18.
(68)
4 minus 12 first, and that total multiplied by 2.

    A. $4 \cdot 12 - 2$ B. $2(12-4)$ C. $12(4-2)$

    D. $2(4-12)$ E. $4 - 12 \cdot 2$

Translate each of the following word problems into an equation. (Don't solve.)

(c) 19.
(69)
There's some number that if you multiply it by 3 first, and then add 7 to the total you get 31.

    A. $3 + 7x = 31$ B. $(3+7)x = 31$ C. $3x + 7 + 31$

    D. $3x + 7 = 31$ E. $3(x+7) = 31$

(d) 20.
(69)
There's some number that if you subtract 9 from it and then multiply that total by 4, the result is -20.

    A. $(9-4)x = -20$ B. $4(x-9) - 20$ C. $4(x-9) = -20$

    D. $x - 9 \cdot 4 = -20$ E. $4x - 9 = -20$

Solve each equation below by undoing. Make sure your answer is fully reduced.

21.
(53)
$\dfrac{1}{2} + x = \dfrac{3}{5}$

22.
(64)
$\dfrac{x}{-7} = -14$

23.
(66)
$25 - x = -39$

Translate the word problem below into an equation; then solve.

(e) 24.
(54)
Stephanie bought some Nappa leather boots at a 20% discount. If the discount saved her $23, what did the boots cost originally?

Lesson 70—Order and the Fraction Bar

In the last couple of lessons we've been learning about the order of operations. But so far we've only done problems that mix multiplication with addition or subtraction. What about division?

Mixing Operations with Division

To see how to handle division, let's go back to the rules.

1.	All multiplications and divisions are done first.
2.	All additions and subtractions are done second.
3.	If a different order is needed, the operations that are supposed to be done first must be put in parentheses.

Rule 1 says that "all multiplications and *divisions* are done first." So according to the rules, division is just like multiplication: it's supposed to be done before addition or subtraction. That means in an expression like $8 + \dfrac{12}{4}$, we should do the division first and the addition second. So to actually do the calculation, we would divide 12 by 4 first to get $8 + 3$. Then we would add 8 and 3 to get 11.

The Fraction Bar Clears Things Up

Now you can understand another reason why we use the fraction bar in algebra instead of the old arithmetic division symbol. Writing 12 divided by 4 as a fraction makes it easy to see that the division is supposed to be done first. Take a close look at the last example.

$$8 + \frac{12}{4}$$

With the problem written this way, nobody would try to add 8 and 12 first. They would have to take the 12 out of the numerator of the fraction, and almost nobody would even think of doing that. So writing the division as a fraction helps us see how to do the operations in the correct order. But if we had used the old division symbol, the problem would have been a lot more confusing.

$$8 + 12 \div 4$$

With the problem written this way, it seems natural to add 8 and 12 first (because we naturally do things from left to right). But that would be wrong according to the order of operations rules. The fraction bar makes it easier to follow the correct order of operations.

Using the Fraction Bar to Change the Order

What if the addition is supposed to come before the division? How should that be written? With parentheses? Actually, no. We use the fraction bar again. If we want the problem to mean "add 8 to 12 first and then divide that total by 4," this is how we should write it.

$$\frac{8+12}{4}$$

We just put the entire addition in the fraction. This makes it really easy to get the order right again. Think about it. Nobody would try to divide 4 into just 12. They would add on top to figure out how big the numerator is first. Then they would divide. So by putting the addition inside the fraction, everybody naturally does the operations in the correct order. That's why we use the fraction bar, instead of parentheses, to show addition before division. We could write it like this: $(8+12) \div 4$. But this isn't as clear.

There is one problem, though. Our rules don't mention using the fraction bar to show a change in the order of operations. We just need to make a small change to rule 3. Instead of saying that to change the order we have to put an operation inside parentheses, we should say that the operation needs to go inside parentheses *or* inside a fraction.

1.	All multiplications and divisions are done first.
2.	All additions and subtractions are done second.
3.	If a different order is needed, the operations that are supposed to be done first must be put in parentheses or *inside a fraction*.

Now the rules cover both multiplication and division.

Mixing Division and Subtraction

When division is mixed with subtraction everything works the same way. Here's an example.

$$14-\frac{10}{2}$$

In this one, we're supposed to divide first, since the subtraction isn't inside the fraction. So to calculate this expression correctly, we divide first. Then we subtract to get an answer of 9.

$$14-5 \qquad \longrightarrow \qquad 9$$

Here's another one.

$$\frac{18}{9-3}$$

This time, the subtraction is in the bottom of the fraction. That means we need to subtract 9 and 3 first and divide second. (Putting the subtraction inside the fraction makes that easy to see.) When you subtract, the bottom turns out to equal 6. Then, the second step is to divide 18 by 6 to get an answer of 3.

$$\frac{18}{6} \qquad \longrightarrow \qquad 3$$

Practice 70

a.
(70)   Calculate the value of the expression $\dfrac{4+8}{2}$. (Make sure to do the operations in the correct order.)

b.
(70)   Translate the following phrase into a mathematical expression: 20 divided by 4 first and then 3 subtracted from that total. (Don't calculate the answer.)

A. $\dfrac{20}{4} - 3$ B. $3 - \dfrac{20}{4}$ C. $\dfrac{20-3}{4}$

D. $\dfrac{20-4}{3}$ E. $\dfrac{20}{4-3}$

c.
(70)   Translate the following phrase into a mathematical expression: 7 added to 8 first and then that total divided by 5. (Don't calculate the answer.)

A. $\dfrac{7}{8+5}$ B. $\dfrac{8}{7+5}$ C. $\dfrac{7}{5} + 8$

D. $7 + \dfrac{8}{5}$ E. $\dfrac{7+8}{5}$

d.
(69)   Translate the following word problem into an equation: There's some number that if you subtract 11 from it first and then multiply that total by 7, the result is 56. (Don't solve.)

A. $7(11-x) = 56$ B. $(11-7)x = 56$ C. $x - 11 \cdot 7 = 56$

D. $7(x-11) = 56$ E. $7x - 11 = 56$

e.
(53)   Translate the word problem below into an equation; then solve.

Terry spent $15.40 on gasoline. If each gallon cost $1.40, how many gallons of gas did he purchase?

Problem Set 70

Tell whether each sentence below is True or False.

1.
(70)   The fraction bar can be used to show the order of operations.

2.
(70)   To show that an addition should be done before a division, the addition should be put inside a fraction.

Answer each question below.

3.
(55)   How far will a mole digging at 3 feet per hour dig in 2 hours?

4.
(55)   How far will a train moving at 42 miles per hour travel in $3\dfrac{1}{2}$ hours?

Add each pair of numbers below.

5.
(59) $-51+(-49)$

6.
(59) $14+(-72)$

Subtract each pair of numbers below.

7.
(60) $-7-(-18)$

8.
(60) $-20-40$

Multiply each pair of numbers below.

9.
(61) $(-4)(11)$

10.
(61) $(-28)(0)$

Divide each pair of numbers below.

11.
(62) $\dfrac{-30}{3}$

12.
(62) $\dfrac{-63}{-9}$

Calculate the value of each expression below. (Make sure to do the operations in the correct order.)

13.
(70) $9+\dfrac{15}{3}$

14.
(68) $12-2\cdot 4$

(a) 15.
(70) $\dfrac{3+7}{2}$

Translate each of the following phrases into a mathematical expression. (Don't calculate the answer.)

16.
(68) 3 and 6 multiplied together first and then 8 subtracted from that total.

A. $3(6-8)$ B. $8-3\cdot 6$ C. $3\cdot 6\cdot 8$

D. $6(3-8)$ E. $3\cdot 6-8$

(b) 17.
(70) 14 divided by 2 first and then 5 subtracted from that total.

A. $\dfrac{14}{5-2}$ B. $\dfrac{14-2}{5}$ C. $\dfrac{14}{2}-5$

D. $\dfrac{14-5}{2}$ E. $5-\dfrac{14}{2}$

(c) 18.
(70) 5 added to 11 first and then that total divided by 8.

A. $\dfrac{5+11}{8}$ B. $\dfrac{11}{5+8}$ C. $\dfrac{5}{11+8}$

D. $\dfrac{5}{8}+11$ E. $5+\dfrac{11}{8}$

312

Translate each of the following word problems into an equation. (Don't solve.)

19.
(69)
There's some number that if you multiply it by 5 first, and then add 3 to the total, the result is 18.

A. $5x \cdot 3 = 18$ B. $5x + 3 = 18$ C. $5x + 3 + 18$

D. $5(x + 3) = 18$ E. $x + 5 \cdot 3 = 18$

(d) 20.
(69)
There's some number that if you subtract 6 from it first and then multiply that total by 3, the result is 45.

A. $3x - 6 = 45$ B. $3(x - 6) = 45$ C. $x - 6 \cdot 3 = 45$

D. $(6 - 3)x = 45$ E. $3(6 - x) = 45$

Solve each equation below by undoing. Make sure your answer is fully reduced.

21. $-5x = -7$
(64)

22. $\dfrac{\frac{x}{2}}{\frac{5}{}} = \dfrac{1}{8}$
(53)

23. $x + (-28) = -96$
(63)

Translate the word problem below into an equation; then solve.

(e) 24.
(53)
Mike spent \$4.55 on Snickers™ bars for him and his road trip buddies. If each Snickers™ bar costs \$0.65, how many did Mike purchase?

Lesson 71—Using the Fraction Bar in Equations

In the last lesson we learned to show the order of operations using the fraction bar. We only did arithmetic problems in the examples, but we can also use the fraction bar to show order in equations. Let's say we want to write an equation for this problem.

> There's some number that if we divide it by 3 first, and then add 7 to that total, we get 14. What's the number?

We're trying to find the missing number, so we should make it x.

$$x = \text{missing number}$$

Notice that the problem says this missing number is divided by 3 first, and then 7 is added second. So the order is division first and addition second. That means we don't need to put the addition inside the fraction. To show that division should come first and addition second, we should write the equation like this.

$$\frac{x}{3} + 7 = 14$$

According to the order of operations rules, division is before addition unless the addition is inside a fraction. The addition is not inside the fraction here, so this equation says exactly what we want it to.

Addition First, Division Second

Let's try another one.

> There's some number that if we add 4 to it first, and then divide that total by 2, we get 18. What's the number?

We'll go through the same process on this one. We'll let x represent the number we're trying to find.

$$x = \text{missing number}$$

Notice the problem says "if you add 4 to it *first*." That means the addition is before the division. So we're going to have to put the addition inside the fraction, like this.

$$\frac{x+4}{2} = 18$$

The equation means "x and 4 are added first, and then the total is divided by 2 to get 18." That's what we want.

Division First, Subtraction Second

Here's an example with subtraction.

> If we divide some number by 5 first, and then subtract that total from 39, the total is 22. What's the number?

In this problem the division is first, so the subtraction doesn't need to be inside the fraction. We divide x and 5 first and then subtract the result from 39.

$$39 - \frac{x}{5} = 22$$

According to the rules, this equation is telling us to divide first (because the subtraction is not inside the fraction) and subtract second. That's exactly what we want. Notice that the x divided by 5 comes after the 39. That's because our problem says to divide those first and then subtract the result *from* 39. If the problem had said take x divided by 5 and subtract 39 from *it*, then we would have had to write it like this: $\frac{x}{5} - 39$. So you have to be really careful when reading a problem to make sure you've translated it into an equation correctly.

See why the order of operations rules are so important? You have to know them to turn a real problem into an equation. And if you can't do that, then you can't really use algebra. But it takes a lot of practice, so don't get frustrated if you're having trouble. It takes a long time to master the process of turning a word problem into an equation. Just keep working at it. You'll be doing a lot more of this in Algebra 1 and even in Algebra 2.

Practice 71

a.
(68)
Translate the following phrase into a mathematical expression: 8 and 3 multiplied together first and than that total subtracted from 14. (Don't calculate the answer.)

    A. $14 - 8 - 3$ B. $14 \cdot 8 - 3$ C. $8 \cdot 3 - 14$

    D. $14 - 8 \cdot 3$ E. $3(14 - 8)$

b.
(71)
Translate the following word problem into an equation: There's some number that if you divide it by 4 first, and then subtract 11 from that total, the result is 32. (Don't solve.)

    A. $\frac{x}{4} - 11 = 32$ B. $11 - \frac{x}{4} = 32$ C. $\frac{x - 11}{4} = 32$

    D. $x - \frac{11}{4} = 32$ E. $\frac{x}{4 - 11} = 32$

c.
(71)
Translate the following word problem into an equation: There's some number that if you add 8 to it first and then divide that total by 3, the result is 27. (Don't solve.)

    A. $\frac{x}{8 + 3} = 27$ B. $\frac{3}{x + 8} = 27$ C. $\frac{x}{8} + 3 = 27$

    D. $\frac{x}{3} + 8 = 27$ E. $\frac{x + 8}{3} = 27$

d.
(66)
Solve the equation $-10 - x = -4$.

e.
(54)
Translate the word problem below into an equation; then solve.

There were 1,500 natural food items in the health food store, but only 6 of them were blue. What percent of the natural foods were blue? (The answer to your equation will be in decimal form. Make sure your final answer is written as a percent.)

Problem Set 71

Add or subtract each pair of fractions below. Make sure your answers are fully reduced.

1.
(10) $\dfrac{1}{7}+\dfrac{3}{7}$

2.
(10) $\dfrac{5}{6}-\dfrac{2}{3}$

Convert each percent below into decimal form.

3.
(25) 57%

4.
(25) 132%

Add each pair of numbers below.

5.
(59) $-15+(-27)$

6.
(59) $61+(-48)$

Subtract each pair of numbers below.

7.
(60) $35-(-11)$

8.
(60) $-83-(-16)$

Multiply each pair of numbers below.

9.
(61) $(-12)(3)$

10.
(61) $(-9)(-11)$

Divide each pair of numbers below.

11.
(62) $\dfrac{-75}{25}$

12.
(62) $\dfrac{-24}{6}$

Calculate the value of each expression below. (Make sure to do the operations in the correct order.)

13.
(70) $\dfrac{45}{4+5}$

14.
(68) $-3(9+2)$

Translate each of the following phrases into a mathematical expression. (Don't calculate the answer.)

15.
(68) -5 added to 13 first and that total multiplied by 4.

A. $-5\cdot4+13$ B. $-5(13+4)$ C. $4(-5+13)$

D. $-5+13\cdot4$ E. $-5\cdot13+4$

16. 14 minus 2 first and then that total divided by 3.
(70)

    A. $14 - \dfrac{2}{3}$ B. $\dfrac{14-2}{3}$ C. $\dfrac{14}{3} - 2$

    D. $\dfrac{14}{3-2}$ E. $\dfrac{3}{14-2}$

(a) 17. 7 and 6 multiplied together first and then that total subtracted from 21.
(68)

    A. $6(21-7)$ B. $21 \cdot 7 - 6$ C. $21 - 7 \cdot 6$

    D. $21 - 7 - 6$ E. $7 \cdot 6 - 21$

Translate each of the following word problems into an equation. (Don't solve.)

18. There's some number that if you multiply it by 2 first, and then subtract 6 from the total, the result is 16.
(69)

    A. $2x - 6 + 16$ B. $2 + x - 6 = 16$ C. $2(x-6) = 16$

    D. $2x - 6 = 16$ E. $6 - 2x = 16$

(b) 19. There's some number that if you divide it by 5 first, and then subtract 14 from that total, the result is 21.
(71)

    A. $\dfrac{x}{5-14} = 21$ B. $x - \dfrac{14}{5} = 21$ C. $\dfrac{x}{5} - 14 = 21$

    D. $\dfrac{x-14}{5} = 21$ E. $14 - \dfrac{x}{5} = 21$

(c) 20. There's some number that if you add 9 to it first and then divide that total by 2, the result is 30.
(71)

    A. $\dfrac{2}{x+9} = 30$ B. $\dfrac{x+9}{2} = 30$ C. $\dfrac{x}{9} + 2 = 30$

    D. $\dfrac{x}{2} + 9 = 30$ E. $\dfrac{x}{9+2} = 30$

Solve each equation below by undoing. Make sure your answer is fully reduced.

21. $\dfrac{1}{3} + x = \dfrac{6}{7}$ **22.** $\dfrac{x}{-9} = 17$ **(d) 23.** $-9 - x = -5$
(53)   (64)   (66)

Translate the word problem below into an equation; then solve.

(e) 24. There were 1,800 different kinds of suits in the men's store, but only 9 of them were yellowish. What
(54) percent of the suits were yellowish? (The answer to your equation will be in decimal form. Make sure your final answer is written as a percent.)

Lesson 72—Undoing in Reverse—Part 1

We've been learning how to write equations with two operations. But so far, we haven't actually solved any of them. In this lesson, we're going to take that next step and actually learn how to solve some two operation equations.

Undoing Addition First

Let's start with an equation that mixes multiplication and addition.

$$2x + 6 = 10$$

To get x by itself here, we have to undo *both* of the operations: the multiplication by 2 and the addition of 6. But which operation should we undo first? It makes a big difference. The rule (and it's a very important one) is that the operations are always undone in reverse order. That means whatever is done to x last, we undo it first. According to the order of operations rules, x is multiplied by 2 first and 6 is added second.[1] To solve the equation, then, we need to undo in reverse, which means addition should be undone first and multiplication second.

$$2x + 6 = 10$$

We undo the addition of 6 in the usual way: by subtracting 6 from both sides.

$$2x + 6 - 6 = 10 - 6 \qquad \textbf{Undoing addition first}$$

The left side looks a little messy, but it just means there's some quantity $2x$ that has 6 added to it, and then 6 subtracted again. So the left side now equals just $2x$. (If someone gave you $6 but then took $6 back again, you'd have the same amount of money you started with.)

$$2x = 10 - 6$$

We should subtract on the right too.

$$2x = 4$$

Now that the addition has been undone first, we're ready to undo the multiplication second. To undo multiplication by 2, we just divide both sides by 2.

$$\frac{2x}{2} = \frac{4}{2} \qquad \textbf{Undoing multiplication second}$$

The left side is now just equal to x.

$$x = \frac{4}{2}$$

Notice we've turned our hard algebra equation with two operations into a simple arithmetic problem. The last step is to divide on the right to get an answer of 2.

$$x = 2$$

So to solve $2x + 6 = 10$ we had to undo both of the operations. But the important thing was that we had to undo the addition first and the multiplication second. That's in reverse order.

---

[1] That's because multiplication is always supposed to be done before addition unless there are parentheses, and this equation doesn't have any.

Checking the Answer

Let's check our answer to make sure it's right. We need to put 2 in for x in the original equation.

$$2x+6=10$$

$$2(2)+6=10$$ **Putting 2 in for x**

Next, we calculate the left side. But since we're just calculating and not undoing, we have to do the operations in the correct order (not in reverse). Reverse order is *only* for undoing. Don't get confused about that. There are no additions or subtractions inside parentheses, so the multiplication should be done first and the addition second.[2] Multiplying 2 and 2 gives us this.

$$4+6=10$$

Now we do the addition by adding 4 and 6.

$$10=10$$

Since the sides are equal, our solution of 2 is correct.

Undoing Multiplication First

Let's look at another example where the x has two operations done to it.

$$3(x-5)=9$$

This equation has both a subtraction and a multiplication. The first step is to figure out the order in which the operations are done to x. The subtraction is in parentheses, so subtraction is first and multiplication is second. So the equation is telling us that there is a missing number, and if we subtract 5 from it first, and multiply the result by 3 second, we'll get 9. To solve the equation, we need to undo those operations in reverse order. That means we undo the multiplication first and the subtraction second. We can undo the multiplication by 3 by dividing both sides by 3. And the way to do it is to put a fraction bar under everything on both sides, like this.

$$\frac{3(x-5)}{3}=\frac{9}{3}$$ **Undoing multiplication first**

The left side looks complicated but it just says that some quantity $x-5$ is multiplied by 3 and divided by 3. Since the division undoes the multiplication, we end up with only $x-5$ on that side.

$$x-5=\frac{9}{3}$$

Now we'll divide on the right side to get 3.

$$x-5=3$$

Since we undid the multiplication first, we can now undo the subtraction second, by adding 5 to both sides.

$$x-5+5=3+5$$ **Undoing subtraction second**

---

[2] The equation does have parentheses. But they're just showing us that 2 and 2 are multiplied. There aren't any operations inside parentheses.

That leaves just x on the left.

$$x = 3 + 5$$

We've turned the algebra equation into an arithmetic problem. The last step is to add on the right to get an answer of 8.

$$x = 8$$

To solve $3(x-5) = 9$, then, we had to undo the multiplication first and the subtraction second. You can check the answer yourself, if you want, by putting 8 back in for x in the original equation and doing the operations in the correct order (not reverse order).

Practice 72

a.
(71)
Translate the following word problem into an equation: There's some number that if you divide it by -6 first and then add 24 to that total, the result is 15. (Don't solve.)

A. $\dfrac{x}{-6} + 24 = 15$
B. $\dfrac{x+24}{-6} = 15$
C. $\dfrac{x}{-6+24} = 15$

D. $\dfrac{x}{24} + (-6) = 15$
E. $\dfrac{-6}{x} + 24 = 15$

b.
(69)
Translate the following word problem into an equation: There's some number that if you subtract 3 from it first, and then multiply that total by 14, the result is 70. (Don't solve.)

A. $14x - 3 = 70$
B. $3 - 14x = 70$
C. $x - 3 \cdot 14 = 70$
D. $14(3 - x) = 70$
E. $14(x - 3) = 70$

c.
(72)
Solve the equation $4x + 5 = 33$.

d.
(72)
Solve the equation $5(x - 2) = 45$.

e.
(55)
Translate the word problem below into an equation; then solve.

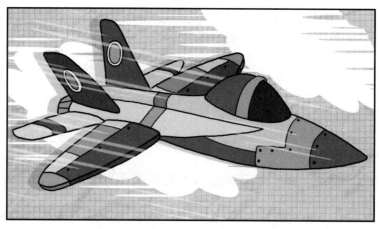

The jet flew for 3 hours, traveling a total of 1,740 miles. How fast did the jet travel in miles per hour?

Problem Set 72

Tell whether each sentence below is True or False.

1.
(72) When solving an equation with two operations, you should undo the operations in reverse order.

2.
(72) In the equation $2(x-7)=16$, the subtraction should be undone first.

Add or subtract (as indicated) each pair of numbers below.

3.
(59) $-29+(-43)$

4.
(60) $-17-(-8)$

5.
(59) $-20+51$

Multiply each pair of numbers below.

6.
(61) $(46)(-2)$

7.
(61) $(-5)(-13)$

Divide each pair of numbers below.

8.
(62) $\dfrac{-7}{3.5}$

9.
(62) $\dfrac{-140}{-20}$

Calculate the value of each expression below. (Make sure to do the operations in the correct order.)

10.
(70) $19-\dfrac{15}{3}$

11.
(68) $5\cdot 2+6$

12.
(70) $\dfrac{8+12}{5}$

Translate each of the following phrases into a mathematical expression. (Don't calculate the answer.)

13.
(68) 7 minus 25 first, and then that total multiplied by -6.

    A. $-6(7-25)$ B. $25(7-6)$ C. $7-25\cdot(-6)$

    D. $25-7\cdot(-6)$ E. $7-25-6$

14.
(70) 28 added to 17 first, and then that total divided by -9.

    A. $\dfrac{28}{-9}+17$ B. $28+\dfrac{17}{-9}$ C. $\dfrac{-9}{28+17}$

    D. $\dfrac{28+17}{-9}$ E. $\dfrac{28+(-9)}{17}$

321

Translate each of the following word problems into an equation. (Don't solve.)

(a) 15.
(71)
There's some number that if you divide it by -8 first, and then add 22 to that total, the result is 13.

    A. $\dfrac{x}{22} + (-8) = 13$ B. $\dfrac{-8}{x} + 22 = 13$ C. $\dfrac{x}{-8 + 22} = 13$

    D. $\dfrac{x + 22}{-8} = 13$ E. $\dfrac{x}{-8} + 22 = 13$

(b) 16.
(69)
There's some number that if you subtract 4 from it first, and then multiply that total by 12, the result is 60.

    A. $x - 4 \cdot 12 = 60$ B. $4 - 12x = 60$ C. $12(x - 4) = 60$

    D. $12(4 - x) = 60$ E. $12x - 4 = 60$

Solve each equation below by undoing. Make sure your answer is fully reduced.

17. $-8x = 3$
(64)

18. $\dfrac{-x}{11} = 2$
(67)

19. $x - (-5) = -12$
(53)

20. $\dfrac{x}{2.5} = -4$
(53)

(c) 21. $3x + 4 = 22$
(72)

(d) 22. $2(x - 3) = 30$
(72)

Translate the word problem below into an equation; then solve.

(e) 23.
(55)
The jalopy sputtered across the desert for 6 hours, traveling a total of 168 miles before it finally broke down. How fast did the jalopy travel in miles per hour?

Lesson 73—Undoing in Reverse—Part 2

In the last lesson, we learned one of the most important rules in all of algebra. It's that equations with more than one operation are solved by undoing in reverse order. Let's use that rule to solve this equation.

$$\frac{x}{2} + 5 = 8$$

The first step is to figure out the order in which the operations are done to x. Here x is divided by 2 first and 5 is added second (because division is before addition unless the addition is inside a fraction, remember).

Undoing Division

To solve, we need to undo those operations in reverse order. That means we should undo the addition first and the division second. Undoing the addition is easy. We just subtract 5 from both sides.

$$\frac{x}{2} + 5 - 5 = 8 - 5 \qquad \textbf{Undoing addition first}$$

On the left we have $\frac{x}{2}$ with 5 added and then 5 subtracted. That's just equal to $\frac{x}{2}$.

$$\frac{x}{2} = 8 - 5$$

On the right we can subtract 8 minus 5.

$$\frac{x}{2} = 3$$

Next, we undo the division by multiplying both sides by 2.

$$2 \cdot \frac{x}{2} = 3 \cdot 2 \qquad \textbf{Undoing division second}$$

On the left side multiplication by 2 undoes division by 2, which leaves just x. And that turns the algebra equation into an arithmetic problem.

$$x = 3 \cdot 2$$

Now we just multiply on the right.

$$x = 6$$

The answer turns out to be 6. So to solve $\frac{x}{2} + 5 = 8$, we had to undo the addition first and the division second, which is undoing in reverse. The main point is that undoing in reverse works on equations with division too.

Undoing When x is Inside a Fraction

Let's try another example.

$$\frac{x - 9}{4} = 7$$

To start, we have to figure out the order in which the operations are done to x. Since the subtraction is inside the fraction, we know from the rules that subtraction is done first and division is done second. To solve, we need to undo in reverse order. That means the division is undone first, by multiplying both sides by 4.

$$4 \cdot \frac{x-9}{4} = 7 \cdot 4 \qquad \textbf{Undoing division first}$$

The left side looks complicated, but it just means that the quantity $x-9$ is divided by 4 and multiplied by 4. The multiplication undoes the division, so the left side becomes $x-9$.

$$x-9 = 7 \cdot 4$$

Now we multiply 7 and 4 to get 28.

$$x-9 = 28$$

Next, we undo the subtraction by adding 9 to both sides.

$$x-9+9 = 28+9 \qquad \textbf{Undoing subtraction second}$$

That makes the left side x.
$$x = 28+9$$

We've turned the algebra equation into an arithmetic problem, and all we have to do now is to add 28 and 9 on the right to get 37.

$$x = 37$$

So to solve harder equations with two operations, we just need to undo in reverse. It doesn't matter if we're mixing multiplication with addition or subtraction, or whether we're mixing division with addition or subtraction. Undoing in reverse works just the same.

Practice 73

a.
(70) Translate the following phrase into a mathematical expression: 20 divided by -4 first, and then that total subtracted from 90. (Don't calculate the answer.)

A. $90 - \dfrac{-4}{20}$ B. $\dfrac{90}{20+(-4)}$ C. $\dfrac{20}{90-(-4)}$

D. $\dfrac{20}{-4} - 90$ E. $90 - \dfrac{20}{-4}$

b.
(71) Translate the following word problem into an equation: There's some number that if you add 17 to it first, and then divide that total by 3, the result is 49. (Don't solve.)

A. $3(x+17) = 49$ B. $\dfrac{3}{x+17} = 49$ C. $\dfrac{x+17}{3} = 49$

D. $x + \dfrac{17}{3} = 49$ E. $\dfrac{x}{3} + 17 = 49$

c. Solve the equation $\dfrac{x}{4} + 3 = 16$.
(73)

d. Solve the equation $\dfrac{x-2}{5} = 18$.
(73)

e. Translate the word problem below into an equation; then solve.
(54)

Wayne was not only foolish enough to waste good money on a pair of camouflage house slippers, he also agreed to pay a 15% shipping and handling charge. If Wayne paid $2.40 in shipping and handling, how much must the house slippers have cost?

Problem Set 73

Multiply or divide each pair of numbers below. Write any remainders in decimal form.

1. $\begin{array}{r} 7.2 \\ \times 6.4 \\ \hline \end{array}$
(20)

2. $9\overline{)8,033}$
(22)

Add or subtract (as indicated) each pair of numbers below.

3. $-6-(-9)$
(60)

4. $59-(-27)$
(60)

5. $94+(-73)$
(59)

Multiply or divide (as indicated) each pair of numbers below.

6. $(-8)(14)$
(61)

7. $\dfrac{-64}{8}$
(62)

8. $\left(-\dfrac{1}{4}\right)(-4)$
(61)

Tell whether each of the following pairs of expressions is equivalent.

9. $\dfrac{7}{-8}$ and $-\dfrac{7}{8}$
(65)

10. $x-(-4)$ and $x+4$
(60)

Calculate the value of each expression below. (Make sure to do the operations in the correct order.)

11. $7(-4+2)$
(68)

12. $\dfrac{35}{5}-4$
(70)

13. $\dfrac{12}{3-9}$
(70)

Translate each of the following phrases into a mathematical expression. (Don't calculate the answer.)

14. -4 multiplied by 8 first, and then 18 added to that total.
(68)

    A. $-4 \cdot 8 \cdot 18$ B. $-4(18)+8$ C. $-4(8+18)$

    D. $-4(8)+18$ E. $8-4+18$

(a) 15. 36 divided by -6 first, and then that total subtracted from 100.
(70)

    A. $\dfrac{36}{-6} - 100$ B. $100 - \dfrac{36}{-6}$ C. $\dfrac{36}{100 - (-6)}$

    D. $\dfrac{100}{36 + (-6)}$ E. $100 - \dfrac{-6}{36}$

Translate each of the following word problems into an equation. (Don't solve.)

16. There's some number that if you multiply it by 2 first, and then subtract 25 from that total, the result is
(69) 38.

    A. $2x - 25 + 38$ B. $25 - 2x = 38$ C. $2(x - 25) = 38$

    D. $x - 2 \cdot 25 = 38$ E. $2x - 25 = 38$

(b) 17. There's some number that if you add 13 to it first, and then divide that total by 9, the result is 54.
(71)

    A. $\dfrac{x + 13}{9} = 54$ B. $9(x + 13) = 54$ C. $x + \dfrac{13}{9} = 54$

    D. $\dfrac{9}{x + 13} = 54$ E. $\dfrac{x}{9} + 13 = 54$

Solve each equation below by undoing. Make sure your answer is fully reduced.

18. $\dfrac{3}{2}x = 15$ **19.** $8 - x = 23$ **20.** $x + \left(-\dfrac{1}{2}\right) = 4$
(53)   **(66)**   **(49)**

21. $\dfrac{x}{-20} = 4.5$ **(c) 22.** $\dfrac{x}{3} + 7 = 19$ **(d) 23.** $\dfrac{x - 9}{2} = 11$
(53)   **(73)**   **(73)**

Translate the word problem below into an equation; then solve.

(e) 24. Sally went souvenir crazy on her trip to Mexico. She not only wasted good money on a sombrero that
(54) had blinking lights on it, she also agreed to pay a special 20% export tax. If Sally paid $9.60 in tax, how much must the sombrero have cost?

Lesson 74—Simplifying First

We've been learning how to solve equations with more than one operation. Here's the longest one yet.

$$3x + 5 + 7 = 18$$

This equation actually has three operations done to x. Here's what it means: "There's a missing number, x, that if we multiply it by 3 first, then add 5 to that, and then add 7 to that, we get 18. What's the number?"

Making Less to Undo

There are two ways to solve this. One way is just to undo everything in reverse order. We could undo the addition of 7 by subtracting 7 from both sides. Then we could undo the addition of 5 by subtracting 5 from both sides, and so on. But there's another method which is faster. What we do is make the equation simpler first. And it's really easy to do. We just add the 5 and 7 first.

$$3x + 12 = 18 \qquad \textbf{Add 5 and 7 first}$$

This is called **simplifying**. We simplified the expression $3x + 5 + 7$ by rewriting it as $3x + 12$. The important thing is that now the equation is easier to undo since there are only two operations instead of three. From here, we can solve by just undoing in reverse order. The multiplication by 3 is done first (since the addition isn't in parentheses), and the addition of 12 is second. So we undo the addition first by subtracting 12 from both sides.

$$3x + 12 - 12 = 18 - 12$$

The subtraction undoes the addition on the left side, so it's just equal to $3x$.

$$3x = 18 - 12$$

Now we subtract on the right.

$$3x = 6$$

Next, we undo the multiplication by dividing both sides by 3.

$$\frac{3x}{3} = \frac{6}{3}$$

The division undoes the multiplication on the left side, which leaves just x.

$$x = \frac{6}{3}$$

The last step is to do the arithmetic on the right for an answer of 2.

$$x = 2$$

Simplifying is a really smart thing to do on longer equations because it reduces the number of operations you have to undo.

Another Example

Let's try another long equation.

$$4x + 3 + 8 = 23$$

We could start undoing in reverse right away, but this equation is so long that it will be easier if we simplify first. All we have to do is add the 3 and 8.

$$4x + 11 = 23 \qquad\qquad \textbf{Simplify by adding 3 and 8}$$

Now the equation is easier to undo, because there are only two operations. As usual, we undo in reverse order. Here the multiplication of x is first and the addition is second (because the addition isn't in parentheses). So to undo in reverse, we should undo the addition first by subtracting 11 from both sides.

$$4x + 11 - 11 = 23 - 11$$

Subtraction undoes addition on the left, leaving just $4x$ on that side. On the right side, $23 - 11$ equals 12.

$$4x = 12$$

Now we undo the multiplication by dividing both sides by 4.

$$\frac{4x}{4} = \frac{12}{4}$$

Division undoes multiplication, making the left side equal x.

$$x = \frac{12}{4}$$

That turns our algebra equation into an arithmetic problem. The last step is to divide on the right to get an answer of 3.

$$x = 3$$

Practice 74

a.
(39)   How many feet are in 5 meters? (There are approximately 39 inches in 1 meter.) Write your answer as a decimal.

b.
(70)   Translate the following phrase into a mathematical expression: 8 subtracted from 14 first, and then that total divided by 3. (Don't calculate the answer.)

A. $14 - \dfrac{8}{3}$ 　　　　　 B. $8 - \dfrac{14}{3}$ 　　　　　 C. $\dfrac{3}{14 - 8}$

D. $\dfrac{14 - 8}{3}$ 　　　　　 E. $\dfrac{8 - 14}{3}$

c. Translate the following word problem into an equation: There's some number that if you subtract 14
(69) from it first, and then multiply that total by 22, the result is 88. (Don't solve.)

    A. $14(x-22)=88$ B. $22(x-14)=88$ C. $x-14\cdot22=88$

    D. $22x-14=88$ E. $14x-22=88$

d. Solve the equation $2x+6+7=19$.
(74)

e. Translate the word problem below into an equation; then solve.
(73)

There is a number that if you add 5 to it first, and then divide that total by 3, you get 8. What's the
number?

Problem Set 74

Tell whether each sentence below is True or False.

1. Longer equations are easier to solve if you simplify them first before undoing.
(74)

2. Simplifying first reduces the number of operations you have to undo.
(74)

Add or subtract each group of numbers below.

3.
(17)
$$\begin{array}{r} 62.81 \\ +47.59 \\ \hline \end{array}$$

4.
(17)
$$\begin{array}{r} 56.95 \\ -39.88 \\ \hline \end{array}$$

Do each unit conversion below.

5. Convert 216 inches to yards.
(34)

(a) 6. How many feet are in 4 meters? (There are approximately 39 inches in 1 meter.)
(39)

Add or subtract (as indicated) each pair of numbers below.

7. $21+(-22)$
(59)

8. $-16-(-33)$
(60)

Multiply or divide (as indicated) each pair of numbers below.

9. $\dfrac{-99}{-9}$
(62)

10. $(6)(-12)$
(61)

11. $\dfrac{65}{-13}$
(62)

Calculate the value of each expression below. (Make sure to do the operations in the correct order.)

12. $40 - 8 \cdot 4$
(68)

13. $\dfrac{-2+16}{7}$
(70)

14. $10(5-9)$
(68)

Translate each of the following phrases into a mathematical expression. (Don't calculate the answer.) Select the best possible choice given.

15. 6 added to 9 first, and then that total multiplied by 3.
(68)

    A. $3(6+9)$ B. $6 \cdot 9 \cdot 3$ C. $3(6)+9$

    D. $6+9+3$ E. $6+9(3)$

(b) 16. 7 subtracted from 12 first, and then that total divided 5.
(70)

    A. $\dfrac{7-12}{5}$ B. $5-\dfrac{12}{7}$ C. $\dfrac{12-7}{5}$

    D. $12-\dfrac{7}{5}$ E. $\dfrac{5}{12-7}$

Translate each of the following word problems into an equation. (Don't solve.) Select the best possible choice given.

17. There's some number that if you divide it by -12 first, and then add 3 to that total, the result is 4.
(71)

    A. $\dfrac{x}{-12}+3=4$ B. $\dfrac{-12}{x}+3=4$ C. $\dfrac{x}{-12+3}=4$

    D. $\dfrac{-12}{x+3}=4$ E. $\dfrac{x+3}{-12}=4$

(c) 18. There's some number that if you subtract 18 from it first, and then multiply that total by 24, the result is 72.
(69)

    A. $24(x-18)=72$ B. $x-18\cdot 24=72$ C. $24x-18=72$

    D. $18(x-24)=72$ E. $18x-24=72$

Solve each equation below by undoing.

19. $-9x=108$
(66)

20. $2x+8=26$
(72)

21. $\dfrac{x+4}{7}=3$
(73)

22. $3x+4+2=21$
(74)

(d) 23. $4x+3+8=35$
(74)

Translate the word problem below into an equation; then solve.

(e) 24. There is a number that if you add 7 to it first, and then divide that total by 4, you get 10. What's the number?
(73)

Lesson 75—More Simplifying First

In the last lesson, we learned to simplify a longer equation first before solving it by undoing. Now take a look at this long equation.

$$8 + 2x + 1 = 19$$

Do you see what's different? The numbers aren't next to each other. There's a $2x$ between them. Can we still simplify by adding the numbers first before undoing? Yes, we can.

Adding In Any Order

Remember the commutative property of addition and the associative property of addition? Those are basic rules about adding numbers in any order. The commutative property applies to two numbers. It's what tells us that $3 + 4$ is the same as $4 + 3$. The associative property applies to more than two numbers. Even though we covered this at the very beginning of the book, here's a quick example: $2 + 7 + 6 + 9$. We can add these in any order we want, and the answer will come out to be 24 every time. That's because of the associative property of addition. Now back to our equation.

$$8 + 2x + 1 = 19$$

Because of the associative property, we know that the three quantities on the left side (8, $2x$, and 1) can be added in any order. So we're allowed to add the 8 and 1, even though they aren't next to each other. That will give us this.

$$2x + 9 = 19 \qquad \textbf{Adding 8 and 1 first}$$

Now there are only two operations to undo. The equation has been simplified, and from here we undo in reverse order. We should undo the addition first by subtracting 9 from both sides.

$$2x + 9 - 9 = 19 - 9$$

Since we've added 9 and then taken 9 away on the left side, it becomes $2x$. And subtracting on the right side gives us 10.

$$2x = 10$$

Next, we undo the multiplication by dividing both sides by 2.

$$\frac{2x}{2} = \frac{10}{2}$$

Because the division undoes the multiplication, the left side becomes x.

$$x = \frac{10}{2}$$

And now we've turned the algebra equation into an arithmetic problem, so all that's left is to divide on the right to get an answer of 5.

$$x = 5$$

The main point is that even when the numbers aren't right next to each other, we can simplify first by adding. And we can do this because of the associative property of addition, which tells us that the order doesn't matter when adding several numbers.[1]

Simplifying With a Subtraction

Let's try another example that's a little harder.

$$1 + 3x - 7 = -16$$

This is another long equation with three operations. The x is multiplied by 3, 1 is added to that, and then 7 is subtracted. It would be nice if we could simplify before beginning to undo. And it's really tempting to add 1 and 7 right away, but that would be wrong. The problem is the 7 is subtracted. We can *add* in any order but we can't *subtract* in any order. So that won't work.

Is there still a way to simplify? Yes, there is. We just have to use our knowledge of negative numbers. Remember we learned that subtraction can be changed to addition of the opposite. So we can change the subtraction of 7 to addition of -7.

$$1 + 3x + (-7) = -16 \qquad \textbf{Change - 7 to + (-7)}$$

Now 1 and -7 are both added, and addition can be done in any order. So there's no problem in adding 1 and -7 on the left to get -6.

$$3x + (-6) = -16 \qquad \textbf{Add 1 and -7 first}$$

We've simplified the equation. From here, we can just undo in reverse order as usual. In this equation the multiplication by 3 is first and the addition of -6 is second. That's because, as you know, multiplication is always done first unless the addition is in parentheses. (And don't get confused by the parentheses around the -6. There's no addition or subtraction inside. The parentheses are just there to show that the negative sign is attached to the 6.) We could undo the addition of -6 by subtracting -6, but that would be kind of messy. The easiest way to undo the addition of a negative number is to add the opposite to both sides. So let's add positive 6 to both sides of the equation.

$$3x + (-6) + 6 = -16 + 6$$

That makes the left side $3x$, and if we do the addition on the right side we get -10.

$$3x = -10$$

Now we undo the multiplication by dividing both sides by 3.

$$\frac{3x}{3} = \frac{-10}{3}$$

The division undoes the multiplication on the left, leaving just x.

---

[1] To show that the associative property of addition will work for all numbers, we use letters: $(a + b) + c = a + (b + c)$. The parentheses say that adding a and b first gives the same answer as adding b and c first.

$$x = \frac{-10}{3}$$

The fraction on the right can't be reduced. So the only thing we need to do is figure out the sign of the entire fraction. Since a negative divided by a positive is a negative, this is the same as negative $\frac{10}{3}$. We show that by just putting the negative sign out in front of the entire fraction.

$$x = -\frac{10}{3}$$

So we end up with an answer of $-\frac{10}{3}$.

The main point is that our rules about adding numbers in any order can help us simplify equations. Even when one of the numbers is subtracted, we can still simplify by changing the subtraction to addition first.

Practice 75

a. Simplify the expression $6+3x+11$. Select the best possible choice.
(75)

    A. $9x+11$ B. $3x+17$ C. $20x$
    D. $3x+5$ E. $6+14x$

b. Simplify the expression $2+7x-6$. Select the best possible choice.
(75)

    A. $3x$ B. $2+x$ C. $9x-6$
    D. $7x+4$ E. $7x+(-4)$

c. Solve the equation $3+5x-10=13$.   **d.** Solve the equation $4+8x-14=-26$.
(75)   (75)

e. Translate the word problem below into an equation; then solve.
(54)

There were 2,400 stamps in the man's collection, but only 15 of them contained pictures of wagons. What percent of the stamps had pictures of wagons on them? (The answer to your equation will be in decimal form. Make sure your final answer is written as a percent.)

Problem Set 75

Tell whether each sentence below is True or False.

1. There's a rule (called the associative property of addition) which says that more than two numbers can
(75) be added in any order without affecting the total.

2. It is impossible to simplify an equation where one of the numbers is subtracted.
(75)

Multiply or divide each pair of numbers below. Make sure your answers are fully reduced.

3.
(13) $\dfrac{3}{10} \cdot \dfrac{20}{36}$

4.
(14) $32 \div \dfrac{8}{11}$

Add or subtract (as indicated) each pair of numbers below.

5.
(59) $50 + (-50)$

6.
(60) $34 - (-27)$

Multiply or divide (as indicated) each pair of numbers below.

7.
(61) $(-16)(3)$

8.
(62) $\dfrac{-18}{-2}$

9.
(61) $\left(\dfrac{1}{4}\right)(-20)$

Calculate the value of each expression below. (Make sure to do the operations in the correct order.)

10.
(70) $-9 + \dfrac{10}{5}$

11.
(68) $8 \cdot 4 - 12$

12.
(68) $-2(6+1)$

Translate each of the following phrases into a mathematical expression. (Don't calculate the answer.)

13.
(68) 6 multiplied by 5 first, and then 18 subtracted from that total.

A. $6 - 5 \cdot 18$ B. $6(18-5)$ C. $18 - 6 \cdot 5$

D. $6 \cdot 5 - 18$ E. $6(5-18)$

14.
(70) -11 added to 3 first, and then that total divided 2.

A. $\dfrac{-11}{2} + 3$ B. $\dfrac{-11}{3+2}$ C. $\dfrac{-11+3}{2}$

D. $\dfrac{2}{-11+3}$ E. $-11 + \dfrac{3}{2}$

Simplify each expression below. Select the best possible choice.

15.
(74) $7x + 2 + 6$

A. $7x + 8$ B. $7 + 8x$ C. $9x + 6$

D. $7x + 4$ E. $15x$

(a) 16.
(75) $5 + 4x + 9$

A. $5 + 13x$ B. $4x + 14$ C. $18x$

D. $9x + 9$ E. $4x + 45$

(b) 17. $3 + 6x - 8$
(75)

      A. $6x + 5$ B. $3 + (-2x)$ C. $6x + (-5)$

      D. x E. $9x - 8$

Solve each equation below by undoing.

18. $\dfrac{x}{-11} = -8$ **19.** $\dfrac{x}{3} + 9 = 17$ **20.** $5(x - 4) = -45$
(64)   (73)   (72)

(c) 21. $4 + 2x - 6 = 16$ **(d) 22.** $3 + 4x - 11 = -32$
(75)   (75)

Translate the word problem below into an equation; then solve.

(e) 23. There were 9,600 tourists on the beach that day, but only 12 of them were buried up to their neck in
(54)   sand. What percent of the tourists were buried up to their neck in sand? (The answer to your equation
    will be in decimal form. Make sure your final answer is written as a percent.)

CHAPTER 10:
COMBINING LIKE TERMS

Lesson 76—Adding *x*'s

We've been learning how to simplify equations first before undoing. In all our examples so far, we've simplified by adding numbers. But sometimes we need to simplify an equation by adding *x*'s. That may seem strange, because how can we add missing numbers?

Two *x*'s that Stand for the Same Thing

We'll show you with an example.

$$4x + 2x = 18$$

Notice that this equation has two *x*'s. A few lessons back, we said that one big difference between algebra and arithmetic is that in algebra the missing number can appear more than once. That's what is going on here. Both *x*'s stand for the same missing number. The equation $4x + 2x = 18$ actually means this: "There's a missing number *x* and if you multiply it by 4 and then multiply that same missing number by 2 and add those results, you'll get 18."

Making Two *x*'s One

Before undoing, we have to simplify the left side so that there's only one *x* showing. And we do that by adding $4x$ and $2x$. The process is actually pretty easy. We just add the numbers 4 and 2 to get 6, and then put that 6 in front of an *x* to get $6x$. So $4x + 2x$ is equivalent to $6x$.

$$6x = 18 \qquad\qquad \textbf{4x + 2x is 6x}$$

See, adding the *x*'s makes our equation a lot simpler because now there's just one operation to undo. From here, we undo multiplication of 6 by dividing both sides by 6.

$$\frac{6x}{6} = \frac{18}{6} \qquad\qquad \textbf{Undo normally}$$

The left side becomes *x*.

$$x = \frac{18}{6}$$

Finally, we do the division on the right, which gives us an answer of 3.

$$x = 3$$

How It Works

You may be wondering how $4x$ and $2x$ can be added to get $6x$. Well, remember that 4 times 3 means $3+3+3+3$. And 2 times 3 means $3+3$. So shouldn't $4x$ (which is just 4 times *x*) mean $x+x+x+x$? And shouldn't $2x$ mean $x+x$? Yes. So $4x + 2x$ is really just $x+x+x+x+x+x$. But that's six *x*'s added, which is the same as $6x$.

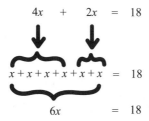

$$4x \quad + \quad 2x \quad = \quad 18$$

$$x + x + x + x + x + x \quad = \quad 18$$

$$6x \qquad = \quad 18$$

That's why we can change $4x + 2x$ to $6x$. And the great thing is that no matter what numbers are multiplied by the x's, all we have to do is add the numbers (and put the total in front of an x). Here are a few other examples.

5x + 3x is equivalent to 8x
2x + 7x is equivalent to 9x
10x + 12x is equivalent to 22x

Some Important Terms

We should also define some new technical terms for you. As it turns out, the numbers that are multiplied by the x's are actually called **coefficients**. So, for example, the coefficient of $7x$ is 7, and the coefficient of $3x$ is 3. Also, instead of saying "add the x's," some people say **combine** the x's. But adding and combining mean basically the same thing, so use whichever word you like. The main point of this lesson, though, is that to solve an equation with more than one x, we simplify first by adding (combining) the x's and then undoing normally.

Practice 76

a.
(69) Translate the following word problem into an equation: There's some number that if you add 7 to it first, and then multiply that total by -2, the result is 36. (Don't solve.)

    A. $7 + (-2x) = 36$ B. $-2(x + 7) = 36$ C. $-2x + 7 = 36$

    D. $x + 7(-2) = 36$ E. $x + 7 - 2 = 36$

b.
(76) Simplify the expression $6x + 2x$. Select the best possible choice.

    A. $16x$ B. $8 + x$ C. $8x$

    D. $x + 4$ E. $4x$

c.
(76) Solve the equation $4x + 3x = 14$.   **d.**
(76) Solve the equation $2x + 8x = 30$.

e. Translate the word problem below into an equation; then solve.
(55)

The rocket flew for 15 seconds, traveling a total of 11,250 meters. How fast did the rocket travel in meters per second?

Problem Set 76

Tell whether each sentence below is True or False.

1. Some equations need to be simplified by adding x's (instead of numbers).
(76)

2. A number multiplied by an x is called a "coefficient."
(76)

3. To add (combine) x's, you just add their coefficients.
(76)

Answer each question below.

4. How far will a sports car traveling at 78 miles per hour go in $4\frac{1}{2}$ hours?
(55)

5. How far will a tree growing at 6 inches per year grow in 3 years?
(55)

Add or subtract (as indicated) each pair of numbers below.

6. $1-(-6)$
(60)

7. $-95+(-105)$
(59)

Multiply or divide (as indicated) each pair of numbers below.

8. $(13)(-9)$
(61)

9. $\dfrac{-42}{-7}$
(62)

Calculate the value of each expression below. (Make sure to do the operations in the correct order.)

10.
(70)
$$\frac{3-27}{2}$$

11.
(68)
$$25-(5)(3)$$

Translate each of the following word problems into an equation. (Don't solve.)

12.
(71)
There's some number that if you divide it by -7 first, and then subtract 11 from that total, the result is 53.

    A. $\dfrac{-7-11}{x}=53$ B. $\dfrac{x}{11-(-7)}=53$ C. $11-\dfrac{x}{-7}=53$

    D. $\dfrac{x}{-7}-11=53$ E. $\dfrac{x}{-7-11}=53$

(a) 13.
(69)
There's some number that if you add 5 to it first, and then multiply that total by -3, the result is 40.

    A. $x+5(-3)=40$ B. $-3x+5=40$ C. $5+(-3x)=40$

    D. $-3(x+5)=40$ E. $x+5-3=40$

Simplify each expression below. Select the best possible choice.

14.
(75)
$1+5x+4$

    A. $5x+5$ B. $5x+3$ C. $6x+4$

    D. $10x$ E. $1+9x$

(b) 15.
(76)
$5x+4x$

    A. $9x$ B. $9+x$ C. x

    D. $x+1$ E. $20x$

Solve each equation below. Make sure your answer is fully reduced.

16.
(66)
$$\frac{2}{3}-x=\frac{5}{6}$$

17.
(53)
$$\frac{1}{2}x=6$$

18.
(71)
$$\frac{x-4}{3}=10$$

19.
(74)
$-2x+3+4=25$

(c) 20.
(76)
$2x+3x=15$

(d) 21.
(76)
$5x+3x=16$

Translate the word problem below into an equation; then solve.

(e) 22.
(55)
The satellite had been on its own for 45 seconds, traveling a total of 5,400 meters. How fast did the satellite travel in meters per second?

Lesson 77—Subtracting x's

In the last lesson, we learned how to solve equations that have more than one x, and if you'll remember the process turned out to be pretty simple. All we did was add (combine) the x's and then undo. Well, now we're going to look at some other equations with more than one x, but this time the x's are subtracted instead of added. Here's an example.

$$8x - 3x = 15$$

Subtracting Coefficients

Before solving this by undoing, we have to subtract the x's. And you can probably guess how it's done. We just *subtract* the coefficients 8 and 3. (Remember, the numbers multiplied by x are called "coefficients.") Since $8 - 3$ equals 5, the left side simplifies to $5x$.

$$5x = 15 \qquad \textbf{8x - 3x is 5x}$$

Now there's just one operation left to undo. Dividing both sides by 5 gives us this.

$$x = \frac{15}{5}$$

Finally, we simplify on the right for an answer of 3.

$$x = 3$$

So to subtract x's, we just subtract the coefficients (the numbers in front of the x's). Here are a few other examples.

> **11x - 4x is equivalent to 7x**
>
> **5x - 2x is equivalent to 3x**
>
> **18x - 10x is equivalent to 8x**

How It Works

You may be wondering how the method of subtracting coefficients works. Basically, it works the same way as adding coefficients. Let's go back to our original example of $8x - 3x$. Remember, $8x$ means eight x's added. And $3x$ means three x's added. So if we have eight x's and take away three x's, that just leaves five x's, which is the same as $5x$.

You know that adding x's is called "combining x's." It turns out that subtracting x's can also be called combining. So we can say that we "combined" $8x - 3x$ to get $5x$. Generally, the word combining applies to both addition and subtraction of x's.

More than One Method

You may have already realized this, but there's actually another way to subtract x's. To show you, let's go back to the equation $8x - 3x = 15$. Instead of subtracting the coefficients, we can change the subtraction to addition of the opposite first like this.

$$8x + (-3x) = 15 \qquad \textbf{Change subtraction}$$
$$\textbf{to addition}$$

Now since the x's are being added, we can combine them by adding their coefficients. But watch what happens when we do that: $8 + (-3) = 5$. We still end up with $5x$.

$$5x = 15$$

So when combining x's that are subtracted, you can either subtract the coefficients or change the subtraction to addition first and then add. Use whichever method you think is easier. Just remember to add coefficients when the x's are added and subtract coefficients when the coefficients are subtracted. It doesn't matter whether the numbers involved are positive or negative.

Negative Coefficients from the Start

Here's an example of an equation where the coefficients are negative to begin with.

$$-9x + (-3x) = 48$$

Before undoing, we have to add (combine) the x's. To do that, we just add the coefficients $-9 + (-3)$ equals -12 so that gives us $-12x$.

$$-12x = 48 \qquad \textbf{Add the coefficients}$$

Now we have just one operation to undo. We need to divide both sides by -12.

$$\frac{-12x}{-12} = \frac{48}{-12}$$

The left side now becomes just x.

$$x = \frac{48}{-12}$$

Finally, we do the division on the right to get our answer of -4.

$$x = -4$$

The main point is that even when the coefficients are negative, we combine the x's in the same way.

Practice 77

a.
(77)
Simplify the expression $7x - 3x$. Select the best possible choice.

    A. $10x$ B. $21x$ C. $-4x$

    D. $4x$ E. $-21x$

b.
(75)   Solve the equation $11 + 3x - 7 = 19$.

c.
(76)   Solve the equation $4x + 7x = 88$.

d.
(77)   Solve the equation $12x - 8x = 24$.

e.
(73)   Translate the word problem below into an equation; then solve.

There is a number that if you subtract 3 from it first, and then divide that total by 8, you get 4. What's the number?

Problem Set 77

Tell whether each sentence below is True or False.

1.
(77)   To subtract x's, you subtract their coefficients.

2.
(77)   Another way to subtract x's is to change the subtraction to addition of the opposite first.

Convert each fraction below into decimal form. Give exact answers (no rounding).

3.
(24) $\dfrac{2}{3}$

4.
(23) $\dfrac{1}{100}$

Add or subtract (as indicated) each pair of numbers below.

5.
(59) $-20 + (-17)$

6.
(60) $-52 - 18$

Multiply or divide (as indicated) each pair of numbers below.

7.
(61) $(-2)(-23)$

8.
(62) $\dfrac{82}{-41}$

Calculate the value of each expression below. (Make sure to do the operations in the correct order.)

9.
(70) $8 + \dfrac{10}{2}$

10.
(68) $4(26 - 19)$

Translate each of the following phrases into a mathematical expression. (Don't calculate the answer.)

11.
(70)
16 divided by 4 first, and that total subtracted from 31.

A. $\dfrac{16}{4-31}$

B. $\dfrac{16}{31}-4$

C. $31-\dfrac{16}{4}$

D. $\dfrac{16}{4}-31$

E. $\dfrac{16}{31-4}$

12.
(68)
15 added to 8 first, and then that total multiplied by 6.

A. $6(15+8)$

B. $15(8+6)$

C. $15+8(6)$

D. $15\cdot8\cdot6$

E. $6\cdot15+8$

Simplify each expression below. Select the best possible choice.

13.
(75)
$6+2x-9$

A. $8x-9$

B. $2x+(-3)$

C. $-x$

D. $2x+3$

E. $6+(-7x)$

14.
(76)
$7x+5x$

A. $35x$

B. $-35x$

C. $2x$

D. $12x$

E. $-12x$

(a) 15.
(77)
$8x-2x$

A. $-6x$

B. $-16x$

C. $10x$

D. $16x$

E. $6x$

Solve each equation below.

16.
(73)
$\dfrac{x}{2.4}=15.1$

17.
(72)
$8(x-2)=96$

18.
(72)
$5x-14=31$

(b) 19.
(75)
$15+4x-9=18$

(c) 20.
(76)
$3x+6x=54$

(d) 21.
(77)
$10x-4x=42$

Translate the word problem below into an equation; then solve.

(e) 22.
(73)
There is a number that if you subtract 6 from it first, and then divide that total by 3, you get 5. What's the number?

Lesson 78—x and 1x

We've been learning how to combine x's, and so far it hasn't been too tough. Remember, all we have to do is add the coefficients if the x's are added or subtract the coefficients if the x's are subtracted. But now take a look at this equation.

$$2x + x = -24$$

This says that there's a missing number and if we multiply it by 2 and then add the same missing number to that total we'll get -24. To solve, we need to combine the x's and then undo as always. But notice that we can't combine the x's by adding their coefficients, because the second x doesn't have a coefficient. What now?

Let's think about this. Since $2x$ means $x + x$, the left side of the equation, $2x + x$, is really the same as $x + x + x$. But aren't three x's added the same as $3x$? Yes, so we can change $2x + x$ to $3x$.

$$3x = -24$$

Now we can solve by undoing. The multiplication can be undone by dividing both sides by 3.

$$\frac{3x}{3} = \frac{-24}{3}$$

That gives us just x on the left.

$$x = \frac{-24}{3}$$

Finally, we divide -24 by 3 to get $x = -8$, which is our answer.

Changing x to 1x

We were able to deal with the x that didn't have a coefficient fairly easily. But wouldn't it be nice if we could use the shortcut of adding the coefficients, even in equations like $2x + x = -24$? Actually, we can. The mathematicians figured out a way to add coefficients even in an equation with just a plain x. Here's how they did it. Any number times 1 is just the number itself. For example, 5 times 1 equals 5, 3 times 1 equals 3, 8 times 1 equals 8. So shouldn't 1 times x equal x? Absolutely. Then why not change $2x + x$ to $2x + 1x$? That won't change the value of the left side one bit, because $1x$ and x are equal.

$$2x + 1x = -24 \qquad\qquad \textbf{Change x to 1x}$$

Now *both* x's have a coefficient, which means we can use the shortcut of adding the coefficients. Since $2 + 1$ is 3, the left side becomes $3x$. And we know that's right. Of course, you don't have to write the coefficient of 1 down on paper. You can just do it in your head. (Every time you see an x, just think $1x$.) The important thing, though, is that you can still use the shortcut of adding the coefficients, even when there's a plain x. You just have to change x to $1x$ first. Here are a few other examples of how to do that.

7x + x is equivalent to 8x
5x + x is equivalent to 6x
10x + x is equivalent to 11x

Subtracting x

It should come as no surprise that we can also *subtract* plain x's. Take a look at this example.

$$5x - x = 9$$

First, we change x to $1x$ again.

$$5x - 1x = 9 \qquad \textbf{Change x to 1x}$$

Now we subtract the coefficients. Since $5-1$ is 4, the left side becomes $4x$, and that leaves just one operation to undo.

$$4x = 9$$

Dividing both sides by 4 gives us an answer of $\dfrac{9}{4}$.

$$\frac{4x}{4} = \frac{9}{4}$$

$$x = \frac{9}{4}$$

So anytime you have a single x subtracted, just change it to $1x$.

Changing -x to -1x

Another way to handle $5x - x = 9$ is to change the subtraction to addition of the opposite.

$$5x + (-x) = 9$$

That gives us $-x$, but what is the coefficient of $-x$? Well, from the rules for multiplying negatives, we know that -1 multiplied by any number is equal to its opposite. For instance, -1 times 6 is -6, -1 times -8 is $+8$, and so on. So -1 times x must be the same as $-x$. Why not change $-x$ to $-1x$ then? That leaves us with this.

$$5x + (-1x) = 9 \qquad \textbf{Change -x to -1x}$$

Now both x's have a coefficient, and we can combine normally by adding their coefficients. Since $5 + (-1)$ equals 4, the left side becomes $4x$, which we know is right. Remember, then, that if you need to combine $-x$, just change it to $-1x$, either in your head or on paper. It's up to you.

Practice 78

a. Simplify the expression $8x + x$. Select the best possible choice.
(78)

    A. $7x$ B. $-9x$ C. $8x$

    D. $9x$ E. $-7x$

b. Simplify the expression $3x - x$. Select the best possible choice.
(78)

    A. $-3x$ B. $2x$ C. $4x$

    D. $-2x$ E. $-4x$

c. Solve the equation $-3x + 11x = 64$.
(76)

d. Solve the equation $5x - x = -28$.
(78)

e. Translate the word problem below into an equation; then solve.
(72)

There is a number that if you multiply it by 4 first, and then subtract 10 from the result, you get 14. What's the number?

Problem Set 78

Tell whether each sentence below is True or False.

1. You can change a single x to $1x$ in order to use the adding coefficients shortcut.
(78)

2. You can change a $-x$ to $-1x$ in order to use the adding coefficients shortcut.
(78)

Add or subtract each pair of numbers below. Make sure your answers are fully reduced.

3. $\dfrac{3}{10} + \dfrac{4}{5}$
(11)

4. $9 - 3\dfrac{1}{4}$
(12)

Add or subtract (as indicated) each pair of numbers below.

5. $82 + (-49)$
(59)

6. $-41 - (-25)$
(60)

Multiply or divide (as indicated) each pair of numbers below.

7. $(-6)(9)$
(61)

8. $\dfrac{40}{-8}$
(62)

Calculate the value of each expression below. (Make sure to do the operations in the correct order.)

9. $-3 + (5)(3)$
(68)

10. $\dfrac{5 - 13}{-2}$
(70)

Translate each of the following word problems into an equation. (Don't solve.)

11. There's some number that if you subtract 14 from it first, and then divide that total by 2, the result is -1.
(71)

A. $\dfrac{14 - x}{2} = -1$

B. $x - \dfrac{14}{2} = -1$

C. $\dfrac{x}{2 - 14} = -1$

D. $\dfrac{x - 14}{2} = -1$

E. $\dfrac{x}{2} - 14 = -1$

12.
(69)
There's some number that if you multiply it by 10 first, and then add 6 to that total, the result is 27.

A. $6x + 10 = 27$ B. $10x + 6 + 27$ C. $10x + 6 = 27$

D. $10(x + 6) = 27$ E. $6(x + 10) = 27$

Simplify each expression below. Select the best possible choice.

13.
(76)
$2x + 13x$

A. $-11x$ B. $26x$ C. $-15x$

D. $15x$ E. $11x$

(a) 14.
(78)
$4x + x$

A. $-5x$ B. $-3x$ C. $4x$

D. $3x$ E. $5x$

(b) 15.
(78)
$7x - x$

A. $6x$ B. $-8x$ C. $-6x$

D. $-7x$ E. $8x$

Solve each equation below. Make sure your answer is fully reduced.

16.
(53)
$\dfrac{3}{5}x = \dfrac{7}{10}$

17.
(75)
$3 + 8x + 2 = 37$

18.
(76)
$13x + 5x = -18$

19.
(77)
$9x - 6x = 21$

(c) 20.
(76)
$-2x + 11x = 81$

(d) 21.
(78)
$9x - x = -16$

Translate the word problem below into an equation; then solve.

(e) 22.
(72)
There is a number that if you multiply it by 7 first, and then subtract 12 from the result, you get 23. What's the number?

Lesson 79—Work Problems

For several lessons now, we've been solving equations with x's that are added or subtracted. But are there any real-world problems that have equations like that? Well, as a matter of fact, there are lots of them. In this lesson, we'll show you one of the simplest (and most common) kinds. Here's an example.

> Gina can paint 3 porcelain dolls per hour and Rosalie can paint 4 porcelain dolls per hour. How long will it take the two of them working together to paint 21 dolls?

This is what's called a work problem, because it involves people working at a job. In a work problem, we're told how long it takes a person to do a certain task. This is called a **rate**. In this case, Gina can paint 3 porcelain dolls per hour, so that's her rate. Rosalie's rate is 4 because she can paint 4 porcelain dolls per hour. A different work problem might be about a person who licks 2 stamps per hour (definitely a slow worker) or a person who digs 5 ditches per day. Those are also rates. Obviously, rates come up all the time in the real world because it's often necessary to calculate how long it will take to finish a job.

Writing the Equation

Now for some bad news. Work problems are useful but they can be tough. In fact, they're too tough for most people to solve using just basic arithmetic. Fortunately, they can be solved quickly with a little algebra. To see what we mean, let's translate our work problem about Gina and Rosalie into an algebra equation.

Since we're trying to find the number of hours it will take the two of them together to paint 21 dolls, that's what we should set equal to x.

$$x = \text{number of hours to paint 21 dolls}$$

After this amount of time (x), the number of dolls Gina has painted plus the number Rosalie has painted should equal 21. So the equation should be set up like this.

$$\text{number of dolls Gina painted } + \text{ number of dolls Rosalie painted} = 21$$

Next, we need to put in the x's and numbers. If Gina can paint 3 dolls per hour, then in 2 hours she can paint 3 times 2, or 6 dolls. In 5 hours she can paint 3 times 5 or 15 dolls. In 7 hours she can paint 3 times 7 or 21 dolls. Get the idea? The rate multiplied by the time always equals the total amount of work done.

rate x time = total amount of work done

So how many dolls should Gina be able to paint in x hours? That's the amount of time we're trying to find. Well, in x hours Gina will have painted 3 times x, or $3x$ dolls. So we need to put $3x$ in for the number of dolls Gina painted. We can follow the same process for the number of dolls Rosalie painted. Since she can paint 4 dolls per hour, in x hours she will have painted $4x$ dolls. That finishes our equation.

$$3x + 4x = 21$$

Solving the Equation

This equation looks familiar, doesn't it? It has two x's that are added. Work problems almost always translate into equations like this. To solve the equation, we first have to simplify the left side by combining the x's. All we have to do is add the coefficients. Since $3 + 4$ is 7, that gives us $7x$.

$$7x = 21$$

Now we can undo the multiplication by dividing both sides by 7.

$$\frac{7x}{7} = \frac{21}{7}$$

Simplifying on the left gives us this.

$$x = \frac{21}{7}$$

Finally, we do the division to get an answer of 3.

$$x = 3$$

That means it will take Gina and Rosalie 3 hours working together to paint 21 dolls. You'll be doing a lot of problems like this throughout the rest of this book. But don't worry. They'll get easier and easier.

Practice 79

a.
(41) How many square feet are in 4 square yards?

b.
(76) Simplify the expression $-4x + (-10x)$. Select the best possible choice.

    A. $14x$ B. $-14x$ C. $40x$
    D. $-6x$ E. $6x$

c.
(78) Solve the equation $6x - x = 35$.

d.
(78) Solve the equation $-x + 8x = 63$.

e.
(79) Translate the word problem below into an equation; then solve.

Toby can make 4 shelves per hour and Brett can make 5 per hour. Working together, how many hours will it take them to make 18 shelves?

Problem Set 79

Tell whether each sentence below is True or False.

1.
(79) Work problems usually translate into an equation with more than one x.

2.
(79) In a work problem, the rate multiplied by the time equals the total amount of work a person does.

Multiply or divide each pair of numbers below. Write any remainders in decimal form.

3.
(20)
$$\begin{array}{r} 250 \\ \times 6.8 \\ \hline \end{array}$$

4.
(4) $22\overline{)14,322}$

351

Do each unit conversion below.

5.
(38) Convert 14 meters into millimeters.

(a) 6.
(41) How many square feet are in 2 square yards?

Add or subtract (as indicated) each pair of numbers below.

7.
(59) $-19+(-65)$

8.
(60) $0-(-5)$

Multiply or divide (as indicated) each pair of numbers below.

9.
(61) $\left(-\dfrac{1}{2}\right)(12)$

10.
(62) $\dfrac{-46}{23}$

Calculate the value of each expression below. (Make sure to do the operations in the correct order.)

11.
(70) $8+\dfrac{100}{50}$

12.
(68) $-9(4+3)$

Translate each of the following phrases into a mathematical expression. (Don't calculate the answer.)

13.
(70) -7 added to -3 first, and that total divided by 5.

    A. $\dfrac{-7+(-3)}{5}$ B. $-7+\dfrac{-3}{5}$ C. $\dfrac{5}{-7+(-3)}$

    D. $\dfrac{-7}{5}-3$ E. $\dfrac{-7}{-3+5}$

14.
(68) 16 multiplied by 2 first, and then 21 subtracted from that total.

    A. $16(21-2)$ B. $16-2\cdot21$ C. $16(2-21)$

    D. $21-16(2)$ E. $16\cdot2-21$

Simplify each expression below. Select the best possible choice.

15.
(75) $5+2x+8$

    A. $2x+13$ B. $15x$ C. $5+10x$

    D. $7x+8$ E. $2x+3$

16. $19x - x$
(78)

    A. $-18x$ B. $-19x$ C. $18x$

    D. $-20x$ E. $20x$

(b) 17. $-5x + (-11x)$
(76)

    A. $16x$ B. $6x$ C. $-16x$

    D. $55x$ E. $-6x$

Solve each equation below.

18. $\dfrac{\frac{x}{2}}{7} = 49$ **19.** $24 - x = -6$ **20.** $8x + 12x = 100$
(73)   (66)   (76)

(c) 21. $5x - x = 44$ **(d) 22.** $-x + 9x = 32$
(78)   (78)

Translate the word problem below into an equation; then solve.

(e) 23. Scott can deliver 10 pizzas per hour and Kenneth can deliver 12 per hour. How many hours will it take
(79)   them to deliver 110 pizzas?

Lesson 80—Fancy Distance Problems

In the last lesson, we learned about work problems. As it turned out, we were able to solve those with equations having more than one x. There are also quite a few distance problems that can be solved with equations with more than one x. Since these distance problems are more complicated than the ones you've been doing, we call them "fancy distance problems." Here's an example.

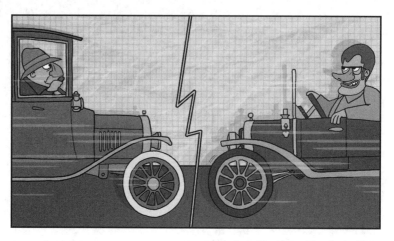

Hal and Larry are headed straight toward each other. Hal is driving at a safe speed of 55 mph, but Larry is driving recklessly at a speed of 75 mph. If the two are 260 miles apart, how many hours will it be before they meet (assuming Larry can keep his car on the road)?

Drawing a Picture then Writing an Equation

What makes this problem a little more complicated is that there are two drivers. Since we're trying to find the number of hours it will take the two to meet, let's make that equal to x.

$$x = \text{number of hours it will take them to meet}$$

Hal and Larry have to meet somewhere, but it won't be in the middle because Larry's going faster than Hal.

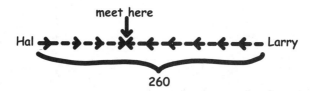

They'll meet somewhere over to the left, as the diagram shows. We don't know how far Hal and Larry will travel individually before meeting. But we do know that the total distance that both will travel must equal 260 miles. That's because Hal and Larry started out 260 miles apart. That's the key piece of information we need to set up the equation. We can add Hal's distance to Larry's distance to get 260.

$$\text{Hal's distance} + \text{Larry's distance} = 260$$

To finish the equation, we just need to put in the x's and numbers. The key to doing this step is to remember that distance is always equal to speed multiplied by time. Since Hal's speed is 55 mph and his time is x hours, speed multiplied by time for Hal is $55x$. The expression for Larry's distance works the same way. His speed is 75 mph and he's going to drive for x hours. So Larry's distance is $75x$. Putting these two expressions into the equation gives us this.

$$55x + 75x = 260$$

Solving for x

Notice the equation has two x's. And now that you've had a lot of practice combining x's by adding coefficients, solving this equation should be simple. Since $55 + 75 = 130$, we can combine $55x$ and $75x$ to get $130x$.

$$130x = 260$$

Next, we can undo the multiplication by dividing both sides by 130.

$$\frac{130x}{130} = \frac{260}{130}$$

That makes the left side x.

$$x = \frac{260}{130}$$

This turns the equation into an arithmetic problem. The last step is to divide on the right.

$$x = 2$$

The answer to our problem is that it will take 2 hours for Hal and Larry to meet.

To do fancy distance problems, you just have to set up expressions for the two people's distances. Those are always going to equal the speed multiplied by the time. Then you add these two distances together to get the total distance that they have to travel to come together (which was 260 miles for Hal and Larry).

Practice 80

a.
(78)
Simplify the expression $-5x + x$. Select the best possible choice.

    A. $-5x$ B. $-6x$ C. $4x$
    D. $6x$ E. $-4x$

b.
(75)
Solve the equation $9 + 2x - 5 = 12$.

c.
(78)
Solve the equation $x + 15x = -80$.

d.
(78)
Solve the equation $-x + 5x = 24$.

e.
(80) Translate the word problem below into an equation; then solve.

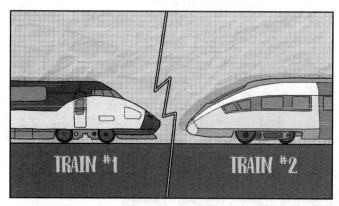

Train #1 and train #2 are headed straight toward each other. Train #1 is traveling at 60 mph, and train #2 is traveling at 68 mph. If the two trains are 512 miles apart, how many hours will it be before they meet?

Problem Set 80

Multiply or divide each pair of fractions below. Make sure your answers are fully reduced.

1.
(13) $\dfrac{5}{12} \cdot \dfrac{3}{10}$

2.
(13) $\dfrac{3}{4} \div \dfrac{1}{16}$

Add or subtract (as indicated) each pair of numbers below.

3.
(59) $-20 + 14$

4.
(60) $-8 - (-1)$

Multiply or divide (as indicated) each pair of numbers below.

5.
(62) $\dfrac{-45}{-5}$

6.
(61) $(-8)(8)$

Calculate the value of each expression below. (Make sure to do the operations in the correct order.)

7.
(68) $4 \cdot 7 - 13$

8.
(70) $14 + \dfrac{12}{-4}$

9.
(68) $5(8 + 6)$

Translate each of the following word problems into an equation. (Don't solve.)

10.
(69) There's some number that if you multiply it by 9 first, and then subtract 7 from that total, the result is 10.

    A. $9x - 7 = 10$ B. $7 - 9x = 10$ C. $9(x - 7) = 10$

    D. $9x(-7) = 10$ E. $7x - 9 = 10$

11.
(71)
There's some number that if you subtract 2 from it first, and then divide that total by 14, the result is −33.

A. $\dfrac{x}{14} - 2 = -33$

B. $\dfrac{2-x}{14} = -33$

C. $\dfrac{x-2}{14} = -33$

D. $\dfrac{x}{14-2} = -33$

E. $x - \dfrac{2}{14} = -33$

Simplify each expression below. Select the best possible choice.

12.
(75)
$-4 + 4x + 7$

A. $4x + 3$

B. $7x$

C. $4x + 11$

D. 7

E. $-4 + 11x$

13.
(76)
$2x + 3x$

A. $5x$

B. $6x$

C. $-5x$

D. $-6x$

E. x

(a) 14.
(78)
$-7x + x$

A. $-8x$

B. $-7x$

C. $-6x$

D. $6x$

E. $8x$

Solve each equation below.

15.
(53)
$\dfrac{1}{2}x = 7$

(b) 16.
(75)
$7 + 3x - 2 = 11$

17.
(64)
$\dfrac{-x}{5} = 8$

18.
(77)
$15x - 9x = 30$

(c) 19.
(78)
$x + 17x = -54$

(d) 20.
(78)
$-x + 6x = 40$

Translate the word problem below into an equation; then solve.

(e) 21.
(80)
Cyclist #1 and cyclist #2 are headed straight toward each other. Cyclist #1 is traveling at 15 mph, and cyclist #2 is traveling at 20 mph. If the two cyclists are 70 miles apart, how many hours will it be before they meet?

Lesson 81—x's on Both Sides

Now that you're getting more comfortable solving equations with two x's, it's time for something new. As it turns out, in some equations the x's are on different sides. Take a look.

$$7 + 5x = 16 + 2x$$

We have a $5x$ on the left side, and then a $2x$ on the right. This equation says that there's a missing number, x, and if we multiply it by 5, then add that to 7, the result is equal to 16 plus the product of 2 and that same missing number. We know that the x's have to be combined before undoing. But how do we combine the x's when they're on different sides? What we have to do is move the $2x$ over to the left side so that both of the x's are together.

Getting the x's on the Same Side

To get the x's on the same side, we can just subtract $2x$ from both sides, like this.

$$7 + 5x - 2x = 16 + 2x - 2x$$ **Subtract 2x from both sides**

You may be wondering if this step is legal. We subtract *numbers* from both sides of an equation all the time. But can we subtract a $2x$? Absolutely. Even though we don't know the value of $2x$ (since x is an unknown number), we're still subtracting the same amount from both sides ($2x$ and $2x$). And that doesn't violate the golden rule of algebra. So subtracting $2x$ is just fine.

The next step is to simplify the right side. Since the subtraction of $2x$ undoes the addition of $2x$, we end up with just 16.

$$7 + 5x - 2x = 16$$ **2x is now on the left**

Now do you see why we subtracted $2x$? That step eliminated the $2x$ from the right side completely and caused it to pop up on the left side, with the $5x$, which is exactly what we wanted. The only thing that's changed, really, is that the $2x$ is now subtracted instead of added. So by subtracting $2x$ from both sides, we were able to move the $2x$ from the right to the left. The next step is to combine $5x$ and $2x$ by subtracting their coefficients. Since $5 - 2 = 3$, we get $3x$.

$$7 + 3x = 16$$

Switch and Undo

This leaves only two operations to undo: a multiplication by 3 and an addition of 7. But since we're not used to seeing a $3x$ written on the inside (near the equals sign) and a plain number on the outside, let's switch the order of the 7 and $3x$ before undoing.

$$3x + 7 = 16$$ **Switch 7 and 3x**

In this case, switching is allowed since the 7 and $3x$ are added, and we can always add two things in any order. It's no different, really, than changing $7 + x$ to $x + 7$, and we do that all the time.

Now we're ready to undo. Since the multiplication is done before the addition, we should undo the addition first by subtracting 7 from both sides.

$$3x + 7 - 7 = 16 - 7$$

The left side becomes $3x$ and the right side 9.

$$3x = 9$$

Next, we undo the multiplication by dividing both sides by 3.

$$\frac{3x}{3} = \frac{9}{3}$$

That makes the left side equal to x. And on the right side, 9 divided by 3 is 3.

$$x = 3$$

Moving a Subtracted x Term

Just to make sure you're catching on, let's do one more problem.

$$5 + 7x = 25 - 3x$$

Notice we have x's on both sides again: a $7x$ on the left and a $3x$ on the right. In order to combine the x's, we need to get them on the same side of the equation. Let's move the $3x$ over to the left side. Notice, though, that the $3x$ is subtracted. Can we still move it by undoing? Absolutely. But instead of subtracting, we need to add $3x$ to both sides.

$$5 + 7x + 3x = 25 - 3x + 3x \qquad \textbf{Add 3x to both sides}$$

On the right, the addition of $3x$ undoes the subtraction of $3x$, leaving just 25.

$$5 + 7x + 3x = 25$$

Now the x's are on the same side, and we can combine them by adding their coefficients. Since $7 + 3 = 10$, we end up with $10x$ on the left.

$$5 + 10x = 25$$

Next, let's switch the order of the 5 and $10x$ before undoing.

$$10x + 5 = 25$$

Finally, we're ready to undo. The x is multiplied by 10 first and then 5 is added second, so we need to undo the addition first, by subtracting 5 from both sides.

$$10x + 5 - 5 = 25 - 5$$

That makes the left side equal to $10x$ and the right side 20.

$$10x = 20$$

From here, we undo the multiplication by dividing both sides by 10.

$$\frac{10x}{10} = \frac{20}{10}$$

The left side becomes just x. And on the right, 20 divided by 10 is 2.

$$x = 2$$

Practice 81

a.
(78)
Simplify the expression $-x + (-6x)$. Select the best possible choice.

A. $5x$ B. $6x$ C. $-5x$

D. $-7x$ E. $7x$

b.
(81)
Solve the equation $5 + 9x = 19 + 2x$.

c.
(81)
Solve the equation $2 + 6x = 7 + 5x$.

d.
(81)
Solve the equation $3 + 2x = 21 - 4x$.

e.
(72)
Translate the word problem below into an equation; then solve.

There is a number that if you add 4 to it, and then multiply the result by 5, you get 60. What's the number?

Problem Set 81

Tell whether each sentence below is True or False.

1.
(81)
To solve an equation with x's on both sides, you have to move the x's to the same side first.

2.
(81)
Undoing can be used to move an x to the other side of an equation.

Add or subtract each group of numbers below.

3.
(17)
$$\begin{array}{r} 5.384 \\ +9.027 \\ \hline \end{array}$$

4.
(17)
$$\begin{array}{r} 7{,}305 \\ -4{,}018 \\ \hline \end{array}$$

Add or subtract (as indicated) each pair of numbers below.

5.
(59)
$-41 + (-9)$

6.
(60)
$-84 - 67$

Multiply or divide (as indicated) each pair of numbers below.

7.
(61)
$(11)(-12)$

8.
(62)
$\dfrac{-70}{-10}$

Calculate the value of each expression below. (Make sure to do the operations in the correct order.)

9.
(68)
$8 - 3 \cdot 9$

10.
(70)
$\dfrac{-56}{5 + 2}$

Translate each of the following phrases into a mathematical expression. (Don't calculate the answer.)

11.
(70)
15 divided by 3 first, and 21 added to that total.

    A. $\dfrac{15}{21}+3$ B. $\dfrac{15}{3+21}$ C. $\dfrac{15}{3}+21$

    D. $15+\dfrac{21}{3}$ E. $\dfrac{15+21}{3}$

12.
(68)
6 minus 4 first, and then that total multiplied by -5.

    A. $6-4(-5)$ B. $6-4\cdot5$ C. $6-4-5$

    D. $6(-5)-4$ E. $-5(6-4)$

Simplify each expression below. Select the best possible choice.

13.
(74)
$25x+5+11$

    A. $25x+16$ B. $41x$ C. $25x+6$

    D. $30x+6$ E. $30x+11$

14.
(77)
$18x-7x$

    A. $126x$ B. $-25x$ C. $25x$

    D. $11x$ E. $-11x$

(a) 15.
(78)
$-x+(-4x)$

    A. $5x$ B. $3x$ C. $-5x$

    D. $-3x$ E. $4x$

Solve each equation below.

16. $9-x=11$ **17.** $5x+3=38$ **18.** $\dfrac{x+6}{2}=-7$
(66)   (53)   (73)

(b) 19. $6+8x=21+3x$ **(c) 20.** $1+5x=7+4x$ **(d) 21.** $4+3x=12-5x$
(81)   (81)   (81)

Translate the word problem below into an equation; then solve.

(e) 22.
(72)
There is a number that if you add it 7 to it, and then multiply the result by 9, you get 81. What's the number?

361

Lesson 82—Refrigerator Repairs

There's no point in learning algebra if you can't use it to solve real-world problems. But what kinds of problems have equations with x's on both sides (which we learned about in the last lesson)? Well, here's an example from the not-so-glamorous (yet certainly important) world of refrigerator repairs.

Poor Richard's Refrigerator Repair Service only charges $25 for a service call (just to come to the house) plus $40 per hour to do the repair job. Snooty Rudy's Refrigerator Repair Service charges $50 for a service call plus $35 per hour to do the repair job. How many hours would a job have to take for the bill of both repair services to be the same?

The first step is to make x equal the thing we're trying to find. We want to know how many hours a job has to take for Rudy's and Richard's bills to be the same. So that's x.

x = number of hours the job has to take for bills to be the same

Writing the Equation

Next, let's set up the equation. We're interested in a job where Richard and Rudy will charge the same amount. That means the equation can be set up like this.

Poor Richard's bill = Snooty Rudy's bill.

Now we have to put in the x's and numbers. How can we write an expression for Poor Richard's bill? He charges $25 just to come out to the house plus $40 per hour to do the repair work. That means if a job takes 2 hours, his bill will be $25 + 40(2)$. If a job takes 3 hours, his bill will be $25 + 40(3)$. But we're interested in a job that takes x hours (that's what we're trying to find). For that job, Richard's bill will be $25 + 40x$. That's the expression we need.

We still need an expression for Snooty Rudy's bill. If Snooty Rudy charges $50 to come out to the house plus $35 per hour to do the work, his bill for a job taking x hours must be $50 + 35x$. It's the same thinking we used for Poor Richard. Putting both expressions in the equation gives us this.

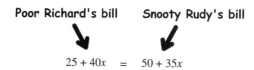

Poor Richard's bill   **Snooty Rudy's bill**

$$25 + 40x \quad = \quad 50 + 35x$$

Getting the x's on the Same Side

This equation has x's on both sides. But after the last lesson, we know how to solve it. We have to move the x's to the same side. Let's move $35x$ to the left side by subtracting $35x$ from both sides.

$$25 + 40x - 35x = 50 + 35x - 35x$$

The subtraction undoes the addition (of $35x$) on the right, leaving just 50.

$$25 + 40x - 35x = 50$$

We've moved the $35x$ over to the left side (only now it's being subtracted). From here, we can combine the x's by subtracting their coefficients. Since $40-35=5$, we end up with a $5x$ on the left.

$$25+5x=50$$

To get ready to undo, let's switch the order of 25 and $5x$.

$$5x+25=50$$

Since addition is the last operation being performed on x, it's the first thing we should undo. So we subtract 25 from both sides.

$$5x+25-25=50-25$$

That leaves $5x$ on the left and 25 on the right.

$$5x=25$$

Next, we undo the multiplication by dividing both sides by 5.

$$\frac{5x}{5}=\frac{25}{5}$$

And that gives us x on the left and 5 on the right.

$$x=5$$

That means Poor Richard's and Snooty Rudy's bill will be exactly the same for a job that takes 5 hours. This was an example of a real-world problem that can be solved with an equation that has x's on both sides.

Practice 82

a. What is $\frac{3}{4}$ of $\frac{8}{9}$? Make sure your answer is fully reduced.
(13)

b. Simplify the expression $4x-6x$. Select the best possible choice.
(77)

     A. $2x$ B. $10x$ C. $-10x$

     D. $-24x$ E. $-2x$

c. Solve the equation $2+8x=6+3x$.
(81)

d. Solve the equation $12+x=2-4x$.
(81)

e. Translate the word problem below into an equation; then solve.
(82)

    Palatial Plumbing only charges \$35 for a service call (just to come to the house) plus \$50 per hour to do the repair job. Perfecto Plumbing charges \$60 for a service call plus \$45 per hour to do the repair job. How many hours would a job have to take for the bills of both plumbing services to be the same?

Problem Set 82

Convert each percent below into decimal form.

1.
(26)   42%

2.
(26)   75.25%

Answer each question below.

3.
(27)   What is 38% of 275? Write your answer as a decimal.

(a) 4.
(13)   What is $\dfrac{5}{6}$ of $\dfrac{7}{10}$? Make sure your answer is fully reduced.

Add or subtract (as indicated) each pair of numbers below.

5.
(59) $-17+31$

6.
(60) $-25-(-43)$

Multiply or divide (as indicated) each pair of numbers below.

7.
(62) $\dfrac{42}{-7}$

8.
(61) $(-7.5)(4)$

Calculate the value of each expression below. (Make sure to do the operations in the correct order.)

9.
(68) $-3(8+5)$

10.
(70) $\dfrac{54}{6}-9$

Translate each of the following word problems into an equation. (Don't solve.)

11.
(71)   There's some number that if you divide it by 4 first, and then add 26 to that total, the result is 89.

    A. $\dfrac{4}{x}+26+89$ B. $\dfrac{x}{4}+26=89$ C. $x+\dfrac{26}{4}=89$

    D. $\dfrac{x}{4+26}=89$ E. $\dfrac{x+4}{26}=89$

12.
(69)   There's some number that if you subtract 3 from it first, and then multiply that total by -7, the result is 21.

    A. $-7(x-3)=21$ B. $x-3+(-7)=21$ C. $-7(3-x)$

    D. $3x+(-7)=21$ E. $x-3(-7)=21$

Simplify each expression below. Select the best possible choice.

13. $9 + x - 4$
(75)

    A. $x - 36$ B. $x + 5$ C. $x + (-13)$

    D. $x + (-5)$ E. $x + 13$

14. $x + 8x$
(78)

    A. $9x$ B. $-9x$ C. $7x$

    D. $-7x$ E. $8x$

(b) 15. $2x - 5x$
(77)

    A. $3x$ B. $-7x$ C. $7x$

    D. $-10x$ E. $-3x$

Solve each equation below.

16. $2(x + 7) = 24$ **17.** $\dfrac{x}{5} - 9 = 3$ **18.** $8x + 11 = 27$
(72)   (73)   (72)

19. $3x + 6x = -81$ **(c) 20.** $2 + 7x = 4 + 2x$ **(d) 21.** $9 + x = 3 - 5x$
(76)   (81)   (81)

Translate the word problem below into an equation; then solve.

(e) 22. Alaskan Air Conditioning only charges $20 for a service call (just to come to the house) plus $30 per
(82) hour to do the repair job. Antarctic Air Conditioning charges $40 for a service call plus $25 per hour to do the repair job. How many hours would a job have to take for the bills of both air conditioning services to be the same?

CHAPTER II:
RATIONAL EXPRESSIONS

Lesson 83—Reducing Fractions with x's

We've been learning all about algebra equations. But now we're going to switch gears, and learn about algebra fractions. Those are fractions with x's. The technical name for them is **rational expressions**. Rational is another word for fraction. We'll begin by learning how to reduce rational expressions (fractions with x's).

Factoring Top and Bottom into Primes

Here's our first example.

$$\frac{18x}{45}$$

This fraction has an x in the top. And at first, you might think the fraction is impossible to reduce. After all, how can we reduce a fraction that contains a missing number? We don't even know the value of the numerator. Well, we can still reduce the fraction. And the process is almost exactly the same one we use to reduce fractions that have only numbers: we factor and cancel. As a first step, let's factor the denominator, 45, into prime numbers: 45 is the same as 9 times 5, and 9 can be changed to 3 times 3, so the bottom becomes $3 \cdot 3 \cdot 5$.

$$\frac{18x}{3 \cdot 3 \cdot 5}$$

Now for the numerator. This is tougher, because the numerator has an x. How do we factor something that has a missing number? All we have to do is treat x as a prime number, which can't be broken down any further. Since 18 is *not* a prime number, it can be broken down as $9 \cdot 2$. Then, 9 can be broken down further to get $3 \cdot 3 \cdot 2$, which means the numerator can be factored as $3 \cdot 3 \cdot 2 \cdot x$.

$$\frac{3 \cdot 3 \cdot 2 \cdot x}{3 \cdot 3 \cdot 5}$$

So an x in a fraction is really no big deal. We just treat it as a prime number and let it sit there. With both the numerator and denominator factored into prime numbers, we're ready to cancel. There are two pairs of 3s that can be canceled.

$$\frac{\cancel{3} \cdot \cancel{3} \cdot 2 \cdot x}{\cancel{3} \cdot \cancel{3} \cdot 5} \qquad\qquad \textbf{Cancel the 3s}$$

That leaves us with a fully reduce fraction of $\dfrac{2x}{5}$.

$$\frac{2 \cdot x}{5} \quad \text{or} \quad \frac{2x}{5}$$

The thing to remember from this first example is that we reduce fractions with x's in basically same way that we reduce fractions that have just numbers: We factor everything into prime numbers and then cancel. Just remember to treat x as a prime number.

Reducing with an x in the Bottom

Let's do another example.

$$\frac{8}{24x}$$

This fraction has an x in the bottom. That's no problem because we can treat the x as a prime number. To reduce $\dfrac{8}{24x}$, we factor the top and bottom into prime numbers first. On top, 8 can be broken down as $2 \cdot 2 \cdot 2$. On bottom, 24 breaks down as $8 \cdot 3$, but then 8 can be broken down further as $2 \cdot 2 \cdot 2$. And then x is just x. So $24x$ is the same as $2 \cdot 2 \cdot 2 \cdot 3 \cdot x$.

$$\frac{2 \cdot 2 \cdot 2}{2 \cdot 2 \cdot 2 \cdot 3 \cdot x}$$

Now we're ready to cancel. There are three pairs of 2s that can be crossed out.

$$\frac{\cancel{2} \cdot \cancel{2} \cdot \cancel{2}}{\cancel{2} \cdot \cancel{2} \cdot \cancel{2} \cdot 3 \cdot x} \qquad \textbf{Cancel the 2s}$$

That leaves us with a $3x$ on bottom. We ended up canceling everything on top, so we put a 1 in the numerator. That's because canceling is the same as dividing, remember. So by canceling the 2s, we were really dividing the top and bottom by 2 three times, which is the same as dividing by 8. And $8 \div 8$ equals 1. So we end up with 1 on top and $3x$ on bottom.

$$\frac{1}{3x}$$

Practice 83

a.
(34) How many feet are in 3.7 miles?

b.
(83) Reduce the fraction $\dfrac{20x}{44}$. Select the best possible choice.

    A. $\dfrac{16x}{40}$ B. $\dfrac{x}{24}$ C. $\dfrac{5x}{11}$

    D. $\dfrac{5}{11}$ E. $\dfrac{x}{64}$

c.
(83) Reduce the fraction $\dfrac{9}{45x}$. Select the best possible choice.

    A. $5x$ B. $\dfrac{1}{54x}$ C. $\dfrac{1}{36x}$

    D. $\dfrac{5}{x}$ E. $\dfrac{1}{5x}$

d.
(81) Solve the equation $3 + 7x = 15 + 5x$.

e.
(79) Translate the word problem below into an equation; then solve.

Eric can paint 4 postcards an hour and Jeremy can paint 5. Working together, how many hours will it take them to paint 54 postcards?

Problem Set 83

Tell whether each sentence below is True or False.

1.
(83) To reduce fractions with x's, you need a completely different method from the one used in basic math.

2.
(83) An x is treated as a prime number when factoring.

Do each unit conversion below.

3.
(38) Convert 5,700 centimeters to meters.

(a) 4.
(34) How many feet are in 2.4 miles?

Add or subtract (as indicated) each pair of numbers below.

5.
(59) $-10+29$

6.
(60) $-62-(-23)$

Multiply or divide (as indicated) each pair of numbers below.

7.
(61) $\left(\dfrac{1}{4}\right)(-12)$

8.
(62) $\dfrac{35}{-7}$

Calculate the value of each expression below. Make sure to do the operations in the correct order.

9.
(68) $14-2\cdot3$

10.
(70) $\dfrac{-5+17}{2}$

Translate each of the following phrases into a mathematical expression. (Don't calculate the answer.)

11.
(70) 31 minus 4 first, and that total divided by 9.

A. $\dfrac{4-31}{9}$ B. $\dfrac{9}{31-4}$ C. $31-\dfrac{4}{9}$

D. $\dfrac{31-4}{9}$ E. $\dfrac{31}{9}-4$

12.
(68) -3 multiplied by 8 first, and then 11 added to that total.

A. $-3(8)+11$ B. $-3(8+11)$ C. $-3(11)+8$

D. $-3+8+11$ E. $8\cdot11+(-3)$

Simplify each expression below. Select the best possible choice.

13.
(74)
$7x+2+5$

    A. $7x+7$ B. $7x+(-3)$ C. $7x+3$

    D. $9x+5$ E. $7x+10$

14.
(77)
$20x-11x$

    A. $-31x$ B. $-220x$ C. $31x$

    D. $-9x$ E. $9x$

Reduce each fraction below. Select the best possible choice.

(b) 15.
(83)
$\dfrac{12x}{42}$

    A. $\dfrac{6x}{36}$ B. $\dfrac{x}{54}$ C. $\dfrac{x}{30}$

    D. $\dfrac{2x}{7}$ E. $\dfrac{2}{7}$

(c) 16.
(83)
$\dfrac{4}{28x}$

    A. $\dfrac{1}{32x}$ B. $\dfrac{1}{7x}$ C. $7x$

    D. $\dfrac{7}{x}$ E. $\dfrac{1}{24x}$

17.
(83)
$\dfrac{5x}{35}$

    A. $\dfrac{x}{40}$ B. $\dfrac{1}{7}$ C. $\dfrac{x}{7}$

    D. $7x$ E. $\dfrac{x}{30}$

Solve each equation below. Make sure your answer is fully reduced.

18.
(73)
$\dfrac{x+15}{2}=13$

19.
(53)
$\dfrac{1}{3}x=\dfrac{5}{9}$

20.
(75)
$7+3x+5=-15$

21.
(76)
$6x+3x=18$

(d) 22.
(81)
$6+8x=18+5x$

Translate the word problem below into an equation; then solve.

(e) 23.
(79)
Lucy can assemble 6 care packages to the troops overseas in an hour. Debra can assemble 10 care packages in an hour. Working together, how many hours will it take them to assemble 128 care packages?

Lesson 84—Canceling x's

In the previous lesson, we learned how to reduce fractions with x's. But did you notice that each of our examples had just one x? Some fractions have more than one x, though. Here's an example.

$$\frac{9x}{15x}$$

This fraction has an x on top and another on bottom. The question is how do we reduce in a case like this? We just factor and cancel, as usual. The numerator, $9x$, can be factored by breaking down 9 as $3 \cdot 3$ and then treating x as a prime number. That gives us $3 \cdot 3 \cdot x$ on top. On bottom, 15 can be factored as $3 \cdot 5$. Then with the x, we have $3 \cdot 5 \cdot x$ on bottom.

$$\frac{3 \cdot 3 \cdot x}{3 \cdot 5 \cdot x} \qquad \textbf{Factor the top and bottom}$$

Cancel x's like Numbers

With everything factored, we're ready to cancel. We'll start by canceling a pair of 3s.

$$\frac{\cancel{3} \cdot 3 \cdot x}{\cancel{3} \cdot 5 \cdot x} \qquad \textbf{Cancel the 3s}$$

What about the x's? Can they be canceled? Absolutely. After all, x just stands for a missing number. And it's the same missing number on top as it is on bottom. So we can cancel x's just as we would any other number. Just cross them out.

$$\frac{\cancel{3} \cdot 3 \cdot \cancel{x}}{\cancel{3} \cdot 5 \cdot \cancel{x}} \qquad \textbf{Cancel the xs}$$

That leaves 3 on top and 5 on bottom. So our fully reduced answer is $\dfrac{3}{5}$.

Another example

Let's do one more example.

$$\frac{5x}{30x}$$

The first step is to factor the numerator and the denominator. In this case, the top has just a 5 and an x, so nothing can be factored any further there. We'll put a dot in between the 5 and the x, just to show that the top is factored. The $30x$ in the denominator can be changed to $6 \cdot 5 \cdot x$. But then 6 can be broken down further as 2 times 3 to get $2 \cdot 3 \cdot 5 \cdot x$ on bottom.

$$\frac{5 \cdot x}{2 \cdot 3 \cdot 5 \cdot x} \qquad \textbf{Factor the top and bottom}$$

Now we're ready to cancel. We can cancel a pair of 5s and a pair of x's.

$$\frac{\cancel{5}\cdot\cancel{x}}{2\cdot3\cdot\cancel{5}\cdot\cancel{x}}$$ Cancel the 5s and xs

Since everything on top has canceled, we need to put a 1 up there. On the bottom, we have 2 times 3, or 6. So we end up with $\frac{1}{2\cdot3}$, or $\frac{1}{6}$, which is fully reduced. The main point of this lesson, then, is that we can cancel x's just as we would any other number.

Practice 84

a.
(84)
Reduce the fraction $\frac{9x}{21x}$. Select the best possible choice.

A. $\frac{3x}{7}$ B. $\frac{3}{7}$ C. $\frac{7x}{3}$

D. $\frac{7}{3}$ E. $\frac{1}{12x}$

b.
(84)
Reduce the fraction $\frac{7x}{63x}$. Select the best possible choice.

A. $\frac{1}{9}$ B. 9   C. $\frac{x}{9}$

D. $\frac{1}{56x}$ E. $9x$

c.
(81)
Solve the equation $8+2x=7-5x$. Make sure your answer is fully reduced.

d.
(81)
Solve the equation $10+11x=-14+3x$.

e.
(80)
Translate the word problem below into an equation; then solve.

Dump truck #1 and dump truck #2 are headed straight toward each other. Truck #1 is traveling at 55 mph, and truck #2 is traveling at 58 mph. If the two are 339 miles apart, how many hours will it be before they meet?

Problem Set 84

Convert each fraction below into decimal form. Give exact answers (no rounding).

1.
(23) $\dfrac{1}{100}$

2.
(24) $\dfrac{2}{9}$

Add or subtract (as indicated) each pair of numbers below. Make sure your answer is fully reduced.

3.
(59) $-\dfrac{1}{5}+\left(-\dfrac{2}{5}\right)$

4.
(60) $74-(-59)$

Multiply or divide (as indicated) each pair of numbers below.

5.
(61) $(-7)(14)$

6.
(62) $\dfrac{-52}{13}$

Calculate the value of each expression below. (Make sure to do the operations in the correct order.)

7.
(70) $\dfrac{60}{12}+18$

8.
(68) $6(1-8)$

Translate each of the following word problems into an equation. (Don't solve.)

9.
(69) There's some number that if you multiply it by -3 first, and then add 15 to that total, the result is 29.

    A. $-3x+15+29$ B. $-3x+15=29$ C. $x-3+15=29$
    D. $-3x(15)=29$ E. $-3(x+15)=29$

10.
(71) There's some number that if you subtract 7 from it first, and then divide that total by 20, the result is -100.

    A. $\dfrac{7-x}{20}=-100$ B. $x-\dfrac{7}{20}=-100$ C. $\dfrac{20}{x-7}=-100$

    D. $\dfrac{x}{20}-7=-100$ E. $\dfrac{x-7}{20}=-100$

Simplify each expression below. Select the best possible choice.

11.
(76) $3x+(-5x)$

    A. $8x$ B. $2x$ C. $-8x$
    D. $-2x$ E. $-15x$

12.
(78)
$-x+4x$

    A. $-3x$ B. $3x$ C. $5x$

    D. $-4x$ E. $-5x$

Reduce each fraction below. Select the best possible choice.

(a) 13.
(84)
$\dfrac{4x}{10x}$

    A. $\dfrac{2x}{5}$ B. $\dfrac{1}{6x}$ C. $\dfrac{5x}{2}$

    D. $\dfrac{5}{2}$ E. $\dfrac{2}{5}$

(b) 14.
(84)
$\dfrac{3x}{12x}$

    A. $\dfrac{1}{4}$ B. $\dfrac{x}{4}$ C. $4x$

    D. 4 E. $\dfrac{1}{9x}$

15.
(83)
$\dfrac{16}{36x}$

    A. $\dfrac{4}{9x}$ B. $\dfrac{1}{20x}$ C. $\dfrac{9}{4x}$

    D. $\dfrac{4}{9}$ E. $\dfrac{9}{4}$

Solve each equation below. Make sure your answer is fully reduced.

16. $-14x = 378$ **17.** $\dfrac{x}{3} + 7 = -3$ **18.** $-4(x+9) = -16$
(64)   (73)   (64)

19. $5x + 2x = 63$ **(c) 20.** $6 + 2x = 5 - 7x$ **(d) 21.** $3 + 10x = -9 + 4x$
(76)   (81)   (81)

Translate the word problem below into an equation; then solve.

(e) 22.
(80)
Motorcycle #1 and motorcycle #2 are headed straight toward each other. Motorcycle #1 is traveling at 55 mph, and motorcycle #2 is traveling at 70 mph. If the two motorcycles are 500 miles apart, how many hours will it be before they meet?

Lesson 85—Fractions and Parentheses—Part 1

We've been learning how to reduce fractions with x's, and so far it probably seems pretty easy. We just treat the x's as numbers, and everything else works just like fractions from arithmetic. Well, in this lesson, things get a little more complicated. Take a look at our first example.

$$\frac{2(x+5)}{4}$$

What's different about this fraction is that it has parentheses in the numerator. Basically, the fraction takes a missing number (x) and adds 5 to it; then 2 is multiplied by that result, and finally that total is divided by 4.

The Top Really is Factored

The question is how do we reduce the fraction? Well, the good news is that we can still use our same method: factor and cancel. As a first step, let's factor the denominator: 4 breaks down as $2 \cdot 2$.

$$\frac{2(x+5)}{2 \cdot 2} \qquad \textbf{Factor the bottom}$$

Now for the numerator. It may seem like the numerator isn't factored, because it has an addition: $x+5$. But actually the numerator is factored. That's because the $x+5$ is inside parentheses. Here's why that matters. The rule says that any quantity that's inside parentheses should be treated as a single number. So we can think of $2(x+5)$ as the number 2 multiplied by another number $(x+5)$. That's a multiplication, so the numerator is technically factored. That means we have both bottom and top factored, and we're ready to cancel.[1]

$$\frac{2 \cdot (x+5)}{2 \cdot 2} \qquad \textbf{Top already factored}$$

We have a 2 and an $(x+5)$ on top and two 2s on bottom. The only thing to cancel is a pair of 2s.

$$\frac{\cancel{2} \cdot (x+5)}{\cancel{2} \cdot 2} \qquad \textbf{Cancel the 2s}$$

All we have left now is the quantity $x+5$ on top (remember, that's supposed to be treated as a single number) and one 2 on bottom. So there's nothing else to cancel. Here's our fully reduced answer.

$$\frac{x+5}{2}$$

Notice that we took off the parentheses. Those can be dropped, because $x+5$ isn't being multiplied by anything anymore.

---

[1] We put a dot between the 2 and the $(x + 5)$ to show that it's been broken down into its factors (just as we did with the 4 on bottom)

Subtraction in Parentheses

Here's a slightly tougher example.

$$\frac{6(x-5)}{12}$$

This fraction also has a quantity inside parentheses, but it's a subtraction instead of an addition. That doesn't change a thing, though. The $x-5$ should be treated as a single number, as in the previous example. And we should start by factoring the top and bottom, as usual. In the bottom, 12 factors as $2\cdot 2\cdot 3$.

$$\frac{6(x-5)}{2\cdot 2\cdot 3}$$ **Factor the bottom**

On top, we have 6 times the quantity inside parentheses: $(x-5)$. The $(x-5)$ has to be treated like a single number, remember. So we have 6 times $(x-5)$, which is factored. But we can break the top down a little further by changing 6 to $2\cdot 3$.

$$\frac{2\cdot 3\cdot (x-5)}{2\cdot 2\cdot 3}$$

Now the top is factored as far as it will go, and we're ready to cancel. There's a pair of 2s that will cancel, and there's also a pair of 3s.

$$\frac{\cancel{2}\cdot\cancel{3}\cdot (x-5)}{\cancel{2}\cdot 2\cdot\cancel{3}}$$ **Cancel the 2s and 3s**

Since $x-5$ is no longer multiplied by anything, we can drop the parentheses. And on bottom, we have just a 2 left.

$$\frac{x-5}{2}$$

The main point is that when reducing fractions, quantities inside parentheses are treated as a single number.

Practice 85

a.
(85) Reduce the fraction $\dfrac{2(x+7)}{4}$. Select the best possible choice.

    A. $6(x+7)$ B. $8(x+7)$ C. $\dfrac{x+7}{6}$

    D. $\dfrac{x+7}{2}$ E. $\dfrac{x+7}{8}$

b.
(85) Reduce the fraction $\dfrac{8(x-3)}{16}$. Select the best possible choice.

    A. $8(x-3)$ B. $24(x-3)$ C. $\dfrac{x-3}{2}$

    D. $\dfrac{x-3}{8}$ E. $\dfrac{x-3}{128}$

c.
(81)
Solve the equation $6 + 7x = 8 + 2x$. Make sure your answer is fully reduced.

d.
(81)
Solve the equation $9 + x = 3 - 4x$. Make sure your answer is fully reduced.

e.
(73)
Translate the word problem below into an equation; then solve.

There is a number that if you divide it by 3, and then add 7 to the result, you get 13. What's the number?

Problem Set 85

Tell whether each sentence below is True or False.

1.
(85)
The method used to reduce fractions with x's is basically the same one used to reduce fractions that have just numbers.

2.
(85)
When reducing fractions, any quantity in parentheses should be treated as a single number.

Add or subtract each group of numbers below.

3.
(18)
$$\begin{array}{r} 297.5 \\ +931.04 \\ \hline \end{array}$$

4.
(17)
$$\begin{array}{r} 0.6359 \\ -0.4836 \\ \hline \end{array}$$

Add or subtract (as indicated) each pair of numbers below.

5.
(59)
$12 + (-25)$

6.
(60)
$-9 - (-13)$

Multiply or divide (as indicated) each pair of numbers below.

7.
(61)
$(10)(-3.5)$

8.
(62)
$\dfrac{-36}{-4}$

Calculate the value of each expression below. (Make sure to do the operations in the correct order.)

9.
(68)
$7 \cdot 3 - 5$

10.
(70)
$\dfrac{2 - 14}{-4}$

Translate each of the following phrases into a mathematical expression. (Don't calculate the answer.)

11.
(68)
-7 added to 6 first, and that total multiplied by 20.

    A. $20(-7 + 6)$ B. $20 \cdot 6 + (-7)$ C. $20(-7) + 6$

    D. $6(-7 + 20)$ E. $-7 + 6(20)$

12.
(70)
-42 divided by 6 first, and then 8 subtracted from that total.

    A. $\dfrac{-42}{8-6}$ B. $\dfrac{-42-8}{6}$ C. $8-\dfrac{-42}{6}$

    D. $\dfrac{-42}{6}-8$ E. $\dfrac{-42}{6-8}$

Simplify each expression below. Select the best possible choice.

13.
(78)
$8x+x$

    A. $-7x$ B. $9x$ C. $8x$

    D. $-9x$ E. $7x$

14.
(76)
$-5x+4x$

    A. x B. $-9x$ C. $9x$

    D. $-x$ E. $-20x$

Reduce each fraction below. Select the best possible choice.

15.
(84)
$\dfrac{3x}{24x}$

    A. $\dfrac{1}{8x}$ B. $8x$ C. 8

    D. $\dfrac{1}{21x}$ E. $\dfrac{1}{8}$

16.
(83)
$\dfrac{27x}{18}$

    A. $-\dfrac{2x}{3}$ B. $9x$ C. $\dfrac{3x}{2}$

    D. $-\dfrac{3x}{2}$ E. $\dfrac{2x}{3}$

(a) 17.
(85)
$\dfrac{3(x+4)}{9}$

    A. $\dfrac{x+4}{27}$ B. $12(x+4)$ C. $\dfrac{x+4}{6}$

    D. $3(x+4)$ E. $\dfrac{x+4}{3}$

(b) 18.
(85)
$\dfrac{10(x-3)}{20}$

    A. $\dfrac{x-3}{2}$ B. $\dfrac{x-3}{10}$ C. $\dfrac{x-3}{30}$

    D. $200(x-3)$ E. $10(x-3)$

Solve each equation below. Make sure your answer is fully reduced.

19.
(53) $4x - 7 = 13$

20.
(73) $\dfrac{x+11}{2} = -14$

(c) 21.
(81) $2 + 6x = 6 + 3x$

(d) 22.
(81) $9 + x = 2 - 5x$

Translate the word problem below into an equation; then solve.

(e) 23.
(73)   There is a number that if you divide it by 6, and then add 4 to the result, you get 12. What's the number?

Lesson 86—Fractions and Parentheses—Part 2

In the last lesson, we learned how to reduce fractions with parentheses. Here's another example like that.

$$\frac{15}{3(x+1)}$$

Notice that this time the parentheses are in the bottom of the fraction. This just means 15 divided by 3 times the sum of x and 1 (in other words, the addition is done before the multiplication). To reduce the fraction, we follow the same method we always use: factor and cancel. The top factors as 3 times 5.

$$\frac{3\cdot5}{3(x+1)}$$

The bottom is already factored, because the quantity in parentheses has to be treated as a single number. So the bottom is the number 3 times some other quantity $(x+1)$.

$$\frac{3\cdot5}{3\cdot(x+1)}$$

With both top and bottom factored, we're ready to cancel. We can cross out a pair of 3s.

$$\frac{\cancel{3}\cdot5}{\cancel{3}\cdot(x+1)} \qquad \textbf{Cancel the 3s}$$

That leaves us with 5 on top and $(x+1)$ on bottom, but we don't need parentheses around the $x+1$ anymore. Here's our final, fully reduced answer.

$$\frac{5}{x+1}$$

Parentheses in Top and Bottom

Now, for the next example.

$$\frac{8(x-7)}{24(x-7)}$$

This fraction has parentheses in both the top and bottom. But we can still reduce by factoring and canceling. The top is already factored, since 8 is multiplied by the quantity $(x-7)$, which is treated as a single number. But we can factor the top even further by breaking down 8 as $2\cdot2\cdot2$.

$$\frac{2\cdot2\cdot2\cdot(x-7)}{24(x-7)}$$

On the bottom, we have 24 multiplied by the quantity $(x-7)$, which is factored. But we can go further by breaking 24 down as $2\cdot12$. Then 12 can be changed to $2\cdot2\cdot3$. So we end up with $2\cdot2\cdot2\cdot3\cdot(x-7)$ on bottom.

$$\frac{2\cdot2\cdot2\cdot(x-7)}{2\cdot2\cdot2\cdot3\cdot(x-7)}$$

Now we're ready to cancel. There are actually three pairs of 2s that can be canceled.

$$\frac{\cancel{2}\cdot\cancel{2}\cdot\cancel{2}\cdot(x-7)}{\cancel{2}\cdot\cancel{2}\cdot\cancel{2}\cdot3\cdot(x-7)}$$

Cancel three pairs of 2s

Canceling Quantities in Parentheses

But what about the $(x-7)$'s? Can they be canceled? Well, remember, anything inside parentheses has to be treated as a single number, so what we have is some number on top, $(x-7)$, and that same number on bottom. Since they're the same, we can cancel them.

$$\frac{\cancel{2}\cdot\cancel{2}\cdot\cancel{2}\cdot\cancel{(x-7)}}{\cancel{2}\cdot\cancel{2}\cdot\cancel{2}\cdot3\cdot\cancel{(x-7)}}$$

Cancel the (x-7)'s too

By the way, what we really did by canceling the $(x-7)$'s was divide the top and bottom by $(x-7)$. Since everything on top has been canceled, we have to put a 1 up there (as always). And there's just a 3 left on bottom. Amazingly, our original messy fraction, $\dfrac{8(x-7)}{24(x-7)}$, has reduced all the way down to $\dfrac{1}{3}$.

$$\frac{1}{3}$$

The main points of this lesson are that quantities in parentheses can be in the top and bottom of a fraction. And, since they're treated as single numbers, they can be canceled just like anything else.

Practice 86

a.
(86) Reduce the fraction $\dfrac{15}{5(x+4)}$. Select the best possible choice.

    A. $10(x+4)$ B. $\dfrac{3}{x+4}$ C. $3(x+4)$

    D. $\dfrac{10}{x+4}$ E. $\dfrac{x+4}{3}$

b.
(86) Reduce the fraction $\dfrac{6(x-9)}{42(x-9)}$. Select the best possible choice.

    A. $\dfrac{1}{7}$ B. $7(x-9)$ C. 7

    D. $\dfrac{x-9}{36}$ E. $\dfrac{x-9}{7}$

c.
(78) Solve the equation $-x+4x=33$.

d.
(81) Solve the equation $7+9x=5+2x$. Make sure your answer is fully reduced.

e. Translate the word problem below into an equation; then solve.
(82)

Sunshine Electrical Repair Service only charges $20 for a service call (just to come to the house) plus $30 per hour to do the repair job. Rainy Day Electrical Repair Service charges $40 for a service call plus $25 per hour to do the repair job. How many hours would a job have to take for the bills of both repair services to be the same?

Problem Set 86

Answer each question below.

1. What is 50% of 1,274?
(27)

2. What is $\frac{3}{4}$ of 230?
(14)

Add or subtract (as indicated) each pair of numbers below.

3. $-83+(-55)$
(59)

4. $-29-14$
(60)

Multiply or divide (as indicated) each pair of numbers below.

5. $(-5)(-16)$
(61)

6. $\dfrac{43}{-43}$
(62)

Calculate the value of each expression below. (Make sure to do the operations in the correct order.)

7. $30+\dfrac{20}{4}$
(70)

8. $9(-11+4)$
(68)

Translate each of the following word problems into an equation. (Don't solve.)

9. There's some number that if you divide it by 8 first, and then subtract 37 from that total, the result is
(71) -91.

    A. $\dfrac{37-x}{8}=-91$ B. $x-\dfrac{37}{8}=-91$ C. $\dfrac{x}{8}-37=-91$

    D. $37-\dfrac{x}{8}=-91$ E. $\dfrac{x-37}{8}=-91$

10. There's some number that if you add 4 to it first, and then multiply that total by -13, the result is 50.
(69)

    A. $4(x-13)=50$ B. $-13(x+4)=50$ C. $-13(4)+x=50$

    D. $x+4(-13)=50$ E. $-13x+4=50$

Simplify each expression below. Select the best possible choice.

11.
(75)

$7+4x+21$

    A. $4x+28$ B. $7+25x$ C. $11x+21$

    D. $32x$ E. $4x+14$

12.
(76)

$6x+9x$

    A. $-15x$ B. $54x$ C. $3x$

    D. $-3x$ E. $15x$

Reduce each fraction below. Select the best possible choice.

13.
(83)

$\dfrac{18}{6x}$

    A. $\dfrac{12}{x}$ B. $\dfrac{x}{3}$ C. $\dfrac{3}{x}$

    D. $3x$ E. $\dfrac{1}{3}$

14.
(84)

$\dfrac{5x}{25x}$

    A. $\dfrac{1}{5}$ B. $\dfrac{1}{5x}$ C. $\dfrac{x}{5}$

    D. $20x$ E. $\dfrac{1}{20x}$

15.
(85)

$\dfrac{4(x-2)}{12}$

    A. $16(x-2)$ B. $8(x-2)$ C. $\dfrac{x-2}{3}$

    D. $\dfrac{x-2}{8}$ E. $\dfrac{x-2}{48}$

(a) 16.
(86)

$\dfrac{14}{7(x+1)}$

    A. $7(x+1)$ B. $\dfrac{7}{x+1}$ C. $\dfrac{x+1}{2}$

    D. $2(x+1)$ E. $\dfrac{2}{x+1}$

(b) 17. $\dfrac{4(x-5)}{24(x-5)}$
(86)

     A. $\dfrac{x-5}{6}$ B. $\dfrac{x-5}{28}$ C. $6(x-5)$

     D. $\dfrac{1}{6}$ E.   6

Solve each equation below. Make sure your answer is fully reduced.

18. $5(x-8)=30$ **19.** $\dfrac{x}{4}+21=19$ **(c) 20.** $-x+5x=48$
(72)   (73)   (78)

(d) 21. $5+11x=3+2x$
(81)

Translate the word problem below into an equation; then solve.

(e) 22.   Four Eyes Computer Repair Service only charges \$40 for a service call (just to come to the house) plus
(82)   \$25 per hour to do the repair job. File Savers Computer Repair Service charges \$50 for a service call plus \$20 per hour to do the repair job. How many hours would a job have to take for the bills of both repair services to be the same?

Lesson 87—Multiplying Fractions with x's

We've learned to reduce fractions with x's. But what about multiplying, dividing, adding, and subtracting fractions with x's? We need to learn to do that too. So for the next few lessons, we'll concentrate on those operations, and we'll start in this lesson with multiplication.

Multiply the Tops and Bottoms

Here's our first example.

$$\frac{6x}{15} \cdot \frac{5}{14x}$$

We have two fractions multiplied and both contain x's. As it turns out, we can multiply these in the same way that we multiply fractions with just numbers. We factor and cancel first and then multiply the tops and the bottoms. The only thing we have to remember is to treat x as a prime number, which means it can't be broken down any further.

As a first step, let's factor everything in the top and bottom of both fractions. Remember, when multiplying fractions we always want to factor and cancel first because it's faster. The top of the first fraction factors as $2 \cdot 3 \cdot x$ and the bottom factors as $3 \cdot 5$.

$$\frac{2 \cdot 3 \cdot x}{3 \cdot 5} \cdot \frac{5}{14x} \qquad \textbf{Factoring first fraction}$$

Now for the second fraction. On top, we have the prime number, 5, which can't be broken down any further. On bottom, we can factor $14x$ as $2 \cdot 7 \cdot x$.

$$\frac{2 \cdot 3 \cdot x}{3 \cdot 5} \cdot \frac{5}{2 \cdot 7 \cdot x} \qquad \textbf{Factoring second fraction}$$

With everything factored in both fractions, we're ready to cancel. And, remember, as with fractions that have only numbers, we can cancel anything on top with anything on bottom, in either fraction. There's a pair of 2s, a pair of 3s, a pair of 5s, and a pair of x's that will cancel.

$$\frac{\overset{1}{2} \cdot \overset{}{3} \cdot \overset{}{x}}{\underset{1}{3 \cdot 5}} \cdot \frac{\overset{1}{5}}{2 \cdot 7 \cdot x} \qquad \textbf{Cancel first}$$

Notice we put ones in place of the numerators and denominator where every factor was canceled. The final step is to multiply the tops and bottoms to get $\dfrac{1}{7}$, which is fully reduced.

$$\frac{1}{1} \cdot \frac{1}{7} \quad \Longrightarrow \quad \frac{1}{7}$$

The great thing about factoring and canceling before multiplying is that we know that our answer is always fully reduced.

One More Time

Let's do one more multiplication example.

$$\frac{9x}{20} \cdot \frac{4x}{18x}$$

The first step is to factor everything in both fractions. The top of the first fraction factors as $3 \cdot 3 \cdot x$, and the 20 on bottom factors as $2 \cdot 2 \cdot 5$.

$$\frac{3 \cdot 3 \cdot x}{2 \cdot 2 \cdot 5} \cdot \frac{4x}{18x} \qquad \textbf{Factoring first fraction}$$

Now for the second fraction. On top, $4x$ factors as $2 \cdot 2 \cdot x$ and on bottom $18x$ factors as $2 \cdot 3 \cdot 3 \cdot x$.

$$\frac{3 \cdot 3 \cdot x}{2 \cdot 2 \cdot 5} \cdot \frac{2 \cdot 2 \cdot x}{2 \cdot 3 \cdot 3 \cdot x} \qquad \textbf{Factoring second fraction}$$

Next, we're ready to cancel. There are two pairs of 2s and two pairs of 3s that will cancel. A pair of x's can be canceled too.

$$\frac{\overset{1}{\cancel{3} \cdot \cancel{3} \cdot \cancel{x}}}{\cancel{2} \cdot \cancel{2} \cdot 5} \cdot \frac{\cancel{2} \cdot \cancel{2} \cdot x}{2 \cdot \cancel{3} \cdot \cancel{3} \cdot \cancel{x}} \qquad \textbf{Cancel in both fractions}$$

The last step is to multiply the tops and bottoms of what is left to get the fully reduced answer of $\frac{x}{10}$.

$$\frac{1}{5} \cdot \frac{x}{2} \quad \longrightarrow \quad \frac{x}{10}$$

The main point is that fractions with x's are multiplied in basically the same way that we multiply fractions with just numbers: factor and cancel, then multiply the tops and bottoms.

Practice 87

a.
(86) Reduce the fraction $\frac{15(x-7)}{20(x-7)}$. Select the best possible choice.

     A. $\frac{10}{15}$ B. $\frac{x-7}{5}$ C. $\frac{4}{3}$

     D. $\frac{3}{4}$ E. $\frac{3(x-7)}{4}$

b.
(87) Multiply the fractions $\frac{4x}{24} \cdot \frac{8}{16x}$. Make sure your answers are fully reduced then select the best possible choice.

     A. $\frac{1}{28x}$ B. $\frac{4x+8}{24+16x}$ C. $\frac{1}{12}$

     D. 12   E. $\frac{1}{8x}$

c.
(87) Multiply the fractions $\dfrac{12x}{26} \cdot \dfrac{13x}{24x}$. Make sure your answers are fully reduced then select the best possible choice.

A. $\dfrac{x}{8}$

B. $\dfrac{x}{2+2x}$

C. $\dfrac{25x}{26+24x}$

D. $\dfrac{1}{4}$

E. $\dfrac{x}{4}$

d.
(81) Solve the equation $5+4x=-19-4x$.

e.
(79) Translate the word problem below into an equation; then solve.

Wendy and Sue are doubles partners. Wendy usually hits about 4 aces per hour, and Sue usually hits about 5 per hour. Together, how many hours should it take them to hit 27 aces?

Problem Set 87

Tell whether each sentence below is True or False.

1.
(87) To multiply fractions with x's, you factor and cancel first.

2.
(87) When multiplying fractions with x's, you factor, cancel, and then add the numerators.

Convert each fraction below into decimal form. Give exact answers (no rounding).

3.
(23) $\dfrac{3}{5}$

4.
(24) $\dfrac{1}{9}$

Add or subtract (as indicated) each pair of numbers below.

5.
(59) $-15+8$

6.
(60) $10-(-10)$

Multiply or divide (as indicated) each pair of numbers below.

7.
(61) $(9)(-9)$

8.
(62) $\dfrac{-60}{-4}$

Calculate the value of each expression below. (Make sure to do the operations in the correct order.)

9.
(68) $10+4(-3)$

10.
(70) $\dfrac{-15}{4-7}$

Translate each of the following phrases into a mathematical expression. (Don't calculate the answer.)

11.
(68)
-7 multiplied by 16 first, and 22 added to that total.

    A. $-7(22)+16$ B. $-7(16)-22$ C. $-7(16)+22$

    D. $-7(16+22)$ E. $16(-7+22)$

12.
(70)
11 minus 4 first, and that total divided by -3.

    A. $\dfrac{11}{-3}-4$ B. $\dfrac{4-11}{-3}$ C. $11-\dfrac{4}{-3}$

    D. $\dfrac{-3}{11-4}$ E. $\dfrac{11-4}{-3}$

Simplify each expression below. Select the best possible choice.

13.
(75)
$5+10x-11$

    A. $10x+(-6)$ B. $5-x$ C. $15x-11$

    D. $10x+(-16)$ E. $10x+6$

14.
(59)
$-8x+(-5x)$

    A. $-3x$ B. $3x$ C. $13x$

    D. $40x$ E. $-13x$

Reduce each fraction below. Select the best possible choice.

15.
(86)
$\dfrac{35}{5(x+11)}$

    A. $\dfrac{1}{7(x+11)}$ B. $\dfrac{7}{x+11}$ C. $\dfrac{30}{x+11}$

    D. $\dfrac{x+11}{7}$ E. $\dfrac{1}{30(x+11)}$

(a) 16.
(86)
$\dfrac{14(x-4)}{21(x-4)}$

    A. $\dfrac{2(x-4)}{3}$ B. $\dfrac{2}{3}$ C. $\dfrac{x-4}{7}$

    D. $\dfrac{3}{2}$ E. $\dfrac{7}{14}$

Multiply each pair of fractions below. Make sure your answers are fully reduced then select the best possible choice.

(b) 17.
(87)
$$\frac{4x}{18} \cdot \frac{6}{12x}$$

    A. $\dfrac{4x+6}{18+12x}$ B. $\dfrac{1}{9}$ C. $\dfrac{1}{6x}$

    D. 9 E. $\dfrac{1}{9x}$

(c) 18.
(87)
$$\frac{10x}{28} \cdot \frac{6x}{15x}$$

    A. $\dfrac{16x}{28+15x}$ B. $\dfrac{x}{7}$ C. $\dfrac{5x}{17}$

    D. $\dfrac{1}{7}$ E. $\dfrac{x}{14}$

Solve each equation below.

19.
(73)
$$\frac{x-5}{8} = -2$$

20.
(77)
$$25x - 17x = -64$$

(d) 21.
(81)
$$4 + 5x = -16 - 5x$$

Translate the word problem below into an equation; then solve.

(e) 22.
(79)
Bud and Lou are on the same bowling team. Bud usually bowls about 6 strikes per hour, and Lou usually bowls about 8 per hour. Together, how many hours should it take them to bowl 56 strikes?

Lesson 88—Dividing Fractions with x's

We've been combining fractions with x's, and in the last lesson we covered multiplication. Now we're going to learn how to divide fractions with x's. Here's our first example.

$$\frac{3x}{10} \div \frac{21x}{8}$$

The Old Division Symbol

First of all, notice that we've used the old arithmetic division symbol. Dividing fractions is one of the few places in algebra where this symbol is still used. It's also okay to use the fraction bar on this kind of problem. With the fraction bar, the problem looks like this.

$$\frac{\dfrac{3x}{10}}{\dfrac{21x}{8}}$$

You can write it the second way too. But most of the time, when fractions with x's are divided, the problem will be written with the old division symbol.

Invert and Multiply

Now let's do the division. It's actually really easy. Everything works the same way as it does when dividing fractions with only numbers. All we have to do is invert the second fraction (which just means flip it over) and then multiply. Flipping over $\dfrac{21x}{8}$, gives us this.

$$\frac{3x}{10} \cdot \frac{8}{21x} \qquad \textbf{Inverting second fraction}$$

If the division had been written with the fraction bar, then we would have inverted the bottom fraction and multiplied.

From here, we just multiply in the usual way. We factor everything in both fractions. On top of the first fraction, 3 and x can't be broken down any further. On bottom, 10 can be factored as $2 \cdot 5$.

$$\frac{3 \cdot x}{2 \cdot 5} \cdot \frac{8}{21x} \qquad \textbf{Factoring first fraction}$$

Now for the second fraction. On top, 8 can be factored as $2 \cdot 2 \cdot 2$. On bottom, $21x$ can be factored as $3 \cdot 7 \cdot x$.

$$\frac{3 \cdot x}{2 \cdot 5} \cdot \frac{2 \cdot 2 \cdot 2}{3 \cdot 7 \cdot x} \qquad \textbf{Factoring second fraction}$$

With everything factored, we're ready to cancel. As usual, we can cancel any factor on top with the same factor on bottom of either fraction. We can cancel one pair of 2s, a pair of 3s, and a pair of x's.

$$\frac{\overset{1}{\cancel{3} \cdot \cancel{x}}}{\cancel{2} \cdot 5} \cdot \frac{\cancel{2} \cdot 2 \cdot 2}{\cancel{3} \cdot 7 \cdot \cancel{x}} \qquad \textbf{Cancel in both fractions}$$

391

The last step is to multiply the tops and bottoms of the remaining factors to get $\frac{4}{35}$.

$$\frac{1}{5} \cdot \frac{2 \cdot 2}{7} \quad \longrightarrow \quad \frac{4}{35}$$

Even though these numbers are pretty big, we don't need to bother trying to reduce our answer. Since we factored and canceled before multiplying, we know the answer has to be fully reduced. The main point is dividing fractions with x's is exactly like dividing fractions in arithmetic. (At least for the fractions that we'll be dividing in Pre-Algebra, that is. It gets a little harder in Algebra 1.)

Practice 88

a.
(61)
Multiply $(-2)(-5)(-6)$

b.
(87)
Multiply the fractions $\frac{5x}{12x} \cdot \frac{14x}{10x}$. Make sure your answers are fully reduced then select the best possible choice.

A. $\frac{7}{10}$ B. $\frac{7x}{8}$ C. $\frac{7}{12x}$

D. $\frac{7}{12}$ E. $\frac{19}{22}$

c.
(88)
Divide the fractions $\frac{4x}{18} \div \frac{16x}{9}$. Make sure your answers are fully reduced then select the best possible choice.

A. $\frac{1}{8}$ B. $\frac{1}{16}$ C. $\frac{32x}{81}$

D. $\frac{20x}{27}$ E. $\frac{1}{8x}$

d.
(88)
Divide the fractions $\dfrac{\frac{5}{6x}}{\frac{10}{16x}}$. Make sure your answers are fully reduced then select the best possible choice.

A. $\frac{3}{4}$ B. $\frac{4}{3}$ C. $\frac{4}{3x}$

D. $\frac{8x}{3}$ E. $\frac{25}{48}$

e.
(80)
Translate the word problem below into an equation; then solve.

Riding lawnmower #1 and riding lawnmower #2 are headed straight toward each other. Mower #1 is traveling at 3 feet per second, and mower #2 is traveling at 4 feet per second. If the two mowers are 77 feet apart, how many seconds will it be before they meet?

Problem Set 88

Answer each question below.

1.
(55) How far will a roller blader skating at 28 miles per hour go in $2\frac{1}{4}$ hours?

2.
(55) How long will a strand of blonde hair growing at 10 inches per year grow in $\frac{1}{2}$ year?

Add or subtract (as indicated) each pair of numbers below.

3. $-70-(-58)$
(60)

4. $-100+82$
(59)

Multiply or divide (as indicated) each group of numbers below.

5. $\dfrac{-1,000}{-50}$
(62)

(a) 6. $(-2)(-3)(-4)$
(61)

Calculate the value of each expression below. (Make sure to do the operations in the correct order.)

7. $\dfrac{-45}{5}-7$
(70)

8. $10(12-8)$
(68)

Translate each of the following word problems into an equation. (Don't solve.)

9.
(69) There's some number that if you multiply it by 14 first, and then add 23 to that total, the result is 101.

A. $14x\cdot23=101$ B. $14+23x=101$ C. $14(x+23)=101$
D. $14x+23=101$ E. $23(x+14)=101$

10.
(71) There's some number that if you subtract 41 from it first, and then divide that total by -5, the result is 26.

A. $\dfrac{x-41}{-5}=26$ B. $x-\dfrac{41}{-5}=26$ C. $\dfrac{41-x}{-5}=26$
D. $\dfrac{x}{-5}-41=26$ E. $\dfrac{-5}{x-41}=26$

Simplify each expression below. Select the best possible choice.

11. $17x+59x$
(76)

A. $-42x$ B. $76x$ C. $42x$
D. $-76x$ E. $1,003x$

12. $10x + (-x)$
(78)

    A. $-11x$ B. $-10x$ C. $-9x$

    D. $9x$ E. $11x$

Reduce each fraction below. Select the best possible choice.

13. $\dfrac{21}{7(x+5)}$
(86)

    A. $\dfrac{3}{x+5}$ B. $\dfrac{28}{x+5}$ C. $\dfrac{14}{x+5}$

    D. $\dfrac{147}{x+5}$ E. $\dfrac{x+5}{3}$

14. $\dfrac{10(x-2)}{18(x-2)}$
(86)

    A. $\dfrac{5}{9}$ B. $\dfrac{1}{9}$ C. $\dfrac{1}{8}$

    D. $\dfrac{5(x-2)}{9}$ E. $\dfrac{5}{9(x-2)}$

Multiply each pair of fractions below. Make sure your answers are fully reduced then select the best possible choice.

15. $\dfrac{32}{27x} \cdot \dfrac{9x}{8}$
(87)

    A. $\dfrac{4}{3x}$ B. $\dfrac{4x}{9}$ C. $\dfrac{4}{3}$

    D. $\dfrac{32+9x}{27x+8}$ E. $\dfrac{3}{4}$

(b) 16. $\dfrac{3x}{14x} \cdot \dfrac{7x}{5x}$
(87)

    A. $\dfrac{10}{19}$ B. $\dfrac{3x}{4}$ C. $\dfrac{3}{10}$

    D. $\dfrac{3}{7}$ E. $\dfrac{3}{10x}$

Divide each pair of fractions below. Make sure your answers are fully reduced then select the best possible choice.

(c) 17.
(88)

$$\frac{2x}{15} \div \frac{8x}{10}$$

    A. 6   B. $\dfrac{1}{12}$ C. $\dfrac{12x}{23}$

    D. $\dfrac{10x}{25}$ E. $\dfrac{1}{6}$

(d) 18.
(88)

$$\frac{\frac{4}{9x}}{\frac{2}{3x}}$$

    A. $\dfrac{3}{2}$ B. $\dfrac{8}{27}$ C. $\dfrac{2}{3x}$

    D. $\dfrac{8x}{3}$ E. $\dfrac{2}{3}$

Solve each equation below.

19. $-9(x+3) = 18$ **20.** $4x - 10 = 6$ **21.** $21x - 13x = 56$
(72)   (53)   (77)

Translate the word problem below into an equation; then solve.

(e) 22.
(80)
Electric scooter #1 and electric scooter #2 are headed straight toward each other. Scooter #1 is traveling at 5 feet per second, and scooter #2 is traveling at 8 feet per second. If the two scooters are 52 feet apart, how many seconds will it be before they meet?

Lesson 89—Adding Fractions with x's

We've covered multiplying and dividing fractions with x's. What about adding them?

Same Denominators

Look at this example.

$$\frac{4}{3x} + \frac{2}{3x}$$

We have two fractions added together. And, for the first time, the denominators have x's. The good news is that all we have to do to add these by adding the numerators. It works just like adding fractions that have only numbers. Since our denominators are the same ($3x$), we just add 4 and 2 to get 6 on top.

$$\frac{4+2}{3x} \quad \text{or} \quad \frac{6}{3x} \qquad \textbf{Add numerators}$$

Now, we have to make sure our answer is fully reduced. And this is where addition of fractions is different from multiplication and division. When multiplying or dividing fractions, we reduce first, which means we don't have to worry about reducing our answer. But when adding fractions, the reducing step comes last. So after getting our answer, we always have to try to reduce it. Let's see if we can reduce $\frac{6}{3x}$. The top factors as $2 \cdot 3$ and the bottom is already broken down as far as it will go as $3 \cdot x$.

$$\frac{2 \cdot 3}{3 \cdot x} \qquad \textbf{Factoring top and bottom}$$

We can cancel the 3s.

$$\frac{2 \cdot \cancel{3}}{\cancel{3} \cdot x} \qquad \textbf{Cancel the 3s.}$$

That gives us our fully reduced answer.

$$\frac{2}{x}$$

Different Denominators

Let's try another one.

$$\frac{5}{2x} + \frac{6}{x}$$

We have x's in the denominators again. But this time the denominators are not the same. As always, we need to make the denominators the same before adding. All we have to do is multiply the bottom and top of the second fraction by 2.

$$\frac{5}{2x} + \frac{2 \cdot 6}{2 \cdot x} \qquad \textbf{Multiply top and bottom}$$
$$\textbf{by 2}$$

$$\frac{5}{2x}+\frac{12}{2x}$$

Now we add the numerators.

$$\frac{17}{2x}$$ **Add the numerators**

Since we're adding (and not multiplying or dividing), we need to make sure that this answer is fully reduced by trying to factor and cancel. On top, 17 is a prime number, so it can't be broken down any further. Nothing can be done on bottom either. It just has the factors 2 and x.

$$\frac{17}{2 \cdot x}$$ **Nothing cancels**

So $\frac{17}{2x}$ is fully reduced, and that's our final answer.

Let's do another example.

$$\frac{3}{5x}+\frac{1}{2x}$$

The denominators are different here too, so we have to make them the same before adding. Only in this case, we need to multiply both fractions. The lowest common denominator is $10x$, which means we should multiply the top and bottom of the first fraction by 2 and the top and bottom of the second fraction by 5.

$$\frac{2\cdot3}{2\cdot5\cdot x}+\frac{5\cdot1}{5\cdot2\cdot x}$$ **Change bottoms to 10x**

Now we can simplify by multiplying in both fractions.

$$\frac{6}{10x}+\frac{5}{10x}$$

With both denominators the same, we add the numerators.

$$\frac{11}{10x}$$

We're not finished yet, though. We still need to try to reduce our answer. Since 11 is a prime number, it can't be broken down. On bottom, $10x$ factors as $2\cdot5\cdot x$.

$$\frac{11}{2\cdot5\cdot x}$$

Since nothing will cancel, $\frac{11}{10x}$ is fully reduced.

So adding fractions with x's is pretty simple. First, we make sure the denominators are the same. If they're not we multiply the top and bottom of one or both fractions by the right numbers. Second, we add the numerators. Last, we reduce the answer (if possible). It's the same exact process we use in arithmetic.

Practice 89

a.
(86)
Reduce the fraction $\dfrac{28(x-6)}{49(x-6)}$. Select the best possible choice.

A. $\dfrac{4}{7}$ B. $\dfrac{4(x-6)}{7}$ C. $\dfrac{21}{42}$

D. $\dfrac{7}{x-6}$ E. $\dfrac{7}{4}$

b.
(87)
Multiply the fractions $\left(\dfrac{16x}{21x}\right)\left(\dfrac{7}{24x}\right)$. Make sure your answers are fully reduced then select the best possible choice.

A. $\dfrac{2}{9x}$ B. $\dfrac{23x}{45}$ C. $\dfrac{1}{3x}$

D. $\dfrac{1}{3}$ E. $\dfrac{2}{9}$

c.
(89)
Add the fractions $\dfrac{2}{5x}+\dfrac{3}{x}$. Make sure your answers are fully reduced then select the best possible choice.

A. $\dfrac{6}{5x}$ B. $\dfrac{2}{15}$ C. $\dfrac{5}{6x}$

D. $\dfrac{1}{x}$ E. $\dfrac{17}{5x}$

d.
(89)
Add the fractions $\dfrac{1}{3x}+\dfrac{2}{7x}$. Make sure your answers are fully reduced then select the best possible choice.

A. $\dfrac{3}{10x}$ B. $\dfrac{1}{4x}$ C. $\dfrac{13}{21x}$

D. $\dfrac{3}{21x}$ E. $\dfrac{2}{21x}$

e.
(72)
Translate the word problem below into an equation; then solve.

There is a number that if you subtract 4 from it, and then multiply the result by 7, you get 42. What's the number?

Problem Set 89

Tell whether each sentence below is True or False.

1.
(89)   To add fractions with x's, you factor and cancel first.

2.
(89)   When adding fractions with x's, once the denominators are the same, you add the numerators.

Multiply or divide each pair of numbers below. Write any remainders in decimal form.

3.
(20)
$$\begin{array}{r} 15.3 \\ \times 4.6 \\ \hline \end{array}$$

4.
(22) $12\overline{)34,254}$

Add or subtract (as indicated) each group of numbers below.

5.
(59) $-4+(-7)+(-8)$

6.
(60) $-19-20$

Multiply or divide (as indicated) each pair of numbers below.

7.
(61) $(6)(-9)$

8.
(62) $\dfrac{-68}{-17}$

Calculate the value of each expression below. (Make sure to do the operations in the correct order.)

9.
(68) $(9)(3)-14$

10.
(70) $\dfrac{7+15}{2}$

Translate each of the following phrases into a mathematical expression. (Don't calculate the answer.)

11.
(68)   12 added to 21 first, and that total multiplied by 3.

A. $12(3+21)$ B. $21(12+3)$ C. $3(12+21)$

D. $12+21(3)$ E. $12(3)+21$

12.
(70)   42 divided by 7 first, and then 5 added to that total.

A. $42+\dfrac{5}{7}$ B. $\dfrac{7}{42+5}$ C. $\dfrac{42+5}{7}$

D. $\dfrac{7}{42}+5$ E. $\dfrac{42}{7}+5$

Reduce each fraction below. Select the best possible choice.

13.
(85)
$$\frac{20(x+7)}{60}$$

A. $\dfrac{x+7}{30}$ B. $\dfrac{x+7}{3}$ C. $\dfrac{x+7}{40}$

D. $3(x+7)$ E. $\dfrac{x+7}{1,200}$

(a) 14.
(86)
$$\frac{32(x-3)}{40(x-3)}$$

A. $\dfrac{4}{5}$ B. $\dfrac{24}{32}$ C. $\dfrac{4(x-3)}{5}$

D. $\dfrac{5}{x-3}$ E. $\dfrac{5}{4}$

Multiply or divide (as indicated) each pair of fractions below. Make sure your answers are fully reduced then select the best possible choice.

15.
(88)
$$\frac{4x}{12} \div \frac{8x}{6}$$

A. $\dfrac{12x}{18}$ B. $\dfrac{10x}{21}$ C. 4

D. $\dfrac{1}{4}$ E. $\dfrac{1}{4x}$

(b) 16.
(87)
$$\left(\frac{20x}{15x}\right)\left(\frac{5}{16x}\right)$$

A. $\dfrac{5}{7}$ B. $\dfrac{5}{12}$ C. $\dfrac{5}{7x}$

D. $\dfrac{5}{12x}$ E. $\dfrac{64x}{15}$

Add each pair of fractions below. Make sure your answers are fully reduced then select the best possible choice.

17.
(89)
$$\frac{5}{2x} + \frac{3}{2x}$$

A. $\dfrac{1}{x}$ B. $\dfrac{2}{x}$ C. $\dfrac{15}{2x}$

D. $\dfrac{x}{4}$ E. $\dfrac{4}{x}$

(c) 18.
(89)
$$\frac{5}{3x} + \frac{3}{x}$$

A. $\dfrac{5}{9}$

B. $5x$

C. $\dfrac{8}{3x}$

D. $\dfrac{14}{3x}$

E. $\dfrac{2}{x}$

(d) 19.
(89)
$$\frac{7}{2x} + \frac{1}{3x}$$

A. $\dfrac{23}{6x}$

B. $\dfrac{7}{6x}$

C. $\dfrac{8}{5x}$

D. $\dfrac{6}{x}$

E. $\dfrac{4}{3x}$

Solve each equation below.

20.
(78)
$3x + (-x) = 14$

21.
(81)
$6 + 7x = -4 + 2x$

Translate the word problem below into an equation; then solve.

(e) 22.
(72)
There is a number that if you subtract 5 from it, and then multiply the result by 8, you get 72. What's the number?

Lesson 90—Subtracting Fractions with x's

We've covered multiplying, dividing, and adding fractions with x's. That just leaves subtraction.

Same Denominators

So let's look at a subtracting fractions example.

$$\frac{9}{8x} - \frac{5}{8x}$$

Since the denominators are already the same, we can just subtract the numerators.

$$\frac{4}{8x}$$ **Subtract the tops**

See, the process works just like subtracting fractions in arithmetic. We're not finished yet, though. We still need to make sure that our answer is fully reduced. (Subtracting fractions is just like adding fractions in this way too: we have to reduce at the end.) The top factors as $2 \cdot 2$ and the bottom factors as $2 \cdot 2 \cdot 2 \cdot x$.

$$\frac{2 \cdot 2}{2 \cdot 2 \cdot 2 \cdot x}$$ **Factor on top and bottom**

Now we can cancel. There are two pairs of 2s that will cancel.

$$\frac{\overset{1}{\cancel{2} \cdot \cancel{2}}}{\cancel{2} \cdot \cancel{2} \cdot 2 \cdot x}$$ **Cancel the 2s**

That leaves $\frac{1}{2x}$, which is fully reduced. So subtracting fractions with x's is pretty easy. It's the same method you learned in basic math.

Different Denominators

Let's do another example that's a little harder.

$$\frac{1}{3x} - \frac{5}{2x}$$

See, this is harder because the denominators are different. But all we have to do is make the denominators the same before subtracting. The lowest common denominator for these two fractions is $6x$. That means we're going to have to multiply both fractions. We should multiply the top and bottom of the first fraction by 2 and the top and bottom of the second fraction by 3.

$$\frac{2 \cdot 1}{2 \cdot 3x} - \frac{3 \cdot 5}{3 \cdot 2x}$$ **Make bottoms equal 6x**

Let's simplify by multiplying everything.

$$\frac{2}{6x} - \frac{15}{6x}$$

Now you can see another reason why this example is a little harder. Subtracting the numerators is going to give us a negative result (since $2-15$ is negative). That's no big deal, though. The numerator comes out to -13.

$$\frac{-13}{6x} \qquad \textbf{Subtracting tops}$$

Next, we have to make sure our answer is fully reduced. Since 13 is a prime number, the top factors only as $(-1)(13)$. On bottom, $6x$ factors as $2 \cdot 3 \cdot x$.

$$\frac{(-1)(13)}{2 \cdot 3 \cdot x} \qquad \textbf{Factoring top and bottom}$$

Everything's factored, but there isn't anything to cancel. So $\frac{-13}{6x}$ is fully reduced. There's still one last step, though. We need to figure out the sign of the fraction as a whole. Since a negative divided by a positive equals a negative, we can put the negative sign out in front of the entire fraction like this.

$$-\frac{13}{6x}$$

And that's our final answer.

x's on Top and Bottom

We'll do one more example, and this one has something new.

$$\frac{7x}{4} - \frac{3x}{2}$$

As you can see, there are x's in the numerators instead of the denominators. At first that might seem hard, but it's really not. We can subtract these fractions in the same way—by subtracting the numerators. We already know how to subtract x's, so those shouldn't be a problem. But before subtracting, we have to make the denominators the same. This time, we only have to multiply the top and bottom of the second fraction by 2.

$$\frac{7x}{4} - \frac{2 \cdot 3x}{2 \cdot 2} \qquad \textbf{Making bottoms the same}$$

And we can simplify by multiplying.

$$\frac{7x}{4} - \frac{6x}{4}$$

Now we're ready to subtract the tops: $7x$ minus $6x$ equals just x. That gives us this.

$$\frac{x}{4} \qquad \textbf{Subtracting the tops}$$

We can try to reduce this answer. But it's pretty obvious that it won't reduce. The x on top can't be broken down at all, and 4 is $2 \cdot 2$, so there's nothing to cancel. Our fully reduced answer, then, is $\dfrac{x}{4}$.

Practice 90

a.
(89) Add the fractions $\dfrac{1}{2x} + \dfrac{2}{6x}$. Make sure your answers are fully reduced then select the best possible choice.

    A. $\dfrac{5x}{6}$ B. $\dfrac{5}{6x}$ C. $\dfrac{1}{3x}$

    D. $\dfrac{1}{2x}$ E. $\dfrac{x}{2}$

b.
(90) Subtract the fractions $\dfrac{8}{3x} - \dfrac{5}{3x}$. Make sure your answers are fully reduced then select the best possible choice.

    A. $\dfrac{1}{x}$ B. $\dfrac{1}{3x}$ C. x

    D. $\dfrac{3}{x}$ E. $\dfrac{13}{3x}$

c.
(90) Subtract the fractions $\dfrac{11x}{9} - \dfrac{2x}{3}$. Make sure your answers are fully reduced then select the best possible choice.

    A. $\dfrac{22x}{9}$ B. $\dfrac{3x}{2}$ C. x

    D. $\dfrac{13x}{9}$ E. $\dfrac{5x}{9}$

d.
(81) Solve the equation $4 + 5x = 20 - 3x$.

e.
(82) Translate the word problem below into an equation; then solve.

The Sound Doctor, an on-site stereo repair service, charges $15 for a service call (just to come to the house) plus $15 per hour to do the repair job. The Audio Cure, another on-site stereo fixer-upper, charges $25 for a service call plus $10 per hour to do the repair job. How many hours would a job have to take for the bills of both repair services to be the same?

Problem Set 90

Convert each percent below into decimal form.

    1.
(26)   3.5%   **2.**
(26)   182%

Add or subtract (as indicated) each pair of numbers below.

3.
(59) $-13 + (-4)$

4.
(60) $-11 - (-8)$

Multiply or divide (as indicated) each group of numbers below.

5.
(62) $\dfrac{62}{-2}$

6.
(61) $(4)(-6)(5)$

Calculate the value of each expression below. (Make sure to do the operations in the correct order.)

7.
(70) $\dfrac{15}{3} + 14$

8.
(68) $2(6 + 8)$

Translate each of the following word problems into an equation. (Don't solve.)

9.
(69) There's some number that if you subtract 7 from it first, and then multiply that total by 5, the result is -3.

    A. $5(7 - x) = -3$ B. $7x - 5 = -3$ C. $5(x - 7) = -3$

    D. $x - 7 \cdot 5 = -3$ E. $7(x - 5) = -3$

10.
(71) There's some number that if you divide it by 9 first, and then add 28 to that total, the result is 40.

    A. $\dfrac{x}{9 + 28} = 40$ B. $x + \dfrac{28}{9} = 40$ C. $\dfrac{x + 28}{9} = 40$

    D. $\dfrac{9}{x} + 28 = 40$ E. $\dfrac{x}{9} + 28 = 40$

Simplify each expression below. Select the best possible choice.

11.
(76) $14x + 5x$

    A. $9x$ B. $70x$ C. $-19x$

    D. $19x$ E. $-9x$

12.
(76) $-3x + (-7x)$

    A. $4x$ B. $-10x$ C. $10x$

    D. $21x$ E. $-4x$

Multiply or divide (as indicated) each pair of fractions below. Make sure your answers are fully reduced then select the best possible choice.

13.
(87)
$$\frac{3x}{25} \cdot \frac{10x}{9x}$$

      A. $\dfrac{1}{4x}$ B. $\dfrac{2x}{15}$ C. $\dfrac{27}{250x}$

      D. $\dfrac{13x}{34}$ E. $\dfrac{7}{15x}$

14.
(88)
$$\frac{4x}{3} \div \frac{16x}{6}$$

      A. $\dfrac{x}{2}$ B. $\dfrac{32x}{9}$ C. $\dfrac{1}{2}$

      D. $\dfrac{1}{6}$ E. $\dfrac{1}{4}$

Add each pair of fractions below. Make sure your answers are fully reduced then select the best possible choice.

15.
(89)
$$\frac{3}{12x} + \frac{1}{12x}$$

      A. $\dfrac{1}{3x}$ B. $\dfrac{x}{4}$ C. $\dfrac{1}{4x}$

      D. $\dfrac{1}{6x}$ E. $\dfrac{x}{3}$

(a) 16.
(89)
$$\frac{1}{2x} + \frac{3}{8x}$$

      A. $\dfrac{3}{16x}$ B. $\dfrac{7x}{8}$ C. $\dfrac{1}{2x}$

      D. $\dfrac{7}{8x}$ E. $\dfrac{x}{2}$

Subtract each pair of fractions below. Make sure your answers are fully reduced then select the best possible choice.

(b) 17.
(90)
$$\frac{7}{2x} - \frac{5}{2x}$$

      A. $\dfrac{6}{x}$ B. $\dfrac{1}{2x}$ C. $\dfrac{1}{x}$

      D. x E. $\dfrac{2}{x}$

(c) 18.
(90)
$\dfrac{13x}{6} - \dfrac{4x}{3}$

    A. $3x$ B. $\dfrac{5x}{6}$ C. $\dfrac{17x}{6}$

    D. $\dfrac{3x}{2}$ E. $\dfrac{52x}{6}$

Solve each equation below.

19.
(73)
$\dfrac{x+3}{2} = 5$

20.
(76)
$4x + 2x = -30$

(d) 21.
(81)
$1 + 8x = 11 - 2x$

Translate the word problem below into an equation; then solve.

(e) 22.
(82)
The Roof Rescue Squad, a roofing repair service, charges $35 for a service call (just to come to the house) plus $35 per hour to do the repair job. The Shingle Masters, another roofing repair service, charges $55 for a service call plus $30 per hour to do the repair job. How many hours would a job have to take for the bills of both repair services to be the same?

CHAPTER 12:
POWERS, POLYNOMIALS, AND RADICALS

Lesson 91—Raising a Number to a Power

So far, we've only worked with the four operations of basic math—addition, subtraction, multiplication, and division. But algebra actually has six operations. For the next few lessons, we're going to learn about the fifth and sixth operations. We'll start with the fifth.

Repeated Multiplication

You already know that multiplication is a short way to write the same number added to itself several times. For example, $(3)(5)$ is really just three 5s added or $5+5+5$. So multiplication is really repeated addition. That's nothing new.

But here's a good question. Is it ever necessary to *multiply* the same number over and over? The answer is yes. We have to do that all the time, especially in more advanced math. For example, we might have to multiply the number 3 seven times, like this.

$$(3)(3)(3)(3)(3)(3)(3) \qquad \textbf{3 multiplied seven times}$$

The problem is that it's a hassle to write all those 3s. It takes up a lot of space too. So just as we have a short way to write repeated addition (multiplication), we also have a short way to write repeated multiplication. And this is the fifth operation of algebra. You've probably seen it before, but here's the short way to write 3 multiplied seven times.

$$3^7$$

Exponents, Bases, and Powers

The little number in the upper right (the 7) is called the **exponent**; the big number down below (the 3) is called the **base.** The exponent tells us how many times the base is multiplied by itself.

When a repeated multiplication is written this way (with an exponent) we say that the number (the base) has been **raised to a power**. So the fifth operation of algebra is raising a number to a power. In our example (3^7) 3 is raised to the seventh power. We pronounce it "3 raised to the 7th power" or just "3 to the 7th power." The entire expression (the 3 and the 7) is also sometimes called a **power**.

Here's another power: 2^5. This is 2 raised to the fifth power. And it means 2 multiplied by itself five times: $(2)(2)(2)(2)(2)$ or 32. The little number, the exponent, always tells us how many times to multiply the big number, the base. Here's another example of a power: 4^3. This is 4 raised to the third power, and it means 4 multiplied by itself three times: $(4)(4)(4)$ or 64.

There are several advantages to writing a repeated multiplication as a power. We already mentioned two: It saves pencil lead and it takes up a lot less space. But another advantage is that we don't have to count a bunch of numbers that are being multiplied repeatedly. We can just read it off the exponent. With really long repeated multiplications this last advantage can be important. What if we had to multiply not seven 3s, but seventeen 3s? Without being able to use powers, we would have to write it like this.

$$(3)(3)(3)(3)(3)(3)(3)(3)(3)(3)(3)(3)(3)(3)(3)(3)(3)$$

Not only is this incredibly long, but you can't even figure out how many 3s there are without counting them. But now look at the same thing written as a power: 3^{17}. It's so nice and short, and we don't have to count the 3s because the exponent tells us how many of them are multiplied.

x's and Powers

It's even possible to raise an x to a power. Here's an example: x^2. This is x raised to the second power, and it means two x's multiplied or $x \cdot x$. We can't actually calculate the value of this because x stands for an unknown number. But whatever that number is, x^2 is that number multiplied twice. And x^3 is x raised to the third power. It means three x's multiplied or $x \cdot x \cdot x$. We can also raise other letters like y or z to powers. It works exactly the same way as with plain numbers. The exponent always tells us how many times the unknown letter is being multiplied.

Math Nicknames

Second powers (with 2 in the exponent) and third powers (with 3 in the exponent) have special nicknames. A second power is also called a **square**. So to multiply 8 two times by writing it as a power (8^2), most people don't say "8 to the second power." It's okay to say it that way. But most people say "8 squared" or "the square of 8." The nickname for a third power is **cube**. For example, 7^3 is not usually called "7 to the third power." It's more often called "7 cubed" or "the cube of 7."

The reason for these nicknames goes way back into history. In ancient times, people used exponents primarily to calculate areas of squares and volumes of cubes. As you know, the area of a square is its length multiplied by its width.

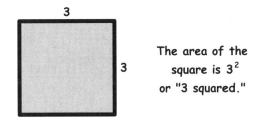

The area of the square is 3^2 or "3 squared."

Of course, all of the sides of a square are equal. That means the area, which is the length times the width, requires us to multiply the side length by itself. The area of the square above is 3 times 3 or 3^2. Since this used to be just about the only time second powers were ever used—to calculate areas of squares—people called 3 raised to the second power "3 squared."

And the same thing happened with cubes. The volume of a cube is its length times its width times its height. And since all those lengths are equal, the volume calculation involves multiplying a number by itself three times, which is a third power. Here's a cube with sides equal to 5, and the volume is (5)(5)(5) or 5^3.

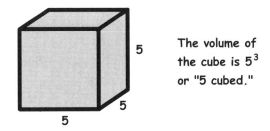

The volume of the cube is 5^3 or "5 cubed."

Since in ancient times, this was the only time people used third powers (to calculate volumes of cubes), they called 5^3 "5 cubed."

Of course, today we use powers for lots of other things besides calculating areas of squares and volumes of cubes. But the old nicknames are still really popular. So if you hear somebody say 4 squared or 6 cubed, you'll know they mean 4^2 and 6^3.

Practice 91

a.
(91)
Calculate the value of 2^6.

b.
(91)
Write $5 \cdot 5 \cdot 5 \cdot 5 \cdot 5 \cdot 5 \cdot 5$ as a power. (Don't calculate the answer.)

c.
(88)
Divide the fractions $\dfrac{\frac{2}{5x}}{\frac{16}{15x}}$. Make sure your answers are fully reduced then select the best possible choice.

A. $\dfrac{9}{10x}$ B. $\dfrac{3}{8}$ C. $\dfrac{17}{21}$

D. $\dfrac{32}{75x}$ E. $\dfrac{8}{3}$

d.
(90)
Subtract the fractions $\dfrac{2}{5x} - \dfrac{3}{x}$. Make sure your answers are fully reduced then select the best possible choice.

A. $-\dfrac{13}{5x}$ B. $-\dfrac{2}{15}$ C. $-\dfrac{1}{5x}$

D. $-\dfrac{1}{x}$ E. $-\dfrac{6}{5x}$

e.
(79)
Translate the word problem below into an equation; then solve.

Bored listener #1 fidgets 12 times each minute. Bored listener #2 fidgets 18 times each minute. Together, how many minutes will it take them to fidget 600 times?

Problem Set 91

Tell whether each sentence below is True or False.

1.
(91)
Raising a number to a power is a short way to write the same number multiplied repeatedly.

2.
(91)
In a power (like 5^3) the little number in the upper right is called the "exponent" and the big number below is called the "base."

Do the indicated operation with each group of numbers below.

3.
(60)
$45 - (-38)$ **4.**
(59)
$-15 + (-7) + 9$ **5.**
(61)
$(-20)(3)$

Calculate the value of each expression below. (Make sure to do the operations in the correct order.)

6.
(68) $11 - 8 \cdot 6$

7.
(70) $\dfrac{28}{9-2}$

Calculate the value of each power below.

8.
(91) 2^4

(a) 9.
(91) 3^5

Write each of the following as a power. (Don't calculate the answer.)

10.
(91)   9 squared

(b) 11.
(91) $4 \cdot 4 \cdot 4 \cdot 4 \cdot 4 \cdot 4$

Translate each of the following phrases into a mathematical expression. (Don't calculate the answer.)

12.
(68)   5 multiplied by -19 first, and 22 subtracted from that total.

   A. $5 \cdot 22 - 19$ B. $22 - (5)(-19)$ C. $(5)(-19) - 22$

   D. $5(-19 - 22)$ E. $5(22 - 19)$

13.
(70)   6 added to 14 first, and then that total divided by -3.

   A. $\dfrac{6}{14+3}$ B. $\dfrac{6+14}{-3}$ C. $\dfrac{-3}{6+14}$

   D. $6 + \dfrac{14}{-3}$ E. $\dfrac{6}{-3} + 14$

Reduce each fraction below. Select the best possible choice.

14.
(85) $\dfrac{3(x-1)}{9}$

   A. $\dfrac{x-1}{3}$ B. $\dfrac{x-1}{12}$ C. $3(x-1)$

   D. $\dfrac{x-1}{27}$ E. $\dfrac{x-1}{6}$

15.
(86) $\dfrac{18(x+5)}{24(x+5)}$

   A. $\dfrac{3(x+5)}{4}$ B. $\dfrac{x+5}{6}$ C. $\dfrac{4}{3}$

   D. $\dfrac{3}{4}$ E. $\dfrac{1}{42}$

Multiply or divide (as indicated) each pair of fractions below. Make sure your answers are fully reduced then select the best possible choice.

16.
(87)
$$\frac{12x}{20} \cdot \frac{15x}{24x}$$

     A. $\dfrac{24}{25}$ B. $\dfrac{3x}{8}$ C. $\dfrac{x}{2}$

     D. $\dfrac{3x}{10}$ E. $\dfrac{27x}{44}$

(c) 17.
(88)
$$\frac{\frac{3}{8x}}{\frac{9}{10x}}$$

     A. $\dfrac{5}{12}$ B. $\dfrac{27}{80x}$ C. $\dfrac{12}{5}$

     D. $\dfrac{13}{17}$ E. $\dfrac{2}{3x}$

Add or subtract (as indicated) each pair of fractions below. Make sure your answers are fully reduced then select the best possible choice.

18.
(89)
$$\frac{4x}{13} + \frac{5x}{13}$$

     A. $\dfrac{5x}{4}$ B. $\dfrac{4}{5}$ C. $\dfrac{20x}{13}$

     D. $\dfrac{x}{13}$ E. $\dfrac{9x}{13}$

(d) 19.
(90)
$$\frac{3}{7x} - \frac{2}{x}$$

     A. $-\dfrac{3}{14}$ B. $\dfrac{5}{7x}$ C. $-\dfrac{6}{7x}$

     D. $\dfrac{1}{7x}$ E. $-\dfrac{11}{7x}$

Solve each equation below.

20. $\dfrac{x}{9} + 14 = 17$ **21.** $-x + 5x = 36$
(73)   (78)

Translate the word problem below into an equation; then solve.

(e) 22.   Nervous speaker #1 says the word "um" 8 times each minute. Nervous speaker #2 says the word "um"
(79)   10 times each minute. Working together, how many minutes will it take them to say the word "um" 270 times?

Lesson 92—Scientific Notation

In this lesson, we're going to see how powers are used in science. Scientists have to deal with really huge numbers all the time. For instance, an astronomer might have to do a calculation involving the distance from the sun to the planet Pluto. Actually, that's nearly 4 *billion* miles.[1]

Shorter and Simpler

The bad thing about big numbers, though, is that all those zeros take up too much space. Another problem is that you have to count the zeros to figure out how big the number is. Without counting, it is hard to tell whether 4,000,000,000 is billions or millions. Scientists got so tired of wrestling with big numbers that they invented a new way to write them. And this new way uses powers. Instead of writing the distance from the sun to Pluto as 4,000,000,000, a scientist would write it like this.

$$4 \times 10^9$$

The number contains a 10 raised to the ninth power. If you do the calculation, 4 times 10 to the ninth power has the exact same value as 4,000,000,000, but it's shorter. Plus we don't have to count zeros at all, because the exponent tells us how many zeros go after the 4. The exponent is 9 and 4 billion has exactly 9 zeros. This way of writing large numbers is called **scientific notation** (because scientists use it so much). Technically, for a number to be in scientific notation it needs to be in the following form:

A number between 1 and 10 times a power with a base of 10

The number 4×10^9 is in proper scientific notation, then, since 4 is between 1 and 10 and 10^9 has a base of 10.

If you're not convinced that 4×10^9 equals 4,000,000,000, we can prove it to you. As you know, when any number is multiplied by 10, its decimal point will move one place to the right (for example 3.2 times 10 is 32.0 or 32). The number 4×10^9 is just 4 or 4.0 multiplied by 10 nine times. If we move the decimal point in 4.0 nine places to the right, one for each multiplication by 10, we end up with the original number, 4,000,000,000.

4.000000000.   **Move 9 places**
to the right

4,000,000,000.   **to get 4 billion.**

---

[1] This picture is not drawn to scale. In reality, Pluto would be much smaller compared to the sun and the space between them would be far greater.

That's why the exponent is equal to the number of zeros. The exponent 9 is really telling you how many times to multiply by 10 to get back to the original number 4 billion.

Another thing you may have noticed about scientific notation is that it uses the old multiplication symbol from arithmetic: 4×10^9. It's not absolutely necessary to write it this way. We could write 4×10^9 as $(4)(10^9)$ or $4 \cdot 10^9$. But most people use the old multiplication symbol.

Writing a Number in Scientific Notation

In order to use scientific notation, you have to be able to put any number that might come up into scientific notation form. How do you actually do that? Well, let's go through the process on another large number.

$$7,200,000,000,000,000,000$$

This is a gigantic number; it's a lot bigger than the distance from the sun to Pluto. This number would definitely be easier to work with if it were in scientific notation. Here's what we do. We know there's really a decimal point to the right of the last zero. We'll put it in.

Putting in the decimal point.

$$7,200,000,000,000,000,000.0$$

Now we move that decimal point to the left. Every place we move it will make the number smaller. We need to move the point until the number gets to be between 1 and 10. That means it should go between the 7 and 2, which makes the number equal to 7.2.

$$7,200,000,000,000,000,000.$$

That's 18 places.

Move the decimal point to between the 7 and 2.

The important thing about this step, though, is that we need to count how many places we've moved the decimal point. We had to move the decimal point 18 places. The next step is easy. We take 7.2 and multiply it by a power with a base of 10 and an exponent equal to however many places we moved that decimal point, which was 18. That gives us this.

$$7.2 \times 10^{18}$$

That's our gigantic number, 7,200,000,000,000,000,000, in scientific notation.

So scientific notation is a great way to write really large numbers. Not only are numbers in scientific notation shorter and easier to read, they're also easier to calculate with. We won't do any calculations with them in this book, though. That's saved for Algebra 1. To finish off the lesson, let's review the two steps for changing a number to scientific notation.

To Put a Number in Scientific Notation

1.	Move the decimal point in the original number to the left as many times as necessary for the number to be between 1 and 10 (and count the number of places).
2.	Take the new smaller number and multiply it by a power of 10 with an exponent equal to the number of places you moved the decimal point.

Practice 92

a.
(92) Rewrite 83,000,000,000,000 in scientific notation.

b.
(91) Write "8 cubed" as a power. (Don't calculate the answer.)

c.
(89) Add the fractions $\dfrac{5x}{12}+\dfrac{7x}{12}$. Make sure your answers are fully reduced then select the best possible choice.

    A. $\dfrac{x}{6}$ B. x C. $\dfrac{12}{x}$

    D. $\dfrac{1}{x}$ E. $\dfrac{x}{12}$

d.
(64) Solve the equation $-3(x+5)=-15$.

e.
(80) Translate the word problem below into an equation; then solve.

Runaway firework #1 and runaway firework #2 are headed straight toward each other. Firework #1 is traveling at 20 feet per second, and firework #2 is traveling at 25 feet per second. If the two fireworks are 405 feet apart, how many seconds will it be before they meet?

Problem Set 92

Tell whether each sentence below is True or False.

1.
(92) Scientific notation is a short way to write very large numbers that is used by scientists.

2.
(92) Scientific notation never includes powers.

Rewrite each number below in scientific notation.

3.
(92) 8,000,000,000

(a) 4.
(92) 57,000,000,000,000

Do the indicated operation with each pair of numbers below.

5.
(60) $-32-44$

6.
(62) $\dfrac{-75}{-25}$

Calculate the value of each expression below. (Make sure to do the operations in the correct order.)

7.
(70) $15-\dfrac{8}{2}$

8.
(68) $5(3+4)$

417

Calculate the value of each power below.

9. 7^2
(91)

10. 5^4
(91)

Write each of the following as a power. (Don't calculate the answer.)

11. $9 \cdot 9 \cdot 9 \cdot 9 \cdot 9$
(91)

(b) 12. 7 cubed
(91)

Translate each of the following word problems into an equation. (Don't solve.)

13. There's some number that if you multiply it by 26 first, and then add 15 to that total, the result is 305.
(69)

A. $15x + 26 = 305$ 　　　　B. $(15)(26)x = 305$ 　　　　C. $26x + 15 = 305$

D. $26(x + 15) = 305$ 　　　　E. $15(x + 26) = 305$

14. There's some number that if you subtract 4 from it first, and then divide that total by 8, the result is 0.
(71)

A. $x - \dfrac{4}{8} = 0$ 　　　　B. $\dfrac{x}{8} - 4 = 0$ 　　　　C. $\dfrac{4 - x}{8} = 0$

D. $\dfrac{8}{x - 4} = 0$ 　　　　E. $\dfrac{x - 4}{8} = 0$

Simplify each expression below. Select the best possible choice.

15. $4 + 7x + 16$
(75)

A. $4 + 23x$ 　　　　B. $7x + 12$ 　　　　C. $7x + 20$

D. $27x$ 　　　　E. $11x + 16$

16. $-5x + (-18x)$
(59)

A. $-23x$ 　　　　B. $23x$ 　　　　C. $-13x$

D. $13x$ 　　　　E. $-90x$

Multiply or divide (as indicated) each pair of fractions below. Make sure your answers are fully reduced then select the best possible choice.

17. $\dfrac{5x}{14} \div \dfrac{15x}{7}$
(88)

A. $\dfrac{1}{6x}$ 　　　　B. $\dfrac{75x}{98}$ 　　　　C. $\dfrac{1}{6}$

D. $\dfrac{1}{5}$ 　　　　E. $\dfrac{20x}{21}$

18.
(87)
$$\frac{8x}{11x} \cdot \frac{22}{24x}$$

A. $\dfrac{2}{3x}$

B. $\dfrac{6}{7}$

C. $\dfrac{1}{6x}$

D. $\dfrac{3x}{2}$

E. $\dfrac{8x+22}{35x}$

Add or subtract (as indicated) each pair of fractions below. Make sure your answers are fully reduced then select the best possible choice.

19.
(89)
$$\frac{5}{3x} + \frac{1}{x}$$

A. $\dfrac{5}{3}$

B. $\dfrac{4}{3x}$

C. $\dfrac{8}{3x}$

D. $\dfrac{5}{3x}$

E. $\dfrac{2}{x}$

(c) 20.
(89)
$$\frac{3x}{10} + \frac{7x}{10}$$

A. x

B. $\dfrac{10}{x}$

C. $\dfrac{2x}{5}$

D. $\dfrac{x}{10}$

E. $\dfrac{1}{x}$

Solve each equation below.

21.
(64)
$-9x+13=-5$

(d) 22.
(64)
$-4(x+3)=-12$

Translate the word problem below into an equation; then solve.

(e) 23.
(80)
Test missile #1 and test missile #2 are headed straight toward each other. Missile #1 is traveling at 950 feet per second, and missile #2 is traveling at 1,000 feet per second. If the two missiles are 7,800 feet apart, how many seconds will it be before they meet?

Lesson 93—Order and Powers

We've been learning about raising a number to a power, which is the fifth operation of algebra. It goes along with the other four: addition, subtraction, multiplication, and division. But if we want to mix powers with the other operations, we need to include powers in our order of operations rules. Otherwise, we'll create a lot of confusion.

Which Way is Right?

For instance, take the expression $2 \cdot 3^2$, which mixes a power with a multiplication. There are actually two ways we might calculate this. We could start on the left and multiply 2 and 3 first to get 6^2. Then we could raise 6 to the second power to get 36. The other way to do the calculation, though, is to do the power first. We could raise 3 to the second power first to get $2 \cdot 9$. Then we could multiply second to get 18.

Multiply first?	Raise power first?
$2 \cdot 3^2$	$2 \cdot 3^2$
6^2	$2 \cdot 9$
36	18

This is confusing because we did the operations in a different order and got two different answers: 36 and 18. To clear up the confusion, we need to include powers in our rules for the order of operations. Here are the new rules with powers included.

Updated Order of Operations Rules

1.	All powers are calculated first.
2.	All multiplications and divisions are done second.
3.	All additions and subtractions are done third.
4.	If a different order is needed, the operations that are supposed to be done first must be put in parentheses (or inside a fraction).

Powers come first, before all the other operations, even before multiplication and division.

With these rules, there's no more confusion about how to calculate $2 \cdot 3^2$. The power should be done first: 3^2 is 9. That gives us $2 \cdot 9$. Then the multiplication is done second to get 18. The correct answer is 18, not 36.

Parentheses and Powers

Notice in rule 4 that if we want to change the usual order so that some other operation is done before a power, we need to use parentheses. That means to write our example so that the multiplication of 2 and 3 was first, we would have to use parentheses: $(2 \cdot 3)^2$. The correct way to do this calculation is to multiply 2 and 3 first to get 6^2. Then we calculate the power second to get 36. Written as $(2 \cdot 3)^2$, the correct answer is 36, not 18.

$$(2 \cdot 3)^2 \qquad \textbf{Multiply first}$$

We can use parentheses to put any of the other operations ahead of a power too. For example, look at this expression: $1+2^3$. Since powers are supposed to be done before additions, the correct way to calculate this is to raise 2 to the third power first to get $1+8$. Then the addition is done second to get 9. But if we wanted the addition to be done before the power, we would need to put parentheses around the addition: $(1+2)^3$. The correct way to calculate this expression is to add 1 and 2 first to get 3^3. Then the power is done second to get 27 ($3 \cdot 3 \cdot 3$ equals 27).

Raise power first	Add first
$1+2^3$	$(1+2)^3$
$1+8$	3^3
9	27

x's Too

Of course, all of these rules still apply when x's are involved. Take $6x^2$, for example. Because of the rule that powers are calculated before multiplications, this means x multiplied by itself first and that total multiplied by 6 second. If we want to show the multiplication first, we would have to put it in parentheses like this: $(6x)^2$. Now the expression means 6 multiplied by x first and then that total raised to the second power, which is the same as $(6x)(6x)$. So the order of operations rules are powers first, multiplications and divisions second, additions and subtractions third. To change that order, we have to use parentheses (or a fraction bar).

Practice 93

a.
(92) Rewrite 340,000,000,000 in scientific notation.

b.
(93) Calculate the value of $(2 \cdot 3)^3$. (Make sure to do the operations in the correct order.)

c.
(93) Calculate the value of $(4+3)^2$. (Make sure to do the operations in the correct order.)

d.
(85) Reduce the fraction $\dfrac{4(x-5)}{12}$. Select the best possible choice.

A. $\dfrac{x-5}{16}$
B. $\dfrac{x-5}{8}$
C. $3(x-5)$

D. $\dfrac{x-5}{3}$
E. $8(x-5)$

e.
(72) Translate the word problem below into an equation; then solve.

There is a number that if you multiply it by 3 first, and then add 7 to the result, you get 43. What's the number?

421

Problem Set 93

Tell whether each sentence below is True or False.

1.
(93)   If they're going to be mixed with other operations, powers need to be included in the order of operations rules.

2.
(93)   In the new order of operations rules, powers are done first unless parentheses (or a fraction) indicate otherwise.

Rewrite each number below in scientific notation.

3.
(92)   2,000,000

(a) 4.
(92)   560,000,000,000

Do the indicated operation with each group of numbers below.

5.
(61) $(5)(2)(-8)$

6.
(59) $7+(-16)$

Calculate the value of each expression below. (Make sure to do the operations in the correct order.)

7.
(68) $24-2\cdot5$

8.
(70) $\dfrac{8+12}{4}$

9.
(93) $5\cdot2^{3}$

(b) 10.
(93) $(2\cdot4)^{3}$

(c) 11.
(93) $(3+1)^{2}$

Write each of the following as a power. (Don't calculate the answer.)

12.
(91)   4 raised to the fifth power

13.
(91) $(8)(8)(8)(8)(8)(8)(8)(8)(8)$

Translate each of the following phrases into a mathematical expression. (Don't calculate the answer.)

14.
(68)   22 added to 16 first, and that total multiplied by 7.

A. $22(16+7)$ B. $22(16)+7$ C. $7(22+16)$
D. $22+16(7)$ E. $7(22)+16$

15.
(70)   42 divided by 6 first, and then that total added to 19.

A. $\dfrac{42}{6+19}$ B. $42+\dfrac{6}{19}$ C. $\dfrac{42+19}{6}$

D. $\dfrac{19}{42+6}$ E. $\dfrac{42}{6}+19$

Reduce each fraction below. Select the best possible choice.

16.
(84) $\dfrac{27x}{45x}$

    A. $\dfrac{5}{9}$ B. $\dfrac{3}{5}$ C. $\dfrac{5}{3}$

    D. $\dfrac{18}{36x}$ E. $\dfrac{4}{5}$

(d) 17.
(85) $\dfrac{9(x-7)}{18}$

    A. $\dfrac{x-7}{9}$ B. $2(x-7)$ C. $\dfrac{x-7}{27}$

    D. $9(x-7)$ E. $\dfrac{x-7}{2}$

Add or subtract (as indicated) each pair of fractions below. Make sure your answers are fully reduced then select the best possible choice.

18.
(90) $\dfrac{2}{x} - \dfrac{3}{4x}$

    A. $\dfrac{3}{2x}$ B. $-\dfrac{5}{4x}$ C. $-\dfrac{1}{4x}$

    D. $\dfrac{4}{5x}$ E. $\dfrac{5}{4x}$

19.
(89) $\dfrac{1}{2x} + \dfrac{4}{5x}$

    A. $\dfrac{3}{10x}$ B. $\dfrac{13}{10x}$ C. $\dfrac{2}{5x}$

    D. $\dfrac{5}{7x}$ E. $\dfrac{1}{2x}$

Solve each equation below.

20.
(73) $\dfrac{x-8}{4} = 5$ **21.** $2 + 5x + 4 = 21$
(75)

Translate the word problem below into an equation; then solve.

(e) 22. There is a number that if you multiply it by 5 first, and then add 6 to the result, you get 91. What's the
(72)   number?

Lesson 94—Adding and Subtracting Powers

A few lessons ago, we learned to add x's. Remember $3x + 2x$ is equal to $5x$. Well, it turns out that it's also possible to add x's that are raised to a power.

Adding Coefficients Again

Here's an example.

$$3x^2 + 2x^2$$

To add these, all we have to do is add the 3 and 2 to get $5x^2$. As you know, 3 and 2 are called coefficients.

$3x^2 + 2x^2$ is equivalent to $5x^2$ **Add coefficients**

So the method is to add the coefficients. It's just like adding plain x's.

You may be wondering why we can add the coefficients even when the x's are raised to powers. Well, $3x^2$ is 3 multiplied by x^2. But that's the same as $x^2 + x^2 + x^2$ because multiplication is just repeated addition. And $2x^2$ is the same as $x^2 + x^2$ for the same reason. So $3x^2 + 2x^2$ is really just $x^2 + x^2 + x^2 + x^2 + x^2$, which is five x^2's added or $5x^2$. That's why it works.

$$
\begin{array}{ccccc}
\overbrace{3x^2} & + & \overbrace{2x^2} & = & 5x^2 \\
x^2 + x^2 + x^2 & + & x^2 + x^2 & = & 5x^2
\end{array}
$$

The same as five x^2's added.

Subtracting Too

We can also subtract x's that are raised to powers in the same way that we subtract plain x's. Here's an example of that.

$$7x^3 - 4x^3$$

All we have to do is subtract the coefficients: $7 - 4$ equals 3. So that gives us $3x^3$. And the reason this works is that $7x^3$ is seven x^3's added, and if we take four of those away, we're left with three x^3's, which is $3x^3$.

Sometimes when we're adding or subtracting x's raised to a power, one of them won't have a coefficient showing. Here's an example of that.

$$5x^2 + x^2$$ **No coefficient showing**

You already know how to handle this. The second x^2 can be written as $1x^2$, so it actually has a coefficient of 1. Now we can add the coefficients to get $6x^2$. It's exactly like combining plain x's. (Remember, you can also say "combine" instead of add or subtract x's.)

Like Terms

The only thing we really have to watch out for when combining x's with powers is to make sure that both x's have the same exponent. For instance, we can't add these two powers.

$$3x^4 + 2x^5$$ **These can't be added**

424

The reason is that one of the x's has an exponent of 4 and the other has an exponent of 5. $3x^4 + 2x^5$ really means $x^4 + x^4 + x^4 + x^5 + x^5$. Obviously, there's not five of any one thing. There are three x^4's and two x^5's, so there's no way to combine.

Actually, x's that have the same exponent are called **like terms**.[1] For instance, $3x^2 + 2x^2$ are like terms, since both x's are squared. But $3x^4 + 2x^5$ are not like terms, because the exponents on the x's are different. The formal rule for adding and subtracting x's raised to a power, then, is that we can only combine like terms. And the method we use is to add or subtract their coefficients.

Another word that will be important to know when you move into higher math is polynomial. A **polynomial** is an expression where x is raised to a whole number exponent. Some polynomials even have several such terms added together. For instance, the expression $3x^4 + 2x^5$ qualifies as a polynomial because both of the x's have exponents that are whole numbers (4 and 5). In fact, most of the expressions we've been using in our algebra problems so far are polynomials. In more advanced courses, you'll learn about expressions with exponents that are not whole numbers. These expressions won't qualify as polynomials.

Practice 94

a.
(93)
Calculate the value of $15 - 3^2$. (Make sure to do the operations in the correct order.)

b.
(94)
Simplify the expression $3x^2 + 4x^2$. Select the best possible choice.

    A. $7x^4$ B. x^2 C. $12x^2$

    D. $7x^2$ E. $14x$

c.
(94)
Simplify the expression $13x^5 + x^5$. Select the best possible choice.

    A. $70x^5$ B. $14x^5$ C. $12x^5$

    D. $14x^{10}$ E. $12x^{10}$

d.
(81)
Solve the equation $9 + 7x = 14 - 6x$. Make sure your answer is fully reduced.

e.
(82)
Translate the word problem below into an equation; then solve.

Better than Spotless, a carpet cleaning service, charges $50 for a service call (just to come to the house) plus $45 per hour to do the cleaning job. Whiter than White, another carpet cleaning service, charges $80 for a service call plus $30 per hour to do the cleaning job. How many hours would a job have to take for the bills of both cleaning services to be the same?

Problem Set 94

Tell whether each sentence below is True or False.

1.
(94)
To add x's raised to a power, you add their coefficients.

2.
(94)
Like terms are x's with the same exponents.

---

[1] Of course, the letters have to be the same also. They both have to be x's or y's whatever. You can't combine $3x^4 + 2y^5$ because the letters are different.

Rewrite each number below in scientific notation.

3. 90,000
(92)

4. 1,800,000,000
(92)

Do the indicated operation with each pair of numbers below.

5. $\dfrac{-24}{6}$
(62)

6. $-5 - (-12)$
(60)

Calculate the value of each expression below. (Make sure to do the operations in the correct order.)

7. $\dfrac{32}{2} - 14$
(70)

8. $3(11 - 6)$
(68)

9. $(3 \cdot 4)^2$
(93)

(a) 10. $19 - 2^3$
(93)

Translate each of the following word problems into an equation. (Don't solve.)

11. There's some number that if you subtract 29 from it first, and then multiply that result by 3, the result is
(69) 41.

    A. $x - 29 \cdot 3 = 41$ B. $29 - 3x = 41$ C. $3(x - 29) = 41$

    D. $3x - 29 = 41$ E. $3(29 - x) = 41$

12. There's some number that if you divide it by 20 first, and then add 52 to that total, the result is 98.
(71)

    A. $\dfrac{20}{x} + 52 = 98$ B. $\dfrac{20 + 52}{x} = 98$ C. $\dfrac{x}{20} + 52 = 98$

    D. $\dfrac{x}{20 + 52} = 98$ E. $\dfrac{x + 52}{20} = 98$

Simplify each expression below. Select the best possible choice.

13. $2x + 15x$
(76)

    A. $17x$ B. $30x$ C. $13x$

    D. 30 E. 17

(b) 14. $4x^2 + 5x^2$
(94)

    A. $9x^4$ B. $18x$ C. $9x^2$

    D. $20x^2$ E. x^2

(c) 15. $10x^5 + x^5$
(94)

    A. $9x^{10}$ B. $55x^5$ C. $9x^5$

    D. $11x^{10}$ E. $11x^5$

Multiply or divide (as indicated) each pair of fractions below. Make sure your answers are fully reduced then select the best possible choice.

16.
(87)
$$\frac{9x}{22} \cdot \frac{11x}{18x}$$

    A. $\dfrac{x}{2}$ B. $\dfrac{3x}{4}$ C. $\dfrac{1}{4x}$

    D. $\dfrac{1}{2}$ E. $\dfrac{x}{4}$

17.
(88)
$$\frac{3}{20x} \div \frac{6}{15x}$$

    A. $\dfrac{3}{8}$ B. $\dfrac{3}{5x}$ C. $\dfrac{3}{8x}$

    D. $\dfrac{9}{35x}$ E. $\dfrac{3}{50x}$

Add or subtract (as indicated) each pair of fractions below. Make sure your answers are fully reduced then select the best possible choice.

18.
(89)
$$\frac{5}{3x} + \frac{7}{6x}$$

    A. $\dfrac{13}{6x}$ B. $\dfrac{1}{3x}$ C. $\dfrac{2}{x}$

    D. $\dfrac{17}{6x}$ E. $\dfrac{35}{18x}$

19.
(90)
$$\frac{7}{20x} - \frac{9}{20x}$$

    A. $-\dfrac{3}{5x}$ B. $\dfrac{4}{5x}$ C. $-\dfrac{1}{10x}$

    D. $-10x$ E. $-\dfrac{10}{x}$

Solve each equation below. Make sure your answer is fully reduced.

20. $4(x+7)=20$ **(d) 21.** $7+8x=13-3x$
(72)   (81)

Translate the word problem below into an equation; then solve.

(e) 22.   Dependable Maids, a housecleaning service, charges $20 for a service call (just to come to the house)
(82)   plus $15 per hour to do the cleaning job. Clean as a Whistle, another housecleaning service, charges $35 for a service call plus $12 per hour to do the cleaning job. How many hours would a job have to take for the bills of both cleaning services to be the same?

Lesson 95—Multiplying Powers

We've learned how to add and subtract powers. In this lesson, we're going to learn how to multiply powers. Let's start with a simple example.

$$4^3 \cdot 4^2$$

We could just follow the order of operations rules. First, we calculate the value of each power.

$$64 \cdot 16$$

Next, we multiply 64 and 16.

$$1,024$$

And that gives us our answer of 1,024.

Just Add the Exponents

But there's another way to do $4^3 \cdot 4^2$. We can just add the exponents. We take $3+2$ which is 5, and that total becomes the exponent of the answer.

$$4^3 \cdot 4^2$$

$$4^{3+2} = 4^5$$ **Adding the exponents**

If you multiply out 4^5, you'll see that it equals 1,024, which is right. So a really easy way to multiply powers is just to add their exponents. Here are some other examples of this technique.

$$2^4 \cdot 2^3 = 2^7 \qquad\qquad 3^5 \cdot 3^4 = 3^9 \qquad\qquad 5^6 \cdot 5^2 = 5^8$$

You may be wondering why this technique works. To explain, let's go back to the first example.

$$4^3 \cdot 4^2$$

We know that 4^3 means $4 \cdot 4 \cdot 4$ and 4^2 means $4 \cdot 4$. So $4^3 \cdot 4^2$ is really just a string of five 4's multiplied or $4 \cdot 4 \cdot 4 \cdot 4 \cdot 4$.

Just five 4s multiplied

But that's the same as 4^5. So that's why we can always add the exponents. By adding the exponents, we're really just counting the number of 4s that are being multiplied.

With x's Too

But why would anyone bother multiplying $4^3 \cdot 4^2$ by adding their exponents? After all, once you get 4^5, you still have to calculate its value and that takes awhile. So the adding exponents method doesn't really seem any faster. But for anybody who knows algebra, adding the exponents still has a big advantage. You can use it to multiply x's that have exponents. Look at this example.

$$x^3 \cdot x^2$$

These powers both have a base (x) that's an unknown number. So we can't calculate the value of each power and then multiply them together. But with the adding exponents method, we can still multiply, even though the bases are unknowns.

$$x^{3+2} = x^5$$

The answer is x^5. The real advantage, then, of the adding exponents method is that it works on x's as well as numbers. Only a person who understands algebra could appreciate that. Here are a few other examples of multiplying x's with exponents.

$$x^2 \cdot x^5 = x^7 \qquad\qquad x^3 \cdot x^6 = x^9 \qquad\qquad x^4 \cdot x^7 = x^{11}$$

A Warning

Before finishing this lesson, we need to give you an important warning. The adding exponents method can only be used to multiply powers when the powers have the same base. That's the way it was with all of our examples. In $4^3 \cdot 4^2$, both powers had a base of 4. In $2^4 \cdot 2^3$, both powers had a base of 2. In $3^5 \cdot 3^4$, the bases were both 3. And, of course, in the examples with x's, (like $x^3 \cdot x^2$) the powers all had a base of x. But if we had powers with different bases, like $4^3 \cdot 7^2$, it would be totally wrong to try and multiply them by adding their exponents to get 4^5 or 7^5. The reason this won't work is that $4^3 \cdot 7^2$ actually means $4 \cdot 4 \cdot 4 \cdot 7 \cdot 7$.

There's not five of
any one thing to multiply

We don't have five of any one number being multiplied. So don't forget that to multiply powers by adding their exponents, those powers have to have the same base.

Practice 95

a.
(41) How many square inches are in 8 square feet?

b.
(94) Simplify $-5x^4 + (-3x^4)$ by adding or subtracting the powers.

    A. $-2x^4$ B. -2 C. $-8x^4$

    D. $-8x^8$ E. $8x^4$

c.
(95) Simplify $6^5 \cdot 6^7$ by multiplying the powers. (Don't calculate the answer.)

    A. 6^{35} B. 36^{12} C. 12^2

    D. 6^2 E. 6^{12}

d. Simplify $x^5 \cdot x^3$ by multiplying the powers.
(95)

    A. x^8 B. x^2 C. $(2x)^8$

    D. $(x^2)^8$ E. x^{15}

e. Translate the word problem below into an equation; then solve.
(79)

Insomniac #1 can count 55 sheep each minute. Insomniac #2 can count 58 sheep each minute. Working together, how many minutes will it take them to count 791 sheep?

Problem Set 95

Tell whether each sentence below is True or False.

1. One way to multiply powers is to add their exponents.
(95)

2. Only powers with the same base can be multiplied with the adding exponents method.
(95)

Do each unit conversion below.

3. Convert 4.8 kilometers to dekameters.
(38)

(a) 4. How many square inches are in 16 square feet?
(41)

Do the indicated operation with each pair of numbers below.

5. $-17 + (-26)$ **6.** $(-31)(4)$
(59)   (61)

Calculate the value of each expression below. (Make sure to do the operations in the correct order.)

7. $\dfrac{16}{5-1}$ **8.** $(2+6)^3$ **9.** $5 \cdot 4^2$
(70)   (93)   (93)

Translate each of the following phrases into a mathematical expression. (Don't calculate the answer.)

10. 3 multiplied by 7 first, and 15 subtracted from that total.
(68)

    A. $3 - 7 \cdot 15$ B. $3 \cdot 7 - 15$ C. $3(7 - 15)$

    D. $15 - 3 \cdot 7$ E. $7(3 - 15)$

11. 14 minus 8 first, and that total divided by 2.
(70)

    A. $\dfrac{2}{14-8}$ B. $\dfrac{8-14}{2}$ C. $14 - \dfrac{8}{2}$

    D. $\dfrac{14-8}{2}$ E. $\dfrac{14}{2} - 8$

Reduce each fraction below. Select the best possible choice.

12.
(83) $\dfrac{18}{24x}$

    A. $\dfrac{4}{3x}$ B. $\dfrac{2}{3x}$ C. $\dfrac{3}{4x}$

    D. $\dfrac{3x}{4}$ E. $\dfrac{1}{6x}$

13.
(86) $\dfrac{15(x-6)}{10(x-6)}$

    A. 5   B. $\dfrac{3}{2}$ C. $\dfrac{2}{3}$

    D. $\dfrac{3(x-6)}{2}$ E. $\dfrac{2}{3(x-6)}$

Add or subtract (as indicated) each pair of fractions below. Make sure your answers are fully reduced then select the best possible choice.

14.
(89) $\dfrac{3x}{16}+\dfrac{7x}{16}$

    A. $\dfrac{5x}{8}$ B. $\dfrac{x}{4}$ C. $\dfrac{21x}{16}$

    D. $\dfrac{3}{4x}$ E. $\dfrac{5}{4x}$

15.
(90) $\dfrac{2}{5x}-\dfrac{4}{x}$

    A. $-\dfrac{7x}{5}$ B. $-\dfrac{8}{5x}$ C. $\dfrac{18}{5x}$

    D. $-\dfrac{18}{5x}$ E. $-\dfrac{2}{5x}$

Simplify each expression below by adding or subtracting (as indicated) the powers.

16.
(94) $8x^3+4x^3$

    A. $32x^9$ B. $12x^3$ C. $4x^3$

    D. $32x^3$ E. $12x^6$

(b) 17.
(94)
$-7x^4 + (-2x^4)$

    A. $-9x^8$ B. $-5x^4$ C. $9x^4$

    D. -5 E. $-9x^4$

Simplify each expression below by multiplying the powers. (Don't calculate the answer.)

(c) 18.
(95)
$4^7 \cdot 4^4$

    A. 4^3 B. 8^3 C. 4^{28}

    D. 4^{11} E. 16^{11}

(d) 19.
(95)
$x^4 \cdot x^2$

    A. x^8 B. $(x^2)^8$ C. x^6

    D. $(2x)^6$ E. x^2

Solve each equation below.

20. $4x - 11 = 13$ **21.** $\dfrac{x+5}{4} = -7$
(53)   (73)

Translate the word problem below into an equation; then solve.

(e) 22.   Ultra chef #1 can ice 42 cakes each hour. Ultra chef #2 can ice 47 cakes each hour. Working together,
(79)   how many hours will it take them to ice 1,068 cakes?

Lesson 96—Multiplying Powers: Tougher Cases

In the last lesson, we learned to multiply powers by adding their exponents. It turns out that we can use that method to multiply even in tougher cases.

Multiply Numbers, Multiply x's

Here's our first example.

$$(5x^3)(6x^2)$$

This is a little tougher because it has both powers with x's and numbers. But all we have to do is multiply the numbers first: 5 times 6 is 30.

$$(30)(x^3)(x^2)$$

Next, we multiply the x's by adding their exponents: $3 + 2$ is 5, so $(x^3)(x^2)$ equals x^5. That gives us this.

$$30x^5$$

Why it Works

It's always important to understand why a method works, so let's analyze what we just did. The expression $(5x^3)(6x^2)$ really means $5 \cdot x \cdot x \cdot x \cdot 6 \cdot x \cdot x$.

You may remember the associative property of multiplication. We learned about that at the beginning of the course. The associative property of multiplication basically says that you can multiply a string of numbers in any order. Technically, it's stated this way. If we have three numbers (a, b, and c), then $(ab)c = a(bc)$. In other words, we can multiply a and b first and then c. Or we can multiply b and c first and then a. You can do it in any order. But getting back to our problem, it's because of the associative property of multiplication that we can multiply the numbers first and then the x's in $(5x^3)(6x^2)$, even though they aren't right next to each other. This problem is really just a string of numbers (and x's) multiplied. And since we're allowed to multiply in any order, why not start with 5 and 6.

Another Example

Now let's try another example.

$$(7x^9)(3x^8)$$

The exponents on these x's are pretty big, but that doesn't matter. Our adding exponents method will still work just fine. We can multiply in any order, so let's multiply the numbers first: 7 times 3 is 21.

$$(21)(x^9)(x^8)$$

Now we can multiply the x's by adding their exponents ($9 + 8 = 17$) to get this.

$$21x^{17}$$

Practice 96

a.
(88)
Divide the fractions $\dfrac{6x}{30x} \div \dfrac{15}{40x}$. Make sure your answers are fully reduced then select the best possible choice.

 A. $\dfrac{6x+15}{70x}$ B. $\dfrac{6x}{15}$ C. $\dfrac{8x}{15}$

 D. $\dfrac{3}{40x}$ E. $\dfrac{x}{120}$

b.
(90)
Subtract the fractions $\dfrac{4}{3x} - \dfrac{5}{2x}$. Make sure your answers are fully reduced then select the best possible choice.

 A. $-\dfrac{7}{6x}$ B. $\dfrac{x}{3}$ C. $-\dfrac{10}{3x}$

 D. $-\dfrac{1}{6x}$ E. $\dfrac{3}{2x}$

c.
(96)
Simplify $(7x^3)(8x^4)$ by multiplying the powers.

 A. x^{12} B. $56x^7$ C. $15x^7$
 D. $56x^{12}$ E. $15x^{12}$

d.
(81)
Solve the equation $6+7x=19+2x$. Make sure your answer is fully reduced.

e.
(80)
Translate the word problem below into an equation; then solve.

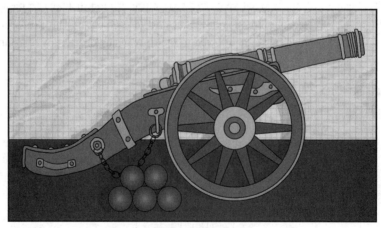

Cannonball #1 and cannonball #2 are headed straight toward each other. Cannonball #1 is traveling 40 meters each second, and cannonball #2 is traveling 45 meters each second. If the two cannonballs are 680 meters apart, how many seconds will it be before they meet?

Problem Set 96

Rewrite each number below in scientific notation.

1.
(92) 200,000,000,000

2.
(92) 93,000,000

Do the indicated operation with each pair of numbers below.

3.
(62) $\dfrac{-96}{-8}$

4.
(60) $-13-(-13)$

Calculate the value of each expression below. (Make sure to do the operations in the correct order.)

5.
(68) $2(5+4)$

6.
(93) $(2\cdot6)^2$

7.
(93) 8^2+15

Translate each of the following word problems into an equation. (Don't solve.)

8.
(69) There's some number that if you multiply it by 8 first, and then add -14, the result is 95.

    A. $8x+(-14)=95$ B. $-14x+8=95$ C. $8x(-14)=95$

    D. $x-8\cdot(-14)=95$ E. $x+8+(-14)=95$

9.
(71) There's some number that if you subtract 3 from it first, and then divide that total by 24, the result is 17.

    A. $\dfrac{3-x}{24}=17$ B. $\dfrac{x-3}{24}=17$ C. $\dfrac{x}{24}-3=17$

    D. $x-\dfrac{3}{24}=17$ E. $\dfrac{24}{x-3}=17$

Multiply or divide (as indicated) each pair of fractions below. Make sure your answers are fully reduced then select the best possible choice.

10.
(87) $\dfrac{14x}{24}\cdot\dfrac{6}{7x}$

    A. $\dfrac{1}{2}$ B. $\dfrac{14x+6}{24+7x}$ C. $\dfrac{1}{2x}$

    D. $\dfrac{1}{4}$ E. 2

(a) 11.
(88)
$$\frac{4x}{20x} \div \frac{10}{30x}$$

     A. $\dfrac{x}{15}$ B. $\dfrac{3x}{10}$ C. $\dfrac{4x+10}{50x}$

     D. $\dfrac{3x}{5}$ E. $\dfrac{1}{15x}$

Add or subtract (as indicated) each pair of fractions below. Make sure your answers are fully reduced then select the best possible choice.

12.
(89)
$$\frac{1}{2x} + \frac{3}{7x}$$

     A. $\dfrac{23}{14x}$ B. $\dfrac{3}{14x}$ C. $\dfrac{13x}{14}$

     D. $\dfrac{13}{14x}$ E. $\dfrac{2}{7x}$

(b) 13.
(90)
$$\frac{5}{4x} - \frac{7}{2x}$$

     A. $\dfrac{3}{2x}$ B. $\dfrac{3}{4x}$ C. $-\dfrac{35}{8x}$

     D. $-\dfrac{1}{4x}$ E. $-\dfrac{9}{4x}$

Simplify each expression below by adding or subtracting (as indicated) the powers.

14.
(94)
$10x^2 + 9x^2$

     A. $19x^2$ B. $90x^2$ C. $90x^4$
     D. x^4 E. $19x^4$

15.
(94)
$4x^8 - x^8$

     A. $-4x^8$ B. 3 C. $-4x^{16}$
     D. $-4x^{64}$ E. $3x^8$

Simplify each expression below by multiplying the powers.

16.
(95)
$x^3 \cdot x^7$

     A. $2x^{10}$ B. $(2x)^{10}$ C. x^{10}
     D. x^{21} E. x^4

17.
(95)

$x^5 \cdot x^9$

A. x^{45} B. $(2x)^{14}$ C. x^4

D. $2x^{45}$ E. x^{14}

(c) 18.
(96)

$(4x^5)(9x^2)$

A. $13x^{10}$ B. $13x^7$ C. $36x^3$

D. $5x^3$ E. $36x^7$

19.
(96)

$(5x^9)(4x^7)$

A. x^{63} B. $20x^{16}$ C. $20x^{63}$

D. $9x^{16}$ E. $9x^{63}$

Solve each equation below. Make sure your answer is fully reduced.

20.
(73)

$\dfrac{x}{8} - 1 = -6$

(d) 21.
(81)

$5 + 8x = 20 + 2x$

Translate the word problem below into an equation; then solve.

(e) 22.
(80)

Meteoroid #1 and meteoroid #2 are headed straight toward each other. Meteoroid #1 is traveling 980 meters each second, and meteoroid #2 is traveling 1,100 meters each second. If the two meteoroids are 6,240 meters apart, how many seconds will it be before they meet?

Lesson 97—Dividing Powers

We've learned how to multiply powers. Now we're going to see how to divide them. Let's start with a numbers-only example. Let's divide 9^5 by 9^3. Since we always show division with a fraction bar, we'll write it like this.

$$\frac{9^5}{9^3}$$

One way to divide here is to write each power as a repeated multiplication. On top, 9^5 just means five 9s multiplied. And on bottom, 9^3 means three 9s multiplied.

$$\frac{9 \cdot 9 \cdot 9 \cdot 9 \cdot 9}{9 \cdot 9 \cdot 9}$$

Now we can cancel. There are three pairs of 9s that can be canceled.

$$\frac{\cancel{9} \cdot \cancel{9} \cdot \cancel{9} \cdot 9 \cdot 9}{\cancel{9} \cdot \cancel{9} \cdot \cancel{9}} \qquad \textbf{Cancel the 9s}$$

That leaves $\dfrac{9 \cdot 9}{1}$ or $9 \cdot 9$, which can also be written as 9^2. So the answer is 9^2 or 81. That's the long way to divide 9^5 by 9^3.

Just Subtract the Exponents

But if there's a long way to divide powers, there has to be a short way. In the last lesson, we learned to multiply powers by adding their exponents. As it turns out, we can divide powers by subtracting their exponents. On $\dfrac{9^5}{9^3}$, all we do is take 5, the exponent on top, and subtract 3, the exponent on bottom. The result becomes the exponent of the answer. We end up with 9^2, which we know is right.

$$\frac{9^5}{9^3} = 9^{5-3} = 9^2 \qquad \textbf{Subtract the exponents}$$

The reason this method works is pretty obvious. The exponent on top tells us how many 9s are in the numerator and the exponent on bottom tells us how many 9s are in the denominator. By subtracting, we're figuring out how many 9s are going to be left over after canceling. So the short method for dividing powers is to subtract their exponents. Here are a few other examples.

$$\frac{3^8}{3^2} = 3^6 \qquad\qquad \frac{5^7}{5^3} = 5^4 \qquad\qquad \frac{8^{11}}{8^6} = 8^5$$

Subtracting Exponents with x's

Of course, we can also use this method to divide powers with x's. And this is where it's really useful. Look at this example.

$$\frac{x^7}{x^2}$$

To divide here, all we have to do is subtract the exponents: $7 - 2 = 5$. Then we make 5 the exponent of our answer.

$$\frac{x^7}{x^2} = x^{7-2} = x^5$$

It's incredibly easy. Here are a few other examples with x's.

$$\frac{x^{10}}{x^4} = x^6 \qquad\qquad \frac{x^8}{x^5} = x^3 \qquad\qquad \frac{x^{15}}{x^6} = x^9$$

Bases Must be the Same

There's one other important point that you've probably already figured out. We can only subtract exponents when the bases are the same. It's just like multiplying, where we can only add exponents when the bases are the same. Here's the reason for this rule. What if we had a division problem like this?

$$\frac{7^5}{4^2}$$

It would make no sense to try and subtract the exponents, $5 - 2 = 3$, and then make the answer 7^3 or 4^3. That would be crazy, because $\frac{7^5}{4^2}$ really means $\frac{7 \cdot 7 \cdot 7 \cdot 7 \cdot 7}{4 \cdot 4}$. This fraction can't be reduced at all, since there's nothing in the numerator and denominator that can be canceled. So there's no way $\frac{7^5}{4^2}$ equals 7^3 or 4^3. Don't forget, then, that to divide powers by subtracting exponents, the bases have to be the same. And to multiply powers by adding exponents, the bases have to be the same as well.

Practice 97

a.
(90) Subtract the fractions $\frac{5x}{2} - \frac{7x}{3}$. Make sure your answers are fully reduced then select the best possible choice.

A. $\dfrac{15x}{14}$ B. $-\dfrac{x}{3}$ C. $-\dfrac{35x}{6}$

D. $\dfrac{x}{6}$ E. $-\dfrac{11x}{6}$

b.
(96) Simplify $(-6x^5)(7x^8)$ by multiplying the powers.

A. x^3 B. $13x^{13}$ C. $-42x^{13}$

D. $-42x^{40}$ E. x^{13}

c.
(97) Simplify $\dfrac{x^9}{x^6}$ by dividing the powers.

A. x^{15} B. $x^{\frac{1}{3}}$ C. x^{54}

D. x^3 E. $x^{\frac{3}{2}}$

d. Solve the equation $4+(-3x)=9-4x$.
(81)

e. Translate the word problem below into an equation; then solve.
(54)

When Ginger special-ordered a book recently, she agreed to pay an 8% shipping and handling charge. If Ginger paid $2.72 in shipping and handling, how much must the book have cost?

Problem Set 97

Tell whether each sentence below is True or False.

1. The short method for dividing powers is to subtract their exponents.
(97)

2. Only powers with the same base can be divided with the subtracting exponents method.
(97)

Convert each fraction below into decimal form. Give exact answers (no rounding).

3. $\dfrac{7}{6}$
(24)

4. $\dfrac{1}{25}$
(23)

Calculate the value of each expression below. (Make sure to do the operations in the correct order.)

5. $15-3\cdot2$
(68)

6. $(3-1)^4$
(93)

Translate each of the following phrases into a mathematical expression. (Don't calculate the answer.)

7. 8 added to 4 first, and that total multiplied by 3.
(68)

A. $3(8+4)$ B. $8\cdot4\cdot3$ C. $8+4(3)$
D. $4+8\cdot3$ E. $8(4+3)$

8. 28 divided by 7 first, and 12 subtracted from that total.
(70)

A. $\dfrac{7}{28}-12$ B. $12-\dfrac{28}{7}$ C. $\dfrac{28-12}{7}$
D. $\dfrac{28}{7}-12$ E. $28-\dfrac{12}{7}$

Multiply or divide (as indicated) each pair of fractions below. Make sure your answers are fully reduced then select the best possible choice.

9.
(87)

$$\frac{8}{14x} \cdot \frac{21x}{12x}$$

A. x　　　　B. $\frac{1}{x}$　　　　C. $\frac{x}{3}$

D. $\frac{1}{3x}$　　　　E. $\frac{8+21x}{28x}$

10.
(88)

$$\frac{6}{45x} \div \frac{15x}{9x}$$

A. $\frac{6+15x}{54x}$　　　　B. $\frac{1}{5x}$　　　　C. $\frac{2}{9x}$

D. $\frac{2x}{27}$　　　　E. $\frac{2}{25x}$

Add or subtract (as indicated) each pair of fractions below. Make sure your answers are fully reduced then select the best possible choice.

11.
(89)

$$\frac{7}{20x} + \frac{9}{20x}$$

A. $\frac{4}{5x}$　　　　B. $\frac{1}{10x}$　　　　C. $\frac{1}{4x}$

D. $\frac{63}{20x}$　　　　E. $\frac{5}{4x}$

(a) 12.
(90)

$$\frac{3x}{7} - \frac{2x}{5}$$

A. $\frac{x}{7}$　　　　B. $\frac{x}{12}$　　　　C. $\frac{x}{35}$

D. $\frac{11x}{35}$　　　　E. $\frac{6x}{35}$

Simplify each expression below. Select the best possible choice.

13.
(75)

$4+5x-9$

A. $4x+5$　　　　B. $4-4x$　　　　C. $5x+(-5)$
D. $9x-9$　　　　E. $5x+13$

14.
(94)

$3x^5 + (-7x^5)$

A. $-4x^5$　　　　B. $10x^5$　　　　C. $-4x^{10}$
D. $4x^5$　　　　E. $-21x^5$

15. $8x^7 + 11x^7$
(94)

    A. $19x^{14}$ B. $19x^7$ C. $3x^7$

    D. $88x^7$ E. $3x^{14}$

Simplify each expression below by multiplying the powers.

16. $x^{10} \cdot x^4$
(95)

    A. $x^{\frac{5}{2}}$ B. $(2x)^{14}$ C. x^{40}

    D. x^{14} E. x^6

17. $(2x^3)(8x^5)$
(96)

    A. $4x^2$ B. $10x^8$ C. $6x^2$

    D. $16x^8$ E. $16x^{15}$

(b) 18. $(-4x^7)(5x^9)$
(96)

    A. $9x^{16}$ B. $-20x^{16}$ C. x^{16}

    D. $-20x^{63}$ E. x^2

Simplify each expression below by dividing the powers. (Don't calculate the answer.)

19. $\dfrac{4^9}{4^4}$
(97)

    A. 4^{36} B. $4^{\frac{1}{3}}$ C. 4^{13}

    D. $4^{\frac{9}{4}}$ E. 4^5

(c) 20. $\dfrac{x^8}{x^2}$
(97)

    A. x^{10} B. $x^{\frac{1}{4}}$ C. x^4

    D. x^{16} E. x^6

Solve each equation below.

21. $-5x + 17x = 48$ **(d) 22.** $1 + (-5x) = 7 - 6x$
(76)   (81)

Translate the word problem below into an equation; then solve.

(e) 23. When Marcia bought an umbrella over the Internet, she agreed to pay a 12% shipping and handling
(54)   charge. If Marcia paid $3.36 in shipping and handling, how much must the umbrella have cost?

Lesson 98—Fractions with Powers

Now that we've learned to divide powers by subtracting their exponents, we can use the method to reduce some pretty complicated fractions.

The Long Way
Look at this example.

$$\frac{4x^7}{4x^2}$$

This fraction has both numbers and x's. And one way to reduce it is to factor everything first. On top, 4 factors as $2 \cdot 2$ and x^7 is the same as seven x's multiplied.

$$\frac{2 \cdot 2 \cdot x \cdot x \cdot x \cdot x \cdot x \cdot x \cdot x}{4x^2}$$ **Factor on top**

On bottom, 4 factors as $2 \cdot 2$ again, and x^2 is the same as two x's multiplied.

$$\frac{2 \cdot 2 \cdot x \cdot x \cdot x \cdot x \cdot x \cdot x \cdot x}{2 \cdot 2 \cdot x \cdot x}$$ **Factor on bottom**

The next step is to cancel. We can cancel two pairs of 2s and two pairs of x's.

$$\frac{\cancel{2} \cdot \cancel{2} \cdot \cancel{x} \cdot \cancel{x} \cdot x \cdot x \cdot x \cdot x \cdot x}{\underset{1}{\cancel{2} \cdot \cancel{2} \cdot \cancel{x} \cdot \cancel{x}}}$$ **Cancel the 2s and x's**

That leaves $\dfrac{x \cdot x \cdot x \cdot x \cdot x}{1}$ or $\dfrac{x^5}{1}$, which is just x^5.

The Short Way

So that's one method for reducing $\dfrac{4x^7}{4x^2}$. But another, faster method is to just factor the numbers.

$$\frac{2 \cdot 2 \cdot x^7}{2 \cdot 2 \cdot x^2}$$ **Just factoring numbers**

Now we can cancel the pairs of 2s.

$$\frac{\cancel{2} \cdot \cancel{2} \cdot x^7}{\cancel{2} \cdot \cancel{2} \cdot x^2}$$ **Cancel the 2s**

That gives us $\dfrac{x^7}{x^2}$. Next, instead of factoring x^7 and x^2 by writing out a bunch of x's, we can just divide them by subtracting their exponents: $7-2=5$, so we end up with x^5. That's the same answer we got before. Only by using the subtracting exponents shortcut, we didn't have to write all those x's![1]

Let's do one more example.

$$\frac{3x^9}{15x^5}$$

First, we factor the numbers: 3 is a prime number, so it can't be broken down any further; 15 factors as 3 times 5.

$$\frac{3 \cdot x^9}{3 \cdot 5 \cdot x^5}$$ **Factor the numbers**

There is one pair of 3s that will cancel.

$$\frac{\cancel{3} \cdot x^9}{\cancel{3} \cdot 5 \cdot x^5}$$ **Cancel the 3s**

That leaves $\dfrac{x^9}{5 \cdot x^5}$. Next, instead of having to write out a bunch of x's, we'll use the subtracting exponents method: $9 - 5 = 4$, so we end up with x^4, which goes on top.

$$\frac{x^4}{5}$$ **Subtracting exponents**

And that's fully reduced. The main point is that dividing powers by subtracting exponents can be a big time saver when reducing more complicated fractions.

Practice 98

a.
(13)
What is $\dfrac{2}{5}$ of $\dfrac{7}{8}$? Make sure your answer is fully reduced.

b.
(98)
Reduce the fraction $\dfrac{8x^7}{8x^5}$. Select the best possible choice.

    A. $x^{\frac{7}{5}}$ B. x^{35} C. x^2

    D. $8x^2$ E. x^{12}

c.
(98)
Reduce the fraction $\dfrac{5x^6}{30x^3}$. Select the best possible choice.

    A. $\dfrac{x^3}{6}$ B. $\dfrac{x^2}{6}$ C. $\dfrac{x^3}{25}$

    D. $\dfrac{x^2}{25}$ E. $\dfrac{1}{6x^3}$

---

[1] Actually, in this case we didn't even have to factor the numbers. We could have just canceled the 4s in the first step.

d. Solve the equation $2x + 3x + 3 = 18$.
(76)

e. Translate the word problem below into an equation; then solve.
(73)

There is a number that if you subtract 6 from it first, and then divide that total by 4, you get 2. What's the number?

Problem Set 98

Rewrite each number below in scientific notation.

1. 8,000
(92)

2. 650,000,000,000,000,000
(92)

Answer each question below. Make sure your answer is fully reduced.

3. What is 70% of 490?
(27)

(a) 4. What is $\frac{2}{3}$ of $\frac{5}{8}$?
(13)

Do the indicated operation with each pair of numbers below.

5. $(-6)(-12)$
(61)

6. $35 + (-43)$
(59)

Calculate the value of each expression below. (Make sure to do the operations in the correct order.)

7. $9(2 + 5)$
(68)

8. $14 - 3^2$
(93)

Translate each of the following word problems into an equation. (Don't solve.)

9. There's some number that if you subtract 28 from it first, and then multiply that total by 7, the result is 0.
(69)

A. $28(x - 7) = 0$ B. $7(28 - x) = 0$ C. $7(x - 28) = 0$

D. $x - 28 \cdot 7 = 0$ E. $28x - 7 = 0$

10. There's some number that if you divide it by 50 first, and then add 41 to that total, the result is -183.
(71)

A. $\dfrac{50}{x + 41} = -183$ B. $\dfrac{x + 41}{50} = -183$ C. $\dfrac{x}{50 + 41} = -183$

D. $\dfrac{x}{50} + 41 = -183$ E. $\dfrac{50}{x} + 41 = -183$

Multiply or divide (as indicated) each pair of fractions below. Make sure your answers are fully reduced then select the best possible choice.

11.
(87)
$$\frac{5x}{24}\cdot\frac{21}{35x}$$

A. $\frac{1}{8}$

B. $8x$

C. $\frac{26}{59}$

D. $\frac{16}{11}$

E. $\frac{1}{56}$

12.
(88)
$$\frac{8}{3x}\div\frac{2}{9x}$$

A. $\frac{16}{27x}$

B. $\frac{3}{4}$

C. 12

D. $\frac{4}{3}$

E. $\frac{10}{9x}$

Simplify each expression below. Select the best possible choice.

13.
(76)
$17x+13x$

A. $30x$

B. $4x$

C. $221x$

D. $4x^2$

E. $30x^2$

14.
(94)
$25x^4-14x^4$

A. $39x^8$

B. $350x^{16}$

C. $11x^4$

D. 11

E. $39x^4$

Simplify each expression below by multiplying the powers.

15.
(95)
$x^4\cdot x^4$

A. 2

B. x^8

C. $2x^4$

D. $2x^{16}$

E. x^{16}

16.
(96)
$(9x^2)(5x^4)$

A. $4x^2$

B. $45x^8$

C. $14x^6$

D. $45x^6$

E. $14x^8$

17.
(96)
$(-4x^8)(12x^2)$

A. $-48x^{10}$

B. $8x^{10}$

C. $-48x^{16}$

D. $-16x^6$

E. $-16x^4$

Reduce each fraction below. Select the best possible choice.

18.
(86)
$$\frac{9(x+2)}{15(x+2)}$$

A. $\dfrac{1}{135}$　　　　B. $\dfrac{3}{5}$　　　　C. $\dfrac{1}{6}$

D. $\dfrac{1}{6(x+2)}$　　　E. $\dfrac{3(x+2)}{5}$

(b) 19.
(98)
$$\frac{6x^9}{6x^5}$$

A. x^{45}　　　　B. $6x^4$　　　　C. x^4

D. $x^{\frac{9}{5}}$　　　E. x^{14}

(c) 20.
(98)
$$\frac{4x^8}{28x^3}$$

A. $\dfrac{x^{\frac{8}{3}}}{24}$　　B. $\dfrac{1}{7x^5}$　　C. $\dfrac{x^{\frac{8}{3}}}{7}$

D. $\dfrac{x^5}{7}$　　　E. $\dfrac{x^5}{24}$

Solve each equation below.

21. $4(x-9)=20$　　　　**(d) 22.** $4x+3x+5=19$
(72)　　　　　　　　　　　　　(76)

Translate the word problem below into an equation; then solve.

(e) 23.
(73)
There is a number that if you subtract 5 from it first, and then divide that total by 3, you get 7. What's the number?

447

Lesson 99—Taking a Root

We've learned all about the fifth operation of algebra, which is raising a number to a power. Now it's time for the sixth operation, which is called taking a **root**. Here's how it works. To take the "second" root of 16, we find the number which when raised to the second power equals 16. Can you think of what number that is? It's 4 because 4 to the second power (4^2 or $4 \cdot 4$) is 16.

Roots and Radical Signs

A root is shown with a funny symbol called a **radical sign**. Here's what it looks like.

$$\sqrt[2]{} \qquad\qquad \textbf{A radical sign}$$

The little 2 means that this is a second root. So we write the second root of 16 as $\sqrt[2]{16} = 4$. Roots are also sometimes called **radicals**, since they're written with radical signs.

Higher Roots

Roots aren't limited to just second roots. There are also third roots. To show you, let's take the "third" root of 27. We just find the number which, when raised to the "third" power, equals 27. That turns out to be 3, since 3^3 equals 27. In mathematical form, the third root of 27 is written like this: $\sqrt[3]{27} = 3$. The little 3 in the upper left means that it's a third root. Second roots and third roots are also called **square roots** and **cube roots**. You already know where those names come from. But we could also say "the *square* root of 16 is 4," and "the *cube* root of 27 is 3."

There are also fourth roots. Let's do one of those. We'll take the fourth root of 16. That's the number that when raised to the fourth power is equal to 16. Since 2^4 equals 16, the fourth root of 16 must be 2. This is written mathematically as $\sqrt[4]{16} = 2$. Of course, the little 4 means fourth root. Are you getting the concept? It's just like powers. There are lots of different powers—second powers, third powers, fourth powers, and all the way up. In the same way, there are lots of different roots—second roots, third roots, fourth roots, and they go on up as well.

Leaving Off the 2

There's something else you should know—if you don't already—about second roots or square roots. These are by far the most common of all the roots. They're so common, in fact, that people usually don't bother to put the little two in the upper left corner of the radical sign. Instead of writing the square root of 16 as $\sqrt[2]{16}$, they just write it as $\sqrt{16}$.

$$\sqrt[2]{16} \text{ is usually written as } \sqrt{16}$$

That's just because people write square roots so much that they started leaving the 2 off. So when a radical sign doesn't have a little number at all, it is supposed to be a square root. That means if you want to show a third root or a fourth root, you'd better put in the little 3 or 4 ($\sqrt[3]{}$ and $\sqrt[4]{}$) or people will think it's a square root.

Practice 99

a.
(94)
Simplify $3x^4 - 11x^4$ by subtracting the powers.

    A. $14x^4$ B. $-8x^4$ C. $-33x^4$

    D. $8x^4$ E. -8

b.
(98)
Reduce the fraction $\dfrac{8x^8}{48x^3}$. Select the best possible choice.

    A. $\dfrac{x^{11}}{6}$ B. $\dfrac{6}{x^5}$ C. $\dfrac{1}{6x^5}$

    D. $\dfrac{x^5}{6}$ E. $\dfrac{x^5}{40}$

c.
(99)
Calculate the root $\sqrt{36}$.
                      d.
(99)
Calculate the root $\sqrt[3]{64}$.

e.
(55)
Translate the word problem below into an equation; then solve.

The experimental train traveled at a whopping speed of 297 miles per hour. At this speed, how many hours would it have taken it to travel 6,237 miles?

Problem Set 99

Tell whether each sentence below is True or False.

1.
(99)
Taking a root is the sixth operation of algebra.

2.
(99)
A root is shown with the symbol $\sqrt{}$, which is called a radical sign.

Calculate the value of each expression below. Make sure to do the operations in the correct order.

3.
(68)
$8 \cdot 5 - 29$
                            4.
(93)
$(4 \cdot 2)^2$

Translate each of the following phrases into a mathematical expression. (Don't calculate the answer.)

5.
(68)
12 and 2 multiplied first, and 16 subtracted from that total.

    A. $12(16-2)$ B. $12 \cdot 2 - 16$ C. $12(2-16)$

    D. $16 - 12 \cdot 2$ E. $16(2) - 12$

6.
(70)
5 added to 94 first, and that total divided by 33.

    A. $\dfrac{5+94}{33}$ B. $\dfrac{33}{5+94}$ C. $\dfrac{5}{94+33}$

    D. $\dfrac{5}{33}+94$ E. $5+\dfrac{94}{33}$

Add or subtract (as indicated) each pair of fractions below. Make sure your answers are fully reduced then select the best possible choice.

7.
(89)
$$\frac{5}{18x} + \frac{11}{18x}$$

    A. $\dfrac{4x}{9}$ B. $\dfrac{8}{9x}$ C. $\dfrac{55}{18x}$

    D. $\dfrac{1}{3x}$ E. $\dfrac{1}{2x}$

8.
(90)
$$\frac{7}{6x} - \frac{1}{2x}$$

    A. $\dfrac{4}{3x}$ B. $\dfrac{x}{2}$ C. $\dfrac{1}{x}$

    D. $\dfrac{2}{3x}$ E. $-\dfrac{7}{6x}$

Simplify each expression below by adding or subtracting (as indicated) the powers.

9.
(94)
$4x^5 + 23x^5$

    A. $92x^{25}$ B. $27x^{10}$ C. $92x^{10}$

    D. $27x^5$ E. $19x^5$

(a) 10.
(94)
$4x^9 - 9x^9$

    A. $5x^9$ B. $-36x^9$ C. -5

    D. $13x^9$ E. $-5x^9$

Simplify each expression below by multiplying the powers.

11.
(95)
$x^{13} \cdot x^6$

    A. $(2x)^{78}$ B. x^{19} C. x^7

    D. x^{78} E. $(2x)^{19}$

12.
(96)
$(-6x^7)(3x^5)$

    A. $-18x^{35}$ B. $18x^{12}$ C. $-3x^{12}$

    D. $-3x^{35}$ E. $-18x^{12}$

Simplify each expression below by dividing the powers.

13.
(97) $\dfrac{x^{11}}{x^2}$

    A. $x^{\frac{2}{11}}$ B. x^9 C. x^{22}

    D. $x^{\frac{11}{2}}$ E. x^{13}

14.
(97) $\dfrac{x^9}{x^7}$

    A. x^{63} B. $x^{\frac{7}{9}}$ C. x^2

    D. $x^{\frac{9}{7}}$ E. x^{16}

Reduce each fraction below. Select the best possible choice.

15.
(98) $\dfrac{2x^5}{2x^2}$

    A. $2x^3$ B. x^3 C. x^7

    D. $\dfrac{x^{10}}{2}$ E. $x^{\frac{5}{2}}$

(b) 16.
(98) $\dfrac{4x^9}{20x^5}$

    A. $\dfrac{x^4}{5}$ B. $\dfrac{1}{5x^4}$ C. $\dfrac{x^4}{16}$

    D. $\dfrac{x^{14}}{5}$ E. $\dfrac{5}{x^4}$

Calculate each root below.

(c) 17.
(99) $\sqrt{25}$ **(d) 18.**
(99) $\sqrt[3]{8}$ **19.**
(99) $\sqrt[3]{27}$

Solve each equation below.

20.
(53) $-5x + 3 = 23$ **21.**
(73) $\dfrac{x-6}{9} = 3$

Translate the word problem below into an equation; then solve.

(e) 22.
(55)   The primitive space capsule traveled at the rather unimpressive speed of 17,830 miles per hour. At this speed, how many hours would it have taken it to travel 160,470 miles?

Lesson 100—Undoing Powers and Roots

In the last lesson, we learned about the sixth operation of algebra: taking a root. But did you notice that taking a root was a lot like raising a number to a power backwards?

Inverse Operations Again

For example, when taking the second (square) root of 25, instead of multiplying the same number twice, we try to figure out what number has to be multiplied twice to get 25. That's going backwards.

The reason a root is like a power backwards is that roots and powers are inverse operations. Remember, inverse operations are operations that undo each other. Addition and subtraction are inverse operations, and so are multiplication and division. That's why we use one to undo the other when solving equations. It's also why subtraction is a lot like doing addition backwards (when subtracting $8-5$, we think "what number has to be added to 5 to get 8?") And division is like doing multiplication backwards too. They're inverse operations.

You already know how to show subtraction undoing addition. Let's say that 5 has 3 added to it: $5+3$. To undo the addition, we subtract 3 like this: $5+3-3$. That gets us back to 5 again. You also know how to show division undoing multiplication. If 8 is multiplied by 4, to undo the multiplication we write it as $\frac{8 \cdot 4}{4}$. That gets us back to 8.

Well, since powers and roots are inverse operations, we can also show a root undoing a power. Let's say we have 5 squared: 5^2. To undo the power, we can just take the square root of 5^2. All we have to do is put a radical sign over the whole thing: $\sqrt{5^2}$.

$$\sqrt{5^2} = 5$$ **Root undoes the power**

That equals 5 because the square root undoes the square. The other way to see this is to remember that 5 squared is 25, so we're really taking the square root of 25, which equals 5. The process would have worked the same way if it had been 4 or 3 or 8 or any other number that was squared (instead of 5). Basically, any square can be undone by taking the square root of the entire power. Here are a few other examples.

$$\sqrt{3^2} = 3 \qquad\qquad \sqrt{7^2} = 7 \qquad\qquad \sqrt{11^2} = 11$$

Undoing Higher Powers

Just as second (square) roots can undo second powers (squares), so can third roots undo third powers. Let's undo the third power 2^3. We just take the third root of the whole thing: $\sqrt[3]{2^3}$. And since the root undoes the power, the result is 2.

$$\sqrt[3]{2^3} = 2$$ **Third root undoes third power**

You can also tell that this is right, because 2 cubed is 8, so we're really taking the third root of 8, which is 2. A fourth power can also be undone by a fourth root.

$$\sqrt[4]{5^4} = 5$$ **Fourth root undoes fourth power**

The root undoes the power and gets us back to 5. Obviously, we could keep going all the way up: fifth roots will undo fifth powers, sixth roots will undo sixth powers, and so on. Therefore, a root will always undo the same degree (kind) of power.

Powers Also Undo Roots

But with inverse operations, both of the operations are supposed to undo each other. Remember, it's not just subtraction that undoes addition. Addition also undoes subtraction. Is the same thing true for powers and roots? Absolutely. If we have a square root, like $\sqrt{4}$, and want to undo it, all we have to do is square the whole thing like this: $(\sqrt{4})^2$. Notice that we use parentheses to show that the entire root is being squared. Since the square undoes the square root, the result is 4.

$$(\sqrt{4})^2 = 4 \qquad \textbf{Power undoes root}$$

It's obvious this has to be true because the square root of 4 is 2. So we're really just squaring 2, and that equals 4.

We can undo a third root with a third power too. Here's an example like that: $\sqrt[3]{27}$. To undo the third root, all we do is raise the whole thing to the third power. That takes us back to 27.

$$(\sqrt[3]{27})^3 = 27 \qquad \textbf{Third power undoes third root}$$

You can see why this works because the third root of 27 is actually 3. So we're really raising 3 to the third power, which is 27. Continuing upward, fourth roots can be undone with fourth powers. Here's a quick example of that.

$$(\sqrt[4]{16})^4 = 16 \qquad \textbf{Fourth power undoes fourth root}$$

Raising the fourth root of 16 to the fourth power undoes the root and gets us back to 16. And we can continue all the way up. Fifth roots can be undone by fifth powers, and sixth roots can be undone by sixth powers, and so on. The main point is that powers and roots are inverse operations so they will undo each other.

Practice 100

a.
(87)
Multiply the fractions $\dfrac{3}{6x^2} \cdot \dfrac{18x^5}{9}$. Make sure your answers are fully reduced then select the best possible choice.

    A. $\dfrac{1}{4x^3}$ B. $\dfrac{3+18x^5}{6x^2+9}$ C. $\dfrac{1}{x^3}$

    D. $\dfrac{1}{2x^3}$ E. x^3

b.
(99)
Calculate the value of the root $\sqrt[4]{81}$.

c.
(100)
Calculate the value of the expression $\sqrt{8^2}$.

d.
(100)
Calculate the value of the expression $(\sqrt[3]{27})^3$.

e.
(54)
Translate the word problem below into an equation; then solve.

There were 130 water slides in the whole state, but only 26 of them were open year-round. What percent of the water slides were open year-round? (The answer to your equation will be in decimal form. Make sure your final answer is written as a percent.)

Problem Set 100

Tell whether each sentence below is True or False.

1.
(100)   Powers and roots are inverse operations.

2.
(100)   Powers can undo roots, and roots can undo powers.

Do the indicated operation with each pair of numbers below.

3. $-37-(-28)$
(60)

4. $\dfrac{20}{-4}$
(62)

Calculate the value of each expression below. (Make sure to do the operations in the correct order.)

5. $14-\dfrac{35}{5}$
(70)

6. $(5-2)^4$
(93)

Translate each of the following word problems into an equation. (Don't solve.)

7.   There's some number that if you multiply it by -4 first, and then add 29 to that total, the result is 45.
(69)

    A. $x-4\cdot29=45$ B. $29x+(-4)=45$ C. $-4(x+29)=45$

    D. $-4x+29=45$ E. $29(x-4)=45$

8.   There's some number that if you subtract 3 from it first, and then divide that total by 17, the result is
(71) -11.

    A. $x-\dfrac{3}{17}=-11$ B. $\dfrac{x-3}{17}=-11$ C. $\dfrac{3-x}{17}=-11$

    D. $\dfrac{17}{x-3}=-11$ E. $\dfrac{x}{17}-3=-11$

Simplify each expression below. Select the best possible choice.

9. $23+x-18$
(75)

    A. $x+5$ B. $6x$ C. $x+(-5)$

    D. $24x-18$ E. $23+17x$

10. $-13x+(-41x)$
(76)

    A. $28x$ B. $-28x$ C. $-54x$

    D. $-54x^2$ E. $54x$

Simplify each expression below by multiplying the powers.

11.
(95) $x^4 \cdot x^9$

      A. $x^{\frac{9}{4}}$ B. x^{13} C. x^{36}

      D. x^5 E. $2x^{13}$

12.
(96) $(-15x^3)(-2x^5)$

      A. $30x^8$ B. $-17x^{15}$ C. $-17x^8$

      D. $30x^{15}$ E. $-30x^8$

Multiply or divide (as indicated) each pair of fractions below. Make sure your answers are fully reduced then select the best possible choice.

13.
(88) $\dfrac{4x}{9} \div \dfrac{8x}{27}$

      A. $\dfrac{12x}{243}$ B. $\dfrac{32x}{243}$ C. $\dfrac{2}{3}$

      D. $\dfrac{4x}{27}$ E. $\dfrac{3}{2}$

(a) 14.
(87) $\dfrac{5}{4x^2} \cdot \dfrac{8x^4}{10}$

      A. $\dfrac{1}{x^2}$ B. $\dfrac{1}{4x^2}$ C. x^2

      D. $\dfrac{1}{2x^2}$ E. $\dfrac{5+8x^4}{4x^2+10}$

Reduce each fraction below. Select the best possible choice.

15.
(98) $\dfrac{34x^6}{34x^3}$

      A. $34x^2$ B. x^9 C. x^2

      D. x^{18} E. x^3

16.
(98) $\dfrac{15x^7}{45x^2}$

      A. $\dfrac{x^5}{3}$ B. $3x^9$ C. $\dfrac{x^5}{30}$

      D. $\dfrac{3x^{14}}{5}$ E. $\dfrac{x^9}{5}$

Calculate each root below.

17.
(99)
$\sqrt{49}$

(b) 18.
(99)
$\sqrt[4]{16}$

Calculate the value of each expression below.

(c) 19.
(100)
$\sqrt{9^2}$

(d) 20.
(100)
$(\sqrt[3]{64})^3$

Solve each equation below.

21.
(76)
$7x + 11x = -54$

22.
(73)
$\dfrac{x}{9} - 6 = 2$

Translate the word problem below into an equation; then solve.

(e) 23.
(54)
There were 68 kinds of ice cream in the freezer, but only 17 of those were some kind of chocolate flavor. What percent were chocolate-flavored? (The answer to your equation will be in decimal form. Make sure your final answer is written as a percent.)

Lesson 101—An Exponent of 1

A few lessons ago, we learned to divide powers by subtracting their exponents. A quick example is $\frac{x^7}{x^2}$. All we do, remember, is take the exponent on top, 7, and subtract the exponent on bottom, 2, to get 5 or x^5.

$$\frac{x^7}{x^2} = x^{7-2} = x^5$$

Back to Dividing Powers

But look at this division: $\frac{x^3}{x^2}$. We've got an exponent of 3 on top and an exponent of 2 on bottom. If we subtract the exponents, we get 3 – 2 or 1, which would be x^1.

$$\frac{x^3}{x^2} = x^{3-2} = x^1 \qquad \textbf{What is } x^1\textbf{?}$$

What could x^1 possibly mean? Exponents are supposed to tell how many times to multiply the base. But we can't multiply one of anything. Even though an exponent of 1 seems strange, it actually makes some sense.

Let's go back to the original problem $\frac{x^3}{x^2}$. Instead of using the subtracting exponent method, let's do it the old way, by factoring and canceling. On top, we have three x's multiplied and on bottom we have two x's multiplied.

$$\frac{x \cdot x \cdot x}{x \cdot x}$$

That gives us two pairs of x's that will cancel, so we end up with $\frac{x}{1}$, which is just x.

$$\frac{\cancel{x} \cdot \cancel{x} \cdot x}{\underset{1}{\cancel{x} \cdot \cancel{x}}} \qquad \textbf{Cancel the x's}$$

$$\frac{x}{1} = x$$

Apparently, when we got x^1, the actual answer was just a single x.

But think about this for a second. Doesn't it make sense that a single x should equal x^1? If x^3 is three x's multiplied and x^2 is two x's multiplied, why can't x^1 be a single x all by itself? More importantly, if we make $x^1 = x$, then we can use the subtracting exponent method even on divisions like $\frac{x^3}{x^2}$, where the answer comes out to just a single x. That's exactly what the mathematicians decided to do. They made $x^1 = x$. Actually, they went further than that. They made any number raised to the first power equal to the number itself. Since this rule works for any number at all, powers with other bases can be handled this way too. Here are some examples with other bases.

457

$$\frac{2^5}{2^4} = 2^1 = 2 \qquad\qquad \frac{5^8}{5^7} = 5^1 = 5 \qquad\qquad \frac{7^4}{7^3} = 7^1 = 7$$

Of course, you don't have to write out the exponent of 1. Once you get the hang of the concept, just do it in your head.

Multiplying with an Exponent of 1

Interestingly, an exponent of 1 isn't just useful for dividing powers. It can also help multiply powers. Look at this multiplication.

$$x^4 \cdot x$$

We know what the answer is here: x^4 represents four x's multiplied. Then, after multiplying by another x, we end up with five x's multiplied or x^5. But what about using the method of adding the exponents? Remember, that's another, faster way to multiply powers. The problem with adding exponents here is that the second x doesn't seem to have an exponent. But if $x^1 = x$, why can't we change $x^4 \cdot x$ to $x^4 \cdot x^1$?

$$x^4 \cdot x \text{ can be changed to } x^4 \cdot x^1$$

That's perfectly legal. Now there are exponents on both x's, and we can add them in the usual way: 4 + 1 is 5, so we get x^5, which we know is right.

$$x^4 \cdot x = x^4 \cdot x^1 = x^5 \qquad\qquad \textbf{Add the exponents}$$

Basically, we can put an exponent of 1 on anything if it helps us multiply. Here are a couple of other examples with different bases.

$$2^5 \cdot 2 = 2^5 \cdot 2^1 = 2^6 \qquad\qquad\qquad 8^3 \cdot 8 = 8^3 \cdot 8^1 = 8^4$$

Practice 101

a.
(90)
Subtract the fractions $\dfrac{5}{2x} - \dfrac{8}{3x}$. Make sure your answers are fully reduced then select the best possible choice.

    A. $-\dfrac{1}{2x}$ B. $-\dfrac{20}{3x}$ C. $\dfrac{13}{6x}$

    D. $\dfrac{3}{x}$ E. $-\dfrac{1}{6x}$

b.
(101)
Simplify $\dfrac{3^8}{3^7}$ by dividing the powers. Select the best possible choice.

    A. 1   B. 3^{15} C. 3^{56}

    D. 3   E. $3^{\frac{8}{7}}$

c.
(101)
Simplify $x^6 \cdot x$ by multiplying the powers. Select the best possible choice.

A. x^5 B. $(2x)^7$ C. x^7

D. $(2x)^5$ E. x^6

d.
(100)
Calculate the value of the expression $(\sqrt[4]{81})^4$.

e.
(82)
Translate the word problem below into an equation; then solve.

Lickety-Split Emergency Care, a private ambulance service, charges $100 for a service call (just to come to the house) plus $60 per hour after that. Super Speedy Sirens, another ambulance firm, charges $120 for a service call plus $50 per hour after that. How many hours would a job have to take for the bill of both ambulance services to be the same?

Problem Set 101

Tell whether each sentence below is True or False.

1.
(101)
Any number raised to the first power is equal to the number itself.

2.
(101)
An exponent of 1 can be used to divide powers, but never to multiply powers.

Rewrite each number below in scientific notation.

3.
(92)
7,000,000,000

4.
(92)
31,800,000

Translate each of the following phrases into a mathematical expression. (Don't calculate the answer.)

5.
(68)
42 and 17 added first, and that total multiplied by 6.

A. $42 + 17 \cdot 6$ B. $17 + 42(6)$ C. $6(42 + 17)$

D. $42 \cdot 17 + 6$ E. $42(17 + 6)$

6.
(70)
18 divided by 3 first, and 5 subtracted from that total.

A. $5 - \dfrac{18}{3}$ B. $\dfrac{3}{18} - 5$ C. $\dfrac{18 - 5}{3}$

D. $\dfrac{3}{18 - 5}$ E. $\dfrac{18}{3} - 5$

Add or subtract (as indicated) each pair of fractions below. Make sure your answers are fully reduced then select the best possible choice.

7.
(89) $\dfrac{7x}{12} + \dfrac{2x}{12}$

        A. $\dfrac{3x}{4}$ B. $\dfrac{4x}{3}$ C. $\dfrac{7x}{6}$

        D. $\dfrac{3x}{2}$ E. $\dfrac{5x}{12}$

(a) 8.
(90) $\dfrac{3}{2x} - \dfrac{8}{5x}$

        A. $-\dfrac{5}{3x}$ B. $-\dfrac{1}{10x}$ C. $\dfrac{11}{10x}$

        D. $-\dfrac{12}{5x}$ E. $-\dfrac{1}{2x}$

Simplify each expression below by adding or subtracting (as indicated) the powers.

9.
(94) $7x^4 + 6x^4$

        A. x^8 B. x^4 C. $13x^8$

        D. $42x^8$ E. $13x^4$

10.
(94) $9x^7 - 4x^7$

        A. 5 B. $5x^7$ C. $-5x^7$

        D. $13x^7$ E. $-36x^7$

Simplify each expression below by dividing the powers.

11.
(97) $\dfrac{x^5}{x^3}$

        A. x^{15} B. $x^{\frac{1}{2}}$ C. x^8

        D. $8x$ E. x^2

(b) 12.
(101) $\dfrac{6^8}{6^7}$

        A. $6^{\frac{8}{7}}$ B. 6^{15} C. 6

        D. 1 E. 6^{56}

13.
(101)
$$\frac{x^4}{x^3}$$

    A. 1   B. x C. x^7

    D. x^{12} E. $\dfrac{1}{x}$

Simplify each expression below by multiplying the powers.

14.
(96)
$(9x^8)(4x^{11})$

    A. $36x^{88}$ B. $13x^{88}$ C. $36x^{19}$

    D. $13x^3$ E. $13x^{19}$

(c) 15.
(101)
$x^7 \cdot x$

    A. x^8 B. x^6 C. $(2x)^6$

    D. $(2x)^8$ E. x^7

Calculate each root below.

16.
(99)
$\sqrt{100}$
                                17.
(99)
$\sqrt[3]{125}$

Calculate the value of each expression below.

18.
(100)
. $\sqrt{7^2}$
                              (d) 19.
(100)
$(\sqrt[4]{16})^4$

Solve each equation below.

20.
(53)
$3(x-4)=15$
                              21.
(78)
$-x+10x=72$

Translate the word problem below into an equation; then solve.

(e) 22.
(82)
Gary's Green Thumb, a professional gardening service, charges $75 for a service call (just to come to the house) plus $60 per hour after that. Luscious Landscapes, another gardening firm, charges $95 for a service call plus $40 per hour after that. How many hours would a job have to take for the bill of both gardening services to be the same?

Lesson 102—An Exponent of 0

We learned about exponents of 1 in the last lesson. The idea probably seemed weird at first, but, if you remember, it turned out to be very useful. In this lesson, we're going to learn about an exponent that's even weirder.

Same Exponent on Top and Bottom

Here's an example: $\dfrac{x^3}{x^3}$. We know this is equal to 1, since anything divided by itself equals 1. The other way to see that the answer has to be 1 is to factor and cancel. If we did that, all the x's on top would cancel with all the x's on bottom and that would give us an answer of 1. But watch what happens when we apply the subtracting exponents method here.

$$\frac{x^3}{x^3} = x^{3-3} = x^0$$

We end up with a 0 exponent. If you thought an exponent of 1 was weird, what about an exponent of 0? But let's think this through. We know the real answer to our problem has to be 1. If we make x^0 equal 1, then we have the right answer. More importantly, we could use the shortcut of subtracting exponents to divide $\dfrac{x^3}{x^3}$. That's why the mathematicians decided to make a rule that any number with an exponent of 0 is automatically equal to 1. And since the rule applies to any number, it can also be used on other divisions. Here are a few examples with different bases.

$$\frac{2^5}{2^5} = 2^0 = 1 \qquad\qquad \frac{4^7}{4^7} = 4^0 = 1 \qquad\qquad \frac{9^2}{9^2} = 9^0 = 1$$

Notice that every time we get an exponent of 0, the actual answer to the division is 1. It has to be that way because the only time the exponent will turn out to be 0 is when the exponent on top is the same as the exponent on bottom, which just means that all the factors are going to cancel.

Be careful, though. One of the most common mistakes that beginners make is thinking that a 0 exponent makes a power equal not 1 but 0. To a beginner, it's just common sense that 2^0 ought to equal 0. But common sense isn't always right. Once again, an exponent of 0 makes a power equal to 1, not 0.

Using a Zero Exponent to Multiply

Here's something else interesting about exponents of 0. They will also work when multiplying powers. Look at this example.

$$x^3 \cdot x^0$$

We have x^3 multiplied by x^0. If we multiply these by adding the exponents, we get this.

$$x^3 \cdot x^0 = x^{3+0} = x^3$$

Is that right? Yes, it is. Remember, any number with an exponent of 0 equals 1. So $x^3 \cdot x^0$ is really just $x^3 \cdot 1$, which equals x^3. So an exponent of 0 even gives the right answer when it's used in a multiplication. The main point is that any number with an exponent of 0 is automatically equal to 1. It doesn't matter whether it's an x or an actual number like 2 or 3.

Practice 102

a.
(102)
Simplify $\dfrac{4^9}{4^9}$ by dividing the powers.

    A. 1   B. 16^9 C. 0

    D. 8^9 E. 4^{18}

b.
(102)
Simplify $x^4 \cdot x^0$ by multiplying the powers.

    A. x^{40} B. x^3 C. 0

    D. x^4 E. 1

c.
(98)
Divide the fractions $\dfrac{4x^8}{7} \div \dfrac{8x^3}{14}$. Make sure your answers are fully reduced then select the best possible choice.

    A. $\dfrac{1}{4x^5}$ B. x^5 C. x^6

    D. $\dfrac{x^5}{2}$ E. $\dfrac{16x^{11}}{49}$

d.
(81)
Solve the equation $5+7x=16+3x$. Make sure your answer is fully reduced.

e.
(79)
Translate the word problem below into an equation; then solve.

Carl can hand-toss 5 pizzas per hour. Eddie can hand-toss 7 pizzas per hour. Working together, how many hours would it take them to hand-toss 156 pizzas?

Problem Set 102

Tell whether each sentence below is True or False.

1.
(102)
Any number with an exponent of 0 is equal to 1.

2.
(102)
A number with an exponent of 0 cannot be used in any actual mathematical calculations.

Answer each question below.

3.
(55)
How far will a chartered bus driving at 78 miles per hour go in 4 hours?

4.
(55)
How far will a riding mower driving at 2 feet per second go in 30 seconds?

Calculate the value of each expression below. (Make sure to do the operations in the correct order.)

5.
(68) $7(9-1)$

6.
(93) $12 \cdot 2^3$

Translate each of the following word problems into an equation. (Don't solve.)

7.
(69)   There's some number that if you subtract 2 from it first, and then multiply that total by 10, the result is 18.

    A. $2(10)-x=18$ B. $2(x-10)=18$ C. $x-2\cdot10=18$

    D. $10(x-2)=18$ E. $10(2-x)=18$

8.
(71)   There's some number that if you divide it by 5 first, and then add 22 to that total, the result is 350.

    A. $\dfrac{x}{5}+22=350$ B. $\dfrac{5}{x+22}=350$ C. $\dfrac{5}{x}+22=350$

    D. $\dfrac{x+5}{22}=350$ E. $\dfrac{x+22}{5}=350$

Simplify each expression below. Select the best possible choice.

9.
(76) $3x+14x$

    A. $17x$ B. $12x$ C. $11x$

    D. $\dfrac{14x}{3}$ E. $42x$

10.
(75) $7+2x+(-5)$

    A. $9x-5$ B. $4x$ C. $7-3x$

    D. $2x+(-2)$ E. $2x+2$

Simplify each expression below by dividing the powers.

11.
(97) $\dfrac{x^{12}}{x^8}$

    A. x^{96} B. $x^{\frac{3}{2}}$ C. x^4

    D. $4x$ E. x^{20}

(a) 12.
(102) $\dfrac{2^9}{2^9}$

    A. 2^{18} B. 1 C. 4^9

    D. 0 E. 4^{18}

13.
(102)
$\dfrac{x^4}{x^4}$

    A. x B. $\dfrac{1}{x}$ C. 0

    D. 1 E. x^4

Simplify each expression below by multiplying the powers.

14.
(101)
$x^2 \cdot x$

    A. x^2 B. x^3 C. x

    D. $2x^2$ E. $\dfrac{1}{x}$

(b) 15.
(102)
$x^6 \cdot x^0$

    A. x^5 B. 1 C. x^{60}

    D. 0 E. x^6

Multiply or divide (as indicated) each pair of fractions below. Make sure your answers are fully reduced then select the best possible choice.

16.
(87)
$\dfrac{7x}{24x} \cdot \dfrac{20x}{14}$

    A. $\dfrac{5}{12x}$ B. $\dfrac{5x}{12}$ C. $\dfrac{27x}{24x+14}$

    D. $\dfrac{5x}{6}$ E. $\dfrac{5x}{8}$

(c) 17.
(98)
$\dfrac{5x^7}{2} \div \dfrac{15x^3}{6}$

    A. $\dfrac{x^4}{3}$ B. x^5 C. x^4

    D. $\dfrac{75x^4}{12}$ E. $\dfrac{1}{9x^4}$

Calculate each root below.

18.
(99)
$\sqrt{9}$ **19.**
(99)
$\sqrt[3]{27}$

Calculate the value of each expression below.

20.
(100) $\sqrt{6^2}$

21.
(100) $(\sqrt[3]{64})^3$

Solve each equation below. Make sure your answer is fully reduced.

22.
(53) $7x+19=23$

(d) 23.
(81) $3+5x=11+2x$

Translate the word problem below into an equation; then solve.

(e) 24.
(79) Robert can do 12 belly-flops per hour. Timmy can do 16 belly-flops per hour. Together, how many hours would it take them to do 112 belly-flops?

CHAPTER 13:
GEOMETRY

Lesson 103—Points, Lines, and Planes

We've been doing a lot of algebra. But now we're going to switch to geometry. You've done geometry in earlier math courses. Geometry is basically the study of shapes, such as squares, circles, and rectangles. All shapes are made up of simple parts. And the simplest part of all is a **point**, which is really just a position or location somewhere in space. Technically, a point doesn't even have any size. Nevertheless, a point is always shown as a dot on paper.

• P

A point is named
with a capital letter.

A point is always named and labeled with a capital letter. The point above is called point P, as you can see.

Lines and Line Segments

Another simple part that's used to make shapes is a line. Technically, a **line** is a group of points that go in opposite directions forever. We don't have room to show a line going forever, obviously. So we put arrows on each end to show that the line actually keeps going in both directions.

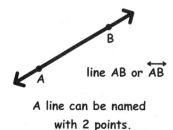

line AB or $\overleftrightarrow{AB}$

A line can be named
with 2 points.

A line has points that run all along it; the points are what make up the line. But in the line above only two of those points are labeled: point A and point B. When two of the points on a line are labeled, those points can be used to name the line. We can call this line AB. The short way to write a line is to place a small line above the two letters that are used to name it: $\overleftrightarrow{AB}$. Notice that the line above the letters has arrows on each end.

Even if none of the points on a line are labeled, the line can still be named. But in this case, you should use a lower case letter. Even though any letter will work, people often use the letters ℓ, n, m, and p. For instance, since the line below isn't showing any points we can just call it line n.

There's also such a thing as a line segment. A **line segment** is part of a line. The line below stops at point A and point B. This is just part of a line, so it qualifies as a line segment. The points are actually called the **end points** of the line segment.

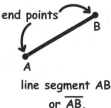

end points

line segment AB
or $\overline{AB}$.

And notice that the short way of writing a line segment is to just put a little segment above the end point letters: $\overline{AB}$. The little line above AB doesn't have arrows; it's a line segment.

Rays

Besides lines and line segments, there are also rays. A **ray** has an end point on one side but then goes on forever in the other direction. Here's an example.

The end point of this ray is point G. There's another point F that's also on the ray, but the ray doesn't stop with F. It keeps going as the arrow shows. We can still use both G and F to name the ray, though. We can just call it ray GF. And it's important that point G be listed first. The end point should always be first when naming a ray. The short way to write a ray is to put a little ray over the two letters used to name it. So the ray above can be written like this: $\overrightarrow{GF}$.

Planes

Another simple part that's used to make shapes is a plane. A plane is basically a flat surface like a table top. The technical definition of a **plane** is a flat surface with no thickness that extends forever in all directions. Here's plane Q.

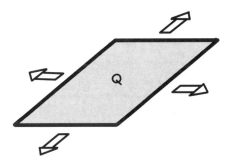

The edges make it look like plane Q stops. But that's just because there isn't room to show it. As the arrows indicate, the edges actually continue forever in all directions. A line is made up of points, but a plane is made up of lines. Plane Q has many lines running along it.

Pairs of Lines

In geometry we also sometimes analyze two lines at once. When two lines cross, we say that they **intersect**. The lines ℓ and m below intersect at point P. So we say that P is the intersection point.

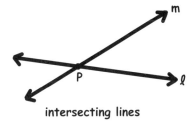

intersecting lines

Parallel lines are lines that lie in the same plane but that don't intersect. Lines *AB* and *CD* below are parallel. They're in the same plane because they're both lying on a page in a book. A page is like a plane.

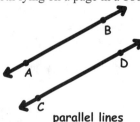

parallel lines

Just because you can't see an intersection point between two lines doesn't necessarily mean they're parallel. For instance, the only reason we can't see an intersection point between lines *p* and *m* below is that there isn't room to extend the lines far enough.

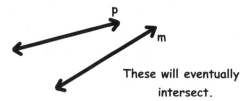

These will eventually
intersect.

These are both lines (notice the arrows on both ends), so they actually go on forever in both directions. If we kept the lines going they would eventually cross. By contrast, parallel lines are slanted in exactly the same way. That's why they won't intersect even if you extend them further.

Skew lines are lines that don't lie on the same plane. It's tough to show skew lines on a book page. But if you look at the box below, you can see that it's made up of parts of planes. *ABEF* is a flat surface. And so is *CDGH*. There are planes on the top and bottom of the box too. The edges of these planes are parallel line segments.

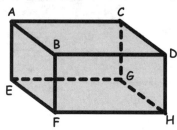

$\overline{AE}$ and $\overline{BD}$ are skew.

But line segments *AE* and *BD* are skew. The reason is they don't lie in the same plane. One way to tell is that it's impossible to run a flat surface (like a table top or sheet of paper) through both of these line segments at the same time. So $\overline{AE}$ and $\overline{BD}$ don't intersect, but they aren't parallel either. That's true of all skew lines.

Practice 103

a.
(103)
Select the correct name for the dashed section below.

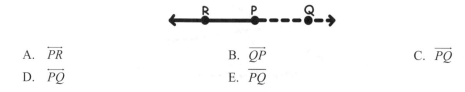

A. $\overrightarrow{PR}$

B. $\overrightarrow{QP}$

C. $\overrightarrow{PQ}$

D. $\overrightarrow{PQ}$

E. $\overline{PQ}$

470

b. Use the figure on the right to select the answer to the question below.
(103)

$\overline{IJ}$ and $\overline{BC}$ _____.

    A. intersect   B. are skew
    C. are parallel   D. are rays
    E. both C and D

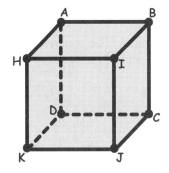

c. Use the picture on the right to tell which two streets appear to intersect.
(103)

    A. 23rd St. and 5th Ave.
    B. Madison Ave. and Canal St.
    C. Houston Ave. and Madison Ave.
    D. Canal St. and Park Ave.
    E. 18th St. and Holland St.

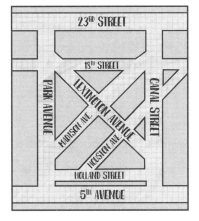

d. Solve the equation $13 + x = 8 - 5x$. Make sure your answer is fully reduced.
(81)

e. Translate the word problem below into an equation; then solve.
(55)

The rocket flew for 12 seconds, traveling a total of 91,224 meters. How fast did the rocket travel in meters per second?

Problem Set 103

Tell whether each sentence below is True or False.

1. A line segment has one end point and goes forever in the opposite direction.
(103)

2. Parallel lines are lines that lie in the same plane but that don't intersect.
(103)

3. A plane is a flat surface with no thickness that extends forever in all directions.
(103)

Answer each question below.

(a) 4. Select the correct name for the dashed section below.
(103)

A. $\overline{AB}$	B. $\overleftrightarrow{AB}$	C. $\overrightarrow{AB}$
D. $\overrightarrow{AC}$	E. $\overrightarrow{BA}$	

5. Name three line segments in the figure below.
(103)

Use the figure on the right to select the answer to each question below.

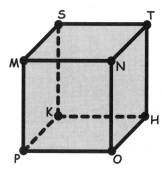

6. $\overline{MP}$ and $\overline{NT}$ _____.
(103)

A. are skew   B. are parallel
C. intersect   D. are rays
E. both B and D

(b) 7. $\overline{MN}$ and $\overline{ST}$ _____.
(103)

A. are skew   B. are parallel
C. intersect   D. are rays
E. Both B and D

Use the picture on the right to answer each question below.

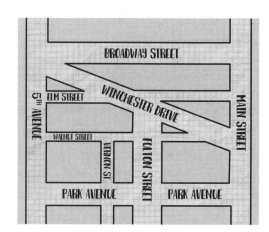

8. Tell which two streets appear to be parallel.
(103)

A. 5th Ave. and Walnut St.
B. Winchester Dr. and Main St.
C. Elm St. and Broadway St.
D. Vernon St. and Park Ave.
E. Fulton St. and Walnut St.

(c) 9. Tell which two streets appear to intersect.
(103)

A. Broadway St. and Winchester Dr.   B. Park Ave. and Walnut St.
C. Main St. and Vernon St.   D. 5th Ave. and Fulton St.
E. Elm St. and Park Ave.

Translate each of the following phrases into a mathematical expression. (Don't calculate the answer.)

10.
(68) 65 minus 42, and that total multiplied by 9.

    A. $9(65) - 42$ B. $42 - 65(9)$ C. $9(65 - 42)$

    D. $65 - 42 \cdot 9$ E. $9(42 - 65)$

11.
(70) 27 divided by 3 first, and 14 added to that total.

    A. $\dfrac{3}{27} + 14$ B. $\dfrac{3}{27 + 14}$ C. $\dfrac{27 + 14}{3}$

    D. $\dfrac{27}{3 + 14}$ E. $\dfrac{27}{3} + 14$

Simplify each expression below by multiplying the powers.

12.
(95) $x^5 \cdot x^7$

    A. x^{35} B. $x^{\frac{1}{2}}$ C. x^2

    D. x^{12} E. $2x$

13.
(96) $(-10x^9)(5x^4)$

    A. $-5x^{36}$ B. $-15x^5$ C. $-50x^{13}$

    D. $-5x^{13}$ E. $-50x^{36}$

Simplify each expression below by dividing the powers.

14.
(101) $\dfrac{x^7}{x}$

    A. x^6 B. x^7 C. $\dfrac{1}{x^6}$

    D. $\dfrac{1}{x^8}$ E. x^8

15.
(102) $\dfrac{15^8}{15^8}$

    A. 15^{16} B. 1 C. 0

    D. 15^4 E. 15^8

Reduce each fraction below. Make sure your answers are fully reduced.

16.
(98)
$$\dfrac{7x^{10}}{7x^2}$$

A. $7x^8$ B. x^5 C. x^{20}
D. x^8 E. x^{12}

17.
(98)
$$\dfrac{8x^3}{16x^2}$$

A. $\dfrac{1}{8x}$ B. $2x$ C. $\dfrac{x}{8}$

D. $\dfrac{x}{2}$ E. $8x$

Calculate the value of each expression below.

18.
(100)
$\sqrt[6]{3^6}$

19.
(100)
$(\sqrt{4})^2$

Solve each equation below. Make sure your answer is fully reduced.

20.
(64)
$\dfrac{x-10}{3} = -4$

(d) 21.
(81)
$11 + x = 7 - 4x$

Translate the word problem below into an equation; then solve.

(e) 22.
(55)
The satellite orbited for 15 seconds, traveling a total of 93,945 meters. How fast did the satellite travel in meters per second?

Lesson 104—Angles

In the last lesson, we learned about points, lines, line segments, rays, and planes. These are all simple parts that are used to make geometry shapes. Another simple part is an angle. An **angle** is made up of two rays that have the same end point. You can see below that $\overrightarrow{AB}$ and $\overrightarrow{AC}$ share the same end point, A. The angle is the space in the middle, between the rays.

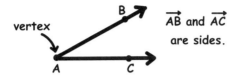

vertex

$\overrightarrow{AB}$ and $\overrightarrow{AC}$
are sides.

The end point where the rays meet is called the **vertex** of the angle. So point A is the vertex of this angle. The rays can also be called the sides of the angle. So we can say that this angle has sides $\overrightarrow{AB}$ and $\overrightarrow{AC}$.

Naming an Angle

How do you name an angle? Let's look at another example. The angle below has three points that are labeled: C, D, and E. One way to name this angle is to use all three of those points. We could call this angle CDE. Notice that the letter representing the vertex (D) is in the middle. That's always the way it works. The vertex letter should always be in the middle. That means we could also name this angle EDC. That's legal, since D, the vertex point, is still in the middle.

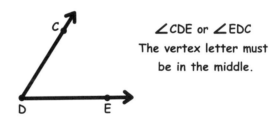

$\angle CDE$ or $\angle EDC$
The vertex letter must
be in the middle.

But it would be wrong to name the angle DCE because C isn't the vertex. The short way to write an angle is to use a little angle symbol in front of the letters. So the proper way to write the angle above would be as $\angle CDE$ or $\angle EDC$.

It's actually possible to name an angle in a simpler way. Instead of using three letters, we can just use the vertex letter. So we could name the angle below $\angle S$. When using only one letter, you must use the vertex letter. It would be wrong to call this $\angle R$ or $\angle T$.

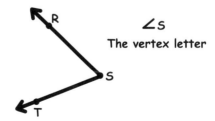

$\angle S$
The vertex letter

The only time we're not allowed to use just the vertex letter to name an angle is if it would cause confusion. Take the diagram below as an example. What if we wanted to name angle *KJL* using just one letter? We couldn't just call it ∠*J* because people would be confused about which angle we were referring to. ∠*J* could mean angle *KJL*, but it could also mean angle *HJK*. In fact, it might even mean angle *HJL*. The problem is all three of these angles have *J* as their vertex.

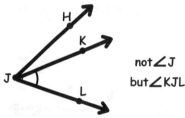

In a case like this, if we want to name angle *KJL*, we're forced to use all three letters: ∠*KJL*. This eliminates the confusion. Another way of communicating which angle you're referring to is to use an arc. An arc is just part of a circle. In the diagram above, ∠*KJL* has a little arc connecting its two sides. This arc shows that ∠*KJL* is the angle that we're discussing.

There is one other way to name an angle. It's the one to use when we don't know any points on the angle. For instance, none of the points on the angle below are labeled, not even the vertex. In such cases, we usually name the angle with a number. This angle is labeled angle 1. You can put the number inside the angle, near the vertex. And you can also just write ∠1 .

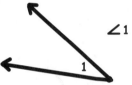

Measuring Angles

Angles come in all different sizes. That's why it's important to be able to measure an angle with a **protractor**. A protractor has two sets of numbers around it. There's a bottom row of numbers and a top row. The bottom row starts with 0 on the right and goes around to 180 on the left. The top row starts with 0 on the left and goes around to 180 on the right. Angles are measured in **degrees**, so the numbers 0 to 180 actually stand for degrees. The reason for the two rows is that we're supposed to use the bottom row to measure an angle that opens to the right and the top row to measure an angle that opens to the left.

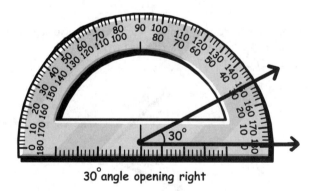

30° angle opening right

The protractor is on top of an angle that's opening toward the right. The way to tell is that the bottom side of the angle is pointing rightward. That means we need to use the bottom row of numbers to measure it. There's a hole at the bottom of the protractor in the middle. This hole should be right on top of the vertex of the angle. And the bottom of the protractor should be horizontal, just like the bottom side of the angle. To measure the angle, we just look at where the top side of the angle crosses the bottom row of numbers. The top side of the angle above crosses at 30, which means this angle measures 30 degrees. The symbol for degrees is a little circle, so 30 degrees is written as 30°.

Below is an angle that opens to the left. Notice the bottom side of the angle is pointing to the left. That means we should use the top row of numbers to measure this angle. We have the protractor in the proper position, with the hole on top of the vertex and the protractor's bottom runs horizontally, along with the bottom side of the angle.

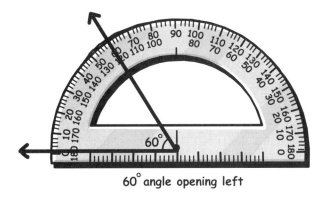

60° angle opening left

To measure the angle we just need to look at where the top side of the angle crosses the top row of numbers. You can see that it crosses at 60, which means this angle measures 60° .

Right Angles

Angles that are less than 90° are also called **acute angles**. Our first example was 30° and the last one was 60° . So both of these were acute angles. But there are also angles that measure exactly 90°. One easy way to recognize a 90° angle is that the angle's sides make the shape of the letter L. Here is an example of a 90° angle.

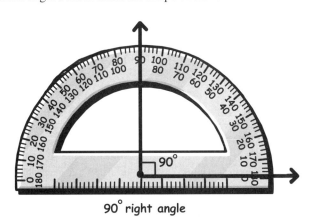

90° right angle

Notice that the upper side of the angle goes through the number 90. And the angle is shaped like an L. A 90° angle is also called a **right angle**. This particular right angle is opening to the right (because the bottom side is pointing in that direction). But a right angle could open to the left as well. Then it would look like a backward L. There's a symbol for a 90° angle that's used quite a bit. People put a box inside the angle, near the vertex. The angle above is labeled with a box. Whenever you see this symbol, you'll know automatically that the angle is a right angle. You don't even have to measure it.

Sometimes two lines will intersect and make right angles. The two lines below are an example.

Perpendicular lines

The angle with the box is a right angle. The other three angles created by the intersecting lines are also right angles. We just don't have them labeled. Lines that intersect to form right angles are called **perpendicular lines**.

Obtuse Angles

There are acute angles that measure less than 90°. There are right angles that measure 90° exactly. And there are also **obtuse angles**. These are angles that measure greater than 90°. The angle below is opening toward the left because its bottom side points in that direction. That means we should measure it using the top row of numbers.

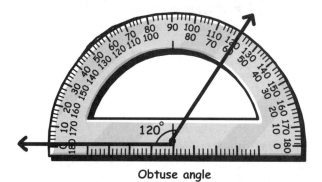

Obtuse angle

The top side of the angle crosses the number 120 in the top row, so this angle measures 120°. And since 120 is greater than 90, this qualifies as an obtuse angle. You can always tell an obtuse angle, because it will be bigger than an L shape. In other words, the sides will be even farther apart than the lines in an L.

Straight Angles

There's also such a thing as a **straight angle**. That's just an angle whose sides make a straight line. The vertex is in its usual place in the middle. If we measure a straight angle with a protractor, both of its sides will cross at 180. We'll assume that in the angle below, the right side is the bottom side. So the angle is opening to the right and it should be measured with the bottom row of numbers. And notice that the other side runs through 180 in the bottom row. The main point is that a straight angle makes a straight line and it measures 180°.

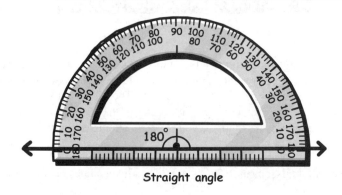

Straight angle

Practice 104

a.
(104)
Select the correct description of the angle to the right.

    A. obtuse   B. right

    C. straight   D. acute

b.
(104)
Name the angle shown by the arc in the simplest possible way.

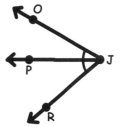

    A. $\angle J$ B. $\angle P$

    C. $\angle OPR$ D. $\angle OJR$

    E. $\angle OJP$

c.
(104)
Tell the measure of the angle on the right.

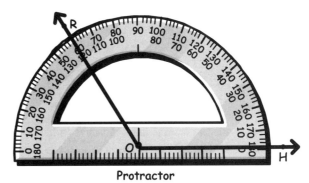

    A. 140°

    B. 120°

    C. 100°

    D. 60°

    E. 20°

Protractor

d.
(94)
Simplify $-2x^2 + (-3x^2)$ by adding the powers.

    A. $-x^2$ B. $5x^2$ C. $6x^4$

    D. 5   E. $-5x^2$

e.
(54)
Translate the word problem below into an equation; then solve.

Dorothy bought a fake crocodile clutch, which is just a small purse that you can easily hold in your hand, at a 35% discount. If the discount saved her $42, what was the clutch's original price?

Problem Set 104

Tell whether each sentence below is True or False.

1.
(104)
An angle is made up of two rays that both have the same end point.

2.
(104)
When naming an angle, the vertex letter should always be first.

Select the best possible choice to fill in the blanks below.

3.
(104)
The point where the two sides of an angle meet is called the _____.

    A. protractor   B. side   C. end point
    D. vertex   E. ray

4.
(104)
A straight angle is always _____.

    A. 45 degrees   B. less than 90 degrees   C. 90 degrees
    D. more than 180 degrees   E. 180 degrees

Answer each question below.

5.
(103)
Select the correct name for the dashed section below.

    A. $\overline{OE}$ B. $\overrightarrow{OP}$ C. $\overline{OP}$
    D. $\overleftrightarrow{OP}$ E. $\overrightarrow{PE}$

6.
(103)
Use the figure on the right to select the answer to the question below.

$\overline{SH}$ and $\overline{IO}$ _____.

    A. are parallel   B. are skew
    C. are rays   D. intersect
    E. both A and C

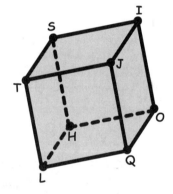

7.
(103)
Tell which two streets appear to be parallel.

    A. Columbus Blvd. and Chelsea St.
    B. 42nd St. and Broadway St.
    C. Lincoln Blvd. and Astor Ln.
    D. Union Ave. and Amsterdam Ave.
    E. Brooklyn St. and Liberty St.

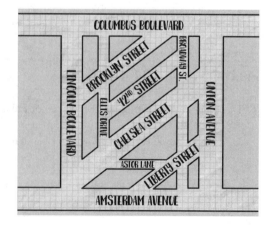

Select the correct description of each angle below.

8.
(104)

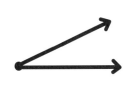

A. right
B. acute
C. obtuse
D. straight

9.
(104)

A. obtuse
B. right
C. straight
D. acute

(a) 10.
(104)

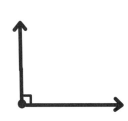

A. acute
B. obtuse
C. straight
D. right

Name each angle shown by the arc in the simplest possible way.

11.
(104)

A. ∠CDB   B. ∠B
C. ∠DBC   D. ∠CBD
E. ∠BCD

(b) 12.
(104)

A. ∠P   B. ∠QRS
C. ∠QPR   D. ∠QPS
E. ∠R

13.
(104)

A. ∠SRN   B. ∠NRS
C. ∠RNS   D. ∠RSN
E. ∠R

Tell the measure of each angle below.

14.
(104)

A. 130°
B. 120°
C. 80°
D. 50°
E. 30°

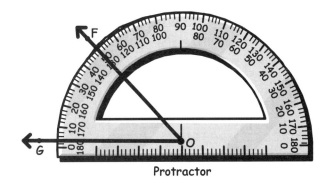

Protractor

(c) 15.
(104)

A. 180°
B. 150°
C. 140°
D. 30°
E. 10°

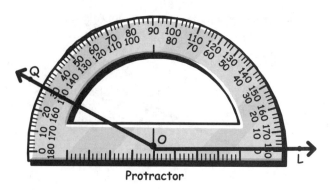

Protractor

Add or subtract each group of numbers below.

16.
(17)
$$\begin{array}{r} 364.85 \\ +729.21 \\ \hline \end{array}$$

17.
(17)
$$\begin{array}{r} 62.03 \\ -47.98 \\ \hline \end{array}$$

Simplify each expression below by adding or subtracting (as indicated) the powers.

(d) 18. $-4x^2 + (-3x^2)$
(94)

     A. $12x^4$ B. $7x^2$ C. $-7x^2$

     D. $-x^2$ E. -7

19. $11x^3 - 2x^3$
(94)

     A.   9   B. $9x^9$ C. $9x^3$

     D. $9x^6$ E. $22x^9$

Calculate each root below.

20. $\sqrt{81}$
(99)

21. $\sqrt[5]{32}$
(100)

Translate the word problem below into math; then solve.

(e) 22.   Winifred bought a bib necklace, which is just a big necklace in the shape of a dinner bib, at a 45%
(54)   discount. If the discount saved her $63, what was the necklace's original price?

482

Lesson 105—Pairs of Angles

We've been learning about angles. Now we're going to concentrate on angles two at a time. In the diagram below, notice the two angles $\angle JGK$ and $\angle KGL$. These are right next to each other. In fact, they have the same vertex (point G). And the angles even share a side. Ray GK is a side of both angles.

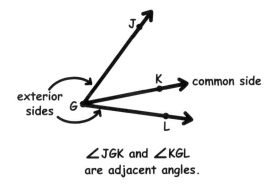

$\angle JGK$ and $\angle KGL$
are adjacent angles.

Adjacent Angles

Angles of this kind are called adjacent angles. The word adjacent just means "right next to each other." Technically, for two angles to qualify as **adjacent angles,** they have to be right next to each other, without overlapping. They have to have the same vertex and they have to share one side. That's called the common side. In our diagram, $\overrightarrow{GK}$ is the common side. The other sides—$\overrightarrow{GL}$ and $\overrightarrow{GJ}$—also have a special name. They're called exterior sides. That's just because they're on the outside or exterior of the angles.

Vertical Angles

There are other kinds of angle pairs besides adjacent angles. There are also **vertical angles**. Those are created by two intersecting lines. For instance, in the diagram below, we have two lines, $\overleftrightarrow{SR}$ and $\overleftrightarrow{QT}$. They intersect at point P. Vertical angles are always on opposite sides of the intersection point of the two lines. So here $\angle QPS$ and $\angle RPT$ are vertical angles.

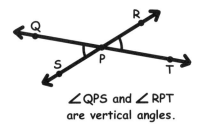

$\angle QPS$ and $\angle RPT$
are vertical angles.

Notice that vertical angles have the same vertex (point P). It's always the intersection point of the two lines. But the angles don't share a side. There's no common side, in other words, because the angles are on opposite sides of P.

Probably the most interesting thing about vertical angles is that they're always equal. If we used a protractor to measure $\angle QPS$ and $\angle RPT$, we would see that they have exactly the same measure. If $\angle QPS$ is $60°$, then $\angle RPT$ also has to be $60°$. Another way of saying that angles are equal is to say that they are **congruent**. So $\angle QPS$ and $\angle RPT$ are congruent. It's written like this: $\angle QPS \cong \angle RPT$.

There's actually another pair of vertical angles in the diagram. It's $\angle QPR$ and $\angle SPT$. They are formed by the same two intersecting lines ($\overleftrightarrow{SR}$ and $\overleftrightarrow{QT}$). They're on opposite sides of the intersection point (P). And they share a vertex (point P again). So $\angle QPR$ and $\angle SPT$ also qualify as vertical angles. That means that $\angle QPR$ and $\angle SPT$ must also have the same measure. If $\angle QPR$ equals $120°$, then $\angle SPT$ also has to equal $120°$. We could write it like this. The little m in front of the angles stands for measure.

If $m\angle QPR = 120$, then $m\angle SPT = 120$

Supplementary Angles

Another interesting thing about this diagram is that $\angle QPS$ and $\angle QPR$ add to equal $180°$. These two angles are adjacent angles with exterior sides, $\overrightarrow{PS}$ and $\overrightarrow{PR}$. But notice that $\overrightarrow{PS}$ and $\overrightarrow{PR}$ make a straight line.

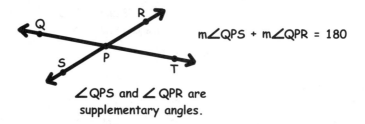

m∠QPS + m∠QPR = 180

∠QPS and ∠QPR are
supplementary angles.

That means that $\angle QPS$ and $\angle QPR$ have to add to equal $180°$. Remember, a straight angle always equals $180°$. Angles that add to equal $180°$ are called **supplementary angles**. So $\angle QPS$ and $\angle QPR$ are supplementary angles. That's another kind of angle pair that you need to know.

Supplementary angles don't always have to be adjacent (next to each other). They can be totally separated. For example, here's another pair of supplementary angles.

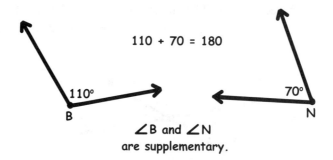

110 + 70 = 180

∠B and ∠N
are supplementary.

These angles aren't touching at all. But notice that $\angle B$ is $110°$ and $\angle N$ is $70°$. And since $110 + 70 = 180$, these angles qualify as supplementary.

Complementary Angles

There's also a special name for angles that add to equal $90°$. They're called **complementary angles**. The diagram below shows two angles, $\angle UVT$ and $\angle TVW$. These are adjacent angles because they have the same vertex (point V) and a common side ($\overrightarrow{VT}$). But notice the measures of the angles also add to $90°$ because $60 + 30 = 90$. That means $\angle UVT$ and $\angle TVW$ qualify as complementary angles.

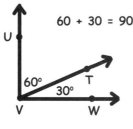

∠UVT and ∠TVW
are complementary.

Just as with supplementary angles, it's not necessary for two angles to be right next to each other in order to be complementary. As long as their measures add to 90°, the angles qualify as complementary. Here are two angles, ∠*DCE* and ∠*FGH*. Or we could just call them ∠*C* and ∠*G*. But even though they're separated, the angles are still complementary because they add to 90°.

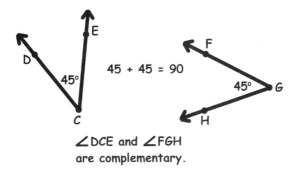

∠DCE and ∠FGH
are complementary.

Solving Angle Problems

Sometimes a problem will tell you that two angles are supplementary and then ask you to find the measure of one of the angles. Here's an example like that.

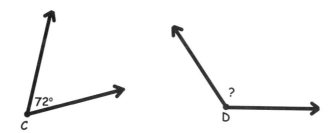

If ∠C and ∠D are supplementary and m∠C=72, what is m∠D?

One way to solve this is to set up an equation. Since ∠*C* and ∠*D* are supplementary, we know their measures have to add to 180.

$$m\angle C + m\angle D = 180$$

But the problem tells us that $m\angle C = 72$, so we can put 72 in for $m\angle C$.

$$72 + m\angle D = 180$$

Now we have an equation with an unknown, $m\angle D$. (We could replace $m\angle D$ with an x. Or we can just leave it as $m\angle D$. It really doesn't matter.)

Let's solve the equation. Since two numbers can be added in any order, we can switch the order of 72 and $m\angle D$. That will make the undoing step a little easier.

$$m\angle D + 72 = 180$$

Now to undo addition of 72, we just subtract 72 from both sides.

$$m\angle D + 72 - 72 = 180 - 72$$

That makes the left side equal just $m\angle D$.

$$m\angle D = 180 - 72$$

The last step is to do the subtraction on the right.

$$m\angle D = 108$$

So $\angle D$ equal 108°. That's an example of how to solve a problem with supplementary angles using an algebra equation. We didn't have to solve the problem with an equation. We could have just subtracted: $180 - 72 = 108$. That would have worked too.

Here's another example of a problem where you have to find a missing angle. Below $\angle R$ and $\angle T$ are complementary. If $m\angle T = 37$, what is $m\angle R$?

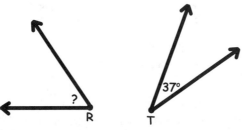

If $\angle R$ and $\angle T$ are complementary and m$\angle$T=37, what is m$\angle$R?

Since the angles are complementary, we know their measures have to add to 90. So we can set up an equation that looks like this.

$$m\angle R + m\angle T = 90$$

Since the problem tells us that $m\angle T = 37$, we can put 37 in for $m\angle T$.

$$m\angle R + 37 = 90$$

Now we just solve for $m\angle R$. We undo the addition by subtracting 37 from both sides.

$$m\angle R + 37 - 37 = 90 - 37$$

After simplifying on the left, we end up with this.

$$m\angle R = 90 - 37$$

The last step is to subtract on the right.

$$m\angle R = 53$$

So $\angle R$ is 53°.

Practice 105

a.
(105)
Use the figure on the right to find the measure of $\angle HON$.

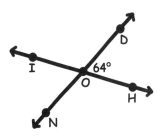

b.
(105)
$\angle F$ and $\angle G$ are supplementary. If $\angle F$ has a measure of $83°$, find the measure of $\angle G$.

c.
(105)
$\angle Q$ and $\angle R$ are complementary. If $\angle R$ has a measure of $26°$, find the measure of $\angle Q$.

d.
(78)
Solve the equation $-x-3x=-9$. Make sure your answer is fully reduced.

e.
(54)
Translate the word problem below into an equation; then solve.

The website stocked 2,200 different kinds of sneakers, but only 22 of those had no laces. What percent of the sneakers had no laces? (The answer to your equation will be in decimal form. Make sure your final answer is written as a percent.)

Problem Set 105

Tell whether each sentence below is True or False.

1.
(105)
Adjacent angles must have the same vertex, a common side, and not overlap.

2.
(105)
Vertical angles are always equal.

Select the correct description of each angle below.

3.
(104)

A. right
B. acute
C. obtuse
D. straight

4.
(104)

A. obtuse
B. right
C. acute
D. straight

Name each angle shown by the arc in the simplest possible way.

5.
(104)

A. $\angle TKM$ B. $\angle MKT$
C. $\angle TMK$ D. $\angle MTK$
E. $\angle K$

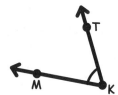

6.
(104)

A. $\angle HJP$ B. $\angle HJV$
C. $\angle J$ D. $\angle PJV$
E. $\angle H$

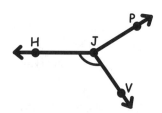

Tell the measure of each angle below.

7.
(104)

A. 5°
B. 10°
C. 20°
D. 40°
E. 160°

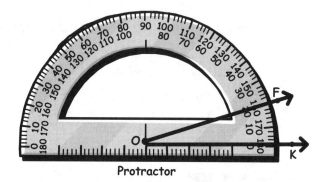

Protractor

8.
(104)

A. 170°
B. 110°
C. 70°
D. 30°
E. 10°

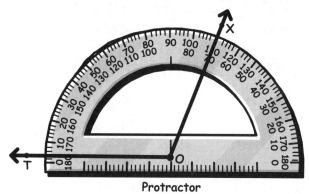

Protractor

Use the figure to find the measure of each angle below.

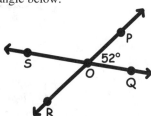

9. $\angle SOR$
(105)

10. $\angle POS$
(105)

(a) 11. $\angle QOR$
(105)

488

Answer each question below by writing and solving an equation.

(b) 12.
(105)
$\angle A$ and $\angle B$ are supplementary. If $\angle A$ has a measure of $75°$, find the measure of $\angle B$.

(c) 13.
(105)
$\angle J$ and $\angle K$ are complementary. If $\angle K$ has a measure of $19°$, find the measure of $\angle J$.

14.
(105)
$m\angle T = 45$ and $\angle T$ and $\angle W$ are complementary. Which of the following must be true?

    A. $m\angle W = 135$ B. $m\angle W = 90$ C. $\angle W \cong \angle T$

    D. The measure of $\angle W$ is twice that of $\angle T$ E. None of the above

15.
(105)
Are $\angle D$ and $\angle E$ complementary, supplementary, or neither?

16.
(105)
Are $\angle J$ and $\angle H$ complementary, supplementary, or neither?

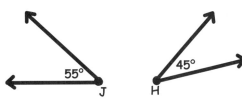

Add or subtract (as indicated) each pair of fractions below. Make sure your answers are fully reduced.

17.
(89)
$\dfrac{5}{9x} + \dfrac{1}{3x}$

    A. $\dfrac{8}{9x}$ B. $\dfrac{10}{9x}$ C. $\dfrac{5}{9x}$

    D. $\dfrac{4}{9x}$ E. $\dfrac{2}{3x}$

18.
(90)
$\dfrac{21}{30x} - \dfrac{11}{30x}$

    A. $\dfrac{10x}{3}$ B. $\dfrac{1}{3x}$ C. $\dfrac{16}{15x}$

    D. $\dfrac{15}{16x}$ E. $\dfrac{231}{30x}$

Simplify each expression below by dividing the powers.

19.
(101)
$\dfrac{x^{11}}{x^{10}}$

   A. x^{21} B. x^{110} C. $\dfrac{1}{x}$

   D. $\dfrac{1}{x^{21}}$ E. x

20.
(101)
$\dfrac{x^3}{x}$

   A. $\dfrac{1}{x^4}$ B. $\dfrac{1}{x^2}$ C. x^4

   D. x^2 E. x^3

Solve each equation below. Make sure your answer is fully reduced.

21. $7 + 3x + 4 = 20$ **(d) 22.** $-x - 2x = -7$
(75)   (78)

Translate the word problem below into an equation; then solve.

(e) 23.   There were 2,500 different kinds of yo-yos at the museum, but only 25 of them had strings that weren't
(54)   white. What percent of the yo-yos had strings that weren't white? (The answer to your equation will be
               in decimal form. Make sure your final answer is written as a percent.)

Lesson 106—Line and Angle Relationships

In the last lesson we learned about pairs of angles. Those can be formed by two intersecting lines. But in some situations, three lines will intersect. In the diagram below, we have two lines ℓ and m with a third line p intersecting them both. A line that intersects two other lines at different points is called a **transversal**. So line p is the transversal in this diagram.

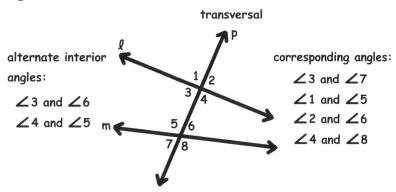

Alternate Interior Angles

The transversal has created eight different angles, which are labeled. Some of them have special names. For instance, $\angle 3$ and $\angle 6$ are called **alternate interior angles**. They're "alternate" because the angles are on opposite sides of the transversal. (Alternate is used to mean opposite here: $\angle 3$ is on the left side and $\angle 6$ is on the right side of the transversal.) The angles are "interior" because they're located inside the two other lines, ℓ and m. (Interior means inside.) There's actually more than one pair of alternate interior angles in this diagram: $\angle 4$ and $\angle 5$ are also alternate interior angles. They're on opposite sides of the transversal (p). And they're both on the inside, between lines ℓ and m.

Corresponding Angles

In the diagram above $\angle 3$ and $\angle 7$ are called corresponding angles. **Corresponding angles** are on the same side of the transversal and in "corresponding" or similar positions: $\angle 3$ is below line ℓ and $\angle 7$ is below line m. Their positions are similar in that way. There's another pair of corresponding angles on the left side of the transversal: $\angle 1$ and $\angle 5$. These qualify as corresponding because they're on the same side of the transversal and they're in corresponding (similar) positions. Specifically, $\angle 1$ is above line ℓ and $\angle 5$ is above line m. There are two more pairs of corresponding angles: $\angle 2$ and $\angle 6$, and also $\angle 4$ and $\angle 8$. Both of these pairs are on the right side of the transversal.

With Two Lines Parallel

Now let's make a change to our diagram. Let's adjust the slant of ℓ and m so that these lines are parallel. We'll keep the transversal, line p, so the points of intersection between the lines still form 8 angles.

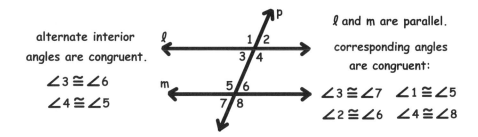

Notice that with lines ℓ and m parallel, the measures of the angles have changed. Specifically, the alternate interior angles are congruent: $\angle 3 \cong \angle 6$ and $\angle 4 \cong \angle 5$.[1] It turns out that this always happens when a transversal intersects parallel lines. Here's the formal rule: When a transversal intersects two parallel lines, alternate interior angles are congruent.

It's not just alternate interior angles that have to be congruent when lines ℓ and m are parallel. As it turns out, the corresponding angles are also congruent. Specifically, $\angle 3 \cong \angle 7$, $\angle 1 \cong \angle 5$, $\angle 2 \cong \angle 6$, and $\angle 4 \cong \angle 8$. And the general rule is that whenever a transversal intersects two parallel lines, the pairs of corresponding angles are congruent.

Now that you know these angle relationships, it's pretty easy to find a missing angle in a diagram with parallel lines and a transversal. Let's look at a slightly different diagram (below). Lines ℓ and m are still parallel. And transversal p creates 8 angles at the intersection points. But this time, we're told that the first angle is $125°$.

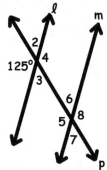

m∠5=125, m∠6=55, m∠3=55

With this one piece of information, we can find the measures of all of the other angles. For instance, since the first angle (that's $125°$) is a corresponding angle with $\angle 5$, we know that those two must have the same measure. We can conclude, then, that $\angle 5$ must also be $125°$. Also, notice that $\angle 5$ and $\angle 6$ are supplementary angles, because together they form a straight angle. If they're supplementary, then these two angles must add to equal $180°$. So $\angle 6$ must equal $180-125$ or $55°$.[2] Now that we know $\angle 6$, we can easily find $\angle 3$. That's because $\angle 6$ and $\angle 3$ are alternate interior angles. And since ℓ and m are parallel, these have to be equal. Angle 3 must also equal $55°$, then. We could continue this process and find all of the other angles, just by using the knowledge of angle pairs that we've learned in the last couple of lessons.

Practice 106

a.
(105) $\quad$ $\angle E$ and $\angle H$ are supplementary. If $\angle E$ has a measure of $156°$, find the measure of $\angle H$.

In the figure below, lines n and h are parallel. Find the measure of each angle below.

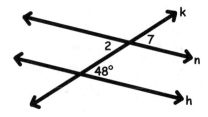

b. $\angle 2$
(106)

c. $\angle 7$
(106)

---

[1] That doesn't mean that all 4 angles are congruent. Angle 3 isn't congruent to $\angle 4$, for instance.

[2] You could also find $\angle 6$ by writing an equation and solving it.

d. Find the measure of ∠SGK in the figure below.
(105)

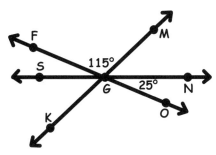

e. Translate the word problem below into an equation; then solve.
(73)

There is a number that if you add 6 to it first, and then divide that total by 4, you get 12. What's the number?

Problem Set 106

Tell whether each sentence below is True or False.

1. A line that intersects two other lines in different points is a transversal.
(106)

2. When a transversal intersects two parallel lines, alternate interior angles are complementary.
(106)

3. When a transversal intersects two parallel lines, corresponding angles are supplementary.
(106)

Answer each question below.

4. Name three line segments in the figure below.
(103)

Use the figure on the right to select the answer to the question below.

5. $\overline{QJ}$ and $\overline{RK}$ _____.
(103)

    A. intersect   B. are skew
    C. are rays   D. are parallel
    E. both C and D

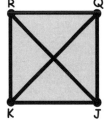

493

Select the correct description of each angle below.

6.
(104)

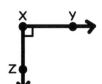

A. obtuse
B. acute
C. straight
D. right

7.
(104)

A. obtuse
B. acute
C. straight
D. right

Answer each question below by writing and solving an equation.

(a) 8. ∠*H* and ∠*D* are supplementary. If ∠*H* has a measure of 128°, find the measure of ∠*D*.
(105)

9. ∠*I* and ∠*N* are complementary. If ∠*N* has a measure of 48°, find the measure of ∠*I*.
(105)

10. $m\angle S = 90$ and ∠*S* and ∠*V* are supplementary. Which of the following must be true?
(105)

    A. ∠*S* ≅ ∠*V*   B. The measure of ∠*S* is twice that of ∠*V*.
    C. $m\angle V = 45$ D. $m\angle V = 0$
    E. None of the above

11. Are ∠*T* and ∠*U* complementary, supplementary, or neither?
(105)

In the figure below, lines *l* and *r* are parallel. Find the measure of each angle below.

(b) 12. ∠5
(106)

14. ∠1
(106)

(c) 13. ∠3
(106)

15. ∠4
(106)

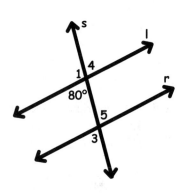

Use the figure to find the measure of each angle below.

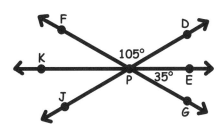

16. $\angle DPE$
(105)

(d) 17. $\angle KPJ$
(105)

Simplify each expression below.

18. $6x - x$
(78)

    A. $-7x$ B. $5 + 2x$ C. $5x$

    D. $7x$ E. $-5x$

19. $12 + 4x + 7$
(75)

    A. $4x + 19$ B. $23x$ C. $16x + 7$

    D. $4x + 5$ E. $12 + 11x$

Calculate each root below.

20. $\sqrt{49}$
(99)

21. $\sqrt[3]{8}$
(100)

Translate the word problem below into an equation; then solve.

(e) 22. There is a number that if you add 3 to it first, and then divide that total by 9, you get 14. What's the
(73)   number?

Lesson 107—Triangles

We said earlier that geometry was all about shapes. But so far we've only talked about lines and angles. That's because shapes are made up of line segments and angles. They're the building blocks. Now it's time for the actual shapes. The simplest shape in geometry is the triangle. Technically, a **triangle** is a figure (shape) with three sides and three angles.

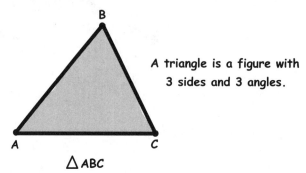

A triangle is a figure with
3 sides and 3 angles.

△ ABC

The sides of this triangle are $\overline{AB}$, $\overline{BC}$, and $\overline{AC}$. The three angles are $\angle A$, $\angle B$, and $\angle C$. As with lines, we can use the labeled points to name the triangle. We can call this triangle ABC. The symbol for a triangle is just a little triangle, so the short way to write it is like this: $\triangle ABC$. Each of the labeled points is called a vertex. So A, B, and C are all vertices of the triangle.[1]

Kinds of Triangles by Sides

There are different kinds of triangles that have special names. Notice that in $\triangle DEF$ below, $\overline{DE}$ has a length of 3 feet, $\overline{EF}$ has a length of 2 feet, and $\overline{DF}$ has a length of 7 inches. Since all three sides have different lengths this is called a scalene triangle. So a **scalene triangle** is a triangle with no equal sides.

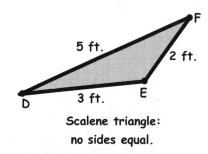

Scalene triangle:
no sides equal.

In some triangles, two of the sides will be equal. Notice in $\triangle LOM$ below, sides $\overline{LO}$ and $\overline{MO}$ both have a length of 9 inches. A triangle with at least two equal sides is called an **isosceles triangle**. Sometimes, people will put a little mark on two sides of a figure to show that they're equal. That's what the little marks below are for. They're called tick marks.

---

[1] The word "vertices" is plural for vertex.

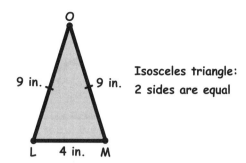

Isosceles triangle:
2 sides are equal

The next kind of triangle is one where all three of the sides are equal. It's called an **equilateral triangle**. Notice in $\triangle ABC$ below that all three of its sides have a length of 7. It could be 7 inches or 7 feet or 7 centimeters. We're not told. But since all of the sides are equal, this qualifies as an equilateral triangle.

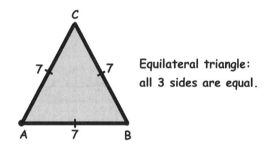

Equilateral triangle:
all 3 sides are equal.

Even if the lengths of the sides of $\triangle ABC$ had not been labeled, we still could have figured out that this triangle was equilateral because of the tick marks on the sides. Those mean that all three sides have the same length.

Kinds of Triangles by Angles

It turns out that triangles also have special names based on their angles. You know that an acute angle is an angle that's less than $90°$. Well, an **acute triangle** is a triangle where all three angles are acute—less than $90°$. In $\triangle ABC$ below, $\angle A$ is $70°$, $\angle B$ is $45°$, and $\angle C$ is $65°$. Those are all acute angles, so $\triangle ABC$ is an acute triangle.

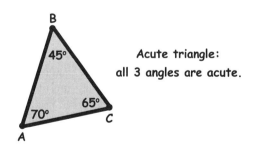

Acute triangle:
all 3 angles are acute.

Another special kind of triangle is a right triangle. Remember, a right angle is an angle that measures $90°$. Well, a **right triangle** is a triangle that has one right angle. Notice in $\triangle UVW$ below, $\angle V$ is a right angle. We know that because of the box. That's the symbol for a right angle. That means $\triangle UVW$ qualifies as a right triangle.

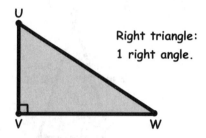

Right triangle:
1 right angle.

The last kind of triangle that's based on angles is an obtuse triangle. An obtuse angle is an angle that's greater than $90°$. As you might guess, then, an **obtuse triangle** is a triangle that has one obtuse angle. An example is $\triangle HPZ$ below. None of the angles are labeled, but it's pretty obvious that $\angle P$ is obtuse (greater than $90°$). Its sides are wider apart than an L. It's actually about $110°$. Because of $\angle P$, though, we know that $\triangle HPZ$ must be an obtuse triangle.

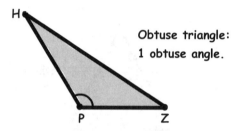

Obtuse triangle:
1 obtuse angle.

Adding Up the Angles

There's another important rule about the angles of a triangle. It turns out that the three angles of any triangle—no matter what its shape—always add to equal $180°$. Take $\triangle AJK$ below as an example. We have the measures of all 3 angles. Adding these together gives us a total of $180°$.

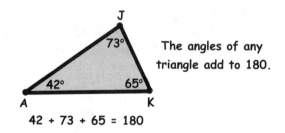

The angles of any triangle add to 180.

42 + 73 + 65 = 180

If you tried to change the measure of just one of these angles, you wouldn't be able to draw a proper triangle. The sides wouldn't fit together right. This rule about the sum of the three angles of a triangle works for any triangle, whether it's acute, right, or obtuse.

You can use the fact that the sum of the angles of a triangle equal 180 to find missing angles. In $\triangle MNP$ below, we know two out of the three angles. Specifically, we know that $\angle M$ is $30°$ and $\angle P$ is $37°$, but we don't know $\angle N$.

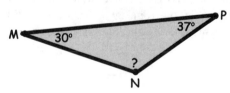

But using the fact that all three angles must add to equal 180, we can set up an equation with $\angle N$ as the unknown. According to our rule, the following must be true.

$$m\angle N + m\angle M + m\angle P = 180$$

Now we just put in 30 and 37 for $m\angle M$ and $m\angle P$.

$$m\angle N + 30 + 37 = 180$$

From here, we solve for $m\angle N$ in the usual way. First, we'll simplify the left side by adding 30 and 37.

$$m\angle N + 67 = 180$$

Next, we undo the addition by subtracting 67 from both sides.

$$m\angle N + 67 - 67 = 180 - 67$$

That makes the left side equal just $m\angle N$.

$$m\angle N = 180 - 67$$

The last step is to do the subtraction on the right.

$$m\angle N = 113$$

So $\angle N$ has to be $113°$.

Practice 107

a.
(105)
Find the measure of $\angle OMQ$ in the figure below.

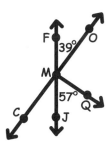

b.
(107)
Tell what kind of triangle is shown below.

A. equilateral
B. isosceles
C. scalene

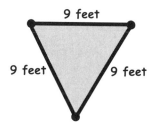

Find the missing angle in each triangle below.

c.
(107)

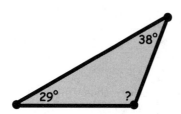

d.
(107)

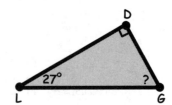

e. Translate the word problem below into an equation; then solve.
(55)

If a fighter jet is traveling at 960 miles per hour, how many hours will it take it to go 5,760 miles?

Problem Set 107

Tell whether each sentence below is True or False.

1. In a scalene triangle all three angles are less than $90°$.
(107)

2. An isosceles triangle has at least two equal sides.
(107)

3. The three angles of any triangle, no matter what it's shape, always add to $360°$.
(107)

Name each angle shown by the arc in the simplest possible way.

4.
(104)

A. ∠SGR   B. ∠R

C. ∠FGS   D. ∠SRF

E. ∠G

5.
(104)

A. ∠OJP   B. ∠O

C. ∠JOP   D. ∠J

E. ∠P

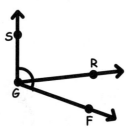

Tell the measure of each angle below.

6.
(104)

A. 180°
B. 150°
C. 140°
D. 60°
E. 40°

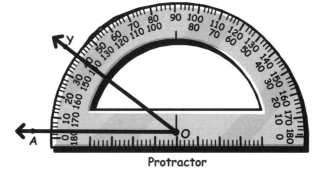

Protractor

7.
(104)

A. 0°
B. 80°
C. 90°
D. 100°
E. 180°

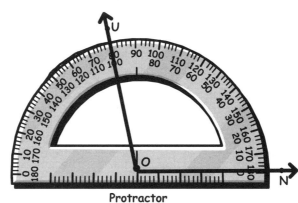

Protractor

In the figure below, lines *f* and *g* are parallel. Find the measure of each angle below.

8. ∠2
(105)

9. ∠5
(106)

10. ∠6
(106)

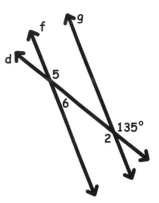

Use the figure to find the measure of each angle below.

11. ∠DFE
(105)

(a) 12. ∠BFC
(105)

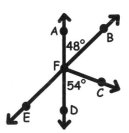

Tell the kind of each triangle below.

13.
(107)

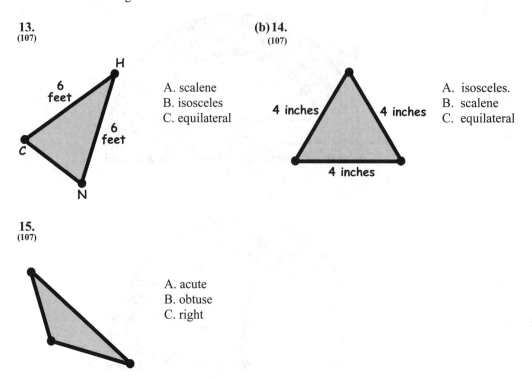

A. scalene
B. isosceles
C. equilateral

(b) 14.
(107)

A. isosceles.
B. scalene
C. equilateral

15.
(107)

A. acute
B. obtuse
C. right

Find the missing angle in each triangle below.

16.
(107)

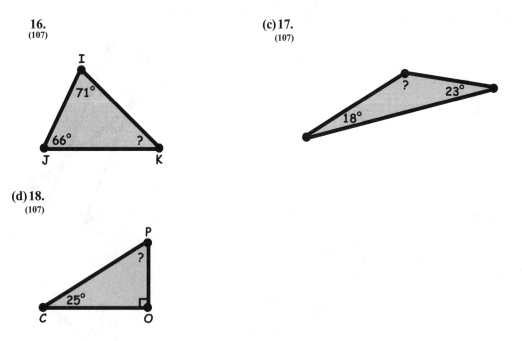

(c) 17.
(107)

(d) 18.
(107)

Translate each of the following phrases into a mathematical expression. (Don't calculate the answer.)

19.
(68)
3 and 6 multiplied first, and 29 subtracted from that total.

    A. $29 \cdot 3 - 6$ B. $3 \cdot 6 - 29$ C. $3(6 - 29)$

    D. $29 - 3(6)$ E. $6(3 - 29)$

20.
(70)
7 added to 8 first, and that total divided by 3.

    A. $\dfrac{7}{3} + 8$ B. $7 + \dfrac{3}{8}$ C. $7 + \dfrac{8}{3}$

    D. $\dfrac{3}{7 + 8}$ E. $\dfrac{7 + 8}{3}$

Simplify each expression below by multiplying the powers.

21.
(102)
$x^8 \cdot x^0$

    A. 0 B. $-x^8$ C. x^7

    D. $\dfrac{1}{x^8}$ E. x^8

22.
(96)
$(12x^3)(13x^4)$

    A. $25x^{12}$ B. $156x^7$ C. $25x^7$

    D. $156x^{81}$ E. $156x^{12}$

Translate the word problem below into an equation; then solve.

(e) 23.
(55)
If a speedboat is traveling at 130 miles per hour, how many hours will it take it to go 1,040 miles?

Lesson 108—Pythagorean Theorem

We've been studying triangles. It turns out there's a very important rule about right triangles, which you've probably heard of. To show you how this rule works, look at right triangle *ABC* below. We know it's a right triangle because ∠*B* is a right angle (notice the box). The lengths of the sides are 3, 4, and 5.

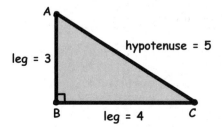

The sides of all right triangles are often given special names, which are labeled here. The longest side of any right triangle is called the **hypotenuse**. In △*ABC*, the hypotenuse is $\overline{AC}$. The two shorter sides are called **legs**. So the legs of △*ABC* are $\overline{AB}$ and $\overline{BC}$. You can always tell in a right triangle which side is the hypotenuse. The longest side will always be opposite the right angle. Notice that $\overline{AC}$ is all the way on the other side of the triangle from ∠*B*, which is the right angle. So even if the side lengths hadn't been labeled, we could have figured out that $\overline{AC}$ was the hypotenuse and that the other two sides were the legs.

The important rule about right triangles is called the Pythagorean Theorem. It's actually pretty simple. The **Pythagorean Theorem** says that for any right triangle (no matter what its specific shape) the square of the two legs added together must equal the square of the hypotenuse.

$$\text{leg}^2 + \text{leg}^2 = \text{hypotenuse}^2$$

Let's check to see if the Pythagorean Theorem works for △*ABC*. All we have to do is put the side lengths into the equation. The legs of the triangle have lengths of 3 and 4, so we should put those into the left side. The hypotenuse has a length of 5, so it should go in the right side.

$$3^2 + 4^2 = 5^2$$

Now simplifying both sides gives us this.

$$9 + 16 = 5^2$$

$$25 = 5^2$$

$$25 = 25$$

It works. When we square the legs and add those together, that equals the square of the hypotenuse. Even more important, the Pythagorean Theorem will work for *any* right triangle. But it does have to be a right triangle. The theorem won't work for a triangle that doesn't have a right angle.

Finding a Missing Side

The Pythagorean Theorem can be used to find a missing side length of a right triangle. Take the right triangle *DEF* below. We know this is a right triangle because ∠*E* is a right angle. That means the Pythagorean Theorem applies.

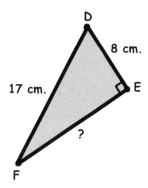

We know that $\overline{DF}$ is the hypotenuse since it's opposite the right angle ($\angle E$). The length of the hypotenuse is 17 centimeters. We're also given the length of the shorter leg, $\overline{DE}$, which is 8 centimeters. We can use the Pythagorean Theorem to find the length of the long leg, $\overline{EF}$. Here's the equation for the theorem again.

$$\text{leg}^2 + \text{leg}^2 = \text{hypotenuse}^2$$

Now let's put in 8 for one of the legs, because $\overline{DE}$ equals 8. And we'll put in 17 for the hypotenuse. That's the length of $\overline{DF}$.

$$\text{leg}^2 + 8^2 = 17^2$$

That leaves just one unknown, the other leg. We can just use x to stand for the unknown, if we want. So x = side EF.

$$x^2 + 8^2 = 17^2$$

Now let's solve this. First, we should calculate the value of the squares.

$$x^2 + 64 = 289$$

From here we just undo the operations. There are actually two operations done to x. It's raised to the second power first, and then 64 is added to that total second. We should reverse that order, which means the addition should be undone first. So we subtract 64 from both sides.

$$x^2 + 64 - 64 = 289 - 64$$

Now we simplify the left and right sides.

$$x^2 = 225$$

The last step is to undo the square. We haven't done this before, but it's actually pretty easy. Since squares and square roots are inverse operations, we can make the left side equal x by taking the square root of x^2. But we don't want to violate the Golden Rule of Algebra, so we have to take the square root of the right side also.

$$\sqrt{x^2} = \sqrt{225}$$

The square root undoes the square and that leaves just x on the left.

$$x = \sqrt{225}$$

The last step is to figure out the square root of 225. That's just the number that when you square it equals 225. The answer turns out to be 15 (since $15 \cdot 15 = 225$).

$$x = 15$$

That means the missing side, $\overline{EF}$, must have a length of 15 centimeters.

With a Calculator

Sometimes when finding a missing side of a right triangle, you have to use a calculator. Let's go through an example like that. Below is a diagram of right triangle *FGH*. The right angle is $\angle G$, which means that $\overline{FH}$ is the hypotenuse (it's opposite the right angle). The hypotenuse has a length of 16 feet.

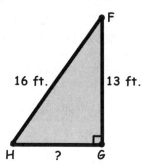

$\overline{FG}$ and $\overline{GH}$ are the legs. And we're given that $\overline{FG}$ is 13 feet long. The missing side is $\overline{GH}$. But we can find it with the Pythagorean Theorem. Here's the equation for the theorem.

$$\text{leg}^2 + \text{leg}^2 = \text{hypotenuse}^2$$

We're allowed to use this equation since ΔFGH is a right triangle. The first step is to put in 16 for the hypotenuse and 13 for one of the legs.

$$\text{leg}^2 + 13^2 = 16^2$$

The other leg, $\overline{GH}$, is unknown. We'll represent it with an *x*.

$$x^2 + 13^2 = 16^2$$

Now we just solve the equation. First, we need to simplify the squares.

$$x^2 + 169 = 256$$

Next, we undo the addition by subtracting 169 from both sides.

$$x^2 + 169 - 169 = 256 - 169$$

Simplifying on both sides gives us this.

$$x^2 = 87$$

The next step is to take the square root of both sides to undo the square.

$$\sqrt{x^2} = \sqrt{87}$$

On the left that gives us just x.

$$x = \sqrt{87}$$

But what's $\sqrt{87}$? This is pretty tough. It has to be less than 10, because 10^2 is 100, which is too big. But it has to be greater than 9, because $9^2 = 81$, which is too low. That means the answer is somewhere between 9 and 10, so it's not a whole number. When a square root doesn't equal a whole number, it's best to use a calculator and get a decimal answer. The decimal won't be the exact answer. But if you take it out to enough decimal places, your answer will be close enough.

To punch a square root into your calculator, first find the square root key. It should look something like this: $\boxed{\sqrt{x}}$. To make sure you're punching it in correctly, you may have to look at the instruction manual. Usually, the instructions will tell you to punch in 87 (whatever number you're taking the square root of) first and then press the square root key. Taken out to quite a few decimal places, $\sqrt{87}$ comes out to 9.327379053. Even this isn't exact. There are even more digits that a typical calculator wouldn't have room to show. As far as our problem is concerned, we don't need much accuracy, so we'll round the answer to tenths. The length of side $\overline{GH}$ in our right triangle, then, is about 9.3 feet. The main point is that when the answer to a square root doesn't come out to be a whole number, you should estimate it with a calculator.

Practice 108

a.
(106) In the figure below, lines k and s are parallel. Find the measure of $\angle KCF$ below.

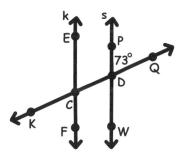

Use the Pythagorean Theorem to find the missing side of each right triangle below. Estimate with a calculator (to one decimal place) any answers that don't simplify to a whole number.

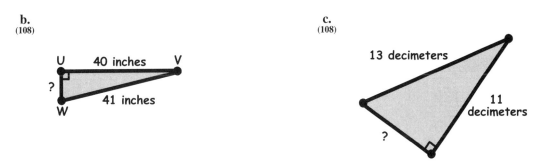

b.
(108)

c.
(108)

507

d. Multiply the fractions $\dfrac{9}{5x^3} \cdot \dfrac{15x^7}{27}$. (Make sure your answer is fully reduced.)
(98)

A. $\dfrac{x^4}{9}$

B. x^{10}

C. $9x^4$

D. $\dfrac{x^4}{3}$

E. x^4

e. Translate the word problem below into an equation; then solve.
(54)

Matthew wants to buy a golf club drink dispenser for $31.25 less than the normal price. If the drink dispenser normally costs $125, by what percent is it being discounted? (Don't forget to convert your answer to a percent.)

Problem Set 108

Tell whether each sentence below is True or False.

1. The longest side of any right triangle is always opposite the right angle.
(108)

2. According to the Pythagorean Theorem, the square of the two legs of a right triangle added together
(108) always has to equal the square of the hypotenuse.

In the figure below, lines d and g are parallel. Find the measure of each angle below.

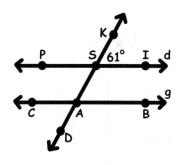

3. $\angle KSP$
(105)

4. $\angle SAB$
(106)

(a) 5. $\angle CAD$
(106)

Answer each question below by writing and solving an equation.

6. $\angle G$ and $\angle B$ are supplementary. If $\angle B$ has a measure of $143°$, find the measure of $\angle G$.
(105)

7. Are $\angle N$ and $\angle R$ complementary, supplementary, or neither?
(105)

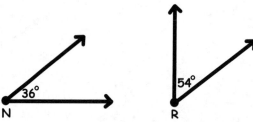

Tell the kind of each triangle below.

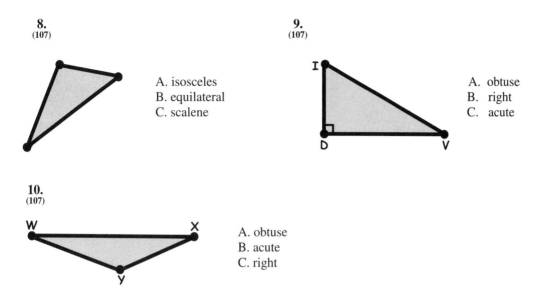

8.
(107)

A. isosceles
B. equilateral
C. scalene

9.
(107)

A. obtuse
B. right
C. acute

10.
(107)

A. obtuse
B. acute
C. right

Find the missing angle in each triangle below.

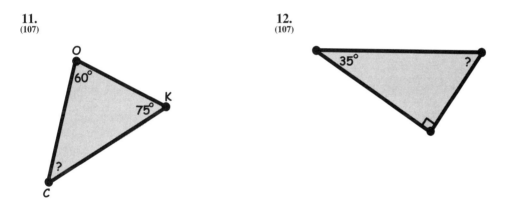

11.
(107)

12.
(107)

Use the Pythagorean Theorem to find the missing side of each right triangle below. Estimate with a calculator (to one decimal place) any answers that don't simplify to a whole number.

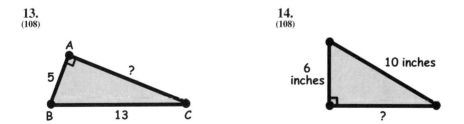

13.
(108)

14.
(108)

509

(b) 15.
(108)

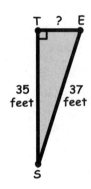

(c) 16.
(108)

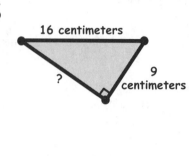

Multiply or divide (as indicated) each pair of fractions below. Make sure your answers are fully reduced.

17.
(88)
$$\frac{4x}{3x} \div \frac{2x}{9}$$

    A. $\dfrac{8x}{27}$ B. $\dfrac{6}{x}$ C. $\dfrac{3}{2x}$

    D. $\dfrac{1}{6x}$ E. $\dfrac{5}{x}$

(d) 18.
(98)
$$\frac{12}{13x^4} \cdot \frac{26x^9}{24}$$

    A. x^{13} B. $\dfrac{x^5}{2}$ C. $\dfrac{x^5}{4}$

    D. x^5 E. $4x^5$

Simplify each expression below by adding or subtracting (as indicated) the powers.

19.
(94)
$$-9x^4 - 2x^4$$

    A. $-11x^8$ B. -7 C. $-11x^4$
    D. $-7x^4$ E. -11

20.
(94)
$$13x^5 + 6x^5$$

    A. $19x^5$ B. $7x^{10}$ C. $19x^{10}$
    D. $7x^5$ E. 19

Calculate the value of each expression below.

21.
(100)
$\sqrt[4]{5^4}$

22.
(100)
$(\sqrt{16})^2$

Translate the word problem below into an equation; then solve.

(e) 23.
(54)
Kevin wants to buy a "no fetch" putting mat for $114.30 less than the normal price. If the putting mat normally costs $254, by what percent is it being discounted? (Don't forget to convert your answer to a percent.)

Lesson 109—Quadrilaterals

We've been studying about triangles, which have three sides. But geometry also has figures with four sides. They're called **quadrilaterals**. "Quad" means four. An example is quadrilateral *ABCD*, which is shown below. Notice it has four sides and also four angles. The points *A*, *B*, *C*, and *D* are the vertices of the quadrilateral.

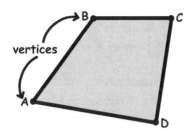

A quadrilateral has 4 sides
and 4 angles.

Trapezoids

Just as there are special kinds of triangles, there are also special kinds of quadrilaterals. The first kind of quadrilateral is called a trapezoid. The figure below is trapezoid *JKLM*. It has two sides that are parallel: $\overline{KL}$ and $\overline{JM}$. They're on opposite sides of the figure.

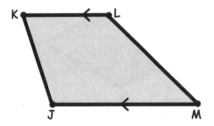

A trapezoid is a quadrilateral
with exactly 1 pair of parallel sides.

The little arrows on $\overline{KL}$ and $\overline{JM}$ are the way we show that two lines (segments) are parallel. Technically, a **trapezoid** is a quadrilateral that has exactly one pair of opposite sides parallel. The other sides, $\overline{KJ}$ and $\overline{LM}$, are *not* parallel. If they were, the figure wouldn't be a trapezoid.

Parallelograms

Another special quadrilateral besides the trapezoid is a parallelogram. The diagram below shows parallelogram *RSTU*. What makes a parallelogram special is that *both* pairs of opposite sides are parallel: $\overline{RU}$ and $\overline{ST}$ are parallel and so are $\overline{RS}$ and $\overline{UT}$.

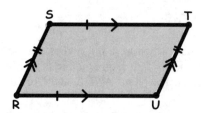

A parallelogram is a quadrilateral
with 2 pairs of parallel sides.

Notice that the top and bottom sides have a single arrow, and the left and right sides have a double arrow. The double arrows show that $\overline{RS}$ and $\overline{UT}$ are parallel to each other, but they're not parallel to $\overline{RU}$ and $\overline{ST}$, since those each have just one arrow. But the main point is that a **parallelogram** is a quadrilateral with two pairs of opposite sides parallel. Even though it's not part of the definition, the opposite sides of a parallelogram are also equal. So $RU = ST$ and $RS = UT$. That's what the tick marks show. And notice that $\overline{RU}$ and $\overline{ST}$ have a single mark to show that they're equal. But $\overline{RS}$ and $\overline{UT}$ have two tick marks. That shows they're equal to each other but not necessarily to $\overline{RU}$ and $\overline{ST}$.

Another special kind of quadrilateral is called a rhombus. The diagram below shows rhombus *STWV*. It's a quadrilateral, because it has four sides. What makes it special, though, is that all four of those sides are equal. (You can see that from the tick marks.)

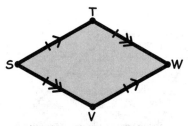

A rhombus is a parallelogram
with 4 equal sides.

It turns out that the only way to make all the sides equal is for the opposite sides to also be parallel. (The arrows show that.) That means a rhombus is also a special kind of parallelogram. Technically, then, a **rhombus** is a parallelogram with four equal sides. Just because the four sides of a rhombus are equal doesn't mean that the angles are necessarily equal. They're not. In the rhombus above, it's pretty obvious that the angles are different. For instance, $\angle T$ is quite a bit bigger than $\angle S$. One good way to recognize a rhombus is that it's shaped like a diamond. A diamond has all four sides equal. But there are fat diamonds and skinny ones because the angles can be of different sizes.

Rectangles and Squares

There are two more special quadrilaterals that are extremely common. They're the rectangle and the square. Below you can see rectangle *ABCD* and square *MNOP*. A rectangle is a quadrilateral where all four of its angles are right angles. Notice angles *A*, *B*, *C*, and *D* are all right angles. The opposite sides of a rectangle are also parallel and equal. That means a rectangle also qualifies as a parallelogram. So the technical definition of a **rectangle** is a parallelogram with four right angles. The basic difference between a plain parallelogram and a rectangle, then, is the angles. The rectangle's four right angles cause it to stand up straight. A plain parallelogram looks tilted.

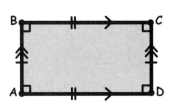

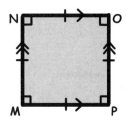

A rectangle is a parallelogram
with 4 right angles.

A square is a parallelogram with
4 equal sides and 4 right angles.

What about a square? A square actually has four right angles and all four equal sides. It's opposite sides are parallel, and, of course, they're equal since all the sides are equal. That means a square is a special kind of parallelogram (and a special kind of rhombus). The technical definition of a **square** is a parallelogram with four equal sides and four right angles.

How Do They Relate?

How do all these different kinds of quadrilaterals relate to one another? First, there's a plain quadrilateral. Anything with four sides qualifies as a plain quadrilateral. Every figure we've talked about in this lesson is a quadrilateral. One special kind of quadrilateral is a trapezoid. In order for a quadrilateral to qualify as a trapezoid, it has to have just one pair of opposite sides parallel. Another special kind of quadrilateral is a parallelogram, which has two pairs of opposite sides parallel. The opposite sides of a parallelogram are also equal.

All the other quadrilaterals we talked about are special kinds of parallelograms. There's a rectangle, which is a parallelogram with four right angles. Not only are all the angles equal, but they're all 90°. The opposite sides of a rectangle are also both parallel and equal. But that's because a rectangle is just a special kind of parallelogram. The next kind of special parallelogram is a rhombus. A rhombus has four equal sides. But since a rhombus is also a parallelogram, the opposite sides are parallel as well. The last special parallelogram is a square. A square actually qualifies as a special kind of rectangle and a special kind of rhombus. A square has four right angles (a requirement of a rectangle). And it also has all four equal sides (a requirement of a rhombus). So a square qualifies as all the other special kinds of quadrilaterals except a trapezoid. The diagram below shows the relationships among all of the different quadrilaterals in this lesson.

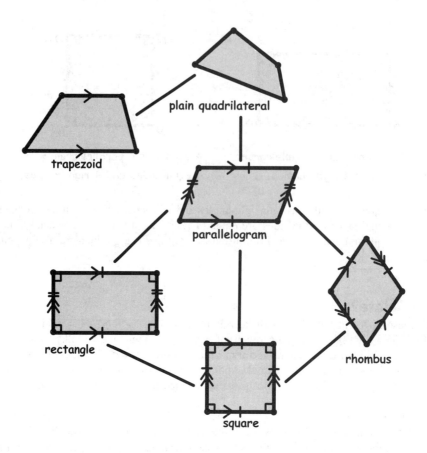

Practice 109

Use the Pythagorean Theorem to find the missing side of each right triangle below. Estimate with a calculator (to one decimal place) any answers that don't simplify to a whole number.

a.
(108)

b.
(108)

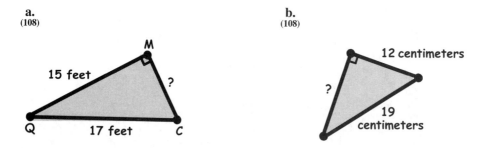

Tell the kind of each quadrilateral below.

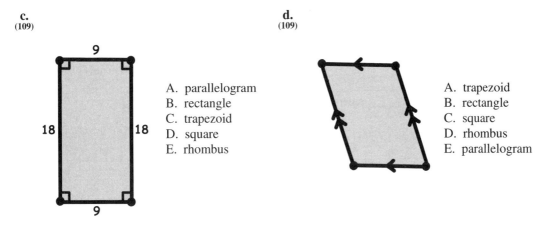

c.
(109)

9

18   18

9

A. parallelogram
B. rectangle
C. trapezoid
D. square
E. rhombus

d.
(109)

A. trapezoid
B. rectangle
C. square
D. rhombus
E. parallelogram

e.
(79)
Translate the word problem below into an equation; then solve.

Renee can make 7 marionettes per hour and Agatha can make 9 per hour. Working together, how many hours will it take them to make 48 marionettes?

Problem Set 109

Tell whether each sentence below is True or False.

1.
(109)
Figures with four sides are called quadrupeds.

2.
(109)
A trapezoid is a quadrilateral with exactly one pair of opposite sides parallel.

Complete each sentence below with the best of the choices given.

3.
(109)
A(n) _____ is a quadrilateral with both pairs of opposite sides parallel.

    A. acute triangle   B. triangle   C. parallelogram
    D. trapezoid   E. right triangle

4.
(109)
A _____ is a parallelogram with four equal sides.

    A. parallelogram   B. rectangle   C. trapezoid
    D. right triangle   E. rhombus

5.
(109)
A _____ is a parallelogram with four right angles.

    A. rhombus   B. parallelogram   C. right triangle
    D. rectangle   E. trapezoid

6.
(109)
A parallelogram is _____ a quadrilateral.

    A. sometimes   B. always   C. never

7. A square is _____ a rhombus.
(109)

    A. sometimes   B. always   C. never

8. A trapezoid is _____ a parallelogram.
(109)

    A. sometimes   B. always   C. never

9. A parallelogram is _____ a rectangle.
(109)

    A. sometimes   B. always   C. never

Find the measure of the missing angle in each figure below.

10.
(105)

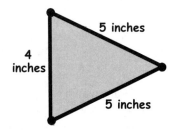

11. In the figure below, lines *r* and
(106)   *s* are parallel.

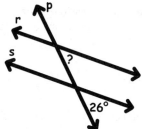

Tell the kind of each triangle below.

12.
(107)

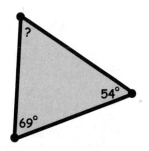

    A. scalene
    B. equilateral
    C. isosceles

13.
(107)

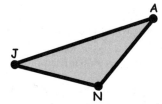

    A. right
    B. obtuse
    C. acute

Find the missing angle in each triangle below.

14.
(107)

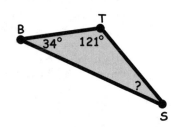

15.
(107)

516

Use the Pythagorean Theorem to find the missing side of each right triangle below. Estimate with a calculator (to one decimal place) any answers that don't simplify to a whole number.

16.
(108)

(a) 17.
(108)

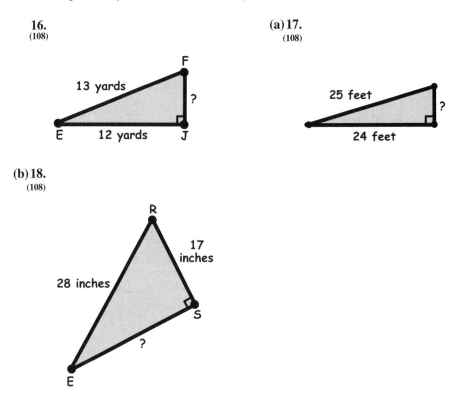

(b) 18.
(108)

Tell the kind of each quadrilateral below.

(c) 19.
(109)

A. trapezoid
B. parallelogram
C. rectangle
D. square
E. rhombus

20.
(109)

A. rectangle
B. square
C. trapezoid
D. rhombus
E. parallelogram

21.
(109)

A. square
B. rhombus
C. trapezoid
D. rectangle
E. parallelogram

(d) 22.
(109)

A. rhombus
B. trapezoid
C. square
D. parallelogram
E. rectangle

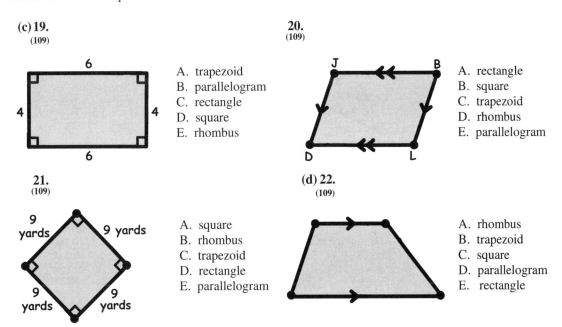

Translate the word problem below into an equation; then solve.

(e) 23. Bridget can ice 17 cupcakes per hour and Pattie can ice 19 per hour. How many hours will it take them
(79)   to ice 180 cupcakes?

Lesson 110—Polygons

Triangles, quadrilaterals and even more complicate figures (with additional sides) are all called polygons. Technically, **a polygon** is a simple, closed figure formed by three or more line segments. Triangles and quadrilaterals both have sides that are line segments. So they're polygons. But here's a figure that does not qualify as a polygon.

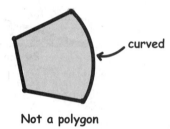

curved

Not a polygon

The problem with this figure is that the right side is curved. It isn't a line segment, so the figure can't be a polygon. All the sides of a polygon must be straight line segments. Here's another figure that's not a polygon.

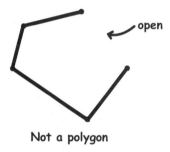

open

Not a polygon

What disqualifies this one is that one of the sides is open. The definition of a polygon is a simple, *closed* figure. There can't be any openings, in other words. Here's another figure that doesn't qualify as a polygon.

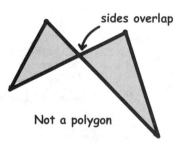

sides overlap

Not a polygon

This has two sides that overlap. A polygon has to be a *simple* figure. That means no overlaps allowed.

Here's an example of a figure that *does* qualify as a polygon, but people often mistakenly think it shouldn't.

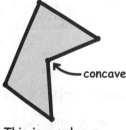

concave

This is a polygon.

518

What's unusual about this figure is that the bottom side is caved in. The technical word for "caved in" is concave. The concave side makes some people think that this shouldn't qualify as a polygon. But polygons are allowed to have concave sides. So this is a polygon. The more typical polygons have convex sides, which just means that the sides push outward instead of caving inward.

Pentagons

Triangles are three-sided polygons and quadrilaterals are four-sided polygons. What about polygons with five sides? Those are called **pentagons**. And here are a couple of examples.

Pentagons have 5 sides.

A six-sided polygon is called a **hexagon**. And a seven-sided polygon is called a **heptagon**.

A hexagon has 6 sides.   A heptagon has 7 sides.

There's also a special name for an eight-sided polygon. It's called an **octagon**.

A octagon has 8 sides.

There are even names for polygons with than eight sides, but they aren't used as often. So we won't learn about those.

Regular Polygons

There's one last thing about polygons that we need to discuss. I've been drawing polygons with sides of different lengths. But there are polygons where all of the sides have the same length. They're called regular polygons. The technical definition of **a regular polygon** is a polygon with all sides equal and all angles equal. To give you some examples, the figure below on the left is a regular hexagon. All six of its sides have exactly the same length. The tick marks show that. In fact, if you measured the six angles with a protractor, they would all be equal as well. Notice that each angle is marked with a single arc. The arcs indicate that all of the angles are equal. When used this way, the arcs are like tick marks. The figure on the right is a regular octagon. It has six sides, and they're all exactly the same length. The angles are all equal as well. If this shape looks familiar, it's because a regular octagon is the same shape as a stop sign.

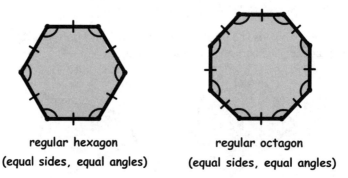

regular hexagon
(equal sides, equal angles)

regular octagon
(equal sides, equal angles)

Even figures with fewer sides can be regular polygons. For example, a "regular triangle" is a triangle with all three sides equal. But that's just an equilateral triangle. So a regular polygon with three sides and an equilateral triangle are the same thing. Also, since it's a regular polygon, an equilateral triangle must also have three equal angles. (see below left) A regular polygon with four sides is a square. (see below right) And, of course, a square has four equal sides and four equal angles (all right angles). So triangles and quadrilaterals also have regular polygons—very well known ones.

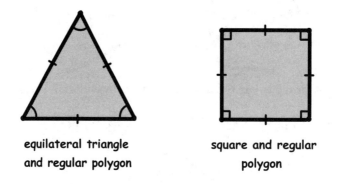

equilateral triangle
and regular polygon

square and regular
polygon

Practice 110

a. Find the missing angle in the figure below.
(107)

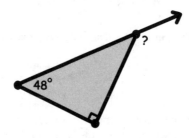

b.
(108) Use the Pythagorean Theorem to find the missing side of the right triangle below. Use a calculator to estimate your answer to one decimal place.

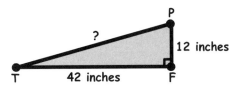

Identify each polygon below.

c.
(110)

A. regular heptagon
B. hexagon
C. regular octagon
D. pentagon
E. quadrilateral

d.
(110)

A. hexagon
B. quadrilateral
C. octagon
D. regular pentagon
E. regular heptagon

e.
(80) Translate the word problem below into an equation; then solve.

Tractor #1 and tractor #2 are headed straight toward each other. Tractor #1 is traveling at 25 feet per second, and tractor #2 is traveling at 30 feet per second. If the two tractors are 220 feet apart, how many seconds will it be before they meet?

Problem Set 110

Tell whether each sentence below is True or False.

1.
(110) A polygon is a simple, closed figure formed by 3 or more line segments.

2.
(110) A regular polygon is a polygon where all the sides are equal and all the angles are equal.

3.
(110) A rhombus is a regular polygon.

Complete each sentence below with the best of the choices given.

4.
(110) A _____ is a polygon with five sides.

A. pentagon   B. hexagon   C. octagon
D. heptagon   E. quadrilateral

5.
(110) A _____ is a polygon with seven sides.

A. quadrilateral   B. pentagon   C. heptagon
D. hexagon   E. octagon

6.
(110)
A _____ is a polygon with eight sides.

    A. heptagon   B. octagon   C. hexagon
    D. quadrilateral   E. pentagon

Select the correct description of each angle below.

7.
(104)

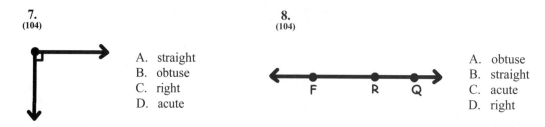

A. straight
B. obtuse
C. right
D. acute

8.
(104)

A. obtuse
B. straight
C. acute
D. right

Name each angle shown by the arc in the simplest possible way.

9.
(104)

    A. $\angle M$ B. $\angle K$
    C. $\angle XMK$ D. $\angle X$
    E. $\angle KMX$

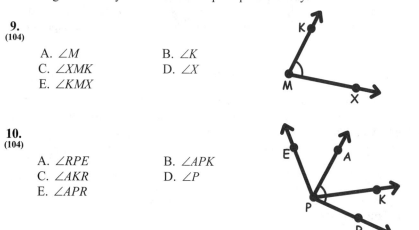

10.
(104)

    A. $\angle RPE$ B. $\angle APK$
    C. $\angle AKR$ D. $\angle P$
    E. $\angle APR$

Find the missing angle in each figure below.

11.
(107)

(a) 12.
(107)

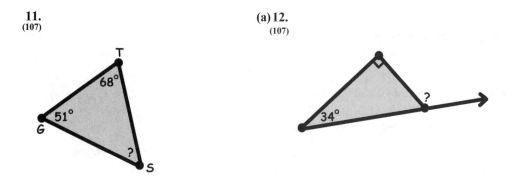

Use the Pythagorean Theorem to find the missing side of each right triangle below. Estimate with a calculator (to one decimal place) any answers that don't simplify to a whole number.

13.
(108)

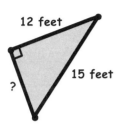

12 feet
15 feet
?

(b) 14.
(108)

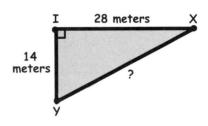

I   28 meters   X
14 meters
?
Y

Identify each polygon below.

15.
(110)

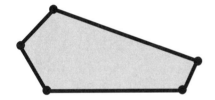

A. quadrilateral
B. pentagon
C. regular octagon
D. regular heptagon
E. hexagon

(c) 16.
(110)

A. regular heptagon
B. pentagon
C. quadrilateral
D. regular hexagon
E. octagon

(d) 17.
(110)

A. regular octagon
B. hexagon
C. regular pentagon
D. heptagon
E. quadrilateral

Simplify each expression below by dividing the powers.

18.
(97) $\dfrac{x^9}{x^3}$

    A. 6   B. $\dfrac{1}{x^6}$ C. x^{12}

    D. x^{27} E. x^6

19.
(102)

$$\frac{9^{12}}{9^{12}}$$

A. $\dfrac{1}{12}$ B. 1 C. 0

D. 9^{24} E. 9

Solve each equation below.

20. $11(x-3) = 44$
(72)

21. $9x + 5x = -28$
(76)

Translate the word problem below into an equation; then solve.

(e) 22. Robot ball #1 and robot ball #2 are headed straight toward each other. Robot ball #1 is traveling at 35
(80) feet per second, and Robot ball #2 is traveling at 40 feet per second. If the two balls are 225 feet apart, how many seconds will it be before they meet?

CHAPTER 14:
MORE ON GEOMETRY

Lesson 111—Congruent Figures

In the last lesson, we learned about a lot of different kinds of polygons. Remember, polygons are geometry figures with straight sides. In geometry, we often compare two polygons. For example, look at the two quadrilaterals below. Since they're exactly the same size and exactly the same shape, they're called **congruent figures**.

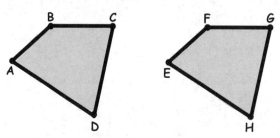

Congruent figures are the exact
same size and shape.

So we say that quadrilateral *ABCD* is congruent to quadrilateral *EFGH*. And it's written like this. (The congruent symbol is the same one we use for angles.)

Quadrilateral *ABCD* ≅ Quadrilateral *EFGH*

Corresponding Sides and Angles

Sometimes it's hard to tell if two figures are actually congruent, because one of them will be turned a different way. For instance, what if our quadrilaterals had been drawn like this?

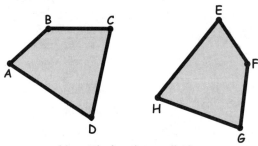

Now it's hard to tell if
these are congruent.

Now it's hard to tell if these two figures are the exact same size and shape. (They still are.) You can't always tell just by looking whether two figures are congruent. Fortunately, there's another way to do it. When two figures are congruent, their corresponding sides must be equal and their corresponding angles must be equal. **Corresponding sides** just means matching sides—that they're in the same position in both figures. For quadrilateral *ABCD* and quadrilateral *EFGH*, side *AB* matches up with side *EF*. They're in the same position in both quadrilaterals. (It's easy to see that in the first diagram.) And sides *BC* and *FG* are also corresponding sides. And so are other *CD* and *GH*, and finally *AD* and *EH*. But when two figures are congruent, each of their corresponding sides must be equal.

$$AB = EF \qquad BC = FG \qquad CD = GH \qquad AD = EH$$

The same thing is true of the **corresponding angles**—those are just pairs of angles that are in the same position. For *ABCD* and *EFGH*, the corresponding angle pairs are ∠*A* and ∠*E*, ∠*B* and ∠*F*, ∠*C* and ∠*G*, ∠*D* and ∠*H*. And when the figures are congruent, the measures of each of these pairs must be equal.

$$m\angle A = m\angle E \qquad m\angle B = m\angle F \qquad m\angle C = m\angle G \qquad m\angle D = m\angle H$$

Here's how we can tell, then, that two figures are congruent without relying on eyesight alone. We can just compare the corresponding sides and the corresponding angles. If all those pairs are the same, then we know the figures have to be congruent.

If we already know that two figures are congruent, there's an easy way to tell which sides and angles match up. The first quadrilateral above was named *ABCD* and the second one was named *EFGH*. The letters could have been in a different order. It could have been *BDCA* and *HGEF* or some other combination. We put the letters in this order deliberately because it showed how the sides and angles matched up. The *A* is first and the *E* is first. That means $\angle A$ and $\angle E$ are corresponding angles and if the quadrilaterals are congruent, $m\angle A = m\angle E$. The letters *B* and *F* are listed second. That means these are also corresponding angles. And if the quadrilaterals are congruent, then $m\angle B = m\angle F$. It works the same way for the other letters. Angle *C* and $\angle G$ are corresponding angles because their letters are listed in the same position. And so are $\angle D$ and $\angle H$. It follows that if the quadrilaterals are congruent, $m\angle C = m\angle G$ and $m\angle D = m\angle H$. The main point is that the order of the letters tells us which angles are corresponding.

The letters in the names of the figures also tell us which *sides* are corresponding. Once again, the first two letters of quadrilateral *ABCD* are *A* and *B*. And the first two letters of quadrilateral *EFGH* are *E* and *F*. That tells us that sides *AB* and *EF* must be corresponding sides. And if the quadrilaterals are congruent, then *AB = EF* . It works the same way for the other letters. Moving one letter down in quadrilateral *ABCD* takes us to the letters *B* and *C*. Moving one letter down in *EFGH* takes us to the letters *F* and *G*. From that we know that *BC* and *FG* are corresponding sides. And if the quadrilaterals are congruent, *BC = FG*. Moving down another letter at a time in both, we can conclude that *CD* and *GH* are corresponding sides. And so are *AD* and *EH*. That means if the quadrilaterals are congruent, then *CD = GH* and *AD = EH* . The main point is that the letters in the names of two figures tell how their angles and sides match up. When the figures are congruent, that makes it easy to tell which sides and which angles are equal. Of course, if the figures aren't congruent, then the corresponding sides and angles won't all be equal.

Finding Missing Sides and Angles

Now let's look at two congruent triangles. The diagram below says that $\triangle MNP$ is congruent to $\triangle RST$. It also tells us that *MN* has a length of 4 inches and $\angle M$ is $58°$. We're supposed to find *RS* and $\angle R$ in the second triangle.

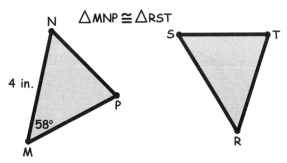

Find RS and ∠R.

Just by looking at the diagram, it's hard to tell how the angles and sides match up; the triangles aren't turned the same way. But we can use the order of the letters. The name of the first triangle is *MNP* and the name of the second is *RST*. Notice *M* is listed first and so is *R*. Also, *M* and *N* are the first two letters listed in $\triangle MNP$ and *R* and *S* are the first two letters listed in $\triangle RST$.

That means $\angle M$ and $\angle R$ are corresponding angles, and sides MN and RS are corresponding sides. And since the triangles are congruent, we can conclude that $m\angle M = m\angle R$ and $MN = RS$. That gives us the information we need to answer the question. The diagram tells us that $\angle M$ is 58°, so we know that $\angle R$ must also be 58°. And since MN is 4 inches, RS must also be 4 inches.

$$m\angle R = 58 \qquad\qquad\qquad RS = 4$$

It didn't really matter that the triangles were turned differently. In fact, we could have found $\angle R$ and RS without even looking at the diagram. We only needed to know the order of the letters and that the triangles were congruent. That's how you can find missing sides and angles using the concept of congruent figures. When two figures are congruent—they have the exact size and shape—you know automatically that all their corresponding (matching) sides and corresponding (matching) angles have to be equal.

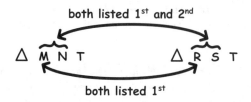

You may be wondering whether congruent figures have any use in the real world. Actually, they do. Just to take one fun example, what if you were running a cookie factory that produced thousands of cookies? You would probably want all the cookies to be the same size because otherwise somebody might feel cheated if he got a smaller cookie than someone else. To avoid that problem you would have to make sure that all the cookies were congruent—the exact same size and shape. You're factory would have to have some way to measure them to make sure. That's just one real world example involving congruent figures.

Practice 111

a.
(107) Find the missing angle in the figure below.

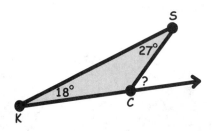

Answer each question below given that Quadrilateral $SEIL \cong$ Quadrilateral $GJFV$.

b. What is the measure of $\angle J$?
(111)

c. What is the measure of $\angle I$?
(111)

d. What is the measure of side LI?
(111)

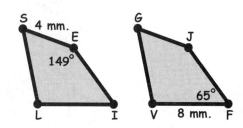

e.
(33)
Translate the word problem below into math; then solve.

Jeremy is 6 feet tall, and the diving board he is standing on is 48 inches high. How many *inches* high is Jeremy plus the diving board?

Problem Set 111

Tell whether each sentence below is True or False.

1.
(111)
Figures that are the exact same size and shape are called congruent figures.

2.
(111)
If two figures are congruent, their corresponding sides are equal and their corresponding angles have to be equal.

Tell the measure of each angle below.

3.
(104)

A. 5°
B. 10°
C. 25°
D. 160°
E. 170°

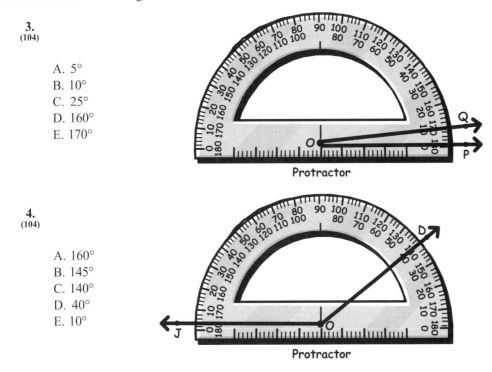

Protractor

4.
(104)

A. 160°
B. 145°
C. 140°
D. 40°
E. 10°

Protractor

Find the missing angle in each figure below.

5.
(107)

(a) **6.**
(107)

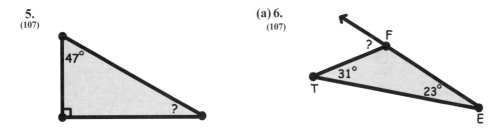

Tell the kind of each quadrilateral below.

7.
(109)

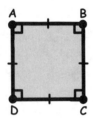

A. rectangle
B. trapezoid
C. rhombus
D. parallelogram
E. square

8.
(109)

A. rhombus
B. parallelogram
C. trapezoid
D. square
E. rectangle

Identify each figure below.

9.
(110)

A. heptagon
B. regular hexagon
C. quadrilateral
D. regular pentagon
E. octagon

10.
(110)

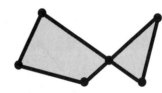

A. regular heptagon
B. pentagon
C. regular octagon
D. hexagon
E. none of the above

Answer each question below given that $\triangle ABC \cong \triangle DEF$.

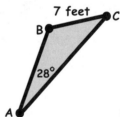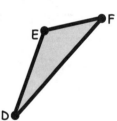

11. Which angle in $\triangle ABC$ must be equal to $\angle E$ in $\triangle DEF$?
(111)

    A. $\angle A$ B. $\angle B$
    C. $\angle C$ D. None of the above

12. Which side in $\triangle DEF$ must be equal to side AB in $\triangle ABC$?
(111)

    A. DF B. EF
    C. DE D. None of the above

13. What is the length of side EF?
(111)

14. What is the measure of $\angle D$?
(111)

15. If side AC has a length of 13 feet, what is the length of side DF?
(111)

Answer each question below given that Quadrilateral $DEFG \cong$ Quadrilateral $QRWV$.

(b) 16. What is the measure of $\angle R$?
(111)

(c) 17. What is the measure of $\angle G$?
(111)

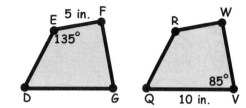

(d) 18. What is the measure of side DG?
(111)

Simplify each expression below by multiplying the powers.

19. $x^4 \cdot x^{10}$
(95)

    A. x^6 B. $x^{10,000}$ C. x^{14}

    D. $14x$ E. x^{40}

20. $(25x^2)(4x^3)$
(96)

    A. $100x^6$ B. $29x^5$ C. $100x^8$

    D. $29x^8$ E. $100x^5$

Calculate each root below.

21. $\sqrt[4]{16}$ **22.** $\sqrt{1}$
(100)   (99)

Translate the word problem below into an equation; then solve.

(e) 23. The boy magician is 5 feet tall, and the stage he is standing on is 72 inches high. How many *inches* high
(33)   is the boy plus the stage?

Lesson 112—Similar Figures

In the last lesson, we learned about congruent figures, which are the exact same size and shape. But there's also such a thing as **similar figures**. Those are figures that are the same shape but not necessarily the same size. It's obvious that the two triangles below are of different sizes. But their shapes are the same. That's why the triangles are similar.

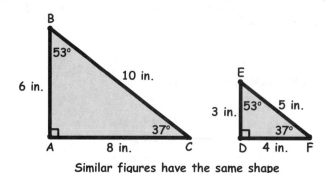

Similar figures have the same shape
but not necessarily the same size.

What makes these triangles have the same shape is that their corresponding angles are the same. The triangles are both right triangles, because they both contain a 90° angle. And they both have a 53° angle on top and a 37° angle on bottom. For all similar figures, every pair of corresponding angles must be equal. That's what gives the figures the same shape.

What about the corresponding sides? Well, these obviously won't always be equal because then similar figures couldn't be of different sizes. Look again at the two similar triangles above. Since the triangle on the left is bigger, its corresponding sides are longer. For instance, side AB is 6 inches, but the corresponding side of the smaller triangle, side DE, is just 3 inches. But here's what's really interesting about the sides of similar figures. Even though they have different lengths, the sides are still connected mathematically. Notice that AB is twice as long as DE: 6 inches is twice 3 inches. This same pattern holds for the other corresponding sides. On the bottom, in the larger triangle, side AC is 8 inches. That's twice the length of the corresponding side, DF, in the smaller triangle: DF is 4 inches long. And the hypotenuse of the larger triangle, BC, is 10 inches. That's twice the hypotenuse of the smaller triangle, EF, which is just 5 inches. In general, each side of $\triangle ABC$ is twice as long as the corresponding side of $\triangle DEF$.

△ABC	△DEF
AB=6	DE=3
AC=8	DF=4
BC=10	EF=5

It turns out that's always the way it works. For similar figures, the lengths of the corresponding sides will always differ by the same factor. In our example, the factor is 2. The larger triangle's sides are twice as long as the smaller triangle's corresponding sides. (You multiply the side from the smaller triangle by 2 to get the side from the larger triangle.) But the factor could be 3 or 4 or any other number.

Just to summarize what we've learned so far. For two similar figures, their corresponding angles are always equal. That's what gives the figures the same shape. And their corresponding sides will be of different lengths. But they will differ by the same factor. Maybe the sides of one figure will be twice as long as the other, or 3 times as long, or 4 times, or something else. The technical way of saying it is that the corresponding sides are proportional.

You've studied ratios and proportions in earlier math courses. A **ratio** is just a fraction. And a **proportion** is two fractions that are equal to each other. With those facts in mind, here's why the corresponding sides of similar figures have to be proportional. We can make ratios (fractions) out of the corresponding sides of our two similar triangles. We'll put the side from the larger triangle on the top of a fraction and its corresponding side from the smaller triangle on the bottom. For sides AB and DE that gives us $\frac{6}{3}$. For sides AC and DF, the fraction is $\frac{8}{4}$. And for sides BC and EF, it's $\frac{10}{5}$.

$$\frac{AB}{DE} = \frac{6}{3} = 2 \qquad\qquad \frac{AC}{DF} = \frac{8}{4} = 2 \qquad\qquad \frac{BC}{EF} = \frac{10}{5} = 2$$

Notice that all three fractions have the same value. This is what it means to say that corresponding sides of similar figures are proportional. If you create ratios of each pair of corresponding sides, those ratios will all be equal. That allows us to create proportions out of the different pairs.

$$\frac{AB}{DE} = \frac{AC}{DF} \qquad\qquad \frac{AC}{DF} = \frac{BC}{EF} \qquad\qquad \frac{AC}{DF} = \frac{BC}{EF}$$

$$\frac{6}{3} = \frac{8}{4} \qquad\qquad\qquad \frac{8}{4} = \frac{10}{5} \qquad\qquad\qquad \frac{8}{4} = \frac{10}{5}$$

We can also show these relationships by setting all three ratios equal like this.

$$\frac{AB}{DE} = \frac{AC}{DF} = \frac{BC}{EF}$$

$$\frac{6}{3} = \frac{8}{4} = \frac{10}{5} = 2$$

In setting up the fractions (ratios) of the sides, we decided to put the side from the larger triangle on top and the side from the smaller triangle on bottom. It's important to be consistent. But we could have done it the other way; we could have put the side from the smaller triangle on top in each fraction. That would have given us this.

$$\frac{DE}{AB} = \frac{DF}{AC} = \frac{EF}{BC}$$

$$\frac{3}{6} = \frac{4}{8} = \frac{5}{10} = \frac{1}{2}$$

The ratios don't equal 2 anymore. They equal the reciprocal of 2, which is $\frac{1}{2}$. But the important thing is the ratios are still all equal to each other. So you can choose to put the sides from the larger or smaller figure on top. It doesn't matter, as long as you're consistent for all of the fractions.

Finding Missing Sides

Now let's use these rules about similar triangles to find a missing side. In the diagram below, we have two similar triangles, $\triangle STV$ and $\triangle DGP$. The squiggly line (~) between $\triangle STV$ and $\triangle DGP$ below is the symbol for "similar."

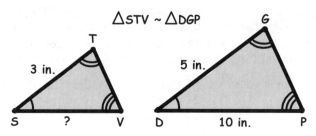

Find the length of SV.

Since the triangles are similar, we know that their corresponding angles have to be equal. That's shown here with arcs. There's a single arc on $\angle S$, and on $\angle D$, indicating that those angles are equal. There are two arcs on $\angle T$ and $\angle G$ showing that those angles are equal. We use two arcs on $\angle T$ and $\angle G$ because we want to make it clear that this pair angles isn't necessarily equal to $\angle S$ and $\angle D$. Following the same approach, there are three arcs on $\angle V$ and $\angle P$, indicating that these are equal to each other as well. We also know the lengths of several sides of the triangles. We know that ST is 3 inches, DP is 10 inches, and DG is 5 inches. We don't know the lengths of the other sides. But we're asked to find the length of side SV.

Our first step is to figure out the ratio of the corresponding sides. Since the triangles are similar, we know that their side lengths have to be proportional. In other words, a fraction made up of one pair of corresponding sides must equal a fraction made up of another pair of corresponding sides. But first we need to find the value of those fractions. What does it equal? Is it 2 or 3 or $\frac{1}{4}$? We were given the length of three sides in the triangles. Two of those—ST and DG—are corresponding. ST and DG are the first two letters in $\triangle STV$ and $\triangle DGP$, which means they match up. (And in this diagram you can also just tell by looking.) All we have to do, then, is set up a fraction (ratio) with ST and DG. We'll put the side from the smaller triangle (ST) on top and the side from the larger triangle (DG) on bottom.[1]

$$\frac{ST}{DG} = \frac{3}{5}$$

We end up with $\frac{3}{5}$. Since the triangles are proportional, we know that the ratios of other pairs of corresponding sides must also equal $\frac{3}{5}$ (as long as we do smaller over larger again).

Now we're ready to find the length of SV. The side in the larger triangle that corresponds to SV is DP. That's because SV and DP are both listed first and third in $\triangle STV$ and $\triangle DGP$. Since they are corresponding sides as well, the ratio of SV and DP should also equal $\frac{3}{5}$. We just need to make sure to put the smaller triangle's side on top, as we did with $\frac{ST}{DG}$. Setting up the ratio gives us this.

$$\frac{SV}{DP} = \frac{3}{5}$$

We also know the length of DP. It's 10 inches. So we can put 10 in for DP.

---

[1] We just as easily could have done it the other way: larger over smaller.

$$\frac{SV}{10} = \frac{3}{5}$$

Now we have an equation with unknown SV that we can solve. We could even put an x in for SV.

$$\frac{x}{10} = \frac{3}{5}$$

Here are the solving steps.

$$10 \cdot \frac{x}{10} = 10 \cdot \frac{3}{5}$$

$$x = 10 \cdot \frac{3}{5}$$

$$x = \frac{30}{5}$$

$$x = 6$$

That means side SV has to be 6 inches long. And the neat thing is we were able to figure that out without measuring anything. We just used algebra.

Cross Multiplying

Remember, a proportion is just two ratios that are equal to each other. So the equation $\frac{x}{10} = \frac{3}{5}$ is a proportion.

Basically, any equation consisting of two fractions separated by an equals sign qualifies as a proportion. It turns out that there's a shortcut for solving proportions (when one of the parts is an unknown). Instead of going through the usual undoing process, we can **cross multiply**. That just means in the first step we multiply the numerator of one fraction by the denominator of the second. Specifically, in $\frac{x}{10} = \frac{3}{5}$ we multiply x and 5 and 3 and 10 and set those equal.

cross multiplying

$$\frac{x}{10} \bowtie \frac{3}{5}$$

$$x \cdot 5 = 3 \cdot 10$$

Most people would go immediately to this simplified version.

$$5x = 30$$

Now we can solve by dividing both sides by 5.

$$\frac{5x}{5} = \frac{30}{5}$$

$$x = 6$$

That's the same answer we got before. But it's a little faster to cross multiply. Just remember that cross multiplying only works with proportions.

Practice 112

a.
(106) In the figure below, lines p and u are parallel. Find the measure of $\angle QPD$.

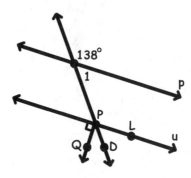

b.
(111) Find the length of side GL given that $\triangle LGF \cong \triangle AHT$.

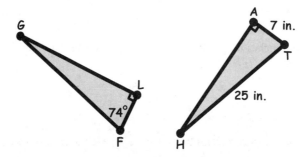

c.
(112) Solve the proportion $\dfrac{x}{4} = \dfrac{3}{25}$. Make sure your answer is fully reduced.

d.
(112) Given that $\triangle OGB \sim \triangle WST$, What is the length of side ST?

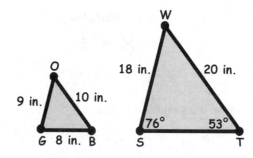

e.
(54) Translate the word problem below into math; then solve.

Salespeople at Music City Utopia earn a 20% commission. How much will Rodney make in commission if he sells a tambourine for $69?

Problem Set 112

Tell whether each sentence below is True or False.

1. Similar figures are figures that have the same shape, but not necessarily the same size.
(112)

2. For similar figures, the ratio of one pair of corresponding sides has to equal the ratio of any other pair of corresponding sides.
(112)

3. For similar figures, each pair of corresponding angles are equal to each other.
(112)

Answer each question below by writing and solving an equation.

4. ∠1 and ∠3 are complementary. If ∠1 has a measure of 39°, find the measure of ∠3.
(105)

5. ∠F and ∠E are supplementary. If ∠E has a measure of 164°, find the measure of ∠F.
(105)

In the figure below, lines *d* and *e* are parallel. Find the measure of each angle below.

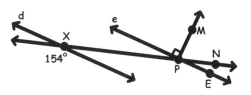

6. ∠EPN   **(a) 7.** ∠MPN
(106)   (106)

Tell the kind of each triangle below.

8.
(107)

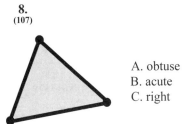

A. obtuse
B. acute
C. right

9.
(107)

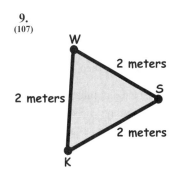

A. equilateral
B. isosceles
C. scalene

537

Answer each question below given that $\triangle ODB \cong \triangle FIL$.

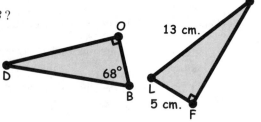

10.
(111)
Which side in $\triangle FIL$ must be equal to side OD in $\triangle ODB$?

A. *FL*   B. *FI*
C. *IL*   D. None of the above

11.
(111)
What is the measure of $\angle L$?

12.
(111)
What is the measure of $\angle I$?

(b) 13.
(111)
What is the length of side OD?

Solve each proportion below. Write your answer as a fully reduced fraction if needed.

14.
(112)
$\dfrac{5}{7} = \dfrac{x}{21}$

15.
(112)
$\dfrac{x}{4} = \dfrac{12}{16}$

(c) 16.
(112)
$\dfrac{x}{3} = \dfrac{2}{15}$

Answer each question below given that $\triangle GER \sim \triangle QKS$.

17.
(112)
What is the measure of $\angle R$?

18.
(112)
What is the measure of $\angle E$?

(d) 19.
(112)
What is the length of side KS?

Calculate the value of each expression below.

20.
(100)
$\sqrt[3]{14^3}$

21.
(100)
$(\sqrt{100})^2$

Translate the word problem below into math; then solve.

(e) 22.
(54)
The salespeople at Killer Gadgets Inc. get paid a 15% commission on everything they sell. How much will Stanley make in commission if he sells a pair of noise-cancelling headphones for $86?

Lesson 113—Perimeter, Symmetry, and Reflections

We've been learning about geometry figures. One important measurement that's used a lot in geometry is perimeter. The **perimeter** is just the distance all the way around a figure. A simple example is finding the perimeter of a rectangle. Look at the rectangle in the diagram below. Since its side lengths are all given, to find the perimeter we can just add up the lengths: $7+12+7+12=38$. So the perimeter is 38 inches. Since the opposite sides of a rectangle are always equal, another way to calculate the perimeter is to use multiplication. We could have done the calculation like this: $2\cdot12+2\cdot7=38$.

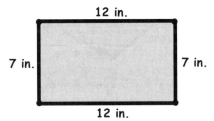

Perimeter = 2 · 7 + 2 · 12 = 38 in.

The answer comes out the same, obviously. In general, the perimeter of any rectangle can be calculated as 2 × width + 2 × length. Perimeter is often represented by the letter P, w is used for width, and l for length. With these letters, the calculation looks like this.

Perimeter of a Rectangle

$$P = 2w + 2l$$

What about perimeters of other figures? Well, the perimeter of a square is extremely easy because all four sides of a square are equal. In the square below, the sides are each 8 feet in length. And the perimeter is 32 feet. You can add up the sides one at a time or just multiply the side length by 4.

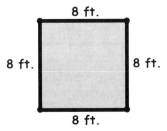

Perimeter = 4 · 8 = 32 ft.

Letting P stand for perimeter again and s for the side length, the perimeter of any square can be calculated like this.

Perimeter of a Square

$$P = 4s$$

539

More Complicated Perimeters

Now let's calculate the perimeter of a more complicated figure. The diagram below is a hexagon. It's not a regular hexagon, because the sides aren't all the same length. But it's still a hexagon since it has six sides. To find the perimeter we just add up all the sides.

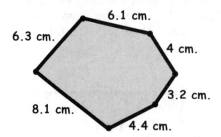

$$P = 6.3 + 6.1 + 4 + 3.2 + 4.4 + 8.1 = 32.1 \text{ cm.}$$

Sometimes we have to calculate the perimeter of a figure that has certain sides missing. Let's calculate the perimeter of the diagram below. Although two side lengths are missing, we can find these lengths using the information given.

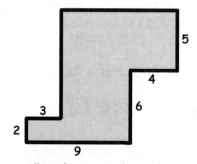

All angles are right angles.

What we have to do is draw a couple of extra line segments. We'll make them dashed to show that they aren't part of the actual figure.

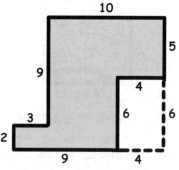

All angles are right angles.

The section on the bottom right that includes the dashed segments is a rectangle. So the dashed segments have lengths of 6 and 4. Remember, opposite sides of a rectangle are always equal. The entire right side, including the vertical dashed segment, has a length of 5+6 or 11. That means the missing side on the left plus the 2 must also equal 11. Therefore, the missing left side must have a length of 9. The bottom, including the horizontal dashed segment, has a length of $9+4$ or 13. The top must equal 13 minus 3, which is the little horizontal section on the bottom left. So the top of the figure must have a length of 10.

Now we have both missing side lengths and we can calculate the perimeter. We can't include the dashed line segments, though. We just drew those to help us find the missing sides. The perimeter of the figure comes out to 48.

$$P = 2+3+9+10+5+4+6+9 = 48$$

We don't know whether that's inches or feet or some other unit. The units aren't labeled in the diagram. But that's how you can find missing sides of a figure in order to do a perimeter calculation.

Symmetry

One thing that makes a perimeter calculation easier is when the figure has symmetry. **Symmetry** means that the two sides of the figure are mirror images of each other. For instance, a rectangle has symmetry because we can run a vertical line through the middle and that line cuts the rectangle into two matching halves.

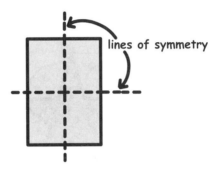

lines of symmetry

When a figure can be cut in half with a line and the halves match up, the figure has **bilateral symmetry**. The dashed line is called the **line of symmetry**. In fact, a rectangle also has bilateral symmetry with its top and bottom halves. Notice the horizontal dashed line also creates matching halves. The horizontal line is another line of symmetry.

Not all figures have both vertical and horizontal lines of symmetry. The figure below on the left can be cut into two matching halves by a horizontal line, but not a vertical line. The star on the right only has a vertical line of symmetry. The vertical dashed line creates two matching halves but a horizontal line would not. But both diagrams have bilateral symmetry because they can both be divided into two matching halves.

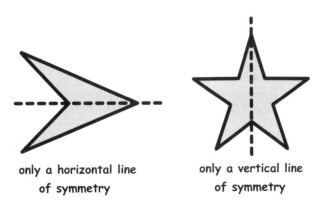

only a horizontal line
of symmetry

only a vertical line
of symmetry

Some figures have a line of symmetry that's not vertical or horizontal. In the square below, diagonal lines cut the figure into matching halves.

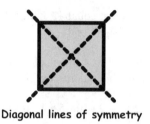

Diagonal lines of symmetry

The halves of each pair are mirror images of each other. So a square actually has four lines of symmetry. It has vertical and horizontal lines of symmetry as well as two diagonal lines.

Technically, the way to tell if a figure has bilateral symmetry is to imagine flipping it. If you could pick up one side of the figure and flip it over the line of symmetry and end up with a figure that looks exactly the same as before, then the figure has bilateral symmetry. Flipping a figure in this way is called a **reflection**. Doing a reflection is the technical way to determine if a figure has bilateral symmetry.

There's another kind of symmetry besides bilateral symmetry. There's also rotational symmetry. We learned earlier that the star below has bilateral symmetry because it can be cut into matching halves with a vertical line. But the star also has rotational symmetry.

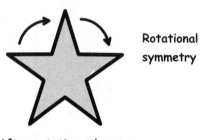

Rotational symmetry

After rotating, the star will look exactly the same.

If instead of flipping the star over a vertical line, what if we rotated it? Just imagine turning the star so that a different point ends up on top. Wouldn't the star look exactly the same? It would. When you can rotate a figure and it doesn't change shape, then the figure has **rotational symmetry**.

Practice 113

a.
(108)   Use the Pythagorean Theorem to find the missing side of the right triangle below. Estimate your answer with a calculator (to one decimal place).

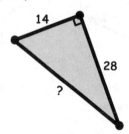

14

28

?

Find the perimeter of each figure below.

b.
(113)

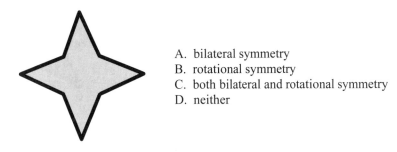

c.
(113)

d. Tell the type of symmetry that the figure below appears to have.
(113)

A. bilateral symmetry
B. rotational symmetry
C. both bilateral and rotational symmetry
D. neither

e. Translate the word problem below into an equation; then solve.
(79)

Catkin can sew 3 stuffed animals an hour and Rosemary can sew 5. Working together, how many hours would it take them to sew 32 stuffed animals?

Problem Set 113

Tell whether each sentence below is True or False.

1. The perimeter is the distance all the way around a figure.
(113)

2. When a figure can be rotated and doesn't change shape then it has rotational symmetry.
(113)

Find the missing angle in each figure below.

3.
(107)

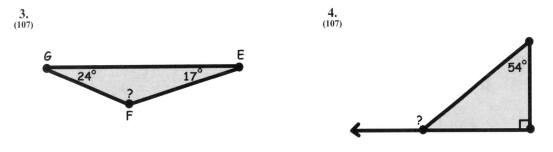

4.
(107)

Use the Pythagorean Theorem to find the missing side of each right triangle below. Estimate with a calculator (to one decimal place) any answers that don't simplify to a whole number.

5.
(108)

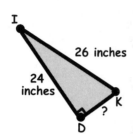

(a) 6.
(108)

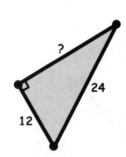

Answer each question below given that $\triangle YDG \cong \triangle EPJ$.

7.
(111)

Which side in $\triangle EPJ$ must be equal to side YD in $\triangle YDG$?

A. PJ B. EP
C. JE D.   None of the above

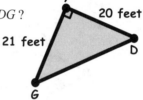
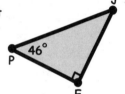

8.
(111)

What is the measure of $\angle D$?

9.
(111)

What is the measure of $\angle G$?

10.
(111)

What is the length of side GD?

Answer each question below given that $\triangle PGS \sim \triangle KEM$.

11.
(112)

What is the measure of $\angle P$?

12.
(112)

What is the length of side EM?

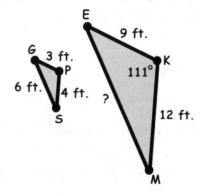

Find the perimeter of each figure below.

13.
(113)

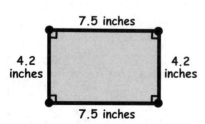

14.
(113)

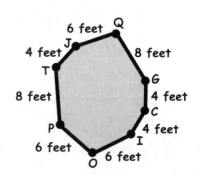

(b) 15.
(113)

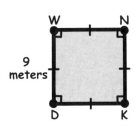

(c) 16.
(113)

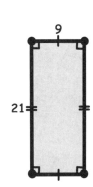

Tell the type of symmetry that each figure below appears to have.

17.
(113)

A. bilateral symmetry
B. rotational symmetry
C. both bilateral and
  rotational symmetry
D. neither

18.
(113)

A. rotational symmetry
B. bilateral symmetry
C. neither
D. both bilateral and
  rotational symmetry

(d) 19.
(113)

A. bilateral symmetry
B. rotational symmetry
C. both bilateral and rotational symmetry
D. neither

Tell how many lines of symmetry each figure below appears to have.

20.
(113)

21.
(113)

545

22.
(113)

Translate the word problem below into an equation; then solve.

(e) 23. Randall can assemble 5 race car tracks in an hour. Diggory can assemble 4 race car tracks in an hour.
(79) Working together, how many hours would it take them to assemble 63 race car tracks?

Lesson 114—Area Calculations

In the last lesson, we covered the concept of perimeter, which is just the distance all the way around a figure. But another important concept from geometry is area. Area is a measure of the space inside a figure. Earlier in the course, we learned how to calculate the area of a rectangle. For instance, the area of the rectangle below is just the number of little 1 foot squares that will fit inside of it.

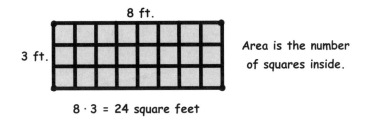

8 · 3 = 24 square feet

We don't actually have to count all the squares, of course. We can just multiply the width by the height. The width is 8 feet and the height is 3 feet, which gives us $8 \cdot 3 = 24$. So the area is 24 square feet.

Area of a Parallelogram

What about calculating the area of figures of different shapes such as quadrilaterals or triangles? Calculating the area of a parallelogram is fairly simple. It's basically the same as calculating the area of a rectangle: width × height. Only with a parallelogram, the height is more difficult to measure because you have to draw a dashed line segment from the top of the figure to the bottom. And the dashed segment must be perpendicular to the bottom of the parallelogram. In other words, it must make a right angle with the bottom. The height is then equal to the length of the dashed segment. As you can see, the parallelogram below is 7 feet wide and 4 feet high.

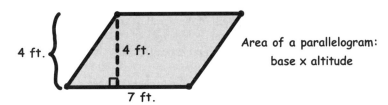

To find the area, we just multiply the width times the height again. Since $7 \cdot 4 = 28$, the area is 28 square feet. That means if we filled all the space inside this parallelogram with little 1 foot squares, there would be room for exactly 28 of them.

The bottom of a parallelogram is actually called the **base**. And the length of the dashed line segment is often called the **altitude** of the parallelogram. So even though it means the same as width × height, the area of a parallelogram can be stated a little differently: base × altitude.

Area of Parallelogram = base × altitude

People often use letters for these. They represent the base with a lower case *b*, and the altitude with a lower case *a*. With the letters, it looks like this.

Area of Parallelogram $= ba$

The diagram below shows another parallelogram with some important lengths labeled. The bottom has a length of 8 inches, so the base is 8. On this problem a lot of people would mistakenly think that the altitude is 7 because the length of the left side is 7 inches.

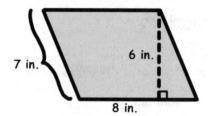

But the altitude is the height of the figure. It's measured by a vertical line segment from the top down to the base. That segment must make a right angle with the base. The altitude is shown on the right. It measures 6 inches. So the area is 8 times 6 or 48 square inches.

$$\text{Area} = ba$$

$$\text{Area} = 8 \cdot 6$$

$$48 \text{ square inches}$$

The diagram below shows another parallelogram. In this one, the vertical dashed segment measuring the altitude has been drawn outside the figure.

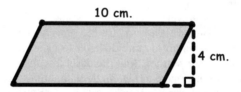

The calculation works the same way, though. The dashed segment still properly measures the height of the parallelogram. It's 4 centimeters. The length of the parallelogram's base isn't labeled. But we know that the opposite sides of all parallelograms are always equal. The length of the top is 10 centimeters, so the base must also have a length of 10 centimeters. The area calculation must be 10 × 4.

$$\text{Area} = ba$$

$$\text{Area} = 10 \cdot 4$$

$$40 \text{ square centimeters}$$

Area of a Triangle

There's also a fast way to calculate the area of a triangle. It's $\frac{1}{2} \times$ base $\times$ altitude. Using the letters b and a, it looks like this.

$$\text{Area of triangle} = \frac{1}{2}ba$$

As an example, let's calculate the area of the triangle below.

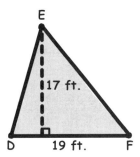

The base is 19 feet. The altitude isn't DE. It's the length of the dashed segment. So the altitude is 17 feet. Doing the calculation gives us an area of 161.5 square feet.

$$\text{Area of } \Delta DEF = \frac{1}{2} \cdot 19 \cdot 17 = 161.5 \text{ square feet}$$

With some triangles, you have to choose which side should be the base. Notice that ΔABC below is rotated a bit. But since we're given the length of side AB—it's 11 inches—we can just make AB the base. That means we need to measure the distance from point C down to the base (AB) to get the altitude. Since the triangle is tilted to the right, we need to extend AB some so the dashed segment can make a right angle with the base. That makes the dashed segment fall outside. But there's nothing wrong with that. The altitude turns out to be 12 inches. The area calculation gives us an answer of 66, so the area of the triangle is 66 square inches.

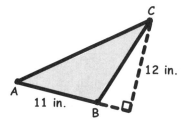

$$\text{Area of } \Delta DEF = \frac{1}{2} \cdot 11 \cdot 12 = 66 \text{ square inches}$$

Area of a Trapezoid

We've calculated the area of a rectangle, parallelogram, and triangle. But what about a trapezoid? Remember, a trapezoid is a quadrilateral that has exactly one pair of parallel sides. The diagram below shows trapezoid $FGHK$. The two parallel sides are GH and FK.

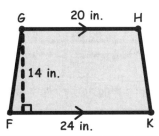

In a trapezoid, both of the parallel sides are considered to be the bases. So GH and FK are the bases here. Notice they have different lengths: GH is 20 inches and FK is 24 inches.

The altitude is still the distance from the top base to the bottom. That's measured by a line that's perpendicular (makes a right angle with) the bottom base. The altitude is 14 inches. As it turns out, the area of a trapezoid equals $\frac{1}{2}$ × the altitude × the sum of the two bases. It's usually written like this.

$$\text{Area of a Trapezoid} = \frac{1}{2} \times \text{altitude} \times (\text{base}_1 + \text{base}_2)$$

Now let's put in the numbers from our example.

$$\text{Area of a } FGHK = \frac{1}{2} \times 14 \times (20 + 24)$$

The parentheses around the bases means the addition should be done first.

$$= \frac{1}{2} \cdot 14 \cdot 44$$

Now we multiply what's left.

$$= 7 \cdot 44$$

$$= 308$$

So the area of the trapezoid is 308 square inches.

Some area problems involve figures that are quite complicated. The best way to find the area of those is to break the figure up into smaller, simpler pieces. The diagram below is an example. To calculate the area, it's best to break this into simpler pieces. We've already done that by drawing a dashed segment which divides the figure into a rectangle and a triangle.

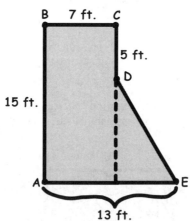

All angles appearing to be right angles are 90°.

Now we can calculate the area of each of these separately (which is easier) and then just add the two areas together to get the area of the total figure. The base and altitude of the rectangle are 7 feet and 15 feet. (Both the top and bottom of the rectangle must have the same length.) So we just multiply those.

$$\text{Area of rectangle} = (7)(15)$$

$$= 105$$

So the area of the rectangle is 105 square feet. Now for the triangle. The base and altitude of the triangle aren't labeled, but we can find them. The entire bottom of the figure is 13 feet. If we subtract the length of the top, which is 7 feet, that leaves 6 feet. This has to be the length of the base of the triangle. As for the altitude, notice that the left side of the entire figure is 15 feet. And CD is 5 feet. Subtracting CD from 15 gives us the altitude of the triangle: $15 - 5 = 10$ square feet. So the altitude is 10 feet. Now we can calculate the area of the triangle.

$$\text{Area of triangle} = \frac{1}{2}ba$$

$$= \frac{1}{2}(6)(10)$$

$$= 30$$

So the area of the triangle is 30 square feet. The last step is to add the area of the rectangle and the area of the triangle.

$$\text{Total Area of Figure} = 105 + 30 = 135$$

So the figure has a total area of 135 square feet. That's how you handle more complicated areas. You break the figure up into simpler pieces that you know how to handle.

We'll look at one more example below. This one's a little tougher. Remember, the strategy is to break up the figure into simpler pieces, calculate the area of each of those, and, finally, add those areas to get the total. There are several different ways to break up this figure up.

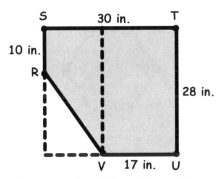

All angles appearing to be right angles are 90°.

One way is to draw only the vertical dashed segment in the middle. This separates the figure into a trapezoid on the left and a rectangle on the right. We know how to calculate the area of both of those. Another approach, though, is to draw two additional segments on the bottom left (which are shown). These turn the entire figure into one big rectangle. With this strategy, we can calculate the area of the big rectangle. Then we can calculate the area of the triangle in the lower left. And, as a last step, we subtract the area of the triangle to get the area of the actual figure. Following this second strategy, the big rectangle has a base of 30 inches and an altitude of 28 inches.

$$\text{Area of Big Rectangle} = ba$$

$$= 30 \cdot 28$$

$$= 840$$

So the area of the big rectangle is 840 square inches. Now let's calculate the area of the triangle. This isn't part of the actual figure, remember, so we'll need to subtract it in the end. To find the base of the triangle, we take 30 inches, the length of the base, and subtract 17 inches. That gives us 13 inches. To find the altitude, we take 28 inches, the altitude of the entire left side, and subtract 10 inches (SR). That leaves 18 inches for the altitude of the triangle. Now we can calculate.

$$\text{Area of Triangle} = \frac{1}{2}ba$$

$$= \frac{1}{2}(13)(18)$$

$$= 117$$

So the area of the triangle is 117 square inches. We have the area of the big rectangle, 840 square inches. And we have the area of the extra triangle space, 117 square inches. The final step is to subtract the two.

$$\text{Area of Actual Figure} = 840 - 117$$

$$= 723$$

So the total area of the figure is 723 square inches.

Practice 114

a.
(113)
Find the perimeter of the figure below.

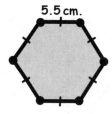

5.5 cm.

Find the area of each figure below. Write your answer as a whole number or decimal.

b.
(114)

c.
(114)

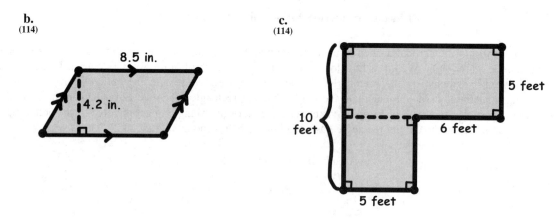

8.5 in.

4.2 in.

5 feet

10 feet

6 feet

5 feet

d.
(114)

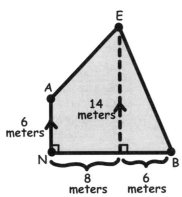

e. Translate the word problem below into an equation; then solve.
(54)

When Chadwick special-ordered a drum major's hat recently, he agreed to pay a 7% shipping and handling charge. If Chadwick paid $3.01 in shipping and handling, how much must the hat have cost?

Problem Set 114

Tell whether each sentence below is True or False.

1. The area of a triangle equals base × altitude.
(114)

2. The area of a trapezoid equals $\frac{1}{2}$ × base × altitude.
(114)

Find the missing angle in each figure below.

3.
(105)

4. In the figure below, lines m and k are parallel.
(106)

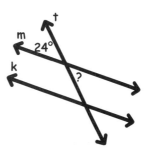

Use the Pythagorean Theorem to find the missing side of each right triangle below. Estimate with a calculator (to one decimal place) any answers that don't simplify to a whole number.

5.
(108)

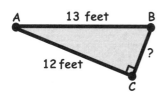

6.
(108)

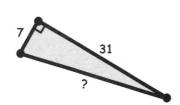

Tell the kind of each quadrilateral below.

7.
(109)

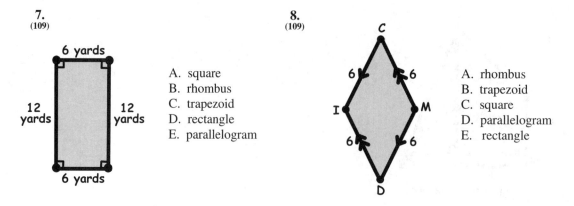

A. square
B. rhombus
C. trapezoid
D. rectangle
E. parallelogram

8.
(109)

A. rhombus
B. trapezoid
C. square
D. parallelogram
E. rectangle

Find the perimeter of each figure below.

9.
(113)

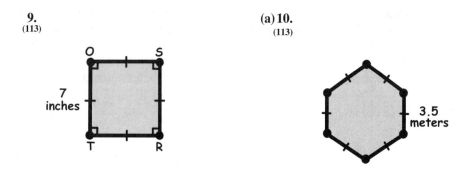

(a) 10.
(113)

Tell the type of symmetry that each figure below appears to have.

11.
(113)

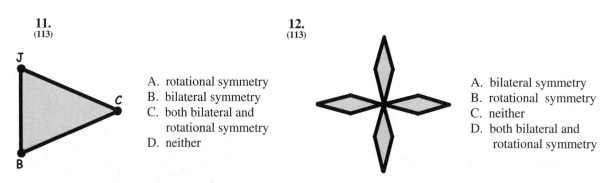

A. rotational symmetry
B. bilateral symmetry
C. both bilateral and
   rotational symmetry
D. neither

12.
(113)

A. bilateral symmetry
B. rotational symmetry
C. neither
D. both bilateral and
   rotational symmetry

Find the area of each figure below. Write your answer as a whole number or decimal.

(b) 13.
(114)

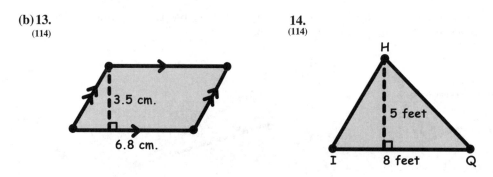

14.
(114)

15.
(114)

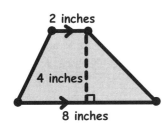

2 inches

4 inches

8 inches

(c) 16.
(114)

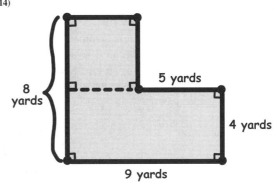

8 yards

5 yards

4 yards

9 yards

(d) 17.
(114)

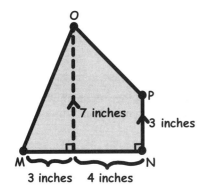

O

P

7 inches

3 inches

M

N

3 inches   4 inches

Simplify each expression below by adding or subtracting (as indicated) the powers.

18. $-7x^3 - 5x^3$
(94)

    A. -2 B. $-12x^6$ C. $-2x^3$

    D. -12 E. $-12x^3$

19. $11x^7 + 4x^7$
(94)

    A. 15 B. $7x^{14}$ C. $15x^7$

    D. $7x^7$ E. $15x^{14}$

Calculate the value of each expression below.

20. $\sqrt[3]{11^3}$
(100)

21. $(\sqrt{49})^2$
(100)

Translate the word problem below into an equation; then solve.

(e) 22. When Owen bought a remote-control helicopter, he agreed to pay a 9% shipping and handling charge. If
(54) Owen paid $4.86 in shipping and handling, how much must the helicopter have cost?

Lesson 115—Circles

We've studied several different geometric figures so far. But one important figure that we left out is the circle. A circle is not a polygon, because it's curved along its edge. A polygon has to have straight sides. Every circle has a center point. Technically, a **circle** is a smooth curve where every point is the same distance from the center point. In the circle below, the center is labeled point *O*. The center point is also used to name the entire circle. So this is circle *O*.

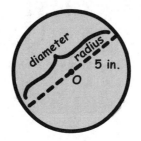

A circle is a smooth curve where every point is the same distance from the center.

Radius, Diameter, Chord

The distance from the center to the edge of the circle is called the **radius**. The distance all the way across the circle, running from one edge of the circle to another through the center is called the **diameter**. It takes two radii (radii is the plural of radius) to make one diameter. In circle *O*, the radius is 5 inches. So that means the diameter must be 10 inches.

Sometimes a circle will have a segment that connects two points on the circle, but that doesn't necessarily run through the center. That's called a **chord**. In circle *Q* below, segment *AB* is a chord. Technically, a diameter also qualifies as a chord. It's just a special chord that does happen to go through the center.

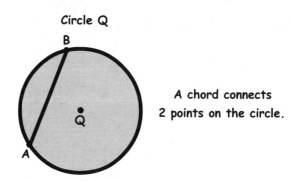

Circle Q

A chord connects 2 points on the circle.

Circumference and π

We learned about perimeter, which is the distance all the way around a figure. The distance around a circle has a different name. Instead of perimeter, it's called the **circumference**.

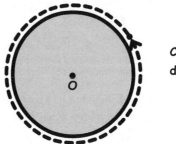

Circumference is the distance all the way around a circle.

There's an important fact relating the circumference and diameter of any circle. If you divide the circumference by the diameter of any circle, you'll always get the same number. That's true regardless of the circle's size. For instance, the circle below has a diameter of 8 inches and a circumference of about 25.12 inches. Notice that when we divide the circumference of this circle by its diameter, the answer comes out to be about 3.14.

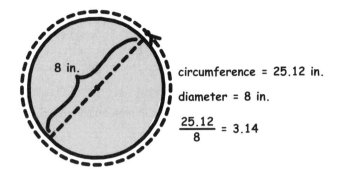

It's "about" 3.14, because the circumference is actually a little bit more than 25.12 inches. But 3.14 is close. So we'll say the circumference divided by diameter of the circle above equals 3.14.

Now look at circle R below. This has a diameter of 24 feet. And the circumference—the distance all the way around the circle—comes out to about 75.36 feet. So this is a much bigger circle than the one in the last example. But when we divide the circumference by the diameter, the answer comes out the same as with the previous circle: 3.14.

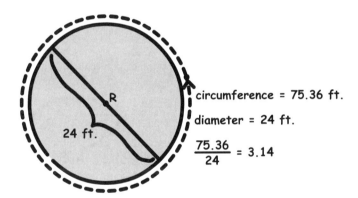

The main point is that the circumference divided by the diameter of *any* circle is always equal to about 3.14.

As it turns out, this number we keep getting (approximately 3.14) is one of the most important in all of math. The number is called pi, which is a Greek letter written like this: π. The reason we use a letter to represent the number, is that it's impossible to write the number π exactly as a whole number, fraction, or decimal. If you try, the digits will keep going forever. They won't even repeat. It's just an endless stream of various digits. Here's π written out to several more digits.

$$\pi = 3.141592654...$$

But we could just keep going and going with these digits.

Since a circle's circumference divided by its diameter is always equal to π, it's possible to use π to calculate the circumference of a circle. The circumference of any circle equals π multiplied by the diameter.

Circumference of a circle = π × diameter

Since the diameter of a circle is equal to 2 × radius, another way to calculate the circumference is just to multiply π by 2 × radius. People usually write it as $2\pi r$, where r stands for radius.

$$\text{Circumference of a Circle} = 2\pi r$$

Here's how we can use $2\pi r$ to calculate the circumference of an actual circle. The circle in the last example had a radius of 12 feet. And the circumference was about 75.36 feet. Let's use $2\pi r$ to calculate the circumference and see if we get the right answer. When doing actual calculations, most people estimate π to 2 decimal places: 3.14. Even though this isn't exact, it's close enough for most real world problems. So the circumference of our circle is equal to 2 times 3.14 times 12 feet.

$$\text{Circumference} = 2\pi r$$

$$= 2(3.14)(12)$$

$$= 75.36$$

We end up with 75.36 feet, which is correct. You can always calculate the circumference of a circle using $2\pi r$.

Area of a Circle

What about calculating the area of a circle? This also involves the number π. The area of any circle is equal to π × radius × radius. But it's always written like this.

$$\text{Area of a circle} = \pi r^2$$

Let's use πr^2 to calculate the area of a circle. The circle below has a radius of 6 inches.

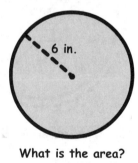

What is the area?

If we estimate π as 3.14 again, we end up with the following.

$$\text{Area} = \pi r^2$$

$$= 3.14 \cdot 6^2$$

$$= 3.14 \cdot 36$$

$$= 113.04$$

So the area of the circle is about 113.04 square inches. This isn't exact, because we rounded π to 3.14. But it's close. That means we can fit a little more than 113 squares with 1 inch sides inside this circle.

Semicircles

We've been talking about full circles, but there's also something called a **semicircle**, which is just half of a circle. The diagram below shows a semicircle that's been taken from a circle with a radius of 3 inches. Let's figure out the perimeter of this semicircle. It's not called circumference. When you're measuring the distance around a semicircle, it's called perimeter.

semicircle

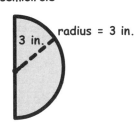

radius = 3 in.

3 in.

What is the perimeter?

If this were a full circle, the distance all the way around the circle (circumference) would equal $2\pi r$. Let start by calculating the circumference of a full circle of this size.

$$\text{Circumference of full circle with radius of 3 inches} = (2)(3.14)(3)$$

$$= 18.84$$

It's about 18.84 inches. Now think about this. The curved part of our semicircle is half of the circumference of the full circle. So the curved part should have a length of half of 18.84.

$$\text{Length of curved part of semicircle} = \frac{18.84}{2}$$

$$= 9.42$$

So the curved part has a length of about 9.42 inches. We're still not done because we need to add the line segment—the left side of the semicircle. We need its length. This segment is actually the diameter of the full circle. If the radius of the full circle is 3 inches, then the diameter must be 6 inches.

$$\text{Length of straight part} = 6 \text{ inches}$$

The last step of calculating the perimeter is to add 9.42 and 6.

$$\text{Perimeter of semicircle} = 9.42 + 6 = 15.42 \text{ inches}$$

So the perimeter of the semicircle is actually 15.42 inches.

Now let's find the area of the semicircle. This is just going to be half of the area of the full circle. Here's the way to calculate the area of a full circle again.

$$\text{Area of a circle} = \pi r^2$$

Since the radius here is 3 inches, we put in 3 for r and then we'll use 3.14 for pi again.

$$\text{Area of circle with radius 3 inches} = 3.14 \cdot 3^2$$

$$= 3.14 \cdot 9$$

$$= 28.26$$

We end up with 28.26 square inches. This is the area of the full circle. The area of the semicircle is half of 28.26. So we need to divide by 2.

$$\text{Area of semicircle} = \frac{28.26}{2}$$

$$= 14.13$$

So the area of the semicircle is about 14.13 square inches. It's not exact, because we rounded π to 3.14.

Complicated Perimeter and Area Problems

Sometimes in a complicated diagram one or more of the sides will include a semicircle. In the diagram below, the top left section is actually a semicircle. We know that because there's a radius drawn. It shows that the radius of the semicircle is 7 inches. That just means that the radius of a full circle of this size would be 7 inches. There's also a dashed horizontal segment; it's a diameter of the semicircle.

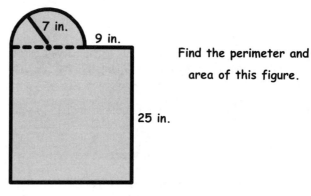

Find the perimeter and area of this figure.

(All angles are right angles.)

Let's calculate the perimeter and area of this figure. We'll start with the perimeter. We need to find the lengths of the missing sides. Since the main section of the figure is a rectangle, we know that the left side has to equal the right side, which is labeled 25 inches. So the left side must also be 25 inches. The bottom side is tougher. The dashed segment on top is the diameter of the semicircle. Since the radius is 7 inches, the diameter must be twice that or 14 inches. The top of the rectangle, then, must be 14+9 or 23 inches. And since opposite sides of a rectangle are equal, the bottom side must also have a length of 23 inches.

We've found the lengths of all the straight sides. But we still need the curved part of the semicircle. This equals half of the circumference of a full circle with a radius of 7 inches. The circumference of a circle equals $2\pi r$. We can put 7 in for r and use 3.14 for π.

$$\text{Circumference of full circle} = 2(3.14)(7)$$

$$= 43.96$$

So the circumference of the full circle is about 43.96 inches. The curved part of our semicircle must equal half of this.

$$\text{Curved part of semicircle} = \frac{43.96}{2}$$

$$= 21.98$$

So the curved part of the semicircle is 21.98 inches.

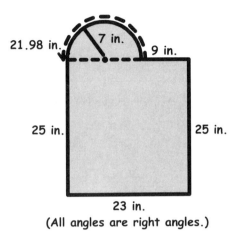

(All angles are right angles.)

Now we have enough information to calculate the perimeter of the entire diagram. Adding the curve of the semicircle to each of the sides gives us this.

$$\text{Perimeter of entire figure} = 21.98 + 9 + 25 + 23 + 25 = 103.98$$

The perimeter of the figure, then, is about 103.98 inches.

That's our first answer. But we still have to find the area. What we do is find the area of the rectangle and add it to the area of the semicircle. The area of the rectangle is the base × altitude. The base is 23 inches and the altitude is 25 inches.

$$\text{Area of rectangle} = 23 \cdot 25$$

$$= 575$$

So the area of the rectangle is 575 square inches. The area of the semicircle is half of the area of a full circle of radius 7 inches. And, remember, the area of a full circle is πr^2.

$$\text{Area of a full circle with radius 7 inches} = 3.14 \cdot 7^2$$

$$= 3.14 \cdot 49$$

$$= 153.86$$

So the area of the full circle is 153.86 square inches. The area of the semicircle equals half of this. So let's divide by 2.

$$\frac{153.86}{2} = 76.93$$

561

The area of the semicircle is 76.93 square inches. The last step is to add the area of the rectangle to the area of the semicircle.

$$\text{Area of total figure} = 575 + 76.93$$

$$= 651.93$$

So the area of the entire figure is 651.93 square inches.

Practice 115

a.
(113) Find the perimeter of the figure below. Write your answer as a decimal.

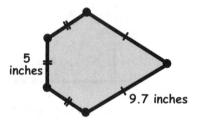

b.
(115) Find the perimeter of the figure below. Use 3.14 for π. Write your answer as a decimal.

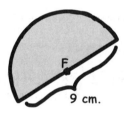

c.
(115) Find the perimeter of the figure below. Use 3.14 for π. Write your answer as a decimal.

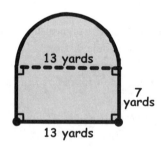

d. Find the area of the figure below. Use 3.14 for π. Write your answer as a decimal.
(115)

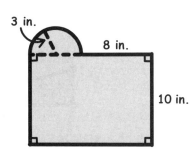

e. Translate the word problem below into math; then solve.
(46)

Super Duper Saver Mart is selling 7-liter coolers of Eckhart's Eco-Friendly Lemonade. How many centiliters are in a cooler?

Problem Set 115

Tell whether each sentence below is True or False.

1. A circle is a smooth curve where every point is the same distance from the center.
(115)

2. The circumference of a circle equals $2\pi r$.
(115)

3. The area of a circle equals $\pi^2 r^2$.
(115)

Find the missing angle in each figure below.

4.
(107)

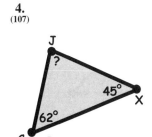

5.
(107)

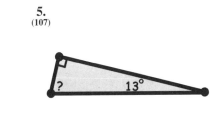

Solve each proportion below. Write your answer as a fully reduced fraction if needed.

6. $\dfrac{1}{8} = \dfrac{x}{24}$
(112)

7. $\dfrac{x}{5} = \dfrac{28}{35}$
(112)

8. $\dfrac{x}{6} = \dfrac{13}{12}$
(112)

Answer each question below given that $\triangle WQA \cong \triangle TGD$.

9.
(111)
Which side in $\triangle WQA$ must be equal to side GD in $\triangle TGD$?

    A. QA B. AW

    C. WQ D. None of the above

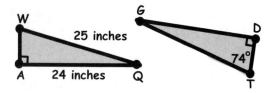

10.
(111)
What is the measure of $\angle W$?

11.
(111)
What is the measure of $\angle Q$?

12.
(111)
What is the length of side DT?

Find the perimeter of each figure below. Write your answer as a decimal.

(a) 13.
(113)

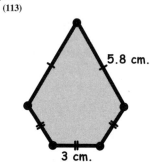

14.
(113)

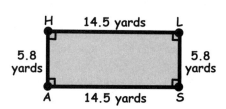

Find the area of each figure below. Write your answer as a decimal.

15.
(114)

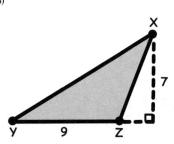

16.
(114)

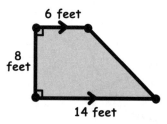

Find the circumference (or perimeter) of each figure below. Use 3.14 for π. Write your answer as a decimal.

17.
(115)

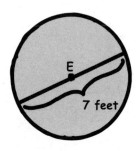

(b) 18.
(115)

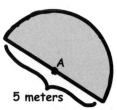

Find the area of each figure below. Use 3.14 for π. Write your answer as a decimal.

19.
(115)

20.
(115)

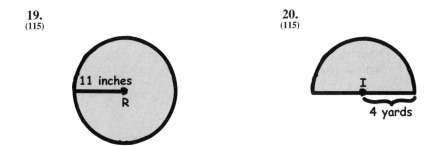

(c) 21. Find the perimeter of the figure below. Use 3.14 for π. Write your answer as a decimal.
(115)

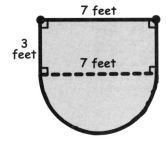

(d) 22. Find the area of the figure below. Use 3.14 for π. Write your answer as a decimal.
(115)

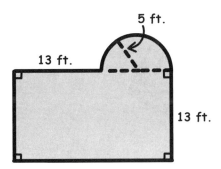

Translate the word problem below into math; then solve.

(e) 23. Super Duper Saver Mart is selling 4-liter jugs of a new item called Swadley's Sweeter than Honey Iced
(46) Tea. How many centiliters are in the jug?

Lesson 116—Solids

Earlier, we learned about units for volume. Volume is a way to measure something like the inside of a box. A box is actually a three dimensional (3-D) geometry figure. It's also called a **solid**. Solids are different from the figures we've been studying. We've been studying two-dimensional (2-D) figures such as rectangles, triangles, and circles. They're two-dimensional because they can fit onto a flat plane like a surface.

Kinds of Solids

In this lesson, we're going to review several different kinds of solids. But there are a few terms we should define first. The sides of a solid are called **faces**. A box actually has six faces.

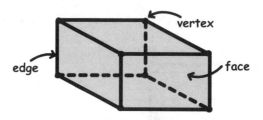

A box is three-dimensional.
It's a solid.

The lines where the faces connect are called edges. The vertices of the box are the points where three edges meet. In a box, all the faces are rectangles. But it's also possible for a solid to have faces with different shapes. Here's a solid where the faces are triangles.

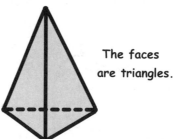

The faces
are triangles.

Another important term that you need to know is polyhedron. Any closed solid figure with polygon faces is called a **polyhedron**. It's like a 3-D version of a polygon. One special kind of polyhedron that's common is a prism. A **prism** is a polyhedron where two of its opposite faces are congruent and parallel. The other faces are parallelograms. The two faces that are parallel and congruent are called **bases**. A box qualifies as a prism. The top and bottom faces are congruent and parallel to each other. The other faces are parallelograms. They're rectangles, actually. But a rectangle is a special kind of parallelogram. So a box is a **rectangular prism**.

A prism could also have bases that are triangles. The diagram below is a **triangular prism** because both of its bases are triangles. The other faces are rectangles, which are parallelograms. So this still qualifies as a prism. The main point is that a lot of solids are polyhedrons. And prisms are a special kind of polyhedron.

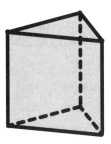

triangular prism

Pyramids are another major kind of polyhedron. Technically, a **pyramid** is a polyhedron where one face (the base) is any polygon and the other faces are all triangles. The base is usually on the bottom of the pyramid.

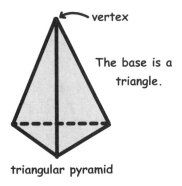

vertex

The base is a triangle.

triangular pyramid

The tip of the pyramid on top, where all the triangles come together, is the vertex. The diagram above is actually a **triangular pyramid** because the base is also a triangle. But it's possible for pyramids to have other kinds of bases. The base can be any polygon. Below is a pyramid with a base that's a rectangle. It's called a **rectangular pyramid**.

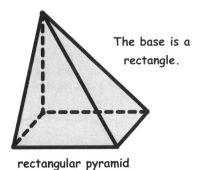

The base is a rectangle.

rectangular pyramid

There's another group of solids called cylinders. You've seen lots of cylinders because the shape is basically the same as a can. A **cylinder** is a solid with two bases that are both circles. The circles are congruent and parallel to each other. The middle part of the cylinder is called the **lateral surface**. The radius of the cylinder is just the radius of the circular bases.

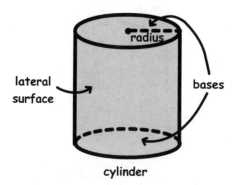

cylinder

There's also a cone. A **cone** is a solid that has just one base that's a circle. The base is usually on bottom. The other end is a single point, the vertex. The middle part is called the lateral surface, as with a cylinder. And the radius of the cone is just the radius of the circle base. A cone looks like an upside down ice cream cone (without the ice cream).

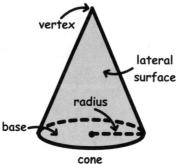

cone

One way to think about the difference between cylinders and cones is that a cylinder is a round version of a prism and a cone is a round version of a pyramid. A prism has two bases that are parallel and congruent. That's also true of a cylinder. But with a cylinder, the bases aren't polygons; they're circles. A pyramid has just one base that's a polygon. A cone has one base as well, only it's a circle.

Another rounded solid—the roundest of all—is the sphere. A sphere is just a ball. Think of it as a 3-D circle. The radius of the sphere is the distance from the center out to the edge. That distance is the same all the way around. The definition of a **sphere** is a round solid where every point is the same distance from the center point.

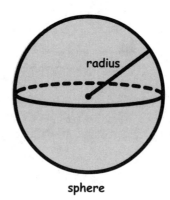

sphere

Volume of a Prism

The volume of a solid is a measure of the space inside of it. Earlier in the course, we learned how to calculate the volume of a box, which is technically a rectangular prism. Let's calculate the volume of the rectangular prism below.

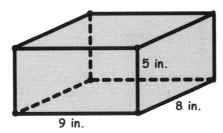

**What is the volume of this
rectangular prism?**

The volume is just length × width × height. The length is 9 inches, the width is 8 inches, and the height (altitude) is 5 inches. So that gives us this.

$$\text{Volume} = 9 \cdot 8 \cdot 5 = 360$$

The volume is 360 cubic inches. That means exactly 360 little cubes with 1 inch sides will fit inside this rectangular prism.

Now let's calculate the volume of a more complicated prism. The diagram below qualifies as a prism, because the two bases are parallel and congruent polygons. But instead of being rectangles, the bases are triangles. So this is a triangular prism.

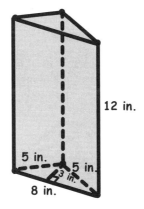

**What is the volume of this
triangular prism?**

We know the height (altitude) is 12 inches. And we know the lengths of several of the other sides on bottom. We can't just multiply 8, 5, and 12, though. That won't give us the volume. The correct calculation is to find the area of either one of the triangular bases. Then we multiply that area by the altitude.

Volume of a Prism = area of base × altitude

$$V = Ba$$

569

In the equation, *B* stands for the area of a base and *a* stands for altitude. It's important not to confuse the base of a triangle with the base of the entire solid. We use the word base for both. But the base of a triangle is one of the triangle's sides; it's a length. The base of a solid is a 2-D figure; it's an area. The main point is that $V = Ba$ can be used to calculate the volume of any prism.[1] Now let's find the volume of our triangular prism. First, we need to calculate the area of one of the triangular bases. Here's how to calculate the area of a triangle again.

$$\text{Area of a Triangle} = \frac{1}{2} \times \text{base} \times \text{altitude}$$

The base in this equation is a length not an area. The diagram above has two sides of the bottom triangle labeled. We'll let the base of the triangle be the 8 inch side in front. The altitude is the small 3 inch dashed segment, which runs from the top of the triangle down to the base. It's perpendicular to the base. Putting these numbers in gives us this.

$$\text{Area of Base } = \frac{1}{2} \cdot 8 \cdot 3$$

$$= 12$$

The area of each base is 12 square inches. Next, we multiply this area by the altitude of the prism.

$$\text{Volume of a Prism} = \text{area of base} \times \text{altitude}$$

$$V = (12)(12)$$

$$= 144$$

The volume of our triangular prism is 144 cubic inches. That's how many little cubes will fit inside the prism exactly.

Surface Area of a Prism

The surface area of a solid is the sum of the area of all of its faces. It's just all the space along the outside of the solid. As an example, let's find the surface area of the triangular prism below. This is the same prism we just calculated the volume of.

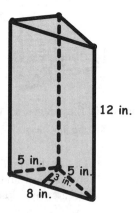

12 in.

5 in.

5 in.

3 in.

8 in.

What is the surface area of this triangular prism?

---

[1] We could have even used it to calculate the volume of the box in our first example.

The first step is to add the area of the two bases. Since they're congruent, we'll just find the area of one base and multiply that by 2. The next step is to add the areas of the other three faces. The faces in the middle are called **lateral faces**. That total equals the surface area of the prism.

Surface Area = 2×area of base + area of lateral face 1 + area of lateral face 2 + area of lateral face 3

Now let's put in the numbers. We already know the area of the bases from the previous example. Each base has an area of 12. Two of the lateral faces are 5 inches wide and 12 inches tall. Since these are rectangles, their areas are $5 \cdot 12$. The last lateral face is at the front. It has a width of 8 inches and an altitude of 12 inches. So its area is $8 \cdot 12$. That gives us the following.

$$\text{Surface Area of Prism} = 2 \times 12 + 5 \cdot 12 + 5 \cdot 12 + 8 \cdot 12$$

$$= 240$$

So the surface area of the prism is 240 square inches. That's the space all around the outside of the prism. Notice that surface area is always in square units. The volume of a solid is in cubic units, but surface area is a measure of flat surfaces, so it's in square units.

Practice 116

a.
(115)
Find the perimeter of the figure below. Use 3.14 for π. Write your answer as a decimal.

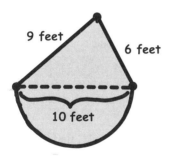

9 feet · 6 feet · 10 feet

b.
(116)
Identify the solid below.

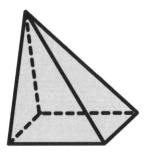

A. triangular pyramid
B. rectangular pyramid
C. triangular prism
D. rectangular prism
E. cone

c.
(116)
Find the volume of the solid below.

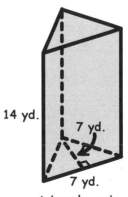

14 yd. · 7 yd. · 7 yd.
triangular prism

d. Find the surface area of the solid below.
(116)

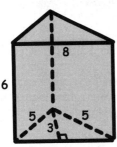

triangular prism

e. Translate the word problem below into an equation; then solve.
(82)

Buddy's Bug Stompers charges $40 for a service call (just to come to the house) plus $35 per hour to do the job. The Pest Police charge $60 for a service call plus $25 per hour to do the job. How many hours would a job have to take for the bills of both bug exterminators to be the same?

Problem Set 116

Tell whether each sentence below is True or False.

1. A cone is a solid with two bases that are congruent and parallel circles.
(116)

2. A cylinder is a polyhedron where two faces are parallel and congruent and the remaining faces are parallelograms.
(116)

Answer each question below by writing and solving an equation.

3. $\angle F$ and $\angle Q$ are complementary. If $\angle F$ has a measure of $54°$, find the measure of $\angle Q$.
(105)

4. $\angle V$ and $\angle O$ are supplementary. If $\angle O$ has a measure of $33°$, find the measure of $\angle V$.
(105)

In the figure below, lines *m* and *n* are parallel. Find the measure of each angle below.

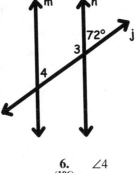

5. $\angle 3$
(105)

6. $\angle 4$
(106)

Find the perimeter of each figure below. Write your answer as a whole number or decimal.

7.
(113)

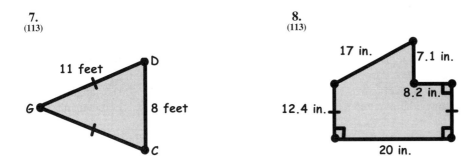

8.
(113)

Find the area of each figure below. Use 3.14 for π. Write your answer as a decimal.

9.
(115)

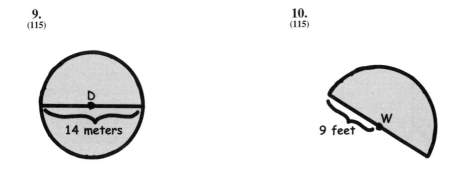

10.
(115)

Find the perimeter of the figure below. Use 3.14 for π. Write your answer as a decimal.

(a) 11.
(115)

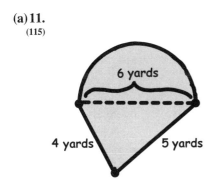

Identify each solid below.

12.
(116)

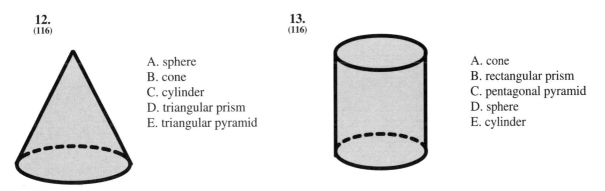

A. sphere
B. cone
C. cylinder
D. triangular prism
E. triangular pyramid

13.
(116)

A. cone
B. rectangular prism
C. pentagonal pyramid
D. sphere
E. cylinder

14.
(116)

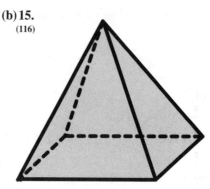

A. rectangular pyramid
B. triangular prism
C. cylinder
D. rectangular prism
E. triangular pyramid

(b) 15.
(116)

A. triangular prism
B. rectangular prism
C. cone
D. triangular pyramid
E. rectangular pyramid

Find the volume of each solid below.

16.
(116)

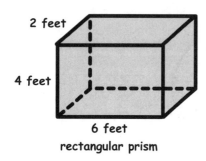

2 feet

4 feet

6 feet

rectangular prism

(c) 17.
(116)

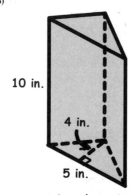

10 in.

4 in.

5 in.

triangular prism

Find the surface area of each solid below.

(d) 18.
(116)

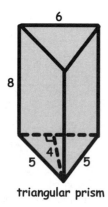

6

8

5   4   5

triangular prism

19.
(116)

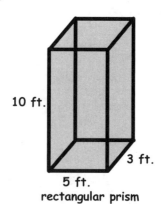

10 ft.

3 ft.

5 ft.

rectangular prism

574

Solve each equation below.

20.
(73) $\dfrac{x+6}{7} = -2$

21.
(81) $22 + x = 4 - 8x$

Translate the word problem below into an equation; then solve.

(e) 22.
(82)   Payless Plumbing Service charges $50 for a service call (just to come to the house) plus $60 per hour to do the job. The Clog Squad charges $80 for a service call plus $50 per hour to do the job. How many hours would a job have to take for the bills of both plumbing services to be the same?

Lesson 117—More on Volume and Surface Area

In the last lesson, we learned how to calculate the volume and surface area of prisms. We're going to continue learning about volume and surface area. For our next example, let's see how to calculate the volume of a cylinder. In the cylinder below, there are 2 bases and they're both circles. That's always the case with a cylinder. The radius of each base is 6 centimeters. The height (altitude) of the cylinder is 17 centimeters.

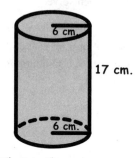

**What is the volume
of this cylinder?**

Volume of a Cylinder

To find the volume, we just need to find the area of the base and multiply it by the altitude.

Volume of a Cylinder = area of base × altitude

It's the same calculation as the volume of a prism. The only difference is the base is a circle this time. The area of a circle is πr^2, remember. So let's put that in for the area of the base.

$$= \pi r^2 \times \text{altitude}$$

Now we can substitute the specific numbers. The radius is 6 centimeters. That should go in for r. We'll use 3.14 for π. And the altitude is 17.

$$= 3.14 \cdot 6^2 \times 17$$

From here, we just simplify the expression.

$$= 3.14 \cdot 36 \times 17$$

$$= 113.04 \times 17$$

$$= 1,921.68$$

The volume of the cylinder is 1,921.68 cubic centimeters.

Surface Area of a Cylinder

Next, let's calculate the surface area of the cylinder. That's just the sum of the areas of all the faces. The bases are congruent circles. So we can just multiply the area of one of the bases by 2 to get the area of both of those. Then we need to add the area of the lateral surface. It's actually called the **lateral area**. For a cylinder, the lateral area is just one continuous piece. But for other solids, it is often several faces. In general, the lateral area is the sum of all the lateral faces, however many there may be.

lateral area = sum of the area of the lateral faces

So the surface area of the cylinder equals the area of the two bases plus the lateral he lateral area.

Surface Area of Cylinder = 2 × area of base + lateral area

But how do we calculate the lateral area here? Imagine taking the cylinder apart by removing the top and bottom and unwrapping the middle section. When you flatten out the section it will have the shape of a rectangle.

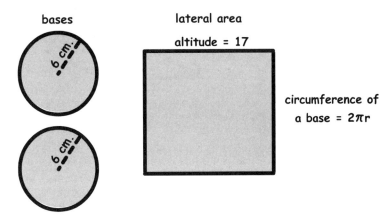

Unwrapping the cylinder

The height of the rectangle will equal the altitude of the cylinder (17 centimeters). The width of the rectangle will equal the circumference of the circles on top and bottom—the bases. That's because the middle section was wrapped all the way around the cylinder. That means the lateral area is a rectangle with a height (altitude) of 17 and a width of the circumference of a base. Multiplying width and height gives us this.

lateral area = circumference of a base × altitude

Now let's put this expression into the calculation for the surface area of the cylinder.

Surface Area of Cylinder = 2 × area of base + circumference of base × altitude

From here, we just put in the numbers and simplify. We already calculated the area of the bases when we found the volume. The area of each base came out to 113.04. The circumference of a circle is $2\pi r$. In this case, $2\pi r$ equals $2 \cdot 3.14 \cdot 6$. And the altitude of the cylinder is 17.

$$\text{Surface Area of Cylinder} = 2(113.04) + 2(3.14)(6)(17)$$

$$= 2(113.04) + (37.68)(17)$$

$$= 226.08 + 640.56$$

$$= 866.64$$

The surface area of the cylinder equals 886.64 square centimeters. It's square units because we're calculating an area not a volume.

Volume of a Pyramid

Now let's find the volume and surface area of a pyramid. We'll start with the volume. The diagram below is a rectangular pyramid because the base is a square. A square qualifies as a rectangle. You might guess that the volume should equal the area of the base multiplied by the altitude, but that's not it.

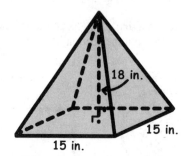

What is the volume of this rectangular pyramid?

Since a pyramid gets skinnier as you go up, the volume is smaller than that. The volume of a pyramid equals $\frac{1}{3}$ of the area of the base multiplied by the altitude.

$$\text{Volume of Pyramid} = \frac{1}{3} \times \text{area of base} \times \text{altitude}$$

For this particular pyramid, the base is a square with side lengths of 15 inches. So the area of the base is $15 \cdot 15$. The altitude is 18 inches. We can just put in the numbers and simplify.

$$\text{Volume of Pyramid} = \frac{1}{3} \times 15 \cdot 15 \times 18$$

$$= \frac{1}{3} \times 225 \times 18$$

$$= 1{,}350$$

The volume of the rectangular pyramid is 1,350 cubic inches.

Surface Area of a Pyramid

Now for the surface area of the pyramid. We just need to add up the areas of all the faces. One face is the square base on bottom. The other faces are the lateral faces around the sides. Those are triangles. The sum of these equals the lateral area. So the surface area calculation should look like this.

Surface Area of Pyramid = area of base + lateral area (sum of area of triangular sides)

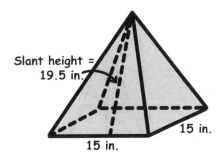

Slant height = 19.5 in.

15 in.

15 in.

What is the surface area of
this rectangular pyramid?

We already know the area of the base is $15 \cdot 15$ or 225 square inches. The lateral faces are four triangles. We need the areas of those. Remember the area of a triangle is $\frac{1}{2} \times$ base $\times$ altitude . We'll take the bottom of each triangle as its base. Each bottom is 15 inches long. The altitude of the triangles is different from the altitude of the pyramid. The triangle altitude is slanted. It runs from the base of each triangle to the vertex (top) of the pyramid. This distance is actually called the **slant height**. The diagram shows that the slant height is 19.5 inches. So the altitude of each triangle is 19.5. The area of each of the triangle faces equals this.

$$\text{Area of each triangular face} = \frac{1}{2} \times \text{base} \times \text{altitude}$$

$$= \frac{1}{2} \times 15 \times 19.5$$

$$= 146.25$$

So each triangular face has an area of 146.25 square inches. Now we're ready to add everything up to get the surface area of the entire pyramid. The area of the square base is 225. We should add the lateral area (the area of the four triangle faces) to that and simplify. Since each of the 4 triangular faces has the same area, we'll just multiply 146.25 by 4.

$$\text{Surface Area of Pyramid} = \text{area of base} + \text{lateral area}$$

$$= 225 + (4)(146.25)$$

$$= 225 + 585$$

$$= 810$$

The surface area of the entire pyramid is 810 square inches.

Volume of a Cone

Now let's find the volume and surface area of a cone. To find the volume of any cone, we take $\frac{1}{3}$ of the area of the base times the altitude. It's the same as calculating the volume of a pyramid, only the base is a circle.

$$\text{Volume of Cone} = \frac{1}{3} \times \text{area of base} \times \text{altitude}$$

The cone below has a radius of 12 inches and an altitude of 30 inches. Since the base is a circle, its area is equal to πr^2.

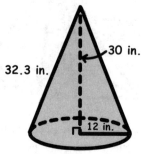

**What is the volume
of this cone?**

Substituting πr^2 in for the area of the base and 30 for the altitude gives us this.

$$\text{Volume} = \frac{1}{3} \times \pi r^2 \times 30$$

We'll use 3.14 for π and the radius of the base is 12 inches.

$$\text{Volume} = \frac{1}{3}(3.14)(12)^2(30)$$

Now we just simplify.

$$= \frac{1}{3}(452.16)(30)$$

$$= (150.72)(30)$$

$$= 4,521.6$$

The volume of the cone is 4,521.6 cubic inches.

Surface Area of a Cone

Now let's quickly calculate the surface area of our cone. The surface area is equal to the area of the base—the circle on the bottom—plus the area of the middle section, which is the lateral area.

Surface Area of a Cone = area of base + lateral area

We already figured out the area of the base. That was πr^2 or $(3.14)(12)^2$, which comes to 452.16 square inches. The lateral area is more difficult because it's just a smooth section all the way around. If we could take the cone apart and unwrap the middle section, it would look like this.

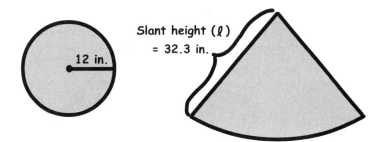

Of course, the circle is the base of the cone. And we know it's radius is 12 inches. The length of the side of the middle section is the slant height. It's represented by the letter ℓ, by the way. But here's how we calculate the area of the middle section—the lateral area. It equals π times the radius of the base (r) times the slant height (ℓ).

$$\text{Lateral area of cone} = \pi r \ell$$

Putting in the numbers and simplifying gives us this.

$$= (3.14)(12)(32.3)$$

$$= 1{,}217.06$$

We end up with 1,217.06 square inches (rounded to two decimal places).

Now to get the surface area of the complete cone, we just need to add the area of the base and the lateral area.

$$\text{Total surface area } = 452.16 + 1{,}217.06$$

$$= 1{,}669.22$$

The surface area of our cone is 1,669.22 square inches. Here again is the complete equation for calculating the surface area of any cone.

$$\text{Surface Area of Cone} = \text{Area of the base } (\pi r^2) + \text{Lateral Area } (\pi r \ell)$$

Practice 117

a.
(117)
Find the volume of the solid below. Use 3.14 for π. Write your answer as a decimal.

b.
(115)
Find the area of the figure below. Use 3.14 for π. Write your answer as a decimal.

11 ft.

5 ft.

cylinder

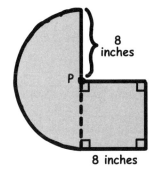

8 inches

P

8 inches

Find the surface area of each solid below. Use 3.14 for π. Write your answer as a decimal.

c.
(117)

cone

d.
(116)

13 ft.

28 ft.

5 ft.   13 ft.

24 ft.
triangular prism

e. Translate the word problem below into an equation; then solve.
(54)

There were 175 kinds of skateboards in the store, but only 21 of them were made from bamboo. What percent of the skateboards were made from bamboo? (The answer to your equation will be in decimal form. Make sure your final answer is written as a percent.)

Problem Set 117

Tell whether each sentence below is True or False.

1. The volume of a cylinder is equal to the area of the base times the altitude.
(117)

2. The volume of a pyramid is equal to the area of the base times the altitude.
(117)

Find the missing angle in each figure below.

3.
(107)

4.
(105)

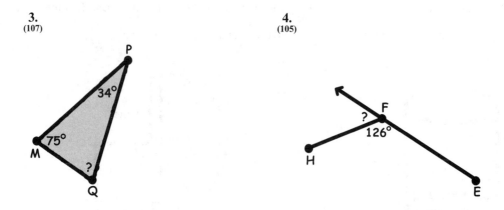

Solve each proportion below. Write your answer as a fully reduced fraction if needed.

5.
(112) $\dfrac{3}{5} = \dfrac{x}{20}$

6.
(112) $\dfrac{x}{7} = \dfrac{12}{56}$

Find the perimeter of each figure below.

7.
(113)

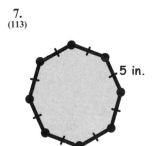

.5 in.

8.
(113)

6 feet

9 feet

15 feet

3 feet

Find the area of each figure below. Write your answer as a whole number or decimal.

9.
(114)

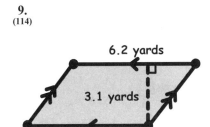

6.2 yards

3.1 yards

10.
(114)

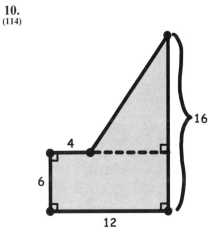

4

16

6

12

Find the circumference (or perimeter) of each figure below. Use 3.14 for π. Write your answer as a decimal.

11.
(115)

D

14 meters

12.
(115)

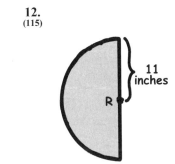

11 inches

R

Identify each solid below.

13.
(116)

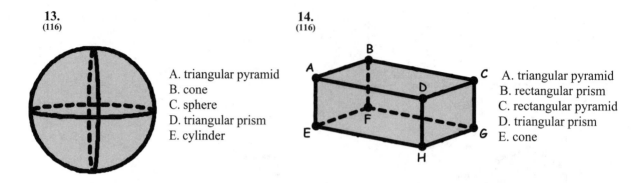

A. triangular pyramid
B. cone
C. sphere
D. triangular prism
E. cylinder

14.
(116)

A. triangular pyramid
B. rectangular prism
C. rectangular pyramid
D. triangular prism
E. cone

Find the volume of each solid below. Use 3.14 for π. Write your answer as a whole number or decimal.

(a) 15.
(117)

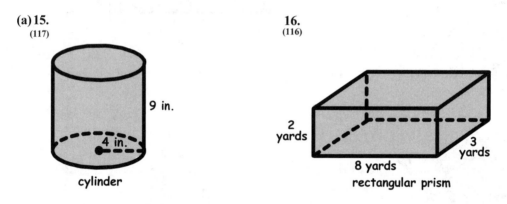

9 in.

4 in.

cylinder

16.
(116)

2 yards

8 yards

3 yards

rectangular prism

Find the area of the figure below. Use 3.14 for π. Write your answer as a decimal.

(b) 17.
(115)

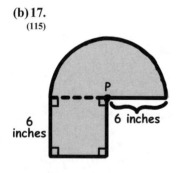

P

6 inches

6 inches

Find the surface area of each solid below. Use 3.14 for π. Write your answer as a decimal.

(c) 18.
(117)

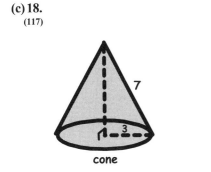

cone

19.
(117)

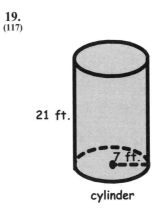

21 ft.

7 ft.

cylinder

(d) 20.
(116)

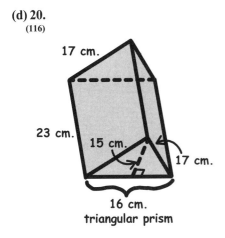

17 cm.

23 cm.

15 cm.

17 cm.

16 cm.
triangular prism

Translate the word problem below into an equation; then solve.

(e) 21.
(54)
There were 120 kinds of dogs in the kennel, but only 18 of those were puppies. What percent were puppies? (The answer to your equation will be in decimal form. Make sure your final answer is written as a percent.)

CHAPTER 15:
RELATIONS, FUNCTIONS, AND GRAPHING

Lesson 118—Relations and Functions

We spent the last two chapters on geometry. Now we're going to go back to some algebra topics. So far, all of our algebra equations have had just one unknown (an x). But some equations have two different unknowns: an x and a y.

Two-Variable Equations

Let's go through a real world example involving a two-unknown equation.

Water is running out of a hose and at a rate of 3 gallons every hour. Show the mathematical relationship between the time that the water runs and the total amount of water that's run out.

Think about how these two quantities time and water will change together. After 1 hour, a total of 3 gallons of water will have run out. After 2 hours, the total will be 6 gallons of water. After 3 hours, the total will be 9 gallons of water. And after 4 hours, it will be 12 gallons, and so on. We could set up a table showing how time and the total amount of water change.

time	water
1	3
2	6
3	9
4	12
5	15
6	18
⋮	⋮

We could keep this table going forever. What is shows, though, is that time and the total amount of water are two changing quantities that are linked together mathematically. As one goes up, the other goes up.

So what does this have to do with equation having two unknowns? Well, what if we let x stand for the time? Then, since the total amount of water is a different quantity, we should use a different letter for it. We could let y stand for the total amount of water.

$$x = \text{time} \qquad\qquad y = \text{total amount of water}$$

Now we have two different unknowns: x and y. And we can use these to write an equation showing how time and the total amount of water are linked together mathematically. It's a pretty simple relationship. The amount of water is always equal to 3 multiplied by the time, because 3 gallons of water run out every hour. That gives us the following equation.

$$\underset{\text{water}}{\text{amount of}} \searrow \quad \overset{\text{time}}{\swarrow}$$
$$y = 3x$$

This equation represents our situation with the water running out of the hose. Here's the way the equation works. What if we wanted to know how many gallons of water would come out in total after 7 hours? What we do is put 7 in for x.

$$y = 3(7)$$

And then calculate y.

$$y = 21$$

Since y equals 21, we know that 21 gallons of water will have run out of the hose after 7 hours. As for the equation, we say that when $x = 7$, the matching value for y is $y = 21$.

Finding a Matching y-Value

The main point is that with a two-unknown equation (like $y = 3x$), we can put in a value for one unknown and find the matching value for the other unknown. Since x and y can have many different values, they're actually called **variables**. The word variable just means that the value of the unknown can "vary." It can change. For instance, x could be 1, 2, 3, or anything. And the same goes for y. Equations of this kind are called **two-variable equations**. Instead of just an x, they have an x and a y. And the variables represent two different quantities that change. Since those quantities are linked together mathematically, we can write an equation with them.

There are actually many situations in the real world that can be represented by two-variable equations. What if you were cutting logs and loading them onto a truck? The greater the number of logs, the heavier the load on the truck. So the number of logs and the weight on the truck would be related mathematically. Those would be the variables. We could let x be the number of logs and y the weight on the truck. And if we knew the details, we could write a two-variable equation to represent that situation. Here's another example. What if you were going to make drapes for a house? The fabric would cost so much per square yard. So the number of yards of fabric and the total price would be linked mathematically. And you could write an equation to represent the relationship between those variables. Whatever equation you came up with would depend on the price. Let's do another example. On this one, we'll actually write the equation.

> A truck driver is traveling from Dallas, Texas to Los Angeles, California. His average speed is 60 miles per hour. Write a two-variable equation to represent his trip.

The first step is to figure out the variables. The two changing quantities in this situation are time and distance traveled. We'll let x stand for the time (in hours), and we'll let y stand for the distance traveled (in miles).

$$x = \text{time (in hours)} \qquad\qquad y = \text{distance (in miles)}$$

Now let's write the equation. Since the truck driver's speed is 60 miles per hour, he must go 60 miles every hour he's on the road. That's 60 miles after 1 hour, 120 miles after 2 hours, 180 miles after 3 hours, and so on. The equation that represents this situation mathematically is $y = 60x$.

Here's how we could use this equation. Let's say we want to know how far the truck will go in 2 hours. All we have to do is put 2 in for x.

$$y = 60x$$

$$y = 60(2)$$

$$y = 120$$

When $x = 2$, $y = 120$. That means after 2 hours, the truck will have traveled 120 miles.

To figure out how far the truck would travel after 4 hours, we just put 4 in for x.

$$y = 60x$$

$$y = 60(4)$$

$$y = 240$$

After 4 hours, the truck will have gone 240 miles.

Finding a Matching x-Value

We've been starting with a number for x and finding a matching value for y. But what if we wanted to reverse things? Let's say we already know the number of miles. So we have a number for y. And we need to find a matching value for x (the time). Specifically, in the last example, what if we wanted to know how many hours it would take the truck to go 480 miles? All we have to do is put 480 in for y.

$$y = 60x$$

$$480 = 60x$$

Now we can find the matching value for x by solving the equation. We can undo the multiplication by dividing both sides by 60.

$$\frac{480}{60} = \frac{60x}{60}$$

Simplifying on the right gives us this.

$$\frac{480}{60} = x$$

The last step is to do the division.

$$8 = x$$

When $y = 480$, $x = 8$. That means it will take 8 hours to go 480 miles. That's how you start with a number for y and then find a matching value for x.

Two Special Words

Relationships between variables such as our first example with the running water (which had the equation $y = 3x$) and the truck driver example (which had the equation $y = 60x$) have a special name. They're called functions. The technical definition of a **function** is a relationship between variables where if you pick a value for x, there's just one matching value for y. We often say that in a function "y depends on x."

Some relationships between variables don't qualify as a function. This table represents a relationship between x and y. We won't worry about the equation for now. But notice the x column.

x	y
9	-3
4	-2
1	-1
0	0
1	1
4	2
9	3

The number 9 shows up twice. At the top, when $x = 9$, $y = -3$. But at the bottom when $x = 9$, $y = 3$. That's two different y values for the same x. A relationship like this doesn't qualify as a function. For each x, there can only be one matching y-value. There's actually a special name for relationships between variables whether or not they qualify as a function. Their called relations. Basically, a **relation** is any relationship between variables. So a function is a special kind of relation—one where each x-value has just one matching y-value.

Why would the mathematicians bother to create a definition for a function? Well, it's because functions show up so often in the real world. Take the function $y = 60x$, for example. This represented a truck going from Dallas to L.A. at 60 miles per hour. What if we were able to put a number like 3 in for x and then get two answers for y? That would be saying that after 3 hours, the truck had gone two different distances: maybe 180 miles and 240 miles. That makes no sense! The relationship between x and y must be a function or it couldn't accurately represent the truck driver problem. The main point is that mathematicians defined functions because they represent so many situations in the real world.

Practice 118

a. Find the volume of the solid below. Use 3.14 for π. Round your answer to two decimal places.
(117)

cone

b. Tell whether the relationship in the table below represents a function.
(118)

x	y
-4	-16
-3	-9
-2	-4
-1	-1
0	0
1	-1

591

c.
(118) For the function $y = 4x + 7$, find the matching y-value when $x = 3$.

d.
(118) For the function $y = -3x + 2$, find the x-value that makes $y = 8$.

e.
(79) Translate the word problem below into an equation; then solve.

Tomas can paint 7 toy soldiers per hour, and Leonard can paint 5 per hour. Together, how many hours should it take them to paint 48 toy soldiers?

Problem Set 118

Tell whether each sentence below is True or False.

1.
(118) A relation is a relationship between two variables such as x and y.

2.
(118) A function is a special kind of relation where if you pick a value for x, there's just one matching value for y.

3.
(118) The equation $y = 60x$ represents a function.

Answer each question below by writing and solving an equation.

4.
(105) $\angle 7$ and $\angle 8$ are complementary. If $\angle 8$ has a measure of $52°$, find the measure of $\angle 7$.

5.
(105) $\angle L$ and $\angle X$ are supplementary. If $\angle L$ has a measure of $86°$, find the measure of $\angle X$.

Find the area of each figure below.

6.
(114)

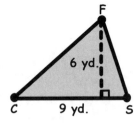

7.
(114)

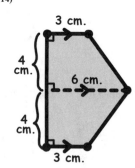

Find the area of each figure below. Use 3.14 for π. Write your answer as a decimal.

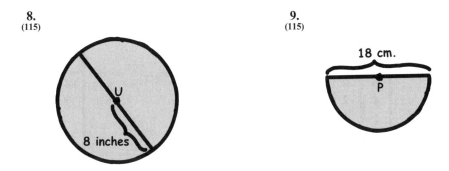

8.
(115)

9.
(115)

18 cm.

P

8 inches

U

Find the volume of each solid below. Use 3.14 for π. Write your answer as a decimal.

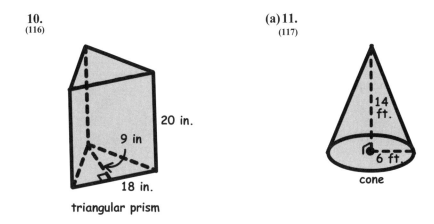

10.
(116)

(a) 11.
(117)

20 in.

9 in

18 in.

triangular prism

14 ft.

6 ft.

cone

Find the surface area of each solid below. Use 3.14 for π. Write your answer as a decimal.

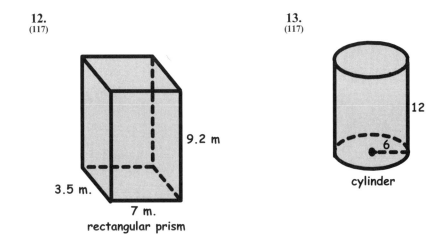

12.
(117)

13.
(117)

9.2 m

3.5 m.

7 m.

rectangular prism

12

6

cylinder

Tell whether the relationship in each table below represents a function.

14.
(118)

y=6x

x	y
0	0
1	6
2	12
3	18
4	24
5	30

15.
(118)

x	y
9	-3
4	-2
1	-1
0	0
1	1
4	2

16.
(118)

y=4x-7

x	y
-2	-15
-1	-11
0	-7
1	-3
2	1
3	5

(b) 17.
(118)

x	y
-4	16
-3	9
-2	4
-1	1
0	0
1	1

Answer each question below.

18. For the function $y = -10x$, find the matching y-value when $x = 3$.
(118)

(c) 19. For the function $y = 5x + 9$, find the matching y-value when $x = 4$.
(118)

20. For the function $y = 6x$, find the x-value that makes $y = 30$.
(118)

(d) 21. For the function $y = -2x + 1$, find the x-value that makes $y = 3$.
(118)

Translate the word problem below into an equation; then solve.

(e) 22. Opal can make 9 beaded bracelets per hour, and Lynette can make 6 per hour. Together, how many
(79) hours should it take them to make 45 beaded bracelets?

Lesson 119—More on Functions

In the last lesson we learned about functions. Remember, a function is a relationship between variables where every x-value has just one matching y-value. Here's a simple example of a function.

x	y
3	26
2	18
1	10
0	2
-1	-6
-2	-14

$y = 8x+2$

The table has several pairs of x and y-values. The equation that represents the entire relationship is $y = 8x+2$. Let's use this equation to figure out what y has to be when $x = -3$. All we have to do is put -3 in for x in the equation and calculate the matching y value.

$$y = 8x+2$$

$$y = 8(-3)+2$$

$$y = -24+2$$

$$y = -22$$

That's how we can add more pairs of numbers to the table. We can just put a number for x in the equation and calculate the matching value for y.

Independent and Dependent Variables

There are a few technical words about functions that you should know. In a function, the variable x is called the **independent variable**. And the variable y is called the **dependent variable**. Here's where these words come from. For the function $y = 8x+2$, the x is independent because we can put any number we want in for x. Earlier, we put -3 in for x, but we could put any number in. That's why we say that x is independent. It can be anything. But the value of y is dependent on whatever is put in for x. After putting in -3 for x, y had to equal -22. So y is the dependent variable. It depends on x.

The letters x and y aren't the only ones that can be used for the variables in a function. In fact, people often prefer to use different letters, especially when they're doing a real world problem. What if we were analyzing how far a car travels after so many hours? We could make $x =$ the time and $y =$ the distance. But a lot of people would rather use the letter t for time and the letter d for distance. That makes it easier to remember what the letters stand for. Then the equation might look something like this: $d = 60t$. This qualifies as a function, because every t has just one matching d-value. And even though this function doesn't have the letters x and y, there's still a dependent and an independent variable: t is independent, and d is dependent. Basically, the variable that's by itself on one side is the dependent variable, and the other variable is the independent variable.

Let's look at the equation $A = 14P+1$. There are two variables: A and P. Since the equation is solved for A, we'll assume that A is the dependent variable and P is the independent variable. We would normally put a number in for P first and then find the matching value for A. Even though that's the normal order, it's possible to put a number in for A first and then find a matching value for P. For instance, we can put 15 in for A.

$$A = 14P + 1$$

$$15 = 14P + 1$$

Now we can find a matching value for P by just solving the equation. Some undoing is required, but we know how to do that. First, we subtract 1 from both sides.

$$15 - 1 = 14P + 1 - 1$$

Next, we simplify on both sides.

$$14 = 14P$$

Now we can undo the multiplication.

$$\frac{14}{14} = \frac{14P}{14}$$

The last step is to simplify again.

$$1 = P$$

So when $A = 15$, $P = 1$.

Domain

Another technical word that's often used with functions is domain. The **domain** of a function consists of all the numbers that can possibly be put in for x, the independent variable. As an example, let's go back to the function $y = 8x + 2$. There's nothing to stop us from putting any number we want in for x in this equation. We could put in any positive number, like 3, 14, or 1,080. Or we could put in any fraction or decimal like $\frac{1}{2}$, $\frac{5}{9}$, or 0.98. We could even put in a negative number, such as -3 or -49, or $-\frac{3}{4}$. All these different kinds of numbers fall under a larger category of numbers called **real numbers**. Since there are no restrictions on what number we can put in for x, we say that the domain of the function $y = 8x + 2$ is all real numbers. That just means we can put any number we want in for the independent variable, x.

$$y = 8x + 2$$

domain = all real numbers

Here's another function: $y = 3x - 1$. We can also put any number we want in for x in this function. That includes positive or negative whole numbers (integers), fractions, decimals, etc. So the domain of this function is also all real numbers.

$$y = 3x - 1$$

domain = all real numbers

You might be wondering what kind of function we would *not* be able to put in any number at all for x. Here's an example of a function with a slightly different domain: $y = \frac{3}{x}$. This qualifies as a function, because when we put a number in for x, we get just one matching value for y. But notice this function contains an x in the bottom of a fraction. That's important, because in basic math we're not allowed to divide by 0. If we tried to put 0 in for x in this function, we would end up with this.

$$y = \frac{3}{0} \qquad \textbf{not allowed}$$

Now the fraction has division by 0 and that's not allowed. So for this function, we can put any number in for x, except 0. That's the domain of this function.

$$y = \frac{3}{0}$$

domain = all real numbers except 0

Here's another function: $y = \dfrac{7}{x-1}$. This doesn't have all real numbers as its domain either. Putting 1 in for x makes the denominator equal 0.

$$y = \frac{7}{1-1}$$

$$y = \frac{7}{0} \qquad \textbf{not allowed}$$

Any other number but 1 will work. But 1 is off limits. So the domain of this function is all real numbers except 1.

$$y = \frac{7}{x-1}$$

domain = all real numbers except 1

Range

Another technical word that goes along with domain is range. The **range** is all the possible numbers that the dependent variable can equal. Let's go back to the function $y = 8x + 2$. Remember, the domain of this function is all real numbers. Well, it turns out that the range is also all real numbers: y can also equal any number. Basically, we can always come up with a number for x that, when it's put into the equation, will make y equal anything. For instance, what if we wanted y to equal 100? We could figure out what x would have to equal in order to do that. We could just put 100 in for y and solve for x.

$$100 = 8x + 2$$

$$100 - 2 = 8x + 2 - 2$$

$$98 = 8x$$

$$12.25 = x$$

Since $x = 12.25$, we know that putting 12.25 in for x will make $y = 100$. So the number 100 is included in the range. We could do that to show that y could equal any other number we wanted. So the range is all real numbers.

$$y = 8x + 2$$

range = all real numbers

Here's another function that we looked at earlier: $y = \dfrac{3}{x}$. Let's see if we can figure out its range. For this function, the range isn't all real numbers because, if you analyze the equation, you'll realize that y can never equal 0. Remember, from basic math that the only way a fraction can equal 0 is when its numerator is 0. (The denominator can never equal 0.) But it's impossible for $\dfrac{3}{x}$ to equal 0 because the numerator already equals 3. If the fraction on the right side of $y = \dfrac{3}{x}$ can never equal 0, then y can never equal 0 either. Since 0 is the only number that's off limits for 0, the range of this function is all real numbers except 0.

$$y = \dfrac{3}{x}$$

range = all real numbers except 0

Practice 119

a.
(117) Find the surface area of the solid below.

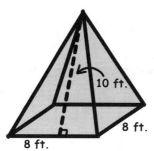

8 ft.

8 ft.

10 ft.

rectangular pyramid

b.
(119) For the function $y = -\dfrac{1}{2}x + 7$, find the matching y-value when $x = -8$.

c.
(119) For the function $y = \dfrac{1}{5}x + 2$, find the x-value that makes $y = -4$.

d.
(119) Select the domain and range of the function $y = \dfrac{8}{x-3}$.

    A. Domain: All real numbers except 3; Range: All real numbers except 8
    B. Domain: All real numbers except 3; Range: All real numbers except 0
    C. Domain: All real numbers except 0; Range: All real numbers except 8
    D. Domain: All real numbers; Range: All real numbers
    E. Domain: All real numbers except 8; Range: All real numbers except 0

e. Translate the word problem below into an equation; then solve.
(55)

If a motor scooter rider traveled for 3 hours at a constant speed and went a distance of 123 miles, at what speed did she travel?

Problem Set 119

Tell whether each sentence below is True or False.

1. In a function, the variable that's by itself on one side is the dependent variable, and the other variable is the independent variable.
(119)

2. The domain of a function is all the numbers that you could possibly put in for the independent variable.
(119)

3. The range of a function is all the numbers that make a denominator equal to 0.
(119)

Find the perimeter of each figure below. Write your answer as a whole number or decimal.

4.
(113)

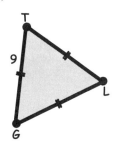

5.
(113)

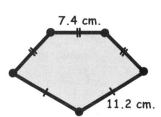

Find the volume of each solid below. Use 3.14 for π. Write your answer as a whole number or decimal.

6.
(116)

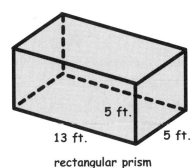

rectangular prism

7.
(117)

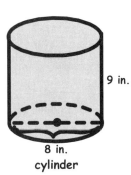

cylinder

Find the surface area of each solid below.

8.
(116)

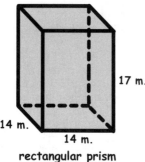

rectangular prism

(a) 9.
(117)

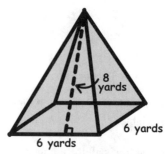

rectangular pyramid

Tell whether the relationship in each table below represents a function.

10.
(118)

y=-2x+9

x	y
-2	13
-1	11
0	9
1	7
2	5
3	3

11.
(118)

x	y
-5	-9
-3	-2
-1	0
0	-1
2	-9
4	-12

Answer each question below.

12.
(119)
For the function $y = 12x - 4$, find the matching y-value when $x = 2$.

(b) 13.
(119)
For the function $y = -\frac{1}{3}x + 5$, find the matching y-value when $x = -6$.

14.
(119)
For the function $y = -5x$, find the x-value that makes $y = 35$.

(c) 15.
(119)
For the function $y = \frac{1}{4}x + 3$, find the x-value that makes $y = -1$.

Give the independent and dependent variable of each function below.

16.
(119)
$y = \frac{1}{2}x + 3$

17.
(119)
$d = \frac{-2}{t + 7}$

18.
(119)
$q = r^2 - 8r - 1$

Select the domain and range of each function below.

19. $y = 11x - 5$
(119)

       A. Domain: All positive real numbers; Range: All positive real numbers
       B. Domain: All real numbers; Range: All real numbers greater than -5
       C. Domain: All real numbers greater than 11; Range: All real numbers greater than -5
       D. Domain: All real numbers; Range: All real numbers
       E. Domain: All real numbers greater than -5; Range: All real numbers

20. $y = \dfrac{9}{x}$
(119)

       A. Domain: All real numbers except 0; Range: All real numbers except 0
       B. Domain: All real numbers except 9; Range: All real numbers except 0
       C. Domain: All real numbers except 0; Range: All real numbers except 9
       D. Domain: All real numbers; Range: All real numbers except 0
       E. Domain: All real numbers; Range: All real numbers

(d) 21. $y = \dfrac{7}{x-2}$
(119)

       A. Domain: All real numbers except 0; Range: All real numbers except 7
       B. Domain: All real numbers except 2; Range: All real numbers except 7
       C. Domain: All real numbers; Range: All real numbers
       D. Domain: All real numbers except 7; Range: All real numbers except 0
       E. Domain: All real numbers except 2; Range: All real numbers except 0

Translate the word problem below into an equation; then solve.

(e) 22. If a truck driver traveled for 5 hours at a constant speed and went a distance of 135 miles, at what speed
(55)   did he travel?

Lesson 120— Functional Notation

We've been learning about functions. It turns out that there are short ways to write functions. For instance, if we were working with the function $y = 8x + 2$, one short way to write it is like this: $y(x)$. It's pronounced "y of x." Notice the dependent variable, y, is listed first and the independent variable, x, is listed second, inside parentheses. The advantage of writing $y(x)$ is it's shorter and simpler than having to write out $y = 8x + 2$ every time. This method of writing a function is called **functional notation**. Notation just means a way of writing something.

Here's a function with different variables: $d = 10t - 4$. To write this in functional notation, we put the independent variable, which is t in this case, inside parentheses. And the dependent variable, d, goes in front, outside parentheses: $d(t)$. This is pronounced "d of t." If we were working with this function, instead of writing out the entire equation repeatedly, we could save time and space by writing $d(t)$ instead.

Putting a Number in for x

Another advantage of functional notation is that it makes it easy to see what number has been put in for the independent variable. Let's go back to the function $y = 8x + 2$. Since y is the dependent variable and x is the independent variable, we could write this function as $y(x)$. But let's say we want to put 1 in for x and find the matching y-value. We could just put 1 in the equation and solve for y like this.

$$y = 8(1) + 2$$

$$y = 8 + 2$$

$$y = 10$$

We end up with $y = 10$. The only problem with this answer is that you can't see what number was put in for x to get $y = 10$. Here's where functional notation comes in. Instead of having just y on the left side of the equation, people write y as $y(x)$.

$$y(x) = 8x + 2$$

Now when they put 1 in for x, the 1 goes in place of the x on the left side too.

$$y(1) = 8(1) + 2$$

The way to pronounce this is "y of 1." This just means that we've put 1 in for the independent variable x. Now after simplifying the right side, we're able to see what number was put in for x to get $y = 10$.

$$y(1) = 10$$

This equation says that if you put 1 in for x in the function $y(x)$, you end up with $y = 10$.

Here's another function: $A = 60t$. To write this in functional notation, A is the dependent variable, so it goes first. And t is the independent variable, so it goes second, inside parentheses. That gives us $A(t)$. Now let's say that we want to put 2 in for t and find the matching A-value. And let's use functional notation to do this. The first step is to write the function like this.

$$A(t) = 60t$$

Now we need to put 2 in for both t's.

$$A(2) = 60(2)$$

From here, we calculate the value of the right side.

$$A(2) = 120$$

The equation $A(2) = 120$ means when $t = 2$, $A = 120$. And notice that when written this way, we can see what number was put in for t to get the answer $A = 120$.

Using Different Letters

Sometimes you will be working with two functions and both of them have the same variables. How do you tell them apart in functional notation? For instance, what if we were working with these two functions?

$$y = 17x \qquad\qquad\qquad y = -6x$$

They both have independent variables x and dependent variables y. But we can't represent both functions as $y(x)$ because we wouldn't be able to tell them apart. What we do is use different letters for the dependent variables. We could represent $y = 17x$ as $f(x)$ and $y = -6x$ as $g(x)$. The letters f and g are used a lot in cases like this. We could work with $f(x)$ and $g(x)$ in the usual ways. What if we want to know the matching value for y in $y = 17x$ when $x = 2$? First, we write the function like this.

$$f(x) = 17x$$

Now we put 2 in for both of the x's and simplify on the right.

$$f(2) = 17(2)$$

$$f(2) = 34$$

The equation $f(2) = 34$ just means that for this function when $x = 2$, $y = 34$.

Practice 120

a. Find the area of the figure below.
(114)

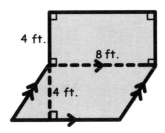

b.
(119)
Select the domain and range of the function $y = \dfrac{-2}{x+5}$.

    A.   Domain: All real numbers except -5; Range: All real numbers except -2

    B.   Domain: All real numbers except -5; Range: All real numbers except 0

    C.   Domain: All real numbers except 0; Range: All real numbers except -2

    D.   Domain: All real numbers; Range: All real numbers

    E.   Domain: All real numbers except -2; Range: All real numbers except 0

Find each value below.

c.
(120)
If $y = 4x - 3$, find $y(7)$.

d.
(120)
If $y = \dfrac{60}{x}$ is represented by $f(x)$, find $f(-20)$.

e.
(55)
Translate the word problem below into an equation; then solve.

If William is driving at 37 miles per hour, how many hours will it take him to travel 15 miles? Round your answer to the nearest tenths place (one decimal place).

Problem Set 120

Tell whether each sentence below is True or False

1.
(120)
Functional notation is a short way of writing functions.

2.
(120)
Functional notation makes it easy to see what number you've put in for the independent variable.

Solve each proportion below. Write your answer as a fully reduced fraction if needed.

3.
(112)
$\dfrac{4}{9} = \dfrac{x}{27}$

4.
(112)
$\dfrac{x}{5} = \dfrac{3}{7}$

Find the area of each figure below.

5.
(114)

(a) 6.
(114)

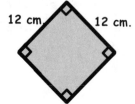

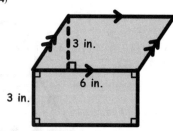

Find the volume of each solid below. Use 3.14 for π. Write your answer as a whole number or decimal.

7.
(117)

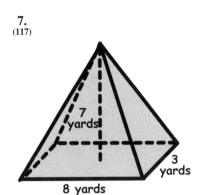

rectangular pyramid

8.
(117)

cone

Tell whether the relationship in each table below represents a function.

9.
(118)

x	y
-4	2
-3	-1
-2	6
0	1
-2	0.5
4	3

10.
(118)

x	y
-1	3.5
0	3
1	2.5
2	2
3	1.5
4	1

Give the independent and dependent variable of each function below.

11. $\quad y = -\dfrac{1}{4}x + \dfrac{1}{2}$
(118)

12. $\quad v = \dfrac{5.1}{s-7}$
(118)

Select the domain and range of each function below.

13. $\quad y = -x + 4$
(119)

      A. Domain: All real numbers greater than -4; Range: All real numbers

      B. Domain: All real numbers; Range: All real numbers

      C. Domain: All real numbers; Range: All real numbers greater than 4

      D. Domain: All real numbers less than 4; Range: All real numbers

      E. Domain: All positive real numbers; Range: All positive real numbers

14.
(119) $y = \dfrac{5}{x}$

    A. Domain: All real numbers except 0; Range: All real numbers except 5
    B. Domain: All real numbers except 5; Range: All real numbers except 0
    C. Domain: All real numbers; Range: All real numbers except 0
    D. Domain: All real numbers; Range: All real numbers
    E. Domain: All real numbers except 0; Range: All real numbers except 0

(b) 15.
(119) $y = \dfrac{-1}{x+3}$

    A. Domain: All real numbers except -1 ; Range: All real numbers except 0
    B. Domain: All real numbers; Range: All real numbers
    C. Domain: All real numbers except -3 ; Range: All real numbers except 0
    D. Domain: All real numbers except -3 ; Range: All real numbers except -1
    E. Domain: All real numbers except 0; Range: All real numbers except -1

Match the functional notation with a function below.

16. $y(x)$
(120)

    A. $y = 5x + 8$

    B. $P = x - 3$

17. $v(t)$
(120)

    C. $v = -9t - 1$

    D. $y = \dfrac{1}{2}T + 4$

18. $P(T)$
(120)

    E. $P = \dfrac{2}{T-5}$

    F. $t = \dfrac{v}{6}$

Find each value below.

(c) 19. If $y = 3x - 1$, find $y(5)$.
(120)

20. If $d = 45t$, find $d(3)$.
(120)

(d) 21. If $y = \dfrac{20}{x}$ is represented by $f(x)$, find $f(-10)$.
(120)

Translate the word problem below into an equation; then solve.

(e) 22. If Leonard is riding his mountain bike at 17 miles per hour, how many hours will it take him to travel 8
(55) miles? Round your answer to the nearest tenths place (one decimal place).

Lesson 121—The Coordinate Plane

We've been learning about functions, which are relationships between variables. It's actually possible to draw a picture of a function. It's a picture of the relationship between the variables x and y. We draw the picture on something called a **coordinate plane**. Here's what a coordinate plane looks like.

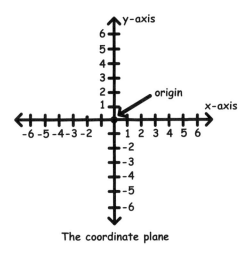

The coordinate plane

It's basically two number lines, one horizontal (x) and one vertical (y). They're called the **x-axis** and **y-axis**. They contain both positive and negative numbers. And the arrows show that the lines go on forever in both directions. The point where the two lines intersect is called the **origin**.

Plotting Points

It turns out that we can take any two numbers and turn the pair into a point on the coordinate plane. Take $x = 3$ and $y = 4$, for instance. To find the point for this pair, we start at the origin, where the x- and y-axis cross. Then, since x equals *positive* 3, we go to the *right* three places along the x-axis to 3. Then since y equals *positive* 4, we go *up* four places until we're directly across from positive 4 on the y-axis.

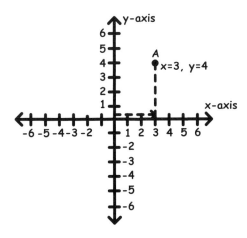

That takes us to this point for $x = 3$ and $y = 4$. That's how it works. We often use a letter to name a point. So we've called this point A, as you can see. Drawing a point for a pair of numbers is called plotting a point. So we just plotted the point for $x = 3$ and $y = 4$.

We can also plot points for negative numbers. Let's plot the point for $x = -1$, $y = -1$. We start at the origin again. Only this time since x is a *negative* number, we go to the *left*. Specifically, we go one place to the left, which takes us to -1 along the x-axis. Then since $y = -1$, we go *down* one place to -1 along the y-axis. And that takes us to the point for $x = -1$, $y = -1$. We'll name this point C.

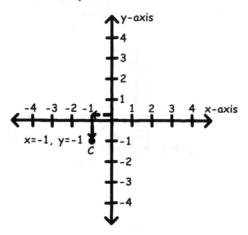

Here's the basic procedure for turning a pair of numbers into a point on the coordinate plane. You start at the origin, then go right or left so many places for x. You go right if x is positive and left if x is negative. From there, you go up or down so many places for y. You go up if y is positive and down if y is negative.

There's not much room on a piece of paper, but a real coordinate plane goes on forever in all directions. That means we could plot points for very large pairs of numbers. For example, we could plot a point for $x = 900,000$, $y = 745,000$. We would start at the origin. Then we would go 900,000 places to the right, and, from there, 745,000 places up. But we would need a much larger piece of paper! We could plot large negative pairs like $x = -1,854,000$, $y = -882,037$ in the same way.

Points on an Axis

Sometimes beginners have a little trouble plotting a point that goes right on top of the x-axis. The point $x = 4$, $y = 0$ is an example. To plot this point, we start at the origin and go four places to the right. Since x is positive, we go right. But since $y = 0$, we don't have to go up or down after that. We just stay on the x-axis.

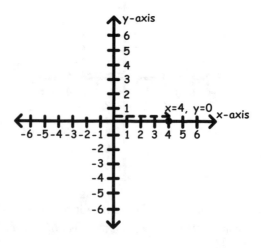

So the point for $x = 4$, $y = 0$ falls right on the x-axis. Actually, any pair of numbers where $y = 0$ will fall on the x-axis. That's because all the points on the x-axis are directly across from 0 on the y-axis. So they all have a y value of 0.

Points can also fall directly on the y-axis. For instance, to plot the point for $x = 0$, $y = 5$, we start at the origin, as usual. But since $x = 0$, we don't go right or left. We just stay at the origin. Then, since $y = 5$, we go up five places. That takes us to a point that falls directly on the y-axis (at 5).

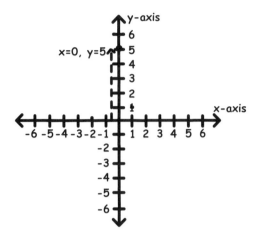

It turns out that all points with $x = 0$ fall on the y-axis. The reason is those points are all directly above or below 0 on the x-axis.

Sometimes we need to plot the point for $x = 0$, $y = 0$. To do that, you start at the origin again. But since both x and y equal 0, you don't go anywhere. You don't go left or right or up or down. That's why the point for $x = 0$, $y = 0$ is the origin itself.

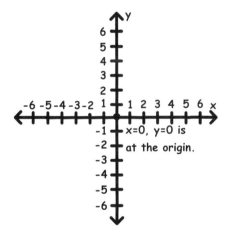

Here are the rules for plotting points that fall on either the x- or y-axis.

Any pair of numbers with y = 0 will be a point on the x-axis.
Any pair of numbers with x = 0 will be a point on the y-axis.

Quadrants

We've learned to plot points. Now let's talk about the coordinate plane itself. The name "coordinate plane" comes from the fact that the plane is flat. Remember, in geometry a plane is flat. And the numbers that go with a point are actually called coordinates. If we plotted the point for $x = 2$, $y = 5$, for instance, we would say that the "x-coordinate" of this point is 2 and the "y-coordinate" is 5. Generally, for any point, the x-value is called the **x-coordinate** and the y-value is called the **y-coordinate**. That's where the name "coordinate" plane comes from.

Because of the way the x-axis and y-axis cross, a coordinate plane can be divided into four sections called **quadrants**, as you can see below. They're labeled with roman numerals. Interestingly, the x- and y-coordinates for all the points in a quadrant always have the same sign.

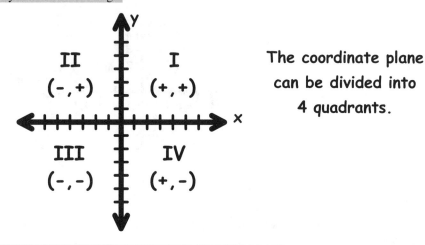

The coordinate plane can be divided into 4 quadrants.

For every single point in the first quadrant, both the x- and y-coordinates are positive. The reason is all the points in the first quadrant are on the right side of the x-axis (to the right of the origin). That's positive territory for x. And they're above the origin, which is positive territory for y. All the points in the second quadrant have a negative x-coordinate and a positive y-coordinate. The reason is these points are to the left of the origin on the x-axis (negative x territory). But they're still above the origin (positive y territory). All the points in the third quadrant have a negative x- and a negative y-coordinate. That's because these points are all to the left of and below the origin. The points in the fourth quadrant all have a positive x- and a negative y-coordinate. These points are to the right of and below the origin.

Ordered Pairs

The x and y-coordinates of a point are often written in parentheses. For instance, when plotting the point for $x = 1$, $y = 4$, people usually just write $(1, 4)$ next to the point. The x-coordinate is always listed first and the y-coordinate is always listed second inside the parentheses. And notice that the two numbers are separated by a comma. Since the numbers are always listed in a certain order, this is called an **ordered pair**.

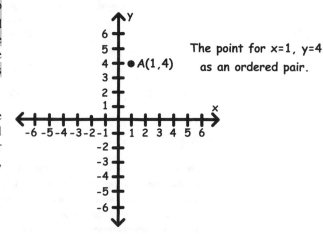

The point for x=1, y=4 as an ordered pair.

Writing it this way just saves space. You don't have write x equals or y equals. Notice that we can still name the point with a letter like A. To help remember what goes first and what goes second in an order pair, people often will write a general ordered pair like this:

$$(x, y)$$

This could stand for any ordered pair. It just shows where x and y should go.

Practice 121

a.
(120) If $y = \dfrac{x-2}{5}$ is represented by $f(x)$, find the x-value that makes $f(x) = -5$.

b.
(121) Plot the point $(0, -6)$ on the coordinate plane below.

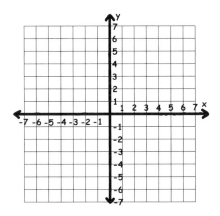

c.
(121) Tell the signs for all the coordinates in the quadrant where point E below is located.

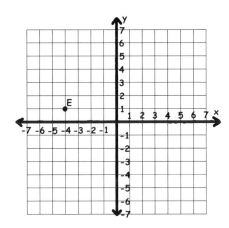

d.
(121) Tell the coordinates of point F shown below.

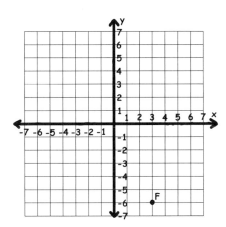

e.
(80)
Translate the word problem below into an equation; then solve.

Train #1 and train #2 are headed straight toward each other. Train #1 is traveling at 73 mph, and train #2 is traveling at 69 mph. If the two trains are 426 miles apart, how many hours will it be before they meet?

Problem Set 121

Tell whether each sentence below is True or False

1.
(121)
On a coordinate plane, any two numbers, such as $x = 2$ and $y = 5$ can be turned into a point.

2.
(121)
In an ordered pair, the y-coordinate is always listed first and the x-coordinate is always listed second.

Find the surface area of each solid below. Use 3.14 for π.

3.
(116)

4.
(117)

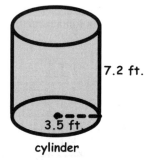

5 m.

12 m.

5 m.

4.3 m.

5 m.

triangular prism

7.2 ft.

3.5 ft.

cylinder

Select the domain and range of each function below.

5.
(119)
$y = -7x$

    A. Domain: All real numbers; Range: All negative real numbers
    B. Domain: All real numbers greater than -7; Range: All real numbers
    C. Domain: All real numbers; Range: All real numbers greater than 0
    D. Domain: All real numbers; Range: All real numbers
    E. Domain: All real numbers less than 0; Range: All real numbers

6.
(119)
$y = \dfrac{4}{x+6}$

    A. Domain: All real numbers except 0; Range: All real numbers except -6
    B. Domain: All real numbers except -6; Range: All real numbers except 0
    C. Domain: All real numbers except -6; Range: All real numbers except 4
    D. Domain: All real numbers; Range: All real numbers
    E. Domain: All real numbers except 4; Range: All real numbers except -6

Match the functional notation with a function below.

7. $x(t)$
(120)

    A. $x = \dfrac{1}{s+2}$

    B. $s = \dfrac{5}{m}$

8. $s(m)$
(120)

    C. $x = 4t - 8$

    D. $m = -\dfrac{1}{7}s + 3$

    E. $y = -3t + 2$

Find each value below.

9.   If $t = -6s + 7$, find $t(3)$.
(120)

10.   If $m = \dfrac{1}{6}n$, find $m(-\dfrac{1}{2})$. Make sure your answer is fully reduced.
(120)

(a) 11.   If $y = \dfrac{x-1}{3}$ is represented by $f(x)$, find the x-value that makes $f(x) = -1$.
(120)

Plot each point on the coordinate plane below.

12. $x = 3,\ y = 6$
(121)

13. $(-1, 7)$
(121)

(b) 14. $(0, -2)$
(121)

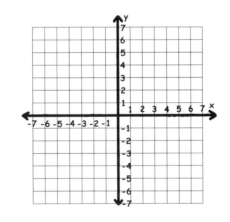

Tell the signs for all the coordinates in the quadrant where each point below is located.

15.   Point A
(121)

16.   Point B
(121)

(c) 17.   Point C
(121)

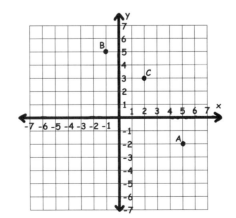

Tell the coordinates of each point shown below.

18. Point *M*
(121)

19. Point *N*
(121)

(d) 20. Point *P*
(121)

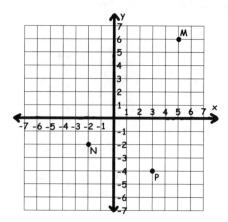

Translate the word problem below into an equation; then solve.

(e) 21. Tugboat #1 and tugboat #2 are headed straight toward each other. Tugboat #1 is traveling at 19 mph,
(80) and tugboat #2 is traveling at 24 mph. If the two tugboats are 215 miles apart, how many hours will it be
before they meet?

Lesson 122—Graphing Equations

In the last lesson, we learned about the coordinate plane. But the real purpose of a coordinate plane is for drawing pictures of functions. The picture is actually called a **graph**. As an example, let's draw the graph for the function $y = 2x$.

Finding Pairs

The equation tells us how y and x are linked together mathematically: y is always twice the size of x. The first step is to use the equation to find several ordered pairs of x and y values. We can just randomly select a few values for x, maybe 1, 2, and 3. Then we can put those into the equation and solve for each matching y-value. Actually, it's a good idea to include some negative values for x as well. So we'll also include x-values of -1 and -2. We just put each x-value into the equation and solve for the matching y-value. These pairs are then put in a table.

x	y
-2	-4
-1	-2
0	0
1	2
2	4
3	6

y = 2x

Now that we have several pairs of x and y-values for the function, the next step is to plot each of these as a point on the coordinate plane. The points are going to be part of the picture of the function. Here are the six points plotted on the plane.

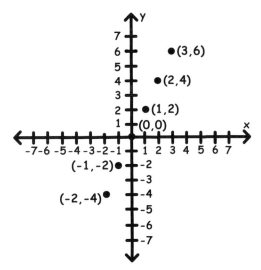

One thing you should understand is there are many more pairs that we could have plotted as points for this function. These aren't the only ones. For instance, we could have put $x = 45$ into the equation ($y = 2x$). The matching value for 45 would have been $y = 90$. Then we could have plotted $(45, 90)$. We won't plot this point because the plane isn't big enough. But there are lots of other pairs of x and y-values for $y = 2x$ besides these six.

Here's what's nice about graphing, though. We don't have to plot all the possible points in order to graph a function. That would take too long. (Actually, we could keep plotting points forever.) We only have to plot enough points to identify a pattern in the graph. If you look carefully at the points already plotted, the pattern is pretty obvious. The points run along a straight line.

It turns out that if we kept plotting more points for $y = 2x$, every point would end up somewhere along a single line. As we plotted more and more points, they would eventually just run together into a solid line. And since the points would go on forever in both directions, so would the line. That's why we need arrows on both ends. The arrows show that the real line goes forever.

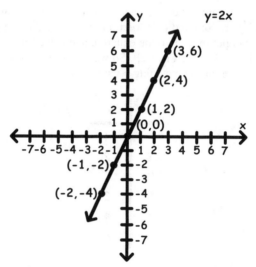

This line is the graph or picture of the function $y = 2x$. It's basically a picture of all the pairs of numbers of the function turned into points on a coordinate plane.

The advantage of having a picture is that it shows you how x and y are linked together. When we move to the right along the line, both the x-values and the y-values of the points are getting bigger. So the graph shows that x and y go up together. When one variable goes up, the other goes up. And if you move to the left along the line, both the x- and y-values are getting smaller. But the variables are still going together.

Let's review the steps for graphing a function. First, we find several pairs of numbers that will solve the function. To do that we just put in a few numbers for x and find their matching y-values. Second, we plot those as points on a coordinate plane. Third, we try to find a pattern with these points. Fourth, once we find the pattern, we connect the points to create the graph (picture) of the function. That picture is actually the pairs of numbers that solve the equation. Those pairs have been turned into points that make a picture.

Graphing a Function

1.	Find several ordered pairs for the function.
2.	Plot those as points on a coordinate plane.
3.	Try to find a pattern with the points.
4.	Finish the graph by drawing through the points according to the pattern.

Practice 122

a.
(120)
If $h = \dfrac{x+9}{3}$ is represented by $h(x)$, find the x-value that makes $h(x) = 2$.

b.
(121)
Plot the point $(-5, 0)$ on the coordinate plane below.

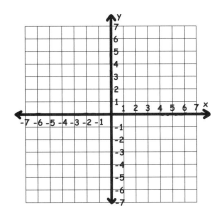

c.
(121)
Tell the coordinates of point E shown below.

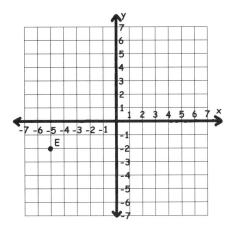

d. Select the graph of the function $y = -3x + 1$.
(122)

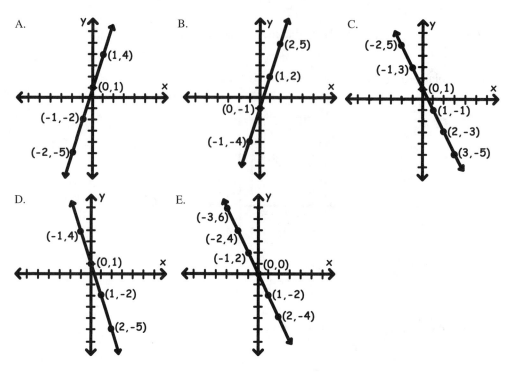

e. Translate the word problem below into an equation; then solve.
(29)

Mr. and Mrs. Gerardi are trying to save enough money to buy some new dining room furniture. They have already saved $900 but that is still not enough. If their $900 in savings is sitting in a bank account that pays 7% in yearly interest.

    i.) How much will Mr. and Mrs. Gerardi have earned in interest one year from now?

    ii.) If they leave their money <u>and</u> interest in the bank for another year, how much interest will they earn for the 2nd year?

Problem Set 122

Tell whether each sentence below is True or False.

1. A coordinate plane can be used to graph (draw a picture of) a function.
(122)

2. A graph is created by turning pairs of x and y values into points on the coordinate plane and drawing through the points according to the pattern.
(122)

Tell whether the relationship in each table below represents a function.

3.
(118)

y=-3x+5

x	y
-1	8
0	5
1	2
2	-1
3	-4
4	-7

4.
(118)

x	y
-4	3
-2	6
-1	-2
0	1
1	9
-4	-4

Find each value below.

5. If $y = \dfrac{1}{3}t - 2$, find $y(9)$.
(120)

(a) 6. If $y = \dfrac{x+7}{2}$ is represented by $g(x)$, find the x-value that makes $g(x) = 1$.
(120)

Plot each point on the coordinate plane below.

7. $x = 4,\ y = 2$
(121)

8. $(-5, 1)$
(121)

(b) 9. $(-3, 0)$
(121)

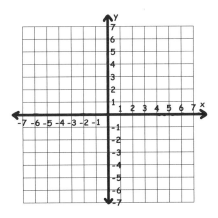

Tell the signs for all the coordinates in the quadrant where each point below is located.

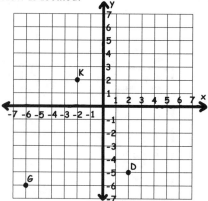

10. Point *G*
(121)

11. Point *D*
(121)

12. Point *K*
(121)

Tell the coordinates of each point shown below.

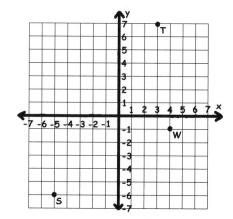

13. Point *S*
(121)

14. Point *T*
(121)

(c)15. Point *W*
(121)

Select the graph of each function below.

16. $y = 3x$
(122)

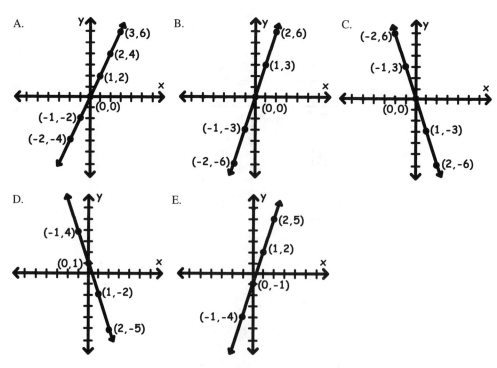

17. $y = 4x - 2$
(122)

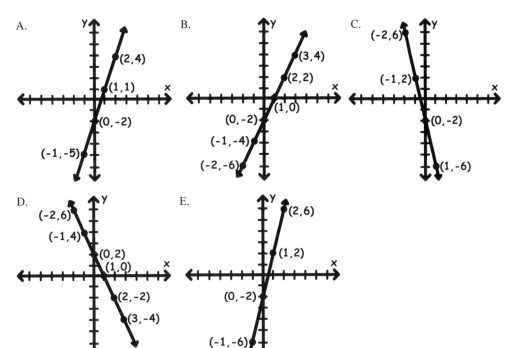

A.

B.

C.

D.

E.

(d) 18. $y = -2x + 3$
(122)

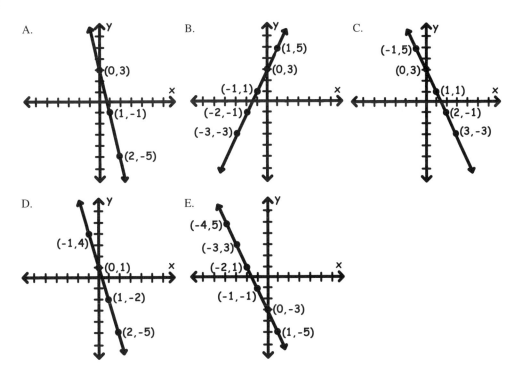

A.

B.

C.

D.

E.

Solve each equation below.

19.
(53)
$$\frac{\frac{x}{4}}{\frac{4}{5}} = 35$$

20.
(78)
$$7x - x = 36$$

Translate the word problem below into an equation; then solve.

(e) 21.
(29)
Mr. Peterson is trying to save enough money to buy a classic sports car. He has already saved $800 but that is still not enough. If his $800 in savings is sitting in a bank account that pays 4% in yearly interest.

    i.) How much will Mr. Peterson have earned in interest one year from now?

    ii.) If he leaves his money <u>and</u> interest in the bank for another year, how much interest will he earn for the 2nd year?

Lesson 123—More on Graphing

In the last lesson, we learned that a graph is basically a picture of a function. It shows how the two variables x and y are linked together mathematically. The graphs we did in the last lesson were straight lines. A function that has a straight line graph is actually called a **linear** function. The word linear just means line. We graphed the equation $y = 2x$, which is a linear function. And, remember, its graph was straight.

Graphing a Curve

It's also possible to have graphs of other shapes. As an example, let's graph the function $y = x^2$. The first step is to find several pairs of x- and y-values. We can just put in a few random numbers for x and find the matching y-values. And, remember, it's best to choose both positive and negative values for x. Here's a table with seven pairs.

x	y
-3	9
-2	4
-1	1
0	0
1	1
2	4
3	9

$y = x^2$

The next step is to plot these as points on a coordinate plane. The plotted points are shown below on the left. And you can see that the pattern is very different from the equations we graphed in the last lesson. Instead of a straight line, the pattern is curved. Connecting the points gives us the curve on the right. It's kind of a U shape that goes up forever on both ends. The technical name of this curve is a **parabola**.

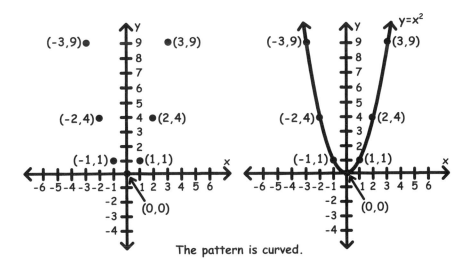

The pattern is curved.

The main point, though, is that this graph has a more complicated pattern than the graphs from the last lesson. The reason is that x and y are linked together in a more complicated way. The graph shows this. Put your pencil on the graph, starting on the left side where x is negative. Then start tracing over the graph. As you move right, x increases (the x-coordinates are getting bigger). But y is actually going down because the curve goes downward on the left side; the y-coordinates get smaller as you move from point to point. But by the time you get to the right side

623

of the curve, the pattern changes. On this side, as you move to the right, x is still increasing, but y is also increasing since the curve is going upward; the y-coordinates are getting bigger from point to point, in other words. On the right side, the x and y values both get bigger as you move along the curve. So the relationship between the variables is more complicated for this function. And that's why it has a more complicated (curved) graph.

Linear = First Degree

It turns out there's a simple way to tell if a function will have a straight line graph (if it's linear). If both x and y are just raised to the first power, then the function has to be linear. Another way of saying it is that x and y are both first degree. Using this rule, we know automatically that the function $y = 2x$ has to be linear, because x and y are both raised to the first power. (Remember, y is the same as y^1 and x is the same as x^1.) That means the graph of $y = 2x$ must be a straight line. By contrast, the last example, $y = x^2$, was not linear because in this equation x is raised to the second power; it's second degree. We can tell just by looking at the equation that the graph has to be curved.

Here's another example: $y = 3x + 5$. We can see immediately that this function is linear and it will have a straight line graph. The reason is that both x and y are raised to the first power—they're first degree. Looking at the graph of $y = 3x + 5$, we see that it is in fact a straight line.

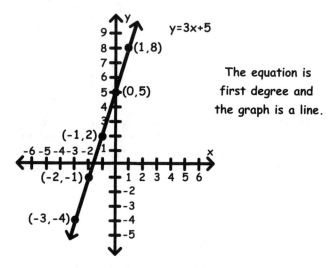

The equation is first degree and the graph is a line.

Let's look at another function: $y = \frac{1}{3}x^2$. Here y is first degree but x is second degree (squared). That means this function is not linear and the graph should be curved instead of straight. Here's the graph and notice that it is U-shaped.

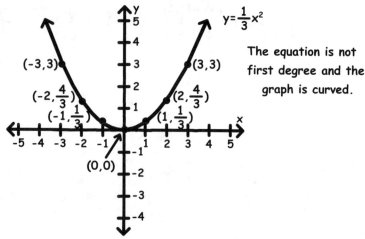

The equation is not first degree and the graph is curved.

Graphing a Line with Just Two Points

Now that you know how to recognize whether a function has a straight line graph—just by looking at the equation—there's a neat graphing shortcut that we can use. What if we needed to graph the function $y = 2x + 1$? Up until now, we would have needed to find quite a few pairs of x and y values. Then we would have plotted those on a coordinate plane to try to identify the pattern in the points. But look carefully at $y = 2x + 1$. Notice both x and y are raised to the first power. That means this is a linear function and the graph has to be a straight line. If that's true, how many points do we really need to plot to do the graph? Think about it. It only takes two points to find exactly where the line should go. Once we have two points on the line, we can just run a line through those and have the finished graph. That's the shortcut.

To do the graph of $y = 2x + 1$, then, we first find just two points. It doesn't matter which two points. Any two will work, as long as they're on the line. To keep things simple, let's just put 1 in for x.[1]

$$y = 2x + 1$$

$$y = 2(1) + 1$$

$$y = 3$$

So when $x = 1$, $y = 3$. That's one point. Now we need another one. We'll put a negative number in for x this time, although we don't really have to use a negative. (Any two points will work, remember.) But let's put in -2 for x.

$$y = 2x + 1$$

$$y = 2(-2) + 1$$

$$y = -3$$

So when $x = -2$, $y = -3$. Now we have our two points, and that's all we need to do the graph. The next step is to plot these points on a coordinate plane and draw a line through them.

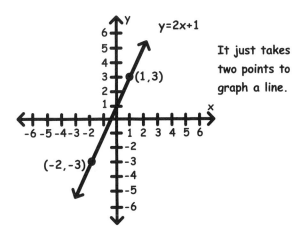

This is the graph of the function $y = 2x + 1$. And it took just two points to draw it. The reason was we knew in advance that the graph had to be a straight line. Plotting two points is a lot faster than plotting five or six.

---

[1] We could have used functional notation and written this as $y(1) = 2(1) + 1$ or $f(1) = 2(1) + 1$.

Here's something else interesting. If we had put two other numbers in for x and found two different points, those would have still fallen on this line. And when we drew the line by connecting the points, it still would have been the same line. So it doesn't matter which two points you use when graphing a line. You'll get the same line every time.

x and y-intercepts

Even though we can use any two points to graph a linear function, there are two special points that are often the easiest to use. One is the point where the graph crosses the y-axis. This point is called the **y-intercept**. The graph of the function $y = -2x - 4$ is shown below on the left. Notice the line crosses the y-axis at $(0, -4)$. That means this point is the y-intercept. And below on the right is the graph of the linear function $y = -2x + 6$. This line crosses the y-axis at $(0, 6)$. That means $(0, 6)$ is the y-intercept of this graph.

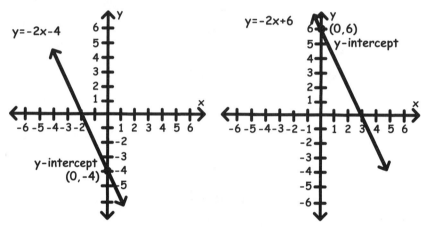

The y-intercept is the point where
the graph crosses the y-axis.

One important thing to remember about the y-intercept is that its x-coordinate is always 0. That's just because the y-intercept point is always on the y-axis. Every point on the y-axis has an x-coordinate of 0. What that means is that if we want to find the y-intercept for a graph, all we have to do is put in 0 for x in the equation and then find the matching y-value. As an example, let's use the equation $y = -2x + 6$ and find the y-intercept of the graph. We just put 0 in for x and find the matching value for y.

$$y = -2(0) + 6$$

$$y = 6$$

When $x = 0$, $y = 6$. That means $(0, 6)$ is the y-intercept. And, of course, that's where the line for this function crosses the y-axis above. One reason the y-intercept is a good point to use when graphing is just that 0 makes the math easy. Putting 0 in for x is simpler than putting in some other number like 7 or 23.

We said that there were two special points that were easy to use when graphing a line. What's the other one? It's the point where the line crosses the x-axis. This is called the **x-intercept**. Here's the graph of $y = -2x + 6$ again.

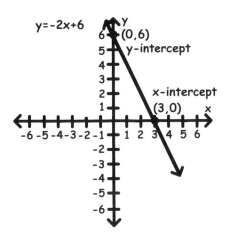

Notice the line crosses the x-axis at $(3,0)$. So this point is the x-intercept. Something else to notice is that the x-intercept has a y-coordinate equal to 0. That's always true. The reason is that all of the points on the x-axis have $y = 0$ since all these points are directly across from 0 on the y-axis. The x-intercept is a good point to use when graphing because all you have to do is put 0 in for y in the equation and solve for the matching x-value. And putting in 0 makes the math easy again.

Let's use the equation $y = -2x + 6$ to find the x-intercept for its graph. First, we put 0 in for y.

$$0 = -2x + 6$$

Now we solve the equation for x. The first step is to undo the addition by subtracting 6 from both sides.

$$0 - 6 = -2x + 6 - 6$$

Simplifying on both sides gives us this.

$$-6 = -2x$$

Next, we undo the multiplication by dividing both sides by –2.

$$\frac{-6}{-2} = \frac{-2x}{-2}$$

Simplifying again gives us an x-value of 3.

$$3 = x$$

When $y = 0$, $x = 3$. So the x-intercept is $(3,0)$. That's how you find the x-intercept using the equation.

As a last example, let's graph the linear function $y = x + 4$. It only takes two points to draw the line on the coordinate plane. But this time instead of just finding two random points, we'll find the x- and y-intercepts. We'll find the y-intercept first. Remember, the y-intercept has to have an x-coordinate equal to 0. So to find the y-coordinate, we put 0 in for x in the equation and find the matching value for y.

$$y = 0 + 4$$

$$y = 4$$

When $x = 0$, $y = 4$. This is the y-intercept of the function. The line will cross the y-axis at $(0,4)$. Now let's find the x-intercept. Remember, the x-intercept—since it's on the x-axis—must have a y-coordinate of 0. To find it, then, we put 0 in for y in the equation and find the matching value for x.

$$y = x + 4$$

$$0 = x + 4$$

$$0 - 4 = x + 4 - 4$$

$$-4 = x$$

When $y = 0$, $x = -4$. This is the x-intercept. The line must cross the x-axis at $(-4,0)$.

Now we have two points on the line. From here, all we have to do is plot both of these on a coordinate plane and run a line through them. And the other nice thing about the x- and y-intercepts is that they're easy to plot as well. You know both points are on an axis.

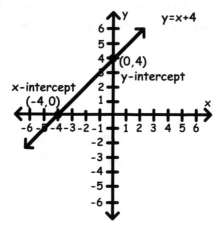

Practice 123

a.
(115) Find the perimeter of the figure below. Use 3.14 for π. Write your answer as a decimal.

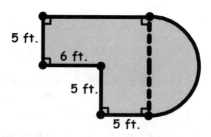

b.
(120) If $s = \dfrac{t}{5} - 6$ is represented by $s(t)$, find the t-value that makes $s(t) = -8$.

c.
(123) Tell whether the pair of x and y-coordinates $x = 2$, $y = 11$ solves the equation $y = 4x + 3$.

628

d. Select the graph of the function $y = -3x + 6$.
(123)

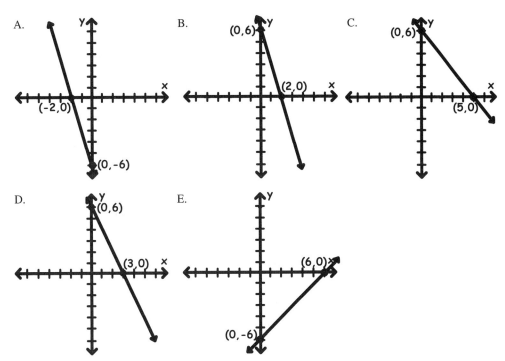

e. Translate the word problem below into an equation; then solve.
(30)

Dwayne wants to buy a samurai sword that is being sold for $35 less than the normal price. If the sword normally costs $400, by what percent is it being discounted? (The answer to your equation will be a decimal. Don't forget to convert it to a percent.)

Problem Set 123

Tell whether each sentence below is True or False

1. A function that has a straight line graph is called a linear function.
(123)

2. The y-intercept is the point where a line crosses the x-axis.
(123)

3. The x-intercept always has a y-coordinate that equals 0.
(123)

Find the missing angle in each diagram below.

4.
(105)

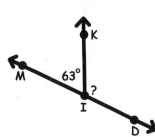

5. In the figure below, lines *f* and *c* are parallel.
(106)

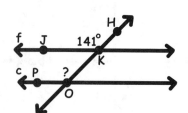

Find the perimeter of each figure below. Use 3.14 for π. Write your answer as a decimal.

6.
(113)

(a) 7.
(115)

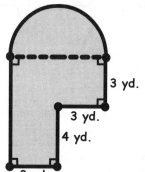

Select the domain and range of each function below.

8. $y = -2x + 3$
(119)

    A. Domain: All real numbers less than 3; Range: All real numbers
    B. Domain: All real numbers greater than -2; Range: All real numbers
    C. Domain: All positive real numbers; Range: All positive real numbers
    D. Domain: All real numbers; Range: All real numbers greater than 3
    E. Domain: All real numbers; Range: All real numbers

9. $y = \dfrac{3}{x+7}$
(119)

    A. Domain: All real numbers; Range: All real numbers
    B. Domain: All real numbers; Range: All real numbers except 0
    C. Domain: All real numbers except -7; Range: All real numbers except 0
    D. Domain: All real numbers except 7; Range: All real numbers except 0
    E. Domain: All real numbers except -7; Range: All real numbers except 3

Find each value below.

10. If $g = -4x + \dfrac{3}{2}$, find $g(5)$. Make sure your answer is fully reduced.
(120)

(b) 11. If $k = \dfrac{t}{4} - 5$ is represented by $k(t)$, find the t-value that makes $k(t) = -8$.
(120)

Plot each point on the coordinate plane below.

12. $x = -1$, $y = 6$ **13.** $(-7, -4)$
(121)   (121)

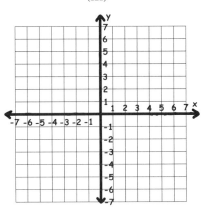

Tell the coordinates of each point shown below.

14. Point Y
(121)

15. Point C
(121)

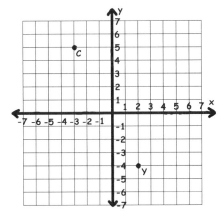

Tell whether each pair of x and y-coordinates below solves the equation $y = 3x + 5$.

16. $x = 3$, $y = 7$ **17.** $x = 1$, $y = 8$
(123)   (123)

(c) 18. $x = -2$, $y = -1$
(123)

Select the graph of each function below.

19.
(123) $y = 3x - 1$

A.
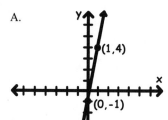

B.
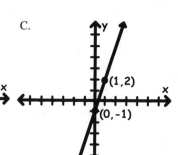

C.

D.
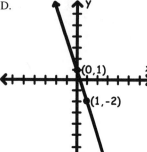

E.
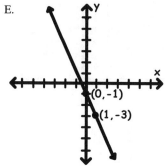

20.
(123) $y = -2x + 4$

A.
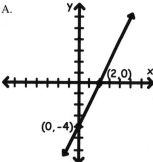

B.
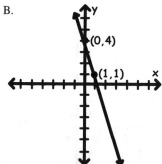

C.
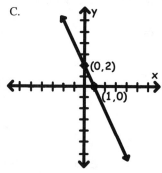

D.
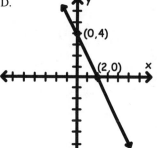

E.
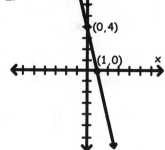

632

(d) 21. $y = -4x - 4$
(123)

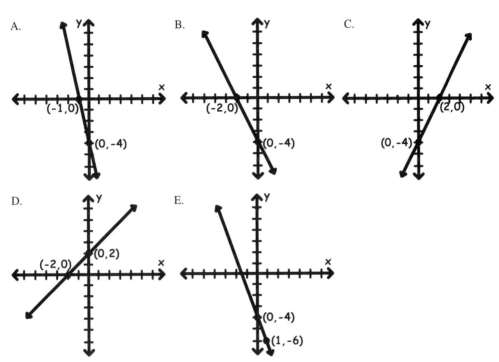

Translate the word problem below into an equation; then solve.

(e) 22. Hannah wants to buy some fake crystal slippers that are being sold for $25 less than the normal price. If
(30) the slippers normally cost $80, by what percent are they being discounted? (The answer to your equation will be a decimal. Don't forget to convert it to a percent.)

Lesson 124—The Slope of a Line

We've been learning how to graph lines. One thing you may have noticed is that lines have different slants. Some are quite steep, while others are more flat. And some lines actually slant downward.

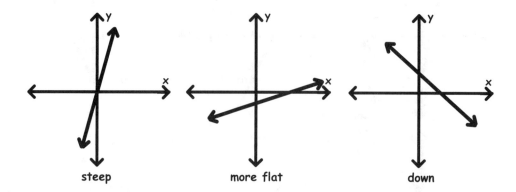

steep   more flat   down

Rise over Run

It turns out there's a way to measure the slant of a line. The measure is called the **slope** of the line. Let's calculate the slope of the line below, which is on a coordinate plane. We know two points on this line. They're the intercepts. The y-intercept is $(0,3)$ and the x-intercept is $(-1,0)$. To calculate the slope of the line, we can actually start with any two points on the line. So the intercepts will work. Then, we divide the vertical distance between those points by the horizontal distance between them.

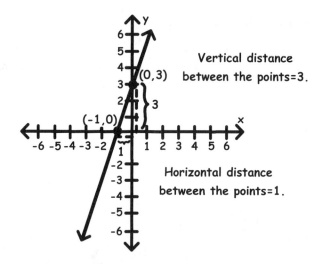

Vertical distance between the points=3.

Horizontal distance between the points=1.

You can see here that the vertical distance between our points is 3 places. That's because the top point, the y-intercept, has a y-coordinate of 3. And the bottom point, the x-intercept, has a y-coordinate of 0. So the points are 3 places away from each other vertically. And the horizontal distance between the points is 1 place because the x-coordinate of the top point is 0 while the x-coordinate of the bottom point is -1. That's a horizontal distance of just 1 place. Now we divide the vertical distance by the horizontal distance.

$$\frac{\text{vertical distance}}{\text{horizontal distance}} = \frac{3}{1} = 3$$

That gives us $\frac{3}{1}$ or just 3. So the slope of this line equals 3. That's the way we measure the slant of a line. Basically, a slope of 3 means that when you're moving along the line, you'll go to the right 1 place for every 3 places that you go up.

There are actually special names for the horizontal and vertical distances between two points. The horizontal distance is often called the "run." So the run of the line above is 1. And the vertical distance is often called the "rise." So the rise of the line above is 3. Just remember that you "run" sideways (horizontally), but you "rise" up (vertically). The vertical distance divided by the horizontal distance is called the "rise over run."

$$\frac{\text{vertical distance}}{\text{horizontal distance}} = \frac{\text{rise}}{\text{run}}$$

Positive or Negative?

We said that the slope of that last line was 3. But technically, the slope was +3. The reason is that the slope of a line can be positive or negative. The way it works is a line has a positive slope if it slants upward from left to right. But a line has a negative slope if it slants downward from left to right.

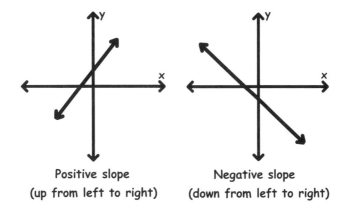

Positive slope   Negative slope
(up from left to right)   (down from left to right)

Let's go through an entire example of calculating the slope of a line with a negative slope. The line below has two points labeled. They're the x- and y-intercepts. The x-intercept is $(2,0)$ and the y-intercept is $(0,4)$. To calculate the slope, we find the vertical distance and the horizontal distance between the two points.

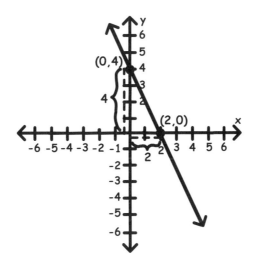

The vertical distance is 4. That makes sense because the *y*-coordinate of $(0,4)$ is 4 while the *y*-coordinate of $(2,0)$ is 0. That's a difference in the *y*-coordinates of 4 places. And the horizontal distance is 2 because the difference in the *x*-coordinates of the two points is 2. The next step is to divide the vertical distance by the horizontal distance. Or we could call it the rise over run.

$$\frac{\text{vertical distance}}{\text{horizontal distance}} = \frac{4}{2} = 2$$

We end up with 2. But 2 isn't the slope because we still have to decide on the sign. Is it $+2$ or -2? The rule is that if the line is slanting upward from left to right, the slope is positive. If the line is slanting downward from left to right, the slope is negative. This line slants downward from left to right. So the slope is -2.

$$\text{Slope of the line} = -2$$

A slope of -2 means that for each 1 place you go to the right, the line actually goes *down* 2 places.

Let's do one last example. On the line below, we have two points labeled. They aren't the *x*- and *y*-intercepts, but we can still use them to calculate the slope. You can calculate slope with *any* two points on a line, remember. We need to calculate the vertical distance divided by the horizontal distance between the points —the rise over run.

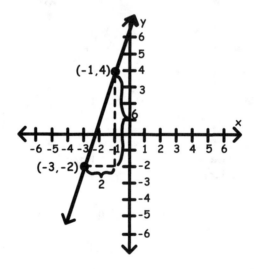

The vertical distance (rise) is 6 places. That has to be right because the *y*-coordinate of $(-1,4)$ is 4 and the *y*-coordinate of $(-3,-2)$ is -2. And 4 and -2 are 6 places apart. The horizontal distance (run) is 2 places because the *x*-coordinates of these points are -3 and -1, which are 2 places apart. That means the rise over run calculation looks like this.

$$\frac{\text{vertical distance}}{\text{horizontal distance}} = \frac{\text{rise}}{\text{run}} = \frac{6}{2} = 3$$

The last step is to figure out the sign. If you look at the line, it's going up from left to right. That means the slope has to be positive. The slope of our line, then, is +3.

$$\text{Slope of the line} = +3$$

Practice 124

a.
(123)   Tell whether the pair of x and y-coordinates $x = -7$, $y = 40$ solves the equation $y = -4x + 12$.

b.
(123)   Select the graph of the function $y = -3x - 3$.

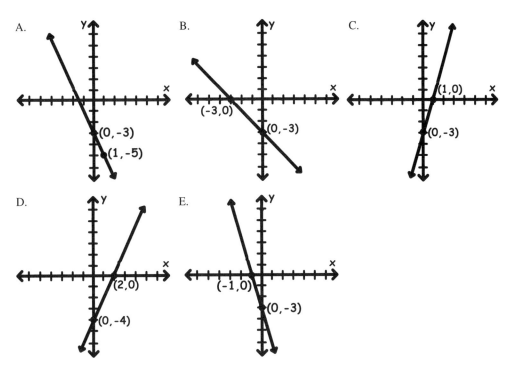

A.   B.   C.   D.   E.

Find the slope of each line below.

c.
(124)   Line *HD*

d.
(124)   Line *SN*

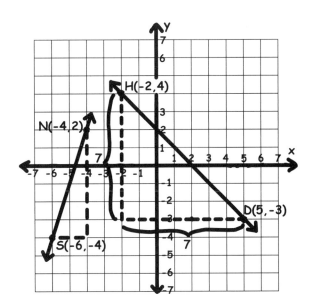

e.
(53)
Translate the word problem below into an equation; then solve.

Today alone, Billy has dipped $2\frac{1}{3}$ gallons of strawberry ice cream out of the case. If there is still $\frac{8}{9}$ of a gallon of strawberry left in the case, how many gallons were in the case to start with? Write your answer as a fraction.

Problem Set 124

Tell whether each sentence below is True or False.

1.
(124)
The measure of the slant of a line is called its slope.

2.
(124)
When calculating the slope of a line, the horizontal distance between two points on the line is called the "rise" and the vertical distance between the points is called the "run."

3.
(124)
The slope of a line is calculated by dividing the rise by the run.

Find the area of each figure below. Use 3.14 for π. Write your answer as a decimal.

4.
(114)

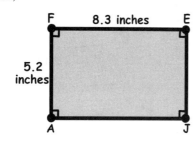

5.
(115)

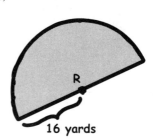

Tell whether the relationship in each table below represents a function.

6.
(118)

x	y
-5	-8
-2	-1
-1	0
0	-1
3	2
4	6

7.
(118)

x	y
-3	12
-1	7
0	0.6
1	-1
4	3
5	3.5

Find each value below.

8.
(120) If $s = \dfrac{1}{4}t - 3$, find $s(8)$.

9.
(120) If $h = \dfrac{x}{6} - 2$ is represented by $h(x)$, find the x-value that makes $h(x) = 1$.

Plot each point on the coordinate plane below.

10.
(121) $x = 3$, $y = -4$

11.
(121) $(2, 5)$

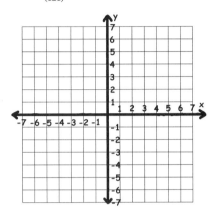

Tell the coordinates of each point shown below.

12.
(121) Point F

13.
(121) Point V

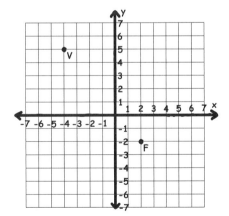

Tell whether each pair of x and y-coordinates below solves the equation $y = -2x + 7$.

14.
(123) $x = 4$, $y = -15$

(a) 15.
(123) $x = -5$, $y = 17$

639

Select the graph of each function below.

16.
(123) $y = 3x - 4$

A.

B.

C.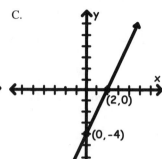

D.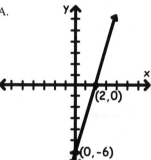

E.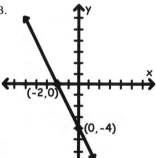

(b) 17.
(123) $y = -2x - 6$

A.

B.

C.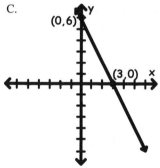

D.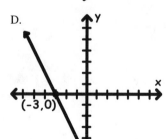

E.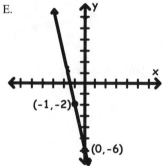

Tell whether the slope of each line below is positive or negative.

18.
(124)

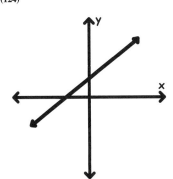

A. Positive
B. Negative

19.
(124)

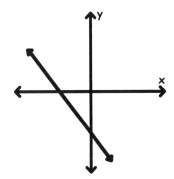

A. Positive
B. Negative

Find the slope of each line below.

20. Line *MN*
(124)

(c) **21.** Line *OP*
(124)

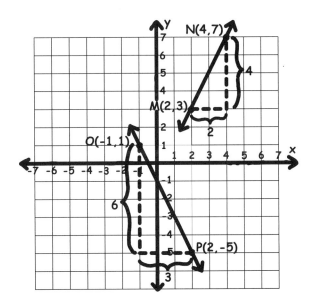

641

22.
(124)   Line *FE*

(d) 23. Line *HJ*
   (124)

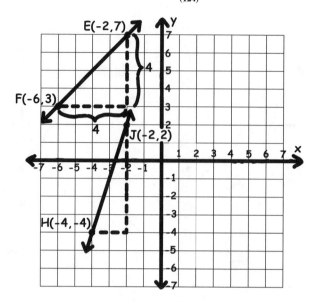

Translate the word problem below into an equation; then solve.

(e) 24.
   (53)   Yesterday, Mrs. Gargantua dipped $3\frac{1}{2}$ gallons out of the tub of sweetened tar that she has at home. If there was still $\frac{5}{8}$ of a gallon left, how many gallons of sweetened tar were in the tub to start with? Write your answer as a fraction.

Lesson 125—Slope-Intercept Form

We've learned how to calculate the slope of a line. So far all of our slopes have been integers—positive or negative whole numbers. But it's also possible for a line to have a slope that's a fraction.

Fractional Slopes

Let's go through an example of a line with a fractional slope. The line below has two points labeled. So we can use these points to calculate the slope. We just find the vertical distance (rise) and the horizontal distance (run) between the points and divide those.

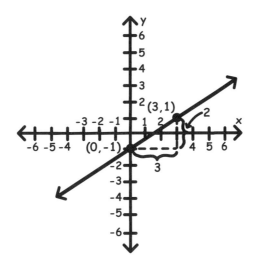

The rise is 2, because $(3,1)$ has a y-coordinate of 1 and $(0,-1)$ has a y-coordinate of -1. And 1 and -1 are 2 places apart. The run is 3 because the x-coordinates of the points are 3 and 0. These are 3 places apart. Now let's calculate the rise over run.

$$\frac{\text{vertical distance}}{\text{horizontal distance}} = \frac{\text{rise}}{\text{run}} = \frac{2}{3}$$

We end up with the fraction $\frac{2}{3}$. But is it positive or negative? Since the line slants slightly upward from left to right, the sign should be positive. So the slope of the line is $+\frac{2}{3}$ or just $\frac{2}{3}$.

$$\text{Slope} = \frac{2}{3}$$

A fractional slope is actually easy to interpret. A slope of $\frac{2}{3}$ means that for every one place you move to the right, the line will go up just $\frac{2}{3}$ of a place. That's not rising very fast, which is why the line is pretty flat.

Let's do another quick example of finding a slope. The line below has two points labeled: $(-2,5)$ and $(1,1)$. The vertical distance (rise) between the points is 4, and the horizontal distance (run) is 3.

643

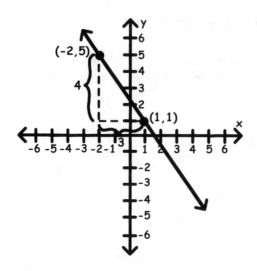

The slope equals the vertical distance divided by the horizontal distance. Rise over run, in other words. That gives us this.

$$\frac{\text{vertical distance}}{\text{horizontal distance}} = \frac{\text{rise}}{\text{run}} = \frac{4}{3}$$

We end up with a fraction again because 4 can't be divided by 3 evenly. The last step is to figure out the sign of the slope. The line slants downward from left to right, so the slope is negative. So the slope of the line is $-\frac{4}{3}$.

$$\text{Slope} = -\frac{4}{3}$$

This means that every time you move one place to the right, the line will go *down* $\frac{4}{3}$ of a place.

Slope-Intercept Form

There's an important fact about slopes and equations that you should know. It's possible to see the slope of a line just by looking at its equation. The line below represents the equation $y = 2x + 4$. There are two points on the line that are labeled; they're actually the x- and y-intercepts. With these two points we can calculate the slope by figuring out the rise over the run. The rise is 4 and the run is 2. So that's a rise over run of $\frac{4}{2}$ or 2. Also, since the line is slanting upward, we know the slope is +2 (or just 2).

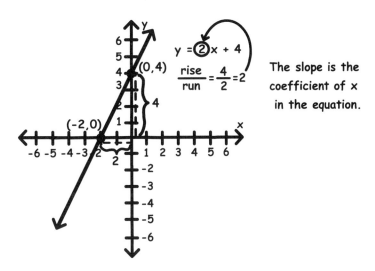

The slope is the coefficient of x in the equation.

But here's what's interesting. The equation for this line is $y = 2x + 4$. Notice that the coefficient of x in the equation is 2. That's not just a coincidence. It turns out that when a linear equation is written in the form below, the coefficient of x is always equal to the slope.

Slope goes here.

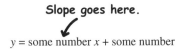

y = some number x + some number

Let's look at another example. Let's see if we can find the slope of the line below. At first you might think we can't calculate the slope because the line doesn't have any points labeled. We can still find the slope, though, by just looking at the equation.

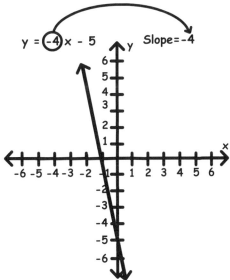

When the equation is solved for y and simplified, the slope is just the coefficient of x. For the equation $y = -4x - 5$, the coefficient of x is -4. So that's the slope.

Now let me show you a linear equation without its graph: $y = -3x + 2$. We know this has a graph that's a straight line because both x and y are raised to just the first power. What's neat, though, is we can figure out the slope without even graphing the equation. The slope is equal to the coefficient of x, which is -3.

$$y = -3x + 2$$

$$\text{Slope} = -3$$

Here's another linear equation: $y = \frac{1}{2}x + 7$. We know this is linear because the variables are both first degree (raised to the first power). That means the graph of the equation is a straight line. To find the slope of that line all we have to do is look at the coefficient of x. The coefficient is $\frac{1}{2}$ and so that's the slope of the line.

$$y = \frac{1}{2}x + 7$$

$$\text{Slope} = \frac{1}{2}$$

Let's find the slope of the graph of another equation: $y = x + 3$. We know the graph is a line because the equation is linear. The slope is supposed to be the coefficient of x. But in this equation, x isn't multiplied by anything. That's not a problem because x is the same as $1x$, remember. So we can change $y = x + 3$ to $y = 1x + 3$. Now the coefficient of 1 is showing, which means that the slope of the equation's line equals 1.

$$y = x + 3 \text{ is the same as } y = 1x + 3$$

$$\text{Slope} = 1$$

The main point is that sometimes, when looking for the slope of a line, you have to rewrite the x-term in order to see the coefficient.

Finding the y-intercept

We've been concentrating on slope, but there's another important piece of information that you can see from a linear equation. You can also see the y-intercept, the point where the line crosses the y-axis. Let's look at the graph of the equation from the last example, $y = x + 3$.

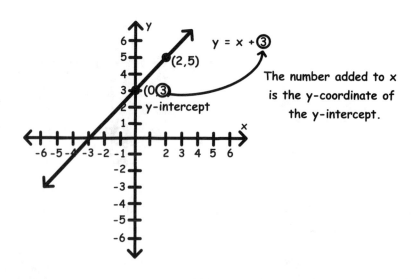

We've labeled two points and one of them is the y-intercept. So the line crosses the y-axis at the point $x=0$, $y=3$. But now look at the equation. The number added to x on the right side is 3. That's the same as the y-coordinate of the y-intercept. That's not just a coincidence. As it turns out, the number that's added to the x in the equation is always the y-coordinate of the y-intercept. It will tell you the y-value of that point. So you can actually figure out the y-intercept of a linear equation without even graphing it. You can read it right off of the equation, in the same way you read the slope.

Let try this technique on another equation: $y=-4x+5$. We know this is linear because x and y are both raised to the first power. So its graph has to be a straight line. And just by looking at the equation, we can see the y-intercept—that's where the line crosses the y-axis. The y-coordinate is the number that's added to the x-term ($-4x$), which in this case is 5. The x-coordinate of the y-intercept is always 0, because every point on the y-axis has an x that's equal to 0. That means the y-intercept is the point $x=0$, $y=5$. We can also figure out the slope of the line just by looking at the equation. The slope is the coefficient of the x-term. The coefficient of $-4x$ is -4. So the slope of the line is -4.

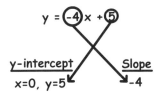

So you can find a lot of information about a line just by looking at the equation. Just remember that the equation has to be written in the form below.

$$y = \text{some number times } x + \text{some number}$$

As long as the equation looks like this, then the slope will be the same as the coefficient of x (the number multiplied by x) and the y-value of the y-intercept will be the number added to x on the far right. Actually, instead of writing "some number," people usually show this form by putting the letter m in the place where the slope should go. And they put the letter b in the place where the y-value of the y-intercept should go.

$$y = mx + b$$

This way of writing a linear equation is called the **slope-intercept form**. That's because in this form, it's easy to see the slope and y-intercept of the line. In a real equation, there would be actual numbers in the m and b places, of course.

Sometimes a linear equation won't be written in slope-intercept form. The equation $y=-x-5$ is not. If we wanted to read the slope and y-value of the y-intercept directly from the equation, we would need to first put the equation into slope-intercept form. That's the form $y=mx+b$. We already have $y=-x-5$ solved for y. But we need to rewrite $-x$ so its coefficient is showing. That's pretty easy because $-x$ is the same as $-1x$. We should also change the subtraction of 5 to addition of the opposite. In slope intercept form, the number on the right should always be added to the x-term. Making both of those changes gives us $y=-1x+(-5)$.

$y=-x-5$ in slope-intercept form looks like this: $y=-1x+(-5)$

Now we can read the slope and the y-intercept directly from the equation. Comparing $y=-1x+(-5)$ with $y=mx+b$, the slope of the equation's line is just the number in the m position (the coefficient of x). That means the slope is -1. And the y-value of the y-intercept is the number in the b position (the number added to the x-term). So the y-coordinate of the y-intercept is -5. Of course, the x-coordinate of the y-intercept is always 0. So the line for $y = -1x + (-5)$ crosses the y-intercept at the point $x = 0$, $y = -5$.

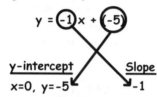

Practice 125

a. Find the area of the figure below.
(114)

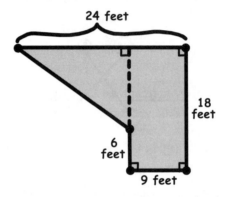

b. Find the slope of line GH below. Make sure your answer is fully reduced.
(125)

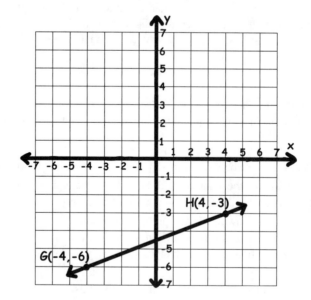

For each linear equation below, find the slope of the line and the y-intercept (where the line crosses the y-axis).

c. $y = \dfrac{2}{5}x + 3$
(125)

d. $y = x - 5$
(125)

e.
(73)
Translate the word problem below into an equation; then solve.

There is a number that if you subtract 7 from it first, and then divide that total by 6, you get 2. What's the number?

Problem Set 125

Tell whether each sentence below is True or False.

1.
(125)
In a linear equation that's written as $y = mx+b$, the number in the m place is the slope of the line and the number in the b place is the y-coordinate of the y-intercept.

2.
(125)
$y = mx+b$ is called the slope-intercept form of a linear equation.

Find the area of each figure below. Write your answer as a whole number or decimal.

3.
(114)

(a) 4.
(114)

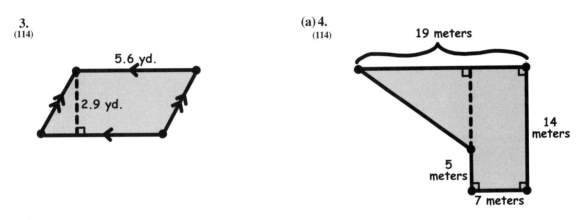

5.6 yd.

2.9 yd.

19 meters

14 meters

5 meters

7 meters

Find the volume of each solid below. Use 3.14 for π. Write your answer as a whole number or decimal.

5.
(117)

6.
(116)

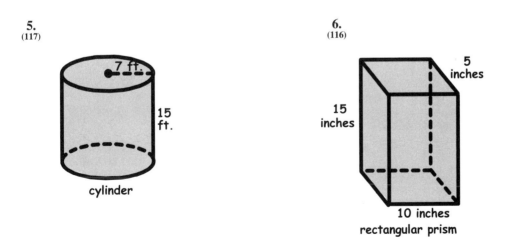

7 ft.

15 ft.

cylinder

5 inches

15 inches

10 inches

rectangular prism

Select the domain and range of each function below.

7.
(119) $y = 8x$

      A. Domain: All real numbers less than 0; Range: All real numbers
      B. Domain: All real numbers; Range: All real numbers
      C. Domain: All real numbers; Range: All negative real numbers
      D. Domain: All real numbers; Range: All real numbers greater than 0
      E. Domain: All real numbers greater than 8 ; Range: All real numbers

8.
(119) $y = \dfrac{1}{2x}$

      A. Domain: All real numbers except 0; Range: All real numbers except 1
      B. Domain: All real numbers except 0 ; Range: All real numbers except 0
      C. Domain: All real numbers except 1; Range: All real numbers except 0
      D. Domain: All real numbers; Range: All real numbers
      E. Domain: All real numbers except $\dfrac{1}{2}$; Range: All real numbers except 0

Find each value below.

9.
(120) If $h = 3x + \dfrac{1}{4}$, find $h\left(\dfrac{1}{8}\right)$. Make sure your answer is fully reduced.

10.
(120) If $Q = \dfrac{k-3}{2}$ is represented by $Q(k)$, find the k-value that makes $Q(k) = -4$.

Tell the coordinates of each point shown below.

11.
(121) Point S

12.
(121) Point W

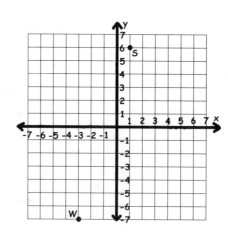

Tell whether each pair of *x* and *y*-coordinates below solves the equation $y = -4x - 8$.

13.　　$x = 6$, $y = -16$
(123)

14.　　$x = -9$, $y = 28$
(123)

Tell whether the slope of each line below is positive or negative.

15.
(124)

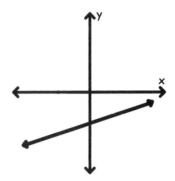

A. Positive
B. Negative

16.
(124)

A. Positive
B. Negative

Find the slope of each line below. Make sure your answer is fully reduced.

17.　　Line *FJ*
(124)

18.　　Line *DE*
(124)

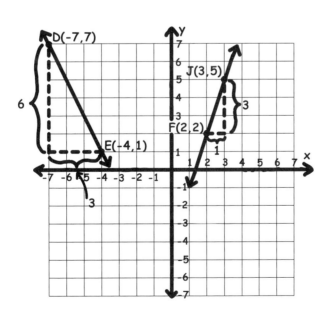

19. Line AC
(125)

(b) 20. Line RK
(125)

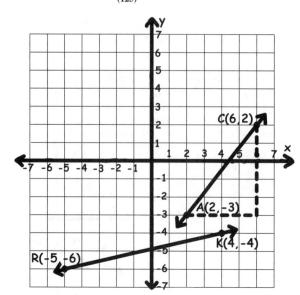

For each linear equation below, find the slope of the line and the y-intercept (where the line crosses the y-axis).

21. $y = -3x + 7$
(125)

(c) 22. $y = \dfrac{2}{3}x + 1$
(125)

(d) 23. $y = x - 2$
(125)

Translate the word problem below into an equation; then solve.

(e) 24. There is a number that if you subtract 9 from it first, and then divide that total by 6, you get 7. What's
(73)   the number?

Lesson 126—Horizontal and Vertical Lines

We've been learning about linear equations, which are equations with straight line graphs. But there are a couple of special linear equations that we haven't yet covered. The first is a horizontal line.

Vertical Distance = 0

As it turns out, all horizontal lines have a slope of 0. To show you why, look at the horizontal line below. This line has two points labeled, $(-2, 3)$ and $(4, 3)$, which we can use to calculate the slope. The horizontal distance between the points is 6 places because the x-coordinates -2 and 4 are 6 apart.

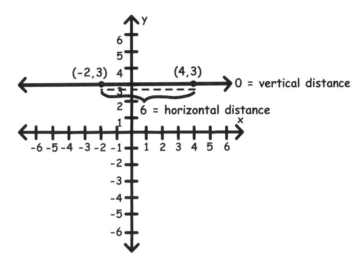

But the vertical distance is 0, which is kind of unusual. It makes sense, though, when you think about it. Since the points are on a horizontal line, they have to be at the same height. That means there's no vertical distance between them at all. You can also see that by looking at the y-coordinates. Both y-coordinates are equal to 3.

Now let's finish the slope calculation. Dividing the vertical distance by the horizontal distance gives us this.

$$\frac{\text{vertical distance}}{\text{horizontal distance}} = \frac{\text{rise}}{\text{run}} = \frac{0}{6} = 0$$

We end up with $\frac{0}{6}$ or 0. But what's interesting is that we would get that same answer for any horizontal line. That's because if the line is horizontal, the points will always be straight across from each other. And that will cause the vertical distance (rise) to equal 0. In basic math, when the numerator of a fraction is 0, the entire fraction has to equal 0.

$$\frac{0}{\text{any number}} = 0$$

So that's why a horizontal line must always have a slope of 0.

Equation for a Horizontal Line

What about the equation for a horizontal line? Well, since the graph is a line, the equation is going to be linear. We can write in the form $y = mx + b$. Remember, this is the slope-intercept form of a linear equation. Let's use this form to write the equation for our horizontal line. The slope is 0, so we should put 0 in the m position. Next is the y-coordinate of the y-intercept. That should go in the b position. The y-intercept wasn't labeled in the graph. But it's not hard to find its y-coordinate. All of the points on the line have a y-coordinate of 3. So the y-coordinate of the y-intercept must also equal 3. That means 3 goes in the b position. So here is the slope-intercept form of the equation.

$$y = 0x + 3$$

Let's write the equation of another horizontal line. The line below has two points labeled: $(-4, -5)$ and $(3, -5)$.

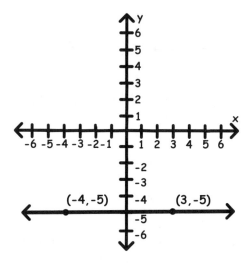

We can set up the equation in slope-intercept form again: $y = mx + b$. Even though the y-intercept isn't labeled on the graph, we know the y-intercept has to be the point $(0, -5)$. That's because all of the points on the line have a y-coordinate of -5. (And any point on the y-axis must have an x-coordinate of 0.) The slope is 0, because every horizontal line has a slope of 0. So we put 0 in the m position. And since the y-coordinate of the y-intercept is -5, that number should go in the b position to get the final equation.

$$y = 0x + (-5)$$

Leaving out 0x

There's something tricky about equations for horizontal lines that you should know. Most people wouldn't write the equation above as $y = 0x + (-5)$. They would write it as just $y = -5$. The reason is no matter what number you put in for x, the term $0x$ will always equal 0. Any number times 0 just equals 0. That means for any value of x, the value of y will always equal -5. That's why people just write the equation as $y = -5$. It makes sense to write the equation this way when you look at the graph too. Every single point on the line has a y-coordinate of -5. So an equation of $y = -5$ tells you that the graph is a horizontal line that goes across at -5 on the y-axis. It works the same way with the equation of any horizontal line. For instance, our earlier horizontal line example had the equation $y = 0x + 3$. But this equation would normally be written without the $0x$ as just $y = 3$. In this form, you can still see that this is a horizontal line crossing the y-axis at 3.

Vertical Lines

Now let's talk about vertical lines. What slope do they have? The graph below is a vertical line with two points labeled, $(2,4)$ and $(2,-3)$. We can try to calculate the slope in the usual way. The vertical distance between the points is 7 places. The y-coordinates are 4 and -3, which are 7 places apart. But the horizontal distance is 0. Since the points are on a vertical line, one is directly above the other. The points both have an x-coordinate of 2.

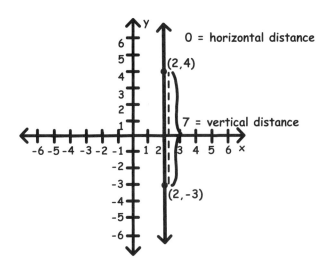

So the vertical distance (rise) over the horizontal distance (run) gives us this.

$$\frac{\text{vertical distance}}{\text{horizontal distance}} = \frac{\text{rise}}{\text{run}} = \frac{7}{0}?$$

We have a problem because the rules of basic math say that you can never divide by 0. It's possible to have 0 in the top of a fraction but never in the bottom. This means that our vertical line doesn't have a slope. The technical way of saying it is that the slope is undefined. In fact, all vertical lines have slopes that are undefined. The reason is that the horizontal distance (run) between their points is always equal to 0. All points on a vertical line will be lined up vertically making the horizontal distance between them 0. But that means for a vertical line the bottom of the rise over run fraction will always equal 0. And since division by 0 isn't allowed in basic math, the slope of any vertical line is undefined.

Equation for a Vertical Line

Does a vertical line have an equation? Even though it doesn't have a slope, a vertical line still has an equation. You can see from the graph of our line above that every point has an x-coordinate of 2. That means x must have a value of 2 no matter what number y equals. The equation should have x on one side and 2 on the other. The equation still needs to have a y, though, since the line is on a coordinate plane with two axes. It turns out the correct equation is $x+0y=2$. If you put different numbers in for 6 in this equation, you'll see that x always equals 2. And, once again, most people leave the $0y$ out since it always equals 0 (no matter what number is put in for y). So $x+0y=2$ is normally written as just $x=2$.

Let's do another vertical line example. The line below shows two points: $(-4,5)$ and $(-4,-6)$. We don't need to bother trying to calculate the slope. Since the line is vertical, we know the slope is undefined.

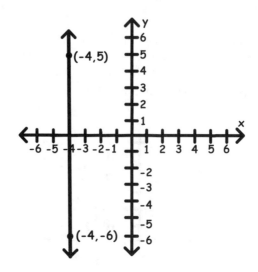

As we learned, the equation has to be in this form: $x + 0y =$ some number. The number on the right is where the vertical line crosses the x-axis. In the last example, that number was 2. But this line crosses the x-axis at -4.[1] So the equation should be $x + 0y = -4$. And we're allowed to drop the $0y$ term and write the equation as just $x = -4$.

The main points of this lesson are that the equation for a horizontal line is in the form $y =$ some number. And the slope will be 0.

Horizontal line equation: y = some number   slope = 0

We could write it as $y = 0x +$ some number, but most people leave out the $0x$.

The equation for a vertical line is $x =$ some number. And vertical lines don't even have a slope. It's undefined.

Vertical line equation: x = some number   slope is undefined

We could write vertical line equations as $x + 0y =$ some number, but people usually leave out $0y$.

Practice 126

    a.   Find the surface area of the solid below. Use 3.14 for π. Write your answer as a decimal.
  (117)

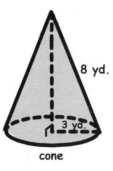

8 yd.

3 yd.

cone

---

[1] Actually, it crosses the x-axis at the point $(-4, 0)$. But only the x-coordinate goes in the equation.

b. Tell whether the slope of line *TM* below is positive, negative, zero or undefined.
(126)

A. Positive
B. Negative
C. Zero
D. Undefined

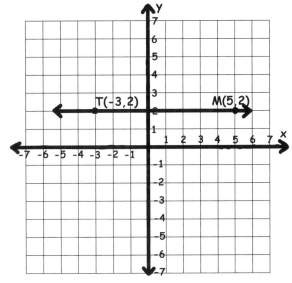

Select the correct equation for each graph below.

c.
(126)

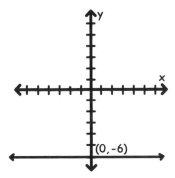

A. $x = -6$ B. $y = -6$

C. $y = -6x$ D. $y = x - 6$

E. $y = 6$

d.
(126)

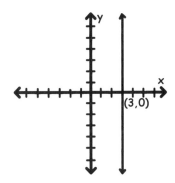

A. $y = 3x$ B. $y = 3$

C. $y = x + 3$ D. $x = \dfrac{1}{3}$

E. $x = 3$

e. Translate the word problem below into an equation; then solve.
(79)

Colleen can make 6 paper pinwheels an hour and Juliet can make 8. Working together, how many hours will it take them to make 84 paper pinwheels?

Problem Set 126

Tell whether each sentence below is True or False

1. The equation for a horizontal line can be written like this: $y =$ some number.
(126)

2. All vertical lines have a slope that equals 0.
(126)

Answer each question below by writing and solving an equation.

3. (105) $\angle T$ and $\angle D$ are complementary. If $\angle T$ has a measure of $26°$, find the measure of $\angle D$.

4. (105) $\angle K$ and $\angle F$ are supplementary. If $\angle F$ has a measure of $83°$, find the measure of $\angle K$.

Solve each proportion below.

5. (112) $\dfrac{7}{6} = \dfrac{56}{x}$

6. (112) $\dfrac{x}{9} = \dfrac{36}{81}$

Find the surface area of each solid below. Use 3.14 for π. Write your answer as a whole number or decimal.

7. (116)

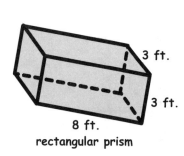

3 ft.

3 ft.

8 ft.

rectangular prism

(a) 8. (117)

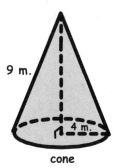

9 m.

4 m.

cone

Tell whether the relationship in each table below represents a function.

9. (118)

x	y
-7	-1
-4	2
-3	0
0	-1
2	4
3	8

10. (118)

x	y
-2	7
-1	5
0	-2
-1	-1
3	0
5	1.5

Plot each point on the coordinate plane on the right.

11. $x = -2$, $y = 5$
(121)

12. $(-4, -6)$
(121)

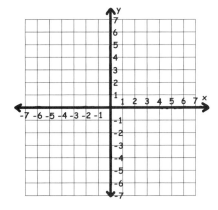

Find the slope of each line below.

13. Line QX
(124)

14. Line PE
(124)

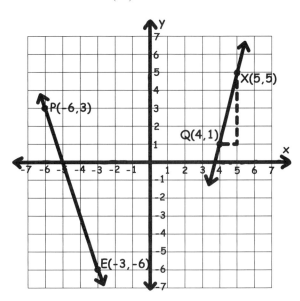

Tell whether the slope of each line below is positive, negative, zero or undefined.

15. Line IK **(b) 16.** Line FD
(126)   (126)

A. Positive
B. Negative
C. Zero
D. Undefined

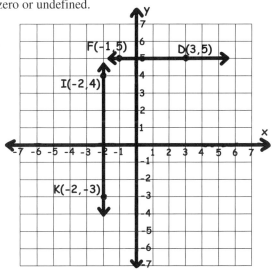

For each linear equation below, find the slope of the line and the *y*-intercept (where the line crosses the *y*-axis).

17. $y = -4x + 2$
(125)

18. $y = \dfrac{1}{7}x - 5$
(125)

19. $y = x + 3$
(125)

Select the correct equation for each graph below.

20.
(126)

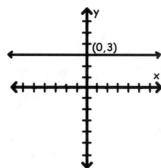

A. $y = 3x$ B. $y = 3$

C. $x = 3$ D. $y = \dfrac{1}{3}x + 3$

E. $y = \dfrac{1}{3}$

(c) 21.
(126)

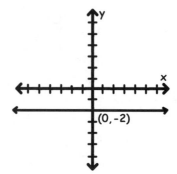

A. $x = -2$ B. $y = x - 2$

C. $y = -2$ D. $y = -2x$

E. $y = 2$

(d) 22.
(126)

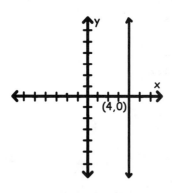

A. $x = \dfrac{1}{4}$ B. $y = 4$

C. $x = 4$ D. $y = 4x$

E. $y = x + 4$

Translate the word problem below into an equation; then solve.

(e) 23. Jennifer can make 5 candleholders an hour and Sheila can make 7. Working together, how many hours
(79)   will it take them to make 48 candleholders?

CHAPTER 16:
STATISTICS, PROBABILITY, AND INEQUALITIES

Lesson 127—Measures of Central Tendency

Statistics is the study of large groups of numbers. People use statistics for all sorts of things. For example, a person might make a list of all the houses that are sold in the country over a year and the price of each. Studying that list might tell them something important about the economy. That's an example of statistics. The technical word for a large group of numbers is **data**. So statistics is the study of data.

Mean

When studying data, people often try to measure the center of a group of numbers. It's called the central tendency of the data. One way to do that is to calculate an average. Let's go through an example just to refresh your memory. Below is a list of the number of video games owned by several people. Let's find the average number of video games that a person on this list owns.

Number of Video Games Owned

Steve:	10	Janice:	3	Paul:	7
Todd:	11	Mark:	16	Chad:	8
Meg:	3	Josh:	8	Tracy:	6
Terry:	5	Andrew:	10	Chris:	10
Aubrey:	10	Ellen:	9	Susan:	4

The first step is to add up all the numbers in the table. The total number of video games is 120. The second step is to divide by the number of people. There are 15 people on the list.

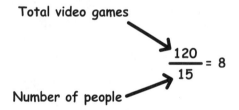

We end up with 8. So the average number of games owned by this group of people is 8 games.

The average is 8 games.

The average is also called the **mean**. That's the technical name. So we could say that the mean of our data equals 8.

Mean = 8

The mean is a way to measure the center of a group of data—the central tendency. The number 8 measures the center because most of the numbers in the table are fairly close to 8.

The mean is usually a good measure of the center of a group of numbers, but not always. Sometimes the mean can be misleading. One of the people in the table is Josh. What if Josh's father owned a video game business and was able to get Josh all the free video games he wanted? Instead of owning 8 video games, Josh might own 200 video games! Let's calculate the mean of the data again assuming that Josh owns 200 video games.

The first step is to add all the numbers. Instead of 120, the total number of video games comes out to 312. The number of people on the list hasn't changed. There are still 15 people. To calculate the new mean, then, we divide 312 by 120.

$$\frac{312}{15} = 20.8$$

The answer comes out to 20.8. So now the mean is 20.8 video games for each person.

$$Mean = 20.8$$

That's a lot higher. But does 20.8 really tell us the central tendency of the data? Does the normal person on this list own about 20 or 21 video games? No. Actually, no one on the list owns anywhere near that many video games other than Josh. Basically, Josh is throwing off the mean calculation because he owns so many video games. The mean isn't really a good measure of the central tendency of the data anymore.

Median

In a situation like this, it's best to use another measure of central tendency called the median. The **median** is the number that's right in the center of the data. It's pretty easy to find. We first need to list all the numbers in the data in order. We can either list the numbers highest to lowest or lowest to highest. Either way. The list below shows the numbers from highest to lowest. The highest number is obviously Josh's. He's the one with 200 video games.

Number of Video Games Owned

1. Josh:	200	6. Andrew:	10	11. Tracy:	6
2. Mark:	16	7. Chris:	10	12. Terry:	5
3. Todd:	11	8. Ellen:	9	13. Susan:	4
4. Steve:	10	9. Chad:	8	14. Janice:	3
5. Aubrey:	10	10. Paul:	7	15. Meg:	3

Since there are 15 numbers, the number that's right in the middle has to be the 8th one. It has 7 numbers higher and 7 numbers lower. Number 8 is Ellen who owns 9 video games. So 9 is the median for this data.

$$Median = 9$$

Obviously, 9 is a better measure of the center of the data than 20.8. Nobody on the list owns anywhere close to 20.8 video games, except Josh, who owns way more than that. But many people own close to 9 video games. In this case, the median is better than the mean. The nice thing about the median is that it's not affected by a very large number (like Josh's 200 games) in the data. The median just takes the number in the middle. Nothing is ever averaged. Even if Josh had owned 1 million video games, the median of the data would still have been 9. That's why the median is best to use when data contain a number that's much bigger or smaller than all the others. Such numbers are called **outliers**. And outliers can seriously distort the mean but not the median.

What if our list had contained 16 people instead of 15? For instance, what if there was one more girl named Julie we had forgotten about. Let's say that Julie owned just 2 video games. She would be number 16 on the list.

Number of Video Games Owned

1. Josh:	200	6. Andrew:	10	11. Tracy:	6	16. Julie:	2
2. Mark:	16	7. Chris:	10	12. Terry:	5		
3. Todd:	11	8. Ellen:	9	13. Susan:	4		
4. Steve:	10	9. Chad:	8	14. Janice:	3		
5. Aubrey:	10	10. Paul:	7	15. Meg:	3		

If we want to find the median of this data we have a slight problem. Since there are 16 numbers on the list and 16 is even, there's no number that's exactly in the middle of the data. Number 8 is Ellen. She isn't in the middle. There are 7 numbers higher than Ellen's but 8 numbers lower. Chad at number 9 isn't in the middle either.

We can still find the median, but we have to find the *two* numbers that are in the middle. It turns out that Ellen and Chad together are exactly in the middle. There are 7 numbers higher than Ellen's and Chad's and 7 numbers lower. To find the median of the data, we have to average the two middle numbers—find the mean, in other words. Ellen owns 9 video games and Chad owns 8. So we add 9 and 8 and divide by 2.

$$9 + 8 = 17$$

$$\frac{17}{2} = 8.5$$

The new median is 8.5 video games.

$$\text{Median} = 8.5$$

That's with the 16th person (Julie) added. The main point is that when a group of data contains an even number of numbers, then you won't have a middle number to be the median. And such cases, you have to find the two middle numbers and calculate the mean of those. That becomes the median of the data.

Mode

There's one more measure of central tendency that we should discuss. It's called the mode and it's easy to find. The **mode** is just the number in the data that appears the most frequently. In our video game data (the version that includes Julie) the number 10 appears four times. That's more frequently than any other number. That means 10 is the mode of the data.

$$\text{Mode} = 10$$

Mode is a good measure to use when there's some special reason why a particular number should come up a lot. For example, in the U.S. a person has to be 16 years old to get a driver's license. If you were looking at data on the age of Americans at the time they first received their driver's license, the number 16 would come up over and over again. Most people want to get their driver's license as soon as possible. In that situation, the mode might be the best measure of central tendency. It would give you a better idea of a "normal" number in the data than either the mean or the median.

Practice 127

a.
(114)   Find the area of the figure below.

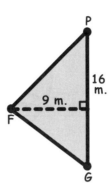

b.
(125)   For the linear equation $y = -x - \dfrac{4}{5}$, find the slope of the line and the y-intercept (where the line crosses the y-axis).

The table below shows the number of hours that a group of professional ballet dancers rehearsed last week.

Number of Hours Per Week

5	20	28	19	34	26
11	10	23	18	9	24
30	15	33	25	27	

c.
(127)   Find the mean of the data above.

d.
(127)   Find the median of the data above.

e.
(54)   Translate the word problem below into an equation; then solve.

There were 6,400 paperweights in Ned's collection but only 24 had insects inside of them. What percent of the paperweights had insects inside of them? (The answer to your equation will be in decimal form. Make sure your final answer is written as a percent.)

Problem Set 127

Tell whether each sentence below is True or False.

1.
(127)   To find the mean, add all the numbers and then divide by however many numbers were added.

2.
(127)   The median is the number that's exactly in the middle of the data.

3.
(127)   The mode is the number in the data that appears the most frequently.

Find the area of each figure below. Use 3.14 for π. Give exact answers.

(a) 4.
(114)

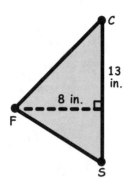

13 in.

8 in.

F

C

S

5.
(115)

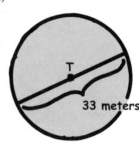

T

33 meters

Find each value below.

6. If $h = -\dfrac{1}{3}c + 5$, find $h(12)$.
(120)

7. If $y = \dfrac{x+3}{5}$ is represented by $f(x)$, find the x-value that makes $f(x) = 2$.
(120)

Tell whether each pair of x and y-coordinates below solves the equation $y = \dfrac{3}{4}x - 6$.

8. $x = 8$, $y = -1$
(123)

9. $x = -16$, $y = -18$
(123)

Find the slope of each line below. Make sure your answer is fully reduced.

10. Line KI
(124)

11. Line BC
(125)

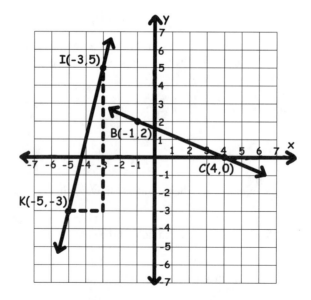

Tell whether the slope of each line below is positive, negative, zero or undefined.

12.
(126)

Line *XY*

13.
(126)

Line *HG*

A. Negative
B. Undefined
C. Zero
D. Positive

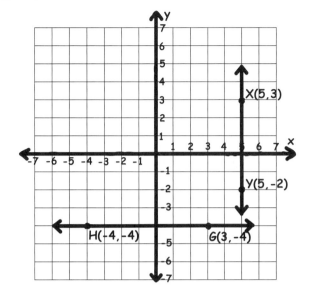

For each linear equation below, find the slope of the line and the *y*-intercept (where the line crosses the *y*-axis).

14.
(125)

$y = \dfrac{1}{4}x + 8$

15.
(125)

$y = -3x - 6$

(b) 16.
(125)

$y = -x - \dfrac{2}{3}$

Select the correct equation for each graph below.

17.
(126)

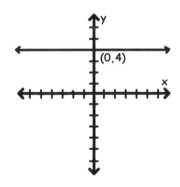

A. $y = \dfrac{1}{4}$

B. $y = 4x$

C. $y = \dfrac{1}{4}x + 4$

D. $y = 4$

E. $x = 4$

18.
(126)

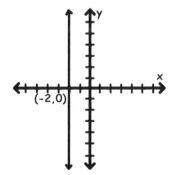

A. $y = -2x$

B. $y = x - 2$

C. $x = 2$

D. $y = -2$

E. $x = -2$

667

The table below shows the annual incomes (in thousands of dollars) of several families in Carson City.

Annual Household Incomes

62	25	54	46	51	70
33	40	24	54	48	63
54	21	32	49	56	

(c) 19. Find the mean of the data above.
(127)

(d) 20. Find the median of the data above.
(127)

21. Find the mode of the data above.
(127)

Translate the word problem below into an equation; then solve.

(e) 22. There were 2,400 military patches in Charlie's collection but only 15 had green dragons on them. What
(54) percent of the patches had green dragons on them? (The answer to your equation will be in decimal form. Make sure your final answer is written as a percent.)

Lesson 128—Range and Stem and Leaf Plots

In the last lesson, we learned about how to find measures of central tendency for a group of data. Mean, median, and mode were the measures we learned about.

Range

It's also important to measure how spread apart a group of numbers are. As an example, here are two groups of numbers.

Set 1	Set 2
23, 25, 27, 28, 32	1, 2, 27, 38, 67

In math, groups of numbers are called sets. So we have Set 1 and Set 2. Let's calculate the mean of each set. To find the mean of Set 1, we first add the numbers to get a total.

$$23 + 25 + 27 + 28 + 32 = 135$$

The total is 135. Now since Set 1 has 5 numbers, we divide 135 by 5.

$$\frac{135}{5} = 27$$

Mean of Set 1 = 27

The mean of Set 1 is 27. Now let's calculate the mean of Set 2. First, we add the numbers in that set.

$$1 + 2 + 26 + 39 + 67 = 135$$

We end up with the same total as before. And since this set also has 5 numbers, we need to divide by 5 again. We already know that the answer equals 27.

$$\frac{135}{5} = 27$$

Mean of Set 2 = 27

Both sets of numbers have the same mean. Yet there's clearly a difference between them. In Set 1, the numbers are a lot closer together. In Set 2 they're more spread out. Finding the median instead of the mean wouldn't help either. Both sets also have the same median: 27. That's the middle number for both.

We need a way to measure how spread apart the numbers are. That would show the difference between Set 1 and Set 2. The spread of the numbers is called the **dispersion**. The simplest measure of dispersion is called the range. The **range** is just the largest number in the data minus the smallest number. Let's calculate the range of Set 1. The largest number in this set is 32 and the smallest number is 23.

Range of Set 1: $32 - 23 = 9$

So the range of Set 1 equals 9. Now let's calculate the range of Set 2.

Range of Set 2: $67 - 1 = 66$

The range of Set 2 is 66. Notice the difference in size of the two ranges: 9 versus 66. That tells us the numbers in set 2 are more dispersed (spread out) than those in Set 1. Even if we had never seen the numbers in either set, these ranges would tell us clearly that the numbers in Set 2 were more widely dispersed than those in Set 1. So range is a measure of dispersion. And it's very simple to calculate.

Stem and Leaf Plot

Unfortunately, the range doesn't tell us anything about what's in between the largest and the smallest numbers. That's why there are other measures of dispersion that give even more information. One of those is called a stem and leaf plot. The way **a stem and leaf plot** works is it splits each number in the data into two separate parts. Then those parts are used to show the dispersion of the data in a table. A stem and leaf plot actually works really well when the numbers in the data are decimals.

Let's go through an example. In the set of data below, the numbers are all decimals. And notice that every number has digits out to the tenths position.

5.2, 7.4, 4.9, 6.7, 2.8, 3.0, 6.8, 4.1, 6.9, 5.2, 1.2, 5.3, 2.2, 5.5, 3.5, 5.6, 4.4, 7.3

The first step is to put the numbers in order from least to greatest.

1.2, 2.2, 2.8, 3.0, 3.5, 4.1, 4.4, 4.9, 5.2, 5.2, 5.3, 5.5, 5.6, 6.7, 6.8, 6.9, 7.3, 7.4

Next, we separate each number into a stem and a leaf. It's a little bit like the stem of a tree and the tree's leaves. We'll make the leaf be the tenths digit in each number—the digit to the right of the decimal point. And we'll make the stem be the ones digit. For example, in the number 1.2, the leaf is 2 and the stem is 1. The next step is to create a table with the stems of the numbers on one side and the leaves on the other. We'll start with the smallest numbers on top and go in order to the largest numbers on the bottom.

	Stem	Leaf	
The stems all stand for ones.	1	2	The leaves all stand for tenths.
	2	2 8	
	3	0 5	
	4	1 4 9	
	5	2 2 3 5 6	
	6	7 8 9	
	7	3 4 ⟵ This row stands for
		1|2 = 1.2	7.3 and 7.4.

The 1 on the top of the stems column represents the 1 in 1.2. The 2 on top of the leaf column represents the 2 in 1.2. The next row down shows a 2 in the stem column, but two different numbers in the leaf column: 2 and 8. That means there are two numbers that start with a 2. If you look back at the data, you'll see that there's a 2.2 and a 2.8. Since both of these have the same ones digit, we just need to list the stem 2 once. Then we show both of the tenths digits on the leaf side. That's how a stem and leaf plot works. Continuing downward, each row represents all of the numbers that start with a particular ones digit: 3 through 7. The highest numbers in the data are 7.3 and 7.4. Those are represented in the bottom row that has a 7 on the left. Also, notice at the very bottom it says 1\|2 = 1.2. This is telling us that having a 1 in the stem column and a 2 in the leaf column equals 1.2. In other words, this line says that all the stems stand for ones and all the leaves stand for tenths in this plot.

Interpreting the Plot

The purpose of a stem and leaf plot is to show the dispersion of a group of numbers—how they're spread out. How does the plot do that? Well, focus on the leaf column. At the top, this column is narrow because the rows don't contain many digits. In the top row (the row with a stem of 1), there's just one digit in the leaf. In the second and third rows, the leaf contains just two digits. But in the fifth row (the row with a stem of 5), the leaf has five digits. That means there are five numbers in the data that start with a 5. So the width of the leaf tells you how many numbers are in the data for particular stems. Since the leaf is wider for the rows with stems of 4 and 5, we know that the data contain more numbers in those categories. That's how a stem and leaf plot shows the dispersion. It provides much more information than the range. The range just tells you how far apart the smallest and largest numbers in the data are. It doesn't tell you anything about the numbers in between.

Practice 128

a.
(127)
The table below shows the number of plastic bottles recycled last week by all of the households in Hartcliff Park.

Number of Plastic Bottles Recycled

19	30	27	4	12	15	22
12	16	8	10	31	13	29

Find the median of the data above. Write your answer as a decimal.

b.
(128)
Calculate the range for the group of numbers: 34, 17, 51, 22, 46, 29, 49, and 195.

Use the stem and leaf plot to answer each question below.

Stem	Leaf
1	0 4 6
2	2 5 7 9 9
3	1 3
4	6 8
5	0 1 1 8
6	2 2 2 3 4 7
7	7 8 8 9
8	0 0
9	6

$1 | 0 = 1.0$

c.
(128)
How many numbers in the data have a 2 in the ones place?

d.
(128)
What ones digit appears the most frequently in the data?

e.
(53)
Translate the word problem below into an equation; then solve.

Hammond spent $44.80 on gasoline. If each gallon cost $2.80, how many gallons of gas did he purchase?

Problem Set 128

Tell whether each sentence below is True or False.

1.
(128)   The range of a group of data equals the largest number minus the smallest number.

2.
(128)   A stem and leaf plot shows how the numbers in a group of data are spread out in the middle.

In the figure below, lines *d* and *t* are parallel. Find the measure of each angle below.

3.   ∠2
(105)

4.   ∠6
(106)

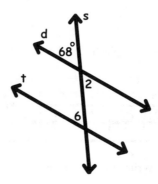

Find the volume of each solid below. Use 3.14 for π. Write your answer as a whole number or decimal.

5.
(117)

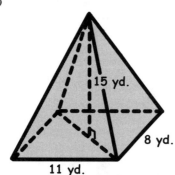

rectangular pyramid

6.
(117)

cone

Select the domain and range of each function below.

7. $y = \dfrac{7}{x}$
(119)

    A.   Domain: All real numbers; Range: All real numbers
    B.   Domain: All real numbers; Range: All real numbers except 0
    C.   Domain: All real numbers except 0; Range: All real numbers except 7
    D.   Domain: All real numbers except 0; Range: All real numbers except 0
    E.   Domain: All real numbers except 7; Range: All real numbers except 0

8. $y = \dfrac{-5}{x+2}$
(119)

    A. Domain: All real numbers; Range: All real numbers
    B. Domain: All real numbers except -2; Range: All real numbers except 0
    C. Domain: All real numbers except -5; Range: All real numbers except 0
    D. Domain: All real numbers except 0; Range: All real numbers except -5
    E. Domain: All real numbers except -2; Range: All real numbers except -5

Find the slope of each line below. Make sure your answer is fully reduced.

9.   Line *DV*   **10.**   Line *SQ*
(124)   (125)

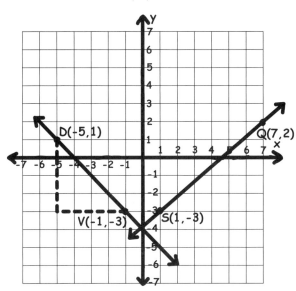

11.   Tell whether the slope of line *BJ* below is positive, negative, zero or undefined.
(126)

    A. Undefined
    B. Zero
    C. Negative
    D. Positive

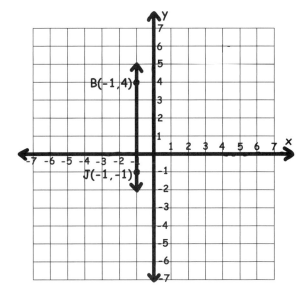

673

For each linear equation below, find the slope of the line and the y-intercept (where the line crosses the y-axis).

12.
(125)
$$y = 4x + \frac{1}{3}$$

13.
(125)
$$y = -7x - 6$$

The table below shows the number of newspapers recycled last week by several neighborhoods in Park Grove. Write your answer as a whole number or decimal.

Number of Newspapers Recycled

24	15	6	31	18	12	10
18	25	23	16	19	20	29

14. Find the mean of the data above.
(127)

(a) 15. Find the median of the data above.
(127)

16. Find the mode of the data above.
(127)

Calculate the range for each group of numbers below.

17. 15, 39, 41, 9, 22, and 17.
(128)

18. 2.6, 1.5, 9.0, 17.6, 15.3, and 4.4.
(128)

(b) 19. 26, 42, 33, 14, 58, 29, 35, and 181.
(128)

Use the stem and leaf plot to answer each question below.

20. How many numbers in the data have a 3 in the ones place?
(128)

(c) 21. How many numbers in the data have a 5 in the ones place?
(128)

22. How many numbers in total are in the data?
(128)

(d) 23. What ones digit appears the most frequently in the data?
(128)

Stem	Leaf
1	2 4 4 5
2	0 3 5
3	8 8 8 9
4	1
5	2 6 7 7 7
6	0 3
7	1 1 2 3
8	0 0 4 5 7 9
9	6 8

1|2 = 1.2

Translate the word problem below into an equation; then solve.

(e) 24. Bromley spent $74.88 on kerosene. If each gallon cost $3.12, how many gallons of kerosene did he purchase?
(53)

Lesson 129—Histograms and Scatter Plots

In the last lesson, we learned about stem and leaf plots. Remember, they show the dispersion of a group of numbers is (how spread out they are). Another way to show dispersion is with something called a histogram. To show you how a histogram works, let's go through an example. What if the mayor of a city wants to analyze the ages of the people on his staff? The mayor could just make a table. He could show the number of staff members within different age ranges. The table below is an example; it would give the mayor a pretty good idea of the dispersion of the staff's ages.

Mayor's Staff

Age Range	Number of Staff Members
20-30	5
30-40	10
40-50	15
50-60	12
60-70	3
70-80	1

But the dispersion would be even easier to see with a histogram. A **histogram** is a graph with bars. The bars show how the numbers in a set of data are dispersed. A histogram for the same data is shown below. Notice that the histogram is similar to a coordinate plane. There are two axes. The vertical axis shows the number of staff members and the horizontal axis shows the age ranges.[1]

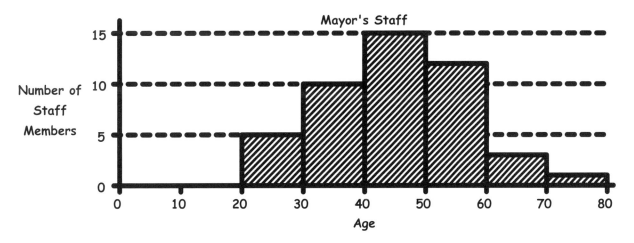

Importantly, every age range is represented by a bar. The first bar represents all the staff members from ages 20 to 30. And notice the top of that bar is directly across from 5 on the vertical axis. That means 5 staff members are in this age range. The second bar represents all of the staff members from ages 30 to 40. The top of this bar is across from 10, which means that 10 people are in the age range of 30 to 40. And the other bars are read in the same way.

---

[1] The axes only show positive numbers, so this is like seeing only the first quadrant of a coordinate plane. The first quadrant has positive values for both variables.

Also, notice that the age ranges along the bottom are all the same. The ranges are all equal. And the bars are squeezed together so there are no gaps between them. All histograms are set up like this. A histogram is a little different from a bar graph. In a bar graph, the bars are usually separated.

Of course, the real advantage of a histogram is that it shows how the numbers in the data are dispersed. It provides much more information than the range of the data. The range just tells you the difference between the largest and smallest number. Just a quick glance at this histogram will tell you that most of the people on the staff are between the ages of 30 and 60. The bars for that age range are the tallest. This kind of information could be very important to the mayor. He might be unpopular with younger voters. After looking at the histogram, the mayor might consider hiring more staff members in their 20s. They might better understand the problems of younger voters. Or the mayor might be unpopular among retired voters. The mayor might see the short bars for the higher age ranges and decide to hire some older staff members.

Scatter Plots

Earlier we learned how to graph a function. Remember, a function is a specific kind of relationship between variables like x and y. We also learned that a linear function has a graph that's a straight line. Sometimes two variables will be somewhat related, but not enough for the graph to come out perfect. As an example, what if we wanted to study the relationship between the value of a car and the car's age? Everybody knows that cars become less valuable the older they get. Here's some data showing the value of Ford Mustangs of different ages.

Age and Values of Ford Mustangs

Age (in Years)	Value
2	$15,900
3	$14,300
4	$13,100
5	$11,600
6	$10,800
8	$9,900
9	$9,700
10	$6,200
12	$5,800
13	$4,000
14	$2,200
15	$1,600

The older cars aren't worth as much. The 2 years old car has a value of $15,900. But the 15 year old car is only worth $1,600. So the price of a car goes down over time, which is no surprise. In fact, we could treat the value of the cars and their age as two variables that are linked together mathematically. We could even graph this data on a coordinate plane. All we have to do is turn each pair of numbers into a point.

Let's set up a graph. Instead of using x and y, we'll make the horizontal axis show the age of the cars and the vertical axis the value of the cars. The numbers labeled on the vertical axis will need to go a lot higher than normal. They should go up to 16,000 since the value of the cars is that high. The horizontal axis only needs to show numbers up to 15 because the oldest car in the data is just 15 years old. We also only need positive numbers on both axes. None of the cars have a negative value and none have a negative age! So we can just show the first quadrant of the graph. The coordinate plane is shown below on the left. Notice there isn't room to label every number on the vertical axis. Only every thousandth number is labeled: 1,000, 2,000, and on up. On the right, the pairs of numbers from the data are plotted as points.

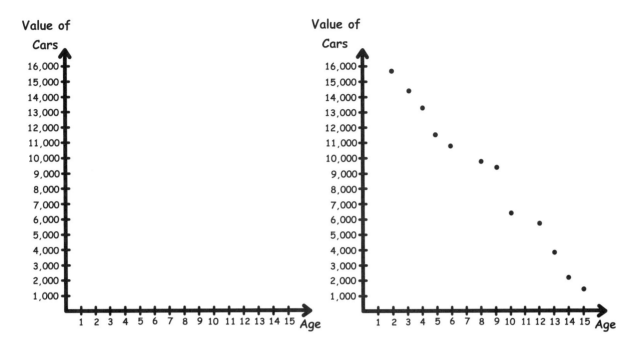

You can see that the points don't fall exactly along a straight line. There are a lot of reasons why the points aren't lined up. Other variables besides age might be impacting the value of a car. For instance, our data doesn't tell us how many miles each car has on it. Mileage can affect a car's value. Another variable that might be important is the condition of the car. A car that's been very well taken care of will be worth more than one that has been treated poorly. So there are a lot of reasons why the points don't line up perfectly. But we can still see that age and the value of a car are related because the points go downward from left to right. That means the mathematical link is that as age goes up, value goes down. There's a clear downward slope. When we plot points and look for a pattern, even though the points don't line up perfectly, the graph is called a **scatter plot**. A scatter plot is used to look for patterns between variables.

Scatter plots are used to predict things. For instance, what if you had a 1 year old Mustang and wanted to know its value? You could look at the scatter plot above and guess where a point that's directly over the 1 year mark should go in order to be consistent with the pattern. To maintain the relationship between the variables, the point would have to be across from about $17,000 on the vertical axis. So you would need to extend the numbers on that axis a bit. The main point is you can use a scatter plot to make predictions. But you have to be careful. A scatter plot prediction may not be accurate.

Another scatter plot is shown below. This scatter plot shows data on the relationship between the number of years of education a person has attained and the amount of money the person earns. Each person's annual income is shown on the vertical axis. And the number of years of education is on the horizontal axis. Each point represents a person in the data.

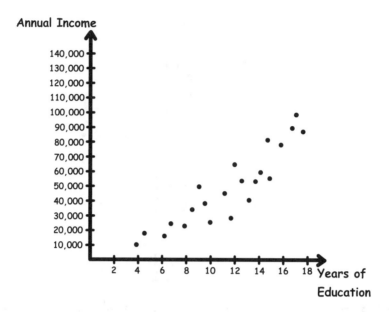

On the left side of the horizontal axis, the years of education are low. And notice that the annual income levels are low on the vertical axis. But as we move to the right horizontally, increasing the years of education, the annual income rises as well. In other words, the scatter plot shows that as education increases, annual income tends to increase. The points show a positive slope; the variables move together. As with the last example, the points don't all fall perfectly along a line. That's because there are a lot of variables that can determine a person's income. But the scatter plot shows that education does tend to increase a person's income.

You could also use this scatter plot to make predictions. What if a person had 18 years of education? That's 12 years through high school plus 4 years of college plus 2 years of graduate school. You could use the scatter plot to try to predict the person's annual income. If you go to 18 on the horizontal axis and then move up until you get in the middle of the points in that region, you'll be close to a $100,000 annual income level. So you might predict that a person with 18 years of education would earn $100,000 annually. That doesn't mean that this prediction would be right. The person could have 18 years of education and $0 income. Maybe the person is unemployed right now. That can happen to anybody, no matter how much education they have. But you can still use the scatter plot to make predictions.

Correlation

In working with scatter plots, three basic patterns come up a lot. Examples of each are shown below. The scatter plots all show a connection between two variables. We don't know what the variables stand for. They're just labeled x and y.

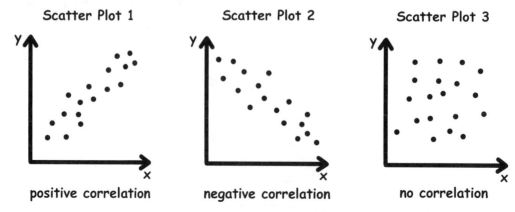

Scatter Plot 1 shows the points going up and to the right. That means both variables are moving in the same direction. In other words, when one variable goes up, the other variable goes up also. The points don't fit perfectly on a line because there are probably other factors affecting the variables. But the basic trend is up and to the right, which means that as x increases y increases also. A real world example of this kind of relationship is the case of education and income. As your education increases, your income tends to increase. The variables move up (or down) together. When two variables move in the same direction, we say there's a **positive correlation** between them. Or we can just say that the variables are "positively correlated." So education and income are positively correlated.

In Scatter Plot 2, the points go downward as you move to the right. That means the variables are going in opposite directions. In other words, when x goes up, y goes down. Again, the points aren't lined up perfectly, but that's the trend. This relationship is similar to our Ford Mustang example. As the age of the cars increases, their value decreases. When two variables move in opposite directions, it is called a **negative correlation.** Or you can just say the variables are negatively correlated.

What about Scatter Plot 3? In this one, the points don't seem to show any pattern. That's because the variables don't have any relationship. They're not linked mathematically at all. A real world example might be something like the month a person was born and the person's height. Obviously, there's no connection between those variables. Just because you're born in July doesn't mean you'll end up really tall! When the variables show no connection, we say that there **no correlation** between them.

Practice 129

a. Use the stem and leaf plot to tell what tens digit appears the most frequently in the data.
(128)

Stem	Leaf
1	4 4 6
2	1 2 2 4
3	6 7 7 7 8 8 9
5	1 3 3 4 5 5 7 7
6	0 2
7	3 3 6
8	2 6
9	1

1|4 = 14

b. The histogram below shows the different range of weights (in pounds) of a group of boxes that were
(129) shipped overseas. Use the histogram to tell the number of boxes that weighed from 12 to 15 pounds.

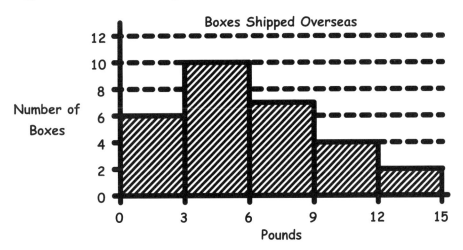

679

c.
(129)
The scatter plot below shows the relationship between the number of hours various employees in a toy factory worked in a week and the number of toys they finished. Use the scatter plot to answer the following question.

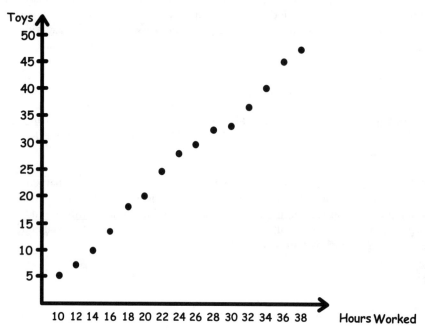

Based on the scatter plot, which would be the best estimate of the toys finished by an employee who worked 36 hours in a week?

A. 25   B. 30   C. 35
D. 40   E. 45

d.
(129)
Tell whether the scatter plot below shows a positive correlation, a negative correlation, or no correlation between the variables.

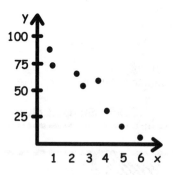

A. Positive correlation
B. Negative correlation
C. No correlation

e.
(55)
Translate the word problem below into an equation; then solve.

If a B-29—that's a type of bomber used during World War II—was traveling at 345 miles per hour, how many hours would it take it to go 690 miles?

Problem Set 129

Tell whether each sentence below is True or False.

1. A histogram is a graph with bars that shows how the numbers in a set of data are dispersed.
(129)

2. A scatter plot is a graph that's used to look for patterns between variables.
(129)

3. Two variables on a scatter plot moving in the same direction are said to have a negative correlation.
(129)

Find the slope of the line in each linear equation below.

4. $y = -\dfrac{4}{7}x + 3$
(125)

5. $y = 8x - \dfrac{2}{5}$
(125)

The table below shows the amount of money (in dollars) raised by each of the members of a church youth group for their inner city Thanksgiving dinner.

Amount of Funds Raised

$53	$74	$120	$36	$24	$90	$61
$36	$52	$44	$21	$30	$13	$36
$74	$39	$52	$110	$96	$132	

6. Find the mean of the data above.
(127)

7. Find the median of the data above.
(127)

8. Find the mode of the data above.
(127)

Calculate the range for each group of numbers below.

9. 36, 81, 53, 74, 29, 65, and 47.
(128)

10. 3.1, 5.5, 4.8, 12.3, 6.2, 7.7, and 2.6.
(128)

11. 54, 39, 265, 54, 27, 30, 61, 76, 21, and 18.
(128)

Use the stem and leaf plot to answer each question below.

12. How many numbers in the data have a 3 in the tens place?
(128)

13. How many numbers in total are in the data?
(128)

(a) 14. What tens digit appears the most frequently in the data?
(128)

Stem	Leaf
1	3 5 6 8
2	4 7 9
3	0 1 1 2 5 6 7 9
4	3 5
6	0 7 8
7	2 2 3 4 6
8	9 9 9
9	2 4

1|3 = 13

681

The histogram below shows ranges for the number of pounds lost by a group of people who agreed to try a new diet for a month. Use the histogram to answer each of the following questions.

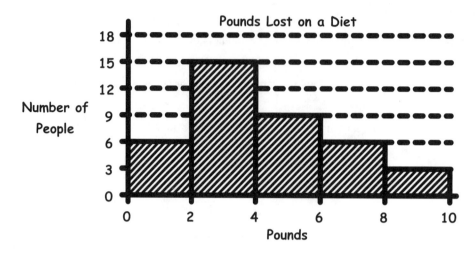

(b) 15. How many people lost from 2 to 4 pounds?
(129)

16. How many people lost from 0 to 2 pounds?
(129)

17. How many people lost from 4 to 8 pounds?
(129)

The scatter plot below shows the relationship between the number of hours studied and the test scores for all the students in a college Calculus class. Use the scatter plot to answer each of the following questions.

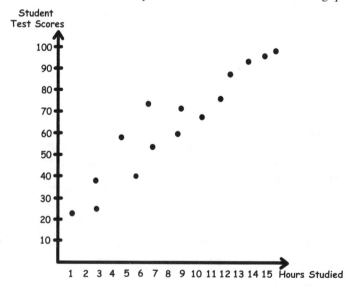

18. Tell whether the scatter plot above shows a positive correlation, a negative correlation, or no correlation
(129) between the variables.

    A. Positive correlation

    B. Negative correlation

    C. No correlation

(c) 19. Based on the scatter plot, which would be the best estimate of the test score for a student who studied 13
(129) hours for the test?

    A. 70   B. 75   C. 80
    D. 90   E. 95

Tell whether each scatter plot below shows a positive correlation, a negative correlation, or no correlation between the variables.

20.
(129)

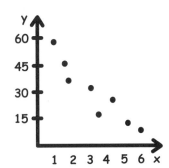

    A. Positive correlation
    B. Negative correlation
    C. No correlation

21.
(129)

    A. No correlation
    B. Positive correlation
    C. Negative correlation

(d) 22.
(129)

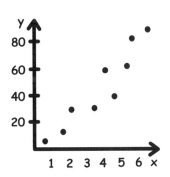

    A. Negative correlation
    B. Positive correlation
    C. No correlation

Translate the word problem below into an equation; then solve.

(e) 23. If a 747—that's a type of plane that ordinary people fly on—was cruising at 565 miles per hour, how
(55) many hours would it take it to go 2,260 miles?

683

Lesson 130—Probability

Probability is basically a measure of how certain something is to happen. So it's used in situations where there is a lot of uncertainty. For example, what if you were doing a chemistry experiment and the instructions said that there was a 30% probability that that chemical compound would blow up! That means if you use that chemical compound in many experiments, it will blow up in about 30% of those. What if you were completely certain that the compound would blow up? Then the probability that it would blow up would be 100%. When something is certain to happen, the probability is always 100%. If there's no chance at all of a blow up, then the probability would be 0%. So a probability can be between 0%, when there's no way that it's going to happen, and 100%, when you're absolutely certain it's going to happen.

People sometimes write a probability as a fraction. So instead of writing the probability as 60%, they might write it as $\frac{60}{100}$ or they could reduce it to $\frac{3}{5}$. It's even possible to write a probability as a decimal. We could write 40% as 0.4, for instance.

Figuring Out Probabilities

How do you actually calculate a probability? We'll go through a simple example. Let's say we were flipping a coin and wanted to figure out the probability of it landing heads. We can do the calculation by creating a fraction. The bottom of the fraction has the total possible outcomes—all the ways that the event can happen. The top of the fraction has the favorable outcomes. That's the number of outcomes that we're trying to calculate the probability of. This fraction equals the probability that the event will take place.

$$\frac{\text{favorable outcomes}}{\text{possible outcomes}} = \text{probability}$$

On our coin flipping example, there are only two possibilities. The coin is either going to land heads or tails. So we should put the number 2 in the bottom of the fraction. The top of the fraction needs the favorable outcomes. That's the number of outcomes that we're trying to calculate the probability of. We're calculating the outcome of the coin landing heads. That's just one outcome, so we need to put a 1 in the top of the fraction.

$$\frac{\text{favorable outcomes}}{\text{possible outcomes}} = \frac{1}{2}$$

The probability of a coin landing heads is therefore $\frac{1}{2}$. We could also write it as 0.5 or 50%. Here is a summary of the steps for calculating a probability.

To Calculate a Probability

1.	Count all the possible outcomes and put that total in the bottom of a fraction.
2.	Count the number of favorable outcomes and put that total in the top of the fraction.
	$\dfrac{\text{favorable outcomes}}{\text{possible outcomes}} = \text{probability}$

The Meaning of Probability

Sometimes people get confused about the meaning of probability. A probability of 50% doesn't mean that a coin is guaranteed to land heads once and tails once. If you flipped a coin twice it might land heads both times or it might land tails both times. That happens a lot. A 50% probability means that when you flip a coin many, many times, it will land heads about 50% of the time. But even then it won't be exact. The more times you flip the coin, however, the closer it should come to 50% heads and 50% tails. For instance, if you flipped a coin 1,000 times, you might get 538 heads and 462 tails. That's how a probability of 50% works.

Let's do another example. You've probably used dice before. You know that dice have six numbers on them: 1, 2, 3, 4, 5, and 6. Also, there is one number on each side, or face. Just one of the dice is called a "die," actually. What if we were rolling a die and wanted to figure out the probability of getting a 2? We can calculate this probability in the usual way. We should set up a fraction.

$$\frac{\text{favorable outcomes}}{\text{possible outcomes}} = \text{probability}$$

The total possible outcomes go in the bottom. And the favorable outcomes go on top. There are six faces on a die. That means we have six possible outcomes. The number of favorable outcomes is the number of outcomes that we're calculating the probability of. We want the probability of rolling a 2. That's just one outcome. So we need a 1 in the top of the fraction.

$$\frac{\text{favorable outcomes}}{\text{possible outcomes}} = \text{probability} = \frac{1}{6}$$

The probability of rolling a 2 is $\frac{1}{6}$. We could convert this to a decimal or a percent. It's actually a repeating decimal. It comes out to 0.1666... As a percent, that equals about 16.7%, rounded to tenths.

Remember, a probability of $\frac{1}{6}$ doesn't mean that if you roll a die six times you're guaranteed of getting a 2 one time out of those six. It means if you roll a die 1,000 times or more, about $\frac{1}{6}$ of those should come out a 2. It won't be exact. The more times you roll, though, the closer it should get to $\frac{1}{6}$. It should be about 16 or 17% of the time. You might roll a 2 around 160 or 170 times out of 1,000.

More Than One Favorable Outcome

Let's do one more probability example. This time we'll figure out the probability of rolling a die and getting an odd number. We need to set up our usual fraction: favorable outcomes over possible outcomes. Since we're rolling a die with six faces, we know that the possible outcomes must equal 6. Now for the favorable outcomes. We're calculating the probability of rolling an odd number. Of the six faces on a die, three of those are odd: 1, 3, and 5. That means the number of favorable outcomes equals 3. Here's our probability.

$$\frac{\text{favorable outcomes}}{\text{possible outcomes}} = \frac{3}{6} = \frac{1}{2}$$

After reducing, we get $\frac{1}{2}$. So the probability of rolling a die and getting an odd number is $\frac{1}{2}$ or 50%. Or you could write it as the decimal 0.5. All three are correct.

Theoretical vs. Experimental

We've been calculating theoretical probabilities so far in this lesson. It's theoretical probability to count the two sides of a coin and conclude that there are two possible outcomes for flipping a coin. It's also theoretical probability to count the six faces of die and conclude that there are six possible outcomes when rolling a die. **Theoretical probability** is worked out by analyzing the particulars of the problem and counting all the possible outcomes, etc.

But some situations are too complicated for theoretical probability. For instance, what if you wanted to find the probability that some person in your town might get a flat tire while driving to work anytime this year? That's an incredibly hard problem. Just think of how many things could cause a flat tire. That would be a huge number of possible outcomes and it would be very difficult to count them all. In such a complicated situation, a better approach is to find the probability by looking at similar data. For instance, you might contact automobile companies to find out how many flat tires drivers tend to get over the course of an entire year. The automobile companies might tell you that out of 100,000 drivers there were 2,014 flat tires in a year. We could then make 100,000 the possible outcomes and 2,014 the favorable outcomes. That gives us a probability of 0.02014 or 2.014%.

$$\frac{\text{favorable outcomes}}{\text{possible outcomes}} = \frac{2,014}{100,000} = 0.02014 = 2.014\%$$

We can just take this as the probability that a person in your town will get a flat tire on the way to work.

$$\text{Probability} = 2.014\%$$

Instead of being based on analyzing the number of sides of a coin or of dice, this probability is based on data—on experience. That's why this kind of probability is called **experimental probability**, and it's used in more complicated situations.

Practice 130

a.
(129)
The histogram below shows ranges for the number of hours that a group of men spent watching sports last week. Use the histogram to tell how many men spent from 0 to 3 hours watching sports.

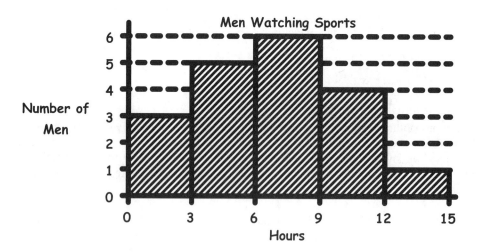

b.
(129)
Tell whether you would expect a positive correlation, negative correlation, or no correlation between the years of education a person has and his/her income.

        A. Negative correlation
        B. Positive correlation
        C. No correlation

c.
(130)
What is the probability of rolling a die and getting an odd number? Write your answer as a fully reduced fraction.

d.
(130)
If a basketball player shot 1,000 blindfolded free throws and made 93 of them, what is the probability that he will make a blindfolded free throw if he shoots again? Write your answer as a decimal, and it's okay to use a calculator.

e.
(80)
Translate the word problem below into an equation; then solve.

Train #1 and train #2 are headed straight toward each other. Train #1 is traveling at 62 mph, and train #2 is traveling at 71 mph. If the two trains are 399 miles apart, how many hours will it be before they meet?

Problem Set 130

Tell whether each sentence below is True or False.

1.
(130)
The probability of an event equals $\dfrac{\text{favorable outcomes}}{\text{possible outcomes}}$.

2.
(130)
Experimental probability is calculated by looking at data to figure out the probability of an event happening.

Find the slope of each line below. Make sure your answer is fully reduced.

3.
(124)
Line *FC*

4.
(125)
Line *GJ*

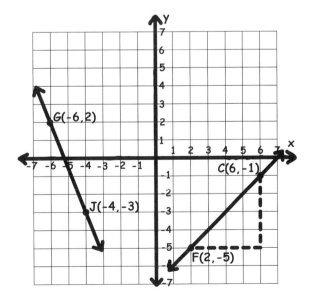

5.
(126)
Tell whether the slope of line AC below is positive, negative, zero or undefined.

A. Undefined
B. Zero
C. Negative
D. Positive

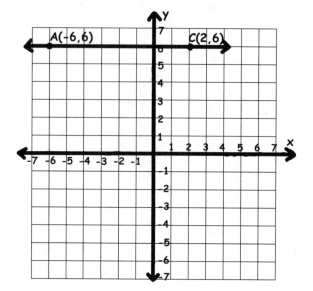

Calculate the range for each group of numbers below.

6.
(128)
46, 24, 15, 77, 98, 61, and 50.

7.
(128)
4.3, 5.2, 8.7, 9.6, 11.0, 7.4, 8.8, 10.6, and 5.3.

Use the stem and leaf plot to answer each question below.

Stem	Leaf
1	2 4 5 5
3	7 8 8 8 9
4	0 0 1
5	6
6	2 3 3 4 7 8
7	1 1 4
8	7 9 9
9	4 5

1|2 = 1.2

8.
(128)
How many numbers in the data have a 3 in the ones place?

9.
(128)
How many numbers in total are in the data?

The histogram below shows ranges for the number of minutes it took a group of students to complete an assignment. Use the histogram to answer each of the following questions.

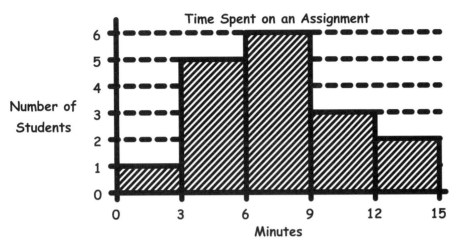

10. How many students took from 0 to 3 minutes?
(129)

11. How many students took from 9 to 12 minutes?
(129)

(a) 12. How many students took from 3 to 9 minutes?
(129)

The scatter plot below shows the relationship between air temperature in Fahrenheit and elevation (in thousands of feet). Use the scatter plot to answer each of the following questions.

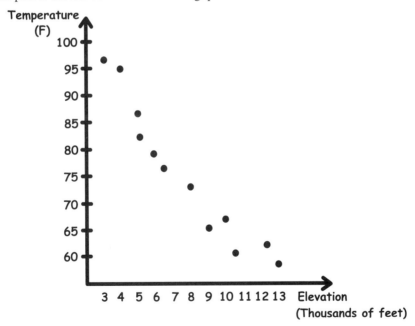

13. Tell whether the scatter plot above shows a positive correlation, a negative correlation, or no correlation
(129) between the variables.

    A. No correlation
    B. Negative correlation
    C. Positive correlation

14.
(129)
Based on the scatter plot, which would be the best estimate of the temperature at a location that has an elevation of 7 thousand feet?

A. 60   B. 65   C. 75
D. 80   E. 85

Tell whether you would expect a positive correlation, negative correlation, or no correlation between each pair of variables described below.

15. Boys' heights and their shoe sizes.   **(b) 16.** The size of a boat and its cost.
(129)   **(129)**

A. No correlation   A. Positive correlation
B. Negative correlation   B. No correlation
C. Positive correlation   C. Negative correlation

17. The month a person is born in and the person's weight.
(129)

A. Negative correlation
B. No correlation
C. Positive correlation

Calculate the probability of each event described below. Write your answer as a fully reduced fraction.

18. What is the probability of flipping a coin and getting tails?
(130)

19. What is the probability of rolling a die and getting a 5?
(130)

(c) 20. What is the probability of rolling a die and getting an even number?
(130)

Use a calculator to find each experimental probability below. Write your answers as decimals.

21. The town of Bedrock has had an earthquake in 14 of the last 100 years. What is the probability that
(130) Bedrock will have an earthquake next year?

(d) 22. The field goal kicker kicked 1,000 field goals from the 50-yard line and made 99 of them. What is the
(130) probability that the kicker will make a goal if he kicks again?

Translate the word problem below into an equation; then solve.

(e) 23. Cyclist #1 and cyclist #2 are headed straight toward each other. Cyclist #1 is traveling at 17 mph, and
(80) cyclist #2 is traveling at 22 mph. If the two cyclists are 78 miles apart, how many hours will it be before they meet?

Lesson 131—Tree Diagrams

In the last lesson, we learned how to calculate probability. The way it works is we count the number of possible outcomes and put that in the bottom of a fraction. Then we count the number of favorable outcomes—those are the outcomes that we're figuring out the probability of—and put that in the top of the fraction. And the fraction equals the probability.

$$\frac{\text{favorable outcomes}}{\text{possible outcomes}} = \text{probability}$$

Three Flips of the Coin

Counting outcomes is easy when it's something simple like flipping a coin or rolling a die. But in more complicated situations, people often draw a picture to count the possible outcomes. Let's go through an example.

> If a coin is flipped 3 times what is the probability that the coin will land heads all 3 times?

It's a little tougher to count the possible outcomes on this problem. It can be done; we don't have to use experimental probability. But counting is harder here. What we can do, though, is draw a picture. The picture is actually called a **tree diagram**. The name comes from the fact that the diagram looks a little like a tree with branches.

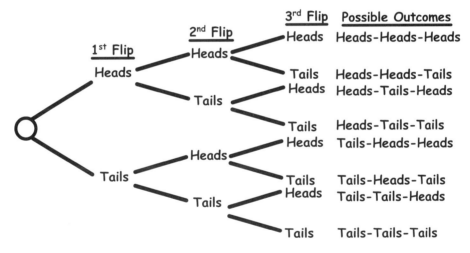

Flipping a coin three times.

This looks complicated, but it's fairly straightforward. We start on the left. The first circle or "node" represents the first flip. And you can see that there are two possible outcomes. In the first flip, the coin can land either heads or tails. And these are shown with "branches" coming out of the node. After that the coin has to be flipped again. There will be two possible outcomes on the second flip. And those will exist whether the coin lands heads or tails on the first flip. So we need two branches coming out of both the node for heads and the node for tails on the first flip. That gives us four possibilities after the second flip. We need to keep going, though. The problem is asking us to find the probability after three flips. There will be two possible outcomes on the third flip. Those will exist for every one of the four branches. So we need two branches coming out of each. That finishes the tree diagram.

Every one of the branches on the far right side of the tree represents a possible outcome for the three flips. The top branch is the outcome where all three flips are heads (heads-heads-heads). The second branch represents the outcome where the first two flips land heads and the third lands tails (heads-heads-tails). And you can continue on down to see what combinations the other branches represent.

We need to know the total possible outcomes for this entire event (of flipping a coin three times). That's equal to the number of branches on the right side of the tree. We can just count those. There are 8 branches. That means there are 8 possible outcomes. That number should go in the bottom of the fraction. Now for the favorable outcomes. We're trying to find the probability of flipping the coin and it landing heads all 3 times. That's the heads-heads-heads scenario. It's the top branch. That's just one of the possible outcomes, which means we should put 1 in the top of the fraction. Now we can calculate the probability.

$$\frac{\text{favorable outcomes}}{\text{possible outcomes}} = \frac{1}{8} = 0.125 = 12.5\%$$

The probability of flipping a coin 3 times and having it land heads all 3 times is equal to $\frac{1}{8}$ or 12.5%. The main point of the example is to show you how to use a tree diagram to count the possible outcomes. Tree diagrams can be helpful on more complicated probability problems.

Simple Problems Too

We could even use a tree diagram to calculate the probability of flipping a coin just once. Most people wouldn't bother because it's a much simpler problem. The entire tree would have only two branches.

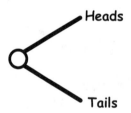

Flipping a coin once.

There are obviously only 2 possible outcomes. To calculate the probability of the coin landing heads, we would have 1 favorable outcome and that would give us an answer of $\frac{1}{2}$.

$$\frac{\text{favorable outcomes}}{\text{possible outcomes}} = \frac{1}{2}$$

We could also use a tree diagram to calculate the probability of rolling a die. Since a die has 6 different faces, the tree would need 6 branches for every time the die is rolled. Here's the tree for 1 roll.

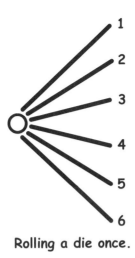

Rolling a die once.

There are 6 possible outcomes. What if we wanted to calculate the probability of rolling a 3 or a 4? That's 2 favorable outcomes, so the probability equals $\frac{2}{6}$ or $\frac{1}{3}$ fully reduced.

$$\frac{\text{favorable outcomes}}{\text{possible outcomes}} = \frac{2}{6} = \frac{1}{3}$$

If we were calculating a probability involving rolling a die twice, the tree diagram would have to be bigger. Each of the 6 branches above would need 6 branches coming from it. That would give us a lot of branches and a very big tree. Even though they can be big, tree diagrams are very helpful for counting the possible outcomes in more complicated situations.

Practice 131

a. The histogram below shows ranges for the number of minutes it took a group of people to eat their lunch.
(129) Use the histogram to tell how many people took from 10 to 25 minutes.

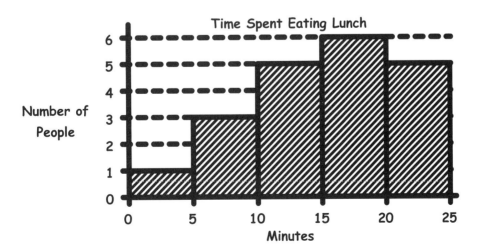

b. Use the tree diagram to find the probability of flipping a coin twice and it landing tails both times?
(131) Write your answer as a fully reduced fraction.

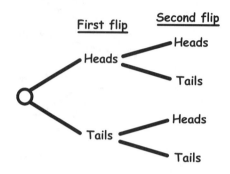

Calculate the probability of each event described below.

c. One green marble and 4 red ones are in a bag. What is the probability of drawing out the green marble
(130) without looking? Write your answer as a decimal.

d. What is the probability of rolling a die and getting a 2 or a 4? Write your answer as a decimal rounded
(130) to two decimal places.

e. Translate the word problem below into an equation; then solve.
(54)

Dirk bought a mini trampoline at a 35% discount. If the discount saved him $21.70, what was the
trampoline's original price?

Problem Set 131

Tell whether each sentence below is True or False.

1. On more complicated probability problems, people may draw a tree diagram to help count the possible
(131) outcomes.

2. You can count the favorable outcomes using a tree diagram.
(131)

Find each value below.

3. If $x = \dfrac{2}{5}t - 4$, find $x(15)$.
(120)

4. If $y = \dfrac{x}{7} - 3$ is represented by $g(x)$, find the x-value that makes $g(x) = -6$.
(120)

The table below shows the number of slurpy drinks sold by a convenience store for the first 16 days of summer.

Number of Slurpy Drinks Sold

72	50	43	86	49	31	66	81
32	90	98	75	50	75	84	50

5. Find the mean of the data above.
(127)

6. Find the median of the data above.
(127)

7. Find the mode of the data above.
(127)

The histogram below shows ranges for the number of minutes it took a group of people to read the morning newspaper. Use the histogram to answer each of the following questions.

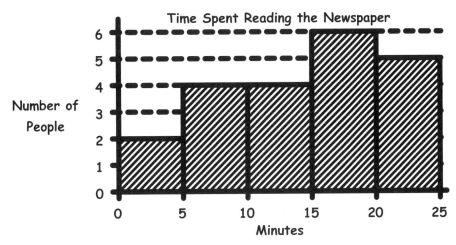

8. How many people took from 0 to 5 minutes?
(129)

9. How many people took from 10 to 15 minutes?
(129)

(a)10. How many people took from 5 to 20 minutes?
(129)

The scatter plot below shows the relationship between the number of months a person has worked and the number of factory rejects he has produced. Use the scatter plot to answer each of the following questions.

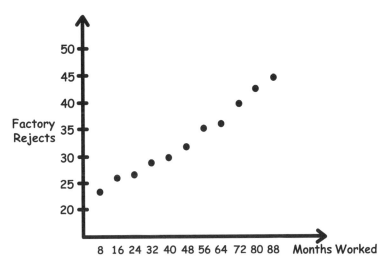

695

11.
(129) Tell whether the scatter plot above shows a positive correlation, a negative correlation, or no correlation between the variables.

    A. Positive correlation
    B. No correlation
    C. Negative correlation

12.
(129) Based on the scatter plot, which would be the best estimate of the factory rejects produced by a person that has worked for 72 months?

    A. 60   B. 55   C. 50
    D. 45   E. 40

Use the tree diagram to answer each question below.

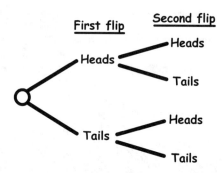

13.
(131) How many total possible outcomes are there when flipping a coin twice?

(b) 14.
(131) What is the probability of flipping a coin twice and it landing heads both times? Write your answer as a fully reduced fraction.

15.
(131) What is the probability of flipping a coin twice and getting tails first and heads second? Write your answer as a fully reduced fraction.

Calculate the probability of each event described below.

(c) 16.
(130) One white tennis ball and 9 yellow ones are in a bag. What is the probability of drawing out the white ball without looking? Write your answer as a decimal.

(d) 17.
(130) What is the probability of rolling a die and getting a 5 or a 6? Write your answer as a decimal rounded to two decimal places.

Tell whether you would expect a positive correlation, negative correlation, or no correlation between each pair of variables described below.

18.
(129) The number of friends you have and the number of phone calls you receive.

    A. Positive correlation
    B. No correlation
    C. Negative correlation

19. The number of times you've been to the beach and the number of sunburns you've had.
(129)

     A. Negative correlation

     B. Positive correlation

     C. No correlation

Use a calculator to find each experimental probability below. Write your answers as decimals.

20. The expert marksman shot at the target 100 times and hit the bullseye 72 of those times. What is the
(130) probability that he will hit the bullseye the next time?

21. The gold prospector panned for gold 1,000 times and actually found some 53 of those times. What is the
(130) probability that he will find gold the next time he pans for it?

Translate the word problem below into an equation; then solve.

(e) 22. Toby bought a pitching machine at a 45% discount. If the discount saved him $38.70, what was the
(54) machine's original price?

Lesson 132—Fundamental Counting Principle

In the last lesson, we learned how to use tree diagrams to count the possible outcomes in a probability problem. There's actually an even faster way to count outcomes where you don't even have to draw anything.

Just Multiply

What if we are going to roll a die twice? Since a die has six faces, with a number on each face, the first roll will have six possibilities. And the second roll will also have six possibilities.

1st roll   2nd roll

6 possibilities   6 possibilities

Instead of drawing a huge tree diagram, we can find the total possible outcomes by multiplying. We just take $6 \cdot 6$ to get 36. That means there are 36 possible outcomes when you roll a die two times.

$$6 \cdot 6 = 36 \text{ possible outcomes}$$

In general, when a situation has two or more separate events, to find the total possible outcomes just multiply the outcomes of each event. This rule is called the **Fundamental Counting Principle**. Here's the technical definition.

Fundamental Counting Principle

If event *A* can occur in *m* ways and event *B* can occur in *n* ways, then event *A* followed by event *B* can occur in *m • n* ways.

Just make sure the two events don't affect each other. In other words, make sure they're **independent events**.

What if we had a magic coin and every time it landed heads the other side would change from tails to heads? That would change the possible outcomes because if the coin landed heads the first time then there would only be one possible outcome on the second flip—both sides would be heads. In this case, we couldn't multiply the possible outcomes ($2 \cdot 2$) to get the total possible outcomes of both flips. That wouldn't work. The reason is the events—the two flips—wouldn't be independent. The main point is that the fundamental counting principle only works when the events are truly independent—when one event has no effect on the other.

Three Rolls of a Die

What if we were going to roll a die three times? Let's figure out all the possible outcomes. We could draw a tree diagram to count them. But it would be a big diagram. A tree diagram for rolling a die just twice requires 36 branches. So a diagram for three rolls would be huge. So drawing a tree is probably not the best strategy. Instead, we can use the fundamental counting principle. The first roll of the die has six possible outcomes because there are six numbers on a die—one number for each face. For the second roll of the die, there are six more possible outcomes. And there are another six outcomes for the third roll. To use the fundamental counting principle, we just need to multiply all three 6s together.

$$\text{Total possible outcomes} = 6 \cdot 6 \cdot 6 = 216$$

That means when rolling a die 3 times, there are 216 possible outcomes in total. But the main point is that on very complicated problems it's often easier to count outcomes by using the fundamental counting principle than by drawing a gigantic tree diagram.

Practice 132

a.
(131)
Use the tree diagram to find the probability of flipping a coin three times and getting heads every time? Write your answer as a fully reduced fraction.

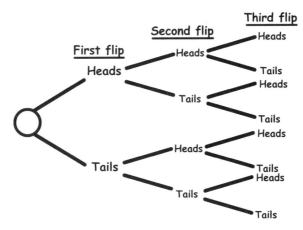

Use the fundamental counting principle to answer each question below.

b.
(132)
There is a special kind of die which has only 4 faces. How many total possible outcomes are there when rolling a 4-faced die five times?

c.
(132)
How many total possible outcomes are there when flipping a coin seven times?

d.
(130)
Three pencils and 9 ink pens are in a box. What is the probability of drawing out one pencil without looking? Write your answer as a decimal with two digits.

e.
(53)
Translate the word problem below into math; then solve.

Linnette's father told her that he would pay her $\frac{1}{3}$ of a penny for every leaf she picked up. How many pennies will Linnette earn after she picks up 63 leaves?

Problem Set 132

Tell whether each sentence below is True or False.

1.
(132)
According to the fundamental counting principle, when a situation has two or more separate events, to find the total possible outcomes just multiply the outcomes of each event.

2.
(132)
Independent events are events that don't affect each other, such as two flips of a coin.

Tell whether each pair of x and y-coordinates below solves the equation $y = \dfrac{5}{2}x + 4$.

3.
(123)
$x = 8$, $y = 24$

4.
(123)
$x = -6$, $y = -19$

Find the y-intercept (where the line crosses the y-axis) for each linear equation below.

5.
(125)
$y = -\dfrac{2}{7}x + 1$

6.
(125)
$y = x - \dfrac{3}{2}$

Calculate the range for each group of numbers below.

7.
(128)
16, 48, 30, 13, 25, 51, and 39.

8.
(128)
5.4, 2.0, 1.7, 8.8, 19.2, 9.6, 8.5, 4.4, and 3.1.

The table below shows the weight (in pounds) of 14 newborn babies at a hospital last week.

Weight of Newborn Babies

6.1	5.2	6.8	7.9	7.0	5.1
7.1	7.0	8.4	6.8	8.9	5.3
6.6	7.0				

9.
(127)
Find the mean of the data above.

10.
(127)
Find the median of the data above.

11.
(127)
Find the mode of the data above.

Use the stem and leaf plot to answer each question below.

Stem	Leaf
2	0 0 2 3
3	1
4	5 6 6 7 9 9
5	0 1 1 3 4 5 6 6
7	2 8
8	1 6 9
9	6 7

2|0 = 20

12. How many numbers in the data have a 4 in the tens place?
(128)

13. How many numbers in total are in the data?
(128)

Use the tree diagram to answer each question below. Write your answers as fractions.

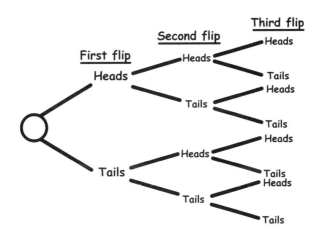

14. What is the probability of flipping a coin twice and getting heads first and tails second?
(131)

(a) 15. What is the probability of flipping a coin three times and getting tails every time?
(131)

Use the fundamental counting principle to answer each question below.

(b) 16. There is a special kind of die which has only 4 faces. How many total possible outcomes are there when
(132) rolling a 4-faced die three times?

(c) 17. How many total possible outcomes are there when flipping a coin six times?
(132)

Calculate the probability of each event described below.

(d) 18.
(130)
Two oranges and 6 apples are in a bag. What is the probability of drawing out one orange without looking? Write your answer as a decimal with two digits.

19.
(130)
What is the probability of rolling a die and getting a 1 or a 6? Write your answer as a decimal rounded to two decimal places.

Tell whether you would expect a positive correlation, negative correlation, or no correlation between each pair of variables described below.

20.
(129)
The number of times a person flosses each week and the number of cavities he or she gets.

     A. Positive correlation
     B. Negative correlation
     C. No correlation

21.
(129)
The weight of a person at birth and the person's IQ (intelligence quotient).

     A. Positive correlation
     B. Negative correlation
     C. No correlation

Translate the word problem below into an equation; then solve.

(e) 22.
(53)
Chase's mother told him that she would pay him $\frac{1}{2}$ of a penny every time he took a bite of spinach. How many pennies will Chase earn if he takes 28 bites of spinach?

Lesson 133—Inequalities

We've learned that algebra is all about equations. That's almost true, but not completely. Algebra also includes other mathematical statements called **inequalities**. Inequalities are similar to equations but they're not exactly the same. We talked some about inequalities at the beginning of the course. Two simple inequalities are shown below. The one on the left means "6 is greater than 4," and the one on the right means "7 is less than 9."

$$6 > 4 \qquad\qquad 7 < 9$$

In an inequality, the pointed end of the inequality symbol is always toward the smaller number, and the open end is always toward the greater number. If you think of the symbol as the mouth of an alligator, the alligator's mouth always opens toward the larger number (because the alligator wants to eat it).

Inequalities with x's

Inequalities can also include x's. The inequality below says that "x is greater than 14" because the open end of the inequality is toward x.

$$x > 14$$

There's an important difference between the equation $x = 14$ and the inequality $x > 14$.

$$x = 14 \qquad\qquad x > 14$$

The equation just has one solution: 14. But the inequality $x > 14$ has lots of solutions: an infinite number of solutions, in fact. Think about it. The number 15 is a solution because if we put 15 in for x, the left side of the inequality will be greater than the right side, the way it's supposed to be.

$$15 > 14$$

But 16 is a solution too because 16 also makes the left side greater than the right side.

$$16 > 14$$

There are a lot of other numbers that will work: 28 is a solution, and so are 42 and 68, for instance.

$$28 > 14 \qquad 42 > 14 \qquad 68 > 14$$

Basically, any number that's above 14 is a solution to the inequality. And that's an infinite number of solutions. However, 14 itself does not qualify as a solution. If we put 14 in for x, we get the inequality below.

$$14 > 14 \qquad\qquad \textbf{This is wrong.}$$

This is wrong because the left side has to be greater than the right side. The two sides can't be equal. The main point is that inequalities with an x can have an infinite number of solutions.

Graphing an Inequality

It's possible to graph an inequality. Let's graph $x > 14$. Since this inequality has just one variable (x) we need to graph it on a single axis: a number line. The way it works is we put a dot or point on the number 14 and then draw a line—it's actually a ray—to the right. The ray shows that all the points to the right of 14, going on forever, are solutions to the inequality.[1]

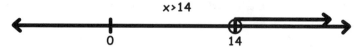

Notice that the point on 14 isn't shaded. It's just white inside. That's because 14 itself is not a solution. The variable x has to be *greater* than 14. The way we show that is to leave the point unshaded.

Now let's graph the inequality $x < -4$. This also has an infinite number of solutions because any number below negative 4 is will solve the inequality. To do the graph, we put an unshaded point on -4. Then we draw a ray to the left of -4. The ray shows that all of the points to the left, going on forever, are solutions to the inequality.

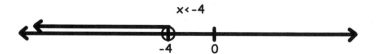

Greater Than or Equal To

You probably know that it's possible to combine an inequality and an equals sign into one symbol. For instance, we can have an inequality like $x \geq 5$. This means "x is greater than or equal to 5." In other words, x can be 5 or it can be any number above 5. What about the graph of $x \geq 5$? Well, it has to be on a single number line again because there's just one variable (x). We need a ray going from 5 to the right showing that all of the numbers up from 5 are solutions. But on this graph the point on the number 5 should be shaded. This shows that 5 itself is a solution to the inequality. In this case, the left side can be greater than 5, but it can also equal 5.

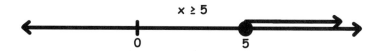

We won't bother doing an example of a "less than or equal to" inequality. The symbol looks like this: $\leq$. And the graph would need a ray going forever to the left of the number. The point, of course would have to be shaded.

Practice 133

a.
(132) Use the fundamental counting principle to find the total possible outcomes when flipping a dime eight times.

b.
(130) Five home decoration magazines and 7 fashion magazines are on a shelf. What is the probability of drawing out one fashion magazine without looking? Write your answer as a decimal rounded to two decimal places.

---

[1] We could have labeled all the other numbers between 0 and 14 (and negative numbers too). We just left off the extra numbers to save space (and ink!).

c. Select the number line below that accurately describes the inequality $x \geq -5$.
(133)

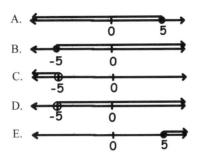

A.
B.
C.
D.
E.

d. Select an inequality for the following statement: A quantity x that can equal -9 or any number above -9.
(133)

A. $x \leq -9$ B. $x > -9$ C. $x \geq -9$
D. $x < -9$ E. $x = -9$

e. Translate the word problem below into an equation; then solve.
(54)

Bradford sells jet skis, and he receives a 9% commission on all that he sells. If Bradford received $27,000 in commissions last year, how many dollars worth of jet skis did he sell?

Problem Set 133

Tell whether each sentence below is True or False.

1. In addition to equations, algebra includes other mathematical statements called inequalities.
(133)

2. Inequalities cannot be graphed.
(133)

Find the area of each figure below. Use 3.14 for π.

3. Assume that $ABCD$ and $DCFE$ are parallelograms.   **4.**
(114)   (115)

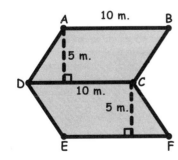

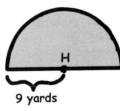

Tell whether the relationship in each table below represents a function.

5.
(118)

x	y
-6	7
-5	4
-1	-3
0	2
-1	-8
3	1

6.
(118)

x	y
-9	0.25
-1	3
0	-1
2	4.5
3	1.5
7	8

Find the slope of each line below. Make sure your answer is fully reduced.

7.   Line *FA*
(124)

8.   Line *EN*
(124)

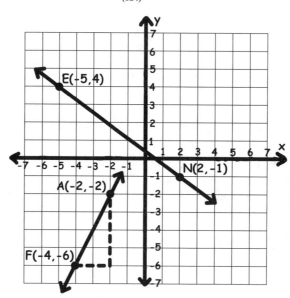

The histogram below shows ranges for the number of minutes it takes a group of commuters to drive to work each morning. Use the histogram to answer each of the following questions.

9.   How many commuters
(129)   take from 20 to 30 minutes to get to work?

10.   How many commuters
(129)   take from 30 to 50 minutes to get to work?

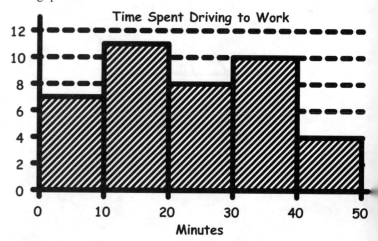

The scatter plot below shows the relationship between the price and the number of carats of various diamonds. Use the scatter plot to answer each of the following questions.

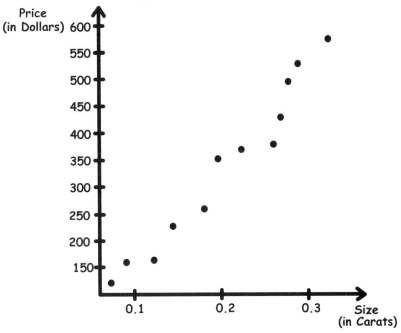

11.
(129)
Tell whether the scatter plot above shows a positive correlation, a negative correlation, or no correlation between the variables.

    A. Positive correlation
    B. Negative correlation
    C. No correlation

12.
(129)
Based on the scatter plot, which would be the best estimate of the price for a 0.3 carat diamond?

    A. $600   B. $550   C. $500
    D. $450   E. $400

Use the fundamental counting principle to answer each question below.

13.
(132)
There is a special kind of die which has only 4 faces. How many total possible outcomes are there when rolling a 4-faced die six times?

(a) 14.
(132)
How many total possible outcomes are there when flipping a nickel nine times?

Calculate the probability of each event described below. Write your answers as decimals rounded to two decimal places.

(b) 15.
(130)
Four cans of orange juice and 7 cans of apple juice are in a sports bag. What is the probability of drawing out one can of apple juice without looking?

16.
(130)
What is the probability of rolling a die and getting a 2 or a 5?

Select the number line that accurately describes each inequality below.

17. $x > 8$
(133)

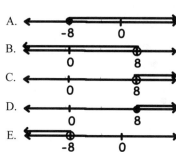

18. $x < -15$
(133)

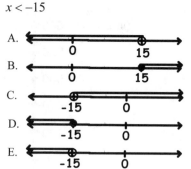

(c) 19. $x \geq -3$
(133)

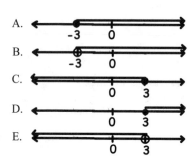

Select an inequality for each statement below.

20. A quantity x that can equal 4 or any number above 4.
(133)

    A. $x < 4$ B. $x > 4$ C. $x \leq 4$
    D. $x = 4$ E. $x \geq 4$

(d) 21. A quantity x that can equal -7 or any number below -7.
(133)

    A. $x \leq -7$ B. $x > -7$ C. $x < -7$
    D. $x \geq -7$ E. $x = -7$

Translate the word problem below into an equation; then solve.

(e) 22. Howard sells used helicopters, and he receives a 3% commission on all that he sells. If Howard received
(54) $42,000 in commissions last year, how many dollars worth of used helicopters did he sell?

Lesson 134—Undoing Inequalities

In the last lesson, we learned about inequalities with x's. The examples were simple. But sometimes inequalities with x's can be a little more complicated. Take a look at this one.

$$x + 4 > 7$$

This inequality has a number added to x. This means "$x + 4$ always has to be greater than 7." To solve the inequality, we have to figure out which numbers are allowed to go in for x.

Undoing Addition and Subtraction

The inequality $x + 4 > 7$ can be solved in the same way we solve equations—by undoing. We just undo the addition of 4 by subtracting.

$$x + 4 - 4 > 7 - 4$$

Simplifying both sides gives us this.

$$x > 3$$

We end up with $x > 3$, which means that any number that's above 3 will solve the original inequality, $x + 4$ is greater than 7. To show you why inequalities can be undone just like equations, let's think of the inequality as a scale.

We used a scale to understand equations. But since this is inequality, the left side is lower than the right side. That shows the left side is greater or "heavier" than the right side, pulling down the scale. Undoing the inequality by subtracting 4 from both sides makes the scale 4 "pounds" lighter on the left. But it also makes the scale 4 pounds lighter on the right. Afterward, the scale looks like this.

Since we took the same amount from both sides, the scale is still tipped in the same way it was before. So x is still heavier than 3. That just means $x > 3$. That's why undoing works with inequalities just as it does with equations. Just make sure you subtract the same amount from both sides.

What if we had an inequality like $x - 9 < 16$? This too can be solved by undoing. We just need to undo the subtraction by adding 9 to both sides.

$$x - 9 + 9 < 16 + 9$$

Simplifying on both sides gives us this.

$$x < 25$$

This means any number that's smaller than 25 will solve the original inequality. We could check by putting in a number for x that's less than 25. Let's put in 21.

$$21 - 9 < 16$$

Now we simplify on the left.

$$12 < 16$$

Since we end up with the true statement that 12 is less than 16, the number 21 worked. And so will any number that's less than 25.

Undoing by Multiplying and Dividing

To undo some inequalities, we have to multiply or divide both sides. As long as we multiply or divide by a positive, everything works just like in equations. Let's go through an example.

$$\frac{x}{2} \le -8$$

To undo the division, we need to multiply both sides by 2.

$$2 \cdot \frac{x}{2} \le (-8)(2)$$

Now we simplify on both sides.

$$x \le -16$$

So x can be any number less than or equal to -16. The main point is that undoing is the same as in equations when multiplying by a positive.

Now let's look at an example of an inequality that has to be undone by dividing both sides.

$$3x > 24$$

We need to divide both sides by 3 to undo the multiplication.

$$\frac{3x}{3} > \frac{24}{3}$$

Simplifying on both sides gives us this.

$$x > 8$$

Any number greater than 8 will solve the original inequality. Undoing inequalities is the same as undoing equations when dividing both sides by a positive number.

    Undoing an inequality by multiplying or dividing by a negative number is trickier. To show you why, look at this simple example involving just numbers.

$$9 > 5$$

Let's multiply both sides of this inequality by positive 2.

$$2(9) > 2(5)$$

$$18 > 10$$

Notice that after multiplying by a positive number, the inequality is still true. The numbers have changed, but the left side is still greater than the right side. Now watch what happens if we multiply both sides by *negative* 2.

$$9 > 5$$

$$-2(9) > -2(5)$$

$$-18 > -10 \qquad \textbf{This is wrong.}$$

After multiplying by a negative, the inequality is wrong. It says that -18 is greater than -10. To avoid this problem when multiplying both sides of an inequality by a negative, we have to flip the inequality symbol. Doing that gives us the correct result.

$$-18 < -10 \qquad \textbf{Flip the inequality symbol.}$$

It works the same way when dividing both sides of an inequality by a negative. We'll show you with an all number example again.

$$8 < 10$$

Let's divide both sides of the inequality by -2.

$$\frac{8}{-2} < \frac{10}{-2}$$

$$-4 < -5 \qquad \textbf{This is wrong.}$$

We get the wrong result again because -4 is actually greater than -5. It's not as far to the left on a number line. So we need to flip the inequality symbol again.

$$-4 > -5 \qquad \textbf{Flip the inequality symbol.}$$

The basic rule is that when multiplying or dividing each side of an inequality by a negative, we should flip the inequality symbol.

x's Too

Importantly, this rule also applies on inequalities with x's. Let's solve the inequality below.

$$-2x \leq 30$$

We need to undo the multiplication by dividing both sides by -2.

$$\frac{-2x}{-2} \leq \frac{30}{-2} \qquad \textbf{This is wrong.}$$

This step looks right, but it's actually not. Since we've divided by a negative number, we need to flip the inequality symbol. It's easy to forget to flip when the inequality contains an x. But the rule still applies.

$$\frac{-2x}{-2} \geq \frac{30}{-2} \qquad \textbf{Flip the inequality symbol.}$$

Now we can continue by simplifying both sides.

$$x \geq -15$$

We end up with x is *greater* than or equal to -15. The main point is just to remember to flip the inequality symbol when you have an x. The symbol has to be flipped every time you either multiply or divide by a negative.

Practice 134

a.
(130)
Eight romantic novels and 6 historical fiction books are on a shelf. What is the probability of drawing out one romantic novel without looking? Write your answer as a decimal rounded to two decimal places.

b.
(133)
Select an inequality for the statement: A quantity v that can equal any number above $\frac{1}{8}$.

A. $v \leq \frac{1}{8}$ 　　　　 B. $v \geq \frac{1}{8}$ 　　　　 C. $v = \frac{1}{8}$

D. $v > \frac{1}{8}$ 　　　　 E. $v < \frac{1}{8}$

c.
(134)
Solve the inequality $x + 9 < 3$. Select your answer along with its graph from the choices given.

A. $x \geq -6$

B. $x < -6$

C. $x > -6$

D. $x \geq 6$

E. $x \leq 6$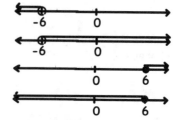

d. Solve the inequality $\dfrac{x}{-4} > 17$. Select your answer along with its graph from the choices given.
(134)

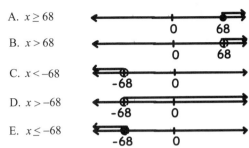

A. $x \geq 68$

B. $x > 68$

C. $x < -68$

D. $x > -68$

E. $x \leq -68$

e. Translate the word problem below into an equation; then solve.
(55)

If a plane flew for 4 hours and traveled a total of 1,904 miles, how fast did the plane travel in miles per hour?

Problem Set 134

Tell whether each sentence below is True or False.

1. When multiplying both sides of an inequality by a negative number, the inequality symbol must be
(134) flipped.

2. When dividing both sides of an inequality by a negative number, the inequality symbol must be flipped.
(134)

Find each value below.

3. If $r = -4x - 17$, find $r(5)$.
(120)

4. If $k = \dfrac{x-2}{4}$ is represented by $k(x)$, find the x-value that makes $k(x) = -3$.
(120)

Calculate the range for each group of numbers below.

5. 52, 79, 36, 44, 90, 71, and 88.
(128)

6. 2.7, 4.0, 5.5, 1.8, 8.0, 9.7, 14.1, 13.3, and 6.6.
(128)

The table below shows the total number of books read last year by the members of a book club.

Number of Books Read

17	10	6	25	11	14	10	21	19
15	13	10	9	13	12	22	18	7

7. Find the mean of the data above.
(127)

8. Find the median of the data above.
(127)

Use the tree diagram to answer each question below. Write your answers as fully reduced fractions.

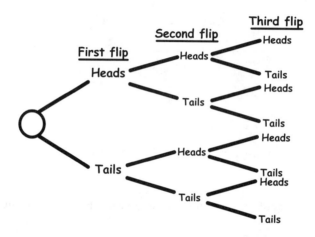

9. What is the probability of flipping a coin three times and getting heads first, tails second and heads third?
(131)

10. What is the probability of flipping a coin three times and it landing heads every time?
(131)

Use the fundamental counting principle to answer each question below.

11. How many total possible outcomes are there when rolling a 6-faced die four times?
(132)

12. How many total possible outcomes are there when flipping a penny five times?
(132)

Calculate the probability of each event described below. Write your answers as decimals rounded to two places.

(a) 13. Nine classical music CDs and 4 jazz music CDs are in a duffle bag. What is the probability of drawing
(130) out one classical music CD without looking?

14. What is the probability of rolling a die and getting a 4 or a 6?
(130)

Select the number line that accurately describes each inequality below.

15. $x > 7$
(133)

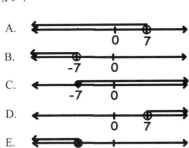

16. $x \leq -2$
(133)

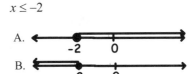

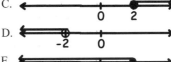

Select an inequality for each statement below.

17. A quantity z that can equal any number below -15.
(133)

     A. $z \geq -15$ B. $z < -15$ C. $z \leq -15$

     D. $z > -15$ E. $z = -15$

(b)18. A quantity t that can equal any number above $\frac{1}{4}$.
(133)

     A. $t < \frac{1}{4}$ B. $t > \frac{1}{4}$ C. $t \geq \frac{1}{4}$

     D. $t \leq \frac{1}{4}$ E. $t = \frac{1}{4}$

Solve each inequality below. Select your answer along with its graph from the choices given.

(c)19. $x + 9 < 4$
(134)

A. $x \leq 5$

B. $x \geq -5$

C. $x < -5$

D. $x < 5$

E. $x \geq 5$

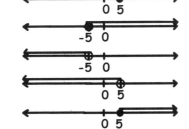

20. $-7x \geq -84$
(134)

A. $x \leq -12$

B. $x \geq 12$

C. $x \geq -12$

D. $x < 12$

E. $x \leq 12$

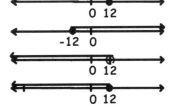

715

(d) 21.
(134)

$$\frac{x}{-3} > 41$$

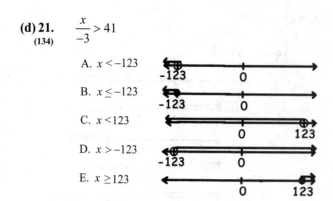

A. $x < -123$

B. $x \leq -123$

C. $x < 123$

D. $x > -123$

E. $x \geq 123$

Translate the word problem below into an equation; then solve.

(e) 22.
(80)
If a plane flew for 5 hours and traveled a total of 2,570 miles, how fast did the plane travel in miles per hour?

Lesson 135—Undoing Inequalities in Reverse Order

In the last lesson, we learned how to undo inequalities. The key concept was that you have to remember to flip the inequality symbol when multiplying or dividing by a negative number. In this lesson, we're going to solve some even tougher inequalities. Here's our first example.

$$-5x + 7 \geq 32$$

This is harder because there are two operations done to x: it's multiplied by 5 first and 7 is added to that total second. We can solve this in basically the same way we solve equations; we undo in reverse order. First, we undo the addition by subtracting 7 from both sides.

$$-5x + 7 - 7 \geq 32 - 7$$

Now we simplify on both sides.

$$-5x \geq 25$$

The next step is to undo the multiplication. But since we're going to have to divide both sides by a negative number (-5) we have to flip the inequality symbol.

$$\frac{-5x}{-5} \leq \frac{25}{-5} \qquad \textbf{Flip the inequality symbol.}$$

The last step is to simplify on both sides again.

$$x \leq -5$$

So the solutions to this inequality are all the numbers -5 and below. You can check that for yourself and see that those number work. The main point is to solve an inequality with more than one operation, just undo in reverse order. Just remember to flip the inequality symbol when multiplying or dividing both sides by a negative.

A Combining x's Example

Let's solve another more complicated inequality.

$$2x + 19 \leq 35 + 6x$$

We have x's on both sides in this inequality. We need to get the x's on the same side and then combine. Let's move $6x$ to the left by subtracting $6x$ from both sides.

$$2x + 19 - 6x \leq 35 + 6x - 6x$$

Now we simplify on the right side. The subtraction of $6x$ undoes the addition of $6x$ and that just leaves 35.

$$2x + 19 - 6x \leq 35$$

Now the x's are on the same side. And we can combine them.

But let's first change the subtraction of $6x$ to addition of the opposite.

$$2x+19+(-6x) \le 35$$

Now we can move everything around. We'll move the x's together.

$$2x+(-6x)+19 \le 35$$

Combining the x's gives us this.

$$-4x+19 \le 35$$

Now we're ready to undo in reverse order. First, we should undo the addition of 19 by subtracting.

$$-4x+19-19 \le 35-19$$

Simplifying on both sides gives us this.

$$-4x \le 16$$

Next, we can undo the multiplication by dividing both sides by -4. Only since we're dividing by a negative, the inequality symbol has to be flipped.

$$\frac{-4x}{-4} \ge \frac{16}{-4}$$

From here, we can just simplify on both sides.

$$x \ge -4$$

So the solutions are -4 and all the numbers above. The main point of the example was that inequalities with x's on both sides can be solved in the normal way.

Practice 135

a.
(130)
Seven red handkerchiefs and 5 white handkerchiefs are in a drawer. What is the probability of drawing out one red handkerchief without looking? Write your answer as a decimal rounded to two decimal places.

Solve each inequality below and select your answer from the choices given.

b.
(135)
$-6x+18 \ge 7+9x$

A. $x \ge \dfrac{11}{15}$

B. $x \le -\dfrac{25}{3}$

C. $x \le \dfrac{11}{15}$

D. $x \le -\dfrac{11}{15}$

E. $x \le -\dfrac{11}{3}$

c.
(135) $\dfrac{x-1}{3} > -7$

    A. $x > -20$ B. $x > -3$ C. $x > -9$

    D. $x > -22$ E. $x < -3$

d.
(135) $6x - 9 \le -41 + 10x$

    A. $x \ge -\dfrac{25}{2}$ B. $x \ge -8$ C. $x \le 8$

    D. $x \ge 8$ E. $x \ge \dfrac{25}{8}$

e.
(29) Translate the word problem below into an equation; then solve.

Mason is saving to buy a dune buggy, and his \$12,000 in savings is sitting in a bank account that pays 7% in yearly interest.

    i.) How much will Mason have earned in interest one year from now?

    ii.) If he leaves his money *and* interest in the bank for another year, how much interest will he earn in the 2nd year?

Problem Set 135

Tell whether each sentence below is True or False.

1.
(135) Inequalities can be solved by undoing in reverse order.

2.
(135) When subtracting both sides of an inequality by a number, the inequality symbol must be flipped.

Find the slope of the line in each linear equation below.

3.
(124) $y = 9x - \dfrac{1}{6}$ **4.**
(124) $y = -\dfrac{2}{3}x + 4$

Find the y-intercept (where the line crosses the y-axis) for each linear equation below.

5.
(125) $y = -3x - 8$ **6.**
(125) $y = x + \dfrac{1}{2}$

Use the stem and leaf plot to answer each question below.

Stem	Leaf
1	1 3 4 4
2	7 9
4	3 3 5 5 5 8 9
6	0 2 7
7	4 6 6 7 7
8	2 8
9	4

1|1 = 1.1

7. How many numbers in the data have a 7 in the ones place?
(128)

8. What ones digit appears the most frequently in the data?
(128)

The histogram below shows ranges for the number of minutes that a group of passengers had to wait to claim their luggage at the airport. Use the histogram to answer each of the following questions.

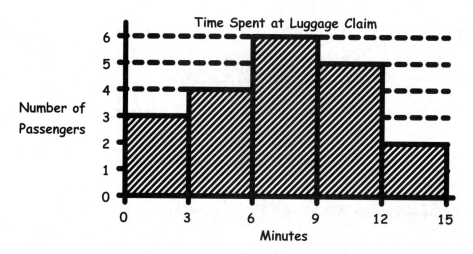

9. How many passengers had to wait from 6 to 9 minutes?
(129)

10. How many passengers had to wait from 0 to 9 minutes?
(129)

Calculate the probability of each event described below.

(a) 11. Eight striped ties and 6 polka dot ties are on a rack in a dark closet. What is the probability of drawing out one polka dot tie? Write your answer as a decimal rounded to two decimal places.
(130)

12. What is the probability of rolling a 4-sided die and getting a 1 or a 3? Write your answer as a fraction.
(130)

Select the number line that accurately describes each inequality below.

13. $x \geq -9$
(133)

14. $x \leq 24$
(133)

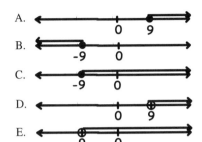

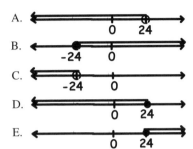

Select an inequality for each statement below.

15. A quantity x that can equal -5 or any number above -5.
(133)

    A. $x = -5$ B. $x \geq -5$ C. $x \leq -5$

    D. $x > -5$ E. $x < -5$

16. A quantity z that can equal any number below $\dfrac{7}{3}$.
(133)

    A. $z > \dfrac{7}{3}$ B. $z \geq \dfrac{7}{3}$ C. $z = \dfrac{7}{3}$

    D. $z \leq \dfrac{7}{3}$ E. $z < \dfrac{7}{3}$

Solve each inequality below and select your answer from the choices given.

17. $\dfrac{x}{3} - 2 < 9$
(135)

    A. $x < 33$ B. $x < 21$ C. $x < \dfrac{11}{3}$

    D. $x > 7$ E. $x < 14$

(b) 18. $-3x + 12 \geq 5 + 8x$
(135)

    A. $x > \dfrac{7}{11}$ B. $x \leq -\dfrac{7}{11}$ C. $x \leq -\dfrac{11}{5}$

    D. $x \leq -\dfrac{17}{5}$ E. $x \leq \dfrac{7}{11}$

(c) 19.
(135)

$$\frac{x-2}{4} > -3$$

A. $x > -3$ B. $x > -10$ C. $x > 3$

D. $x > -14$ E. $x < 3$

(d) 20.
(135)

$$4x - 7 \le -32 + 9x$$

A. $x \ge \dfrac{39}{13}$ B. $x \ge -\dfrac{25}{13}$ C. $x \ge -5$

D. $x \le 5$ E. $x \ge 5$

Translate the word problem below into an equation; then solve.

(e) 21.
(29)

Belinda is saving to buy a sailboat, and her $5,000 in savings is sitting in a bank account that pays 6% in yearly interest.

i.) How much will Belinda have earned in interest one year from now?

ii.) If she leaves her money and interest in the bank for another year, how much interest will she earn for the 2nd year?

CHAPTER 17:
ADDITIONAL TOPICS

Lesson 136—Equations and the Distributive Property

We've been working on inequalities, but in this lesson we're going to switch back to equations. We've solved a lot of equations by combining x's. One example is the equation $5x + 3x = 24$. To solve this, we would have to combine $5x$ and $3x$ first. Then, we could undo. Another example is $7x - 4 = 18 + 2x$. Here we would have to move x's to the same side of the equation first before combining.

Distributing

It turns out that with some equations, the x's can't be combined until one x is taken out of parentheses. Here's an example like that.

$$2(x+3)+4x = -6$$

We have two x's, but the first one is trapped inside parentheses. That's stopping us from combining. We can free the x from parentheses by using the **distributive property**, which is a basic rule of arithmetic. The way it works is we "distribute" the 2 to the x and the 3 by multiplying. We take $2 \cdot x$ and $2 \cdot 3$.

$$2(x+3)+4x = -6 \qquad \textbf{Distributing}$$

And we add $2 \cdot x$ and $2 \cdot 3$.

$$2 \cdot x + 2 \cdot 3 + 4x = -6$$

Simplifying gives us $2x + 6$ on the far left.

$$2x + 6 + 4x = -6$$

Now the x isn't trapped inside parentheses anymore. It's free. And we can combine x's. First, though, let's switch the positions of the 6 and $4x$. Since those are added together, we're allowed to do that.

$$2x + 4x + 6 = -6$$

Now we can combine the x's.

$$6x + 6 = -6$$

From here we can undo in reverse order. We can undo the addition by subtracting on both sides.

$$6x + 6 - 6 = -6 - 6$$

Simplifying on the left side gives us this.

$$6x = -6 - 6$$

On the right, let's change subtraction to addition of the opposite and then add.

$$6x = -6 + (-6)$$

$$6x = -12$$

724

The last undoing step is to divide both sides by 6.

$$\frac{6x}{6} = \frac{-12}{6}$$

Finally, we simplify on both sides.

$$x = -2$$

So the solution to the equation is -2. The main point is that we can get an x out of parentheses by using the distributive property. And, once again, to distribute, you multiply the number on the outside of the parentheses by each of the numbers inside. And then you add those totals. Here's the distributive property using letters.

$$a(b+c) \text{ is the same as } ab+ac.$$

Let's do another equation where we have to distribute.

$$7(x+2) - 5x = 4$$

We need to combine the two x's. But the first x is trapped inside parentheses. To get it out, we can just "distribute" the 7.

$$7(x+2) - 5x = 4 \qquad \textbf{Distributing}$$

$$7 \cdot x + 7 \cdot 2 - 5x = 4$$

$$7x + 14 - 5x = 4$$

Since we followed the distributive property, we know that $7(x+2)$ is the same as $7x+14$. They have the same value. But now we can combine the x's and solve the equation normally.

$$7x + 14 + (-5x) = 4$$

$$2x + 14 = 4 \qquad \textbf{Combining x's}$$

$$2x + 14 - 14 = 4 - 14 \qquad \textbf{Undoing}$$

$$2x = -10$$

$$\frac{2x}{2} = \frac{-10}{2} \qquad \textbf{Undoing}$$

$$x = -5$$

The main point of the example was just to show you another equation that requires distributing to free the trapped x.

How it Works

It's actually kind of interesting to see that distributing always works, even with just numbers. Let's do an experiment on expression that has only numbers (no x's).

$$4(5+2)$$

We've calculated the value of a lot of expressions like this. We're supposed to use the order of operations rules. Remember, the parentheses means do the addition first. So we're supposed to add first and multiply that total by 4 second. If we follow the correct order, here's what we get.

$$4(7)$$

$$28$$

The value of the expression is 28.

We didn't need to distribute the 4 because we knew both of the numbers inside parentheses. Neither one of the numbers was an x. That's why we didn't have to distribute to get rid of the parentheses. But there's nothing to stop us from distributing in $4(5+2)$. It's legal. Let's just distribute the 4.

$$4(5+2)$$

$$4 \cdot 5 + 4 \cdot 2$$

$$20 + 8$$

$$28$$

We end up with the same answer that we got before. The main point is distributing will always give you the right answer. But you don't usually have to distribute unless an x is trapped inside the parentheses, as with an equation like $7(x+2)-5x=4$.

Distributing with Subtraction

It's also possible to distribute when the numbers inside parentheses are subtracted. Look at this equation.

$$3(x-1)+2x=7$$

We need to combine the two x's, but the first one is trapped inside parentheses. Even though the x and 1 are subtracted, that doesn't change much. We still distribute the 3 by multiplying.

$$3(x-1)+2x=7$$

$$3x-3+2x=7$$

Notice that the $3x$ and the 3 are subtracted. The reason is that the x and the 1 were subtracted inside the parentheses. That's the rule. When distributing, when the numbers inside parentheses are added, we add after multiplying. But when the numbers inside parentheses are subtracted, we subtract after multiplying. And here's what it looks like using letters.

$$a(b-c) \text{ is the same as } ab-ac.$$

LESSON 136: EQUATIONS AND THE DISTRIBUTIVE PROPERTY

We won't bother to finish solving the equation. The purpose of the example was just to show you the distributing step.

Practice 136

a. After distributing, $6(x+3)$ is the same as which expression below?
(136)

    A. $6x+3$ B. $x+9$ C. $x+18$

    D. $6x+18$ E. $6x+9$

b. After distributing, $5(x-7)$ is the same as which expression below?
(136)

    A. $5x-7$ B. $5x-35$ C. $x-2$

    D. $5x-12$ E. $5x-2$

Solve each equation below.

c. $7(x+3)+2x=39$ **d.** $3(x-5)+4x=41$
(136)   (136)

e. Translate the word problem below into an equation; then solve.
(79)

Tristan thinks he can play 8 instruments at once. Right now, he is only playing 2. What percent of his goal has been achieved?

Problem Set 136

Tell whether each sentence below is True or False.

1. An x can be taken out of parentheses by using the distributive property.
(136)

2. After distributing, $3(x+2)$ can be changed to $3x+2$.
(136)

Calculate the range for each group of numbers below.

3. 35, 44, 17, 60, 21, 111, and 96   **4.** 4.8, 2.7, 3.9, 19.7, 20.1, 8.8, 15.9, and 12.6
(128)   (128)

A sporting goods store sells 17 different kinds of football jerseys. The table below shows how many of each kind of jersey was sold last month.

Number of Jerseys Sold

45	83	37	72	66	50	45	51	73
59	41	63	62	43	42	55	82	

5. Find the mean of the data above.   **6.** Find the median of the data above.
(127)   (127)

Calculate the probability of each event described below. Write your answers as decimals rounded to two decimal places.

7.
(130)
Sarah has 8 red M&M's and 7 yellow M&M's in her pocket. If Sarah reaches in that pocket for a tiny snack, what is the probability that she'll take out 1 red M&M?

8.
(130)
What is the probability of rolling a 6-sided die and getting a 3 or a 4?

Answer each question below.

(a) 9.
(136)
After distributing, $5(x+4)$ is the same as which expression below?

    A. $x+9$ B. $x+20$ C. $5x+9$
    D. $5x+1$ E. $5x+20$

10.
(136)
After distributing, $2(x+9)$ is the same as which expression below?

    A. $2x+7$ B. $x+11$ C. $2x+18$
    D. $x+18$ E. $2x+11$

(b) 11.
(136)
After distributing, $3(x-2)$ is the same as which expression below?

    A. $3x-6$ B. $x+1$ C. $3x-2$
    D. $3x+1$ E. $3x-5$

Solve each equation below.

(c) 12.
(136)
$3(x+2)+2x=21$

13.
(136)
$6(x+3)-4x=10$

(d) 14.
(136)
$2(x-4)+3x=17$

Find the slope of each line below. Make sure your answer is fully reduced.

15. Line AG
(124)

16. Line NK
(125)

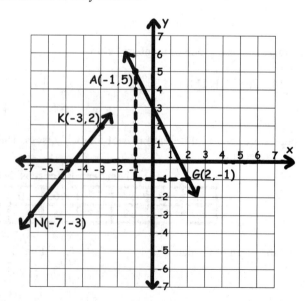

Select an inequality for each statement below.

17.
(133) A quantity x that can equal -9 or any number above -9.

     A. $x > -9$ B. $x < -9$ C. $x = -9$

     D. $x \leq -9$ E. $x \geq -9$

18.
(133) A quantity y that can equal any number below $\dfrac{3}{7}$.

     A. $y < \dfrac{3}{7}$ B. $y = \dfrac{3}{7}$ C. $y \leq \dfrac{3}{7}$

     D. $y \geq \dfrac{3}{7}$ E. $y > \dfrac{3}{7}$

Solve each inequality below and select your answer from the choices given.

19.
(134) $9x < 13$

     A. $x < \dfrac{9}{13}$ B. $x < 22$ C. $x < \dfrac{13}{9}$

     D. $x > 4$ E. $x < 4$

20.
(135) $-8x + 3 \leq 19$

     A. $x \leq 2$ B. $x \geq -2$ C. $x \geq 2$

     D. $x \leq -2$ E. $x \geq -\dfrac{11}{4}$

21.
(134) $\dfrac{x}{2} \geq -5$

     A. $x \leq -\dfrac{5}{2}$ B. $x \geq -3$ C. $x \leq -10$

     D. $x \geq -10$ E. $x \geq -\dfrac{5}{2}$

22.
(135) $\dfrac{x + 78}{7} > 5$

     A. $x > -66$ B. $x > -43$ C. $x > -3$

     D. $x > 3$ E. $x > 73$

Translate the word problem below into an equation; then solve.

(e) 23.
(79) Logan says he can eat 5 foot-long chili dogs in one sitting (without getting sick). So far he has eaten 2. What percent of his goal has been achieved?

Lesson 137—Absolute Value

In the real world we often have to measure things. We usually use a ruler, a yardstick, or a tape measure. These all have numbers on them, which makes measuring easy. Sometimes the best way to measure the length of an object is to subtract. For instance, what if we wanted to use a tape measure to find the length of the running shoe below? We might just hold the tape measure up so that the shoe is in the middle.

Since the shoe starts at 9 inches and goes to 22 inches, we could measure by subtracting.

$$22 - 9 = 13 \text{ inches}$$

The shoe must be 13 inches long.

Some people might be in a hurry and do the subtraction as $9 - 22$, since 9 is on the left side of the tape measure. That might cause them to do the problem like this.

$$9 - 22 = -13$$

The answer comes out to -13 inches, which doesn't make a lot of sense. But most people would realize that the negative was caused by the order of the numbers: $9 - 22$ instead of $22 - 9$. And they would just take the answer to be 13 inches. They would just ignore the negative sign, in other words.

Ignoring the Negative

When measuring a distance by subtracting, we're only interested in the difference between the two numbers—how far apart they are. We don't really care whether the answer comes out negative or positive. There's a special word in math for finding the difference between two numbers and then taking the positive of the answer. It's called **absolute value**. To write absolute value, we put little lines or bars on each side of the subtraction. Here's the absolute value of the quantity $9 - 22$.

$$|9 - 22|$$

The bars mean "calculate $9 - 22$ and take the positive of your answer." We can do it in two steps. First, we figure out $9 - 22$.

$$|-13|$$

Now, to get the absolute value, we just take the positive of the number between the bars. The positive of -13 is 13.

$$|9-22| = 13$$

So the absolute value of $9-22$ is 13. If we had used absolute value to measure the running shoe, we would have gotten the right answer no matter which number we listed first. That's because the absolute value of $9-22$ is the same as the absolute value of $22-9$.

$$|9-22| = |22-9|$$

Either way the answer is 13.

Let's do another absolute value calculation. Here's the absolute value of the quantity $2-11$.

$$|2-11|$$

The first step is to calculate $2-11$. That equals -9.

$$|-9|$$

Next, we take the positive of -9, which is just 9.

$$9$$

So $|2-11| = 9$.

Another example is the absolute value of the quantity $15-10$.

$$|15-10|$$

The first step is to calculate $15-10$. That equals 5.

$$|5|$$

The next step is to take the positive of 5, which is, of course, still 5.

$$5$$

That tells us that $|15-10| = 5$.

We can also have the absolute value of just a single number. Here's the absolute value of -6.

$$|-6|$$

To find the answer, we just take the positive of the number inside the absolute value bars. The positive of -6 is just 6.

$$|-6| = 6$$

All you have to do is take the positive of the number inside the absolute value bars. The positive of negative 6 is just 6. So basically the absolute value of a number is just the positive of that number.

Here's another example. This is the absolute value of 35. Since 35 is already positive, the answer is just 35.

$$|35|$$

$$35$$

Absolute Value and Inequalities

Sometimes absolute value will be in an inequality. Here's an example like that.

$$|-7| > 5$$

At first, you might think this is wrong, because a negative number can't be greater than a positive. But the *absolute value* of -7 is the same as positive 7.

$$7 > 5$$

And positive 7 *is* greater than 5. So this is inequality is correct.

Here's another example of an inequality with an absolute value.

$$17 > |-16|$$

To see if this is correct, first we simplify the absolute value: $|-16|$ is equal to 16.

$$17 > 16$$

Since 17 is greater than 16, the inequality is true.

Absolute Value and Arithmetic

An absolute value can also be inside an arithmetic problem. Here's an example.

$$|-9| + 5$$

The first step is to calculate the absolute value. The absolute value of -9 is 9.

$$9 + 5$$

Now we add the numbers.

$$14$$

Here's another one that's a little tougher.

$$|-12| - |-7|$$

We start out by figuring out both absolute values. The absolute value of -12 is 12. And the absolute value of -7 is 7.

$$12 - 7$$

Now we can just subtract to get an answer of 5.

$$12 - 7 = 5$$

Here's one last problem that's a little tricky.

$$8 + |0|$$

We said earlier that the absolute value of a number equals the positive of that number. But 0 is neither positive nor negative. Remember, it doesn't have a sign. It turns out that the absolute value of 0 is just 0. So this is just $8 + 0$ or 8.

$$8 + 0 = 8$$

Practice 137

a.
(137)
Calculate $|-14| + 6$.

b.
(137)
Select the correct symbol for the problem $17 \_\_\_\_ |-13|$.

    A. $<$ B. $>$ C. $=$

c.
(136)
Solve the equation $9(x + 2) + 4x = 22$. Make sure your answer is fully reduced.

d.
(135)
Solve the inequality $-6x - 7 \geq -52 + 9x$ and select your answer from the choices given.

    A. $x \geq -3$ B. $x \leq 3$ C. $x \leq 30$

    D. $x \leq 15$ E. $x \leq \dfrac{59}{15}$

e.
(82)
Translate the word problem below into an equation; then solve.

Grandpa Fix-It, a handyman service, charges \$60 for a service call (just to come to the house) plus \$55 per hour to do the job. Reggie's Repairs, another handyman service, charges \$90 for a service call plus \$40 per hour to do the job. How many hours would a job have to take for the bills of both services to be the same?

Problem Set 137

Tell whether each sentence below is True or False.

1.
(137)
Finding the difference between two numbers and taking the positive of the answer is called absolute value.

2.
(137)
The absolute value of a number will always be either positive or 0.

Calculate the probability of each event described below.

3.
(130) Nine ice cream sandwiches and 4 popsicles are buried in an ice chest. What is the probability of drawing out 1 popsicle? Write your answer as a decimal rounded to two decimal places.

4.
(132) How many total possible outcomes are there when flipping a quarter four times?

Answer each question below.

5.
(136) After distributing, $9(x+3)$ is the same as which expression below?

    A. $x+27$ B. $9x+6$ C. $9x+27$
    D. $x+12$ E. $9x+12$

6.
(136) After distributing, $6(x-4)$ is the same as which expression below?

    A. $6x+2$ B. $x+2$ C. $6x-10$
    D. $6x-4$ E. $6x-24$

Calculate the value of each expression below.

7.
(137) $|11-3|$ **8.**
(137) $|-2|$ **9.**
(137) $|6-7|$

(a) 10.
(137) $|-12|+8$

Select the correct symbol for each problem below.

(b) 11.
(137) $15 \underline{\hspace{1cm}} |-12|$

    A. $<$ B. $>$ C. $=$

12.
(137) $|-10| \underline{\hspace{1cm}} 7$

    A. $<$ B. $>$ C. $=$

13.
(137) $4 \underline{\hspace{1cm}} |-4|$

    A. $<$ B. $>$ C. $=$

Solve each equation below. Make sure your answer is fully reduced.

14.
(136) $4(x+2)-3x=7$ **15.**
(136) $5(x-6)+2x=-16$

(c) 16.
(136) $6(x+1)+3x=11$

734

Select the number line that accurately describes each inequality below.

17. $x \geq 11$
(133)

18. $x < -20$
(133)

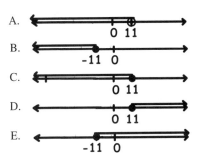

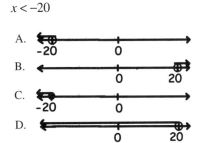

Solve each inequality below and select your answer from the choices given.

19. $7x \geq 21$
(134)

    A. $x \geq 3$ B. $x \geq 147$ C. $x \leq 3$

    D. $x \geq 28$ E. $x \geq 14$

20. $-6x + 4 < -38$
(135)

    A. $x < 4$ B. $x > 48$ C. $x > 7$

    D. $x > \dfrac{17}{3}$ E. $x > -36$

(d) 21. $-4x - 3 \geq -31 + 10x$
(135)

    A. $x \leq \dfrac{14}{3}$ B. $x \leq 14$ C. $x \geq -2$

    D. $x \leq 2$ E. $x \leq 42$

Translate the word problem below into an equation; then solve.

(e) 22. Paradise Plumbing charges $65 for a service call (just to come to the house) plus $40 per hour to do the
(82)   job. The Plunger Pros, another plumbing service, charges $100 for a service call plus $35 per hour to do
    the job. How many hours would a job have to take for the bills of both services to be the same?

Lesson 138—Distance Formula

In this lesson, we're going to learn how to find the distance between two points on a coordinate plane. Remember, we use a coordinate plane to graph functions. Every pair of x and y values of the function is turned into a point on the coordinate plane. That's how graphing works.

Distance between Two Points

Sometimes when working with a coordinate plane, you need to measure the distance between two points. The coordinate plane below shows the points $(4, 7)$ and $(4, 2)$. Since these points are lined up vertically, it's not hard to tell the distance between them. The points are 5 places apart.

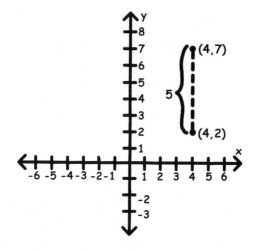

We really didn't even need the graph to find the distance between these points. We can tell that the points are lined up vertically because their x-coordinates are the same. They both have an x-coordinate of 4. Then, to find the distance between the points, we can just subtract the y-coordinates: $7 - 2 = 5$.

Same x-coordinates means
points line up vertically.

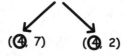

To find the distance between them,
subtract the y-coordinates.

7-2=5 places

Finding the distance between two points that are lined up horizontally is also pretty easy. For instance, the coordinate plane below shows the points $(-5, -3)$ and $(2, -3)$, which are lined up horizontally. We can also just count to see how far apart these points are. They're 7 places apart.

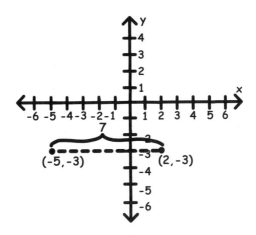

Again, we could have figured out the distance even without using a coordinate plane. Since the points have the same y-coordinates, we know that they're lined up horizontally. Then to find the distance between them we can subtract the x-coordinates: $-5-2=-7$. We end up with -7, which just means that the points are 7 places apart. Technically, when finding the distance between points by subtracting you should take the absolute value. You're just measuring the distance; you don't care about the sign. So the calculation would be $|-5-2|$, which equals 7. The answer comes out the same if the order of the coordinates is switched: $|2-(-5)|=7$.

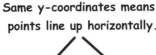

Same y-coordinates means
points line up horizontally.

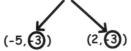

To find the distance between them,
subtract the x-coordinates.

$|-5-2|$ = 7 places

The previous example should really be done the same way. When subtracting the y-coordinates, we take the absolute value: $|7-2|=5$. You still get the right answer if the order of the coordinates is switched: $|2-7|=5$. But the main point of both examples is that it's easy to find the distance between two points when they're lined up vertically or horizontally.

Points that Aren't Lined Up

What about when two points on a coordinate plane aren't lined up? On the coordinate plane below, we have two points, $(1,2)$ and $(5,5)$. These are also named with the letters A and B. The points aren't lined up vertically or horizontally. That means it's harder to calculate the distance between them. We can't just count the places. There aren't any marks between the two points to count. The line segment between them is slanted. Here's how we can figure out the distance. We can create a right triangle with the distance between our points as the hypotenuse.

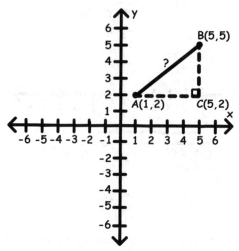

**We can find the distance between
(1,2) and (5,5) using the Pythagorean theorem.**

Point C has to be at $(5,2)$ because it's directly below point B and directly across from point A. Otherwise, we wouldn't have a right triangle. Now to find the distance between A and B, we just need to find the length of the hypotenuse of the right triangle. The lengths of the legs of the triangle are easy to find because they're lined up vertically and horizontally. The distance between points B and C is 3 places. You can either count them or subtract the y-coordinates (since the points are lined up vertically). And the distance between A and C is 4 places. Again you can count or subtract the x-coordinates because these points are lined up horizontally.

So now we know the lengths of both legs of the right triangle. That means we can find the hypotenuse, which is the distance we want, by using the Pythagorean Theorem. Remember, the Pythagorean Theorem says that for any right triangle the square of the hypotenuse has to equal the square of each of the legs added together. Here's the equation.

$$\text{hypotenuse}^2 = \text{leg}^2 + \text{leg}^2$$

We know the lengths of the legs: 4 and 3. So let's put those in.

$$\text{hypotenuse}^2 = 4^2 + 3^2$$

Now we have an equation with just one unknown—the hypotenuse. We can put an x in for the word hypotenuse.

$$x^2 = 4^2 + 3^2$$

From here, we just solve the equation for x. First, we'll simplify the right side.

$$x^2 = 16 + 9$$

$$x^2 = 25$$

Now we undo the square by taking the square root of both sides.

$$\sqrt{x^2} = \sqrt{25}$$

The square root undoes the square and that leaves just x on the left.

$$x = \sqrt{25}$$

The last step is to figure out the square root of 25. Remember, that's just the number that when you square it—when you multiply it by itself—equals 25. That's 5.[1]

$$x = 5$$

The length of the hypotenuse is 5, which means that the distance between our two points is 5 places.

The distance between $(1,2)$ and $(5,5)$ is 5 places.

That's how you can find the distance between two points, even when the points aren't lined up horizontally or vertically. You use the Pythagorean Theorem.

Solving for the Hypotenuse

There's a special way of writing the Pythagorean Theorem that makes it easier to use when finding the distance between points on a coordinate plane. Here's the equation for the Pythagorean Theorem again.

$$\text{hypotenuse}^2 = \text{leg}^2 + \text{leg}^2$$

We start by putting the letter d in for the hypotenuse. When we're using the theorem to find the distance between points, the hypotenuse is that distance. So d stands for distance.

$$d^2 = \text{leg}^2 + \text{leg}^2$$

Now the length of the legs can be calculated by subtracting the coordinates of the points. We could have found the length of the horizontal leg by subtracting the x-coordinates of the two points we're finding the distance between, $A(1,2)$ and $B(5,5)$. That gives us $5-1$ which equals 4 places. We could have found the length of the vertical leg by subtracting the y-coordinates of the points $A(1,2)$ and $B(5,5)$. That gives us $5-2$ or 3 places. If you look back at the diagram you can see why that works. These are the same as the lengths of the two legs of the right triangle. But since we can do the leg calculations this way, in the equation we can write the length of the legs using their coordinates. The first leg is the horizontal leg. It equals the x-coordinates subtracted. The second leg is the vertical leg. It equals the y-coordinates subtracted.

$$d^2 = (x_2 - x_1)^2 + (y_2 - y_1)^2$$

The little numbers below the x's aren't exponents. They just help us tell the difference between the two x coordinates. The x_2 stands for the x-coordinate of the second point, B. That's 5. And x_1 stands for the x-coordinate of the first point, A, which is 1. That means $x_2 - x_1$ equals $5-1$, the length of the horizontal leg. It works the same way for the vertical leg. Specifically, y_2 stands for the y-coordinate of the second point, B and y_1 stands for the y-coordinate of the first point, A. So $y_2 - y_1$ equals $5-2$ or 3. And that's the length of the vertical leg. The equation looks complicated, but it's really not. It's just a special way of writing the Pythagorean Theorem to make it easier to use when finding the distance between two points.

---

[1] Numbers actually have two square roots. The square root of 25 can be both 5 and -5 because $(5)(5)$ equals 25 but so does $(-5)(-5)$. We'll learn more about negative square roots in Algebra 1.

The last step is to solve the equation for d. We're going to use the equation to find distance, so we should get d by itself on one side. To solve, we take the square root of both sides. The radical sign needs to go over everything on the right.

$$\sqrt{d^2} = \sqrt{(x_2 - x_1)^2 + (y_2 - y_1)^2}$$

The square root undoes the square on the left and leaves just d.

$$d = \sqrt{(x_2 - x_1)^2 + (y_2 - y_1)^2} \qquad \textbf{distance formula}$$

This is called the **distance formula**. Obviously, that's because we can use it to find the distance between any two points on a coordinate plane. But it's really just the Pythagorean Theorem.

Once you've had a little practice, using the distance formula is easy. Let's go through our last example again. But this time, we'll use the distance formula. We were trying to find the distance between the points $A(1,2)$ and $B(5,5)$. Instead of wasting time plotting the points, drawing a triangle, and measuring the length of the legs, we can just put the coordinates into the distance formula.

$$d = \sqrt{(x_2 - x_1)^2 + (y_2 - y_1)^2}$$

We'll let $A(1,2)$ be the first point, which means $x_1 = 1$ and $y_1 = 2$. And we'll let $B(5,5)$ be the second point, so $x_2 = 5$ and $y_2 = 5$.[2] Now we just put the numbers in.

$$d = \sqrt{(5-1)^2 + (5-2)^2}$$

Now we just calculate the value of the right side. We'll simplify inside the parentheses first.

$$d = \sqrt{4^2 + 3^2}$$

Next, we calculate the squares and add.

$$d = \sqrt{16 + 9}$$

$$d = \sqrt{25}$$

After taking the square root of 25 we get the same answer as before.

$$d = 5$$

The distance between $A(1,2)$ and $B(5,5)$ is 5 places. We already knew that. But doing the problem with the distance formula was a lot simpler and faster.

---

[2] It doesn't matter which point is first or second. The formula works either way.

Practice 138

a.
(136)
Solve the equation $8(x-3)+4x=-19$. Make sure your answer is fully reduced.

b.
(135)
Solve the inequality $-4x+7\le-71+9x$ and select your answer from the choices given.

A. $x\ge-\dfrac{64}{5}$

B. $x\ge-65$

C. $x\ge6$

D. $x\ge4$

E. $x\le-65$

Use the coordinate plane below to answer each of the following questions.

c.
(138)
Find the length of line segment *NM*.

d.
(138)
Use the distance formula to find the length of line segment *PM*.

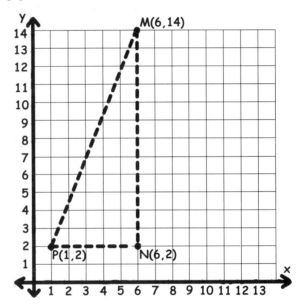

e.
(79)
Translate the word problem below into an equation; then solve.

Whistle #1 blows 6 times each minute. Whistle #2 blows 10 times each minute. Together, how many minutes will it take them to blow 192 times?

Problem Set 138

Tell whether each sentence below is True or False.

1.
(138)
The distance formula is a special way of writing the Pythagorean Theorem.

2.
(138)
The distance formula is easy to use when finding the distance between points on a coordinate plane.

Find the *y*-intercept (where the line crosses the *y*-axis) for each linear equation below.

3.
(125)
$y=4x-12$

4.
(125)
$y=-\dfrac{3}{4}x+1$

The histogram below shows ranges for the number of minutes a group of people exercise each morning. Use the histogram to answer each question below.

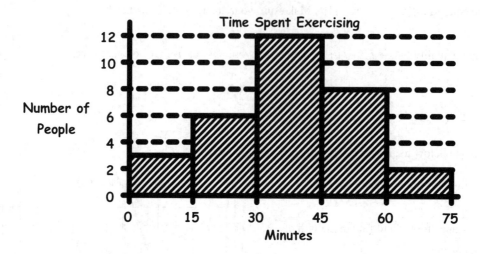

5.
(129) How many people spend from 15 and 45 minutes exercising?

6.
(129) How many people spend from 30 and 75 minutes exercising?

Answer each question below.

7.
(136) After distributing, $8(x+6)$ is the same as which expression below?

      A. $8x+14$ B. $8x+2$ C. $x+48$

      D. $8x+48$ E. $x+14$

8.
(136) After distributing, $5(x-9)$ is the same as which expression below?

      A. $5x-45$ B. $5x-9$ C. $5x+4$

      D. $5x-14$ E. $x-4$

Calculate the value of each expression below.

9.
(137) $|-6|$

10.
(137) $|1-8|$

11.
(137) $|-12|-5$

Select the correct symbol for each problem below.

12.
(137) 14 _____ $|-18|$

      A. <   B. >   C. =

13.
(137) $|-16|$ _____ 9

      A. <   B. >   C. =

Solve each equation below. Make sure your answer is fully reduced.

14.
(136) $6(x+1)+5x=39$

15.
(136) $8(x+3)-2x=0$

(a) 16.
(136) $5(x-2)+10x=-6$

Solve each inequality below and select your answer from the choices given.

17.
(134) $-9x<36$

    A. $x>4$
    B. $x<27$
    C. $x<-4$
    D. $x<-45$
    E. $x>-4$

18.
(135) $\dfrac{x}{4}+1\geq-3$

    A. $x\geq-16$
    B. $x\leq-\dfrac{1}{2}$
    C. $x\geq-8$
    D. $x\geq-1$
    E. $x\leq-8$

(b) 19.
(135) $-6x+8\geq-58+5x$

    A. $x\leq-55$
    B. $x\leq6$
    C. $x\geq4$
    D. $x\geq-50$
    E. $x\geq6$

Use the coordinate plane below to answer each of the following questions.

(c) 20.
(138) Find the length of line segment *BA*.

21.
(138) Find the length of line segment *CB*.

(d) 22.
(138) Use the distance formula to find the length of line segment *CA*.

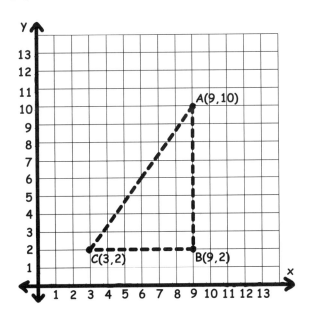

Translate the word problem below into an equation; then solve.

(e) 23.
(79) Faucet #1 is dripping 4 times each minute. Faucet #2 is dripping 5 times each minute. Together, how many minutes will it take them to drip 162 times?

Lesson 139—More on Formulas

In the last lesson, we learned about the distance formula. Remember, the distance formula is just the Pythagorean Theorem after it's been solved for the hypotenuse (represented by the letter d). We sometimes write the Pythagorean Theorem that way to make it easier to find the distance between two points on a coordinate plane.

Distance Formula and Calculator

When using the distance formula, the answer will often come out messy. Let's look at an example. The coordinate plane below shows two points: $A(-5,-2)$ and $B(1,7)$. Since the points aren't lined up vertically or horizontally, we can't find the distance by just counting the places between them. But we can use the distance formula.

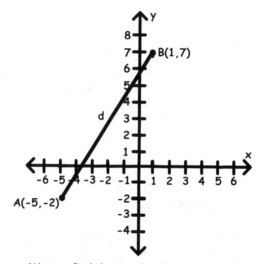

We can find d using the distance formula.

And the nice thing about the distance formula is that we don't need to draw a right triangle in order to calculate the distance between the points. Remember, we could create a right triangle where the distance between A and B is the hypotenuse. But with the distance formula, we don't have to go through that process. Here's the formula again.

$$d = \sqrt{(x_2 - x_1)^2 + (y_2 - y_1)^2}$$

The d stands for distance. The quantity $x_2 - x_1$ is the difference between the x-coordinates of the two points. The quantity $y_2 - y_1$ is the distance between the y-coordinates of the points. We'll make B the first point and A the second point. It doesn't matter which point is first or second. You just have to be consistent for both the x's and the y's. Since we're making B the first point, we should put the x-coordinate of point B in for x_1 and the y-coordinate for B goes in for y_1.

$$d = \sqrt{(x_2 - 1)^2 + (y_2 - 7)^2}$$

Since A is the second point, we put the x-coordinate for A in for x_2 and the y-coordinate for A in for y_2.

$$d = \sqrt{(-5 - 1)^2 + (-2 - 7)^2}$$

Now we can just calculate the right side. We'll do the arithmetic inside parentheses first.

$$d = \sqrt{(-5 + -1)^2 + (-2 + -7)^2}$$

$$d = \sqrt{(-6)^2 + (-9)^2}$$

It may seem strange that these numbers are negatives. Remember, the squared quantities are supposed to represent the legs of a right triangle (whose hypotenuse is d). Here's what happened. We listed the negative coordinates first, because point A was the second point. That caused −5 and −2 to be listed first, which made the quantities inside parentheses come out negative. The lengths of the legs of the right triangle are really equal to the absolute value of −6 and −9 (which are 6 and 9). We could change the negatives to positive, but we really don't have to because when we calculate the squares in the next step, the negatives will go away on their own.

$$d = \sqrt{36 + 81}$$

That always happens when you square a negative number. So you don't have to worry if the legs of the right triangle come out to be negatives, when using the distance formula. You can choose either point to be first. You'll get the right answer with the distance formula either way. The next simplifying step is to add underneath the square root.

$$d = \sqrt{117}$$

We end up with $\sqrt{117}$. It turns out there's no whole number that when multiplied it by itself equals exactly 117. The answer is somewhere between 10 and 11. So this is a messy answer. In a situation like this, we need to use a calculator to estimate $\sqrt{117}$. We just punch in 117 and the square root symbol. When we do that and round the answer to one decimal place, it comes out to 10.8.

d is equal to about 10.8.

That's the distance between our two points. Or we could say that 10.8 is the length of line segment AB. You can think of it either way. Just remember that when using the distance formula, if you get a square root that doesn't come out to equal a whole number, estimate it with a calculator.

Midpoint Formula

There's one last concept we need to cover before finishing this lesson. Sometimes we need to find the point that's exactly in the middle between two points on a coordinate plane. Let's look at a simple example. On the coordinate plane below, we have points $A(-3, 4)$ and $B(6, 2)$. What if we wanted to know the coordinates of the point that's exactly in the middle between A and B?

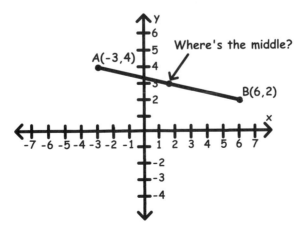

You might think we would have to use the distance formula then cut our answer in half or something like that. But there's actually an easier way to do it. All we have to do is add the coordinates of the two points and divide by 2. We add the x's together and divide by 2, and then add the y's together and divide by 2. The x-coordinate of point A is -3 and the x-coordinate of point B is 6. So we take the quantity $-3+6$ divided by 2. Since we're dividing the whole quantity, the fraction bar has to go underneath the entire addition.

$$\frac{-3+6}{2} = \frac{3}{2}$$

After simplifying we end up with $\frac{3}{2}$. This is the x-coordinate of the midpoint.

$$x\text{-coordinate of midpoint} = \frac{3}{2}$$

To find the y-coordinate of the midpoint we do the same thing. We add the y-coordinates of points A and B, which are 4 and 2, then we divide by 2.

$$\frac{4+2}{2} = \frac{6}{2} = 3$$

After simplifying, we end up with 3. That means the y-coordinate of the midpoint is 3.

$$y\text{-coordinate of midpoint} = 3.$$

So the midpoint is $x = \frac{3}{2}$ and $y = 3$.

$$\text{The midpoint between } A \text{ and } B \text{ is } (\frac{3}{2}, 3)$$

This point is exactly in the middle of $(-3,4)$ and $(6,2)$. Or we could call this the midpoint of line segment AB. That means the same thing. Basically, the method for finding a midpoint involves taking the mean (average) of the coordinates of the two points. Adding two numbers and dividing the sum by 2 is the same as finding the mean.

Here's the midpoint calculation using letters. If we have two points on the coordinate plane (x_1, y_1) and (x_2, y_2), we can add the x's and divide by 2 and add the y's and divide by 2 to get the coordinates of the midpoint.

$$\text{The midpoint between } (x_1, y_1) \text{ and } (x_2, y_2) \text{ is } (\frac{x_1+x_2}{2}, \frac{y_1+y_2}{2}).$$

Practice 139

a.
(135) Solve the inequality $4x - 15 \geq -8 + x$ and select your answer from the choices given.

A. $x \geq \frac{7}{3}$ B. $x \geq \frac{7}{4}$ C. $x \geq \frac{3}{7}$

D. $x \leq -\frac{23}{3}$ E. $x \geq 2$

b.
(138) Use the distance formula to find the length of line segment *HJ* below. If your answer turns out to be a square root that does not equal a whole number, estimate it to one decimal place.

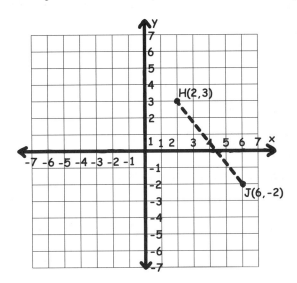

Use the coordinate plane below to answer each of the following questions.

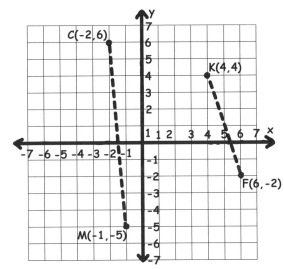

c.
(139) Use the midpoint formula to select the midpoint of line segment *FK*.

    A. (1, 3)   B. (5, 1)   C. (3, 1)

    D. (1, 5)   E. (1, −3)

d.
(139) Use the midpoint formula to select the midpoint of line segment *MC*.

    A. $\left(-\dfrac{3}{2}, \dfrac{1}{2}\right)$ B. $\left(\dfrac{3}{2}, \dfrac{1}{2}\right)$ C. (−3, 1)

    D. $\left(-\dfrac{1}{2}, \dfrac{1}{2}\right)$ E. $\left(-\dfrac{3}{2}, -\dfrac{11}{2}\right)$

e.
(54)
Translate the word problem below into an equation; then solve.

Kyle paid 7% in sales tax on his new fancy fishing rod. If Kyle paid $18.55 in sales tax on the fishing rod, what was the pre-tax price?

Problem Set 139

Tell whether each sentence below is True or False.

1.
(139)
When using the distance formula to find the distance between two points, your answer will always turn out to be a whole number.

2.
(139)
To find the midpoint between two points, take the average of the x-coordinates and the average of the y-coordinates.

Use a calculator to find each experimental probability below. Write your answers as decimals.

3.
(130)
In a batch of 100 key chains, 17 are nervous. What is the probability that the next key chain will be nervous?

4.
(130)
A safety engineer performed an experiment 1,000 times and the collapse occurred only 49 times. What is the probability that the collapse will occur the next time?

Calculate the value of each expression below.

5.
(137)
$|-5|$

6.
(137)
$|9-18|$

7.
(137)
$5-|-3|$

Select the correct symbol for each problem below.

8.
(137)
$|-64|$ _____ 61

    A. $<$ B. $>$ C. $=$

9.
(137)
11 _____ $|-11|$

    A. $<$ B. $>$ C. $=$

Solve each equation below.

10.
(136)
$4(x+5)-3x=12$

11.
(136)
$7(x-3)+2x=24$

Select an inequality for each statement below.

12.
(133)
A quantity t that can equal any number below -7.

    A. $t \le -7$ B. $t < -7$ C. $t > -7$

    D. $t = -7$ E. $t \ge -7$

13. A quantity y that can equal $\frac{5}{6}$ or any number above $\frac{5}{6}$.
(133)

    A. $\;y > \frac{5}{6}$ B. $\;y < \frac{5}{6}$ C. $\;y \le \frac{5}{6}$

    D. $\;y = \frac{5}{6}$ E. $\;y \ge \frac{5}{6}$

Solve each inequality below and select your answer from the choices given.

14. $x - 6 \ge -3$
(134)

    A. $\;x \ge 9$ B. $\;x \le -3$ C. $\;x \ge -9$

    D. $\;x \ge -3$ E. $\;x \ge 3$

15. $-2x + 7 < -1$
(135)

    A. $\;x < -6$ B. $\;x > 3$ C. $\;x > 4$

    D. $\;x < -3$ E. $\;x > -4$

(a) 16. $6x - 17 \ge -9 + x$
(135)

    A. $\;x \ge \frac{5}{8}$ B. $\;x \ge 2$ C. $\;x \ge \frac{6}{5}$

    D. $\;x \ge \frac{8}{5}$ E. $\;x \le -\frac{26}{5}$

Use the coordinate plane below to answer each of the following questions. If your answer turns out to be a square root that does not equal a whole number, estimate it to one decimal place.

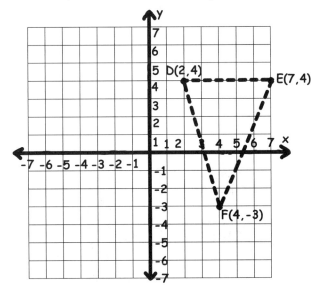

17. Find the length of line segment DE.
(138)

18. Use the distance formula to find the length of line segment FE.
(138)

(b) 19. Use the distance formula to find the length of line segment DF.
(138)

Use the coordinate plane below to answer each of the following questions.

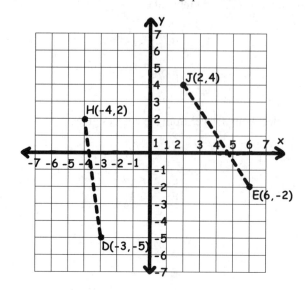

(c) 20. Use the midpoint formula to select the midpoint of line segment *EJ*.
(139)

    A. $(1,4)$ B. $(3,2)$ C. $(4,3)$

    D. $(4,1)$ E. $(2,-3)$

(d) 21. Use the midpoint formula to select the midpoint of line segment *DH*.
(139)

    A. $(-7,-3)$ B. $\left(-\dfrac{7}{2},-\dfrac{7}{2}\right)$ C. $\left(-\dfrac{7}{2},\dfrac{3}{2}\right)$

    D. $\left(-\dfrac{1}{2},-\dfrac{3}{2}\right)$ E. $\left(-\dfrac{7}{2},-\dfrac{3}{2}\right)$

Translate the word problem below into an equation; then solve.

(e) 22. Loni paid 9% in sales tax on her seashell necklace. If Loni paid $34.56 in sales tax on the necklace,
(54) what was its pre-tax price?

APPENDICES

Appendix A—Basic Math

Divisibility Rules

Rule for 2: Even numbers can all be divided evenly by 2.

Rule for 3: For a number to be divisible by 3, the sum of the number's digits must divide evenly by 3.

Rule for 4: To be divisible by 4, the last two digits of the number must divide evenly by 4.

Rule for 5: Numbers ending in 0 or 5 can all be divided evenly by 5.

Rule for 6: For a number to be divisible by 6, the number must be even and the sum of the number's digits must equal a number that's divisible by 3.

Rule for 8: For a number to be divisible by 8, the last three digits must divide evenly by 8.

Rule for 9: For a number to be divisible by 9, the sum of the number's digits must divide evenly by 9.

Rule for 10: Numbers ending in 0 can all be divided evenly by 10.

Commutative Properties

Addition: You can add two numbers in any order: $a + b = b + a$.

Multiplication: You can multiply two numbers in any order: $a \times b = b \times a$.

Associative Properties

Addition: You can add more than two numbers in any order: $(a + b) + c = a + (b + c)$

Multiplication: You can multiply more than two numbers in any order: $(a \times b) \times c = a \times (b \times c)$

Fractions

Adding and subtracting fractions:

Make the denominators the same and then add (or subtract) the numerators. Make sure your answer is fully reduced.

$$\frac{1}{3} + \frac{2}{5} \quad \Rightarrow \quad \frac{1 \times 5}{1 \times 3} + \frac{2 \times 3}{5 \times 3} \quad \Rightarrow \quad \frac{5}{15} + \frac{6}{15} \quad \Rightarrow \quad \frac{11}{15}$$

Multiplying fractions:

Reduce first by factoring and canceling. Then multiply the tops and bottoms.

$$\frac{3}{4} \times \frac{2}{21} \quad \Rightarrow \quad \frac{\cancel{3}}{2 \times \cancel{2}} \times \frac{\cancel{2}}{\cancel{3} \times 7} \quad \Rightarrow \quad \frac{1}{2} \times \frac{1}{7} \quad \Rightarrow \quad \frac{1}{14}$$

Dividing fractions:

Invert (flip over) the second fraction and multiply normally.

$$\frac{5}{6} \div \frac{7}{8} \quad \Rightarrow \quad \frac{5}{6} \times \frac{8}{7} \quad \Rightarrow \quad \frac{5}{\cancel{2} \times 3} \times \frac{\cancel{2} \times 2 \times 2}{7} \quad \Rightarrow \quad \frac{5}{3} \times \frac{2 \times 2}{7} \quad \Rightarrow \quad \frac{20}{21}$$

Multiplying fraction and whole number:

Turn the whole number into a fraction by putting it over 1. Then multiply normally.

$$\frac{3}{5} \times 10 \quad \Rightarrow \quad \frac{3}{5} \times \frac{10}{1} \quad \Rightarrow \quad \frac{3}{\cancel{5}} \times \frac{2 \times \cancel{5}}{1} \quad \Rightarrow \quad \frac{3}{1} \times \frac{2}{1} \quad \Rightarrow \quad 6$$

Dividing fraction and whole number:

Turn the whole number into a fraction by putting it over 1. Then divide normally.

$$\frac{2}{7} \div 6 \;\rightarrow\; \frac{2}{7} \div \frac{6}{1} \;\rightarrow\; \frac{2}{7} \times \frac{1}{6} \;\rightarrow\; \frac{2}{7} \times \frac{1}{2 \times 3} \;\rightarrow\; \frac{1}{7} \times \frac{1}{3} \;\rightarrow\; \frac{1}{21}$$

Decimals

Adding and subtracting decimals:

Line up the decimal points and add or subtract the columns normally.

$$
\begin{array}{r}
^{11}\\
25.81\\
+\,14.73\\
\hline
\mathbf{40.54}
\end{array}
$$

Multiplying decimals:

Line up the numbers on the right. Ignore the decimal points and do normal long multiplication. Then add up the total number of digits that are to the right of both decimal points. Place the decimal point in the answer so that the same number of digits are to the right of the decimal point.

$$
\begin{array}{r}
5.34\\
\times\,2.2\\
\hline
1068\\
10680\\
\hline
11.748
\end{array}
$$

Dividing decimals:

Move the decimal point in the number on the outside (the divisor) until it becomes a whole number. Move the decimal point in the number inside the box (the dividend) the same number of places. Put the decimal point in the answer directly above. Then do normal long division.

$$
2.5\overline{)15.75} \quad\rightarrow\quad
\begin{array}{r}
63\\
25\overline{)157.5}\\
150\downarrow\\
\hline
75\\
75\\
\hline
0
\end{array}
$$

Converting Fraction to Decimal: Divide the denominator into the numerator using long division. Keep dividing until the remainder is 0 or you get a repeating digit.

$$
\frac{1}{8} \quad\rightarrow\quad
\begin{array}{r}
.125\\
8\overline{)1.000}\\
-8\downarrow\\
\hline
20\\
-16\downarrow\\
\hline
40\\
-40\\
\hline
0
\end{array}
$$

Converting Decimal to Fraction: Rewrite the decimal as a fraction with a denominator of 10, 100, 1,000, etc.

$$\frac{17}{50} \;\rightarrow\; \frac{17 \times 2}{50 \times 2} \;\rightarrow\; \frac{42}{100} \;\rightarrow\; 0.42$$

Percents

Converting Percent to Decimal:
Drop the percent symbol and move the decimal point two places to the left.

$$19\% \;\longrightarrow\; 19.0\% \;\longrightarrow\; 0.19$$

Converting Decimal to Percent:
Move the decimal point two places to the right and put in a percent symbol.

$$0.19 \;\longrightarrow\; 19.0\% \;\longrightarrow\; 19\%$$

Percent of a number:
Convert the percent to a decimal then multiply.

$$24\% \text{ of } 150 \;\longrightarrow\; 0.24 \times 150 \;\longrightarrow\; 36$$

Common (English) Units of Measurement

Common units for length:
    mile
    yard
    foot
    inch

Common length conversion factors:

1 mile	=	1,760 yards
1 yard	=	3 feet
1 foot	=	12 inches

Common units for area:
    square miles
    square yards
    square feet
    square inches

Common area conversion factors:[1]

1 square mile	=	3,097,600 square yards
1 square yard	=	9 square feet
1 square foot	=	144 square inches

[1]To get the conversion factors for area, take each conversion factor for length and multiply it by itself (square it). For instance, to get the conversion factor for square feet to square inches you multiply by 12×12 or 144.

Common units for volume:
    cubic miles
    cubic yards
    cubic feet
    cubic inches

Common volume conversion factors:[2]

1 cubic mile	=	5,451,776,000 cubic yards
1 cubic yard	=	27 cubic feet
1 cubic foot	=	1,728 cubic inches

[2]To get the conversion factors for volume, just take each conversion factor for length and multiply it three times (cube it). For instance, to get the conversion factor for cubic feet to cubic inches you multiply by $12 \times 12 \times 12$ or 1,728.

Common units for liquid measure:
    gallon
    quart
    pint
    fluid ounce

Common liquid measure conversion factors:
    1 gallon = 4 quarts
    1 quart = 2 pints
    1 pint = 16 fluid ounces

Metric Units of Measurement

Metric units for length (from small to large):

kilometer
hectometer
dekameter
meter
decimeter
centimeter
millimeter

Metric length conversion factors:

1 kilometer = 10 hectometers
1 hectometer = 10 dekameters
1 dekameter = 10 meters
1 meter = 10 decimeters
1 decimeter =10 centimeters
1 centimeter = 10 millimeters

Metric units for area (from small to large):

square kilometers
square hectometers
square dekameters
square meters
square decimeters
square centimeters
square millimeters

Metric area conversion factors:[3]

1 square kilometer	=	100 square hectometers
1 square hectometer	=	100 square dekameters
1 square dekameter	=	100 square meters
1 square meter	=	100 square decimeters
1 square decimeter	=	100 square centimeters
1 square centimeter	=	100 square millimeters

[3]To get the conversion factors for area, just take each conversion factor for length and multiply it by itself. Since all conversion factors for length are 10, all of the area conversion factors are 10×10 or 100.

Metric units for volume:

kiloliter
hectoliter
dekaliter
liter
deciliter
centiliter
milliliter

Metric volume conversion factors:[4]

1 kiloliter = 10 hectoliters
1 hectoliter = 10 dekaliters
1 dekaliter = 10 liters
1 liter = 10 deciliters
1 deciliter =10 centiliters
1 centiliter = 10 milliliters

[4]For volume, the metric system doesn't use units such as cubic meters. It uses a new group of units based on the liter.

Converting between common and metric units for length:

1 inch	=	2.54 centimeters
1 meter	=	1.0936 yards
1 mile	=	1.069 kilometers

Appendix B: Geometry

Simple Parts of Figures

<u>Point</u>:

A •

A point is a position
or location in space.

<u>Line</u>:

$\overleftrightarrow{AB}$

A line is a group of
points that go in
opposite directions forever.

<u>Line segment</u>:

end points

$\overline{DE}$

A line segment is part of
a line, and has end points
on both sides.

<u>Ray</u>:

$\overrightarrow{GF}$

A ray has an end point
on one side but goes
forever in the other direction.

<u>Plane</u>:

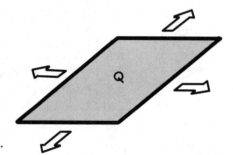

A plane is a flat surface with
no thickness that extends
forever in all directions.

Angles

<u>Angle Sizes</u>:

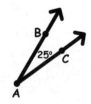

An acute angle is
less than 90°.

A right angle is
exactly 90°.

An obtuse angle is
greater than 90°.

A straight angle is
exactly 180°.

Angle Pairs:

Adjacent angles are right next to each other but don't overlap. They must have the same vertex and share one side called the common side.

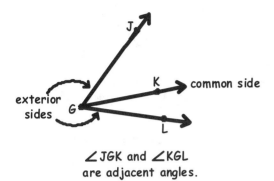

∠JGK and ∠KGL
are adjacent angles.

Vertical angles are created by two intersecting lines, and they are on opposite sides of the intersection point. Vertical angles are always equal.

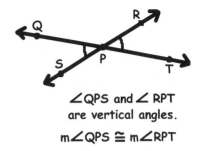

∠QPS and ∠RPT
are vertical angles.

m∠QPS ≅ m∠RPT

Supplementary angles add to 180°.

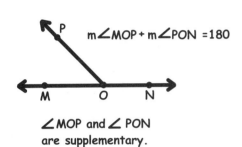

m∠MOP + m∠PON =180

∠MOP and ∠PON
are supplementary.

Complementary angles add to 90°.

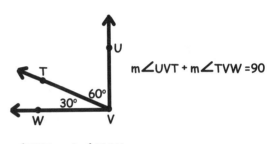

m∠UVT + m∠TVW =90

∠UVT and ∠TVW
are complementary.

Angles and Parallel Lines:

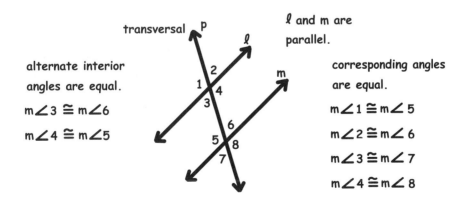

transversal

alternate interior
angles are equal.

m∠3 ≅ m∠6

m∠4 ≅ m∠5

ℓ and m are
parallel.

corresponding angles
are equal.

m∠1 ≅ m∠5

m∠2 ≅ m∠6

m∠3 ≅ m∠7

m∠4 ≅ m∠8

Triangles

by side length:

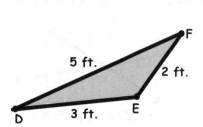
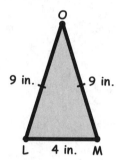
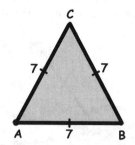

| Scalene triangle: | Isosceles triangle: | Equilateral triangle: |
| no sides equal. | 2 sides are equal | all 3 sides are equal. |

by angle measure:

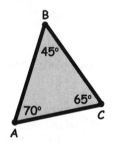
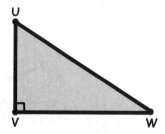
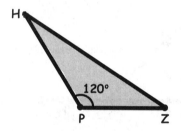

| Acute triangle: | Right triangle: | Obtuse triangle: |
| all 3 angles are acute. | 1 right angle. | 1 obtuse angle. |

Adding the angles of a triangle:

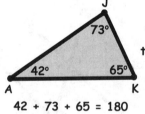

The angles of any triangle add to 180.

$$42 + 73 + 65 = 180$$

Pythagorean Theorem:

For any right triangle, $\text{leg}^2 + \text{leg}^2 = \text{hypotenuse}^2$

$$3^2 + 4^2 = 5^2$$

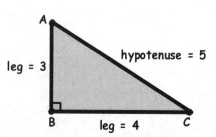

Area of a Triangle:

$$\text{Area of Triangle} = \frac{1}{2} \times \text{base} \times \text{altitude}$$

Quadrilaterals

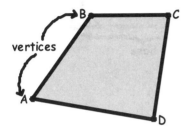

A quadrilateral has 4 sides
and 4 angles.

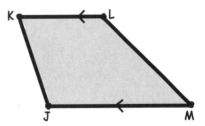

A trapezoid is a quadrilateral
with exactly 1 pair of parallel sides.

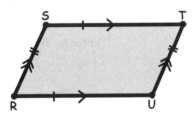

A parallelogram is a quadrilateral
with 2 pairs of parallel sides.

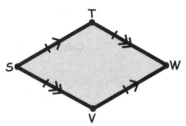

A rhombus is a parallelogram
with 4 equal sides.

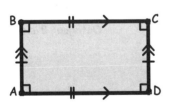

A rectangle is a parallelogram
with 4 right angles.

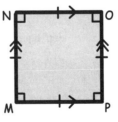

A square is a parallelogram with
4 equal sides and 4 right angles.

Area of a Quadrilateral:

$$\text{Area of a Trapezoid} = \frac{1}{2} \times \text{altitude} \times (\text{base}_1 + \text{base}_2)$$

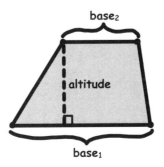

759

Area of a Parallelogram = base × altitude

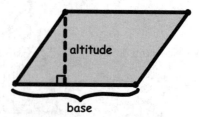

Area of a Rectangle = base × altitude

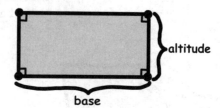

Polygons

Types:

Triangle: 3 sides

Quadrilateral: 4 sides

Pentagon: 5 sides

Hexagon: 6 sides

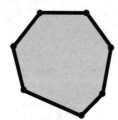

Heptagon: 7 sides

Octagon: 8 sides

Regular Polygons:

A **polygon** with all angles equal and all sides equal.

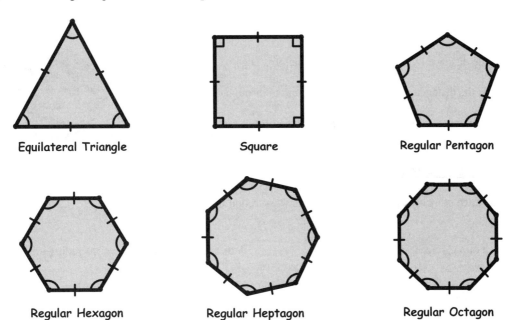

Equilateral Triangle	Square	Regular Pentagon
Regular Hexagon	Regular Heptagon	Regular Octagon

Congruent and Similar Figures

Definitions:

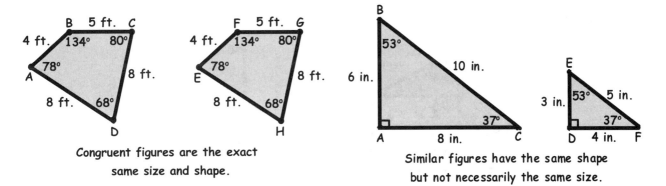

Congruent figures are the exact
same size and shape.

Similar figures have the same shape
but not necessarily the same size.

Corresponding Parts of Congruent Figures:

When two figures are congruent, their corresponding
sides must be equal and their corresponding angles
must be equal.

Corresponding Parts of Similar Figures:

When two figures are similar, their corresponding
angles must be equal and their corresponding
sides must be proportional:

$$\frac{AB}{DE} = \frac{BC}{EF} = \frac{AC}{DF}.$$

Circles

Definition:

A **circle** is a smooth curve where every point is the same distance from the center.

The radius is the distance from the center of a circle to its edge.

The diameter is the distance all the way across the circle through the center.

A chord is a segment that connects two points on the circle.

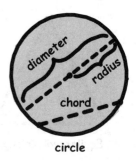

circle

Circumference of a Circle:

The **circumference** of a circle is the distance all the way around it.

Circumference of a Circle = $2 \times \pi \times \text{radius}$

π = about 3.14

Perimeter of a Semicircle = $\pi \times \text{radius} + \text{diameter}$

Area:

Area of a Circle = $\pi \times \text{radius}^2$

Area of a Semicircle = $\dfrac{\pi \times \text{radius}^2}{2}$

Solids

Types of Solids:

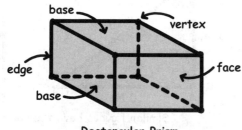

Rectangular Prism

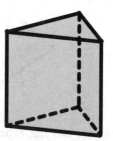

Triangular Prism

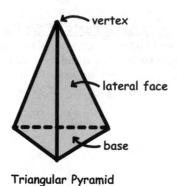

Triangular Pyramid

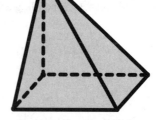

Rectangular Pyramid

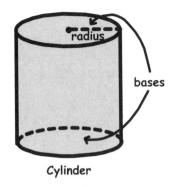

Cylinder

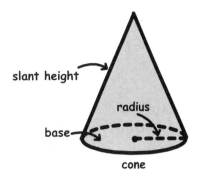

cone

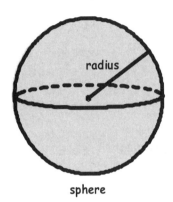

sphere

Volume and Surface Area of Solids:

Volume of a Prism = area of base $\times$ altitude

Surface Area of a Prism= $2\times$area of base + lateral area (sum of the area of the lateral faces)

Volume of a Pyramid = $\dfrac{1}{3}$ $\times$ area of base $\times$ altitude

Surface Area of Pyramid = area of base + lateral area

Volume of a Cylinder = $\pi r^2 \times$ altitude

Surface Area of Cylinder = $2\times\pi\times\text{radius}^2 + 2\times\pi\times\text{radius}\times\text{altitude}$

Volume of Cone = $\dfrac{1}{3}\times\pi\times\text{radius}^2\times\text{altitude}$

Surface Area of Cone = $\pi\times\text{radius}^2 + \pi\times\text{radius}\times\text{slant height}$

Volume of Sphere = $\dfrac{4}{3}\times\pi\times\text{radius}^3$

Surface Area of Sphere = $4\times\pi\times\text{radius}^2$

Appendix C: Algebra, Etc.

Rules for Integers

Adding:

Two positives always equal a positive: $7 + 3 = 10$

Two negatives always equal a negative: $-3 + (-9) = -12$

For a negative plus a positive, subtract the magnitudes of the numbers (ignoring signs) and make the answer the sign of the larger: $-15 + 7 = -8 \qquad 6 + (-11) = -5$

Subtracting:

Change the subtraction to addition of the opposite and add normally:

$$-5 - (-4) \quad \longrightarrow \quad -5 + 4 \quad \longrightarrow \quad -1$$

$$-2 - 9 \quad \longrightarrow \quad -2 + (-9) \quad \longrightarrow \quad -11$$

Multiplying:

$\text{positive} \times \text{positive} = \text{positive} \qquad (3)(4) = 12$

$\text{negative} \times \text{positive} = \text{negative} \qquad (-2)(5) = -10$

$\text{positive} \times \text{negative} = \text{negative} \qquad (7)(-3) = -21$

$\text{negative} \times \text{negative} = \text{positive} \qquad (-6)(-4) = 24$

Dividing:

$\dfrac{\text{positive}}{\text{positive}} = \text{positive} \qquad \dfrac{15}{3} = 5$

$\dfrac{\text{negative}}{\text{positive}} = \text{negative} \qquad \dfrac{-28}{7} = -4$

$\dfrac{\text{positive}}{\text{negative}} = \text{negative} \qquad \dfrac{63}{-9} = -7$

$\dfrac{\text{negative}}{\text{negative}} = \text{positive} \qquad \dfrac{-32}{-8} = 4$

Order of Operations

Rules:
1) All powers are calculated first from left to right.
2) All multiplications and divisions are done second from left to right
3) All additions and subtractions are done third from left to right.
4) If a different order is needed, the operations that are done first must be put in parentheses or inside a fraction.

Examples:

$$17 - 3 \cdot 2 \quad \longrightarrow \quad 17 - 6 \quad \longrightarrow \quad 11$$

$$4 + \frac{10}{2} \quad \longrightarrow \quad 4 + 5 \quad \longrightarrow \quad 9$$

$$3(14 - 9) \quad \longrightarrow \quad 3(5) \quad \longrightarrow \quad 15$$

$$\frac{13-4}{3} + 1 \quad \longrightarrow \quad \frac{9}{3} + 1 \quad \longrightarrow \quad 3 + 1 \quad \longrightarrow \quad 4$$

$$7 \cdot 2^3 \quad \longrightarrow \quad 7 \cdot 8 \quad \longrightarrow \quad 56$$

$$(5 - 1)^2 \quad \longrightarrow \quad 4^2 \quad \longrightarrow \quad 16$$

Solving Equations and Inequalities

Golden Rule of Algebra:
If you change the value of one side of an equation, you have to change the value of the other side by the same amount. In the equation below, we have to subtract 3 from *both* sides.

$$5x + 3 = 18 \quad \longrightarrow \quad 5x + 3 - 3 = 18 - 3$$

Undoing in Reverse Order:
To solve an equation, we undo the operations on x in reverse order. In the equation $5x + 3 = 18$, since x is multiplied by 5 first and 3 is added second, we undo addition first and multiplication second.

$$5x + 3 - 3 = 18 - 3 \quad \longrightarrow \quad 5x = 18 \quad \longrightarrow \quad \frac{5x}{5} = \frac{15}{5} \quad \longrightarrow \quad x = 3$$

Solving Inequalities:
To solve an inequality, you undo in reverse order. But when multiplying or dividing the inequality by a negative number, you must flip the inequality symbol.

$$-8x - 5 \geq 11 \quad \longrightarrow \quad -8x - 5 + 5 \geq 11 + 5 \quad \longrightarrow \quad -8x \geq 16 \quad \longrightarrow \quad \frac{-8x}{-8} \leq \frac{16}{-8} \quad \longrightarrow \quad x \leq -2$$

Powers
Combining Like Terms:
When the variables and exponents are the same, add their coefficients: $3x^4 + 2x^4 \longrightarrow 5x^4$

When the variables and exponents are the same, subtract their coefficients: $9x^2 - 3x^2 \longrightarrow 6x^2$

Multiplying Powers:
When the bases are the same, we can multiply powers by adding their exponents: $5^2 \cdot 5^7 = 5^{2+7} = 5^9$

When the bases are the same, we can divide powers by subtracting their exponents: $\frac{3^8}{3^2} = 3^{8-2} = 3^6$

Powers of 1 and 0:
Any number raised to the first power equals the number itself: $2^1 = 2$

Any number raised to the zero power equals 1: $4^0 = 1$

Functions and Relations

Definitions:
A **relation** is any relationship between variables (such as x and y).

A **function** is a relation where if you pick a value for x, there's just one matching value for y. One example is $y = 3x$. When $x = 4$, there's just one matching y value: 12.

In the function $y = 3x$, x is the **independent variable** because you usually put a number in for it first. And y is the **dependent variable** because y's value depends on x.

The **domain** of a function is all of the possible numbers that you can put in for the independent variable (x).

The **range** of a function is all of the possible numbers that the dependent variable (y) can equal.

Using **functional notation**, we can save space by writing the function $y = 7x - 9$ as $y(x)$.

Graphing Functions

Graphing a line:
Find two pairs of solutions, plot them on the coordinate plane, and draw a line through them.

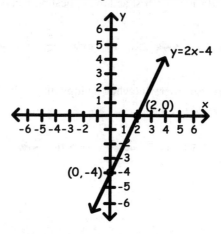

Intercepts:
The **x-intercept** is the point where the line crosses the x-axis.

The **y-intercept** is the point where the line crosses the y-axis.

Slope-Intercept Form of a Linear Equation:
$$y = mx + b \text{ (where } m = \text{slope and } b = y\text{-coordinate of } y\text{-intercept)}$$

Slope calculation:
To find the slope of a line, take any two points on the line and calculate the vertical distance divided by the horizontal distance between them. The calculation is also called "the rise over the run."

$$\text{Slope} = \frac{\text{vertical distance}}{\text{horizontal distance}} = \frac{\text{rise}}{\text{run}}$$

If the two points on the line are $(2, 5)$ and $(-3, 1)$, then the slope calculation works like this

$$\text{Slope} = \frac{5-1}{2-(-3)} = \frac{4}{2+3} = \frac{4}{5}$$

Horizontal lines:
All horizontal lines have a slope of 0.

The equation for any horizontal line has the form $y = 0x + b$ (where m = slope and b = y-coordinate of y-intercept).

Normally, the x-term is left out, since $0x$ always equals 0. So the equation is written as $y = b$. A specific example is $y = 0x + 3$ or $y = 3$.

Vertical lines:

Vertical lines do not have a slope. The slope is undefined.

The equation for any vertical line has the form $x = 0y + a$ (where m = slope and a = x-coordinate of x-intercept).

Normally, the y-term is left out, since $0y$ always equals 0. So the equation is written as $x = a$. A specific example is $x = 0y + 5$ or $x = 5$.

Statistics

Measures of Central Tendency:

The **mean** (or average) of a group of data is the sum of the numbers divided by however many numbers are contained in the data.

The **median** of a group of data is the number exactly in the middle of the data. If no number is in the middle, the median is the mean of the *two* middle numbers.

The **mode** is the number in the data that appears the most frequently.

Measures of Dispersion:

The **range** is the largest number in the data minus the smallest number.

A stem and leaf plot like the one below shows how the numbers in a group of data are dispersed.

Stem	Leaf
1	2
2	2 8
3	0 5
4	1 4 9
5	2 2 3 5 6
6	7 8 9
7	3 4

The stems all stand for ones.

The leaves all stand for tenths.

$1|2 = 1.2$

This row stands for 7.3 and 7.4.

A histogram also shows the dispersion of the numbers in a group of data. The horizontal axis shows several ranges, such as the age ranges below.

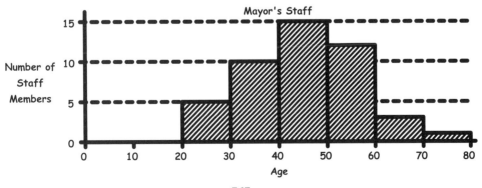

767

Probability

Definition:
Probability is a measure of how certain something is to happen.

Calculating Probability:
Probability is calculated by setting up a fraction with the total possible outcomes on bottom and the favorable outcomes on top.

$$\text{probability} = \frac{\text{favorable outcomes}}{\text{possible outcomes}}$$

Tree Diagrams:
A tree diagram like the one below can be used to count the total possible outcomes.

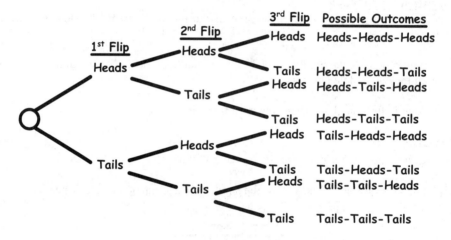

Flipping a coin three times.

Fundamental Counting Principle:
When a situation has two or more separate events, to find the total possible outcomes just multiply the outcomes of each event.

Additional Topics

Distributive Property:
You can free an x from parentheses by distributing. In $7(x+2)-3x=20$, the first x can be freed by distributing the 7 to the x and the 2.

$$7(x+2)-3x=20 \quad \Longrightarrow \quad 7x+14-3x=20$$

Absolute Value:
The **absolute value** of a quantity is the positive of that quantity. Absolute value is shown with little bars on either side of the quantity.

$$|-6| \quad \longrightarrow \quad 6 \qquad\qquad |-9+5| \quad \longrightarrow \quad |-4| \quad \longrightarrow \quad 4$$

Distance Formula:

The distance formula can be used to find the distance between any two points on a coordinate plane.

If the two points are represented as (x_1, y_1) and (x_2, y_2), then the distance (d) is calculated like this:

$$d = \sqrt{(x_2 - x_1)^2 + (y_2 - y_1)^2}$$

Midpoint Formula:

You can find the point exactly in the middle of any two points on a coordinate plane by calculating the mean (average) of the x-coordinates and the mean (average) of the y-coordinates of those points. The answers are the x and y-coordinates of the midpoint.

The midpoint between (x_1, y_1) and (x_2, y_2) is $(\dfrac{x_1 + x_2}{2}, \dfrac{y_1 + y_2}{2})$.

Index

A

Absolute Value
  and arithmetic, 730-733
  defined, 730
Acute angle, 477
Acute triangle, 497
Addend, 12
Addition
  associative property of,
  (see Commutative
  Property)
  carrying in, 11, 92
  commutative property of,
  12, 231, 291, 331
  of decimals, 92
  of fractions, 55
  of integers (negatives),
  262-264
  of like terms, 424-425
  of mixed numbers, 92
  of rational expressions,
  396-397
  of whole numbers, 11
  undoing, 222, 280-281,
  318, 709
  of x's, 338-39, 343, 346-
  347
Adjacent angles, 483
Alternate interior angles,
  491
Algebra
  defined, 214
  steps for solving real-
  world problem with, 219
Altitude
  of cone, 579-580
  of cylinder, 576-577
  defined, 547
  of parallelogram, 547-
  548
  of prism, 569-571
  of pyramid, 578-579
  of rectangle, 547
  of trapezoid, 549-550
  of triangle, 549
Angles
  acute, 477
  adjacent, 483
  alternate interior, 491
  congruent, 483

complementary, 484
corresponding, 491, 526
defined, 475
obtuse, 478
right, 477
straight, 478
supplementary, 485
vertex of, 475
vertical, 483
Applications
  absolute value, 730
  banking, 138
  measurements, 730
  calculating a grade, 145
  common units of
  measurement, 150-151,
  184-185, 196, 199, 203-
  204
  compound interest, 138
  distance problems with
  algebra, 247-248, 354-
  355
  functions used, 588-591
  interest, 138
  metric system, 165-166
  money and decimals, 99
  negatives used, 259
  percents and banking,
  138
  percent problems with
  algebra, 243-244
  refrigerator repairs, 362-
  363
  statistics and probability,
  662-664, 671, 675-678,
  685-686
  work problems, 350
Approximately equal to,
  557
Area
  of circle, 558
  common units of, 185,
  188-189
  of complex figure, 550
  defined, 184, 547
  metric units of, 192
  of parallelogram, 547
  of rectangle, 184, 196,
  547, 561
  of semicircle, 559

of surface, 569-571, 576-
  577, 578-581
of triangle, 548
Associative Property
  of addition, 12, 331
  of multiplication, 18, 433

B

Banking, 138
Base
  of cone, 568, 579-581
  of cylinder, 567, 576-577
  of exponent, 410
  of parallelogram, 547
  of prism, 566, 569-571
  of pyramid, 567, 578-
  579
  of rectangle, 550-551
  of trapezoid, 549-550
  of triangle, 549
Bilateral symmetry, 541

C

Calculator
  and missing side of
  triangle, 506-507
  and distance formula,
  745
Canceling
  in fractions, 47, 50-51,
  70-71, 368-369, 372
  x's, 372-373
  quantities in parentheses,
  382
Centiliter, 208
Centimeter, 170
Circle
  area of, 558
  center of, 556
  chord of, 556
  circumference of, 556-
  558
  diameter, 556
  pi, 557
  radius of, 556
Circumference, 556
Coefficients
  of 1, 346-347
  adding, 338-339

defined, 339
negative, 343
subtracting, 342-343
Combining like terms, 425
Combining x's, 338-339, 342-343
Compound interest, 138
Common system
cubic units, 196
defined, 165
inch, 151, 154, 158, 161
foot, 151, 154, 158, 161
mile, 158, 161
yard, 151, 158, 161
square units, 184-185, 188-189
Commutative Property
of Addition, 12, 331
of Multiplication, 18
Comparing fractions, 41
Complementary Angles, 484
Cone
altitude of, (See Altitude)
base of, (See Base)
defined, 568
surface area of, 580-581
volume of, 579-580
Congruent angles, 483
Congruent figures
corresponding angles of, 491, 526
corresponding sides of, 526-527, 532-533
defined, 526
Converting
decimal to fraction, 116-117
decimal to percent, 127
fraction to decimal, 85-86, 88-89, 115
converting mixed number to improper fraction, 66-67
percent to decimal, 127-128
Coordinate plane
x and y-axis, 607
origin, 607
quadrants of, 610
Coordinates, 610
Correlation
positive, 678-679
negative, 678-679
no, 678-679

Corresponding angles, 491, 526
Corresponding sides, 526-527, 532-533
Cross multiply, 535
Cylinder
altitude of, (See Altitude)
bases of (See Base)
defined, 567
surface area of, 576-577
volume of, 576
Cube
as power, 411
in volume, 196, 569-570
Cubic units (See Units of Volume)
Cube root (third root), 448

D
Data, 662
Decimal point, 85
Decimals
adding, 92
converting to fractions (See Converting)
converting to percents (See Converting)
defined, 84
dividing, 107-109
multiplying, 102-104
as remainders, 111-112
repeating, 119
rounding, 120-121
subtracting, 93
terminating, 119
Degrees, 476
Deciliter, 208
Decimeter, 170-171
Dekaliter, 208
Dekameter, 170-171
Denominator
common denominator, 61
defined, 32
lowest common denominator, 61
Difference, 12
Digit, 6
Dispersion, 669
Distance
how to calculate, 247
algebra word problems, 247, 354-355

Distance formula, 740
Distributive property, 725
Dividend, 21
Division
of decimals, 107-109
defined, 21
fraction bar as symbol, 234
of fractions, 72
of integers (negatives), 275
long, 21-22
of rational expressions, 391
of whole numbers, 21-22
with zeros, 21
Divisor, 21
Divisibility
defined, 25
rules, 25-28
Domain, 596
Dot (·)
as multiplication symbol, 234

E
English system
(See Common system)
Even numbers, 26
Equation
combining like terms in, 425
checking solution of, 223
defined, 218
distributing in, 724-726
graphing, 615-616, 623-628
for horizontal line, 654
with negatives, 279-282, 284, 287-288, 291-292, 295-296
simplifying, 327-328, 331-333
solving, 219
slope-intercept form of, 647
translating words into, 218
two-variable, 589
undoing addition, 222
undoing subtraction, 224
undoing multiplication, 227
undoing division, 228

undoing a power, 452-453
undoing a root, 453
undoing in reverse order, 318-320, 323-324
for vertical line, 655
with –x, 291-292, 295-296
with x's on both sides, 358-359
Equilateral triangle, 497
Equivalent fractions
defined, 39
Law of, 41
Exponents
defined, 410
of 1, 457-458
of 0, 462
Expressions
defined 218
factoring 368
evaluating 292
rational 368
rewriting 231
simplifying 327-328, 331-333

F

Factor
in multiplication, 18
of a number, 46
Factoring
and canceling, 46
defined, 46
to reduce fractions, 46, 50-51
Foot, 151
Fractions
adding, 55
common denominator of, 61
comparing, 41-42
converting to decimals, 85-86, 88-89, 115
defined, 32
denominator of, 32
dividing, 72
improper, 35
lowest common denominator (LCD), 61
multiplying, 70-71
and negatives, 255-256, 287-288
numerator of, 32

reciprocal of, 72
reducing, 42
subtraction of, 55-58
Fraction bar
as division symbol, 234
and order of operations, 309-310, 314-315
Function
defined, 590
domain of, 596
graphing, 616
linear, 623
nonlinear, 624
range of, 597
Functional notation, 602
Fundamental counting principle, 698

G

Gallons, 203-204
Geometric figures
circle, 556
parallelogram, 511
pentagon, 519
heptagon, 519
hexagon, 519
polygon, 518
quadrilateral, 511
rectangle, 512-513
regular polygon, 519-520
rhombus, 512
square, 512-513
trapezoid, 513
triangle, 496
Geometric solids
cone, 568
cylinder, 567
defined, 566
polyhedron, 566
prism, 566
pyramid, 567
sphere, 568
Geometry, 468-469, 475, 496, 511, 526, 566, 610
Golden Rule of Algebra, 223
Graph
bar, 675
histogram, 675
of function, 615-616, 623-628
of inequality, 704
Stem and Leaf Plot, 670

H

Hectoliter, 208-209
Hectometer, 170-171, 174
Height (See Altitude)
Heptagon, 519
Hexagon, 519
Hindu-Arabic numbers, 7
Histogram, 675
Horizontal Line
equation of, 654
graphing, 654
slope of, 654
Hundredths, 84, 88-89
Hypotenuse, 504

I

Improper fractions
converting to mixed number, 67
defined, 36
Inch, 154-155
Independent events, 698
Inequalities
algebraic (with x's), 703
graphing, 704
symbols, 41, 703
Integers
addition of, 11, 262-264
defined, 256
division of, 275-277
multiplication of, 271-273
subtraction of, 267-268
Interest, 138
Inverse operations
addition-subtraction, 222, 224
defined, 224
multiplication-division, 227-228
powers-roots, 452-453
Inverting and multiplying, 72
Isosceles triangle, 496

K

Kiloliter, 208
Kilometer, 170-171, 174-175

L

Law of Equivalent Fractions, 41
Lateral
  area, 576
  face, 571
  surface, 567-568, 576
Lowest common denominator (LCD), 61
Least common multiple, 63
Legs (of a right triangle), 504
Like terms, 425
Line
  defined, 468
  horizontal, 654
  intersecting, 469
  parallel, 470
  perpendicular, 478
  skew, 470
  slope of, 634-636
  vertical, 655-656
Linear function, 623
Line segments, 468
Liquid Measure, 203-204
Liter, 208-209

M

Mean, 662
Median, 663
Metric system
  Centimeter (See Centimeter)
  cubic units for volume, 207-209
  decimeter (See Decimeter)
  dekameter (See Dekameter)
  hectometer (See Hectometer)
  kilometer (See Kilometer meter)
  millimeter (See Millimeter)
  square units for area, 192-193
Midpoint formula, 745-746
Mile, 155, 158-159, 161
Milliliter, 208
Millimeter, 170-171, 174-175

Missing number, 214-215, 243-244, 305
Mixed numbers
  converting to improper fraction, 66
  defined, 66
Mode, 664
Money, 99
Multiplication
  associative property of (See Associative Property)
  carrying, 17, 18
  commutative property of (See Commutative Property)
  of decimals, 102-104
  defined, 16
  of fractions, 70-71
  of fraction and whole number, 75
  of integers (negatives), 271-273
  long, 16
  of rational expressions, 386-387
  symbols (in algebra), 234
  of whole numbers, 16-18
  with zeros, 15

N

Negative numbers,
  coefficients and, 343
  defined, 252
  exponents and fractions and, 287-288
  purpose of, 259
Numbers
  beginnings, 6-8
  even (See Even numbers)
  Hindu-Arabic, 7
  integers, 256
  mixed, 66
  negative, 252
  odd, 26
  positive, 252
  rational, 255
  Roman numerals, 6-7
  Whole, 11
  writing in words, 8

Number line
  with inequalities, 704
  with integers, 255-256
Numerator, 32

O

Obtuse angle, 478
Obtuse triangle, 498
Octagon, 519
Odd numbers, 26
Operations
  addition, 11
  defined, 214
  division, 21
  multiplication, 16
  powers, 410
  roots, 448
  subtraction, 11-12
  undoing, 224, 228, 452-453
Opposites, 256
Order of operations, 300, 309, 310
Ordered pairs, 610
Origin, 607
Ounces, 204
Outliers, 663

P

Parentheses
  as multiplication symbol, 234
  and order of operations, 305-306
Parabola, 623
Parallel lines, 470
Parallelogram
  altitude of (See Altitude)
  area of, 547
  base of, (See Base)
  defined, 512
Pentagon, 519
Percent
  algebra word problems, 243-244
  of any number, 131-132
  calculating, 127-129
  converted into a decimal, 127-128
  converted into a fraction, 127
  defined, 124
  fractional, 134-135

one number of another, 141-142

with repeating decimal, 135

Perimeter

of complicated figures, 540

defined, 539

of rectangle, 539

of square, 539

Perpendicular lines, 478

Pi, 557

Pints, 203-204

Place value system, 7

Plane, 469

Points

defined, 468

finding slope with, 636

plotting, 607-608

writing equation with, 644-648

Polygon

heptagon (See Heptagon)

hexagon (See Hexagon)

octagon (See Octagon)

pentagon (See Pentagon)

quadrilateral as, 518

triangle as, 518

Polyhedron, 566

Polynomial

defined, 425

used in expressions, 429, 433, 439, 443-444, 457-458, 462

Positive Numbers

defined, 252

positive signs and, 253

Powers

base of, 410

exponent of, 410

defined, 410

dividing, 438-439

multiplying, 428-429, 433

and order of operations, 420

raised to a, 411

Prime factors, 52

Prime numbers, 51

Prism

altitude of (See Altitude)

base of (See Base)

defined, 566

rectangular, 566

surface area of, 570-571

triangular, 566

volume of, 569-570

Probability

defined, 684

experimental, 686

theoretical, 686

Product, 18

Profit, 259

Proper fractions, 36

Proportion

defined, 532

cross multiply with (See Cross Multiply)

Protractor, 476

Purpose of algebra, 218

Pyramid

altitude of (See Altitude)

base of (See Base)

defined, 567

rectangular, 567

surface area of, 578-579

triangular, 567

volume of, 578

Pythagorean Theorem 504

Q

Quadrant

in coordinate plane, 610

in metric system, 166

Quadrilateral

defined, 511

as polygon, 518

special, 511-514

Quarts, 203-204

Quotient, 22

R

Radical (also See Roots)

defined, 448

sign, 448

Radius

of circle, 556

of cone, 568

of cylinder, 567-568

Raising a number to a power (See Powers)

Range

of function, 597

of set of data, 669

Rate, 350

Rate of change (See slope)

Ratio, 533

Rational expressions

adding, 396-398

canceling x's, 372-373

defined, 368

dividing, 391-392

multiplying, 386-387

reducing, 368-369

subtracting, 402-404

Rational number, 255

Ray, 469

Real numbers, 596

Reciprocal, 72

Rectangle

area of, 184, 196, 547, 561

altitude of (See Altitude)

base of (See Base)

defined, 512

Rectangular prism, 566

Rectangular pyramid, 567

Reducing fractions

by dividing, 42

by factoring and canceling, 46-48

Reflection, 542

Regrouping (borrowing), 12

Regular polygon, 519

Relation, 591

Remainder

defined, 22

as fraction, 66-67

as decimal, 111-112

Rewriting an expression, 231

Rhombus

defined, 512

Right angles, 477

Right triangle, 497

Rise over run (See Slope)

Roman numerals, 6-7

Roots

cube, 448

defined, 448

square, 448

Rotational symmetry, 542

Rounding, 120-121

S

Scalene triangle, 496

Scatter plot, 676-678

Scientific notation, 415-416

Secondary standards, 151

Semicircle, 559

Similar figures
corresponding angles of, 532
corresponding sides of, 533
defined, 532
Simplifying, 327-328, 331-333
Slant height, 579
Slope
defined, 634
fractional, 643
positive, 635
negative, 635
Slope-intercept form, 644-645
Solution, 219
Speed, 247-248
Square
as power, 411
as geometric figure, 513
perimeter of, 539
Square units (See Units of Area)
Square root, 448
Standard measures, 151
Statistics, 662
Stem and Leaf Plot, 670-671
Straight angle, 478
Substituting a number for *x*, 223
Subtraction
of decimals, 93
of fractions, 55-58
of integers (negatives) , 267-268
of rational expressions, 402-404
undoing, 224, 709
of whole numbers, 11
of *x*'s, 342-343, 347
Sum, 12
Supplementary angles, 485
Surface area, 569-571, 576-577, 578-581
Symmetry
bilateral, 541
defined, 541
line, of 541
rotational, 542

T
Taking a root (See Roots)
Tenths, 84-86
Thousandths, 88-89
Terms
combining, 338-339, 342-343
like, 425
Transversal, 491
Trapezoid
altitude of (See Altitude)
area of, 549-550
bases of (See Base)
defined, 511
Tree diagrams, 691-693
Triangle
acute, 497
altitude of (See Altitude)
area of, 548
defined, 496
equilateral, 497
isosceles, 496
obtuse, 498
as polygon, 518
right, 497
scalene, 496
sum of the angles of, 498
Triangular Prism, 566
Triangular Pyramid, 567
Two-variable equation (See Equation)

U
Undoing
addition in equations, 222
division in equations, 228
equations with negatives, 279-282, 284
multiplication in equations, 227
subtraction in equations, 224
inequalities, 709-712
Undoing in reverse order
equations, 318-320, 323-324
inequalities, 717-718
Units of area (common) , 184
Units of Area (metric) , 192-193

Unit Conversion
common to metric, 178-179
factors (common) , 155
table (common) , 161
table (metric) , 175
Units of Length (common) , 155
Units of Length (metric), 170-171
Units of Liquid Measure, 203-204
Units of volume (common), 199-200
Units of volume (metric), 207-209

V
Variable
defined, 589
dependent, 595
independent, 595
Vertex, 475
Vertical angles, 483
Vertical lines
equation of, 656
graphing, 656
slope of, 656
Volume
of box, 196
of cone, 579
of cylinder, 576
defined, 196
of prism, 569
of pyramid, 578
unit conversions for, 199

W
Whole numbers
addition of, 11
multiplication of, 16-18
division of, 21-22
subtraction of, 12
Work problems, 350-351

X
x, 215
x-axis, 607
x-coordinate, 610
x-intercept, 626

x's on both sides equations,
    358-359

Y

y, 215
Yard, 150
y-**axis**, 607
y-**coordinate**, 610
y-**intercept**, 626

Z

Zero, 7